Henry Cow
The World is a Problem
Benjamin Piekut

Paperback: *Price: $29.95/£23.99*
                      ISBN: 978-1-4780-0466-0
Library cloth: *Price: $114.95/£95.00*
                      ISBN: 978-1-4780-0405-9
E-book: *Price: $29.95/£23.99*
                      ISBN: 978-1-4780-0551-3

Prices subject to change.
Pages: 520 (estimate), 63 illustrations
Publication date: September 2019

For additional information contact:

Laura Sell
Publicity
Ph: 919-687-3639
Fax: 919-688-4391
lsell@dukepress.edu
www.dukeupress.edu

Duke University Press
905 West Main St.
Suite 18B
Durham, NC 27701

D1526360

HENRY COW

BENJAMIN PIEKUT

HENRY COW

THE WORLD IS
A PROBLEM

DUKE UNIVERSITY PRESS
Durham and London
2019

© 2019 DUKE UNIVERSITY PRESS
Printed in the United States of America on acid-free paper ∞
Designed by Matthew Tauch
Typeset in Warnock Pro by Typesetter, Inc.
Library of Congress Cataloging-in-Publication Data

Contents

vii   Preface

xi   Acknowledgments

1   **Introduction**   Feral Experimentalism

29   **1**   You Can't Play This Music at Cambridge | 1968–73

76   **2**   Faust and the Virgins | 1973

119   **3**   Contentment Is Hopeless, Unrest Is Progress | 1974

157   **4**   Death to the Individual: Slapp Happy | 1974–75

199   **5**   Europa | 1975–76

242   **6**   The Roads Leading to Rome | 1976–77

293   **7**   No Joy Anymore | London 1977

345   **8**   Henry Cow Always Had to Be Henry Cow | 1978

387   **Afterword**   The Vernacular Avant-Garde

409   Notes

455   Bibliography

000   Index

Preface

Henry Cow—it's impossible to explain. It's certainly impossible to explain without writing a fat book.

Tim Hodgkinson, 1981

I have written one of those fat books, but many things will still go unexplained. I realized that this would be the case during my research, when a member of the band remarked upon all the things that we hadn't seemed to cover in our conversations. That surprised me, because we had already recorded twenty-five hours of interviews. But I took the point: when you tell somebody else's story, you are bound to accent wrong beats and drop notes here and there. Furthermore, my relentless interrogations occasionally forced my collaborators to articulate things that may never before have been spoken, about events that took place forty or more years ago, when they were just out of university or around that age. I cannot imagine what that is like, but it must feel odd at best, vulnerable and violating at worst.

Nevertheless, these people have been gracious, generous, trusting, and kind to me. They have also been a real pain in the ass now and then, but I've learned enough from them to return that favor in kind, as I'm sure any would testify. Indeed, the substance of their example has worked its way deep into the weave of my own life; I doubt any other research project will ever have such a drastic, bracing impact on how I relate to others and to the future. It will take some time to come to terms with that, but for now, I must credit my consultants with edging me into states of uncertainty I would have found scarcely imaginable before we began.

Readers looking for smooth illustrations of parboiled theory will be disappointed by *The World Is a Problem*. I have found nothing but ambivalence, contradiction, and entanglement—the stuff that attends all practical critique. As a writer, that is the space into which I wish to move further, into more contradiction, greater ambivalence, deeper tangles. Although I aim to remain supportively skeptical of my interlocutors, as they were to each other, I will not reproduce the muted hostility that I have discovered in presenting material from this study. Academic (and some general) audiences have surprised me over the years with responses to Henry Cow's activities that often reach dismissiveness but sometimes approach contempt. After detailing the large, diverse audiences they found in Italy, I might be asked, "But were all those people *really* there to hear Henry Cow?" Or, after hearing my description of what they heard in the rock ethos, someone might object, "But they came from Cambridge!" Or, after recounting their internal debates over the possibility of joining the Communist Party of Great Britain, I might hear a comment like, "How could they have taken themselves so seriously?" It's as if many of these respondents are searching for a technicality through which to toss out the whole topic. How contemporary observers have made it to a point where seriousness of endeavor has been rendered quixotic is a matter best left for other occasions, but it does call to mind Mackenzie Wark's observation: "The authorities on this period delight in drawing attention to the follies then committed, as if their own complacency of thought was in some sense a higher achievement."[1]

Motivating the hostile responses to Henry Cow's endeavors would appear to be naive notions of politics, authenticity, or populism—as if a communist rock band must only come from the working classes, as if the only audience that counts would line up attentively and parse correctly their obscure lyrics, as if significance is granted only upon the disclosure of receipts documenting the sale of greater than fifty thousand units—indeed, as if real significance is measured only by an absence of contradiction. I hope that the kind of account I offer here—one that attempts to preserve "the richest intimacy with facts," as William James would say—will contribute to a more realistic picture of what things like politics, critique, experiment, and collectivism look and sound like.[2] While we might search for the perfect historical case of "correct" cultural politics, a torrent of more "imperfect" ventures rushes further into the past. I have attempted to arrest momentarily a small part of that torrent.

In establishing certain plot points in these stories, I have relied on interviews with my historical subjects, supplementing these accounts with textual evidence from their personal archives, published journalism, and audio evidence from the bootleg archive that circulates on the internet. I have not always singled out specific sources because there are cases (such as the summer of 1975) where texts and memories disagree, and only by reading many of them together and against one another has it been possible to determine what actually happened with any accuracy. Recounting my steps in print would be tedious. When I haven't been able to make precise determinations, my writing reflects this ambiguity. Usually, it isn't a big deal. Some bits of information were confirmed by close reading of the personal notebooks of various band members, particularly those of Tim Hodgkinson. I could have added a reference to the page, but these sources are not available in a public archive and are unpaginated anyway, so I decided to leave it unreferenced and tell you about this decision up front.

When someone speaks in this book and that speech has no footnoted reference, then I am quoting my own interviews with that person. There are also several passages of dialogue interpolated into the prose, originating in different kinds of sources: published and unpublished interviews from the time; later archival conversations; my own double interview with Hodgkinson and Georgina Born; the band's meeting minutes, recorded in shorthand by Lindsay Cooper; and reported speech from one of my own interviews with band members and associates. Wherever possible, I have seized these opportunities to break up my own control of the text; the dialogues have also helped me with plot, characterization, and voice. Someone like Hayden White might complain that I have chosen to work in an outmoded literary style in this history, but I will consider it a distinguishing achievement if there is any style at all.

Lindsay Cooper is the only major player in these stories who couldn't speak for herself during the years of my research, so I wish to express clearly how I represent her in the pages that follow. I met her twice at her apartment in Camdentown; on the first occasion, Sally Potter introduced us. Lindsay had not been able to speak for many years, but she listened intently to me as I described the project and told her a little about myself. I have been told that, in its late stages, multiple sclerosis works its way into the brain; aural comprehension still takes place, but slowly. My experience accorded with this description: Lindsay met my gaze and listened to what I had to say, but any muted reactions might have been delayed by ten seconds or more. Nonetheless, I had the strong impression that she knew what was going on; she participated to the best of her ability during the interview that I subsequently conducted with Potter about Cooper's life and her time in Henry Cow. That evening, Sally and I spent some hours going through the large boxes of materials that Lindsay had put together before her paralysis grew incapacitating. In addition to scores and parts, they included letters to family and friends, datebooks, press cuttings, and other ephemera. The letters and postcards, in particular, have been very important, because she didn't tend to take (or be given) a strong vocal role in band interviews at the time. On my second visit, her caregiver, Astrida Gorkusa, told me that Lindsay had been excited all day because she knew I would be returning to photograph the documents that I hadn't collected on my previous visit—so excited, in fact, that she had completely tired herself out, and wasn't in a state to receive greetings face to face.

Even though Lindsay had been ill for many years, her death in September 2013 came as a nasty surprise. I hope it will not appear sentimental or gratuitous to state the truth as I see it at the end of my time on this project: of all my interlocutors, only Cooper has garnered universal fondness from the others. I do not mean to imply that there were no conflicts, or that she couldn't hold her own in a battle of wills. But she seems to have had the most "liberated" personality of anyone in these stories—a loyal friend, a funny writer, a committed artist, and a passionate thinker. This book is dedicated to her memory. I wish I had known her.

Acknowledgments

I am grateful to all my interview subjects for sharing their time, trust, objections, and clarifications; Tim Hodgkinson, Chris Cutler, and Fred Frith, in particular, have been gracious and generous over a long time span of research and writing. Sally Potter, Astrida Gorkusa, and Mandy Merck were critically important in helping me to integrate Lindsay Cooper's voice into this history.

Countless individuals helped with introductions, services, advice, queries, and materials: Virginia Anderson, Ed Baxter, Steve Beresford, Valentina Bertolani, Chris Brown, Martin Davidson, Steve Feigenbaum, Andy Fry, Trond Garmo, Adrian Haegele, Malcolm Heyhoe, Ian Hoare, Branden Joseph, Wolfram Knauer, Caroline Kraabel, Dave Laing, Cathryn Lane, Richard Leigh, Aymeric Leroy, Sarah Maude, Mandy Merck, Paul Merrill, Paul Miller, Frank Perry, Joanna Poethig, Sally Potter, Ianthe and Malise Ruthven, Victor Schonfield, Irène Schweizer, Nuala Sheehan, Pwyll ap Siôn, Penny Souster, James Spinazzola, Veit Stauffer, David Toop, Ben Walton, D-M Withers, Robert Worby, and Seymour Wright.

At Cornell, I benefited from the assistance of the Student Technology Assistant Program and its director, Amy Cheadle. I also wish to thank the Olin Library's interlibrary loan staff, and, in the Department of Music and the Cox Music Library, Bill Cowdery, Eric Feinstein, Colette Larkin, Fumi Nagasaki-Pracel, Chris Riley, and Lenora Schneller. Colleagues provided help of all kinds, particularly Rebecca Harris-Warrick, Andrew Hicks, Patricia Keller, Roger Moseley, Steve Pond, Judith Peraino, and Trevor Pinch. At the University of Southampton, Mark Everist, Jeanice Brooks, and David Nicholls were supportive of the project from its very beginning. In 1994, Professor Dan Warner assigned *File under Popular* to his students in "experimental music" at Hampshire College, and I still have my copy.

Many graduate and undergraduate students stepped up for me. I received translation help from Thomas Hilder, Sergio Ospina, Evan Cortens, Amanda Recupero, and Andrew Zhou, and research assistance from Joshua Barber, Samuel Dwinell, Charlotte Bentley, and Orit Hilewicz. Barry Sharp lent his sharp ear and fleet notation skills to many of the musical transcriptions. XXXXXXX XXXXXXX assisted with the index. Two individuals deserve special mention: Jordan Musser helped me sound out ideas big and small, and David Marquiss created extraordinary databases and explained how to use them.

My work would have been impossible without the complementary labors of professional and amateur archivists, among them Liz Broekmann, Alexis Chevrier, Rob Cohen, Chris Cotton, David Cursons, Nicola Hudson, Chris Marsh, Juanjo Sanchez, Andrea Zarza, and the staff archivists for the Arts Council of Great Britain. Ian Hoare came through with a last-minute rescue with scans.

Throughout this project, I sounded out ideas with Michael Ashkin, Leslie Brack, Amy Cimini, Chris Corsano, Charles Curtis, John Dieterich, Eric Drott, Miguel Galperin, Bernard Gendron, David Grubbs, Brían Hanrahan, Annie Lewandowski, Yasi Perera, Evan Rapport, Marina Rosenfeld, Greg Saunier, and D-M Withers. Julia Bryan-Wilson read most of this manuscript and improved it dramatically; I would be lost without her friendship. I am particularly in her debt for comments on the afterword. Michael Gallope, Bernard Gendron, Branden Joseph, Fumi Okiji, and Christopher Smith also read that chapter and provided me with invaluable suggestions, while Charles Curtis, Eric Drott, Ellie Hisama, Evan Rapport, and Barry Shank graciously read other excerpts. My colleagues in Henry Cow studies, Aymeric Leroy and Veit Stauffer, saved me from making numerous errors in the manuscript.

I would have been adrift without ongoing conversations about the insanities of academic life with Robert Adlington, Jo Applin, G. Douglas Barrett, Tamar Barzel, Amy Beal, Andrea Bohlman, Marcus Boon, Georgina Born, Julia Bryan-Wilson, Austin Bunn, Amy Cimini, James Currie, James Davies, Eric Drott, Eva Ehninger, Brían Hanrahan, Ellie Hisama, Michael Gallope, Bernard Gendron, Bill Girard, Russell Greenberg, Branden Joseph, Miki Kaneda, Charlie Kronengold, Tim Lawrence, Richard Leppert, Tamara Levitz, George Lewis, Alejandro Madrid, Nick Mathew, Myra Melford, Roger Moseley, Fumi Okiji, Kate van Orden, Gascia Ouzounian, Judith Peraino, Trevor Pinch, Nancy Rao, Evan Rapport, Rich Robinson, Maryanne Smart, Jason Stanyek, Gavin Steingo, Jonathan Sterne, Lucie Vágnerová, Carol Vernallis, Marianne Wheeldon, and David Yearsley.

Others supplied support of a more fundamental nature: Sylvia Algire, Leila Awada, Keiko Beers, Michael Carreira, John Dieterich, Blake Doherty, Ed Finegan, Kate Fruchey, Miguel Galperin, Bill Girard, Eric King, Dan

Lewis, Nueng Nantika, Conor Prischmann, Dennis Stein, Shannon Vogt, the Lewandowski family, my parents, and my sister, Jennifer Moreland. Marina Rosenfeld's intelligence, humor, empathy, and care—her uncounterfeit happiness—were essential in the late stages of completion. Tamara Levitz, Jason Stanyek, and Jamie Currie were there for me when I needed them.

I thank Ken Wissoker at Duke University Press for his support of this project and his intellectual involvement with it over many years, and I'm also grateful to Elizabeth Ault, Stephanie Gomez Menzies, Sara Leone, Chad Royal, and Joshua Tranen at the press. Ray Smith generously provided the painting that appears on the cover, and Catriona Smith provided vital support in sharing digital files; I hope it succeeds as a small tribute to Ray's memory. All of the photographers who provided images have my deepest gratitude, and I am especially thankful to Takumba RiA Lawal for her generosity.

It would have taken me longer to finish this manuscript without my semester of sabbatical leave from Cornell, as well as the assistance of an Early Career Fellowship from the Arts and Humanities Research Council (United Kingdom); Mark Everist was instrumental in improving my application for it. I also owe a debt of gratitude to Anne Currie and the Faculty of the Humanities at the University of Southampton for awarding me an Annual Adventures in Research grant, which jumpstarted this project at its inception. Finally, I thank the National Endowment for the Humanities for giving me a Summer Stipend in 2011; any views, findings, conclusions, or recommendations expressed in this book do not necessarily reflect those of the National Endowment for the Humanities.

A Note to the Scholarly Reader

This book takes a somewhat unusual, hybrid form combining collective biography and argument-driven cultural history. For that reason, some scholarly readers expecting the customary survey of the contemporary literature at the head of this study will feel unsatisfied. I've stuck that wedge in the afterword. I have taken some inspiration for this ordering from Berthold Brecht, who wrote, "In the epic theatre moral arguments only took second place. Its aim was less to moralize than to observe. That is to say it observed, and then the thick end of the wedge followed: the story's moral."

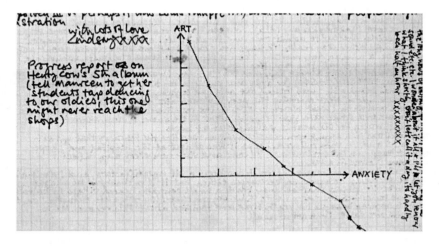

Frontispiece The relationship of art to anxiety, from a letter by Lindsay Cooper, January 1978. COURTESY OF THE LINDSAY COOPER ESTATE.

Introduction

Feral Experimentalism

With this book, I intend to make a small contribution to a large project that would take the form of a rigorous documentation and analysis of adventurous music and sound work in the twenty-first century, and how we got here over the last seventy years. I refer to the related and frequently overlapping contemporary sonic practices of indeterminacy, improvisation, noise, live electronics and coding, field recording, sound art, installation, graphic notation, text scores, and new instruments. Curious and exploratory, this global network of artists stretches across and against the genre formations of notated composition, jazz, rock, dub, electronic music, hip-hop, noise, and folk; it also occasionally stakes positions in contemporary art, theatre, cinema, and new media. If this "foment of activity," as David Toop would call it, wears "looser ties to the ethics, methodology and materials established for free improvisation," it has also stretched far its fetters to the Cagean school of score-based composers in the postwar decades.[1] I sense that this contemporary, mixed formation of experimental music making began to take shape in the late 1960s; though an analysis of these many branching and bunching genealogies would exceed the capabilities of any single book, I hope that Henry Cow will serve as one example of how this congeries of expanded experimentalism sounded in the field of rock.

Genre will vibrate as a pronounced undertone in the story that follows. "Henry Cow is nothing if not a band that tries to step across the dividing lines between jazz, contemporary music, rock, and so on," the band's drummer Chris Cutler told me. "There was a moment in which the fringes of all of those previously highly separate discourses got close together, and, up to a point, communicated. We didn't see much of [composer] Tim Souster, but when we played together somewhere, we got on fine. There wasn't any kind of formal coming together, but when we played with the Art Ensemble of Chicago, they liked us, we liked them, and we got on just fine. The musical languages were compatible but not the same." In this introduction, I will concern myself less with these questions of genre—fascinating though they are—than I will with documenting the historical conditions of the 1960s and 1970s that provided the backdrop for Henry Cow's activities in the rock field.[2] In the afterword, I will pass through this terrain a second time, with a view to illuminating the implications of this history for the theory of the avant-garde. Throughout this book, I will use the word *avant-garde* in this sort of theoretical and conceptual register, counter to another influential approach that posits a historical, aesthetic, and social split between an "experimental" composer like John Cage and an "avant-garde" one like Pierre Boulez.[3] The avant-garde, I will maintain, is irreducible to any single conjunctural milieu, as important as futurism, Dadaism, and surrealism have been in articulating its themes. By contrast, I will use *experimentalism* to refer to a historically specific network, one that does not necessarily express a radical political imagination; indeed, experimental music's genealogical embroilment with science-and-technology discourses has often disinclined it from developing an overt political project.[4] (In those moments when it does develop such a project, I regard it as an avant-garde, too.)

Experimentalism underwent significant expansion in the late 1960s, when composers, improvisers, and rockers came to share several aesthetic concerns—chief among them sound and spontaneity. Journalists and artists held in common the notion that these musical lineages were coming together in some broad manner, even if there persisted disagreements among them. I will occasionally refer to writers in the United States and Europe, but the British conversation about these musics will take center stage. And because popular music has garnered the smallest amount of scholarly discussion in relation to experimentalism, I will spend some extra time with rock, specifically the British reception of German rock.[5] This music instigated a specific formation of the experimental strongly linked to rock's technological apparatus, its loose collectivism, and its spontaneity. It efficaciously disentangled a rock-based, electrified, collective improvisation from the practice's then-recent history in blues jams and guitar solos, an aesthetic transformation that couldn't but draw on and solidify historical associations of avant-gardism as a white European/European American endeavor. I will conclude these introductory observations by zooming out from musical performance to consider how improvisation functioned at multiple scales in the life of Henry Cow, as a general stance or mode of relating certainty to uncertainty. Die-hard fans of the band might find the most satisfaction by jumping directly to the narrative history that begins in chapter 1.

Clive Bell, an early friend of Henry Cow in Cambridge who would develop into a gifted improviser in his own right, recalls the presentation of a new work for piano by Roger Smalley, the composer-in-residence at King's College, Cambridge, during their time there in the late 1960s. It began with the composer drawing complex mathematical diagrams on a blackboard for several minutes. "And then he went over to the piano and played this completely wild piece that might as well have been totally improvised, as far as I was concerned," Bell recalls. "I just thought it was kind of hilarious, that all these diagrams led to this flailing, Cecil Taylor freak-out." Bell's experience represents an increasingly common one for listeners of his generation, especially those rooted in the recording-intensive traditions of African American music such as jazz and rock 'n' roll. His ears moved transversally across relatively distinct historical networks by identifying shared musical properties such as intensity, gesture, and timbre, in spite of whatever formalisms might operate in the work of Smalley or Taylor. At the level of individual listening, Bell could draw musical connections that existed far more problematically in social space; the differences between a Taylor and a Smalley were forged and reforged by educational institutions, economic support networks, critical establishments, and performance contexts.

As for Henry Cow, no amount of stylistic adventure could unseat them from their home genre formation. They may have engaged in open improvisation, but, as the critic Richard Williams noted at the time, "they only have the monopoly on it insofar as they're a rock 'n' roll band."[6] But what drew this popular-music act together with colleagues such as Smalley, Souster, and the Art Ensemble into the space of "compatible but not the same"? Many things, but I would like to begin by taking note of the cohesion of a popular music aesthetics and intellectual vernacular, first with bebop in the early 1940s and then, more quickly, with rock in the 1960s.[7] These discourses established new frameworks of judgment for musics entwined in the commercial marketplace, distinct from numerical popularity and long-standing taste formations perpetuated through the educational institutions of the ruling classes.

Popular music aesthetics did much more than invert or blur the line between high and low culture. Instead, it provided the grounds for a thorough fracturing of those two positions into a new, intricate system of orders and relations. In rock alone, artists could stake their status claims on the poetic and moral gravitas of folk (Bob Dylan), the virtuosity of jazz soloing (Cream), the ambitions of Western classical music (Emerson, Lake, and Palmer), the political stridency of free jazz (MC5), or the shock tactics of the avant-garde (Velvet Underground). In other words, many different high positions opened up in the rock field within a few short years (all buttressed by the privileges of white masculinity, as the above list makes clear). The one that occupies me here nudged rock tropes toward a kind of expanded experimentalism that was gathered around spontaneity and held in common with art-music and free-jazz networks.

Divisions played out among critics, too. The first wave of highbrow commentary on bands such as the Beatles struggled to place them in relation to the legitimated, timeless works of the Western art music canon. Tony Palmer, for example, wrote, "Pop music, if it is ever to achieve any respect at all, has to be made to stand on its own feet alongside such as Schubert and Beethoven."[8] But even by the time Palmer published this condescending caution in 1970, younger critics were comparing new rock laterally to the work of John Cage, Cecil Taylor, Karlheinz Stockhausen, and Morton Feldman. For example, Ian MacDonald's comments about the tape experiments of one band, Faust, indicate this transverse perspective as well as a certain exasperation with the superseded judgment of the older generation of critics, such as Palmer or the *Times'* William Mann. He wrote, "The fact that hardly anyone in the world has found a theory and an integrated role in music for electronically-produced or altered sound except this German rock group is much more of a cultural vindication for our music than William Mann's acceptance of *Sergeant Pepper*—because here rock has outstripped mainstream music, not imitated or genuflected to it, as Tony Palmer believes it should."[9]

These feral high musics grew wild, feeding on LP records and reproducing by the same means. Accordingly, any account of advanced music making after World War II has to leave what Richard Taruskin would call the "literate tradition."[10] In Chris Cutler's schematic history of musical memory systems, recording passed through an initial stage of commercial exploitation by the capitalist entertainment industries before its specific aesthetic and social possibilities were explored by later artists. These musicians—a stylistically diverse wave that would stretch from the Ronettes to Merzbow, rooted in practice-based and phonographic aesthetics—would probe different qualities of working-class, immigrant, and rural musics waxed in the first decades of the century: an expressive egalitarianism, collective compositional process, and precise timbral and rhythmic variation.

With recordings, these exchanges could take place through the ear, upending many established structures of training and accreditation. Recalling his youthful audition of records by the Shadows, Cutler points out, "Every small thing they do is a huge thing if you don't know [music theory], so it was exactly geared to the perceptive level of people of my age and generation, who hadn't learned music, hadn't been taught to play an instrument, who weren't musicians." Masami Akita attempted to create "Merzbow music" for the first time after having his mind blown by Pierre Schaeffer and Pierre Henry's *Symphonie pour un homme seul* on the radio, and former underground rock musicians constitute the "the main forces" in contemporary Chinese sound art, according to sound studies scholar Jing Wang.[11] The examples are endless: Olivia Block, Kaffe Matthews, Otomo Yoshihide, David Grubbs, Ikue Mori, Chris Watson, Maria Chavez, Jessica Rylan, Kim Gordon, Christian Marclay, and many others came to the innovative forms of postwar experimentalism from popular musical practices thoroughly imbricated with the recorded form. In doing so, they extend the lateral and processual movements of what Georgina Born calls "the jazz assemblage,"[12] one of the many ways in which the social histories of Afro-diasporic folk and popular musics have suffused global sonic production in the postwar period. Moreover, the vinyl LP recording tends to encourage promiscuous listening practices in its standardization (for more on these practices, see the afterword), and the very abjection of popular music in its early history has also helped it to absorb materials and techniques from other traditions once alternative systems of evaluation began to emerge in the second half of the twentieth century.

The cross-fertilization of experimental musics surged in the second half of the 1960s, owing not only to the many flavors of cultural accreditation acquired by rock or the proliferation of new musics available on LP. These years also saw musicians in the post–John Cage and post–Ornette Coleman networks looking outward for kindred spirits, assimilable strategies, and unprecedented collaborations. "Any person in today's music scene knows that rock, classical, folk and jazz are all yesterday's titles," Coleman wrote in the liner notes to 1977's *Dancing in Your Head*. "I feel that the music world is getting closer to being a singular expression."[13] Although persistent (and novel) asymmetries in prestige and resources would continue to disenable that singular expression, the late 1960s moment differed substantially from earlier ones such as Third Stream, because the latter, as George E. Lewis explains, "failed to realize or support the complexity of black musical culture's independent development of a black experimentalism that, while in dialogue with white high culture, was . . . strongly insistent upon the inclusion of the black vernacular."[14] Furthermore, Lewis continues, the post-Coleman developments "challenged the centrality of pan-Europeanism" to the existing definition of experimentalism, advancing in its place a notion of experimental music that was becoming creolized. In the emergent British arrangement that set the terms for Henry Cow's activities in the mid-1970s, jazz-affiliated experimentalism was supplemented and twisted by one associated with rock; sharing roots in black vernacular music making, both contributed to the creolization named by Lewis.

Improvised Encounters that Meet in This Moment

All of these musics wended themselves into the contact zone of spontaneity, but each took a different route.[15] Cage may have disavowed improvisation well into the 1960s, but his performances with David Tudor exercised many parts of that faculty in all but name.[16] Once Tudor developed into a designer of electronic systems, he served as an important bridge figure to a new generation with fewer anxieties about calling their work improvisation.[17] And the generation of experimentalists who followed Coleman and John Coltrane abstracted the practice from its circumscribed function in soloing and comping into a general mode of constant interaction, combining it with new compositional techniques, experiments in form, instrumental invention, and electronic elaboration.[18] Meanwhile, by 1965 the British R&B groups improvised long, noisy explorations in concert and occasionally on record. Pink Floyd, Soft Machine, and other psychedelic bands would extend these breaks into longer and longer "freak-outs," a term originally popularized by Frank Zappa.[19]

If these three routes met in the contact zone of spontaneity, this convergence gave rise to some other characteristics that have endured. Their shared improvisational strategies tended to distribute authorship among all the participants in a performance—a relaxation that created more friction for the post-Cageans than it did for those emerging from jazz or rock, both of which had longer histories of shared authorship to draw on.[20] At the same time, paradoxically, sound grew increasingly linked to the body of its creator, who, bypassing the way station of the definitive score, would focus more directly on the empirical means of sound production and its preservation in recordings. One might formulate this change as the passage from a repertory-work model to a database model: musicians build up an ever-expanding individual database of instrumental techniques, technical setups, stylistic and aesthetic tendencies, standalone compositions, and highly personal approaches to improvisation, some or all of which might be drawn on and recombined in a given performance. Concerts are less often occasions to present experimental "works" than they are reports from an ongoing investigation.[21]

English-language music journalism—and British discourse in particular—refracted these sympathies and cross-fertilizations. One strong theme concerned performer freedom and self-expression in spontaneous musics. In the United States, Cage and his associates had been strict about limiting a performer's liberties, and Cage extended credit only to preapproved borrowers of his musical aesthetic, chief among them Tudor.[22] This apprehension was never as strongly expressed in the United Kingdom. Largely through Cornelius Cardew's proselytizing and interpretation, Cagean indeterminacy there was understood to offer a kind of emancipation; it was a tool, in the words of one critic, "to overcome the tame subservience of the modern performer."[23] Such language was very common in the British discourse about this music by the late 1960s. Michael Parsons wrote that Cage, Feldman, and Christian Wolff "have given up some measure of control" in order to "preserve and extend the performer's role."[24] But Cardew had gone one step further, he wrote: "He regards notation more as a stimulus to the players' imagination than a blueprint for exact sounds."[25] These "indeterminists," according to Victor Schonfield in 1967, "want composers to stop telling performers what to do, and start forcing them to be creative."[26] In a striking contrast to Cage, Cardew was equally committed to the emotional dimension of this creativity. He described his little opera, *Schooltime Compositions*, as "a matrix to draw out an interpreter's feelings about certain topics or materials."[27] He was, in short, "committed to a music which is going wild again."[28]

Cardew's preference for performer creativity created a specifically British elaboration of Cagean indeterminacy along the lines of improvisation. As early as 1962, Cardew wrote, "For performances of such pieces a high degree of awareness is required. . . . The ability to react spontaneously within situations that are familiar and yet always fresh in detail is a skill that has to be acquired."[29] Once Cardew joined the free improvisation group AMM in spring 1966, the emphasis on spontaneity became even stronger, and by the end of the decade the story was set: free improvisation was the "logical end" of indeterminate music. In a review of AMM's debut album, the *Times*' critic Stanley Sadie wrote, "Possibly the idea seems far-fetched, but it is a perfectly logical extension of the recognized and accepted processes of aleatory music."[30] Tim Souster, too, advanced a view of experimental music history that ended up at free improvisation. For him, Cage's use of live electronics had led to many new groups "dedicated to the exploration of new sound worlds and holding to no preconceived notions of method or form." He continued, "In America almost every university now has a free improvisation group and in this country a growing field is led by the AMM."[31] For this British writer, then, Cage was a pioneer of live electronics and open exploration, not merely chance operations.

The author of a survey of "free music" in *Time Out* favored jazz in his appraisal of contemporary improvisation, but in a measure of how jumbled up the categories had become by 1972, he also noted that "Cage is probably the greatest influence on free music."[32] For this author, the American had become the progenitor not only of Cardew's Scratch Orchestra and AMM but also of the free improvisation of saxophonist Evan Parker, drummers John Stevens and Frank Perry, and vocalist Maggie Nicols. Given its importance in the jazz tradition, and its culmination there in the form of free jazz, it was no surprise that free music would develop among jazz players. But, the author pointed out, "straight" musicians were reaching the same conclusions: "We might as well just play, eliminating the composer," he reasoned.

When authoring a profile of the Music Improvisation Company (MIC) in 1970, Michael Walters encountered a similar interpretation of recent music history, particularly from the electronic musician Hugh Davies, who had been an assistant to Karlheinz Stockhausen in Cologne, and who improvised on electronic instruments of his own design. "Davies detects certain differences in working with the Music Improvisation Company from improvising in a contemporary classical background, but feels that they are not great, and that the group operates 'at a point where the two different backgrounds meet,'" Walters wrote.[33] Nonetheless, there were differences of opinion among the members of MIC: Parker and Muir still thought of what they did as part of the jazz tradition, while Bailey was adamant about the value of pursuing no tradition, no goals, and no expectations. The point is not about absolute agreement, but rather how this meeting of the worlds was posed as a shared problematic: it was now a question that needed to be addressed, though often with different responses. And the notion of convergence was not only regarded as a salutary development. The *Times'* Miles Kington, for example, agreed that "labels are no longer of any use," but that did not mean that he was bursting with affection for the Spontaneous Music Ensemble: "It does not matter that they no longer play jazz; what makes their music difficult to approach is that they offer the listener no alternative point of contact. What must seem wholly absorbing to them seems self-indulgent to the outsider."[34]

"The concept of improvisation has become highly distorted in recent years," wrote the critic Stanley Myers in 1968. "It doesn't mean memorising

Herr X's cadenza for a Mozart concerto. . . . Nor Herr Y permitting the performers to play the sections of Kontakt-Lens IX in any order they choose. Nor even Soul-Brother Z running through his best twenty-five choruses on the chords of 'Sweet Sue.' When Sonny Rollins was last in London, he opened his performance—there was no rehearsal—by telling the bassist to play something. Just like that. The player was in shock for a few moments, and then began what turned out to be a half-hour trio."[35] As this passage indicates, one of the "distortions" produced by improvisation was that formerly distinct traditions were now held in the same critical space, even if distinctions continued to be marked.

If this discourse on the protean qualities of improvisation tended to enroll mostly critics of jazz and "serious" music, other writers pulled the conversation toward an engagement with questions of high and low. As the US critic Alan Rich wrote in 1967, "For whatever reason the sociologists care to advance, there has been an interesting rapprochement taking place between the so-called popular and the so-called serious worlds, with results that are all around us."[36] The spur to Rich's speculation was Ornette Coleman, who had composed several chamber works in the early 1960s, likely in a bid to shed the restrictions imposed by the "jazz" label. Even with his prodigious talent for writing melodies, Coleman might not be the first name that comes to mind when one hears the word *pop*, and other writers engaged more directly with commercial popular musics in their accounts of "the gradual drawing together and overlapping of the various areas of contemporary musical activity," in the words of Russell Unwin.[37] Unwin noted the omnivorous appetites of new jazz and progressive rock in incorporating aspects of the other's work, as well as those of contemporary classical music. "One can't help observing how sophisticated the taste of the average rock audiences have become recently," he wrote, "and how open they are for the acceptance of new, varied ideas and fresh direction."[38] The audience to which he refers, presumably, would be the one that gave Musica Elettronica Viva the opportunity to work "as happily in pop contexts as concert-halls."[39] Indeed, by 1971, pop's tastes had grown elastic enough that *Melody Maker* could devote a long feature to Yoko Ono's ten-year retrospective show at the Everson Museum of Art in Syracuse, the only such coverage of an art event I've seen in that publication.[40] In 1976, Stockhausen explained to *Melody Maker*'s Steve Lake that he had chosen to release *Ceylon/Bird of Paradise* on the rock label Chrysalis because their young audience was more receptive to his "free" musics.[41]

In the jazz magazine *Down Beat*, Michael Zwerin considered the conundrum of Soft Machine, who were "not part of anybody's musical establishment": they were too rocky for jazz, not commercial enough for pop, and not legitimate enough for serious musicians. Yet, Zwerin wrote, "Soft Machine is unique and satisfying, an impressive synthesis of various elements from Karl-Heinz [*sic*] Stockhausen, John Cage, Ornette Coleman, Cecil Taylor, and rock itself."[42] In jazz criticism of the 1960s, the serious discourse—having to do with politics, civil rights, spirituality, and so on—accrued generally to post-Coltrane free jazz. It was notable, therefore, that radical white critics such as Frank Kofsky, Ralph Gleason, and John Sinclair turned their attention to rock around 1967, praising the improvisational prowess and compositional ambitions of Frank Zappa, Jefferson Airplane, the Grateful Dead, and the MC5. Important to this story is the difference between this moment, when rock gets pulled into comparisons with its contemporaries in classical music and cutting-edge jazz, and the one just a few years prior, when, as Bernard Gendron has shown, highbrow commentators discussed the Beatles and Bob Dylan but hardly viewed them as coequal participants in the latest historical developments.[43] And like the politically minded French critics analyzed by Eric Drott, these Anglophone commentators understood the transformations and convergences in genre space to reflect analogous transformations in social relations; therefore, a loosening of genre restriction could index the white desire for a transcendence of racial barriers.[44]

In the United Kingdom, the composer and critic Tim Souster outpaced all of his classical peers when it came to engaging with rock.[45] In 1969, he surveyed a scene that had piled up the pop DJ John Peel, Anton Webern, Roland Kirk, the Soft Machine, Luciano Berio, the Swingle Singers, and Richard Wagner, and asked, "To what extent is all this overlapping a superficial and passing mutual flirtation, and to what extent is it evidence of a profound convergence of the 'serious' and 'popular' branches of music?"[46] For Souster, the overlaps of the late 1960s differed profoundly from earlier efforts such as that "most miserable" example, Third Stream jazz. He credited "a general creative atmosphere in which numerous factors—electronics, the emphasis on performance and on sheer sound and the idea of music-making as a social activity—are common to 'pop' and 'serious' music." With close analyses of La Monte Young, Terry Riley, Cardew, the Soft Machine, the Who, and the Velvet Underground, Souster sketched out an emergent grouping of like-minded musics. His recommendation of "some records to try out" gives a good sense of this mixed category of adventurous music:

White Light/White Heat by the Velvet Underground, *In C* by Terry Riley, *The Marble Index* by Nico, *Variations IV* by John Cage, and a six-LP Deutsche Grammophone set, "The New Music," that featured works by Stockhausen, Earle Brown, Krzystof Penderecki, and Henri Pousseur.

Souster's list suggested that the convergence of various traditions might represent the beginning of a new advanced music rather than simply a telos in itself. He shared this sense of historicity with other writers, even though they didn't necessarily agree on what the new music might sound like.[47] For example, in a 1968 dispatch on AMM, their promoter, Victor Schonfield writes, "Perhaps a new music could result only if jazz and European music had both evolved to a point where they were committed to the same things—in which case the new language would surely exist without anyone trying to bring it about. The jazz musicians and European musicians who united as AMM evolved over two years ago to a point where they speak a common language, call it neither 'jazz' nor 'European music' but simply 'AMM music.'"[48] In a conversation with Schonfield in the underground newspaper *International Times*, Evan Parker voiced a similar confidence that his form of open, collective improvisation could serve as the next step in modern music history: "There has to be a music that is post-Cage, and of course I'm committed to the idea that group improvisation will be that music. This involves to some extent a reappraisal of Cage's idea that sounds are just sounds. Instead we act in a system of sound relationships which we have selected . . . for qualities which transcend the sum of the parts, the individual sound components."[49]

Indeed, as Parker told a meeting of the Society for the Promotion of New Music in 1973, his "music in the future" would be made by groups of musicians who choose to improvise with each other. "If anyone in the production of a music event is dispensable, it is the score-maker or 'composer' as he is often called."[50] For the younger improvisers associated with *Musics* magazine (founded in 1975), any music of the future had to replace the subject position of the composer with something more egalitarian (a few authors in the early issues of *Musics* specifically mentioned the issue of royalties). As Branden Joseph has persuasively argued, this understanding of real-time sonic collaboration was shared by a whole generation of artists working with Cage's reformulation of the avant-garde around practices of listening.[51]

From his perspective in jazz and rock, critic Richard Williams was much more interested in the convergence of those two traditions, which he considered to be "the most cataclysmic" example of musical cross-pollination.[52] However, nothing had arisen by 1970 in fusion jazz to capture his respect, he explained. A transfusion of other energy was needed. "From where will it come? My guess is from the experimental modern music world of composers like Terry Riley and Karlheinz Stockhausen. This might sound terribly serious and straight, but I think that the advanced compositional techniques of these two and many others will be adapted to form a new music of the Seventies and Eighties."[53] He predicted that two qualities—sound and indeterminacy—would be explored thoroughly by future-oriented rock and jazz musicians. Elsewhere, Williams shared his list of "prophecies for the distant future of music": Nico's *Marble Index*, Riley's *In C*, and "practically everything played by Derek Bailey."[54]

If notated, work-based composition no longer defined the leading edge of music history, as these artists and critics proposed, then the unchallenged authority of Cage and Stockhausen to pronounce judgment on jazz or rock (usually after professing ignorance of the topic) wouldn't last.[55] In the early 1970s, various musicians and critics would turn the tables and issue their own evaluations of contemporary composition. For example, the noted jazz writer Max Harrison argued for the value of "slow yet natural growth" across the "stylistic barriers that once rigidly divided the musical terrain," rather than "enforced confrontations" that merely combine idioms.[56] He took the composer Roger Smalley's *Beat Music* (1971), commissioned by the BBC, to represent "the worst features" of pop and art music; the Spontaneous Music Ensemble, on the other hand, seemed to be forging a genuinely unprecedented path to the future, according to the critic. In conversation with Williams, John Cale compared the "stunning effect" that rock had had on modern classical musicians. "Those guys have got a lot to learn," he said, "and Stockhausen's electronic things didn't affect rock a bit."[57] In *Melody Maker*, Unwin wondered whether "the whole atmosphere of some [music] colleges seems to be fast becoming an anachronism," and worried over reports that the electronic music studio at one college has been threatened with closure by the authorities, who "have reason to believe that the studio attracts undesirables having subversive political views, long hair and weird clothes."[58]

All of this talk of comminglement shadowed the shared aesthetic practices of artists working in different networks and forging new ones. It also gestured toward efforts at the material reconfiguration of presentation and distribution, as promoters such as Schonfield (Music Now) arranged concerts and tours in the United Kingdom for a heterogeneous mix of experimental and improvised music practitioners.[59] And, as we will see, small-time operators like the young Henry Cow produced their own concerts and invited collaborators across London's mixed avant-garde to join them. The

Arts Council of Great Britain struggled to respond to the fusions I have discussed, despite the efforts of the arts administrators, grant applicants, and outside panelists to transform a state agency originally established to support notated composition and opera—slowly, imperfectly, and with great friction—into something that might recognize innovations in open improvisation and even rock.[60] New record labels (Obscure, Incus) and journals (*Microphone, Musics, Impetus, The Wire, ReR Quarterly, Audion, Rubberneck*) devoted to this emergent mixture would be established in the 1970s and 1980s.

Strange Tensions in German Rock

Yet the "interswamp" of academic and popular musics, as Robert Wyatt colorfully described it in 1975, always roiled with residual tensions—the admixture was never total, never free from historical patterns of inequality and other sorting protocols.[61] And that fertile ecology was itself historical, always in motion. The period of fervent cross-pollination that began in the second half of the 1960s partially closed about ten years later for a number of reasons, a few of which I have described elsewhere.[62] One lasting document of this period, Michael Nyman's *Experimental Music: Cage and Beyond* (1974), which joined Cage's *Silence* as an essential—indeed foundational—text for students of this music, neglected to include discussion of any jazz-affiliated British improvisers, despite their prominence on the London scene; that absence was registered by the improvisers at the time and in the years since. Two years later, *Melody Maker*'s survey of avant-garde "prophets, seers, and sages" offered up the kind of salmagundi that we've come to expect, but likewise found no place for post-Coleman improvisers.[63] The article's authors—rock critics Karl Dallas and Steve Lake—introduced traditional precursors such as Erik Satie, Charles Ives, Edgard Varèse, Pierre Schaeffer, and Arnold Schoenberg alongside newer figures such as Cage, Cardew, and György Ligeti, and such minimalists as La Monte Young, Terry Riley, Steve Reich, and Philip Glass. To this list, they added the Velvet Underground, Soft Machine, Gong, Mike Oldfield, Faust, and Can, but no improvisers; the closest they came was Henry Cow, "the world's only genuine experimental rock band," who are offered as exemplars of not improvisation but revolutionary ideals. In a few short years, we had come a long way from that pre-Nyman assertion in *Time Out* that Cage was "the greatest influence on free music."[64]

One might interpret this reterritorialization as evidence of "the degree to which even European free jazz musicians, with few or no African Americans around, still experience the reception of their art through the modalities of race," as Lewis has observed.[65] Like any avant-garde moment, this one repeats old patterns of race difference while creating subtly new ones, but its defining trope of convergence (and therefore, hybridity), not to mention its engagement with afro-diasporic vernacular styles, draws a double line under color. Even if the mixing of traditions in the British context was enabled or eased by the racial homogeneity of its white participants, a progressive, liberal discourse of race subtended the optimism and daring of the earlier, late-1960s visions of convergence. For example, Schonfield would comment in 1970, "I discovered there was room for a [concert presenting] society which would devote itself to contemporary music and which did not have an artistic colour bar."[66] His endeavors on behalf of Sun Ra and Ornette Coleman expressed not only a devotion to their music but also a commitment to place it alongside the work of the pan-European avant-garde, "who are comparable artistically but who've got white skins and letters after their names."[67]

In the light of this explicit race consciousness, the omissions of Nyman, Dallas, and Lake would seem to confirm a widely held, "perhaps unconscious, formulation of the avant-garde as necessarily not black," as Fred Moten has put it. At the same time, certainly by the 1970s, and definitely in music, it would grow increasingly difficult to deny Moten's alternative suggestion that "the avant-garde is a black thing."[68] So these were only partial closures, and journals like *Musics* and *Impetus* continued to feature free improvisation and jazz-affiliated innovators throughout the 1970s; *Impetus*, for example, routinely mixed in articles on Annette Peacock, Johnny Dyani, and Anthony Braxton with others on Henry Cow, Reich, Penderecki, and Klaus Schultz. In fact, the race politics of rock—those bands named in "Prophets, Seers and Sages," or Brian Eno, who remarked (also in 1976) that he thought "the borderline between rock and experimental is a very interesting one"—were overdetermined in the 1970s: it was regarded as a white genre even as its largely white practitioners continued to draw liberally on blues tropes.[69] (This contradiction gained special momentum with punk, another self-consciously "advanced" form of rock that staked its legitimacy claim, at least partially, on a supposed transcendence of its blues roots that has proven difficult to substantiate musically, as Evan Rapport has made clear.)[70] Although Eno might have deracinated rock by grafting it to indeterminacy and ambient music, his musical activities throughout the 1970s demonstrate an ongoing engagement with Afro-diasporic tropes at the low end of the mix.

This strange tension regarding the blues influence—and the extent to which a discourse of disavowal corresponded to formations of the experimental—courses through the British reception of the new rock coming from Germany after 1970. Following the initial burst of salmagundic energy in the late 1960s, British journalists turned with great enthusiasm to krautrock, as they called it. In surveying this very specific discourse of experimentalism, I wish to show how it represented for British (and some French) critics a historically advanced form of rock that was distinct from other contemporaneous, elevated formations such as jazz rock or the more bombastic progressive bands.[71] Seen by commentators as the natural successors to Wyatt-era Soft Machine, early Pink Floyd, the Velvet Underground, and Frank Zappa, the German bands helped to define a rock end of experimentalism for the 1970s along fine lines of distinction that would also apply to Henry Cow. Charles Shaar Murray's declaration about the Cow, "This is *not* the new jazz-rock," found its echo in Kenneth Ansell's distinguishing language on Tangerine Dream: "Their music is far removed from the likes of ELP's electronic histrionics, having a far greater empathy with Terry Riley's gentle format."[72] The assiduities of these critics and their colleagues testify not only to their discriminations of the ear but also to their desire to demarcate an enduring network of experimentalism that shared concerns across classical, jazz, and rock lineages.

"German rock seems to these ears to be the most accomplished in Europe in the experimental area," wrote *Melody Maker*'s Michael Watts in early 1972.[73] Indeed, critics and musicians frequently used this term, or *avant-garde*, to describe these bands.[74] Even the protestations of someone like Uwe Nettelbeck, the manager of Faust, nonetheless recirculated these terms in the popular press. "I want it to be popular music," he told an interviewer. "As far as terms are concerned I wouldn't like to have it in that bag with Stockhausen, Cage and all that, what you call experimental music. . . . Just because some things we are doing nobody else is doing, it puts us in a position to be avant-garde but that's just accidentally. I don't rate such terms very high. . . . I would rather like it to be considered as rock."[75] Regardless of Nettelbeck's comments, Faust was widely held to occupy a vanguard position, but critics identified comparable qualities in Can, Amon Düül II, Tangerine Dream, Xhol Caravan, Neu!, and Kraftwerk, among others. Their commentary animated all those themes associated with convergence I outlined earlier, namely, a transverse critical view of the contemporary music landscape, a progressive sense of historicity, sound itself (and, specifically, electronically mediated sound), distributed authorship, and, above all, improvisation.

Farther from the Mississippi Delta than that of any new style in rock history, krautrock's point of origin elicited much discussion of roots. "They are completely different from yours," Can's Irmin Schmidt told an Anglo interviewer. "They are not the direct relationship with pop music and US blues roots. I think they're a compound of classical, folk music and the eastern influence."[76] Several journalists concurred, in spite of ample musical evidence to the contrary.[77] John Peel's comments about Neu! encapsulate this contradiction: "Their music, which, as everyone observes with an air of punditry, is not based on the Anglo-American rhythm-'n'-blues foundation, is still undoubtedly rock music."[78] Exactly. Critics seemed to want to retain the informality and populism of rock while shedding the lower associations of black R&B, especially when more elevated comparisons to "European Classical and Romantic music" were in the offing.[79] Only the astute Richard Williams called it like he heard it; reviewing Can, "the most talented and consistent experimental rock group in Europe," he noted that their rhythm section "has obviously been watching what the best avant-garde R&B musicians are currently doing."[80] (Williams's is the only reference I've ever seen to "avant-garde R&B" in the British press.)

For the most part, British observers on krautrock compared it to those other experimental artists in the post-Cage, post-Coleman, and post-VU networks. They noted that members of various Northern European bands (Can, Guru Guru, Burnin' Red Ivanhoe [of Denmark]) had played previously with such jazz-associated ensembles as the Gunter Hampel Ensemble, the Manfred Schoof Quartet, the Irène Schweizer Trio, and John Tchicai's Cadential Nova Danica.[81] They compared Amon Düül II, Can, and Xhol Caravan to the "teutonic thumping" of the Velvet Underground or the extended forms of the Soft Machine.[82] Edgar Froese was described as "a failed heavy rock guitarist who saw the light after repeated exposure to the music of Ligeti and the Pink Floyd."[83] The first outside reference in Williams's early profile of Roxy Music—occasionally folded into the "experimental rock" grouping—was to "the heavier German bands," and is followed thereafter by mentions of John Cage and Morton Feldman.[84] Writers also invoked Terry Riley now and then.[85]

Perhaps the most common "influence" cited by musicians and journalists alike was Stockhausen.[86] Reviewers often noted that Schmidt and Holger

Czukay of Can were former students of the composer, who functioned as a benevolent, validating presence for many of the German bands. "In fact," Barry Miles wrote in 1975, "with most German groups, the influence of Stockhausen's Electronic Music Studio is enormous, lurking in the background in the way that Chuck Berry and Elvis do here."[87] Interviewing members of Amon Düül II, Watts found his comparisons with Stockhausen welcomed more than those with Pink Floyd. "We're trying to get back to the concepts of Beethoven, but on a popular level, of course," John Weinzierl told him.[88]

But not every group necessarily idolized the Cologne-based cosmic warrior; Tangerine Dream's Chris Franke, for example, weighed in on his colleague's work in 1975: "I have to say—electronic music before 1970 was really very primitive. There were just a few generators around and you had to do a million tape cuts to get a primitive musical result. People like Stockhausen and the French studio people did it and the music was really horrible!"[89] (He didn't care for US electronic music, either: "It's like a factory. You can get electronic music in pieces, buy it by the hour, by the day, but it all sounds really similar.") Karl Dallas opined that Tangerine Dream's use of the Mellotron made them "an uneasy hybrid between the two kinds of electronic music, the Parisian and the Kolnisch," but took Stockhausen to task for allowing "concrete sounds to intrude into an electronic passage, as with the voice which intones 'les jeux sont faites' during the fourth region of his otherwise brilliant 'Hymnen,'" because "it destroys the sublimity of what has gone below and reduces it to the banal."[90] (He even quotes Stockhausen in *Die Reihe*.) By 1973, Can's Schmidt lamented the emphasis that journalists had placed on Stockhausen, not because he upstaged the group, but because he had overestimated his own importance. "When one of those 'Darmstadt heroes' discovered some underrated composer from 50 years ago, they took it all so seriously. They thought they moved the world—but they didn't move anything," Schmidt told Williams.[91]

In addition to these judgments on other electronic music, the German musicians and their boosters cultivated a strong historical consciousness. Critics compared krautrock to other vanguard moments in rock history, like the British invasion and the US West Coast scene of 1967.[92] To some extent, these writers were following the lead of the artists, many of whom had a strong nationalist sense of their contribution to contemporary music. "The end of the English scene is the beginning of the German," remarked Weinzierl in 1970.[93] Indeed, the search for new beginnings offered one shared point of contact between the rock intelligentsia in its post-Beatles caesura and the young Germans who continually highlighted their comparative lack of roots. Beginning from zero, German rock could overthrow "all the crusty pillars of rock and contemporary music," according to one critic.[94] For the Rhinelandish dreamers, "starting fresh" was underscored ideologically by the rejection of what they saw as the compromised morality of the previous generation, so the frequent observations that West Germany had few recording studios, few gifted rock producers, and no real touring circuit seemed also to say something about their distance and disconnection from the Nazi past. "You see, you have a musical tradition in England as far as rock music goes," Weinzierl explained. "But in Germany there is not one because it's more political, and we, the young people, have finished with what our parents stood for. The pendulum . . . has now swung towards us, and we aren't concerned with the ideas of our parents."[95] In music, as in other arenas of public life, they were starting from zero.[96]

By 1972, Anglo critics were reaching a climax in their drumbeat for German rock, and Virgin Mailorder continued to supply the goods. There seemed to be a never-ending supply. Rolf-Ulrich Kaiser, the founder of Ohr Records and a prominent spokesperson for the scene, told one journalist, "There are thousands of groups over here, of which about 150 are under contract. Two hundred records will be released this year [1972] alone," a factoid that was picked up and retweeted (in a pre-Twitter kind of way) by the French critic Jean-Pierre Lentin in *Actuel* one month later.[97] By early 1974, Nick Kent could look back on these frothy days of yore with a tone of scorn: "Remember back in 1972 when it was the bees knees to get rapped up in dialectics about how the krauts really knew what was going on and how all those niticlistic [*sic*] electronic landscapes they were droning their way through interminably, were nothing more or less than the music of the future?" Well, in Kent's view, the future turned out to be boring, even if this perspective was apparently not widely shared. "Still, Virgin records has kept its Krautrock section intact in their catalogue while balding intellectuals like Ian MacDonald can be heard occasionally muttering earnestly about the undeveloped potential inherent in the contemporary German music culture."[98]

More potential inhered in Faust than any other band, if the critical consensus is to be believed. Steve Peacock averred that Faust were the first band to justify the interest in Eurorock.[99] "At present they are the most avant-garde group in Germany, if not the world," raved Lebrun.[100] "Faust are already unquestionably more advanced than any of their fellow-countrymen. They've mastered the nuances of electro-acoustic sound and employ this knowledge with audacity."[101] Indeed, critics were fascinated by krautrock's use of electronics, synthesizers, and tape work; according to Gerald O'Connell of *Let It Rock*, the "sole common thread running through German rock" was "a fascination for pure sound and its electronic manipulation in music."[102] Tangerine Dream, Can, and Kraftwerk were all noted for their electronics, and references to mechanicity peppered journalistic accounts. Nettelbeck told one journalist, "Basically, Faust is a machine, but everybody is sitting on the machine and trying to get freedom out of it."[103] Phillipe Paringaux declared that Faust's first album "could have been subtitled 'An Application of Technology to Rock'n'Roll.'"[104] Accounts of Can often detailed their creative process, which proceeded, somewhat in the *Bitches Brew* manner, by recording hours of improvisation and then cutting together all the good parts and adding some overdubs.[105] Like Faust, their writing process depended on possessing their own studio and keeping the tape running.[106]

Not surprisingly, critics dwelled on the musical practices of spontaneity in krautrock. The British writers understood free-form, extended improvisation to offer a kind of escape hatch from the limited vessel of rock aesthetics, toward a more open field of progressive exploration. "There is a Berlin group, Tangerine Dream, who carry on where Pink Floyd stop, i.e. minus the tunes," wrote a *Melody Maker* critic in 1971.[107] Artists like Cluster, Can, and Klaus Schultz eschewed the frameworks of blues, folk, jazz, or classical, according to another critic, in favor of simpler format, "a superstructure of open-ended improvisation."[108] For example, Michael Watts described Can's music as one "whose emphasis is strongly instrumental, but aleatory and free-form in a jazz sense."[109] The more adventurous groups, such as Cluster and Tangerine Dream, occasionally made do without a tonal center or rhythmic pulse. "It's safe to say that, within the Anglo-American sphere of influence, not even the Third-Ear Band has laid down three-quarters of an hour of music without key or regular pulse," wrote Ian MacDonald in *NME*. "In Germany such blatantly avant-garde proceedings are taken for granted by ordinary rock audiences."[110]

Furthermore, like the British free improvisers, many of these German artists and their English listeners prized improvisation for the potential it had to level the relations between musical collaborators by eliminating the composer figure. As Can's Schmidt told a critic in 1972, "Now the music is improvised collectively. There's nobody dominating, nobody writing."[111] This utopian political model possessed an added virtue: it could signal the remoteness of the German bands from the celebrity culture of Anglo-American pop in the economic domain. For example, Faust's plan "was to have a band which is not featuring anyone in particular but has a combined sort of sound, just like one instrument, playing in a very wide range of sounds and styles. . . . And we definitely won't have a stage act in which somebody is in the spotlight."[112] Such a description imbued anonymity with both aesthetic and political valences in relation to the culture industry, and led one critic to cite Germany as the only site "to have achieved any kind of rapprochement between the socialist principles of rock culture and its dependence upon a capitalist set-up which continually mocks and thwarts them."[113] It achieved this state by preserving amateurism (everybody is a star), ignoring virtuosity (no guitar heroes), and eschewing recognizable songs (songwriter implies leader). "Translated, this means a lot of simultaneous jamming on one chord," he summed up.[114]

If all of these characteristics—the discursive co-location of academic and popular traditions, a sense of historicity and vanguard status, the use of electronics to work directly on sound, the virtues of anonymity—attuned German rock to the other experimental networks that were converging in the late 1960s, it was improvisation that provided the strongest connection. In a rock context in the late 1960s, that term would have referred primarily to the extended guitar solos in groups such as the Jefferson Airplane, the Mothers of Invention, the Grateful Dead, and Cream. In contrast to this variant of jazz performance (demonstrating liveness, virtuosity, authenticity, self-expression, and fleet-footed formalism), krautrock built on the collective diffusion of psychedelic freak-outs to undercut assertions of individuality, and it used recording and editing to find new ways of organizing time outside of the framing structures of a song or a chord progression. Accordingly, their music had an almost spatial quality that arose in the absence of strong directionality. This quality, along with the use of electronic signal processing and a fine ear for timbre, marked out a specific trajectory through the contact zone of improvisation. Although I would not argue that Henry Cow emulated krautrock in particular (their network attachments to Faust are detailed in chapters to come), their open improvisations did trace a similar trajectory, often in combination with other routes through improvisation sampled from free jazz and indeterminacy. Yet rock was their home. "Oh come on, bass, drums, guitar, organ, riffs, solos—it's loud—we like to play loud y'know—turn 'em up to ten. Road managers. And besides we get written about in rock papers," replied one band member to the challenges of a journalist.[115]

Quests for Uncertainty

Popular music illuminated another, unique facet of postwar spontaneity worth dwelling on. Rock 'n' roll, R&B, and countless other popular musics have always imbued their performances with spontaneous shouts and the like. But I wish to follow Ian MacDonald, who—twenty years after his Faust fixation of 1973—pointed to a different kind of spontaneity: "Indeed, the format of modern pop—its fast turnover, high wastage-rate, and close link with fads and styles—is intrinsically instantaneous."[116] In his writing on the Beatles, MacDonald offered a nuanced understanding of momentariness, of the band's "casually voracious 'nowness.'"[117] He detects this sensibility in Lennon's refusal to learn how to play an instrument "properly" (so that he could move "straight to expressing himself"), or McCartney's displeasure when his demands for new studio innovations were delayed by the practicalities of rejiggering the necessary equipment. "Waiting killed the spontaneity they so prized, taking them back into the patient, postponed, *slow* world of their parents."[118] Outside of musical settings, the band's freshness owed to the lack of calculation they brought to their press appearances, even if this directness produced some of their worst foibles (Lennon on Jesus, McCartney on LSD). MacDonald writes, "The Beatles *felt* their way through life, acting or expressing first, thinking, if at all, later."[119]

By surrounding themselves with the ephemera of the daily press—magazines, newspapers, tabloids, TV and radio broadcasts in the background—the Beatles forced action from their environment. They chased a response, not thought. "Apart from the fact that it amused them to live like this—relishing the coincidences and clashes of high and low style that it entailed—they valued simultaneity for its random cross-references which suggested ideas that might otherwise not have occurred to them."[120] The Beatles did not simply integrate the now into their music but instead used it to find unanticipated possibilities and avenues toward the future; "now" was a site for unexpected encounter, a launching pad, a melting iceberg, a broken bridge to somewhere else, hopefully somewhere better.

MacDonald portrays this instant as the point at which one meets uncertainty—one *divines* uncertainty, one *fosters* uncertainty, one *values* and *investigates* it. One rushes into the future by means of it. The goal of this quest is never chaos itself but rather the oscillation between states of uncertainty and certainty, the conversion of *chronos* into *kairos*, or the expansion of the gap between a cause and its consequence. Nothing describes Henry Cow's arts of music and living better than this quest for uncertainty.

What's next? That was the question. As Peter Blegvad, a short-term member of Henry Cow we will meet in the pages to come, wrote in his notebook at the time, "In action you escape [the] limiting sense of limitations."[121] A committed 'pataphysician, Blegvad prized the science of the singular, the exceptional, the particular rather than that of the general.[122] Likewise, his bandmates persistently endorsed the role of practice, risk, and experiment in the development of theory and the continuous determination of limits. Their intelligence manifested as thinking in and through action, in this moment and in this spot.

According to Andrew Pickering, this kind of intelligence can be readily found in the history of British cybernetics, which was above all concerned with how the brain exists as an active, performative entity, rather than a calculating, "thinking" one. Or, it is actually more complicated than that; for Pickering, the cyberneticians were interested in thinking *as action*. He quotes some jottings of the important brain scientist Ross Ashby, who pursued the idea of adaptability across several fields:

> [When] one is uncomfortable [there] is nothing other than to get restless. (3) Do not suffer in silence: start knocking the env[ironmen]t about, & watch what happens to the discomfort. (4) This is nothing other than 'experimenting': *forcing* the environment to reveal itself. (5) Only by starting a war can one force the revelation of which are friends & which are foes. (6) Such a machine does *not* solve it problems by thinking, just the opposite: it solves them by forcing action. . . . So, in war, does one patrol to force the enemy to reveal himself and his characteristics.[123]

Adaptation, the bringing into alignment of the interior state of the mind with the exterior state of the environment, is one way for thinking about improvisation.[124] As Ashby makes clear in this excerpt from his personal journal, it is a strategy to create disequilibrium in a system so that one might learn something new about the environment, and then turn that new piece of information into a tool for creating a new state of equilibrium. And in this experiment, the outcome is unknown, because any exceedingly complex system—the brain, the weather, a rock band—seems to enact an emergent kind of ontology, one that comes into being with unforeseeable causes and untraceable effects.[125]

Especially during their early years, Henry Cow knocked its environment about to see what would happen. I am thinking, for example, about the Cabaret Voltaire (1972) and Explorer's Club (1973) concert series, two theaters of experimental collaboration. In the case of the latter, they made contact with musicians in the free improvisation scene because they thought they had something to say in that world, but the only way to discover what it actually was was to force that environment to reveal itself. A group of skilled improvisers builds up trust in its ability to handle whatever is revealed—not just handle but enjoy, improve, prolong, or delight in the threshold instant between states of stability and instability. Not blind chance, but good fortune. Likewise, Henry Cow's reinvention of their setlist on a nightly basis surfaced a commitment to disturb any equilibrium they may have achieved in favor of these threshold moments; the disruption not only made things fresh but also allowed them to think with their ears, lungs, hands, and feet. Keeping certain important elements of a performance underspecified—how to get from "Ottawa Song" to "Ruins," or how to begin the concert at all—provided a highly charged theater for observing and encouraging new musical formations that could not have been predicted. The improviser creates these kinds of situations so that she forces action before thought, or action *as* thought.

This kind of creativity was best expressed on stage in the course of an open improvisation. It is a commonplace in conversations about improvisation to remark on how the performers attune themselves to the acoustic profile of the space that holds them. All musicians, if they are any good, adapt their playing to the immediate environment. It is implied, though, that improvisers do this particularly well, but what does this mean in practice? I think the improvising rock band provides a good field for investigating this question, because the small exchanges between musician and environment are amplified, literally. One could say that when Henry Cow improvised acoustically, what we hear is the sonic evidence of an encounter between two exceedingly complex systems: a rock band and the world around them. By "exceedingly complex," I refer to cybernetician Stafford Beers's term for a system whose inner dynamics are unpredictable and generative; an exceedingly complex system organizes itself in ways that are beyond our powers of total comprehension, but we can still interact with it. And it's not only unpredictable but also creative: new things happen.

Calibrating the encounter between a rock band and the world is the PA system that sits between them, and that is why the role of sound engineer was so important to the collective and why disagreements about live sound carried such weight. The subtleties of this job create an inscrutable balancing act in performance. Certain frequencies in a given space will become nodes for screeching feedback, but some of these frequencies (different in every hall) will also be essential to the tone quality of, say, Dagmar Krause's voice. Bringing down the level of the voice to prevent feedback, however, now means that the guitar and drums are too loud, so the engineer must attenuate those instruments in the mains, but this adjustment brings about another consequence: the guitar is now too loud on stage—without the extra oomph in the loudspeakers, Krause is having a hard time hearing herself with Frith's guitar amplifier blaring behind her. In some photos from 1977, Krause holds and sings into two microphones at once—this strange setup may have been an improvised solution to a similar kind of problem.

These interconnected actions and responses are the visual and audible evidence of a constantly fluctuating exchange of effects across different human and technological participants. That's life. The improviser, I would think, distinguishes herself with a heightened awareness of these exchanges and a motivation to highlight, counter, or prolong some of them to hear where they might lead. A certain action risks intended and unintended consequences, and then one responds to this new arrangement of sound in an open-ended negotiation. Engineer Neil Sandford, for example, recalls that Cutler would circle one drumstick high above his head whenever he sensed that the amplification was becoming dangerously unstable and liable to feed back. If everything was going according to plan, Sandford would notice this signal and drop the main level (or perhaps just the troublemakers that had been identified earlier in the soundcheck). If he didn't notice it, or even if he did, but his response came a bit too late, then the musicians would have to make their own adjustments, which involves a bit of improvisation even if they're playing a thoroughly composed piece.

The improvisational sensibility marked more than Henry Cow's live performances—they also approached the studio scenario as another local problem to be solved creatively. What could they do here, in this situation and with these resources, that they couldn't do elsewhere? Particularly in the case of their first album, recorded when the band was still green, such an approach to on-the-spot creativity took courage. And although the recording process for their follow-up, *Unrest,* at least partially owed to the lack of time they had to write new material, it was also a measure of confidence in their ability to enter a new environment, knock it about, and reveal possibilities for elaboration.

A related point that I want to make concerns the isomorphism of this improvisational logic—the same kind of process gets reproduced at different scalar levels of organization. When John Greaves lightly drops a billiard ball from his left hand onto the strings of his bass near its pickups, he does so without full knowledge of how the resulting sound will play out, but his foot is poised on a volume pedal and his right hand grips the tone knob to modulate the sonic response when it comes. Likewise, when Greaves and his bass participate in a group improvisation with the rest of Henry Cow, they sound out their collaborators and explore the possibilities in what comes back. Henry Cow, in turn, improvises with an ear for how their sounds sit acoustically in the room and how their amplifiers and loudspeakers are affecting what they do—they interact with both of these exceedingly complex systems, but they do so from a position of unknowability: feedback, audibility onstage, crowd noise, and the adjustments of their sound engineer can be predicted only within certain limits during the course of the performance.

But the gig itself—let's say it was in Genoa—came about through the same type of process. While the band is parked in Rome for a few weeks in 1975, Cooper might be out in a cafe when a friend introduces her to an organizer for Partito Radicale, who are putting on a festival in Piacenza in four days. The pay isn't great, but there is the possibility of a few more gigs in the days after, and they need to be in Verona later in the week, so at least it would be on the way. She brings this news back to the band, who each sound out their own contacts in the city to determine whether this is a good idea. They decide to take the opportunity, but they don't really know what awaits them, what time they'll play, or who is actually paying them. Uncertainty is a persistent quality of the band's affairs, but they balance it with their own abilities to adapt to whatever situation will present itself.

I sense this improvisational attitude at key moments of Henry Cow's history. The 1974 merger with Slapp Happy, for example, was not a likely course of events, but Krause's description of the ill-fated project—"not undoable, . . . a tryout"—indicates how willing the musicians were to experiment. Several such moments in the band's career should be interpreted in these improvisational terms: Henry Cow embraced opportunities to disturb equilibrium so that they could find new states of temporary stability that could not have been predicted in advance. In each of these specific situations—a musician and his instrument, a musician and other musicians, a band and their sound system, an organization and its planning—we see the same kind of improvisational approach. We can even find this approach at the institutional level with Virgin Records, at least until their housecleaning in 1976: what more was Simon Draper's decision to "suspend disbelief" in signing Henry Cow than a commitment to explore an unknown future, to find and foster emerging orders that exceed the ones in view?

This is a book about open improvisation, but enthusiasts of that style might not entirely recognize or endorse the way that I am approaching it.

(I will use the term *open improvisation* to refer to the musical practice of improvisation without a plan or necessary telos. I want to find a path out of the aporias of "freedom" and "structure" that shadow so many conversations about *free improvisation*. For the most part, I'll use this latter term as a narrower genre marker referring to John Stevens, Derek Bailey, and their European confreres.) In this study, I am highlighting an orientation toward the world that could be described as improvisational; this orientation is not only one about saxophonists, guitarists, and percussionists creating spur-of-the-moment musical works. It is also about seeking out surprising encounters, or beginning from a state of unknowability, or looking out at the world and seeing an array of possible human and nonhuman collaborators. Open improvisation, as I trace it through the worlds of Henry Cow, appears as a kind of concerted movement toward a future that remains underspecified, and thus uncertain.

The political valences of this quest for uncertainty were clear enough: for Henry Cow, the world was a problem, not a given.[126] No matter how perdurable a set of musical, technical, economic, historical, or social arrangements might have appeared, band members habituated themselves to the task of tumbling such certainties into uncertainty—imperfectly but relentlessly. If those habits exacted a toll, the bill for a certain ugliness, it was taken from the collective as a whole. Indeed, perhaps the most pronounced problem that they investigated was collectivism itself, and how one might practice it. That experiment, we will see, proceeded through many trials in the areas of authorship, decision making, labor, language, gender, and commerce. Reopened and rendered as a problem, rock collectivism yielded new possibilities for the distribution of creative labor, not only in open improvisational contexts but also in the composition of notated music and the collaborative authorship made possible by the recording apparatus.

"The most useful description of the inner life of a group," wrote Tim Hodgkinson soon after the dissolution of his own, "is orientated towards showing that its music is every bit a product of work—with all the implied complications of working intensely over a period of time with the same people—and not a product of some mystery or sentiment. . . . On the other hand, a description limited to the work-process itself would leave out the fact that being & working in a group with other people is an art in itself."[127] Pragmatic and unsentimental, the Marxists in Henry Cow concentrated their powers of analysis on artistic labor to a far greater extent than they did on the arts of living. However, their rock collectivism performed a living inversion of its laboring quests for uncertainty in the trials of the road:

collective decision making, autonomous organization, and the cruel co-habitations of touring. Accordingly, I have included in these pages some discussion of those travails, occasionally to the chagrin but always with the permission and cooperation of my interlocutors.

When I began this project, I assumed that "private" or "personal" matters would impinge on my narrative of the band's public actions; initially informed by my reading in actor-network theory but generically true of all proper research, this position declines to designate distinct scenarios of analysis in advance, allowing surprising and heterogeneous ecologies to emerge in their specificity—less "liminal" than "not what I expected." That is how one approaches the granularity of living: a rock band hosts as many affective exchanges as it does musical ones; occasionally, they coincide. Now, however, I understand that any endeavor pressing on the line between art and life risks its own dissolution in the negligence of either side of its dialectic. Therefore, as Hodgkinson surmised over thirty years ago, any critical description of an avant-garde "limited to the work-process itself" might succeed only by half measures. I will leave it to the reader to judge the success of the current study, but I would submit that, whatever its problems, half measures is not one of them.

1 You Can't Play This Music at Cambridge | 1968–73

The first time that Tim Hodgkinson and Fred Frith performed together, in the winter of 1968, Henry Cow did not yet exist. Hodgkinson's friend, Roger Bacon, had choreographed a dance on the subject of the bombing of Hiroshima and asked the pair to provide musical accompaniment. They had met at the Cambridge Folk Club during the previous term, their first as students at Cambridge University. "Fred had been quick off the mark at Cambridge," Hodgkinson remembers. "I think he'd already had one band, so he knew that you could put a band together, and he thought, for some reason, 'I want a band with Tim in it.'" When they met with Bacon to discuss the project in his rooms at Cambridge, Frith might have mistaken the neck strap Hodgkinson was wearing as the mark of a serious saxophonist, when it signaled nothing more than the absentmindedness of a young hippy recently unleashed on the city.

The performance itself—entirely improvised to the movements of the dancers—was a revelation for both, because, in Frith's memory, "we stood up together and played really intense music coming out of nothing except one word [*Hiroshima*], without any experience of each other as players, and me playing an instrument [violin] that I had never used in that way before. . . . And it was really powerful. It was like coincidentally discovering improvisation." It wasn't quite a coincidence, as Frith would later learn, because Hodgkinson had been a devotee of free jazz for many years, bringing his knowledge of Ornette Coleman, John Coltrane, and Albert Ayler into the performance. Frith remarks, "My jazz education up to that point had been much more mainstream, ending with Miles. A little bit of Coltrane. But he introduced me to the more avant-garde stuff." Frith's decision to play violin rather than guitar signaled his own listening habits, which had led him, by chance, to Krzysztof Penderecki's *Threnody for the Victims of Hiroshima*, which the composer had scored for a large ensemble of strings using extended techniques. "I was buying contemporary music records randomly, because there would be these compilations of contemporary music series, put out by cut-price labels. . . . There would be a label with Cage, Berio, Maderna, something or other, and then there would be electronic music with Mimaroglu, and then there was one which had the Penderecki piece on it. . . . I was just curious, you know?" The dance lasted about twenty minutes, a span of time the musicians filled with scrapes, squeals, and squawks of great energy.

Aspects of this proto–Henry Cow performance will return many times in the text to come. First, it was entirely improvised. Second, it was collaborative and dialogical. Third, it was conditioned by the generative capacity of the LP form to make technically advanced music widely available for emulation. Fourth, it was conceived outside of accredited institutions of transmission, sparked by a meeting at a folk club and taking place in a student production without the legitimating support of teachers, a seminar, or a score. Of course, almost any student band—and Henry Cow was no different in its early years—held many of these qualities by dint of their low status and skill level: improvisation is a tactic for dealing with rough-edged musicianship, rock has always found its home in nonaccredited spaces, and pop and jazz musicians had long used recordings to extend their instrumental imaginations and model new possibilities. Yet for Henry Cow, along with many other groups we will encounter in this study, the aspirational nature of their LP emulations distinguished their sort of modeling from a more common sort directed at the mastery of an idiom (though they did plenty of that, too). One must mark the difference between listening to recordings in order to learn open-ended yet firmly established codes (like the electric blues) and doing so to reprogram those codes and unsettle the behaviors they normalize. Anthony Braxton would frame this difference as one between "traditionalism" and "restructuralism."[1] Moreover, as the members of Henry Cow cultivated their intellectual and musical capacities in the years to follow, they did not continue merely to improvise and to collaborate, but rather staged improvisation and collaboration as sites of investigation in themselves—that is, as problems to test, doubt, revise, proclaim, and resist. So the early performance of Hiroshima music offers an utterly mundane example of vernacular experimentation even as it secrets some kernels of an unfamiliar story that will grow increasingly specific and unusual.

Born in 1949, Hodgkinson was preceded by a sister (Ianthe) and brother (Peter). Both of his parents had grown up in large houses with full-time, live-in servants, but that wasn't quite the life that Hodgkinson would know. His father, a former naval officer, had begun a career as an educator after the war;

in 1955, he was named the headmaster of the Milton Abbey School, a private boys' school in Dorset, remaining in the post until retirement. The family took only occasional help with cleaning and childcare until the older children went to school, but the house grew grander when they were fully installed in the headmaster's quarters at Milton Abbey, which presented more occasions for formal dinners. A French governess who had been with some other branch of the family for many years joined the household and instructed Hodgkinson until he was eight years old, when he was packed off to Abberley Hall School in Worcestershire, followed by Winchester College at age thirteen. An acclaimed cornerstone of Britain's depraved private school culture, Winchester enjoyed a more intellectual reputation than Eton or Harrow, but, in Hodgkinson's memory, it still functioned like "a North Korean brainwashing system for producing upper-class imperial functionaries."

Hodgkinson began to develop a musical personality at college. His piano teacher at Abberley had been sufficiently creepy and uninspiring to motivate a change to the clarinet, which he continued to study at Winchester. Peter was a big jazz fan, particularly trad jazz. Hodgkinson was too young to participate fully in his brother's passion, but he did get to listen to his records and would continue to benefit from Peter's example when the latter became involved with *New Departures*, the important journal of the British beat poetry movement. But it was a record that Ianthe brought home on a break—John Coltrane's *Africa/Brass*—that really turned him around. That one, and a perplexing Charlie Parker album, had him realizing "that it might be possible to play like that, with absolutely no idea of how to get there, of course." His sister would also assist with two more highly consequential kindnesses. First, her friend met and accompanied the young Hodgkinson when he stepped off the train in London in search of a saxophone, which (post-Coltrane and -Parker) he had decided to add to his studies. Second, she took him to an AMM gig at London's Conway Hall, part of the Destruction in Art Symposium in September 1966. Otherwise, he was on his own finding LPs and learning about music. Coltrane was his North Star; eventually, he found a record shop in King's Cross that imported the Impulse! catalogue, and he ordered many albums knowing nothing of their contents—a good strategy, given the quality of the label's mid-1960s releases. He even put together a combo in the mold of the Coltrane quartet. Meanwhile, Hodgkinson's classmates were getting into R&B and the blues, but he was a bit slower to develop an interest in these genres, and by the time he finished at Winchester in 1966, he was just beginning to come to grips with the artier side of rock (Dylan, *Revolver*, soon Beefheart).

Figure 1.1 Tim Hodgkinson during the
earliest months of Henry Cow, c. 1968.
COURTESY OF TIM HODGKINSON.

At a place like Winchester College, one drifts toward Cambridge University incrementally but ineluctably. Hodgkinson's schoolmaster asked him what he wanted to study, and the vague ensuing conversation resulted in his admission to the course in "moral sciences." Although it would take over his life by the end of his time at university, music was not a big factor in the move to Cambridge; he hadn't even done a music A-level.

Before he matriculated, however, Hodgkinson took a gap year and toured India. His parents, nonconformist in their way, supported the decision. The father of one of his classmates was the dean of Windsor, prominent in the Anglican Church, and he arranged for Hodgkinson and some friends to deliver a Land Rover to a school in Pakistan, staying with missionaries along the way. They made their way to Peshawar, where they taught in a school for the spring term, after which time Hodgkinson traveled to Varanasi and Kathmandu. He returned to England via public transportation in the late summer, arriving in Cambridge in time for the autumn term.

By the time of the "Hiroshima" performance, Frith had been, as he puts it, "a guitar player who happened to be at school" for many years.[2] He came to Cambridge from Yorkshire, where the family had moved in 1953 (from London) so that Frith's father could take up the same kind of job as Hodgkinson's: headmaster of the Richmond School. Born in 1949, Frith was the middle of five siblings. By the late 1950s, the family had relocated to York, where Frith's father had taken another headmaster position, at Archbishop Holgate's Grammar School.

Born Jeremy Webster Frith, Fred had been nicknamed at school after the famous motorcycle racer Freddie Frith; the nickname stuck once he started performing under it. He had been a good student until about age nine or ten, when he passed the eleven-plus exam one year early. That good fortune put him into his father's grammar school, where his interest in academics plummeted and his interest in music soared. He had taken up the violin at age five, and wouldn't switch to the guitar until he was thirteen years old, when he was packed off to a private school, The Leys, in Cambridge, where his older brothers had both studied on scholarship; the chip had been placed on Fred's shoulder when he failed to win the same for music. In the memory of one of his classmates, Christopher Hitchens, The Leys School enjoyed a rather intellectual reputation, and its location lent it an esteem that other fancy schools lacked. Hitchens wrote, "English public schools have names like Radley and Repton and Charterhouse and Sherborne and Stowe . . . , and it was quite the done thing to debate the relative merits of these status-conscious destinations. 'Hah, Pugh is going to Sedbergh—moldy old prison.'

'Oh yes, well *you're* going to Sherborne, which is full of snobs.' When my turn came, I would portentously say: 'I'm going to Cambridge.' That shut them up. Cambridge these little bastards had heard of."[3] In that learned city, Frith, too, would come into his own, but not without the kind of self-doubt that would accompany any grammar school boy from Yorkshire now in the company of Huxleys and Keyneses.

Strong in science, The Leyes had a weak music program, but Frith sang in the choir and founded a band, the Chaperones, after seeing a Shadows imitator in concert. "I was completely entranced at once and decided immediately that I would have to start to learn guitar. I was so determined that I went out and got a book called *One Hundred Chords* and learned every single one so that I could get into a band too."[4] The Chaperones played your basic British pop until about 1964, when Frith discovered Alexis Korner and followed him into the blues. His hip girlfriend, Jean Stokes, steered him from Muddy Waters to Mississippi John Hurt and other more obscure artists. She also taught Frith how to play clawhammer guitar. He bought every US blues record he could find, transforming the Chaperones into a blues band by 1965. As his facility on the instrument grew, his listening took him to John Renbourn and Bert Jansch, and, like those two adventurous folk guitarists, Frith cultivated a stylistically diverse frame of reference. "Technically, I was a jack-of-all-trades, just copying everything immaculately, kind of making these soulless copies of all my heroes."[5]

At The Leys, Frith's marks indicated a certain lack of commitment, but his inspiring English teacher, Colin Wilcockson, worked closely with him in preparation for Cambridge University's entrance exam. Because he had been a year ahead in school, the guitarist had a long time to ready himself for the test, and his hard work paid off: he was offered a spot to read English at Christ's College, where his father and brother Christopher had both already studied.

Frith and Hodgkinson grew quickly during the 1967–68 school year. A gifted student, Hodgkinson was ensconced at Trinity College, one of the largest and most powerful in the university. Nonetheless, his course in moral sciences failed to stir him; he would switch to social anthropology in his second year. In the meantime, he practiced the saxophone and clarinet and involved himself in the radical theatre and performance scene. He met his future spouse, Caroline Ayerst, that autumn, when she knocked on his door collecting money for a political cause. Their political educations were intertwined for much of the next fifteen years, but began when they played lunatics in a Cambridge production of Peter Weiss's *Marat/Sade* directed

Figure 1.2 David Perry, Fred Frith, and Liza White in Cambridge, c. 1970.
PHOTOGRAPH BY GRAHAM RITCHIE.

by then-student Bruce Birchall. A socially committed teacher in training at nearby Homerton College, Ayerst soon spurned Hodgkinson, and he spent the next year without her, moving further to the left, dropping drugs, and attending meetings and demonstrations. (Following one meeting of the Angry Brigade, he thought, "Hmm, maybe this is not quite my cup of tea.")

He was among the Cambridge group who welcomed a delegation of *soixante-huitards* from Nanterre in the late spring of 1968; they took one look around the sleepy quadrangles and concluded, correctly, that nothing would happen there. But Hodgkinson was in the middle of a personal political transformation that would stick—an experience shared with countless others in the days of Paris, Saigon, Prague, and Chicago. He explains, "There'd been a moment of history where the world paused for a second, and it was possible, foolishly, to believe that anything was possible. . . . And then, suddenly, you realized that there was actually this huge fucking great big weight of stuff that was against you, that had violent force at its disposal." Among other things, that sudden realization also pertained to his own family—perhaps his father, running an upper-class private school, was functioning like a cog in the British class system. A distance opened up.

Eventually, this political consciousness would thread itself through almost every turn in the Henry Cow story, but Hodgkinson's first year or two saw an expansion of his musical horizons in a manner distinct from the political radicalization. He listened to a lot of records. And he shared them with Frith, who was swiftly establishing himself on the Cambridge music scene as a soloist at the Folk Club and an occasional member of student bands such as Blues Roar and The Nasty (the names say it all).[6] Together, the pair made their way through Frank Zappa, Beefheart, Pink Floyd, Vilayat Khan, Charles Mingus, John Coltrane, Messiaen, Luciano Berio, Béla Bartók, and Karlheinz Stockhausen. Frith's brother, Simon, was now enrolled in the sociology graduate program at UC Berkeley, and posted his brother LPs by West Coast groups like Jefferson Airplane and Country Joe and the Fish. Somebody at the Folk Club slipped the guitarist a copy of John Cage's *Silence*, and he soon began reconceptualizing his instrument as a sound-producing mechanism rather than a vehicle for straight self-expression.

In the spring of 1968, Frith and Hodgkinson performed now and then at the Folk Club, where the example of Renbourn, Jansch, Davy Graham, and other progressive folkies had established an open atmosphere.[7] Hardly purists, they played arrangements of Coltrane and generic "Indian" orientalia. By spring, they had enlisted four friends (mostly Cambridge students)— David Attwooll, drums; Andy Spooner, harmonica; Joss Graham, bass; and Rob Brooks, guitar—to form a blues band called Henry Cow. (The obvious reference is the US composer Henry Cowell [1897–1965], but there is no deeper story beyond that, despite Frith and Hodgkinson's occasional evasiveness on this question over the years.) As early setlists make clear (see figure 1.3), their repertoire consisted mostly of standard-issue, white-boy electric blues. But there were a few curveballs, including some classic blues (Bessie Smith's "Judge Judge"), country blues (Skip James's "Hard Time Killin' Floor"), and modern jazz (Hancock, Coltrane, and Adderley). And they also had a few originals; one that would stick for a while was "Amnesia," which was their catchall title for a bout of hypnotic solo improvisations over a pulsing drone. During gigs—they played a handful, mostly dances or parties between May 1968 and September or October—they got up to some

Figure 1.3 Henry Cow setlist, 1968. COURTESY OF FRED FRITH.

LIST.

1. Wee Wee Baby (Big Joe Turner)
2. Watermelon Man (Herbie Hancock, Jon Hendricks)
3. Henry Cow (Henry Cow)
4. Questionnaire (~~ ~~ Snooks Eaglin)
5. Evil (Howlin' Wolf)
6. Interludes
7. 900 miles (traditional)
8. Worksong (Cannonball Adderley)
9. Thing
10. Shake your moneymaker. (Elmore James)

---

1. Rock me baby (traditional)
2. When the lights go out (Willie Dixon)
3. Toys & real grey horses (Henry Cow)
4. Andy
5. Equinox (John Coltrane)
6. Judge judge (Bessie Smith)
7. Mama don't tear my clothes (traditional)
8. Rain Blues (~~ ~~ traditional)
9. 2 Bass hit (Henry Cow)
10. All night long (skip James)
11. It's my own fault (Otis Rush)
12. Hard time Killin' Floor (Skip James)
13. Amnesia (Henry Cow)

hijinks: maybe somebody would start shaving, or an alarm clock would suddenly blare out from a stool on stage.

At an early moment in the autumn term of 1968, Henry Cow played a show to an audience that included members of Pink Floyd and their friend, Andrew Powell. (Henry Cow had opened for Pink Floyd in a gig a few months before.) The previous May, when Henry Cow was just getting started, Powell had put together The Nasty—with himself on bass, Frith on guitar, and Attwooll on drums—to perform at the May Ball at King's College, where he was reading music. At the Henry Cow gig, Powell and the Pink Floyd members heckled the band without mercy, directing their attention toward Graham in particular (in Frith's memory, he had been playing out of tune). Powell heckled with a sense of purpose: he wanted to replace Graham on bass, and he would do just that in the days following the gig.

Powell had a decisive impact on the group. Within a few weeks, he had convinced Frith and Hodgkinson to expel the other members and begin writing more unusual music for the band. Born in 1949, Powell had been composing since age six or seven, eventually encouraged by an adventurous head of music, Noel Long, at the private school he attended in Wimbledon, where the music appreciation modules included world music and postwar composers such as Pierre Boulez; his orchestra performed works by Luigi Dallapiccola and Elisabeth Lutyens, and his piano teacher, Malcolm Troup, introduced him to Olivier Messiaen and the German/Austrian classics. As a composition student, he attended Harrison Birtwistle's Wardour Castle Summer School in 1965, where he heard Roger Smalley perform works by Messiaen, Cornelius Cardew, and Karlheinz Stockhausen.[8] Subsequently, he took a few lessons with Cardew and saw him perform with AMM; he also studied for a spell with David Bedford, a genre-skeptical composer with a passion for The Who.[9] Powell also attended the Darmstadt summer courses in 1967, where he took lessons with Earle Brown, György Ligeti, Henri Pousseur, and Stockhausen, whose *Mikrophonie I* and *Prozession* exposed Powell to some new currents in live electronic music.

As these biographical details indicate, Powell was a preternaturally informed first-year composition student at King's. In collaboration with his main partner in crime, Smalley, only six years older and by chance at King's as composer-in-residence for the 1967–68 academic year (he would remain for one more year as a research fellow), Powell created a few tiny uproars by presenting piano pieces by Tim Souster and a performance of Cardew's indeterminate work, *Octet '61*. "I'd already also done some of the Stockhausen *Klavierstücke*, which were complete mysteries to most of my fellow music students," he remembers. In other words, despite Powell's position as a music concentrator at the university, his most exciting musical engagements happened in spite of his staid tutors and classmates, and not with them. Smalley, too, criticized how students and professors studied music at Cambridge; he agitated for more exposure to non-European musics, and advocated replacing the mandatory exam on acoustics with one on electronics.[10]

By the end of his first year, Powell had already befriended Pink Floyd and Soft Machine. (They shared a contact in Earle Brown, who had met the Softs in Saint-Tropez while participating in Jean-Jacques Lebel's Festival Libre in 1967; he enjoyed them enough that he was rumored to be writing a piece for the band.[11]) A mercurial London hotshot who seemed to know everybody, Powell possessed a commanding musical authority. In Hodgkinson's memory, "He was a whiz-kid—a precocious, very clever young guy who had gotten around with a lot of contemporary music very fast. He had lots of stuff to impress us with. . . . He's absolutely crucial. You could say, maybe, we wouldn't be sitting here without him." Through Powell's record collection, Frith and Hodgkinson began to learn about contemporary composed music, live electronics, Cardew, Stockhausen, and Soft Machine.

What Powell didn't have was a feeling for jazz or the blues, and these styles began dropping out of the trio's repertory. Powell soon switched to drums, and he and Frith convinced Hodgkinson to buy a Farfisa Compact Duo organ in January 1969—in such a small configuration, they needed something that could play multiple lines and chords. Both Powell and Frith wrote for the trio (Hodgkinson was likely learning how to play an organ), and they played one or two Soft Machine covers. The original music has not survived, but all three members recall an emerging devotion to unusual and mixed time signatures—in any case, it was a change from their earlier blues predilection.

They had a busy spring in 1969, performing a handful of gigs in early March at the Corn Exchange, the King's discotheque, and a few other rooms in town, and then a second set of four concerts in June, at Homerton College, the Cambridge Midsummer Pop Festival, and May balls at Trinity and Peterhouse Colleges.[12] They also provided the music for a production of *Tom Paine*, written by Paul Foster in 1967 in close collaboration with the La Mama theatre troupe in New York.[13] Their director, Jonathan Chadwick, was a Cambridge classmate and Brecht enthusiast.

These performance opportunities for the Cow were sprinkled about a calendar packed with all kinds of exciting events, including a series of informal discussions on modern music hosted by Smalley. "He was very nonjudgmental about stuff," remembers Frith, who attended many of these

Figure 1.4 One of the earliest photos of Henry Cow: Fred Frith, Andrew Powell, and Tim Hodgkinson rehearse in the basement of King's College, Cambridge, c. 1968. COURTESY OF ANDREW POWELL.

discussions. "There wasn't any snobbery at all. And I was used to having huge snobbery from classical musicians, so it was very refreshing to have somebody who was just, you know, doing the work." In May, Hodgkinson, Frith, and Powell all attended Cardew's performance of Terry Riley's *In C* in Smalley's rooms at King's—the work had had its UK premiere in London the previous year. The Cows further supplemented their learning with concerts that spring by Davy Graham, Guy Warren, the Incredible String Band, B. B. King, and Champion Jack Dupree, for whom Frith played bass when he appeared at the city's Blues Club.[14] (Concurrently with Henry Cow's development into a trio, Frith had continued to perform solo at the Folk Club.) In early March, they all headed to Lady Mitchell Hall to hear an "International Avant-garde Concert Workshop" advertised under the name "Natural Music." It featured group improvisations from Yoko Ono, John Lennon, Willem Breuker, John Tchicai, Chris McGregor, John Stevens, Maggie Nicols, Barre Phillips, Johnny Dyani, Mongezi Feza, and several others.[15] As I noted in the introduction, concerts like this one represented a common impulse in the late 1960s; one observer wrote of the event: "Certainly it is true that there is an increasing readiness of artists in all fields to work in ways and combinations which are new and exciting—and, in music, wholly different from the effete chamber 'poetry and jazz' games coming out of the desperation of bourgeois art at the dead end it has built for itself."[16]

After the run of May balls, however, the trio began to grow unworkable. "I think we had got to a stage where Tim and Fred both wanted to do something slightly different than what I was wanting to do," Powell explains. While Powell grew increasingly fascinated by the possibilities of rock, his bandmates continued to dedicate themselves to open improvisation and compositional complexity. And Powell's prodigious talents also threw up some roadblocks for the budding composers; mainly a keyboardist and guitarist, he had gotten the hang of drums quickly. And yet, Frith recalls, "when he was with Henry Cow as a drummer, you knew he could do the music, but he never did the same thing twice. It became really untenable compositionally." They split that summer.

Powell moved directly on to Intermodulation, a live-electronic ensemble founded by Smalley and his friend, Tim Souster, who had recently replaced Smalley as composer-in-residence at King's. Born in 1943 (like Smalley), Souster read music at Oxford and studied briefly with Richard Rodney Bennett before joining the BBC's Third Programme, where he produced portrait concerts of figures like Morton Feldman, Luciano Berio, John Cage, and Karlheinz Stockhausen. In addition to his musical and administrative labors, Souster wrote criticism for the *Financial Times*, the *Observer*, and the *Listener*, the widely circulated BBC weekly. His publications after 1967 ranged freely across contemporary art music, electronics, improvisation, and rock. For Powell and the other Cows, Souster's catholic tastes provided a model of adventurous, analytical listening across genres. And his dash of iconoclasm—shared with Smalley—likely didn't hurt. "It's well known that people, as they become older, are less able to tolerate loud sounds," Smalley told an interviewer in autumn 1969. "I like loud sounds."[17] For his part, Souster contributed one of the earliest direct discussions of loudness as an emerging compositional element in the work of groups like Cream. "At their volume," Souster wrote, "harmony, melody and even rhythm become subordinated to a *sound* which build up into massive formal blocks reminiscent of the medieval *organa* of Léonin and Pérotin."[18] No doubt to Souster and Smalley's delight, Pete Townshend himself had lent and set up the PA for the first concert of the group that would become Intermodulation, giving them access to the kind of amplitude customarily restricted to rock musicians and fans.[19]

Armed with a £800 equipment loan from King's and a list of "inspirations" that included Stockhausen's intuitive music, Soft Machine, AMM,

Cage, Cardew, Riley, Cream, The Who, and Sonic Arts Union, Intermodulation began rehearsing in autumn 1969 and played their first concerts the following spring. They developed a repertoire around selections from Stockhausen's text pieces, *Aus den sieben Tagen,* plus works by Riley, Cardew, Cage, Frederic Rzewski, Christian Wolff, Souster, and Smalley, among others.[20] Their run of gigs in early 1970 culminated, on August 13, in a shared bill with Soft Machine for a Proms concert at the Royal Albert Hall.

Contracting back to their duo formation, Frith and Hodgkinson continued to see Powell in Intermodulation, attending the occasional rehearsal and a few concerts. Henry Cow's music never showed much influence from the amplified minimalism that featured in Intermodulation's repertoire, but the latter group surely offered Frith and Hodgkinson an important early example of live electro-acoustic free improvisation. "We were no longer looking at blues and free jazz, or jazz, as the basic improvisational model, but understanding that there were other models, and exploring them," Frith explains. For the next few years, however, Henry Cow kept their improvisations more firmly rooted in the recent African American practices of free-blowing coming out of New York; it would take Chris Cutler's fascination with raw electronic sound, as well as Frith's eventual mechanical and electronic modification of the guitar, to usher Henry Cow into a new improvisational soundworld. In the meantime, the pair continued to test themselves compositionally against the irregular meters and nonstrophic forms of Soft Machine, the contrapuntal entwinement of Beefheart, and the limits of their own musicianship. As Frith later explained, "It was at that time we formulated the approach whereby we started to write music that we couldn't play and used it to teach us to play instruments."[21]

The compositions they worked on—Frith's "Hieronymo's Mad Again" and Hodgkinson's "Poglith Drives a Vauxhall Viva"—show evidence of a certain stretching (they were both about ten minutes long). While "Hieronymo" has Frith trying out a fast, jazzy melody in unison and then establishing some patterns for two long solos (sax and guitar), the more single-minded "Poglith" refracts a simple motif through continually varying metrical expansions; its author had evidently been studying Henry Cowell's *New Musical Resources,* but the piece also bears a strong resemblance to sections of Soft Machine's "10:30 Returns to the Bedroom."[22]

Henry Cow may have performed again as a duo once or twice before they began searching for new members later in autumn 1969. Their posters advertised an "experimental rock ↔ jazz group," seeking a bassist, electrician, drummer, or trumpeter.[23] (The reference to an electrician wasn't entirely facetious: musical electronics were not yet available off the rack in Cambridge in 1969, and a certain amount of DIY was necessary.) According to Hodgkinson's notes, several people auditioned, but it was a second-year student, John Greaves, who would most impress the Cows with his musicianship. And, as Hodgkinson recorded in his notes from the sessions, Greaves had his "own gear." The latter remembers, "I think my Epiphone Rivioli bass was probably more famous than I was."

Frith's friend, David Perry, recalls Frith growing "very enthused about John, and saying, 'This is the guy.' We went round to John's rooms in Pembroke once, and he wasn't in, so Fred left him a note. And there was already a note on his desk from someone else, saying, 'Can you come to such and such gig?'" As this memory indicates, Greaves enjoyed a certain reputation as an experienced working musician, even though he had played only a couple of shows during his time in Cambridge and was still adjusting to the immense affluence of Cambridge after his first year. "You arrive there, coming from where I was coming from, and it's flagrant. It was just five hundred years of upper class privilege thrown right in your face. . . . You don't have to be a Marxist-Leninist—which I certainly wasn't—to feel the old chip on the shoulder." Although he soaked in the culture of the place through films, concerts, theatre, and poetry, he also devoted many hours to shrugging off that chip at the pub. "I didn't attend rehearsals with Henry Cow very often; I was into drinking a lot of the time," he told an interviewer a few years later.[24]

You Can't Play This Music at Cambridge: John Greaves

Greaves may have struck a glib tone about his Cambridge experience years later, but Perry remembers "a very quiet guy, very well behaved" and dedicated to his studies. This serious attitude toward the opportunities presented by a Cambridge education communicates much about the precarity of Greaves's achievement: he came from a family where nobody took university study itself—much less Cambridge—for granted. Greaves's ancestors came from in a village in the Black Country north of Birmingham toward Staffordshire. His parents settled in Wrexham, Wales, where John Sr. directed a dance band called "The Ray Irving Orchestra." In 1950, Greaves jokes, "I was conceived, and that sort of put an end to my father's career." Touring was out of the question, but Greaves's father did establish and maintain his career on the local level—he was the only professional

Figure 1.5 John Greaves, c. 1964. COURTESY OF JOHN GREAVES.

musician in a band otherwise composed of semipro lads who spent the majority of their days in the mines.

Greaves started piano lessons enthusiastically when he was seven or so, and made it through grade five or six despite an awful piano teacher whom he regarded with contempt. He ceased his "formal" training on the piano around the time that he passed his eleven-plus exam and headed to grammar school. Also around this time—1961 or 1962—his father bought him an electric bass guitar. After the bass player in his orchestra had passed away, John Sr. saw an opportunity to streamline the operation after years of hauling a double bass on the roof rack of his car. Greaves was in the band one week later. As one might imagine about a twelve-year-old bass player in a dance band from the north of Wales, Greaves possessed eclectic musical tastes: Mel Tormé, Frank Sinatra, and the Merseyside beat groups—

Liverpool was only forty miles away. His father had educated him in classic jazz, not only through records but also by taking him to the large halls in Liverpool and Birmingham, where they heard the big US bands.

The young Greaves gigged with the Ray Irving Orchestra three to five nights a week until he was eighteen, when he left for Cambridge. Alongside this commitment to his father's band, he started his own beat group called The Jades with a school chum; Greaves played bass and sang. John Sr. keenly supported The Jades; the dance halls had begun to book beat groups for the young people but were unsure about the staying power of the new music, and so they kept the older bands around just in case. Greaves retains memories of local dance halls booking his father's band to open for the Searchers or Gerry and the Pacemakers, down from Liverpool: "You'd have half the audience still dressed in their frocks, and then this other lot—still too young to tear the place up . . . —waiting for the beat group to come on. And there's us in the middle, my father's band, playing arrangements of this new pop music stuff!"

Greaves was not exactly an eager student in school (he showed up late a lot, owing to his other commitments as a musician), but he did well on exams and wanted desperately to escape Wrexham. His young uncle Norman, first in the family to attend university (in London), served as a role model in this regard. When a letter offering Greaves admission to read English literature at Cambridge's Pembroke College arrived in their postbox in 1968, his mother ran across the road waving it madly. He would be the same kind of student at university that he had been at school: a bit on the lazy side, not particularly passionate about literary criticism, but able to write an essay and perform adequately on tests. ("You can't play this music at Cambridge!" warned the father of a friend, aware of the class distinctions soon to come into play.)

The Jades had folded by the time Greaves moved east, but, like Hodgkinson and Frith, Greaves continued to expand his musical tastes across popular culture, coming to terms with Bob Dylan and witnessing the Incredible String Band perform in town. "That was another turning point, where I could appreciate music like that. A year before, I would have said, 'These people can't play music—they're all out of tune, out of time. That's not music!'" In his first year he grew out his hair and encountered the music of John Fahey and Pink Floyd. Soon, Frith was loaning him records by Zappa, Mingus, Stockhausen, and Berio.

Once Greaves committed fully to Henry Cow, the trio rehearsed with alacrity. He remembers "being dazzled by the time signatures," and excited to learn how to play them. And he took his first steps toward open improvisation, a totally new territory defined in part by new objects—a billiard ball, for example—and new modifications like volume pedals and a fuzz box. "A more open, free approach to the instrument, yes, is presumably what I was attempting to achieve. I don't remember it being traumatic, I don't remember it being easy, either. I guess I do remember being . . . thoroughly open and willing to experiment, and being encouraged by Fred and Tim to do so." Their lack of a drummer to mitigate the disarray of tricky meters forced the trio to strengthen their timing, their coordination, and their listening skills. It would be over a year before they found a fourth member.

From late 1969 until early 1971, according to their university friend and fellow musician, Clive Bell, the band presented their unusual, intimate, and complex chamber rock. "The group's reputation preceded them," Bell later wrote, "in the sense that they annoyed the hell out of several people I knew. It was rock music of a sort, but . . . they played sitting down. An exciting riff would appear, only to be dismissed after four bars in favour of a Webernian atonal melody in 13/8 time."[25] They retained some of the earlier hijinks, like the alarm clocks, but also acquired a habit of waving off the performance when somebody had messed up the timing. "They were quite fond of that," friend David Perry would recall. "I think that was a way of indicating that they were serious musicians, and they weren't just letting it all hang out." Many years later, Bell explained that "there was a lot of conservative rock opinion in Cambridge that felt utterly betrayed by a band like Henry Cow, who were just not playing rock 'properly.' . . . Meanwhile, the jazz people . . . had no time for them, either, because they weren't doing jazz 'properly,' either." These skeptical, almost moralistic, responses to somewhat unusual music would continue to arise during the course of Henry Cow's career.

Before Greaves had even joined the band, the Cows gained an intellectual reputation around town, "more interested in their own musical development than in party gigs."[26] By the autumn of 1970, despite the purists described by Bell, Henry Cow were noted in the local press as "really interesting" and generating "so many good reports."[27] They had played a handful of concerts, and continued to forge cross-media collaborations when they presented a ballet, "Trapezium," in late 1969 with the Cambridge Contemporary Dance Group, a local amateur company under the direction of Liebe Klug.[28] Scant details of this initial production survive, but about a year later, in the autumn of 1970, Henry Cow developed a new piece for the CCDG by Hodgkinson, "Dance Monster to My Soft Song," which consisted of "a tightly controlled overall structure containing two passages of improvisation."[29]

For most of 1970, the Cow played few or no concerts, owing to the demands of their studies. That summer, Frith married Liza White, whom he had met at the end of his first year, around the time of the first Henry Cow gigs. A self-described "lazy student" who had grown up in southwest London and attended St. Paul's School for Girls, White had chosen a teacher-training course at Homerton College after getting steered away from university by her uninspiring tutors. Her focus was art, but she also liked the Rolling Stones and often hung out at the Blues Club. Like Frith, she completed her schooling in 1970, and began her probationary teaching year at a school in Cambridge. The newlyweds moved into a house on Victoria Street that would become home to the Cows, their spouses, and many of their friends over the next two years.

By the end of 1970, Hodgkinson, Frith, and Greaves had established a solid musical rapport, created new works for dance, gained some critical notice, and committed to cohabitation. A new energy flowed into their circle with the arrival of two individuals who would take on significant roles in the years to follow. Sarah Baker Smith had lived in Cambridge since she was five years old; her double-barrel surname signaled some kind of inheritance situation in the past, not an elevated class position in the present. She did well on her eleven-plus exam and attended the Cambridge Grammar School for Girls until age sixteen, when she moved into a bedsit with a friend, studied for her A-levels in English and French, and pursued the delights of the late 1960s until deciding to drop out. In the late summer of 1970, she traveled to India with a boyfriend for three months, "got dumped in Delhi," and returned home with a clean slate. She met Greaves at a local pub in December and began hanging out in earnest with him and the other Cows at the Footlights, a Cambridge institution for comedic and theatrical performers. A few short months later, she moved into the Victoria Street house and wed Greaves in June 1971. She would begin mixing Henry Cow's live sound about a year later, in the meantime contributing her labor as a committed listener, occasional roadie, and supportive friend. "I was *absorbing* as much as anything else," she later recalled of her introduction to Soft Machine, Beefheart, and other new music in the company of the Cows.

Another new resident at Victoria Street would end up, by 1978, with more months on the Henry Cow payroll than anyone, save Hodgkinson, Frith, and Chris Cutler. One of three children, Jack Balchin was born in Guildford in 1948. Politically conservative, his parents took a light touch in childrearing; propelled by a hatred of book learning, Balchin gravitated to the local beatnik hangout, the Signet Cafe, where he got into drinking at a young age, formed an appreciation for folk music, and got pushed to join the Campaign for Nuclear Disarmament.

By age fifteen, he had left school; his father found him a job at a plastic coating factory. "Just working on the factory floor, you know, 'cause I really didn't know what I wanted to do—I just wanted to get out. That's all that was on my mind: get out." And he would—by fixing up an old junker and driving north to Edinburgh, the first stop in a multiyear, picaresque series of engagements that took him to several cities, through many short-term jobs, and eventually to carpentry work for a straight theatre in York, where the folk club served beer until midnight. Balchin was there, drinking, when he saw Frith, home on break from Cambridge, perform a set that swerved from traditional tunes to originals to "squeaky bonk shit, good and proper. . . . Hearing that was pretty exciting." The two spent the weekend playing music together at Frith's parents' house and vowed to stay in touch. A few months later, by the end of 1969, Balchin turned up in Cambridge.

"My social skills were not vast, and I didn't worry about shit like that," he later recalls of his initial contact with the Henry Cow trio. "And these people were just way out of my league, but they were just damn interesting. . . . Their wit, their speed—all that shit. Everything I wanted to be." Ducking and diving, Balchin avoided a straight job in Cambridge but began lending his skills as a tinkerer and fixit man to the band. He moved into a room in the Victoria Street house and immersed himself in the Cow's music. To Balchin, its balance of chaos and control resonated in powerful ways. "It was something that I kind of felt myself, you know? [There's] nothing like a bit of chaos, and understanding it. . . . It kept me out of trouble, could be one way of describing it. Because if I wasn't listening to that, I'd be out getting wrecked and smashing things up, probably."

In their memories of Balchin's contributions to Henry Cow, musicians and other crew members paint a portrait of a slightly wild but infinitely energetic hustler, completely devoted to the band and passionate about their shared project. His joie de vivre occasionally led him astray, but more often he worked, rock-solid, at the center of the action. Hodgkinson particularly valued the forward momentum he brought with him: "He was essential, and, in terms of his energy as a person . . . , he would listen to us having these arguments, and he'd stay out. But then whatever [was decided], he'd push and pull it through to the next stage." Balchin's checkered employment history had bestowed him with a certain wisdom of the bricoleur; he had gained skills in carpentry, electric and chemical engineering, engine repair, audio electronics, and stage management. Crucially important to what would become the Henry Cow ethos was his complete comfort in an improvisational state of making do, and he developed into a genius of frugality.

Balchin was around in late 1969 when the band started auditioning drummers, a process that seems to have begun before Greaves's arrival, and would remain ongoing until 1971. One visitor was Frank Perry, who arrived at a rehearsal with his father from nearby Milden sometime in 1969, set up a massive drum kit, and joined the band for some jamming and attempts at "Hieronymo" and "Poglith." Already making a name for himself in London's free improvisation community, Perry would soon relocate to that city to advance his aesthetic prospects.[30] The Cows, meanwhile, found a more permanent drummer in Sean Jenkins, a Birmingham-based musician whom Greaves knew from his professional contacts in that area. A bit of a "hotshot," according to Frith, Jenkins required a fee to play with the band. "We weren't friends or anything—we were hiring him, and he helped us to solidify even further. . . . He was a very good drummer—the first time we had a really good drummer."

Writing in early May 1971, critic James Cannon praised the Cow as "probably the best in Cambridge at the moment," noting that Jenkins brought "a new tightness to the group."[31] His participation also contributed to a growing dedication to promotion, as their earliest publicity materials date to Jenkins's time in the band (see figure 1.6). Sometime that spring, Greaves visited the BBC's headquarters in London, located the office of John Walters, the producer of John Peel's influential Top Gear program, and handed him a Henry Cow rehearsal tape. The disc jockey and his producer liked what they heard, and invited Henry Cow to the BBC's Maida Vale studio to record a session as winners of the "Rockatunity Knocks" competition for unsigned bands. "We were terrified," Greaves later reported of the May 4 recording date, but the Cows turned in respectable performances of their A material: "Hieronymo," "Poglith," and a more recent Greaves number, "Bloody Hair."[32] The latter, a bluesy slow jam reminiscent of Cream, dispensed with tricky time signatures but retained the extended chords and harmonic suspensions of a jazz sophisticate. Like Frith's "Hieronymo," "Bloody Hair" made room for improvised solos with repetitive grooves in the rhythm section; Greaves sang the verses and chorus.

By the time of the Peel session, it had already been decided that Jenkins would be moving on. Two weeks later, some of Frith's Cambridge music connections had led them to a jazzier young drummer named Martin Ditcham, who joined the Cow in time for their slate of summer gigs, including some local engagements, a couple of parties, and festivals in York, Nottingham,

HENRY COW

Henry Cow started as an unruly seven-piece blues band. In the three years since they were formed their playing has become carefully structured and often very complex; nevertheless they retain their early humour and excitement. Although such diverse influences as Messiaen, Barre Philips, Zappa and Chico Hamilton have made themselves felt, the striking characteristic of **Henry Cow's** music is its originality.

Fred Frith, 22, guitar and violin.
Tim Hodgkinson, 21, organ and alto sax.
John Greaves, 21, bass guitar.
Sean Jenkins, 20, drums.

Hieronimo Goes Mad Again, written by Fred Frith, consists of variations on a basic jazz-like theme. The time signature changes from bar to bar according to the sequence : 7/8, 6/8, 8/8, 5/8, 9/8, 4/8.

Poglith Drives A Vauxhall Viva, by Tim Hodgkinson, is an early piece written as an exploration into rhythm-patterns using a simple melody.

Dance Monster To My Soft Song was the first ballet to be written and performed by a rock-group in this country. It consists of a tightly controlled overall structure containing two passages of improvisation and was written by Tim Hodgkinson.

CAMBRIDGE 64263

Figure 1.6 Henry Cow promotional leaflet, 1971. COURTESY OF TIM HODGKINSON.

and Glastonbury. The Glastonbury Fair gig represented a certain pinnacle, since it was only the second installment of that festival and featured performances by David Bowie, Hawkwind, and Traffic; on the final day of the event, June 24, Henry Cow shared the bill with Gilberto Gil and Fairport Convention (among five other bands). After the last of these summer gigs (Sylvia Hallett's eighteenth birthday party, in Sussex), Ditcham accepted an offer to join Ian Carr's Nucleus, one of the United Kingdom's best-known jazz-fusion groups, and was gone after only about three months in the band.

On their way home from the Nottingham Festival gig that July, a friend of the band, Nicky Graves, made a cutting intervention in the course of Henry Cow's affairs. "Yeah, I remember that as being an important moment because the whole thing was a kind of let-down," Hodgkinson later recalled.

"The gig itself was a disaster, and then we talked . . . ," Frith said.

"Peel sort of built us up," Hodgkinson interrupted, "and then we did this gig and we knew it was really bad, and Nicky Graves was very sharply critical, and then we talked with her on the way home . . ."

"On the way home."

"... Suddenly a whole lot of things fell into place about having to work seriously on something and criticize it and develop."

"Yeah, she was actually very important at that time. The things that she was saying, that was the first time I'd been confronted with the idea that what I was doing could be serious, by somebody on the outside."

"Mmm-hmm."

"And she was extremely sharp."[33]

As it happened, Graves's censure would spur the Cows to dedicate themselves more seriously to their musical work together. In fact, they were already moving in this direction, as indicated by their new publicity materials and Greaves's active promotion of the group to Peel in the first place. Frith had spent the 1970–71 academic year not only earning a master's degree (in English literature) while working odd jobs and waiting for Hodgkinson and Greaves to finish their BAS, but also woodshedding on his instrument and developing the delicate two-handed tapping technique that would become a distinctive marker of his style by late 1973; a friend from Cambridge, Charles Fletcher, had built him a second pickup that he could attach to the headstock of his guitar, thereby amplifying the nut side of a resonating string. It would take Frith a few years of practice to make full use of this bit of technology, but he still uses it to this day. Hodgkinson, too, set himself to improving as a keyboardist, and asked a friend to build an effects unit, with distortion and ring modulation, that he would use for the rest of his time in Henry Cow. With the help and encouragement of Frith, Greaves augmented his instrument with volume and fuzz pedals. Another Cambridge friend, Rich Fry, custom built a twelve-channel mixer with Neve circuitry for the band at about this time, and Balchin—who had begun to handle live sound—oversaw the gradual assembly of a PA system. Hodgkinson and Frith both acquired an amplifier and cabinet from HH Electronics, a local firm that had recently gone into business and cut them a deal for advertising purposes. They hauled all this stuff in a longnose Bedford ambulance that Balchin had prized from an RAF scrapyard for £5. It still had a bell.

Let's Play Some Row: Chris Cutler

The final piece of serious arrived in the person of Chris Cutler, who began playing drums with Henry Cow soon after Ditcham's departure and would make his first public appearance with the band when they opened for the (post-Cale, post-Reed, post-Morrison) Velvet Underground in Cambridge on October 8, 1971. They found him through an unlikely classified advertisement that caught their eye: "DRUMMER: Varese/Wyatt, odd times and Counterpoint."[34] "Everything changes at that point," Frith says. A few years older than the rest of the group, Cutler displayed a formidable intellect and a commanding eloquence. Hodgkinson remembers Cutler kicking his drum set roughly into position for their first rehearsal and thinking, "Right, this guy's got attitude." Cutler's unusual style struck Balchin immediately; he recalls, "He was absolutely mind-blowing as a drummer. . . . And the way the band responded was really bizarre, because what are you supposed to do? You're auditioning a drummer, you expect a beat! No, not with Cutler." Indeed, Cutler brought an idiosyncratic drumming style that was almost conversational and rarely repetitive.

Cutler was born in 1947 in Washington, DC, where his father, Philip, a British intelligence analyst, had been seconded after the war. His mother had come from a wealthy Jewish family in Vienna, and when they returned to London a few years later, Philip took a job with TASS, the Russian news agency. By the time Cutler's younger brother, Peter, was born in 1953, the family had settled in Sutton, south London. Multiloquent and engaged, the household encouraged political activism and serious argumentation. Cutler joined the Young Communist League on his own initiative (even though it didn't last long), and marched with the Campaign for Nuclear Disarmament and against apartheid. With two well-educated parents (his mother had studied economics at the University of Vienna), he was expected to attend university and become a lawyer. He loathed grammar school, however, and completed his O-levels with gritted teeth before attending a local sixth form. He worked on his A-levels there but had by then—age sixteen or seventeen—already begun to play in rock bands, and, furthermore, had decided to become a writer. A gifted and dedicated autodidact, he gave university the slip and moved away from home with the support of his parents.

In the 1950s, Cutler had listened to Radio Luxemburg on a crystal radio set, tape recording his favorite songs. In grammar school, he acquired a trumpet from an older classmate, Geoff Leigh (who later joined him in Henry Cow), and also played the banjo in a skiffle band. By about 1960 or 1961, the Shadows instigated a mass exodus among Cutler's generation from skiffle to the electric guitar and beat music, and the young Suttoner would follow. "It was 'our music,' because we hadn't been taught and educated in it by anybody else. And they all hated it, which made it even better." In his first pop group, which concentrated on Shadows-style instrumentals, Cutler had made the permanent switch to drums.

Figure 1.7 Chris Cutler, 1973. PHOTOGRAPH BY BRIAN COOKE.

That group—which was called Kraal, then Pavlov's Dogs, and eventually Louise—changed rapidly with the times.[35] "I evolved with popular music," Cutler remarks. "So I evolved from the Shadows to the Beatles and R&B, and R&B evolves into psychedelia." With his bandmates, Cutler heard The Who, the Yardbirds, and some Merseybeat bands at Sutton's Wallington Public Hall; in concert, these R&B groups often stretched out into long, open, and noisy instrumental explorations that barely survive in recorded form but pushed impressionable listeners like Cutler into a variety of open improvisation that was native to rock—noisy, loud, electronic. They wedged these freak-outs between pop songs, which soon dwindled in number. In Louise, Cutler recalls, "the music got too weird and nobody invited us to play in dances anymore. And so we just rehearsed every week in the coop hall . . . and people started coming to our rehearsals." At about this time, they ventured up to London to hear an unrecorded band called Pink Floyd at the UFO Club, and were amazed by what they found. Stuck in Sutton, they had no clue that other musicians in the London underground scene were interested in similar experiments; once this world had opened up, the band and their friends explored further. "We were probably all completely in awe of Soft Machine at the time," recalls band associate Jane Colling, who designed Louise's band posters and costumes (and would later do the same for Henry Cow).

Louise continued until the spring of 1968, when its members began to drift apart. Cutler played in a few pick-up bands but remained basically unattached and searching for the right permanent group over a couple of years. In the course of his wanderings, he met many talented artists who wrote music but weren't members of a band.[36] After meeting one of these composers, Anthony Marshall, Cutler thought, "It's crazy—he's not in a band and nobody's playing his stuff. Why don't we put a Rock Composers Orchestra together like the Jazz Composers Orchestra? Everybody can compose for it, there'll be a pool of musicians who can play in it." With his friend, Dave Stewart of the band Egg, Cutler soon founded the Ottawa Music Company, a large ensemble of floating players that included former members of Louise, current members of Egg, and several other free agents (there were up to twenty-two players). They self-produced seven concerts from September 1971 until December 1972, though at least of two of these would be cobilled as Henry Cow events. After the first Ottawa concert, Frith, Hodgkinson, and Greaves had been pulled into the London orbit by their new drummer and participated in all subsequent OMC events. The large group broke up into different chamber configurations to present original music by many of its members. They did a few Henry Cow numbers, including an early version of Frith's "Teenbeat" and Greaves's "Would You Prefer Us to Lie?." And they performed new arrangements of songs by Robert Wyatt and Frank Zappa.

In the years after 1968, Cutler had added LPs of modern orchestral music and the recent avant-garde to his pop and psych listening habits. Yet after their first meeting, the other Cows waffled about Cutler. Hodgkinson recalls, "We all thought he spent a lot of time moving around over the drums, but not actually hitting them. . . . We all thought, 'Well, this is somebody interesting and original. We're not sure.'" Soon, however, it was Cutler who developed the cold feet. Although he was a huge fan of Sun Ra, he hadn't really cultivated a taste for jazz, and the long solo sections of "Hieronymo" and "Bloody Hair" did not grip him. (As Balchin would shout, "That's not improvisation. It's jamming!") Cutler was more interested in amplified open improvisation, which he called "row"—"Let's play some *row*," he would suggest. After a few sessions together, Cutler told the Cows that he had decided not to join them; he later wrote, "That set off a long discussion during which everybody's reservations, criticisms and aspirations were thoroughly wrung through."[37] Among those aspirations was Cutler's strong desire for a more pronounced pop tendency, in response to which Frith produced two songs he had been writing on the side, "Rapt in a Blanket" and "Came to See You." Cutler explains, "We began work on them at once—and the practical, collective, business of figuring

Figure 1.8 Henry Cow performing with the Ottawa Music Company, 1972.
PHOTOGRAPH BY KIM FYSON.

out how to put them together obliged us to take a different approach to the
band, the work, the material, and to one another."[38] This challenge—of collective creative process—persuaded Cutler to stick around.

A pensive and intimate song, "Rapt in a Blanket," with lyrics by Frith,
who also sang it, revealed his aptitude for writing unusual melodies that can
float over more complicated changes underneath. The opening tune begins
on the fifth scale degree, skips up an octave, and then settles back down in a
casual bit of syncopation that reinforces the metrical tensions underneath.
Greaves supplies many of these tensions in a delicate, syncopated counter-
melody played in natural harmonics. One might also note the polyrhythms
in the B section, which shifts the meter from 7/4 in the previous verse to
first 5/4 and then a deceptive 4/4 that counts better in groups of eight, divided in 5 + 3. In these sections (1:25 on the *Henry Cow Fortieth Anniversary
Box Set*, disc 1), Cutler establishes a duple back beat with a syncopated snare
hit after beat two in each eight-beat phrase, but keeps us guessing in the rest
of that unit by dissolving into long, loose fills that interact unpredictably
with the patterns in the guitars.[39] Hodgkinson contributes a gentle clarinet
solo that exploits the instrument's sylvan chalumeau register.

If "Rapt" offered a basic song form, "Came to See You" was more ambitious and quirkier, written by somebody who had spent more than a few

hours with the first two Soft Machine albums. I count nine distinct little sections that Frith has stuffed into the first 1:50 of the song, articulated by often-drastic changes in tempo, texture, or meter. He leads the band through these changes with his vocal line, which emulates Robert Wyatt's conversational delivery. The middle of the tune, like Frith's other pieces of the time, opens out into some jamming for the rhythm section while Hodgkinson solos (first on organ, then on alto). They jammed in 13/8, which they referred to as "fast 13s" or "slow 13s," depending on which side of a tempo change they had in mind.[40] These sections showcased Greaves's melodic grooving as much as they did Hodgkinson's solos; as Keith Richards later remarked of Charlie Watts, "He knows the schmaltz."

Cutler didn't drive but played a large instrument, so the new Henry Cow quartet soon moved their rehearsals to Cutler's home in London. The drummer had landed in Ladbroke Grove after getting planted with drugs by a detective in Sutton, a nasty charge that he successfully fought with the help of his family. Fearing a reprisal, he beat feet for Fulham and then Notting Hill, eventually finding a home in Ladbroke Grove through his friends, Bill and Vicky Ridgers, who, though only a few years older than Cutler and the other Cows, would serve as benevolent role models and supporters of the younger artists in the years to come. In Greaves's memory, "They were much more practically involved in politics than us arty-farty musicians," and indeed their political commitments soon rubbed off on the Cows.

Cutler had met Bill working a Christmas job at the post office, and grew closer to the pair—both community activists and sociology students—a year or two earlier, when he showed up on Bill's doorstep with the flu and no place to stay. "That's [just] what you did," Ridgers later recalled. "My parents locked their door. My door was never locked—anybody could come in." In 1970, Bill had moved into a house on Walmer Road with the artist David Nash and the Release activist Rufus Harris. (Vicky would soon join Bill in the house, as well.) A gathering place for the rag-and-bone men who collected scrap metal (still!) in their horse-drawn carts, the dead-end street was located in a slum that had been targeted for demolition by the municipal authorities. One future resident of the house, Cathy Williams, described their living conditions as "absolutely Dickensian." By the time Cutler had joined Henry Cow, he was living there and using the covered rear yard as a rehearsal space. In the basement, Vicky kept a printing press for local radical organizations, and Henry Cow used it periodically to produce their posters and programs. Until the house was finally torn down in 1975, it would serve as a home for a rotating cast of Cows and associates: the Greaveses, Balchin, Geoff Leigh, Cathy Williams, Steve Hillage, Lindsay Cooper, and Maggie Thomas.

Doing This Thing Seriously: To London

Between September 1971 and January 1972, all the Cambridge Cows and their spouses moved house to London. In Hodgkinson's words, "If we were going to do this thing seriously, we were going to go to London. Chris may have added to the general shove." Ayerst and White, newly credentialed, found teaching assignments, and Sarah Greaves landed an office job; the three effectively supported their husbands for the next stage of their careers. For the next year and a half, until they signed with Virgin Records in May 1973, Henry Cow rehearsed in the Walmer Road house with an intensity unmatched before or after. Their new rehearsal space allowed them to leave the equipment set up (essential), and their new drummer gave them a certain leeway to indulge in obsessiveness. "We had no concept of how efficient rehearsals worked, so we tended to work for eight, nine hours with not much break in between," Frith explains. Because Cutler did not read music, he worked out his parts to Frith and Hodgkinson's tricky music through a painstaking process of repetition: the other three musicians would repeat a given, difficult phrase for hours while Cutler created and mastered his percussion parts, which tended to avoid strict repetition (and, because of the frequent meter changes, had to). A byproduct of this endless repetition was a greater coordination and fluidity among the other musicians, who couldn't help but learn their parts well enough to relax into them.

Furthermore, Cutler's commitment to collective creative work loosened the band's sense of ownership over individual compositional ideas. Particularly with Frith and Greaves, the band acquired the habit of switching the order of individual sections and testing different arrangements of short, portable modules that they came to term "Fred Frags" in tribute to Frith's talent for writing and working with them. Although he contributed to and enjoyed these activities, Hodgkinson was less enthused to offer up his own works for such treatment. A more cerebral planner, he had taught himself music and composition from the ground up with books and his own ear. Without as much body knowledge and bandstand musicality as Frith or Greaves had, Hodgkinson tended to control his writing to a greater extent; he wanted a good reason for every new development in a given piece. That's

Example 1.1 Fred Frith and John Greaves, "Teenbeat" tune (*Leg End*, track 4, 0:00); transcription by the author, with assistance from Fred Frith.

why the best example of Henry Cow's new working method was Frith and Greaves's "Teenbeat," rather than Hodgkinson's newest piece, "Amygdala."

Frith later wrote that "['Teenbeat'] basically consists of various bits and pieces that John and I composed that the band then wrestled into form by endless trial and error, and then continued to mess with for years, a beautiful living and breathing beast that was always fun to play and had all kinds of hidden subtleties."[41] Especially in its earliest stages, the piece functioned as a kind of repository for Frith's compositional ideas and the group's strategies for messing with them. (As Frith indicates above, it would also gather contributions from Greaves, which we will survey in the next chapter's discussion of their eventual studio recording of the piece.) Fragments and motives that might have begun as parts of "Teenbeat" would later migrate into Frith's next big piece, "With the Yellow Half-Moon and Blue Star," a ballet that he would assemble in 1972, as well as "Ruins," recorded in 1974. In performance, the piece would make a virtue of its very fragmentariness—a setlist/plan from March 1972 (written for the benefit of a guest musician, Ann Rosenthal, whom Henry Cow had met in the Ottawa Music Company—see figure 1.9) as well as their BBC/Peel recording of the piece one month earlier show that Henry Cow built three distinct "interruptions" into the flow of more strictly written modules. These interludes consisted of sudden, conversational crowd chatter onstage (likely accompanied by some theatrical clowning) or bouts of open improvisation (see figure 1.9: "a certain amount of free expression" and "ANYTHING COULD HAPPEN"). All of these bits of open and closed music eventually cohered around a broad melody that, in Frith's words, "finally turned 'Teenbeat' into a piece." The "Teenbeat tune," as the band would refer to it, opened the piece and returned now and then in later sections (see example 1.1).

"Teenbeat" showcases another predominant concern of the band after Cutler had joined. No longer challenged by odd time signatures shared by

---

Figure 1.9 Henry Cow setlist, March 16, 1972. COURTESY OF FRED FRITH.

<u>ANN</u> — Essex 16-3-72

<u>Narrative</u> laying out for the boys and girls
the inevitable course the evening is to take

(1) First little bit of <u>Tim's new piece</u> (silent) (clever music)

(2) bizarre ¹²/₈ <u>saxophone improvisation</u> [vocal embellishments] (avant-garde music)

(3) '<u>Hieronymo is mad again</u>' (modern jazz)
in which, after the saxophone improvisation,
you sing the following words

"My name is Ann
my teacher says my singing's betting getter
oh gosh I get so tongue-tied
wish I'd stayed at home
with my mum
I must confess
I think the tunes
are getting rather ....."

(4) '<u>Rapt in a blanket</u>' (a popular song)
in the last verse of which you play sustained notes in the key of (G) ← (concert)
upon the clarinet

Interlude in which the inevitable is foreseen
attempts are made to prevent it
they fail [vocal embellishments pt. 2]

(5) <u>TEENBEAT</u> (the meaning of the universe)

(a) sing or play the <u>opening tune</u>
(b) sing the <u>descant</u> that follows (unison with the bass)
(c) <u>FIVES</u> (silent)
(d) heavy <u>Stravinsky</u> section (silent)
(e) <u>interlude</u> in which, with other members of the group, you give vent to
a certain amount of <u>free expression</u>
(f) <u>Teenbeat</u> — the inner core of the piece expressed in music (<u>dance</u>)
(g) <u>sexy guitar solo</u> (silent)

(h) gtr. solo part two (")
(i) frenetic saxophone stylings (clarinet strictly together with sax)
(j) bizarre violin melody (silent)
(k) bar of ¹¹/₈ followed by some science fiction music (vocals?) [drum breaks ANYTHING COULD HAPPEN]
(l) fast organ/violin unison and three over fours (silent)
(m) <u>teenbeat</u> pt two — play some friendly tunes
(n) heavy ⁴/₄ ending - (further vocal embellishments)

all the musicians, they began experimenting with multiple meters simultaneously. One clear and relatively simple example—they get much more complex—can be found in the winking "dance" theme that Frith referred to at the time (jokingly) as "the inner core of the piece."[42] The snippet has the guitar and saxophone playing a melodic phrase of 10 beats, subdivided into 3 + 3+4; they sound this swinging tune three times, with the third extended via Cutler's drum fill into a full 12 beats before launching into the next section of the piece. Meanwhile, the bass plays a walking line in four straight 8-beat phrases that cycle independently from what's happening on top; on drums, Cutler accentuates this 4 + 4 feel rather than the 3 + 3+4 division in the melody. Taken together, these two parts traverse the same 32-beat interval of time, but segment it into smaller cycles in two different ways. This type of rhythmic and contrapuntal complexity would characterize much of the Cow's music for the next few years.

Hodgkinson's "Amygdala" is more inscrutable. At the time, the composer wanted to take a step beyond "Poglith," which put the band through endless meter changes but never stratified the individual parts into a more complex unity. "Amygdala" swung far in the opposite direction by fitting together an intricate patchwork of individual lines that strive for a related kind of independence. In a retrospective analysis, Hodgkinson later wrote, "It's clear that I'm very limited by the actual way I did it: despite the fugues and counterpoints, I cling to a series of chords throughout, because writing it was all wrapped up with playing it to myself: chords with the left hand, tune with the right."[43] There are, nonetheless, some moments when the constant harmonic supports give way to a freer exchange of melody, contour, or rhythmic sequence across the instruments, with phrases overlapping and tumbling into those that follow. As Hodgkinson points out, the piece fails to achieve the thematic development he had intended, and occasionally unfolds without a strong sense of direction.

At the end of more than a year's worth of experimentation, rehearsal, and revision, Hodgkinson would create a full score of "Amygdala," but the band rehearsed it entirely from individual parts, and these parts often had the players operating in different meters for the same sections of music; in other words, one could not request to take it from bar 58, because the guitar's bar 58 came at a different point in the piece than the organ's bar 58. Such a strange approach, probably intended to make individual lines appear more clearly, contributed to a very challenging rehearsal scenario. "Chris is sort of flabbergasted by it," Hodgkinson recalls. "He doesn't know how to get to grips with it at all. I think in fact he said that it was impossible." For his part, Cutler remembers that the instrumental parts seemed to create a constant tension in their interaction, so he struggled to create a drum part that would maintain the balance. It took him a good six months to fix the part, but once he did, it was as fixed as anybody else's. Uninterested in continually de- and recomposing his ideas, Hodgkinson "wanted to write pieces that were totalities, that were autonomous." The tension between modularity and autonomy would run through the rest of Henry Cow's existence, lining up with other qualities such as speed of execution. "I think we both were a little bit annoyed with each other over the years cause I always felt like I hadn't got the chops to write a big, long piece through-composed and he felt like he didn't have the flexibility to come up with stuff on a dime which is what I was good at," Frith explains.

With their newest material—"Teenbeat," "Rapt in a Blanket," and "Came to See You"—Henry Cow returned by invitation to record a Peel session at London's Playhouse Theatre on February 28, 1972. If the first session was an exciting surprise opportunity produced from Greaves's cold call, the second felt more like validation for a band that had committed themselves to their musical work, and to finding more of it. Their wave of publicity materials in 1972 begins with rather straight press releases from Cambridge (that is, from Henry Cow itself as well as from Aardvark Management, a short-lived relationship) and ends with the elliptical, whimsical style that Cutler brought to the group. It doesn't get more businesslike than their early appeal to university social secretaries: "The band's intention is to work the university circuit independently of agencies, thereby cutting costs whilst maintaining business efficiency and reliability. They offer good original music at prices that can be negotiated according to the financial situation of your Union."[44] By the end of the year, their promo sheets included scratched-out words, snatches of poetry, and little surrealist drawings, and Hodgkinson's situationist promises "to liberate *music* from its role as opiate . . . attacking the merchants of contentment and the accomplices of vast hallucinations."[45] They now sent out these communiqués, complete with artwork by Jane Colling, from Walmer Road and "Hollywood Tibet" (sometimes "Thibet"), the catchall production outfit for Cutler's various activities.

Henry Cow reached a new level of publicity when they were asked by director Rob Walker to provide the music for his production of Euripides's *The Bacchae* at the Watford Palace Theatre, a repertory house in the London suburb. (He had probably found them through their old theatre friends, Bruce Birchall and Jon Chadwick.) The Arts Council–funded job, which included one week each of intensive rehearsals and performances in April, paid the band a small but meaningful fee, and gave them a good excuse to dig into serious work. "It made us concentrate," Greaves remembers. "We were scouting around, making demos and sending out demos . . . , in order to achieve that goal of making a record. So having not achieved that yet, and [with] the possibility of three months or whatever it was paid work . . . , we'd got this body of work to complete." They threw themselves into the project. Although Frith and Hodgkinson composed much of the music, everyone contributed ideas and arguments about how their component of the drama should function (Hodgkinson's notebooks contain two dozen pages of notes from these discussions). Hodgkinson had devised two pitch systems balanced a tritone apart to represent the Dionysian and the Apollonian tendencies of the play. "You can't go to E minor, Fred—it's not part of the system," he would say.

In a statement included in the program, Henry Cow explained that they interpreted the play as an exercise in black irony, and that Euripides intended to use audience expectations "as part of the argument."[46] Therefore, they designed music to comment on and "to make independent points at varying distances from the physical action, even to the extent of being entirely subversive." Walker took a similarly Brechtian approach to direction, folding in slow, stylized movements from Noh theatre and occasionally cutting the chorus's lines to a single word. The clearest example of this distanciation came at the drama's climax, when the maenads rip apart Pentheus: instead of thrashing, violent sound, Henry Cow set the episode to a cool, slow melody on the organ with soft guitar accompaniment; the frag had originated in a large piece that Frith had attempted to write for the Ottawa Music Company, and would pop up again a few years later, forty seconds into "Muddy Mouse (c)" on Robert Wyatt's *Ruth Is Stranger Than Richard,* when Wyatt wah-wahs what had been Hodgkinson's organ line.[47]

The collective compositional work on *The Bacchae* wasn't the only major expansion of Henry Cow's musical practice in 1972. On the suggestion of saxophonist Lol Coxhill, whom Frith remembers meeting in late 1971, the guitarist sought out a concert by Derek Bailey at the Little Theatre, where, in Frith's memory, he constituted the entire audience. The period around 1972 was one of Bailey's most adventurous, when he experimented with a widely spaced stereo amplification system through two volume pedals, as well as a nineteen-string guitar complete with bass strings attached to his feet.[48] Frith was as impressed by Bailey's welcoming attitude as he was by the guitarist's unprecedented technique; the elder musician invited Frith over for tea, and the two continued meeting occasionally to discuss music, improvisation, and the guitar. Feeling in over his head as a newly arrived Northerner to the slick metropolis, Frith valued Bailey as a role model. "He represented somebody from Yorkshire who'd moved to London, as I had at that time just done. So he felt like home to me. He spoke like the people I grew up with." Frith began studying Bailey's records, attending his concerts, and emulating some of his techniques, particularly his use of harmonics and his nimble facility with the volume pedal. As Hodgkinson observes in retrospect, Frith also likely began to acquire a "nonsequential" approach to the guitar; if a significant portion of his final year in Cambridge had been devoted to mastering all scales and chords, Bailey offered a more spatial, pointillistic aesthetic.

The Ebullient Geoff Leigh

Bailey's "nonidiomatic" playing wasn't the only new form of improvisation drifting into the Cow's orbit. In early 1971, Cutler ran into an old class-mate from Sutton, Geoff Leigh, who played saxophones and flute in a high-energy, free jazz style. They stayed in touch, and Cutler eventually invited him to play on one of the later Ottawa Music Company programs. Several months later, in May 1972, Henry Cow had convinced Leigh to join as their fifth member. Upwardly mobile—he was the first in his family to attend grammar school or university—Leigh's family was rooted in the Northern working class. He was born in 1945 in London, but his family moved around—to Manchester and Canada—for a few years before returning to Sutton, South London, in the early 1950s.

Leigh's father cut an unusual jib in town, a *New Yorker*–reading, zoot-suited bebopper who booked modern jazz gigs in the local dance hall with one condition: that he be permitted to scat with the band. He took Geoff with him to concerts, including the second "Jazz at the Philharmonic" tour in 1957, where Leigh heard Ella Fitzgerald and the Jimmy Giuffre Trio. A few years later, Leigh heard the John Coltrane quartet open for Dizzy Gillespie in 1960, an event that sparked his self-education in hard bop and led directly to the acquisition of a saxophone. From the local library, he checked out all the Blue Note albums he could find and took lessons for about a year.

By this time, the early 1960s, Leigh had developed a keen interest in politics and served as secretary for the Youth Campaign for Nuclear Disarmament, through which activity he grew friendly with Cutler's parents. (Cutler himself was a year or two behind him in school, and they weren't particularly close.) The gift of Jack Kerouac's *Dharma Bums* from his father inadvertently, but unsurprisingly, introduced Leigh to the drugs that attended jazz culture, and Leigh began to experiment with marijuana. When his father was recalled to Manchester by his employer in 1964, the family decided to leave Leigh behind with some friends so that he could finish his final year of school in Sutton. They sent money to support him, but he spent most of it at the local pub, cultivating an attitude of antiauthoritarianism and mixing with an arty crowd of jazz- and poetry-loving beats, socialists, communists, and anarchists. "That last year of school was one big party for me, which was the death of my academic future."

Eventually, Leigh enrolled at South London Polytechnic in late 1966, but a few months into his studies he decided to pursue music on a full-time basis, thereupon joining a succession of funky soul bands in the Graham Bond/Alexis Korner tradition. One of these, Crazy Mabel, had real management and booking, which allowed Leigh to sharpen his skills (and pick up the flute) on their extensive European tours and club residencies. After a year or more with the band, however, he had learned that busking on the street earned him far more money. By then a full-blown hippy, he was playing on Portobello Road in 1969 when Gerry Fitz-Gerald, an imposing Scots guitarist, approached him with an invitation to play flute and saxophone on the album of psychedelic, progressive music that he was planning, called *Mouseproof*. It would be the first time Leigh had played in a progressive rock setting, with guitars, tape work, sound processing, synthesizers, and some freak-outs.[49] Fitz-Gerald's project never took off as a performing band, however, and Leigh continued to busk on the street until an acquaintance, Amanda Parsons, told him about the Ottawa Music Company, of which she was a member. He went along, heard one or two of their concerts, caught up with Cutler, and eventually joined the group.

Once the other Cows had joined Ottawa, they liked what they heard, and invited Leigh to guest on their February 1972 Peel session. Soon, they asked him to join Henry Cow; initially, he declined, but in April he heard them in *The Bacchae* and, impressed by their dedication and cohesion, rang Cutler and offered his services. At the time, he thought, "Well, this is going to be like going back to school, but maybe that's not such a bad thing." The street-smart, anarchist-leaning hippy was something of an odd fit for the more bookish Cows. Of Cutler, Leigh remembers, "He knew I was into smoking dope, and maybe in his particular way of thinking he liked that idea, as something I might add to the dynamic tension within the group." But he added other things, such as the alto and tenor saxophones, as well as the flute, and his performing and touring experience outstripped that of his new younger bandmates.[50] Through his friendship with Fitz-Gerald, he had met the poet Lady June and the Canterbury scene of post–Soft Machine figures such as Robert Wyatt, Kevin Ayers, and Daevid Allen; given the high esteem in which the Cows held those musicians, Leigh likely offered an intriguing possibility. And he was an ebullient performer, who would soon show the Cow how to relate more directly to their audiences. As Frith puts it, "He allowed us to loosen those edges a little bit, so that we could imagine not [only] going in a precisely choreographed way."

Once Leigh joined Henry Cow, they sprang to a series of gigs that summer, including one that took them out of the country for the first time to support Lady June at Amsterdam's Paradiso club. For a week in late July, they presented nightly concerts at Edinburgh's Traverse Theatre after the evenings' comedic productions; they had devised two continuous programs to present on alternate nights, titled "A Metaphysical Guide to Hollywood Tibet" and "Guider Tells of Silent Airborne Machine."[51] The evenings shared much music, including "Teenbeat," "Amygdala," various excerpts from *The Bacchae*, and some open sections in which improvisation might take them anywhere, but the sequence and transitions between them varied considerably. Both also featured fragments of a new long piece by Frith, "With the Yellow Half-Moon and Blue Star," and among the other new material that dotted the setlists was a tune by Greaves they called "York," which would eventually metamorphose, seven years later, into the quizzical melody for his (post–Henry Cow) song "Kew. Rhone." They also played his "Don't Disturb Me," which shows up spliced onto the end of Henry Cow's "Deluge" (*Unrest*, 1974), and a fast groove frag, "John's 15s," that the band would soon suture into "Teenbeat" (at 2:05 on the *Leg End* recording). Hodgkinson contributed three numbers, two that are now lost ("May 68" and "God Knows") and "Nine Funerals of the Citizen King," his first with vocals.

In these concerts and others during the summer and into the autumn, the Cows adorned themselves with fantastic costumes and makeup. "We are starting to experiment with performance styles," Hodgkinson explains. "I mean, we have the idea of the gig as the unique, unforgettable occasion. . . . The connection between dance and theatre was obviously fruitful in that regard: John gets this tube of gold makeup, probably from the Watford Theatre, and starts covering his face in gold makeup. We start dressing up." Colling, who was generally if informally charged with the band's graphics, recalls painting Frith to look like a tiger, or Leigh as Britannia. She made up Cutler with a white face, dark eyes, and stripes (a look nicked from the

Figure 1.10 Henry Cow—Geoff Leigh, Tim Hodgkinson, and Fred Frith—at the Explorers Club, London School of Economics, 1973. COURTESY OF CHRIS CUTLER.

early Soft Machine, he recalls). Hodgkinson might wear a blue velvet dress. These sartorial choices reflected a kind of wacky, theatrical stage presentation that they'd begun to cultivate in *The Bacchae*, where they were set up on stage with the actors. In the memories of the Cows, "Guider" and "Hollywood" both contained some dramatic episodes (everybody looking off into the distance together or wandering into the audience while improvising), some of which might have been inspired by the antics of Arthur Brown and other British pop musicians who drew on music hall shenanigans. Photographs of the band from later in the year indicate that Leigh provided a push in this direction (see figure 1.10), but the others were already in that mindset. For example, their performance with the Ottawa Music Company in Watford on April 30, 1972, took the form of the large group arguing and "breaking up" in the first half, and then performing in smaller splinter bands for the rest of the event. These sorts of loose programs or narratives would structure many of Henry Cow's concerts into 1973.

This theatrical, dada mode of performance continued the next month, when Henry Cow returned to Edinburgh with Klug's Cambridge Contemporary Dance Group to present another week of performances (August 22–26) in the gymnasium of St. Patrick's School, as part of the fringe festival. According to the choreographer, they gave four performances

Example 1.2 Fred Frith, "With the Yellow Half-Moon and Blue Star," Factory 15s theme, which also appears in "Teenbeat" and "Ruins"; transcription by the author.

per day: a dance in the morning, a Henry Cow concert at lunchtime, and two dance performances in the evening. To join their lunchtime shows they invited a Cambridge friend, Tony Wilkes, who made noise with his synthesizer across their entire set (having not fully learned the pieces ahead of time). The band invited another university pal, the artist Ray Smith, to design stage costumes, but he also offered to perform "activities" (as they were designated on the event poster); they would take a few different forms over the coming year, but in Edinburgh he sat at the front edge of the stage, motionless, during their concert. Smith also designed simple outfits—green tights and leotards under gym skirts—for the dancers that echoed the gym space in which they performed.[52] The set, too, would be created by Smith, who recalls, "There was no money. So what I decided to do was simply to define the space that they operated in, by photocopying a whole series of arrows. These simply would be attached to the wall, or the curtain or wherever it was. The whole of the interior space had its space revealed to it by the use of these arrows, which said 'Look at this line, here.'"

The evening concerts consisted of some shorter pieces, such as a "Rope Ballet" that literally tied each Cow to a dancer onstage, and the longer work, "Yellow Half-Moon," that Frith had written at Klug's request. A multipart suite, "Yellow Half-Moon," collected more than a dozen snatches of music into four large parts totaling twenty minutes, though it probably stretched longer with solos in performance. In their internal planning shorthand, the band referred to its two main melodies as the first and second "Hollywood themes," suggesting that these formed an important part of the earlier "Metaphysical Introduction to Hollywood Tibet."[53] Frith's expanding musical ambition manifests in the three-voice fugue that opens the piece, as well as the mensural canons that pop up later in sections that Henry Cow referred to as "cycles" or "the factory" (and which I would label "Factory 15s," because the recurring cell is in 15/8—see example 1.2). At its most canonically complex, this "factory" section combines four cycles in different meters and even tempi: a simple bassline in 5/4, the factory 15s in 15/8 (doubling the quarter-note ictus of the bass), a twenty-beat melody that matches the bass ictus, and a second layer of factory 15s unfolding at a one-third faster tempo.[54] They built up the ability to play such complicated rhythms through endless rehearsal, Cutler later explained. "We'd think of numbers and play every variation and internal subdivision imaginable, dreaming up different possibilities and then running them, with or against one another, until we could all feel all of the rhythms at once and not be distracted by whatever else was going on."[55] In October, Henry Cow would record "Yellow Half-Moon" in full for their third Peel session.

With "Yellow Half-Moon," the other new fixture in the band's live set was Hodgkinson's "Nine Funerals of the Citizen King." Hodgkinson's lyrics communicated his recent reading of situationist texts (his notebook from the time includes a written index of the first issue of the *Internationale Situationniste*, and he had also been reading Guy Debord's *Society of the Spectacle* and Raoul Vaneigem's *Revolution of Everyday Life*—see figure 1.11). His lyrical reference to Gertrude Stein in the arresting "chorus" section— surrounded as it was by a text otherwise devoted to themes of consumerism and the spectacle—effectively stages the point around which Henry Cow pivoted in 1972 and into 1973: from a zany fascination with the historical avant-garde of dada and surrealism to a more sober, Marxist analysis of contemporary society and a Brechtian relationship to artistic production.

Compositionally, the piece shows substantial progress for someone who had begun writing only three years earlier. Hodgkinson strips away some of the fussy counterpoint of earlier works, and the verse-chorus songform keeps the music from wandering without aim; with repetition, lines of shifting meters that might otherwise be difficult to retain grow more familiar. The texture remains clear throughout: three-part vocal writing, supported by simple chords in the organ, eventually expanding to include violin, bass, and saxophone. The eight measures I consider to be the "chorus" ("But a rose is a rose is a rose") offer some of the sweetest harmonic writing in the Henry Cow repertoire (though sticklers might note that Stein's text does not begin with an indefinite article). Hodgkinson casts a strange spell here by descending from B in the melody while simultaneously ascending from E in the bass with what should be the same pitches (see example 1.3). On the third "rose" they cross at G-sharp with a surprising pentatonic chord that is reinforced by the top vocal line, which Hodgkinson does not notate in the score but sings on D-sharp above the C-sharp written in the middle voice. After the bass and melody intersect, however, the bass moves up to A instead of the A-sharp that had previously taken the melody down to the crossroads. This unadorned A permits a pivot to a simple D–E9–F-sharp progression that feels like a resolution because of the F-sharp suspen-

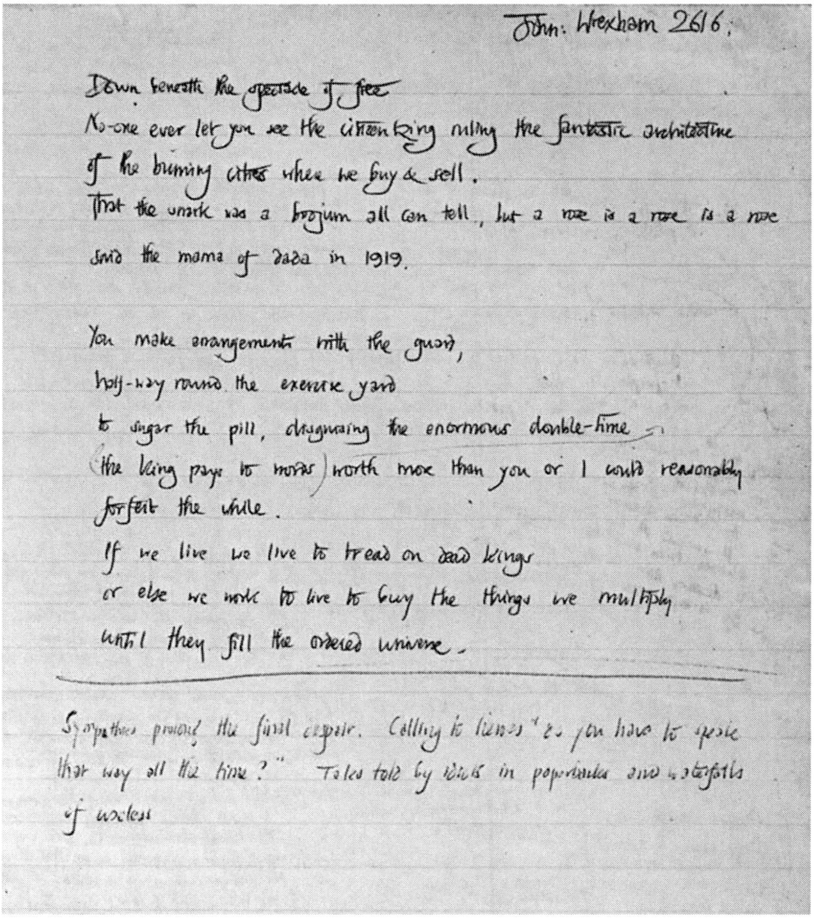

John: Wrexham 2616;

Down beneath the spectacle of free
No-one ever let you see the citizen king ruling the fantastic architecture
of the burning cities where we buy & sell.
That the world was a bogium all can tell, but a rose is a rose is a rose
said the mama of dada in 1919.

You make arrangements with the guard,
half-way round the exercise yard
to sugar the pill, disguising the enormous double-time
(the king pays to moves) worth more than you or I could reasonably
forfeit the while.
If we live we live to tread on dead kings
or else we work to live to buy the things we multiply
until they fill the ordered universe.

Sympathies proving the final despair. Calling to listen "... you have to spoke
that way all the time?" Tales told by ... in popular ... and waterfalls
of useless

Figure 1.11 Lyrics to "Nine Funerals of the Citizen King," by Tim Hodgkinson, from Notebook 3 (1973). COURTESY OF TIM HODGKINSON.

sion that had been hanging over the entire phrase from the beginning. The little tail ("as long ago as 1919") unfolds the work of the previous few bars by taking us back to the minor mode in preparation for a repeat. Overall, Hodgkinson seems to be channeling Bartók by way of Wagner: a deformed symmetry (two lines crossing the same pitch space, slightly differently) and floating kind of harmonic progression in stasis, based on persisting common tones and partial transformation of one or two notes at a time.

For the rest of the year and into 1973, Henry Cow sharpened this repertoire in concert. Several tunes—"Poglith," "Rapt in a Blanket," and

Example 1.3 Tim Hodgkinson, "Nine Funerals of the Citizen King," chorus (*Leg End*, track 8, 0:43); transcription by the author.

the full version of "Came to See You"—had already dropped out of the set, and frags from "Hieronymo" would soon follow. As we have already noted, the group enjoyed working together to create a unique set for each performance, a strategy available only to bands with a lot of rehearsal time. Their array of frags and finished pieces could feel like a diagram or flowchart of possibilities—zones of certainty that also outline possible passages through uncertainty (see figure 1.12). Greaves comments, "My favorite bits in all that, once we had these pieces more or less worked out, were doing all these links. I think those were always the best bits. They were so fresh and spontaneous, and more collective, really." The links also meant that they could assemble long, continuous sets (common for soul and dance bands, but also for Soft Machine, the Art Ensemble of Chicago, and other improvising groups in the late 1960s), because, in Cutler's words, "as with theatre, we wanted to maintain a sense of inward trawl, of

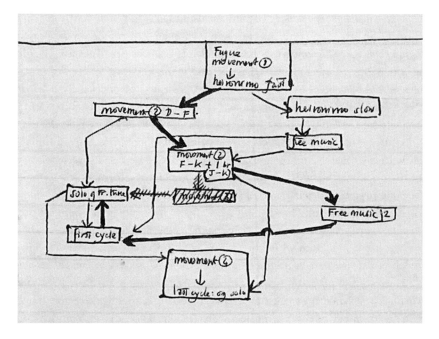

Figure 1.12 Diagram of a possible Henry Cow set (c. 1972), by Tim Hodgkinson.
COURTESY OF TIM HODGKINSON.

unbroken concentration, to draw ourselves and our listeners deeper into our world."[56]

But their improvisational practice, as Frith points out, was "all framed by composed pieces, which tends to reduce its impact as improvisation in a certain way." In other words, improvisations cannot become truly open when they come from one zone of certainty and move by plan to another. "This is not satisfactory," says Cutler. "We have to do pieces where we start from nothing, and which are not going anywhere, and just stop when they're done. So, then I remember Henry Cow particularly would do pieces where we would just do a piece that started and ended without having to come from anywhere or go anywhere. And they got longer and longer." Their increasing familiarity with the improvised music scene, through Derek Bailey, surely contributed to this attempt at "purifying" the practice.

Meanwhile, at some point in 1972, Henry Cow had drafted an old Cambridge friend, Phil Preston, to handle their live sound and help out as a road manager (he accompanied them to Edinburgh). Balchin occasionally mixed, but the band wasn't convinced that he shared their aesthetic and thought he provided better support as a technician and roadie. According to Sarah Greaves, one concert that autumn led to a shake-up: "That was the gig at which Phil . . . was found to be asleep on the mixing desk. . . . He was probably bored to death!" In the pub afterward, a discussion ensued about what to do next. Sarah Greaves continues, "I was sitting back and listening, and I actually said, 'Well why don't I do it?'" Frith and John Greaves liked the idea and pushed hard in support of her. "My only qualification was my familiarity with the music." And indeed, she would prove to be a dedicated member of the organization, writing out cue sheets for each performance. After she became pregnant in early 1973, a threatened miscarriage left her bedridden on doctors' orders until her twelfth week. By then a resident at Walmer Road (in early 1973), Sarah continued rehearsing from a horizontal position in her second-floor bedroom while the Cow played in the covered garden below; Balchin had run leads from the band up to the mixing desk on her floor.[57]

Henry Cow played a few dozen concerts between autumn 1972 and spring 1973, when they set themselves to getting signed by a record label. Garnering most of their attention were two series, Cabaret Voltaire and the Explorers Club, which they produced entirely on their own at the Kensington Town Hall and the Old Theatre at the London School of Economics (LSE), respectively.

Cabaret Voltaire, *Kensington Town Hall*

OCTOBER 6, 1972	Kevin Ayers with Archie Legget
OCTOBER 27, 1972	Khan (Steve Hillage), Bob Bery, Ray Smith
NOVEMBER 17, 1972	Jack Monck, Lady June, Anthony Marshall, Tony Wilkes, Ray Smith, DJ Perry
DECEMBER 5, 1972	Ottawa Music Company, Ray Smith, DJ Perry

Explorers Club, *London School of Economics, Old Theatre*

MARCH 14, 1973	Derek Bailey and Lol Coxhill
APRIL 27, 1973	Rain in the Face, Ray Smith, DJ Perry
MAY 4, 1973	Ron Geesin, Mont Campbell Wind Quartet, Ray Smith, DJ Perry

MAY 11, 1973	Derek Bailey, Christine Jeffries, Scratch Orchestra, Ray Smith, DJ Perry
MAY 18, 1973	Ivor Cutler, Lol Coxhill, Ray Smith, DJ Perry

"Chris had a long history of entrepreneurial attitude to putting on things. . . . Because of his experience in Ottawa, we came to understand that we could do anything we wanted," Frith explains. In the Cabaret Voltaire events, they shared bills with some new friends (Ayers, Lady June), as well as some older ones from London and Cambridge, including former members of the Ottawa Music Company. Significantly, Henry Cow continued their collaboration with Smith, who developed new "activities" in some of these concerts and most of the Explorers' Club. These included drawing on a blackboard, running around the hall at top speed for the duration of Henry Cow's set (perhaps an echo of Carolee Schneemann's *Lateral Splay*), building houses of cards on the side of the stage, performing a puppet show, and enlisting others to repeat his human statuary routine (Leigh's spouse, Cathy Williams, recalls performing this duty on at least one occasion). The band also played in front of one of Smith's films, *Thirty Black Lace Angels*.

Posters for these events situated them clearly in the visual language of dada and 'pataphysics, with cutout typography and other collages, found text and imagery, and explicit references to Zurich and 1916. In his favorable review of the Ayers concert on October 6, the *New Musical Express* critic Ian MacDonald noticed and mentioned these dada associations, and also praised the carefully curated scene: "It was a success in that it managed to maintain its anti-superstar, we're-all-people-not-performing-paypackets ambiance without straying into either earnest solemnity or heady whimsicality."[58] An old classmate of the band's from Cambridge, MacDonald also provided their first exposure in the national music rags, calling them "one of the most resilient and obstinate of that range of groups normally ignored by the popular music press," and commending their "graceful, intricate, and completely uncompromising sets."[59]

Judging from the explanatory text on a flyer, Henry Cow seems to have shut down Cabaret Voltaire after its fourth installment in December because of some dissatisfaction with the Kensington Town Hall and their inability to control every aspect of the programs. (In his review, MacDonald noted some problems with the PA.) Four months later, they restarted their activities at the LSE, where Cutler had some friends who booked the hall. As the list of participants in the Explorers Club makes clear, this series presented "a different set of people," as Greaves says. "These were serious improvisers. The Ottawa and Cabaret things were what they were: they were cabaret entertainment. Fred had met Derek [Bailey], in the meantime, and he became a kind of guru. That's what made us go full-footed down the improvisational path—doing gigs with him and with Lol [Coxhill]." Henry Cow's portion of these evenings consisted of a loose program narrated through a poem written and recited by their Cambridge pal David Perry (who had previously contributed poetry readings to the Cabaret Voltaire gigs). His text told the story of a group of explorers who grow increasingly lost, their state mirrored in the slow fragmentation of the text into modernist opacity. Each evening had a printed program, usually with poetic texts by Cutler or his brother. In some cases—particularly with Bailey and Coxhill—Henry Cow enticed their invitees to join them during segments of open improvisation. "I think we were all aware of the dangers of being insular, and pretty ready to open things out whenever possible," Greaves recalls. "It wasn't a spoken ideology, but it was certainly practically true." In fact, the ideology was spoken, or at least written, on the program of the third installment of the series, which explained that the point of the club was to encourage exploration rather than reminiscence, "where performers play FOR and WITH the peoples present rather than AT them."[60]

When Cutler wrote a letter of invitation to composer Cornelius Cardew and the Scratch Orchestra, he might have had in mind the shambolic ensemble of amateur and professional improvisers from a few years prior; showing up instead were "six stony-faced singers," in Hodgkinson's memory, who gave a talk called "The Role of the Revolutionary in the Conditions in England and the World Today" and then sang nineteenth-century revolutionary songs.[61] Another guest deserving special mention is Rain in the Face, an interesting duo comprising Paul Burwell on drums and David Toop on electric guitar, flutes, and voice. They had, like Henry Cow, been developing a modest kind of rock free improvisation since 1971. They played short numbers, rather than sprawling sets. A "song" might be a loose collection of resources—guitar with alligator clips, Burwell up on the cymbals, then Toop transitioning to a little motive of three or four pitches on a bamboo flute—that allowed some coherence but was relatively underdetermined. Cutler had invited them to appear at the Explorers Club after hearing them perform at the Architect's Association.

In the midst of the Explorers Club, Henry Cow recorded their fourth Peel session, where they played "Teenbeat," "Nine Funerals," and a new number, "Nirvana for Mice." This date, in Frith's recollection, "was the one that got us the record deal." Before we turn to their Virgin period in the next chapter, let us pause to highlight a few themes that had emerged by early 1973. They collaborated energetically, searching out new partners in different media, and also maintained a certain direct address toward the audience. We might say that their tactic consisted of throwing themselves into and against new situations to produce unpredictable results: a commitment to finding the unknown instead of repeating the known. At the same time, their hermetic rehearsal schedule and intricate written music forged a more closed system that would grow increasingly impenetrable.

Moreover, as Hodgkinson put it many years later, they had found themselves stuck between the visual and performative ambiguities of dada/surrealism and the sharper science of Marxist analysis. "So there was this kind of confusion with registers. . . . And we hadn't quite found the fork point yet between those two things." They would soon find that point, taking the second path. Indeed, Hodgkinson's notebooks from late 1972 into 1973 evince a growing doubt over the whimsical imagery of Hollywood Tibet. Their goal, he reasoned, had to be communication with the audience, but that meaningful exchange could remain clear and open only if they could avoid the manipulations of advertising. Their form of communication should be "nonauthoritative" and based upon the will and intelligence of their interlocutors in the audience. As a group "playing music that tries to break down the walls between highbrow and popular," Henry Cow sought to turn the world into a problem, "but without reserving this truth for the rich and 'cultured.'"[62] Wary of offering mere entertainment, which "reaffirms the status quo," the band would seek more transformative interventions; as we will see, however, those interventions would gain greater force and greater complexity once they moved into the heart of the culture industry itself: a record contract would make it so.

2 Faust and the Virgins | 1973

By the beginning of summer 1973, Henry Cow would sign to Virgin Records, the latest venture from a twenty-two-year-old entrepreneur named Richard Branson. Before he started Virgin mail order and the record label, Branson published a fairly successful magazine called *Student*, which he founded when he was still at school and eventually printed four times a year. (The first issue appeared in January 1968).[1] For a sixteen-year-old nobody, his accomplishment was impressive; he secured interviews with the likes of Vanessa Redgrave, Mick Jagger, John Lennon, and R. D. Laing, and his contributors included Bertrand Russell, James Baldwin, and Jean-Paul Sartre. The *Guardian* reported in 1970 that *Student*'s circulation was over 100,000.[2] It may be difficult to imagine the brash billionaire we know today publishing Sartre and conversing with Laing about experimental psychology, but the young prototycoon, though not exactly an intellectual, spent a lot of his time advocating for socially progressive causes.

"We didn't start the magazine with a social conscience. The social side just sort of happened," he told a reporter in 1970.[3] The most significant part of that social side was the Student Advisory Centre (SAC), which Branson founded in the spring of 1968, around the same time that Tim Hodgkinson and Fred Frith had begun to think of themselves as bandmates. When his girlfriend became unexpectedly pregnant, Branson experienced first- and secondhand how difficult and costly it was to get an abortion. He started SAC as a kind of resource list for young people who might require assistance with similar issues—not only abortion but also mental illness, venereal disease, and temporary housing needs for runaways. He and his *Student* team handed out leaflets across London with a single number to call for any of these problems, and the hotline would help anyone in need find a friendly doctor, counselor, or even barrister if necessary. Branson was arrested and taken to court in 1970 on an obscure public decency charge, which only strengthened his youthful streak of antiauthoritarianism. "I suppose I am Left-wing—well, only to the extent that I think Left-wing views are sane and rational," he remarked.[4]

But the magazine and the hotline weren't making money, so Branson hatched a plan to capitalize on the *Student* demographic's rabid love for the newest rock music: he would sell albums by mail at a discount price. The music bug had been planted in his ear by Tom Newman, whose girlfriend, Jacqui Byford, worked part-time on *Student*. After the breakup of his band, the psych outfit July, in 1969, Newman grew very interested in recording equipment, but it was too expensive to acquire on his own; Byford suggested he drop by the *Student* house to meet Branson, who already had a reputation as a go-getter. Newman later recalled, "I had this quite long chat with him, where I suggested that, with this magazine being distributed, he should be selling records. You know, it's the perfect kind of stepping-off point to start a bit of a thing in the music business. And he should start a recording studio!"

Eventually, Branson would hire Newman to set up the studio, but first he concentrated on mail order. In the summer of 1969, the United Kingdom's major record companies withdrew their case to maintain resale price maintenance, which was a long-standing trade practice that effectively allowed manufacturers to set the prices for their own products at the retail end.[5] Shop owners feared an ensuing price war, but it never came. Noticing that nobody was selling records at discount prices, Branson stepped into the breach, advertising in the final issue of *Student* (in spring 1970) and distributing leaflets along Oxford Street in London. He called the new company "Virgin," to reflect the fact that he and his staff had zero experience with this type of business. Virgin would place advertisements in *Melody Maker* offering the latest cool records for a few shillings less than the High Street shops charged; people sent them their requests and cash by post, and then Virgin would acquire those records and mail them to the customer. (In fact, the first advertisement, in *Student*, didn't even list albums that were available. Instead, it directed its reader to simply "Name any record you want and we'll sell it to you 10% to 25% cheaper than anybody else."[6]) The advantage of this process was that it offered a lot of cash up front, but the profit margins were tiny.

It was an improvised enterprise. In the blunt words of Sue Steward, an early employee of the business, "Nobody knew anything." But the mail order really thrived, only running into trouble when the postal service went on strike in early 1971. Meanwhile, Branson's unknown second cousin, Simon Draper, was finishing up his undergraduate degree at Natal University in Durban, South Africa, where he fed his music addiction with six-week-old copies of *Melody Maker* and *New Musical Express*. Draper favored rock— "as avant-garde as I could get." To him, that meant English bands such as The Who, Pretty Things, and the Soft Machine, and American ones like the

Mothers of Invention and Captain Beefheart, all of which he acquired from a shop that imported LPs from the United Kingdom, thereby sidestepping the apartheid government's censorship program. (As was the case for many followers of these bands, he was also conversant in the outer regions of jazz.)

Intending to take a brief pause before continuing his postgraduate studies at an English university, Draper traveled to London in late 1970. One family connection led to the next, and he soon found himself having lunch with Branson in the early days of the new year. Branson was impressed by his cousin's mastery of the contemporary popular music scene, which far outstripped his own limited knowledge. "If I heard a record, I knew whether I liked it or not, but I couldn't compare it with some other band. . . . It seemed to me that Simon had listened to every record released by every band," he later wrote.[7] By the end of this first meeting, Branson had hired Draper to be the record buyer for the first Virgin retail shop, which was slated to open the following week.

Due to the postal strike, Virgin was suffering serious cash-flow problems, and the shop was the only way they could get the business moving again. It also allowed Branson to engage in a bit of experiential marketing. He later wrote, "Although rock music was very exciting, none of that feeling of excitement or vague interest filtered through to the shops that sold the records. The dowdy staff registered no approval or interest if you bought the new Jefferson Airplane; they just rang it up on the till as if you had bought Mantovani or Perry Como."[8] Taking a different approach, the staff at Virgin encouraged customers to hang out and listen to records in the store, covering the floors with cushions and passing joints throughout the day. They soon established a loyal customer base with their cool vibe.

One drawback was the fact that its owner was not cool. "Richard Branson had no musical taste whatsoever," Newman told me. Aware of his own limitations, Branson readily acknowledged the importance of Draper: "Simon's taste in music quickly became the single most critical element of the Virgin ethos. A record shop is not just a record shop, it is an arbiter of taste itself."[9] Soon, Draper bought records not just for the Virgin shop but for the whole mail-order operation. He cultivated an image for Virgin as *the* place to get cool rock LPs that were hard to obtain in the United Kingdom, whether they came from the United States or Europe. "I realized that, although our list, as published in *Melody Maker*, was very good—it had all the hit records of the moment—the only thing that really set it apart was that the records were cheaper than anyone else's, because we were discounting. . . . And I tried to inject more esoteric stuff, particularly imports from America." This esoteric stuff from the States included the Velvet Underground catalogue, the Mothers, Beefheart, the Grateful Dead, John Fahey, John Cale, and Terry Riley. One early success for Virgin was Van der Graaf Generator's *Aerosole Grey Machine*, which had been released by Mercury in the United States but had not come out in the United Kingdom. In cases like this, Virgin found small distributors in the United States and bought up their stock of the album. In other cases, Virgin and the other import shops sold albums that were *going to be* released soon in the United Kingdom but had only come out in foreign markets; the American versions of such albums as John Lennon's *Imagine* or The Band's *Cahoots* were routinely sold to superfans months before their British release dates. As a *Melody Maker* writer explained at the time, the imports market was fueled initially by followers of US West Coast progressive music in the mid-1960s (Dr. John, Jefferson Airplane, Zappa), which didn't enjoy wide UK releases. Some years later, even after these records (and others by groups like the Velvet Underground) were issued by British companies, many enthusiasts preferred the American versions, which often had different artwork and a sturdier sleeve.[10]

By May 1971, Virgin could declare in their weekly advertisement, "Virgin Records now have larger stocks of imports than anyone else."[11] Under Draper's stewardship, the business became more of a connoisseur's shop, stocking live bootlegs under the counter and snatching up recordings that were going out of stock and getting dumped by the big companies. He occasionally slipped in a few domestic releases of special interest: Lol Coxhill's *Ear of the Beholder*, or the first few records on Derek Bailey and Evan Parker's Incus label. Because he had a constant kind of feedback from his mail-order customers, Draper had a good sense of which records had some residual demand from their customer base.

But it was the "esoteric stuff" that really made their name.[12] One representative artist was Gong, whose first few records were released by the French label BYG, otherwise known as Europe's premier source of US second-wave free jazz. Led by former Soft Machine guitarist Daevid Allen, Gong had the exact kind of pedigree that attracted aficionados like Draper. By 1972, however, German rock began to dominate the mail-order list (as well as the shelves in Virgin's expanding set of shops). Although Amon Düül II had been a fixture on the Virgin list since late 1970, customers began to request Can and Tangerine Dream, too. "So we made the investigations and got the entire catalog of Ohr Records, who had Tangerine Dream, and I spent a weekend in my flat . . . listening to all these records. Most of them, we were laughing at—the names, like 'Grogschnitt' [Grobschnitt].

But people wanted the records, so we imported the whole lot, pretty much." Although they didn't invent the term *krautrock* (Popo Management had used it in an April 3, 1971, advertisement in *Melody Maker*), they certainly popularized the appellation, which was finally cemented by a song of the same name on *Faust IV* in autumn 1973.[13]

Virgin's creation of a special section dedicated to new German rock reflected and responded to consumer demand, which was produced in part by a flood of reportage that began in early 1972, though the British music weeklies had published a few earlier features.[14] United Artists began releasing albums by Can and Amon Düül II in England, and eventually these bands—and then Faust—toured the United Kingdom (Can in spring 1972, Amon Düül II in June and December 1972, and Faust in summer and autumn 1973). Other bands, such as Kraan and Embryo, performed at British festivals during this period.[15] This activity led to at least ten album and concert reviews in this interval, as well as a steady trickle of news items, letters to the editor, reader queries, and full-page advertisements about the German bands. John Peel championed Neu! on Top Gear, and invited Can, Amon Düül II, and Faust to perform live on his show during 1973.[16]

The target consumers for Virgin's product were young fans like Julian Cope, who later characterized this batch of German imports as "a blaze of white lightning in the early '70s when all around us was the artless dry-wank of ELP, the spiritual airbrushing of Yes and by far the worst of all, the formica-mantras of Dark Side of the Moon–period Pink Floyd."[17] Indeed, this taste formation shared by Draper, Cope, and so many other characters in this story was built around the appreciation of a particular kind of artiness circa 1970, one that favored meandering tunes, amateurish execution, explorative improvisation, and other hints of the post-68 demos—all a far cry from the bombast and polish of Yes, Pink Floyd, or ELP.

In the introduction, I surveyed the critical discourse on German rock in the British weeklies. The wave of attention to this music culminated in Ian MacDonald's 9,000-word, three-part series, "Germany Calling," which the *NME* published in December 1972. (To judge from his acknowledgments at the end of the third installment, the honchos of several German labels whispered in his ear, as did Simon Draper of Virgin.) MacDonald provided the first detailed examination of the movement as a whole, including Can, Amon Düül I and II, Birth Control, Ash Ra Tempel, Mythos, Kraftwerk, Neu!, Tangerine Dream, Klaus Schulze, Guru Guru, Eruption, Wolfgang Dauner, Popol Vuh, Cluster, and a host of other talents who have faded into history. But this list of 25 bands was just an extended warm-up for the real object of Macdonald's attention: Hamburg's Faust. "The best, you'll be relieved to hear, has been reserved for last," he wrote in the final installment of the series.[18] Faust would come to symbolize all of the tropes of German rock for discerning UK (and French) listeners, and they would benefit more than any of their compatriots from the publicity drumbeat slowly gaining momentum in the rock rags. This attention made them, in the words of one *Melody Maker* critic, "the hottest word-of-mouth group to emerge out of the Common Market mists of Eurorock" by early 1973;[19] they reached as high as number 12 on Virgin's "Top 50" sales list in an eight-week run during spring 1973. But before we explore the ramifications of Faust's word-of-mouth fame, let us back up a few years and relive the post-68 moment from their perspective.

Faust: A Complete Improvisation

Faust formed in Hamburg in late 1970.[20] Jean-Hervé Peron (bass and vocals), Rudolf Sosna (guitar), and Gunter Wüsthoff (saxophone) had been playing in a group called Nukleus, which was song-oriented and enjoyed a few connections to the Hamburg underground film scene—most notably through the filmmaker Helmuth Costard, who had asked the band to provide some music for his films. The other half of what would become Faust— Zappi Diermaier (drums), Arnulf Meifert (drums), and Hans-Joachim Irmler (keyboards)—had another band, Campylognatus Citelli, which favored abstract sonic freak-outs and noise explorations. As Andy Wilson details, there is some disagreement about how the halves came together, but the overall shape of the story is clear enough.[21] According to Irmler, the two groups amalgamated and made a radical pact to recede from public performance and develop a whole new approach to rock. When they began looking for a record company, the only connection they had to a media industry of any kind was the Hamburg Filmmakers Cooperative, where they were soon introduced to a critically important figure, Uwe Nettelbeck.[22]

The path that took Nettelbeck to Faust is circuitous but worth recounting in some detail, because of what it exemplifies about the post-1968 moment in the rock music industry, when renegade, youthful producers spent record company money on whatever they thought might lead to wild, overnight success. The signing of Henry Cow makes little sense without some understanding of this speculation. Nettelbeck had been the chief film critic at *Die Zeit* in the 1960s, before briefly assuming the editorship of *konkret* after that paper's biggest star, Ulrike Meinhof, had resigned to become an urban guerrilla and foment revolution with the Red Army Faction.[23] His wife, Petra, was a former actress who had become a beloved television presenter after breaking her back in a fall.

In the summer of 1968, Nettelbeck traveled to London to research an article on that city's underground scene, where he met Joe Boyd, an American at the center of British counterculture. Along with the photographer John "Hoppy" Hopkins, Boyd ran the important UFO Club, home to Pink Floyd, Soft Machine, and other leading lights of the London psych scene. He had also produced Pink Floyd's "Arnold Layne" single, as well as records by Fairport Convention and the Incredible String Band, and he would soon break another Cambridge native, Nick Drake. Boyd and the Nettelbecks met at a Hyde Park rally to legalize marijuana, and they got on famously.

The chance meeting with Boyd would turn out to be auspicious, because the American ex-pat was a close associate of Polydor's UK A&R man, Horst Schmolzi, who had put Polydor on the map by signing a heap of huge artists in the late 1960s: Jimi Hendrix, Cream, the Bee Gees, and The Who (by distributing their in-house label, Track). He also set up more informal relationships with producers such as Boyd, whose walk-around cash and studio time with Fairport Convention were being supplied, *sans* contract, by Polydor via their London representative. Later in 1968, Boyd traveled to Hamburg to meet with Schmolzi and to try to persuade him to issue a contract for the young Nick Drake. (Schmolzi had been recalled to the city by nervous suits at Polydor, worried that he might be spending too much of their cash at late-night soirees at the UFO Club.) He was also interested in catching up with the Nettelbecks. After their meeting at Polydor (which was unproductive—Schmolzi's wings had been clipped, according to Boyd's recollection), Boyd and Schmolzi connected with their new German friends. "For Horst, the Nettelbecks provided him with an entrée to the kind of Bohemian world he had been missing since his exile from London," Boyd explains. "Soon Uwe had a production deal with Polydor."[24] Slapp Happy's Peter Blegvad, whom Nettelbeck would soon sign to Polydor, explains, "Uwe had been hired as a kind of maverick tastemaker by PolyGram—'find us the next new thing!' And what he found was Faust." Nettelbeck later recalled, "I said to Schmolzi, why not? Could be fun. I'll give it a try."[25]

According to Wilson, Polydor's pitch "was simple. They wanted a völkisch Rolling Stones, Kinks or Small Faces, a German super-group to compete at the pinnacle of the market internationally. Better still, they wanted an electronic Beatles" (Polydor had let the Beat Brothers slip through their hands in 1962).[26] Faust, it turned out, would be the unlikely horse they bet on. The band insisted that they needed to be self-sufficient and isolated in order to practice the innovation they promised, so Nettelbeck persuaded the record company to buy an old schoolhouse in Wümme, outside of Hamburg, and convert it into a living space and recording studio. According to a 1973 press release, Faust moved into the studio in February 1971, and lived there together for the next few years, recording anything and everything, experimenting with magnetic tape, and, eventually, compiling material for three albums.[27] This desire for artistic and technical autonomy—crossed with the communalism of late hippydom—provided one basis for Faust's affinity with Henry Cow. The two bands also shared an acute interest in the possibilities of electronic technologies to extend creativity and uncertainty at the time of performance. As Hodgkinson later recalled, "We were very interested in the way that Faust did things. That was more interesting than the results . . . , the way they recorded everything—recording as the creative process and not the documentation process."

Faust had the gall and the good fortune to ask for—and receive—a live-in audio engineer at Wümme, so that their recording equipment would be ready whenever inspiration struck. Kurt Graupner had been previously employed at Deutsche Grammophon (DG), where he had worked in postproduction; his main project for the company had been cleaning up the Furt-wängler back catalogue and converting it to stereo.[28] At Wümme, Graupner built the studio with unused equipment from DG: an eight-track tape deck, an eight-channel mixer, and an additional submixer for further inputs and headphone mixes. "I can say we experimented with all the resources we had in the most comprehensive way," he later told Chris Cutler. The band was very interested in the effects boxes that had been recently coming onto the market, but these small electronic devices had drawbacks: each offered only a single effect, such as phasing, distortion, or delay, and they were usually too noisy once they were strung together in a series. Moreover, the more technically minded members of the band wanted each musician to be able to affect the sound of anyone else in the group during performance, and they also wanted to be able to move their sounds around the room with an array of loudspeakers. Such a dynamic technical arrangement was not commercially available (obviously!), so Graupner took detailed notes of the band's wishes and went back to the experimental workshop at DG, of which he had been the director during his time at the company. Graupner remembers, "Whenever I came back to do something, they helped me because they had the OK from the management to support Graupner. I would draw them plans and they would build it."[29]

What did they build? "Everyone ended up with a box a metre long with 20 controls—they could set up basic sound configurations with it, and change them as they played. On top of the box was a patch-bay, so they could send their signals to different channels. It was quite sophisticated, it worked very well."[30] After two years of testing and construction, they had their final boxes in 1973.[31] The band used these electronics to control their own sounds and those of their comrades on the fly, and when Graupner manned the control room during a jam, he would add effects such as delay, reverb, and equalization to individual instruments and send the wet signals back into their headphones, creating a feedback loop of sorts. All the electronic effects came out of the live performance scenario. At times, the band recorded by themselves, but because the converted schoolhouse didn't have a proper control room window, their technician would often sneak in without them knowing so that he could manipulate their sound. "The best recordings were made that way, when they were playing for themselves," Graupner recalled.[32]

With their boxes and their sneaky engineer, Faust created a complex, uncertain ecosystem for themselves—at any moment, one's instrument could be dropped out of the mix, or dunked into a deep tank of reverb, or shot across the room to an unexpected loudspeaker. "Actually it should be the equipment which should be in the spotlight," Nettelbeck averred.[33] As I argued in the introduction, this constant deflection and redistribution of agency—to another musician, or the engineer, or a piece of equipment—characterizes a mode of rock improvisation distinct from the heroic mode of the guitar solo. Jerry Garcia or George Harrison improvised in order to affirm their smooth mastery of form (what, in a related context, Ralph Ellison called the "recognition of manhood"), but the musicians of Faust continually interrupted their own flow, setting up obstacles and detours that barred the assertion of personality as often as they enabled it.[34] If the heroic guitar solo drew on the afro-logics of jazz, then the diffuse, impersonal musical environment fostered by Faust seemed to animate the Cagean logics of indeterminacy, even as that band simultaneously cultivated the black diasporic musical tropes of repetition and groove. The 1973 "manifesto" of the band, written by fill-in guitarist Peter Blegvad, specified this understanding of human-machine relations by listing tropes of open-ended interaction in a state of unknowing. He wrote, "A list called 'thus' on which you and Faust appear [i.e., at a concert] also includes the Heisenberg principle, . . . relativity, . . . cybernetics, D.N.A., game theory, etc."[35]

Uncertainty leads to failure as often as it leads to surprise, and this observation brings us to Faust's live debut on November 23, 1971, a promotional event that Polydor crowed "could change the face of rock music for the next decade."[36] Because they hadn't yet performed or issued any recordings, the following that showed up at Hamburg's Musikhalle that night must have been generated though word-of-mouth and previous connections, not to mention Nettelbeck's spirited hustling. Graupner and the band had planned to re-create the surround-sound environment they had been experimenting in back at the schoolhouse; Dynacord supplied an array of loudspeakers.[37] But the wiring was very complicated and they couldn't get anything to work in the relatively short amount of time they had been given to set up. Eight o'clock came and went. Faust soldered on, but the audience grew restless. After a hastily convened rehearsal backstage, the band attempted to perform their set a cappella, each member humming his own part. Still more time was needed. They sent the audience away for an hour or two, and by the time they returned, Faust could get some peeps out of the equipment. It didn't last, however, and soon the audience joined them onstage to kick around the wall of empty tin cans that had been built for the concert. Bassist Jean-Hervé Peron recalled, "We were so nervous and it was such a drama—so bad it was good again."[38] By most accounts, it did not go well. Another member of the group, Hans-Joachim Irmler, was more sanguine in his appraisal of the event: "It was no disaster; in my opinion it was the only true concert we ever did. . . . A complete improvisation. . . . I don't know what the others think, but I never wanted to be a rock band; I wanted to create something completely different and new. And this concert was completely different."[39]

The self-titled album they were promoting was pretty different, too. Released on the continent in early 1972 and in the United Kingdom several months later, Faust's debut was printed on clear vinyl and packaged in a striking, transparent sleeve. In the record's opening gesture, a ragged, buzzing drone of noise swishes in and out over a quiet organ fifth for a while, until a snippet of the Stones' "(I Can't Get No) Satisfaction" squiggles out of the mix, only to be answered shortly by the Beatles' "All You Need Is Love." They sound like bittersweet echoes of a pop landscape long burned away. The ensuing eight-minute song, "Why Don't You Eat Carrots," sounds like a medley of short piano interludes, an odd, loping waltz complete with trumpet solo, and a drunken football chant. Sometimes these fragments go away and sometimes they return, but they're always haloed by a ring of noisy, gurgling sound effects. The second half of side A, another paste-up job called "Meadow Meal," begins with some intrapiano noodling and thwacking that has been augmented with heavy delay—an improvisation, clearly. We then hear a songlike combination of guitar, keyboard, and vocals that imply a fevered kind of paranoia, but this tension soon gives way to a funky, fuzzed-out groove for the whole band. Eventually, Faust halts the proceedings for a field recording of a thunderstorm, which soon cross-fades into a wistful calliope solo that manages to charm in spite of its menacing background buzz.

The second side of *Faust* is occupied by a single track, "Miss Fortune," that blasts off with an amiable jam for a couple of minutes before unraveling into a long stretch of slack, atmospheric noodling. Another eupeptic groove delivers the listener to a second stretch of the giggles. The opus draws to a close with maudlin acoustic guitar arpeggios and a bit of poetry. Despite these frequent changes of speed, texture, and style, Faust's debut sounds remarkably unified. It issues a constant flow of burbling susurrations, and the band exploits the stereo field with great alacrity—every little squeak and smear gets its own place in the mix, and most of these sounds slither around continuously from left to right and back again. Above all, the record is unpredictable. You never know what is going to come next, whether a bit of melody might come back again in four or five minutes; there is little of the directionality that is otherwise so important to rock music. Instead, Faust seize on interruption, distraction, and witty non sequiturs.

In his table-setting review of *Faust,* Philipe Paringaux enthused, "All the resources of the studio and electronics are exploited here with a devouring curiosity, but also with a remarkable sense of proportion."[40] Beyond charismatic and energetic singing, beyond clever or catchy lyrics, and beyond instrumental virtuosity or rear-end-shifting rhythms, Paringaux wrote, Faust "has chosen to retain from all the elements of rock just that which is most neglected today: the investigation of sound, an area which is given so much attention on this album that it becomes the album's essential feature. Sound. Electronic and acoustic."[41] And yet, even as he labeled *Faust* as a kind of elemental return to the essence of rock (in the form of sonic exploration), he also worried that the genre wasn't "adequate to describe something which transcends all the limits of contemporary music." By now, this dissatisfaction with inherited groupings was a familiar theme in post-68 rock experimentalism. For Paringaux, though, such dissatisfaction couldn't get in the way of proclaiming the album to be one of the most innovative in the history of rock.

Years later, Nettelbeck told Cutler, "Even in the early 70's, . . . to play something like that first record to an A&R man meant that you had to sit through a lot of long lunches and dinners afterwards." It hadn't sold well, and the producer was beginning to feel some heat from the higher-ups at Polydor. "I was in Hamburg three times a week, making excuses."[42] Nettelbeck exerted more control over Faust's second album, *So Far*, which was released in an all-black, embossed sleeve in the summer of 1972. This one offered easily recognizable, standalone songs, even if they were often on the long side and surrounded with more wanderative dawdles. The opener, "It's a Rainy Day, Sunshine Girl," was a standout track that recalled the Velvet Underground in its bare-bones drum part (a single low tom struck on every beat), long harmonic stasis, and lyrics—in English—that were delivered somewhere between singing and speaking. Other tunes, such as "No Harm" and "I Got My Car and My TV," showcase a very funky rhythm section (of Peron and Diermaier) that was swiftly developing into Faust's secret weapon. The critics remained interested, but reviews of *So Far* were ambivalent.[43] Faust did find a strong supporter in John Peel, who played the B-side to their only single, "It's a Bit of a Pain," frequently on his radio show. Although *So Far* had not yet been released when he published a column about them in *Disc* magazine, Peel advised his audience "to hear the LP though because it must be one of the most important of the past few years. It's not often that you hear a band that is heading off in a totally new direction."[44]

Many years later, Nettelbeck recalled, "The second record came out. Still no sales—and the problems really came to a head. Nothing sold, ever. There was no distribution."[45] Because Faust was a project of Polydor International, the German executives felt that their authority had been undercut, and therefore they felt little obligation to get behind the release. Nettelbeck continued, "So, the record never really came onto the market. We survived a little longer, thanks to another rule: once you have spent money, you spend more—so as not to lose the original investment. It took another year before Polydor decided that it would be better to cut their losses. Then it was officially over."[46]

Bigger than the Beatles: Faust and Virgin

It was over with Polydor, yes, but not for Nettelbeck and Faust. In the spring of 1973, shortly after getting dumped, Nettelbeck discovered that Richard Branson and Simon Draper were scouting for bands. Now that Virgin had a successful mail-order operation and about fifteen shops across the United Kingdom, they had decided to capitalize on this infrastructure by founding a record label. They had already established a recording studio. In the middle of 1971, Branson bought a country manor house in Shipton-on-Cherwell, five miles north of Oxford, for £30,000. The Manor, as it came to be known, was set up and staffed by Tom Newman over the course of about a year. The house had fifteen bedrooms, a billiards lounge, and a formal dining room. Newman and the other engineers—Phil Newell, Phil Becque, and Simon Heyworth—installed the studio itself in a barn that had been converted into a squash court. The first band to record there was the Bonzo Dog Band in November 1971, followed shortly thereafter by John Cale.[47]

With the label itself, Virgin decided to stick with the bands and styles that were performing well in mail order but not yet represented by British labels. Can and Amon Düül II were already signed to United Artists in London, so that left Tangerine Dream and Faust among their big sellers. After Rolf Kaiser insisted that Draper take all of his Ohr Records slate along with Tangerine Dream, a condition that Virgin would never accept, Draper knew that the immediate future would lie with Faust, "the other band that I think must be the best in Germany," he commented at the time.[48] (Virgin would indeed eventually sign Tangerine Dream, alone, in 1973.) Draper later recalled, "We contacted Uwe and went to Hamburg. He invited us to stay the night. . . . We got on really well with him. Nearly all of our connection to Faust was through him." Nettelbeck made his pitch: "I told them that a good idea to launch Virgin would be to make a very cheap record. Not free, nobody takes something that's free. They liked that, and I gave them *The Faust Tapes*."[49]

This record, Faust's third long-player, was a kind of sampler that Nettelbeck had put together from bits of tape the band had recorded over the last few years. Virgin created a lot of hype by pricing it at only 48p (most LPs went for more than £2), and *The Faust Tapes* therefore became one of the best-selling LPs of experimental music ever released. Julian Cope recalled, "Everybody bought it. Not everybody loved it."[50] Although Bridget Riley's "Crest" graced the cover, I find the verso to be more interesting: it was essentially a press package condensed onto a single, text-heavy twelve-by-twelve surface that made its pitch in blazing capitals: "Since British interest in the group has been unusually great, it has been decided to make some of this unofficial material available to the public in this country. . . . *The Faust Tapes* [is] a unique glimpse behind the scenes of a group which European and British critics have hailed as one of the most exciting and exploratory in the world."

And to leave no doubt about the opinion of those all-important critics, Virgin reprinted excerpts of the reviews and features that had appeared in *Best, Rock and Folk, Sounds, Disc, Extra, Pop Music,* and *NME* throughout 1972. The album reported on its own hype while also producing more of it.

Many anecdotal sources attest to *The Faust Tapes'* high sales in the summer of 1973; *Music Week* reported that Virgin had sold out of its initial pressing—40,000 copies—in the first week, and final estimates range from 80,000 to 100,000 sales.[51] The album even made it onto *Melody Maker's* Pop 30 charts for a few weeks during the summer, and it was pegged at number 1 on the Virgin bestseller list for the better part of June and July. Eventually, Virgin said they were forced to delete it from the catalogue, because they claimed to be losing money with each sale.[52]

What did it sound like? On balance, it was closer to *Faust* than it was to *So Far*. There are a couple of tunes-with-lyrics floating around on the two untitled sides, but they aren't separated and labeled as such. Otherwise, *The Faust Tapes* consists of many short sound experiments: masses of organs moving at different speeds, looped drum phrases or vocal outbursts that become the basis for more improvisations on top, bits and bobs of homemade, Cologne-style electronic music, and casual convivialities seemingly captured by a single microphone across the room. The album advances a strong impression of heightened electronic intervention. Unlike the first side of *Faust*, the fragments here are spliced together roughly, usually without transition or overlap. These bare cuts, as well as the frequent manipulations of tape speed, the prominent loops, and even the title itself, emphasized the work's medium.

Richard Williams used the album as an occasion to assess "the claims made for Faust's importance in the wider scheme of avant-garde rock music."[53] He concluded that their "cerebral" experiments left him emotionally unsatisfied. Ian MacDonald, on the other hand, thought it was as good as *So Far*, and occasionally reached the heights of the first record. "For an album that was never meant for general release, it's excellent—and for 48p, it's ridiculous."[54]

The view from forty years later makes it extremely difficult to imagine how Virgin could have heard sales potential in this music, but we cannot underestimate the hype surrounding Faust in 1973 nor the importance of MacDonald as a tastemaker in London during these years. MacDonald, whom Draper calls "the all powerful avant-garde journalist on the scene," had been a classmate of Henry Cow at Cambridge in the late 1960s. John Greaves says, "I remember being very impressed; he was the first real intellectual I met. He was only nineteen, but you could see this fierce intellect bursting all over the place." In 1972, he had joined the *New Musical Express* as part of the team of critics that would help *NME* overtake *Melody Maker* in circulation by 1975.

In "Germany Calling," MacDonald reserved his highest praise for Faust, "[who] are a single-handed justification of all the ballyhoo that's been kicked up about krautrock in recent years."[55] Upon hearing an advance copy of *The Faust Tapes*, he predicted "a masterpiece." Over the next few months (into the spring of 1973), MacDonald published several articles and reviews favorable to the band. In one piece, "Common Market Rock," he wrote that their debut "gets more awesome on every hearing and could be among the most important rock records ever made."[56] And, although his review of *So Far* was tepid by comparison, he still used the occasion to hype them: "There must be something in the new album that I've missed, since it's selling like hot cakes. Better hear it yourself."

Polydor certainly didn't think that *So Far* was selling like hotcakes, so one might wonder where MacDonald was getting his information. One important source, it turns out, was Nettelbeck. "I . . . told him that he had to write that Faust was the biggest thing ever—otherwise no more Faust. He did it. . . . And with those two pages in a major music paper, Faust the biggest thing since the Beatles, no other band that ingenious, I was able to reopen negotiations. I should add that I didn't bribe Ian, he really did love Faust and the record.[57]" Love Faust he certainly did. One of his most vertiginous raves is worth reproducing at length:

> Noting all the minor innovations in rock since Lennon and McCartney hauled the music bodily out of the twelve-bar trap of rock-and-roll and rhythm-and-blues—noting Brian Wilson's visionary production job on "Good Vibrations," noting the experiments half-completed by the Velvet Underground and the United States of America into the sound-limits of a Late Sixties rock-group, noting Captain Beefheart's casually suggested fusion of primitive blues with free jazz ("free rock," in fact) on "Trout Mask Replica," and forgetting neither "A Day In the Life," "Tomorrow Never Knows," or "I Am The Walrus"—taking all of these contributions into account, I have to say that the *implications* of what Faust are doing form the most significant conceptual revolution in rock for ten years.[58]

Yes, MacDonald thought that Faust were more important than any of those other innovators on the rock connoisseur's list, including the Beach Boys, the Velvet Underground, the United States of America, and Captain Beefheart. "The most significant conceptual revolution in rock for ten years": they were the biggest thing since the Beatles!

The conceptual revolution MacDonald had in mind was Faust's collaging technique. Unlike Zappa, that other skilled cut-up artist, Faust snipped at long takes of organically emerging improvisation, rather than pasting together individually composed frags. For MacDonald, this difference constituted a significant advance in the evolution of the rock form. (And, although he admitted that "the element of rock in the group's work is neither crucial, nor particularly salient," he still thought that "the rock consciousness" pervaded their output.) MacDonald wrote, "How did Faust arrive at this concept? By simply investigating the technology of the rock medium in the same way that they arrived at synthesizing, not one sound or instrument, but the whole group; by really looking at the art and meaning of magnetic tape-editing, and then cross-indexing this with the naturally interrupted continuity of everyday experience."[59] The mediation of magnetic tape, therefore, was crucially important to their aesthetic, according to MacDonald, because it created the possibility for both the documentation of open improvisation as well as the interruptive cuts that were such a pronounced feature of their records.

So Faust had good buzz when Virgin decided to sign them: plenty of coverage in the press, radio airplay, and healthy sales in mail order and the shops. John Peel's producer, John Walters, told Karl Dallas that he hadn't received so much listener mail about a new band since the sixties, even though Polydor hadn't widely publicized the first two records.[60] Draper recalled, "There's definitely a factor there—Ian MacDonald's belief that they were more important than the Beatles. He actually said that. At the same, I thought if rock artists sang in an exaggerated or even discernible foreign way, they were doomed to disappointment and neglect."[61] Nonetheless, the enthusiasm of Virgin's mail-order customers for all these German bands convinced him that Faust had a real chance. "I must have thought that Faust's instrumental thing was so powerful that that would [overcome the foreign accent]. . . . Tangerine Dream were totally safe, because they didn't sing."

Okay, Corral: Henry Cow Signs to Virgin

The Faust Tapes was one of a few releases that Draper and Branson chose to launch their new label, an enterprise to which Draper had devoted the lion's share of his time since June 1972.[62] As we've already seen, Draper had well-honed instincts for what would sell, given his experience with the mail-order and retail business. He surmised that they would have to concentrate on English and European artists, even though his own tastes went toward US bands. "That sort of music wasn't being made in Britain. What we were already doing, of course, was importing records for our mail order customers [from] the sort of New European scene, records by Gong, for example. . . . So it became fairly obvious that this was going to be our own special little area to develop."[63]

In addition to *The Faust Tapes*, Virgin released *Flying Teapot*, the fourth long-player by Gong. Draper recalls, "I was very, very much a fan of Soft Machine, so when I started looking for bands to sign, I looked around at what was happening, and I didn't like much of the contemporary British music. . . . So I went back to what I'd liked a few years before, and which I still like, which is Soft Machine." They attempted to sign Robert Wyatt, but were unsuccessful until the following year (when they landed his stone classic, *Rock Bottom*); they likewise struck out with Kevin Ayers, who was already signed to EMI's Harvest imprint. But Draper did find Mike Oldfield, a young guitarist who played in the Ayers's band, The Whole World. Oldfield had been living at the Manor and supporting himself by assisting Newman in engineering duties for visiting bands. As we'll see, Oldfield's breakaway success with *Tubular Bells* would provide the capital and publicity to keep Virgin's less successful artists afloat for a few years.

After the initial releases of Faust, Gong, and Oldfield in the late spring of 1973, Virgin signed acts that would cement their reputation for quirky, complicated rock for discerning tastes: Henry Cow, Kevin Coyne, Hatfield and the North, Robert Wyatt, and Comus. They even signed Captain Beefheart, but ended up with the duds *Unconditionally Guaranteed* and *Moonbeams and Bluejeans*. Draper comments, "What I was interested in . . . was to make impact. At the time, what was more important to me was that people who I respected, like Ian MacDonald, . . . thought we were hard-hitting, a label with integrity." Integrity comes in many forms, of course, and part of Virgin's appeal in these early years was its embrace of less commercially viable artists; these included the funny poet/songwriter Ivor Cutler and Lady June, whose 1974 disc of poetry and music, *Linguistic Leprosy*, featured Ayers and Brian Eno. Beyond these rock bands and literary loonies, Virgin continued to operate in that post-67, vernacular avant-garde, with releases of electronic music by Tangerine Dream, Klaus Schulze, David Bedford, and White Noise.[64] They also struck up licensing deals with labels such as JCOA, which allowed them to distribute albums by Carla Bley, Mike Mantler, and Don Cherry.

Virgin further cemented their reputation as a sophisticated alternative to the mainstream labels by releasing very few singles, though the success of Wyatt's cover of "I'm a Believer" in 1974 might have caused them to rethink this strategy. One might take as evidence of this reputation the actions of David Toop, who, as we have already observed, was thinking hard about a rock-affiliated kind of open improvisation during these years. And he wanted a record deal, so he took his best tapes of Rain in the Face to Simon Draper in early 1973. The Virgin honcho wasn't impressed. "He thought it was commercial, . . . and it wasn't," Draper comments. According to Toop, Draper continued, "'Let me play you this thing that we're releasing,' and it was *Tubular Bells*. [pause] What can you say?" Toop's implied eye roll illustrates an important point: the taste communities that circulated around Virgin were certainly not homogeneous. As we will shortly see, *Tubular Bells* may have sounded some of the qualities that were associated with rock experimentalism of the post-67 years, but that didn't ensure a uniformity of reception for the music. Indeed, the best we could say is that Virgin produced its own partial, particular translations of experimentalism into the vernacular domain—as was the case with any associated band, label, institution, or artist of the time. But the particularity of these offerings—and their limited sales potential—was built into Virgin's business plan. Draper told a journalist at the time, "As Henry Cow say, and I agree with them, if you want a particular kind of music, then Henry Cow are the only band who're playing that kind of music. That's what we aimed for in each of our groups, that kind of uniqueness, and I do think it's given the label a strong identity."[65]

To Henry Cow and others, Virgin represented an alternative kind of business culture. In 1977, Draper's comments to an interviewer indicate the possible extent of this perceived difference: "Early on our ambitions for the label were quite modest, in keeping with the spirit of Virgin at that time we wanted to establish maybe some kind of a co-operative, working with people who probably wouldn't get record deals otherwise."[66] Although this sense of the young company might be little more than an example of renegade marketing, a strategy that is particularly common in the creative and lifestyle industries, it was pervasive in the early years. Branson was a picture of idealism in the press, telling the readers of *Sounds* in 1974 that "there are certain people who simply wouldn't get a deal at all if we didn't sign them— when you know that it's hard to say no."[67] When combined with Draper's good taste, this kind of idealism created the perception that Virgin was just different. For example, Peacock asserted that Virgin bands were luckier than most: "In the main they get good deals, more rope than most, and a record company team who are young and enthusiastic about their work, which is more than you can say for the majority of companies."[68] Stories about the label—then and now—rarely fail to mention the flat-rate salary of £20 per week (or £12, or £30—accounts vary) that every employee earned, including its founder and A&R man. (This arrangement certainly did not last forever, but Henry Cow did the same in their organization after 1973.[69])

The Cow had already made some unsuccessful attempts at landing a contract. Hodgkinson recalls that—in the summer of 1971 or even earlier (i.e., pre-Cutler)—they recorded a demo for a label that seemed on the cusp of offering them a big-money deal. "I remember it being pretty tough," Hodgkinson remarks, "in the sense that we were just ordered about by these middle-aged guys, who didn't even want us to listen to what we'd recorded. . . . We were these total greenhorns, and they were completely de-fining the situation." Hodgkinson, Frith, Geoff Leigh, and John Greaves each retain the strong impression that another interested label—the name has faded from memory—had been set up as the avant-garde wing of a major company that wished to use it primarily as a tax-write-off. "Sign bands like Henry Cow and lose money!" Leigh explained. In the end, the encounter went nowhere, but left a bad taste in the Cow mouth. "The idea of being dis-enchanted with record labels was an ongoing topic of conversation amongst musicians," Frith said. In any case, it would take a good year and a half until the band seriously considered recording an album. In late 1972 or early 1973, they had tapes circulating among RCA, CBS, Barclay, Chrysalis, Island, MCA, ATV Music, and Liberty; nothing came of these, but members of Cow seem to have met in person with Polydor, Chrysalis, Virgin, and CBS in Febru-ary 1973. One month earlier, the French label Barclay wrote to Leigh, "Quite unfortunately, your beautiful music is a bit far out for our very square in-clined music market."[70]

Virgin quickly emerged as the best and only option—they were certainly not middle-aged powerbrokers. Hodgkinson remembers, "They were really good at dealing with you as if everything was really laid back and informal." And Faust—whose name said it all, and who were portrayed in the press as a unique kind of problem for the commodity-obsessed star machine of the culture industry—had already signed.[71] That was a good precedent: if Virgin was good enough for them, why not for Henry Cow? Daevid Allen, Robert Wyatt, Lol Coxhill, Ian MacDonald, and Steve Lake (of *Melody Maker*) all whispered into Virgin's ear on Henry Cow's behalf. Inside the band, it ap-pears that the two most biz-minded Cows took the lead. Greaves recalls, "We'd done a lot of courting of Virgin, through Simon Draper, who was our man. Richard never had anything to do with anything, really, except he would say 'yes' or 'no' at the end." They'd all been in and out of Draper's office in Notting Hill, but Greaves was perhaps the most committed to that particular project. Leigh also played a direct role at an important juncture. In January 1973, Gong ran out of dope at the Manor, where they were recording *Flying Teapot*. Steve Hillage, who had moved out of the Walmer Road house when he joined the group, rang up Leigh, who enjoyed a reputation as a solid source. Gong's manager, Bob Benamou, was in London for the day—could Leigh hook them up? Sensing an opportunity—Benamou was a consummate networker, and his close associate, Jean Georgakarakos, ran the BYG label in Paris—Leigh had a copy of their Peel session tape ready to hand when Benamou knocked on the door.

"So how's it going up at the Manor?" Leigh asked.

"Oh, it's fantastic, man! Everybody's up there—Richard and Simon, too."

"If everyone is up there, can you take this tape and play it to them?"[72]

Draper apparently liked what he heard, and Henry Cow had a few "official" meetings with the label in February before visiting the Manor on April 7–11 to record some initial probings. The Cows took advantage of their time, recording an early version of what would become the entire first side of their debut LP.[73]

Although things seemed to be going well—and the Cows were *very* interested in pursuing Virgin—they continued to harbor suspicions about how signing a recording contract would restrict their freedom and compromise their position as independent operators. There was also a certain safety in remaining off the big stage that a label might provide. As Hodgkinson put it, "We were right and they were wrong. We were out and they were straight. That starts to happen. You say, 'That's why we're not raking it in. It's because those capitalist motherfuckers don't know what they're missing.'" Without a contract and its attendant promotion and publicity, focus on sales figures, and critical attention, the *artistes* in the band could stay above the fray.

These concerns were readily apparent in a group interview with a film crew from the French program Rockenstock, who visited the Manor after Henry Cow had signed in 1973. Frith told them, "Groups tend to sign up with record companies before they know what the record contract is going to mean to them. And as a result, they don't have very much of a nice time. They lose a lot . . ."

"Not only that," Hodgkinson interjected, "but record companies have, in a normal situation, the power to completely alter what you're doing and convert it into what they're doing, which is . . ."

"Yes, most record companies, you'll join the record company, and they'll try and persuade you to get a girl singer, or change your mind toward doing this and that, whereas with Virgin we do have complete freedom."

"They package your stuff, as well, in such a way that denies any . . ."

So was it simply a matter of Henry Cow finally finding a record company that would allow them to do what they want?

"It wasn't entirely that," Hodgkinson responded.

Frith said, "We wouldn't have signed with anybody."

Hodgkinson continued, "It was partly a choice: you've got a choice on the one hand of trying to stay completely outside of things—you're distanced—and the choice of accepting that they are there, and they do control the means of getting [your music] to audiences, and engaging with them and finding out what they're about. And I think for a long time we really just didn't want to have anything to do with them at all."

"And we didn't," added Cutler.

"And we didn't."

But how did they live without going hungry?

"We starved," Cutler said with a grin.[74]

In fact, Draper had even floated the idea that Henry Cow put out their album on Virgin's boutique subsidiary, Caroline. He told a journalist in 1974, "We were thinking of setting up a label where we could offer people the facility of making a record and we would distribute it only through our shops. It was based on my experience with Incus and seeing what is possible on a very limited basis with records which are very esoteric and have very limited appeal."[75] It turned out that their distribution deal with Island ruled out Virgin's plan to distribute Caroline themselves, but they retained the imprint for one-off, low-cost albums. (The first LP on Caroline was Tony Conrad's *Outside the Dream Syndicate*, which he had recorded in 1972 with Faust at their studio in Wümme. At the time, Draper commented, "I think its the sort of record that not more than a couple of thousand people are really going to want so it would be senseless to spend too much money on it.") In the end, Henry Cow decided against the Caroline option, and elected to try their luck in the big leagues. Many years later, Draper comments, "This is definitely hindsight, but I suspect that they thought they were important, and therefore, they had to be very careful. I think they were overestimating their real sales potential."

Figure 2.1 Henry Cow recording *Leg End* at the Manor, Oxfordshire, 1973. Tom Newman can be seen in the middle frame of the right column, and Ian MacDonald waves from the second row. These photos are among the very few that show Henry Cow in the recording studio. COURTESY OF CHRIS CUTLER.

Henry Cow signed the contract on May 10, 1973. It specified two albums per year for three years, and Virgin had the option to extend the arrangement for two more years in 1976. They could expect to work "at such first class studio as the Company may select," and the contract offered the Manor at reduced rates for this purpose; the company would recoup the costs of these sessions from royalties. Virgin retained copyright of Henry Cow's music. (To this day, Virgin gets paid whenever a Cow composition is sold.) In return, they paid the band an advance of £1,500, and agreed not to "alter the order of tracks, re-mix, edit, or otherwise alter" the masters submitted by the band for release.[76]

For all their concerns about retaining control, Henry Cow had a made serious mistake in giving up copyright. Cutler clarifies, "Instead of looking at the bit where it said, 'The band will be paid nothing and will pay for all of the bills incurred in the making'—we didn't spot that—we spotted the bit that said, 'Virgin shall be able to take out bar 97 if it doesn't feel right.' We said, 'No, we're not having any of that!'" As Hodgkinson and Cutler now realize, it never occurred to the band at the time to borrow money, rent a studio, record and press their own album, and then distribute it themselves. "We didn't *even* secure our own publishing—that's how naive we were," said Cutler. So, without realizing the extent to which they had given up the game by signing away copyright, the band stressed their artistic freedom in their early encounters with the rock press. In his first ardent puff piece on the Cow, Lake wrote, "Almost alone in the executive-cluttered rock business, Henry Cow have retained control over nearly every facet of their activities." They make their own bookings, have final say on all advertisements and covers, and "even wrote their own press release."[77] Wow!

Not everyone was gung ho about signing the contract. Leigh recalls, "I didn't *really* want to sign this contract. I *knew* it was a bad contract." During his time with Mouseproof, he had met an attorney named Robert Allen, "a high-flying lawyer who had been one of the co-founders of Release, the pro-cannabis legalisation lobby group. He did Gerry [Fitz-Gerald]'s contract, probably one of the few times a contract favoured the artist rather than the record company."[78] Leigh had a strong wish to call on Allen's expertise, but the other Cows didn't think it was necessary. While Frith, Hodgkinson, and Cutler were most concerned with securing their creative freedom, their road-hardened reeds man had his eye on the bottom line. "Based on my previous experiences, I was not the kind of person who was going to be super friendly to Richard Branson, Simon Draper, and these people, because—despite everything—in the back of my mind I thought,

'Yeah, they're coming across as being very cool people, but they're just like the rest of them, probably. In the end, you always lose, they always win.'"

But with his relatively straightforward personal history in the music business, Greaves enjoyed an untroubled relationship with Virgin. "I love the fact that we were on Virgin: it was a complete anomaly. It shouldn't have happened, and it wouldn't happen again. Those records—whatever they are—they're anomalous to any kind of major label's career prospects! And the fact that we're having full-page spreads in *Melody Maker* around this stuff. . . . Doors were open which closed *immediately* afterwards." Indeed, the importance of this post-1967 openness cannot be overstated. Bands, listeners, critics, and label honchos cultivated a willingness to push into uncertainty and work with whatever they found or created there. Draper recalls, "Initially, I just thought they are very sure of their own destiny, they have a very strong sense of their own identity. I don't know what's going to happen, but they're gonna make some sort of positive impact, that could turn into sales. It's all just as vague as that, really. . . . I was willing to suspend disbelief. . . . I thought it was important to make an impact, be different, and somehow from that, it would all flow. I signed Henry Cow in that spirit."

The Politics of Reverb: Recording *Leg End*

Have you ever been in a professional recording studio? It can be a profoundly alienating experience. You're wearing huge, heavy headphones that convey a weird, imbalanced mix to your ears with an almost perverse intimacy—you find yourself simultaneously closer to and farther from the "real" sound than you ever wanted to be. A heavy cord dangles down your side, occasionally tangling up your left hand while you play, or hanging free like a dead weight that gradually tugs the phones down one side of your face; in the middle of a seven-minute take, you may find yourself wishing you had bunched up or coiled that heft on top of a nearby amp, but it's too late now, and why the hell are you thinking about the cord when you should really be concentrating on staying in time with the kick drum? That would be a lot easier if you could actually *see* the drummer, but he's on the other side of two baffles; you can barely make out his right shoulder from time to time if you crane your neck (but that just pulls the headphones even further down). Oh, by the way, it's 3:30 in the afternoon, and you are hacking your way through the fourth take of a solo that's supposed to be "searing," but it's difficult to summon the inspiration when the audience comprises a technician futzing with a lead by your feet and two engineers peering at you with wooden dispassion from the darkened control room. They look like half the cover of *Meet the Beatles*. When it's finished, you break the silence to suggest adjustments to your comrades, but halfway through your first sentence, a sharp screech ricochets through the headphones. You wonder if this interruption is related to what you overheard the technician ask his co-workers yesterday: "Why don't they just stop fucking talking, and get fucking on with it!" Anyway, the screech is gone before you even have time to remove the phones, so you continue to articulate your analysis of the preceding performance until you realize that two of your bandmates are also voicing some suggestions; none of you knew the others were talking because nobody can hear anything with headphones on. Meanwhile, the head of the label has dropped by, which only reminds you of what is at stake, and the band is paying a daily fee to work here. Tick tock, tick tock.

I do not mean to imply that Henry Cow uniformly had such a dispiriting experience when they recorded *Leg End*, but as a young band still relatively new to the studio, there might have been moments like these. The BBC sessions had been only about sonic capture—set up, roll tape, record performance. Same day. Now, however, Henry Cow were camped at the Manor for more than a month. (They were there from May 12 to June 14, with frequent breaks for one-off gigs, Explorer's Club events, and rehearsals.) They would need to learn how to compose and arrange under the pressures of the studio environment.

A shaggy old country home, the Manor offered big bedrooms with fireplaces, a large dining room, and pleasantly overgrown gardens for walks in the afternoon. Its gender politics offered no revolution: four or five young women handled cooking, cleaning, and laundry duties. One of them, Maggie Thomas, would (in about a year) begin a relationship with Cutler and join the Cows as cook, roadie, and live sound engineer. At the Manor in 1973, however, she dedicated herself to daily tasks, like everybody else. "What was she doing? You never knew what *anybody* was supposed to be doing," Hodgkinson laughs. Newman was ostensibly the boss, but nobody was really in charge in those early years; people just got on with the work that needed to be done. "There weren't bosses and workers at the Manor," recalled Philip Newell, the chief engineer there. The women prepared a vegetarian feast every night for the staff and band, who had no trouble adjusting to their temporary change in circumstances. Buddies such as Jeremy Baines and Ian MacDonald dropped by, and Branson was around, of course; Greaves had caught a ride up to the Manor in the boss's Bentley.

The creature comforts and conviviality were great, but Henry Cow were embarking on a new kind of creative process and felt some trepidation as a result. The discomfort apparently manifested as arrogance. Frith said, "It's very hard to make a realized record when six people are involved in a learning process at the same time. . . . We always thought that we were much more knowledgeable, and better, than other people, or at least that's the way we were perceived."[79] All things considered, however, Henry Cow could not have asked for a more welcoming introduction, or a more enthusiastic collaborator, than what they got with Newman. He knew what he was doing, but he hadn't had loads of experience; the first record he produced had been *Tubular Bells*. A rather straight-ahead rock 'n' roller, he nonetheless took to them right away. "I suddenly got introduced to a whole area of music that I just didn't know existed. The concept of having kind of a 'rock-and-roll band' lineup . . . , and then playing stuff that was like a bar of 16/7 and a bar of 3/9—you know, fantastically complex time signatures. I was just gobsmacked at watching these guys playing, because to my ignorant ear, it was chaotic. But I was amazed that they could repeat the chaos, you know? Repeatable chaos! I count Henry Cow as a wonderful tutor for me." From the band's perspective, Newman was that rare example of a nonproprietorial recording engineer; he gave them access to all the equipment and was never concerned with protecting his status. And, just as importantly, he was open to experimentation. While the BBC professionals, for example, were set in their ways—the drum mikes go here, the amplifiers go there—Newman could be coaxed into trying new things.

"Can you get more top in the bass sound?" Hodgkinson might have asked.

"Not really, no," Newman would have responded.

"Oh."

Pause. "Well, it's the pickups. If you turn the treble on the amp up, it would just make a lot of noise."

"Well what happens if you put a microphone very close to the bass guitar strings?"

"You don't want to do that."

"Why not?"

"Well, I suppose we could try it."[80]

This kind of conversation would not have taken place in many other recording scenarios. Henry Cow *enjoyed* being skeptical about the received ways of doing things. They liked to question conventional wisdom and experiment with their own solutions, to attempt to redefine the limits of what was possible in a given situation. For the most part, Newman was flexible enough to join them in this approach.

The same could not be said for Newell, who was more technically gifted but less artistically adventurous than Newman. Once the Cows had laid down a good group take of one particular track, they would work individually at different times throughout the day or night, adding overdubs or correcting little errors in execution. This working method meant that Newell and Oldfield also took on considerable engineering responsibilities during the session. Newell couldn't relate to the more cerebral style of Henry Cow. Newman explains, "He didn't like them, because he saw them as posey intellectuals with no rock and roll soul. . . . He saw them as monstrous procrastinators and prevaricators." (Newell, it should be noted, was the source of the quote above: "Why don't they just stop fucking talking, and get fucking on with it!")

What were Henry Cow going on about? The collective memory has yielded two strong contenders: reverb and balance. "Reverb would have been a point of discussion. The politics of reverb," Hodgkinson comments. He adds, "It might have been my idea [laughter]. . . . It's just an attempt to gloss over difference. It's an attempt to add scale or an attempt to 'big up' sound, therefore it might be associated with pomposity, exaggeration—an effect. 'Effects.' Artifice. 'Effects are bourgeois,' right? It's kind of fake." But, although his principles might have led him to one position on reverb, his ears probably led him to another, because rock recording conventions were (and are) surprisingly strong. Ignore them, and the resulting album will feel off in some vaguely undefined way. Newman recalls that he was not "able to convince them that reverb gives you an extra dimension. It gives you distance, in a way that you can't get just by turning it down. If everything's flat and you turn it down, it just becomes small." Eventually, Newman did convince the band to add some reverb here and there, but *Leg End* remains an unusually dry record.

It is also unusually busy, because Henry Cow tended to insist that all the instrumental parts were of equal importance, and each had to be audibly present to the same degree as the next. Newman says, "They appeared to me to have very rigid, unbendable ideas about balance. . . . Everybody in the band felt that their parts were equally important, and everything had to be the same level of loudness, all the way through. It was almost a kind of communist principle . . . : everybody's got to be heard, all the time." At some moments, this principle of equality manifested in a comic scenario: in mixing, each member of the band controlling his own fader, five bodies (plus

Newman) huddled around the mixing desk in a convoluted choreography of fingers and elbows.

The problem of proper balance and the equality of all instrumental voices was a sharp point of contradiction between social and aesthetic values. There were two aspects to this problem. First, as Newman would put it, "the brain wants to be led by a single instrument at a time," meaning that "well recorded" rock necessarily produced a certain kind of sonic hierarchy—if the second guitar line isn't making a clear contribution to the texture, just drop it. While this kind of decision concerned aesthetic judgments about the group's music, the second aspect of the problem had more to do with who could be invested with the power to make such judgments. Perhaps the recording scenario worked best if there were a single discerning producer to silence the endless logorrhea, the procrastination and prevarication, of collective decision making? Such questions would continue to shadow the band in future recording sessions, posed and answered in various ways.

Although Henry Cow had not yet developed a clear analysis of the twin problems of aesthetic and social hierarchy, they did enter the studio in 1973 with a strong commitment to open improvisation. They wanted it on the record. When they needed a break from tracking the more complicated compositions, they would record a few chunks of improvisation, and assembled "The Tenth Chaffinch" from these episodes of downtime dithering. The general consensus among the Cows was that the track wasn't successful. In fact, little of the resulting tape satisfied them. One has the same impression of the introduction to "Teenbeat," where the band sought inspiration from a standing start, and the slow, five-minute crescendo of activity evidences a certain forced feel.

The general air of dissatisfaction extended from "The Tenth Chaffinch" to *Leg End* as a whole.[81] Henry Cow was in good spirits throughout the recording process, but on certain points, they couldn't reach any satisfying end. The drum sound is a good example; it feels like a missed opportunity for some Cows. Rock drums—live or recorded—are always the hardest thing to get right, owing to the material heterogeneity of the instrument (which must be overcome in service of a unified sound) and the rigid conventions of the genre. There is nothing natural about how drums sound on a rock record, but the artifice is highly specific. Cutler did not play like most drummers would, underneath the band on the bottom of the sound. Instead, he almost floated on top of the texture—but how do you record *those* drums? Given the intricacy of Cutler's parts, a big, thumping kick drum wouldn't work, nor would you want too much of a boomy, live sound. But then one risks the opposite problem: a small, tight sound that feels squeezed by itself into a narrow frequency band. (To my ear, this is how the drums ended up in the final mix.) Cutler was no better equipped to solve this question than was anybody else, but it becomes difficult to insist on more tweaks to the sound when the band has already spent a day and a half hearing nothing but the sound of one snare whacking. In addition to the matter of small drums, the multitrack masters reveal odd equalization, instruments jumping around on the tracks, and strange miking techniques.

The problem of fitting "Amygdala" into the flow of connected material was another source of some tension, according to Hodgkinson. The band wanted to retain the fluidity of their live show in some form on the record itself, so they spent considerable time discussing how to stitch together their preconceived material into larger, sidelong chunks. "Amygdala," however, was conceived as a progressively structured totality, rather than a collection of frags, so any possible segue had the potential to corrupt its autonomy—it wasn't meant to be supplemented. This problem arose with respect to the live show as well as the recording. Hodgkinson was against the idea of linking "Amygdala" at all, not putting up too much of a stink but certainly refraining from an enthusiastic agreement. On *Leg End*, the conclusion of "Amygdala" leads into an open improvisation that eventually culminates in "Teenbeat."

Also at issue was the more general problem of determining the relationship between the Cows' live set and the recording they were making. Until they arrived at the Manor in May 1973, Henry Cow had been working and reworking an enormous flux of material in a kind of constant improvisation. Each separate occasion—a concert, a radio broadcast, and now an album—was an opportunity to create something unique, special, and specific to the situation at hand. "I mean you're constantly trying to make a necessity of a contingency, as they say," Hodgkinson explains. "It's almost like you're trying to take care of the possibility already that something will be different from how it is by having your diagram with arrows going all over the place" (see figure 1.12). The recording of *Leg End* achieved its status as "definitive" only because of its material durability on vinyl; at the time, the sequence and arrangements contained therein were no more definitive than those of any other occasion. In fact, plenty of other material was being considered by the band: cycles of 13 from the middle of "I Came to See You Today"; the first chorus from *The Bacchae*; bits from "Hieronymo's Mad Again"; and possibly a piano or organ solo, according to the jottings in Hodgkinson's notebooks from the time.

The album's opener, Frith's "Nirvana for Mice," coalesced into its then-current form a few months before. In a 1984 interview, Hodgkinson guessed that the composition originated with the large work that Frith had written for the Ottawa Music Company earlier in 1972; they never played the whole thing, according to his memory, but enjoyed taking it apart and tinkering with the bits.[82] For his part, Frith had been reading John Cage's *Silence* and wondering about the possibility of using chance operations himself, so he generated the main melody using playing cards to determine pitches and their duration. Once that line had been established, he composed a counter-melody using the same method to determine pitch. He then used his own ear to fill in chords below and to provide a general phrase structure for the rhythm section. Following this expansive opening theme, the group fell into the habit of playing an ensuing section that consisted of a tenor solo in 7/4 (or—to be pedantic—21/8, because the beat is subdivided in three, not two). For *Leg End*, Frith sutured the two sections with a tricky jigsaw connection (at 0:54) that simultaneously introduced and obscured the time signature of the jam section. While the drums and bass thump out in unison a jerky pattern scattered across two bars of 21/8, the guitars wait out two eights and then repeat a lopsided pattern of eighths (11 + 10, then 11 + 8). In the end, they come out together and launch the band into Leigh's solo, a showcase not only for the saxophonist but also for Greaves's rear-end shifting work down below and Cutler's dizzying whirls up top. Organ and guitar flutter and weave in the background for a couple of minutes, but then Frith sneaks in his pattern (at 3:52, now regularized to 11 + 10 [i.e., 21]) to signal the long transition to the coda. (If you're paying attention, you'll notice that Greaves, too, has crept back to the 21-beat pattern that made up the second half of his part in the tricky jigsaw.) Long horn chords shout out a fanfare above the mess, and then chatter away in unison while the rhythm section restates the second half of its jigsaw thumpery. A long pause in the form of an organ drone leads directly to the final fillip—a little vocal frag ("Sweet mystery of life") with hocketed accompaniment that probably also originated in the Ottawa Music Company days. Overall, then, "Nirvana for Mice" was a patchwork of different compositional techniques: chance operations, solo improvisation over a rhythmic pattern, metrical puzzles, and other odds-n-ends.

For reasons already discussed, there is no segue between the opener and "Amygdala," which appears here in its full, unaltered form. It ends with a link to the boozy saxophone duet that kicks off what would be called "Teenbeat Introduction" on *Leg End*. It's basically a five-minute-long open improvisation that builds into the "Teenbeat" opening tune. On this occasion, the band was augmented by a chorus of Maggie Thomas, Sarah Greaves, and Cathy Williams. The rest of the track is a leaner, revised version of the universe of bits they'd been playing with since 1971: the usual 5/4 contra-puntal material up front, leading not to the conversational interlude (which was probably eliminated because it didn't translate well to nonvisual perfor-mance) but straight into the corny, swinging dance (at 1:53). Soon, however, the band jump-cuts straight into a new section that replaced what had been the final six or seven minutes of the piece. An urgent groove in 15/8, this one came mostly from Greaves, who dropped onto his deceptively com-plex bassline little snippets of early Greavesiana: here's the "Kew. Rhone." melody in the guitar, there's "Would You Prefer Us to Lie?" in the organ. The fast 15 pulse allows for an easy graft of the "Factory 15s" from "Yellow Half-Moon," which lead to a lovely and lively little ditty shared between the violin and organ. It skitters all over the place, metrically (but remains in 15 if you count carefully). A return of the Factory 15s at 3:17 means it's cycle time again: the organ and guitar doggedly beat out 43 repetitions of the 15-beat cycle, while bass and (overdubbed) alto saxophone overlay 30 cycles of a new 23-beat pattern that sounds a lot like a slow 5 (fast 10), followed by the 13s from "Came to See You." The 15- and 23-beat cycles match up only twice, on beats 345 and 690 of the section. At that point, the piece draws to a close with a pensive clarinet solo supported by acoustic guitar chords.

Side 2 begins with a subdued reprise of the chance-determined tune from "Nirvana for Mice," now played on three guitars—it could almost be a demo recording. From here, we are taken straight to the opening of "With the Yellow Half-Moon and Blue Star": fugal exposition, Factory 15s tran-sition, and First Hollywood Theme (somewhat obscured by endless over-dubs). It's a nice little break, complete with softer touches on violin and flute. The pause is over after just three and a half minutes, however, when we are thrust back into the cooking solo section of "Teenbeat." This time, however, Henry Cow returns to the older guitar solo that once followed the corny "inner core" of the piece. Much of this reprise plays around with duple and triple feels—the bass might play in groups of three eighths while the guitar strums out chords in groups of four. At 4:10, the organ begins the slow build that signals the final stretch of the track; Frith plays the "Teen-beat" tune on the violin, and then the song wraps up quickly with a bound-ing bridge to nowhere.

"Nowhere" once consisted of an eerie, tremolo-heavy and tightly voiced chord progression in the organ, which supported some very high, pensive artificial harmonics and glissandi in Frith's violin; the latter referred to this texture as "science fiction music" in early 1972, when it was still a part of "Teenbeat." Now, however, we hear the same organ drones and fiddle whistles, but the track is "The Tenth Chaffinch," the band's experiment with recorded and edited improvisation.[83] (This overlap is not a coincidence; in the old days, Henry Cow would follow this organ/violin texture with an interlude of conversation and sparse improvisation from the band; on the record, then, the break filled by "The Tenth Chaffinch" served the same purpose.) Finally, and in keeping with Hodgkinson's aesthetic preferences, "Nine Funerals of the Citizen King" closed the album with no alterations.

A Minor Milestone in Contemporary Rock

While Henry Cow was in the studio recording *Leg End*, Virgin released *Tubular Bells*, *Flying Teapot*, and *The Faust Tapes*. Although the continental rock groups both sold well, it was the twenty-year-old Oldfield whose album would buoy the young label through its first three years. Beginning with a repetitive electric-piano figure that calls to mind Terry Riley (a comparison drawn by many at the time), the album, largely instrumental, moves through a series of linked episodes scored with an expansive rock instrumentarium. Draper later commented, "Tubular Bells sold phenomenally and Faust did well. The impact was not only in England but also in Europe where we were greeted as 'an avant-garde label with ideals' which formed the basis for all our subsequent success, particularly in France."[84] Oldfield's album received an enormous boost when William Friedkin used its opening as the theme music for *The Exorcist*, which was released in late 1973. One year later, *Tubular Bells* had sold five million copies worldwide.[85] But it had enjoyed enough early success that Branson nudged Oldfield to produce a live concert version in Queen Elizabeth Hall in June 1973. Everybody got a slice of the ham. Frith, Greaves, Hodgkinson, Leigh, Sarah Greaves, and Cathy Williams all performed in the ensemble, along with a host of London's rock luminaries: Viv Stanshall, David Bedford, Mick Taylor, and Steve Hillage, among others.[86]

In their first Virgin press release, Henry Cow mentioned the *Tubular Bells* concert in a list of notable engagements that accented their versatility and engagement with multiple scenes, settings, and styles. The list also included their invitation to appear on the "Changing Face of Jazz/Rock" series at the Roundhouse (with Mike Westbrook's Solid Gold Cadillac and Keith Tippett, among others), their upcoming collaboration with Jonathan Chadwick on *The Tempest* at the Watford Palace Theatre, their performance at the Bath International Music Festival ("the only rock group to play at this prestigious classical music festival," they explained), and their Explorer's Club gigs with Derek Bailey and Lol Coxhill. Read between the lines, and they seemed to be saying, "We do jazz, theater, classical, and free." But in spite of this emphasis on multistylism, Henry Cow finished the press release with a firm statement of allegiance to their new home at Virgin: "Like Syd Barrett, the Magic Band and the Mothers, HENRY COW are among the few rock musicians who have been prepared to break the rules, starting again with their audiences but at the same time remaining definitely a rock group."[87]

Now a welcomed member of the Virgin family, Henry Cow was hanging out with the Rolling Stones (or near them, at least) and kicking back on Richard Branson's houseboat in London's Little Venice. "It was a pretty blissful summer," says Sarah Greaves. *Leg End* was finished and would be released in a couple of weeks; they'd contracted their old Cambridge friend, Ray Smith, to create artwork for the cover. It turned out to be iconic: a single stocking, woven from strands of paint that bore an uncanny likeness to electrical wiring. (To explain the album's title, a stocking is what fits onto the end of your leg, or your "leg end.") Smith had developed his striking technique by using a pastry bag to squeeze acrylic paint into long strips on sheets of polyethylene. Once it had dried, he peeled off the film and wove together strands of blue, red, black, and off-white acrylic into the sock shape. Smith also created evocative print advertisements that ran in *Melody Maker* in September.

Indeed, the only blemish on the surface of that blissful summer appeared at a wild party held by Lady June in her London apartment on June 1, when an inebriated Robert Wyatt attempted to climb out of a bathroom window and onto the roof of the building. Instead, he fell from the fourth floor and broke his back. This ugly incident put an end to Matching Mole, the post-Softs band Wyatt was in the process of reforming in the spring of 1973. In the weeks that followed the accident, it became clear that he would be paralyzed below the waist for the rest of his life.[88]

In the midst of these exciting and terrible developments, Henry Cow began to use their Virgin advance money to put together a PA system and touring setup; in general, it was important to them to have a certain level of autonomy in the presentation of their music, and in particular, they needed to get ready for an autumn tour supporting Faust. They took another step by hiring their first employee, Charles Fletcher. (Of course, they had already received concert support from Jack Balchin, Phil Preston, and Sarah

Figure 2.2 Henry Cow, sound checking in late 1973.
PHOTOGRAPH BY BRIAN COOKE.

Greaves, but I see no evidence in the accounts that any of these close associates actually received a wage prior to the Virgin period. None of the band members ever received a wage either, but their rent, food, and expenses were partially covered by earnings.) Fletcher was another Cambridge acquaintance; he had studied engineering at Clare College from 1967 to 1970, and heard Henry Cow for the first time at Glastonbury in June 1971. Two years later, Henry Cow began paying him £5 per week to sort out the PA situation, build road enclosures for their delicate Altec Lansing speakers, and procure a new vehicle. Eventually, they would ask him to do the live sound, too—likely because Sarah Greaves was getting further into her pregnancy and couldn't be expected to carry equipment in the coming months, and the newborn would doubtlessly make sound engineering an impossible occupation for the near future. (In a February 1974 column on the band, Fletcher is identified as Henry Cow's road manager.[89])

A reliable and highly competent worker (he'd earned a double-first at university), Fletcher also shared Henry Cow's disciplined, no-nonsense approach to the work of running a band. He was also, like the Cow, aware of the limits of his own knowledge but confident in his ability to expand those limits by figuring things out for himself. He told me, "To say, 'We know it all'—that's the wrong approach. But it's a very healthy approach to be skeptical of traditional ways of doing things." Frith recalls that the band appreciated both his technical acumen as well as his sober, suspicious personality.

In August, Fletcher purchased a three-ton Commer commercial walk-through van. Slightly larger than the Bedford ambulance, this vehicle had the cargo capacity for a larger PA, and Fletcher customized it further by installing two rows of airline seats in front of the equipment. During the final days of mixing for *Leg End*, he visited the Manor to discuss PA systems with the professionals, Newman and Phil Becque; he needed their advice on what to buy and how to set it up. Based on his own conversations with the band, Newman told him that Henry Cow probably didn't desire a conventional sound, preferring instead "a very clear sound, rather than a big thumping bass sound that a lot of rock bands would go for. It didn't have to be especially loud. A hi-fi sound." They eventually settled on two 2×15 JBL bins with MacLab speakers, JBL horns and tweeters, and two Crown DC150 amplifiers.[90] Along with cables, a few new microphones and stands, and modifications to their mixer by Rich Fry, all of this equipment represented a substantial purchase—one they needed to consider very carefully. Imagine the band's surprise, then, when the huge, wardrobe-size JBL bins, speakers, and amps arrived unexpectedly at the Walmer Road house, looming over the front door on the sidewalk outside. According to Greaves, "Tim looked at it and said, 'I'm leaving the group. This is not happening. . . . This is not what we're about.' . . . The weight of his compromise with capitalism was represented by these black, massive . . . speakers, which were stuck on the pavement in front of the house—you couldn't get into the bloody door!"

Hodgkinson was eventually persuaded to stick around—they had acquired complete sonic autonomy, after all—but they still didn't know where the system came from. It turns out that Newman had been tasked with ordering the PA for Oldfield's QEH concert (still in its infancy, Virgin had no PA of its own yet), and used the opportunity to give a rather expensive gift to his new friends in Henry Cow. In the long list of multicore cables, crossovers, reflectors, and other gizmos, Newman figured, nobody would notice a few extra speaker cabinets and amplifiers, especially if they were delivered straight to a crumbling abode in the middle of Ladbroke Grove. He was right. "We were pretty happy living in the heart of that beast," Greaves maintains, even if some of his bandmates expressed misgivings about their new patrons. (At the time he made this decision, Newman was angry with Branson because the latter had not credited him as the producer of *Tubular Bells*, which had been released on May 25; this change—Newman was instead credited with "sound"—represented the loss of a lot of royalty payments. Branson corrected his moral lapse after several decades.)

Virgin released *Leg End* in early September 1973, to numerous, generally positive reviews.[91] Listeners heard a predictable range of influences (Zappa, Beefheart, Matching Mole) as well as some less predictable ones (Derek Bailey and the Mahavishnu Orchestra). But most often, they heard Soft Machine. By 1973, that band had become something quite different from what they'd been in the late 1960s, and a few reviewers took pains to note that Henry Cow "will avoid becoming boring like the Soft Machine did."[92] In addition to these comparisons to specific bands, writers did their best to label the Cows according to genre, including contemporary composition, modern jazz, rock, cabaret, and avant-garde jazz. Some critics assured the consumer that this record was not "jazz-rock," as if that fairly recent grouping had already passed its sell-by date. Others heard *Leg End* as a representative of its label's good taste: "Virgin have come up with another uncompromising masterpiece,"[93] wrote one journalist, while another observed, "This album sits nicely beside 'Faust Tapes' and 'Tubular Bells.'"[94]

Although nobody panned the album, a handful of professional listeners expressed some reservations.[95] For example, *Let It Rock*'s John Hoyland admired their integrity and commitment but expressed a hope that the free improvisations didn't cause fans to dismiss Henry Cow as rock eccentrics.[96] Other reviewers worried that the band hadn't yet developed a strong identity, or that their exciting live show wasn't translating properly to the recorded format.[97] MacDonald articulated this latter view most conspicuously in the pages of *NME*.[98] He thought the second side of *Leg End*, in particular, evidenced a dull mix, and wagged his pen at "the periods of florid musical isometrics in which plenty happens but little stays to make a lasting impact. . . . However, remember one thing. It's only worth going on and on about the failings of something if it's basically good. Henry Cow are basically very good indeed." Basically good: not exactly gushing praise, but it was good enough, especially when it appeared in the *NME*.

Nonetheless, MacDonald's appraisal wasn't even the most important to appear that autumn. Steve Lake was the new guy at *Melody Maker*, and—having stepped into the big shoes of Richard Williams, who had left the magazine to join Island Records—he needed a project of his own to champion. He pronounced *Leg End* a "salvation for anybody with well-worn copies of the first two Soft Machine epics." Lake wore his discernment on his sleeveless T-shirt, dropping references to Sun Ra, Elisabeth Lutyens, David Bedford, Derek Bailey, and the Art Ensemble of Chicago in the small space of four hundred words. He loved the album, though, predicting that it "should make the cognoscenti think, that's for sure."[99]

Lake followed up his review of *Leg End* with a very positive feature article in *Melody Maker*.[100] It was the first serious attention the band had received in print. "This is Henry Cow, the latest and best outfit yet from the Virgin Records stable, a band whose on-stage good humour and apparently casual attitude belies the intensity and sophistication of its musical approach," he wrote. Running through the rock-interview routine about influences, Cutler mixed the usual references with ones a bit further afield: Wyatt and John French (Magic Band), but also Sun Ra and Edgard Varèse, "from whom I ripped off a whole stack of things. Great bloke, Edgar [*sic*]. He really liberated orchestral percussionists." Lake was particularly keen to compare Henry Cow with Roxy Music, who had come onto the scene the previous year with frequent references to John Cage and other US experimentalists, but who, in Lake's opinion, had never delivered on that promise. In addition to providing a short history of the Cow going all the way back to the Cambridge days, Lake engaged Cutler in a conversation about the limits of categorization and the comparative freedom and opportunity that the rock network could offer. Cutler remarked, "The trouble with people like Derek Bailey and Han Bennink is that, because of what they are, and what they appear to be to the general public, they seldom get the chance to play to large audiences. The area that they are working in is so contained that it is ultimately stifling. What we are trying to do we want to do for as many people as possible."[101]

In the wake of signing with a record company, performing at the Queen Elizabeth Hall, and procuring a PA that was the size of walk-in closet, Cutler and the rest of the Cows were carefully weighing the advantages of their new affiliations, and how those affiliations might change their relation to the audience. On the strength of the evidence from Virgin—Faust, Gong, Oldfield—Cutler was convinced that listeners could be interested in unusual musics. These conclusions further underscored the fact that, for all the daunting complexity of some of their music, Henry Cow were not aloof avant-gardists. They craved the encounter with new listeners, a desire I will investigate in increasing depth in the coming chapters. "Basically, a performance is an argument. A criticism, a strong statement. It's also fun, of course," Cutler said. They could certainly count on the support of Lake, who proclaimed them to be "a potentially major rock band, destined to be hugely influential.[102]"

No More Faust

Meanwhile, Faust was in country. They landed at Plymouth, whose Guild-hall was the site of their first British performance, on May 19, 1973, an event that, for MacDonald, "established them beyond any question as the doyen of the German bands."[103] Faust had already performed live on John Peel's radio show in March, and would do so again in May, and they followed the Plymouth concert with a short, ten-date tour of England that summer.[104] *The Faust Tapes* was selling like mad, and Virgin had arranged a longer tour of England in September and October; Henry Cow was the opening act.

The fans were out in force, but Faust was in total disarray. "It was chaos, right from the word *go*," Leigh remembers. Those familiar with the Faust lineup might have been surprised to discover that Rudolf Sosna and Hans-Joachim Irmler had grown tired of the United Kingdom and elected to re-turn home. As bassist Jean-Hervé Peron told Cutler many years later, "We had a code of honour that said: no compromises; we do absolutely what we feel like with no respect for anybody and no consideration of any conse-quences no matter what."[105] The band replaced their missing members with Uli Trepte of Guru Guru and the American Peter Blegvad. At some point during the seventeen-date tour, Irmler and Sosna decided to come back, and Faust fired Blegvad and Trepte.[106] Trepte was stranded in the country because he hadn't even been paid enough to make it back to Germany with his equipment. (Blegvad hung around on the tour, but mainly to spend time with his new friends in Henry Cow. He was scared of Faust.)

"We do absolutely what we feel like with no respect for anybody." As much a formula for the male id as it was a "code of honor," Peron's program helps to explain Faust's naughty behavior during their English sojourn. They drank gallons of alcohol and reportedly took a lot of drugs. In Leigh's tell-ing, "Their soundchecks were fantastic. Great soundchecks. By the time they came to the gig, they were always so drunk and God knows what, that everything went up to 10, and it was horrendous. We'd have to get out of the building—the whole building would be shaking." The celebratory vibe extended to Blegvad, who enjoyed a legendarily soaked autumn. Greaves remembers fondly, "I've seen a lot of people fall or be carried *off*, but the first person being carried *on* stage in a blind, drunken stupor, was Peter at this gig with Faust."

While Leigh had very little contact with the group, and remembers them even as a bit stand-offish, the other Cows enjoyed their company. Cutler recalls that when Henry Cow turned up to the first gig at the Reading Town

Hall, they hadn't yet met Faust and didn't know what they looked like. Some burly fellows materialized and helped hump the gear into the hall, and only later did Cutler discover that they were Faust. Hodgkinson says, "The head-lining musicians had come and carried our amps out of our van." Fletcher was there, of course, but Balchin stayed away on this tour—and, indeed, he was missing for most of Henry Cow's events in the second half of 1973. The reason, in hindsight, was simple. According to Balchin, "He was mixing, and I wasn't." Balchin had already watched Sarah Greaves take over mixing duties from Phil Preston in 1972, and now Fletcher had become the third novice to be given the responsibility for live sound. The Reading concert on September 21 was only his second gig behind the desk, and Fletcher was definitely learning on the job.[107]

Faust, however, had brought along Graupner, who was a professional. By this point, they had long ditched their dream of playing with a surround-sound system, but their black boxes still necessitated some odd work-arounds, such as the big headphone monitors the band members wore during the performance. Graupner explained, "It looked rather strange, but how else could they hear themselves? . . . We did it our way, and it worked."[108] The newest addition to their instrumentarium was a jackhammer, which they used (occasionally enlisting Frith) to break up bits of concrete on stage. They also had a couple of color TV sets around the stage, and two pinball machines placed off to the side; they were wired into the electronics, but because there was rarely a one-to-one correspondence between electronic input and sonic output, some observers mistakenly thought the machines were there for the band's amusement. It was hard to tell what was going on anyway, because Faust usually played in total darkness (save the eerie flicker of the TVs). Lake asked, "How do you assess the stage presence of a band that you can't see?" As for the music, he drew the Cagean conclusion that it "seemed to be based on the old Zen premise that says if something is boring for sixteen minutes, try it for thirty-two."[109] At least retrospectively, and probably contemporaneously, the members of Henry Cow were unimpressed by Faust's live show. "Their strength as a group was what Uwe Nettelbeck did with them in the studio," Frith explains. "And I think that is really important and critically forward-thinking stuff, and I think it hasn't been matched in many ways. . . . But what they did live had nothing to do with that. They were much more standard 'krautrock.'"[110]

Not everyone yawned at their antics. The young Julian Cope was simply blown away. "It was 1973, and musicians usually soloed and looked to the audience for applause, and great ugly guys nanced around in cheese-cloth singing about fucking nothing at all. And then Faust walked on. . . . I couldn't believe it. . . . It was epic, it was brilliant, it had attitude enough to raze cities and it ruined every show I went to for at least two years after."[111] Cope was less struck by Henry Cow. "They played their wacky Cambridge University Degree music on bassoons and time-changes galore, and the guitarist went to the side of the stage and put headphones on, and pretended to listen to the band in a jolly way. Ho-hum."[112] Cope may have favored the more visceral music of Faust over the intellectual pleasures of the opening act, but his account of the October 5 concert at Birmingham Town Hall agrees with several other descriptions of the Cow's stage presentation during this tour. One critic enjoyed their "fooling about on the stage and the seats behind," while another expressed misgivings about their "miscellaneous foolery. The diversions are more theatrical than musical."[113]

Yuks aside, Henry Cow played a loose and dynamic set on this tour, one that aimed to delight but also to surprise, to engage, to upset, or to jolt. Their mode was still theatrical. Cutler recalls, "It was a social, nice social atmosphere. We were still running out into the audience in the middle of the gig. You know, it's what we used to do." In Wolverhampton, Faust cancelled, and Henry Cow got to play two sets, as they would do in the old days. A reviewer for *Music Scene* reported that Leigh brought the second portion to a raucous close by "leading a chain of stomping people round the hall,"[114] and then Frith gave an impromptu solo performance on acoustic guitar, away from the new PA. They were constantly trying to persuade Faust to join them in these open-ended forays into audience involvement, succeeding only on October 14 in Chelmsford. By this point in the tour, Faust were down to only three members; when Hodgkinson (alto), Leigh (tenor), and Blegvad (clarinet) invaded the stage during Faust's performance, Peron surrendered his bass in favor of a trumpet and joined the Cows' procession to the foyer of the theater, much to the crowd's delight but also to his bandmates' dissatisfaction.[115] At a show in Liverpool, a few Cows inadvertently took the stage wearing the colors of a rival club, which ignited a wave of noisy protest in the crowd. Rather than taking it silently, one member of the group went straight to a microphone and yelled back. Frith recalls, "So the whole of the first five minutes of the concert we are basically shouting at them as they're shouting at us and this kind of nonpluses them a little bit. They're not quite sure what they're supposed to do with that. And it becomes the improvisation that we start with." As band members peeled off to their instruments, one by one, they rode the adrenaline of the confrontation to play one of the strongest sets of the tour, winning over the audience in the process.[116]

Figure 2.3 Henry Cow performing at the Rainbow Theatre, London, October 21, 1973. Visible at left is performance artist Ray Smith. PHOTOGRAPH BY BRIAN COOKE.

Although it wasn't the final date on the tour, the October 21 concert at the Rainbow Theatre was a culminating event for the Cows. According to Frith, "We were building towards the Rainbow, all the time. The Rainbow was the biggest stage we'd had to do it on." The 3,500-seater in Finsbury Park was one of London's most acclaimed rock venues at the time, and Henry Cow invited many of their local friends to help put on a good show for the home crowd.[117] The trio of Lol Coxhill, Phil Minton, and Mike Westbrook greeted the audience in the foyer and led them into the theatre, where the evening began with an introductory text by old pal D. J. Perry, accompanied by Greaves on piano. He soon improvised his way through to the "Kew. Rhone." melody, when he was joined by his bandmates, eventually ending up in an open improvisation around a bass-violin-piano trio. More recitation, then Henry Cow performed "Amygdala." Meanwhile, the artist Ray Smith had materialized onstage next to the band; in his unwavering deadpan, he went through the motions of ironing paper cutouts in the shape of clothing and then hanging them on a drying rack. When they finished "Amygdala," the first big bit of chaos broke out, in the form of a platoon of more than a dozen wind players scattered about the auditorium. Springing up, they began a freeform exploration—in motion—that climaxed into the "Teenbeat" tune, which the reeds (Coxhill, Gary Windo, Gary James, Elton Dean, Peter Blegvad, and John Miles, plus Leigh and Hodgkinson) sounded from the front of the stage. After more poetry from Perry, Henry Cow played some new music from their upcoming production of *The Tempest* (see the next chapter), and then presented an early version of a vamp from "Beautiful as the Moon—Terrible as an Army with Banners." As his solo drew to a close, the saxophonists on stage joined in. Their gaggle eventually petered out, whereupon they exited the stage while the Cow went into "Nirvana for Mice." This time, the solo section was given over to the auxiliary brass players, who had by this point come to the front: Jean-Hervé Peron, Marc Charig, Edward Ray Smith, Nick Evans, Minton, and Westbrook.

Throughout the show an experimental acting group, Lumiere and Son Theatre Company, prowled around the house in a kind of wordless ritual. Their co-leader (with Hilary Westlake), David Gale, later wrote, "The tastes of the partnership were apparent in the deployment in the theatre aisles of performers in ill-fitting suits and summer dresses carrying wooden platters bearing severed sheep's heads."[118] Among the fifteen or so performers was a young Rose English, who would become a notable force in British film and theatre by the 1980s. (She would become a close collaborator and friend of Lindsay Cooper.[119]) After Henry Cow and its musical guests had finished "Nirvana for Mice," the actors burst into a more direct engagement with the audience. As Frith wrote in his directions for the event, "EVERYONE beings to TALK, WAIL, SING etc. dispersing into audience who can be encouraged to join in." Once things died down, Henry Cow went back into a reprise of "Teenbeat" (indeed, an interruption of chatter in the audience was usually linked in performance to this piece—the Cows had always figured out ways to improvise some text in the breaks of "Teenbeat"). The set came to a dramatic close, with a "frenzied and magnificent" improvisation terminating with five sustained chords for the whole ensemble cued by Perry from the stage.

Henry Cow's program had finished, but excitement of a different sort continued with Faust. The Virgin PA that they had been using died during their sound check, so they were forced to commandeer the more delicate Henry Cow system, according to Fletcher. It could barely cope. Meanwhile,

Faust had waited until there were two thousand people in the hall to issue a demand to Richard Branson: increase their fee, or they weren't going on. He eventually relented, but there was still the matter of the puny PA. Peron reached a sensible, if extreme, conclusion. If Faust could have only half the wattage their music required, then Peron would perform with only half his clothes.[120] Upon removing his trousers and underwear, he was restrained by Rainbow security before he could make it onstage, and there ensued an exchange of fisticuffs with the ferine Faust roadies. The next morning, Branson cancelled their contract. No more Faust.

At this point in our story, Faust makes their exit. Their only new Virgin album, *Faust IV*, would be released that autumn to generally positive reviews, but the band began to fall apart, the pieces scattering back to Germany.[121] And for Henry Cow, the tour had a number of outcomes. As Cutler observed years later, it "certainly helped establish us as a Rock Group."[122] They had begun to move on from their previous environs of theaters and university arts centers. Although the onstage theatrics continued throughout the tour, they would soon fade from the band's concert presentation as they moved more squarely into the live rock infrastructure. In that circuit, they began to meet larger audiences in the United Kingdom, and, judging from the limited press, those audiences seemed to like them. Blegvad certainly did, reporting later that he was "transported and dazzled" the first time he heard them.[123] Indeed, this fortuitous affinity with Blegvad would turn out to be perhaps the most important outcome of Henry Cow's time with Faust, because it set the stage for a dramatic moment in the band's history: their merger with Slapp Happy, the subsequent acquisition of a "girl singer," and Greaves's eventual departure from the group. But that is getting ahead of the story. In the autumn of 1973, Henry Cow were gearing up for their first tour on the continent, preparing for what they hoped would be another successful theater collaboration, and enjoying the copious press attention given to their debut album. But there were also significant disruptions on the horizon, and 1974 would turn out to be the band's darkest year until the end.

3 Contentment Is Hopeless, Unrest Is Progress | 1974

Henry Cow's spirits were high coming off the Faust tour, even if the headliner had entered "self-destruct" mode. A letter that Tim Hodgkinson wrote to Caroline Ayerst captures the mood in the group following the Faust concerts: "We're the only people to profit from't & there's talk of our own tour soon w. Tangerine Dream supporting. Everyone at Virgin knocked out by Rainbow concert, Mick Taylor digs the album a lot, Simon [Draper]'s got U.S.A. deal for Faust but secretly trying to substitute us, as Virgin want to get rid of them. So we may get out in the States after all."[1] The growing antagonism between the label and Faust, who had trashed the Manor when they recorded *Faust IV* there earlier in the summer, indeed seems to have led Simon Draper and the Virgin PR team to shift their attentions to Cow. A few days later, Hodgkinson gave Ayerst another status update: Richard Branson had secured a US licensing deal through Atlantic, who would now be releasing *Leg End* in the second batch of Virgin releases after *Tubular Bells*. Hodgkinson wrote, "This is a great coup & Virgin have evidently shifted their main attention from Faust to us."[2]

In fact, evidence for this shift in attention had already surfaced in the glorious full-page advertisement for Henry Cow that Virgin placed in *Melody Maker* at the end of October.[3] Among no fewer than six photographs of the band, Virgin's designer scattered excerpts from *Leg End*'s most favorable reviews along with endorsements by highbrow rock luminaries such as Hugh Hopper, Lol Coxhill, David Bedford, and Robert Wyatt, the sovereign in that world. "Me favourite band in the world," he pronounced. Virgin's fortunes were rising on the sales of *Tubular Bells*, and that meant that everybody in the Virgin family might benefit. Branson wanted to produce four or five big concerts of the Oldfield piece in the United States, and Henry Cow were on the roster of performers; they thought they might get their own North American tour out of it, too (neither happened).[4]

About a week after this advertisement appeared, Henry Cow returned to the Manor for a single-day recording session. On October 8, they had been slated to participate in a benefit concert at Dingwall's in Camden. The charity, Greasy Truckers, had already released one high-profile double-LP in 1972, and they planned to feature live recordings of Henry Cow and three other bands on the newest volume. However, the organizers ran the event so poorly that Cow didn't take the stage until 2:10 in the morning and had to finish twenty minutes later; their set wasn't even recorded. As recompense, they were given a free day at the Manor to record their contribution. The music they produced was quite distinct from that of the *Leg End* date—"a huge turning point for us," according to Fred Frith. Hodgkinson recorded his impression in a letter to Ayerst shortly after: "We are elated about the recording: it has a feel about it that the first one lacks & it is a great deal more developed & uncompromising."[5]

Henry Cow made an attempt at recording an early, incomplete version of Greaves's "Half Asleep, Half Awake," but his complicated composition would take a long time to perfect, so they eventually abandoned it. Nonetheless, Frith noted at the time, "We recorded an absolutely massive amount of material, considering it was all done in one day."[6] Engineer Tom Newman was ill, so he gave them the full run of the place, and they turned on all the microphones in the live room and began to improvise.

Their approach did not entirely owe to the limited time that was available. Hodgkinson, for one, recalls the rather wild mood of the band that evening. Because they had been wronged at the Dingwall's date, he remembers, "We were feeling a bit Bolshie. 'Okay, we're with these other bands [on the LP] that are all doing pretty homely rock. . . . Let's make a lot of weird racket in an ambient studio and just come up with something.'" Much of the racket originated in the piano, prepared by Hodgkinson with nails, screws, and billiard balls. The other predominant instrumental presence is Frith's double pickup, which he used to great effect in the first two tracks; with remarkable precision and speed, he employed a two-handed hammer-on technique while using volume pedals to shift rapidly between the guitar's headstock and body pickups. Greaves, too, contributes an impressive improvised duet with Frith, and Cutler experiments with a more free-jazz drumming style full of gesture and surprise.

Although there are a few overdubs in the final recording, the group mainly used live takes. Because they recorded their performances on multitrack tape, however, they did sculpt those improvisations at the mixdown stage by muting voices here and there. The musicians offer plenty of repetition, but there are no tape loops. Their decisions about microphone placement and mixing helped them create a recording of great depth and detail, with the implied point of audition zooming in and out across the four improvisations.

We do not hear much of Geoff Leigh, however. "If I'm not mistaken, that was the beginning of my disgruntlement with improvised music," he commented in 2011. Ever the free blower, he had little feeling for the spacious and quiet ambience of the Greasy Truckers material. Other factors exacerbated his alienation—weeks of long rehearsals with Henry Cow plus a demanding recording session with Hatfield and the North had left him with a nasty flu, and, as a loud player, he was leaking into the other instrumental microphones to such a degree that he often had to sit out—but Leigh was drifting away at the same time that his comrades were revising their musical frame of reference. This divergence would also manifest in *The Tempest*, which had opened just a few days before the Greasy Truckers session.

The Watford Palace Theatre, host of the Cow's successful 1972 production of *The Bacchae*, asked them in 1973 to provide the music for Shakespeare's musically rich *The Tempest*. They agreed, but on the condition that they could choose the director. "We wanted a Brecht guy," explains Hodgkinson. "And so this was gonna be like a communist Shakespeare." They asked Jonathan Chadwick, an old mate from Cambridge who had directed the UK premiere of Brecht's *The Mother* at the Half Moon Theatre and the Roundhouse earlier that year.

Virgin's press release (which I surmise was written by Hodgkinson and/or Cutler) explained that the play premiered in 1611, "when the merchant capitalists of Western Europe were colonising the world. The play describes Prospero's 'magical machinations' to restore himself as Duke of Milan and in general justifies the ownership of property by the 'property' owner. As with 'The Bacchae,' the music will have far from its customary subsidiary role being instead critical, argumentative, continuous and mobile."

Indeed, their Brecht guy was a willing collaborator in the critical mission; Chadwick had actors changing costumes onstage and boldly rearranged the play's form, at Henry Cow's suggestion: they began with the final scene, when Prospero puts his affairs together and prepares to return to his dukedom, then proceeded to the actual opening scene and Prospero's magically conjured storm. The twist came at the end, when they repeated the final scene in its proper place, but this time Prospero's speech was drowned out by the auditory storm of Henry Cow's music. As Hodgkinson put it, "So the first time [P]rospero's resolution is successful, without music, the second time it's destroyed by the real tempest, the revolutionary struggle."[7] The

Cows were already familiar with Brecht's writings, and Frith had performed music for two Brecht productions during his student days. They likely took this production as an opportunity to deepen their knowledge; Hodgkinson had copied two poems—"In Praise of Communism" and "In Praise of Learning"—into his notebook in the run-up to rehearsals.[8]

Opening night was October 31; because Henry Cow was taking such an active role in the production, they spent much of October rehearsing at the theatre in Watford, a good hour's drive from London. It was a punishing schedule—their datebooks show only three days off between September 28 and December 11. If they weren't playing a date with Faust, they were packing up the gear for a morning rehearsal at the theatre and returning to London in the evening, when they unpacked the truck and fit in another few hours of rehearsal. This marathon of work put a tremendous strain on the Greaveses, whose son, Ben, had been born on September 16. In the memory of Leigh's spouse, Cathy Williams, the band had some trouble coming to terms with one of their own now having other draws on his time. "With the Cow discipline, it was like you do not let emotion get in the way of anything. This is *the* work, *the* discipline, and I know John was really upset at times."

Nobody had more than four or five hours of sleep per night. There was no time to write new music, so the band struggled with their contribution. In his contemporaneous analysis of the project, Hodgkinson noted that having a director who agreed with their interpretation of Prospero meant that Henry Cow's music was often rendered redundant by Chadwick's direction. For a time, they developed an approach to the music that seems to have been inspired by Brecht's "In Praise of Learning": they actually tried to rehearse onstage *during* the play—that is, arriving at the beginning, unpacking, tuning up, and developing a new piece of music every night. The idea was that, through a real process of collective learning and struggle, they could come to understand Prospero's trickery, thereby demystifying it. In practice, though, music and action interfered with each other and obscured the meaning of their interpretation. Plus, nobody could hear the words (and, unlike in *The Bacchae*, there were a lot of them). In the end, Henry Cow improvised a lot of quiet "island sounds." "We are playing an extremely subdued role in the production," Hodgkinson informed Ayerst. "There is absolutely no rock/jazz & at no point do we all play together except for about 90 seconds at the end."[9]

Despite their high hopes and ambitions, everyone appears to have been dissatisfied. "An artistic failure," Greaves recalls. "I think you could apply the word *hubris* to it." Unlike with *The Bacchae*, the Cows have no memories of working together pleasurably on music; only "Solemn Music" stayed in their repertoire, and even that short piece appears to have been stitched together from other fragments that Frith wrote for the project.[10] Writing in the *Guardian*, Nicholas de Jongh reminded his readers of the high quality of Henry Cow's *Bacchae* score, but was less impressed by their *Tempest*: "Here the group provides a kind of episodic, fragmented and irrelevant score. Sometimes it accompanies the players and reduces them to inaudibility."[11] Hodgkinson reported at the time that Henry Cow fans showed up occasionally throughout the three-week run in November, only to be disappointed. He wrote to Ayerst, "The play stumbles on, the good nights succeeding the bad. . . . We remain on our platform, sometimes dozing off, sometimes engaged. . . . A sense of unreality in setting off to Watford after dark for another performance, as if one feels fortunate to have remembered to keep the appointment."

New challenges presented themselves almost immediately, however, so the Cows couldn't linger on the failure. Six concerts around southern England rushed straight into three days of rehearsals for a BBC taping of Oldfield's *Tubular Bells*, which Branson and Draper had been promoting heavily. Frith, Hodgkinson, Greaves, and Leigh joined several rock standouts, such as Mike Ratledge, Mick Taylor, and Steve Hillage, in the TV recording for the BBC's 2nd House program (it aired in early January). The next morning, they were off to a seven-date tour of Holland, where Leigh's contacts there had been instrumental in setting up gigs. Henry Cow was excited to get back to touring on their own, but this one had not been well organized and, to make matters worse, began in frigid weather.

The Holland tour also proceeded with a certain level of anxiety because Leigh had informed the group before they embarked that he would be leaving them at its conclusion. He'd planned his exit for a month or two but hung in during the rehearsals and performances of *The Tempest* because he feared the disruption it would create for his comrades if he jumped out in the middle of things. Beyond the second album, however, there was nothing scheduled after the Dutch tour, so the time was right to make a change.

Leigh had many reasons for leaving Henry Cow, and the list started with the Virgin contract. He recalled, "Once that bit of paper was signed, it was like the whole vibe changed." Virgin had insisted that Henry Cow project a film of the *Tubular Bells* BBC special before each of their sets in Holland. Leigh surely chafed at this minor indignity, which was just one part of a general transformation since the spring.[12] The level of seriousness increased, the group had become more important than its individual members, and he

Figure 3.1 Geoff Leigh, 1973.
PHOTOGRAPH BY BRIAN COOKE.

thought his comrades were writing music that was complicated for its own sake. Their improvisational orientation was shifting, too. While Leigh continued to love the high energy of free jazz jamming, Henry Cow had begun to explore more diffuse, ambient textures, and, unlike their saxophonist, they were adding more electrification. Not only was Frith relying more heavily on his headstock pickup, but Cutler had begun to employ contact microphones on and around his drum set during improvisations, and Hodgkinson was developing a noisier, electronic vocabulary on the organ. For these musical reasons, Leigh often felt isolated during collective improvisations.

In addition to these musical differences, others emerged along the political axis. More anarchist-minded than his bandmates, Leigh had begun to wonder if the Cows, especially Hodgkinson and Cutler, were devoting too much of their attention to the theoretical analysis of their changing circumstances at the expense of a practical response on the local level. He comments, "I felt like I spent my political time in the real world, and these guys are just armchair philosophers. Rightly or wrongly—but at the time, this was [my] feeling."

Finally, Leigh had found a promising and rewarding musical partner in Cathy Williams, who shared his love for free jazz, performance art, and busking on the street. Although she didn't push him to leave the band, she did listen to and validate his expressions of dissatisfaction; some friends urged Geoff to think of his career and stick it out with Henry Cow, but Williams merely pointed out that if it was making him unhappy, there was no reason to stay. In any case, despite these many differences that led Leigh out of Henry Cow, the two parties parted company amicably.

Once they returned from the tour and Leigh had left, the remaining Cows could observe more closely the workings of their record label. It may have been exciting to be Virgin's number one experimental group now that Faust was out of the picture, but the beast had to be fed. Henry Cow owed it two albums a year, according to their contract, so even though the long Faust tour and *The Tempest* had kept them from crafting and refining new material, they would have to produce something whether they wanted to or not. Considering the fact that the band had been honing the material on *Leg End* for years, the quick turnaround to its follow-up felt even shorter. Is this how life would be?

They also began to put together a fuller picture of how the music industry worked. Frith explains, "It shouldn't be underestimated the enormous impact that Virgin's advertising had for us. It opened up all the doors—we could tour all over Europe for the first time. We had support, we had advertising, we had the building of an audience." But the efficacy of Virgin's PR machine surprised the Cows, even breeding a certain disquiet. "They were crowing whenever a journalist would actually write, word-for-word, what they said in their press releases—that would be a victory. In other words, they were controlling the agenda by telling the journalists what to say," Frith continued.

The music weeklies did publish a heap of Cow-related material from late 1973 into 1974. Steve Lake pronounced *Leg End* his number one album of the year on December 22, 1973, and, in an accompanying "crystal ball" column in the following issue, he praised their "brilliant musicianship, honesty, originality, [and] good humour," while also opining that they "frequently upstaged the Germans" on the Faust tour. Perhaps hyperbolically, he even said that Henry Cow was better than Pink Floyd or Soft Machine *had ever* been.[13] A couple of weeks later, *Melody Maker* ran "The Henry Cow File," a kind of primer on the band that gave a brief history of personnel along with a rundown of their equipment, management, influences, tastes, and musical training.[14] The following month, Lake published another column, this time profiling Cutler and his drumming style.[15] In keeping with the pattern of positive critical attention, MacDonald even went so far as to revise his lukewarm appraisal of *Leg End* in a March 1974 review of the Greasy Truckers material. He wrote, "And I'd like to take this opportunity to own up that, immediately after giving it a rather cool review, I realised that the band's album 'The Henry Cow Legend' was quite beautiful and one of the most outstanding debuts by a British band since 'The Soft Machine.' Sorry, lads—my mind was on vacation at the time."[16]

What's Next? Lindsay Cooper

Once Leigh was gone, the Cows collectively considered what and whom they might add in his place. Cutler liked the idea of trombone or harp, but in the end their discussions were rather brief, because a strong candidate rose quickly to the top of the list. About six months earlier, Frith and Cutler had attended a performance by the Ritual Theatre, a free improvisation group that combined movement, gesture, vocalization, and music. (Although the group had been based in Huddersfield, they had begun staging performances in London in 1973.) Their old Cambridge mate, Clive Bell, one of the musicians in Ritual Theatre, had invited them to the gig.[17] The Cows were struck by the musicality of the bassoonist, a twenty-two-year-old named Lindsay Cooper, and Cutler recalled seeing her play with another group, the folk-rock band Comus, a year or two before. In any event, the memory of Cooper's performance that night stayed with them, and Frith rang her up on New Year's Eve. The two improvised together and played through some written music, after which he delivered an eager endorsement to his bandmates.[18] Two weeks later, she was rehearsing at Walmer Road.

Cooper was born in March 1951, in Hornsey, and she grew up in a middle-class family in Middlesex.[19] According to Sally Potter, the family had pulled itself up to this position from the lower-middle class; Cooper's father worked as a publicist for the Royal Festival Hall, where he took Cooper to concerts and ballets from as early as she could remember. At home, the family listened to mainstream classical music (and, like any English child of her age, she followed closely the mid-sixties developments in pop). She began violin lessons at age nine, soon adding piano and, at thirteen or fourteen, fell in love with the bassoon over the protests of her father. Passionate about the instrument, she had also developed a sharp ear and progressed rapidly through the grades.

Figure 3.2 Lindsay Cooper, a multi-instrumentalist from a young age, c. 1973.
COURTESY OF THE LINDSAY COOPER ESTATE.

Cooper attended grammar school at the Notting Hill and Ealing High School. "Once I got to that school, my life in many ways took off," she later wrote.[20] She devoted her life to music, performing with the National Youth Orchestra, composing occasionally, and learning about new traditions, chief among them African music. In her final year at the school, she participated in an educational cruise to West Africa, where she met local musicians and studied drumming patterns. The clutches of Western art music were beginning to loosen. Cooper's excellent performance on the final graded exam in bassoon performance won her a coveted scholarship to the Royal Academy of Music, but, perhaps sensing that it would not make a pleasurable match, she deferred her admission for a year and instead matriculated at the Dartington College of Arts in Devon.

"I used my bassoon as a way to escape from home," she later explained. Although her parents were supportive of her studies, Cooper strongly desired role models for an artistic life, one that was worlds away from a "very cold family where most of the people were severely damaged." She found them at Dartington, a radical institution that encouraged its students to learn about contemporary art practice and to work across disciplines. In the year she spent there, Cooper studied contemporary and early music, continued learning about Ghanaian music, and began improvising in a collaboration with a dancer. Just as significantly, she realized that she was primarily attracted to women. For Cooper, all of these new interests seemed to militate against the buttoned-up world of the Royal Academy.

But she went anyway, drawn there in 1969 by her "addiction to achievement" and the prestigious opportunity that the scholarship represented.[21] Bucking against the parochial views of the institution, Cooper picked fights with the principal over inviting an African friend to teach drumming, and with her teacher, Gwydion Brooke, over the boring and conservative repertoire she had to play for her end-of-year exam. The values inculcated by any conservatory—obedience, uniformity, hierarchy—seemed to contradict directly the ones that had proven so attractive at Dartington—autonomy, exploration, play, creativity, individuality. "The size of orchestras meant that you didn't really have a voice. Sure, I could have done chamber music, but I found the repertoire not very interesting. And I found that endless reproduction of other people's music, and not *really* having much choice over what you played and what you didn't play—I found that a really daunting prospect. I didn't really feel terribly at home with the sort of people who do classical music."[22] At the end of her first year, Cooper had reached her limit, and dropped out. (She recalls that it was a disgraceful exit, because she held the most distinguished scholarship at the academy.)

Liberated, Cooper hitchhiked across Europe that summer and then visited her half-brother in New York City, where she eventually persuaded the principal bassoonist for the New York Philharmonic, Harold Goltzer, to give her lessons. Her commitment to the instrument and to music had not wavered, but she was searching for the right environment to cultivate her gifts. When she returned to London in 1971, she found that environment in the band Comus, which she joined in August of that year.[23] Cooper replaced one of the founding members, Rob Young, quickly learning the oboe and flute in order to cover his parts. Although Comus would eventually come apart one year later, Cooper gained valuable experience touring with them through northern Europe.

Soon after Comus disbanded, Cooper joined the Ritual Theatre, which had been founded earlier in 1972 by the director Barry Edwards. The group presented completely improvised performances, with three "actuals" (rather than "actors") and three musicians appearing together onstage in very loosely structured, abstract rituals without dialogue. Her musical cohort was composed of Billy Currie (viola) and Bell (flute and shakuhachi); with them, Cooper was able to explore free improvisation in a manner similar to her earliest experiences with the practice at Dartington, where dancers provided a visual element that helped to stimulate musical decision-making. She was eventually replaced by the cellist Colin Wood in the summer of 1973, but not before Frith and Cutler heard her perform with the group.

In the interval between her departure from the Ritual Theatre and her invitation to join Henry Cow, Cooper kept her improvising skills sharp by participating in Maggie Nicols's workshops at the Oval House. A respected and experienced jazz singer, Nicols had moved into improvised music in 1968, when she joined drummer John Stevens's Spontaneous Music Ensemble. By the early 1970s, she had followed his example and begun leading workshops based partially on Stevens's exercises; at these meetings, Cooper would have been given the opportunity to experiment with the post-jazz language of British free improvisation.[24]

Cooper's formidable skills as a musician impressed the members of Henry Cow and excited them to perform with and write music for her. Leigh had been every bit the professional that Cooper was, but the shift in tradition from jazz and soul to Western art music (however far Cooper had fallen from that empyrean realm) would spark an equally substantial change in the group's sound. "This was serious," Greaves put it. "She's got an oboe, and she knows what to do with it." Eight years in the practice room had created an excellent sight-reader, even though she had not yet developed an expertise in contemporary extended techniques like multiphonics—that would come later. But in her phrasing and intervallic vocabulary, she would draw a new series of reference points for Henry Cow's improvisations. Hodgkinson remembers, "And she did things like—I remember pretty early on, probably in a rehearsal—she said to Chris, 'Could I just try your drum set out for a minute?' And she played some free drums, and I think we all thought, 'Wow, she's got the knack, hasn't she?'" This combination of bravery, chutzpah, and brio endeared her to the boys quickly and made it easy to join—and reroute—the musical flow. Sitting on an amp and listening to one of her first rehearsals, Jack Balchin loved that Cooper was simply not afraid to fail. "All of a sudden there's this gangly girl with all these bassoons and oboes, and it was mighty impressive. It was fearless. . . . I'd hear how they'd interact, and what she was saying was fresh and exciting. . . . I just remember at the end of that thing, there was just this really nice sensation of 'Yeah—what's next?' That's the big deal, always. . . . When you get something done, what's next?" It was like she had thrown open new doors, left and right.

Socially, all four Cows were smitten with her, as Cutler put it. She wasn't just talented but personable, fun, an intellectual; and she was easy to imagine touring with—in her short career, Cooper had played countless concerts and seemed utterly comfortable in her own skin. Moreover, they loved the fact that she was a woman, a rare sight in the world of rock instrumentalists. Once Cooper had discovered her sexuality at Dartington, she explored it with vigor, cultivating an erotic charisma somewhere between coquettish and assertive—"a bit scary," in the words of one observer. "Oh, I wouldn't say Lindsay had a light touch," Frith adds. "I think Lindsay brought a pile driver of energy in several directions at once." Sue Steward still remembers the first time Cooper walked into the Virgin office as a member of Henry Cow. She recounts, "When they'd gone from the meeting, somebody said, 'You know she's bi-sexual?' And I didn't even know what *bi-sexual* was. I'd never heard of the word. . . . Gay liberation . . . hadn't even started up properly—it was going but not for women. And so this became a fascinating thing for us, a woman in the band—and she's *bi-sexual*." Cooper was constantly attracting attention. As a different member of the group told me, she was the member most likely to remove her shirt in public or disappear with a groupie on tour. "She sort of flirted with us in different ways," Hodgkinson remembers. "Of course we knew that she was a lesbian, but this seemed slightly complicated by the fact that we fairly quickly found out that there was something happening with Fred. I then connected that back to his description of their first meeting, which, in retrospect, seemed to be like one of those stories of the sexual dangers of music from Victorian times."

The two began having sex soon after Cooper joined Henry Cow. Although one cannot dismiss the very rockist structure of male sexual predation, Cooper was more likely to have understood the pairing through the lens of radical feminism, which she was learning about in Shulamith Firestone's classic, *The Dialectic of Sex*, among many other important texts. For Firestone, the patriarchal, biological family was a wellspring for all varieties of oppression; sexual liberation, in her view, would free individuals to pursue physical pleasure independent of the exploitative institution of marriage. "Unlike a lot of women, I never had all this love and marriage business instilled into me, which I'm very grateful for," Cooper later explained. "I never for a minute saw it in the romantic terms they hope women are going to see it. . . . Unlike a lot of other revolutionary analyses, feminist politics have got to deal with love because, I mean, the basis of women's oppression is to do with their relationship with men, although it's obviously economic oppression as well."[25]

This frank and assertive brand of feminist sexuality distinguished Cooper from the other women connected to Henry Cow. Caroline Ayerst, for example, had arrived at her feminism through consciousness-raising groups, where she and her friends helped each other recognize shared patterns of oppression or negative stereotypes that had confined them to predictable gender roles. She continues, "I kind of felt that Lindsay bypassed all that, . . . and was quite powerful with both men and women. She wasn't struggling against negative stereotypes, in a way that Sarah [Greaves], myself, and Dagmar [Krause, who later joined the band] might have been." Indeed, for Sarah Greaves, who had already married and born a child at a young age, Cooper was the sole source of her growing feminist consciousness, not only through the trove of books she shared with her but also through her exemplification of a kind of nonheteronormative sexual womanhood.

These subtleties among subject positions were largely lost on the men of Henry Cow. For them, Cooper brought "feminism" into the group, and this meant little more at the beginning than a dawning awareness of the power of everyday language to reinforce power arrangements. As Frith recalls, "We were all preconditioned males just like everybody else. So that was the beginning of a whole education." Eventually, according to Hodgkinson, that education would lead him and his mates to realize "how dodgy the whole hippy thing had been from the feminist perspective," and, indeed, how dodgy most leftwing or countercultural institutions had been. For example, in Cooper's memory, that supposed haven of unconventional thinking, Virgin Records, also harbored its share of unreconstructed sexists.[26] Nevertheless, she said, "the rock world, or certainly the kind of strange twilight zone of the rock world that I was a part of, . . . was kind of a home for outsiders of all kinds, generally. So although it's certainly true to say that sexism was not absent, it felt like there was more room to maneuver, as a woman, and that there was more chance for one's voice as a woman to be heard."[27] She recognized the limitations of the rock world, but always in comparison with the wider field: "You had to be a certain way as a woman in classical music. You had to be pretty straight—in all senses of the word—and I found it intolerable." Rock may have felt alienating at times, but certainly no more alienating than being in a symphony orchestra "and having the sexism take polite forms," Cooper concluded.

As for Henry Cow itself, Cooper was more interested in the stylistic and generic possibilities evident in the band's work than she was in their political sympathies. "I liked them very much, as people, and I found them very, very interesting, musically, because I think it was really about the first time that I could see the possibility of doing something that engaged me musically, but wasn't classical music and wasn't pop music, and wasn't jazz. I mean Henry Cow was a very unplaceable sort of group."[28] An artist, Cooper drew the bottom line at musical promise.

Ruins and Unrest

The Cows worried in the weeks before they arrived at the Manor on February 14 to record their second album. Although Cooper had added a lot of new energy, the group had scheduled only the first two weeks of January for composing, and then needed to assemble a live set with their new member for a handful of shows around London and in Bristol. Once the gigs were out of the way, they had just ten days to rehearse for the session—twelve-hour days in the freezing back addition of the Walmer Road house. The shorter numbers they had ready wouldn't be too difficult, but the weighty compositions would require serious effort, and they felt rushed by the label. "We were disturbed and 'uneasy,'" Cutler remembered in 1981. Greaves was having serious doubts about his future in the band, and his bandmates had begun—perhaps harshly—to question his "commitment" (an ongoing Cow keyword).

To make matters worse, a dentist had extracted Cooper's wisdom teeth on February 5. Her physically altered embouchure—not to mention the pain—contributed to their struggles. She spent days piecing together her rendering on oboe of what had been Leigh's soprano sax line for Greaves's "Half Asleep, Half Awake." While she negotiated the piece's fiendish rhythms, the Manor's recording engineers sniggered at her in the booth. Persevering, she turned in an impressive solo in the tune's second half, one that growls almost like a tenor saxophone. The episodic and fleet-handed composition, which Greaves himself opens and closes with his searching, cocktail-piano style, bears the final vestiges of *Leg End*'s jazz-rock flavor.

The record's opening track was a Frith fillip called "Bittern Storm over Ulm." Essentially an electric blues guitar solo, the two-minute song was based on a mutilated version of the bassline from the Yardbirds' "Got to Hurry." Frith also composed the opener to side two, "Solemn Music," some distinctive counterpoint for oboe, organ, and guitar over a bass pedal that had been scavenged from *The Tempest*.

His major contribution, however, was the twelve-minute "Ruins." It was new enough that the band was still unable to perform it when they arrived at the Manor, so the recording proceeded in piecemeal fashion. After a pensive introduction of droning organ chords punctured by unison stabs from the piano and triangle, the band launches into some composed bits cribbed from Frith's sections of "Teenbeat" and "Under the Yellow Half Moon." Soon, they drop into the distinctive cycle of the piece: a two-chord pattern (E-11–13 and D-11–13) that alternates six times in varying durations of eighth-notes ([6–4][5–3][3–2][7–3][7–3][4–8]) that add up to 55. The bass and piano play this pattern while Cutler slashes along, together forming the basis of a Hodgkinson organ solo that scrapes and crackles for seven 55-beat cycles; in it, the keyboardist explores the different noise possibilities of a fuzz box and the separate fuzz control on his H&H amplifier, where he also had access to a noise gate that could be finely controlled to produce a sputtering kind of broken sustain. The middle section of "Ruins" opens out onto an unhurried interlude of acoustic chamber music. In this part, Frith announces each of a series of plaintive dialogues—violin and bass-bassoon; bassoon and violin-bass; xylophone-bass-drums and bassoon-violin—with fanfares in the winds that call to mind the 55-beat cycle, but not exactly. This same grouping of winds then takes over the actual 55-beat cycle while Frith delivers the second improvised solo, his nimble performance making the most of the stereo guitar set up first committed to tape on the Greasy Truckers date. The solo is eventually overtaken by a violin melody that, on repetition, assumes the role of a 55-beat cantus firmus when oboe, piano and bass, another oboe, and finally drums fill out the counterpoint. Frith signals the end with a more "rock"-sounding section of distorted, sustaining guitar and clarinet melodies over active bass and drums; the coda consists of a droning guitar sustain and one more round of chords in the winds.

The composition sprawled but possessed an intuitive form: two solos around a chamber music core, the whole thing bracketed by rock intro and outro. "Ruins" soon became a centerpiece of the band's live set for years to come; the 55-beat "Ruins riff" was fun to play and made a versatile bed for solo improvisation on its own. At the time, though, recording it took forever because they still hadn't fully learned the piece.[29] "This was a mistake," Cutler wrote a few years later. "We should have delayed the record. But we were sure the challenge would 'bring out the best' in us. On the written side I think we were wrong here, but on the 2nd side, I am glad we took the risk."[30]

With only one side's worth of material, the band was indeed taking a risk, and their uncertainty about side two contributed to the rancorous environment in the studio. They recorded reels and reels of failed improvisations— false starts and dead ends. Half-days of work produced nothing but friction. At times, nobody knew what to try next. (Indeed, it even seems that they

entertained the possibility of asking Robert Wyatt to come sing for them.[31])
These small failures were painful for Henry Cow, but they also made them
a pain to work with. Andy Morris had to take over engineering duties when
Phil Newell gave up in exasperation.

Newell remembers the atomized recording process the band had settled
into, partially out of desperation in the face of the ticking clock. One musician would improvise a track, and then another would record a second part
on top. A third musician would improvise yet another part, but only while
monitoring one of the previous two takes, and so on. After several improvisations had been layered in this fashion, the whole group (or this subsection
of it) would listen back to everything combined and discuss possibilities for
mixing or editing. For the band, this process was a way to get as much out of
the Manor as they possibly could; some Cows could always been recording
while others took breaks. In Newell's opinion, such fragmentation only contributed to the intellectual character of the group's sound: none of the Virgin
staff, in his memory, could make an emotional connection to the work.

But for Henry Cow, the atomization of the band would itself produce the
theme (and title) of the album: unrest. As the session wore on, they gained
confidence in their abilities to combine improvisation, written composition, and various forms of musique concrète in the service of representing
this theme. For Frith, their confidence in the face of difficulty was a measure of Leigh's lasting influence on the band: "It's not an accident that even
though Geoff had left the group by the time we did *Unrest* . . . , we spent [a]
week in the studio only doing improvisation and nothing else."

After their first two weeks of recording, Henry Cow remained in a certain state of unrest about the new album. Hodgkinson remembers, "I think
when we left the studio on February 28th we were feeling a bit anxious
about whether it was going to work out or not. We had sort of inchoate
musical aspirations that were not being met by what we were hearing on
playback." They took a few weeks, played a few gigs, had a few rehearsals,
and then reconvened at the Manor for the last thirteen days of March, when
the second side finally took shape. A few years later, Cutler wrote, "For instance with 'Linguaphonie,' we began with several tapes of improvisations,
we listened carefully & selected parts to splice together with a view to making a coherent structure upon which to build. . . . we tried to find the *content* of the music, to find a message or meaning which we could bring out of
it."[32] The inability to communicate: this was the meaning of "Linguaphonie."
It featured short bits of French rhyme recited in unison by a small mixed

choir, interspersed with sudden changes of instrumentation and variations in texture that remind me of György Ligeti's *Aventures*.

Cutler continued, "We had to become sensitive to what we *felt* as we improvised & put down the basic material. [Our] mood was dark, & so it was the darkness we brought out & gave shape to."[33] The second track, "Upon Entering the Hotel Adlon," offered a scene from German high society in the mid-1930s: "Desperate monsters who danced & swilled champagne as murder stalked the streets & who turned thier [*sic*] backs to the insatiable spectre of war." It's a frenzied dance of distorted guitar, discombobulated bass, and clamorous drums. Over the top rings a fanfare for winds that calls to mind "Ruins." A noir theme is offered by the next piece, "Arcades," which the band imagined as a cool, rainy night in the city. A more peaceful number that begins with a distant echo (in the chromatic ascent of the bassoon) of Stravinsky's "Ritual of the Ancestors," the piece featured a soulful alto solo by Hodgkinson over plangent ringing in Frith's guitar.

Henry Cow reached the album's crowning achievement in the final composition, "Deluge," which was built on the ground of a sparse, forty-second loop that threaded its fifty-foot path through the control room around wine bottles and the capstans of three tape machines. Guitar, bass, and drums sound continuously through every pass of the loop while other tracks of squeaking saxophone, additional guitar, and a mournful violin line are added and subtracted from the flow. After a few minutes, they fade in a bit from the end of "Ruins" played at half-speed; a few minutes more, and this long sample eventually takes over, augmented by new harmonies added in violin, bassoon, and flute. A sudden cut conjures Greaves at the piano, where he sings a chestnut from the old days, "Don't Disturb Me." Behind him, Cutler wrote, "all the sounds of the worlds [*sic*] end: Downpour, debris, thunder, desolation."[34] The ambient room sound is straight out of Faust's playbook: he's been captured by a single microphone on the other side of the studio. A faint murmur of rain cushions the scene, which closes on the aural image of an orchestra tuning up, "preparing for the future. A small hope, but a hope. At the time this took on a very important meaning for us."

As Frith notes, by 1974 Henry Cow had been improvising together for several years, but those improvisations had been relatively contained by available forms: the jazz or rock solo, or the high-energy free-jazz blow. "I think it got radical quite quickly after *Unrest*," he explains. "Clearly you can hear that the improvisation on *Unrest* has gone way beyond what we were doing before." Indeed, the second side, and especially "Deluge," marked a significant feat: it built up a kind of rock improvisation that eluded the heroics of the guitar solo or the ecstasis of the psychedelic freak-out—a new kind of improvisation that took its route through the tape recorder. Faust couldn't have been far in the background. Of course, Miles Davis had been working with the extended improvisational modality of tape, but Teo Macero's lone assembly of the edits was indeed a far cry from the distributed, multiagent creativity that Henry Cow discovered at the Manor, where they improvised with recordings, added new, composed arrangements, and manipulated tape by varying record and playback speed, making cuts, and fashioning loops. The creative success of this material also seemed to validate their intuition that they could face an uncertainty like not having enough material and rise to the challenge while remaining in the interstice between improvisation and recording technology.

The band took a mix to the Virgin offices on Portobello Road to share this breakthrough. "We were still under the illusion that Virgin was a hip, friendly company and would be interested," Cutler recalls. "So we invited Simon, Jumbo, Sue—in fact, all of the staff—to come and listen to it as if we were one big happy family and, of course, we were really disappointed when they didn't jump up and down, shouting, 'By golly, I think you've *really* done it!' They just looked nonplussed."

This Is Not What This Band Is Made For: Captain
Beefheart and the Tragic Band

But there wasn't much time to worry about their reaction, because the Virgin Agency (for concert booking) had put together a short tour of France supporting Kevin Coyne, after which Henry Cow returned to London and hit the woodshed—they needed to learn their new music and assemble sets that would play to the strengths of their new reeds player. A one-day session they cut for John Peel's "Top Gear" program on April 25 gives some indication that their rehearsals had paid off. "We're feeling good by then, I think," Hodgkinson recalls. Cooper took control right off the top: the fifteen-minute continuous performance began with a cracking oboe solo that boldly announced the change in their sound. Cooper trilled serpentine lines, unfolding in surprising phrases that were many things, none of them jazz-rock. For Greaves, the difference was striking: "I began to see our improvisations on that kind of stage. Maybe it's just my own maturity, or perhaps the maturity of the group in our improvising: we weren't jamming anymore. Lindsay don't jam." The rest of the set that day—"Ruins," "Half Asleep," and "Bittern Storm"—nonetheless had the feel of old Henry Cow. The band broke up "Ruins," eliding the long chamber music section in the middle by abutting the organ and guitar solos before jump-cutting straight into Greaves's composition. Surprisingly, they then concluded "Half Asleep" with a return to the end of "Ruins." They drew the set to a close with a comparatively straight-forward rendering of "Bittern Storm." The April Peel session portrays a band hitting its performing stride, which was auspicious timing given the next big undertaking that lay ahead: a twenty-five date tour in support of one of their heroes, Captain Beefheart, that would begin in France and then take them to England, Scotland, and eventually the Netherlands.

Recently signed to Virgin, Beefheart was touring to generate publicity for his new record, *Unconditionally Guaranteed*. As biographer Mike Barnes has noted, few albums have possessed such an ironic title; often regarded as the low point in Beefheart's career, *Unconditionally Guaranteed* suffered further when his Magic Band quit en masse five days before the start of their North American tour in April.[35] (An abusive bandleader, Beefheart had pushed his musicians over the edge.) Scrambling in response to this dramatic turn of events, Beefheart assembled a new group of session musicians who did their best but had little feel for the elasticity and angularity of the repertoire; history would dub this temporary ensemble the Tragic Band. (Greaves remembers sitting on the bus with one of these musicians, who queried with a pained look, "What do you do—de-tune your guitar? I mean, you guys know about weird shit—how do you do this? 'Cause it's what he wants!" Legend has it that some of these musicians had never heard Beefheart's music before the tour began.)

Despite these significant difficulties, the tour was a major event in the UK rock world and placed Henry Cow in front of the largest audiences of their career. *Unrest* may have consternated the staff at Virgin, but they persevered in promoting Henry Cow despite ample time to swap them out for a more commercially promising opening act. Simon Draper remembers, "We put them on the Captain Beefheart tour. We treated them in every way as if they were a potentially successful rock band. . . . It was only later that I thought, 'God, we were very optimistic to think that we could ever sell that.'"

As captured on a live concert recording from the tour, the band's set bore some similarities to the April Peel session. They opened with a bit of free improvisation, then moved on to "Amygdala" and a jumble of material from "Yellow Half-Moon" and "Teenbeat," before drawing to a close with the "Ruins"–"Half Asleep"–"Ruins"–"Bittern Storm" medley. Band members recall that audiences were divided in their reaction to Henry Cow's music. There was a certain amount of disinterest, which is the case for every supporting band. One attendee referred to the "cathartic surge" that ran through the crowd in Leeds once the headliner took the stage.[36] But occasionally, audiences grew vocal, a response that spurred the band on to some of their more memorable and energized performances. As Frith explained in an interview that summer, "It's much more of a challenge playing to people who basically aren't interested in seeing you at all." If half the audience generally hated their music, he continued, "the other half are polarised into liking it far more than they probably would normally. And that makes the whole thing extreme and exciting."[37]

This charge of direct dialogue with their listeners would become one of the few lasting positive memories of the experience, however. "Which is ironic when you think of how badly we played on the Beefheart tour," Frith said some years later. "This was our production-line tour where everything should've been smoother . . . , but those were some of the worst gigs I remember us ever doing, from a purely competent, technical point of view. I mean we were out of time with each other . . ."

Cutler interjected, "out of tune . . ."

". . . breaking down in the middle of songs . . . ," Frith continued with a laugh.

Hodgkinson added, "Lindsay was permanently out of tune."[38]

Furthermore, Charles Fletcher struggled with the live sound, and he and the band members disagreed frequently about whether a given night's performance had been sonically successful or not. (Tom Newman, who was handling live sound for Beefheart, also participated in these confabs.) Working conditions fell short of optimal. As the opener, Henry Cow rarely enjoyed sufficient time to set up or sound check, and, most disconcertingly, they felt as if their ability to direct their own affairs had been taken away; the Beefheart road managers told them when and where to go, when to take breaks, and how long they could play. The endless series of "hideous," identical Holiday Inns "eat away at your mental fibre," Greaves explained.[39] Most dispiriting were Beefheart's managers, the DiMartino brothers, who had a reputation as shady hustlers; many observers had come to the conclusion that they were exploiting Beefheart, who was already at loose ends dealing with the Tragic Band. Although the Cows got to spend a lot of time with Beefheart, his desperate straights and accompanying depression left the band with grave concerns about the music industry.

When they finally came off the road in late June, Henry Cow were shell-shocked. Although they had enjoyed playing in the somewhat masochistic terms suggested by Frith, the social and organizational reality of the big-business tour felt more like a "warning," to use Cutler's word.[40] Hodgkinson agrees; by the end of the tour, they had "experienced from the inside the standard model of the successful or rising band. We've gone from getting a record contract to *that* in that space of time, and we think, well, 'No. . . . This is not what this band was made for.'" Their most pressing concern during the tour or shortly thereafter was to revise or terminate their arrangement with the Virgin Agency, which was a separate entity from Virgin Records. As for the latter, Cutler recalled, "They were doing their best by us. They were trying to push a band they thought maybe *could* break through if they just had a few more fans. So the association with Beefheart seemed like a good strategy to them." By contrast, the concert agency couldn't match the band's expectations for touring. "We were effectively relegated to the status of support band for other Virgin artists' tours, which was hardly what we wanted. And doing a gig every day. . . . I think that was one of the things that overwhelmed us: having no gigs for the most part, and then more in a block than we were ready to handle."

In any case, they had no gigs in the foreseeable future, and wanted to keep it that way until they felt like they had a handle on their affairs. By the end of the summer, they began to plan a six-night series of concerts at the ICA (like the Cabaret Voltaire or the Explorer's Club) with Robert Wyatt, Derek Bailey, Lol Coxhill, Gilli Smyth, Daevid Allen, and the Radar Favourites, Geoff Leigh and Cathy Williams's new band; "Back to things being organized by us," Cutler told an interviewer at the time. "It's not a record company promotion or anything like that. It's entirely our affair."[41] They wanted the evenings to be relaxed, casual, anarchic, and progressive—in short, everything the Beefheart tour wasn't. But when they asked the Virgin Agency for £150 to cover the expenses of their guests, the company refused; the band didn't want to ask their friends to play for free, given Henry Cow's position in the heart of the beast.[42] They scuttled their plans, and there effectively ended the relationship with the Virgin Agency.

Meanwhile, *Unrest* had appeared in record stores toward the end of the Beefheart dates, clad in a sleeve that featured a second Ray Smith sock painting of stormy black and brown tones. The record vexed the critics.[43] Although they outnumbered the negative reviews, even the positive ones evinced a lack of confidence in their judgment—the album was "perhaps an important contribution,"[44] or it "may in retrospect turn out to be a very important and influential LP."[45] Most often, critics observed that *Unrest* was difficult to pin down in terms of genre, and that might explain the hesitation about judgment—did they feel unqualified to evaluate music that was somewhat remote from their assumed area of expertise? (Writers mentioned the predictable references—*Trout Mask Replica, Uncle Meat*, Soft Machine—but also "modern classical," Derek Bailey, Stockhausen, "avant-garde jazz," "free form blowing," the Portsmouth Sinfonia, Lol Coxhill, and electronic music.) As MacDonald put it, Henry Cow was "on the borderland of rock and Something Else." Although one critic referred to their "solid rock foundation,"[46] another heard roots "clearly in jazz,"[47] while a third clarified that "this is only rock by virtue of using bass and drums and being marketed in the appropriate manner."[48] For the *Morning Star*, Henry Cow was "still basically an experimental group."[49] In his enthusiastically positive *Melody Maker* review, Steve Lake averred that "it's not rock," but the album's marketing as such would help take it to larger audiences.[50] He wrote, "Were Henry Cow called the Walmer Road New Music Ensemble, for example, in keeping with the occasionally almost academic seriousness of their music, there's no way they'd ever play to mass audiences."

The size of Henry Cow's likely audience emerged as another prevalent theme in the reviews of *Unrest*. For many critics, this music spoke to minority tastes; it wasn't for everybody, they noted. MacDonald, the band's old friend and sometime booster, damned them with praise in his *NME* review. They were "painfully altruistic and enormously demanding," he wrote, "remorselessly, uncompromisingly austere." Their virtuosity and sophistication will make them too pedantic to appeal beyond cerebral listeners, he intimated. In other words, you might like them, but you'll have to work for it.

It Sure Ain't No Rock 'n' Roll: Compulsory Accessibility

MacDonald may have thought Henry Cow were "Britain's most technically dazzling rock outfit," but by playing up their "almost cultivated inaccessibility," he touched a nerve with the band. He wasn't the only one to have done so. In the following issue of *NME*, a different critic, Neil Spencer, labeled the Cows "determinedly inaccessible" in a review that provoked a letter to the editor from Cutler.[51] By asserting that Henry Cow were *trying* to erect a barrier between them and their audience, he wrote, Spencer was "imputing to us a complicity in precisely that attitude of irresponsible cynicism that we exist to destroy."[52] On the contrary, he continued, Spencer was simply attempting to pin his own cynicism onto the band, "and, of course, in so doing help to actually create that very antisocial effect you are pretending to criticise in us." (In response, Spencer pointed out that he had stressed that half the audience enjoyed the Cow's performance, but chose not to mention the other half who shouted rude comments and headed to the bar.)

The drummer continued his counterattack a few weeks later in a full-page profile and interview by Charles Shaar Murray.[53] "'Inaccessible' doesn't mean a thing when you think about it," he told the writer. "It just means that they find it hard to listen to, thereby being responsible for a lot of other people not listening to it, implying 'I can understand it but a lot of other people can't.'" Although the *NME* and Henry Cow seemed to be going through a rocky patch, Murray did offer a sympathetic and lengthy portrait of the group, somehow smarmy and complimentary at the same time. Meanwhile Henry Cow could always count on Steve Lake at *Melody Maker* for damage control; he wrote, "Henry Cow are very much a people's band, and at root are very unpretentious people."[54] In the group interview, Frith, Greaves, and Cutler tried to make clear that they were being misrepresented by the press, and, moreover, that those writers were in fact prejudicing potential listeners by telling them that *Unrest* and their live show were only for minority tastes, a charge to which Frith responded, "We're proving those claims wrong ten times out of ten." At the same time, however, if the Cows intended to disprove the false impression that they were brainy and aloof, they didn't entirely help their cause. For example, Frith opined to Lake that "most rock music these days is a lot of shit. The general standard of playing is better now than it ever has been but as a result groups have become far more uniform," while Cutler informed Murray that "Linguaphonie" was "referring to Stockhausen's microphone work [*Mikrophonie I*] and all that stuff."

Murray's smirking response—"Well thanks, Chris. Personally, I'm not hip to Stockhausen, seeing how Mott The Hoople are more my shot"—represented just one small cog in a much bigger process, namely the increasing balkanization of the commercial music markets in the mid-1970s. The capacious rock culture of 1967 and after—like that of the adventurous jazz- and classical-affiliated experimentalisms of the same period—was indeed growing narrower, and this transition was signaled nowhere more clearly than in pronouncements such as the following by Neil Spencer: "Whatever Henry Cow's music is, it sure ain't no rock 'n' roll."[55] Rock, of course, had for years been patrolled by a battalion of critics whose utterances said as much about the right to judge that inhered in white masculinity as they did about, say, Eric Clapton's position in the pantheon. But policing the borders of rock itself appeared to be a novel turn—perhaps those voices, after welcoming Miles Davis into the rock fold around 1970, decided next to emulate instead the critics who had excoriated the trumpeter's supposedly callous violation of jazz's sanctity.

At any rate, these charges of inaccessibility, coldness, and sterility indicate rock's paradoxical nature; it is at once an open genre that pulls material and techniques from anywhere and also a closed one that eagerly polices its edges. A given piece of music might be bad in one of several discourses, but it is only regarded as a betrayal of the form itself or a personal affront in the afrological musics of jazz and rock. Hodgkinson muses, "There's something about the rock group—on the one hand there's the expectations and on the other hand there are the means to shatter those expectations in interesting ways. . . . Whatever I do as a 'contemporary composer,' I can never be shocking. I mean the only thing I could do . . . [would be] to write [a] piece with pornographic films being projected as part of the piece."

Frith's negotiation of these increasingly conservative expectations within the rock genre extended into a series of ten essays on the electric guitar that he began to publish in the NME at precisely this time. His investigation of the instrument's technical history was probably at variance with the wishes of the periodical, who titled the series "Great Rock Solos of Our Time." The magazine might have hoped for a celebratory catalogue of guitar gods, but Frith made clear from the outset that he was not interested in "the ability to play fast or cleanly, or the ability to play impossible chords in ten different positions or any of those things." His definition of virtuosity, he countered, "stretches to include the simplest folk playing and the farthest out use of electronics."[56] Although he had been assigned the topic of *rock* electric guitar, which ruled out discussion of other guitar innovators like Snooks Eaglin or Mississippi John Hurt (to name two Frith heroes), this kind of distancing language signaled a sharp awareness of the frame he'd been tasked. Thus holding the rock genre at arm's length, he would instead conceive of the instrument as a matrix of possibilities; he wanted to discuss those artists who had contributed to "expanding what a guitar can do."[57]

In the next installment, he again cautioned that, despite the NME's title for his essays, "my aims are far more to do with a broad discussion of guitar-playing and music in general than with analysing particular solos or teaching people how to play them."[58] Frith was not entirely above issuing gushing prose, but he largely eschewed the vocabulary of "greatness" in his survey of the figures he considered innovators: Dave Davies, Jimi Hendrix, George

Harrison, Jeff Beck, Frank Zappa, Pete Townshend, Kevin Ayers, Lou Reed, Roger McGuinn, Syd Barrett, and Zoot Horn Rollo and Antennae Jimmy Semens (Magic Band).

In his final installment, however, Frith argued that the radical innovations on the electric guitar were no longer taking place in rock. Jazz-associated players like Larry Coryell and John McLaughlin had brought that genre up to date with the possibilities of an electronically altered guitar, but their rock emulators had reduced these contributions to a mere style based on vacuous chops. In the rock of 1974, he wrote, "the total situation at the moment appears to be one of conservatism, a Fear of taking risks or of committing one self to any other than known paths."[59] The drive for novelty in early pop and rock had produced the most interesting initial uses of the electric guitar, but the industry was an essentially conservative force based on the commodity form, "created and packaged by the record companies and disseminated through magazines like NME." Buttressed by critical sentinels who apply the word *intellectual* as a put-down, Frith averred, the record companies had assembled a system that militated against the ability of regular listeners to explore new tastes. "All of which is a lengthy way of demonstrating why experimentalists tend to work away from rock," he concluded. Instead, he suggested, readers should check out Derek Bailey, David Toop, Ian Brighton, Keith Rowe, and Hans Reichel. Like Cutler, however, Frith was measured in his enthusiasm for free improvised music. "Playing radical music is one thing, but it's very easy to fall into a kind of rarified atmosphere of nonacceptance, playing to one's own converted." For a member of Henry Cow, an artist had to pursue confrontation, challenge, and engagement.

Engagement was exactly what Frith sought—the NME articles were just one aspect of his growing public profile in 1974. He played many instruments on Tom Newman's *Fine Old Tom*, and viola on Robert Wyatt's *Rock Bottom*; his contributions to Wyatt's cover of "I'm a Believer" even led to an appearance on *Top of the Pops*. He also began to gig in London apart from Henry Cow, including Wyatt's September concert at Drury Lane, a couple of concerts in a trio with Lindsay Cooper and Clive Bell, a few more with Lol Coxhill, and even a solo show in November. With Cutler, Frith presented David Bedford's *Star's End* with the London Philharmonic and the Berlin Radio Orchestra in November and December.

Combined with the unrest of the February recording session, the disillusionment of the Beefheart tour, and the frustrations with the music press, Frith's freelancing exerted a destabilizing influence on Henry Cow. For more than a year, the group occasionally wondered if he would break off on his own; the most serious threat had come in spring 1973, when the Cows were close to signing with Virgin. Wyatt had asked Frith to join a new lineup of his band Matching Mole, but the guitarist would eventually decline the invitation.

Frith also remembers that Virgin had in mind to transform him into a solo artist. Sometime around the end of 1973, they offered to release a solo guitar record whenever he might be interested. He took his time, but eventually agreed when the Cows returned to London after the Beefheart tour. The record, eventually titled *Guitar Solos*, would be released on the subsidiary Caroline label, so there was essentially no recording budget; Frith booked four days in July at David Vorhaus's Kaleidophon Studios, perhaps the foremost electronic music studio in the United Kingdom outside the BBC Radiophonic Workshop.[60] "Virgin were trying to turn me into a star, which is what record companies try to do," Frith recalled, "and doing *Guitar Solos* was almost the antithesis of what that would have required." Indeed, he showed *them*.

Listeners to "Bittern Storm over Ulm" know that Frith could still slice off a wedge of electric cheese, but on the new record "rather than do the kind of guitar rock hero record, which is what they were imagining, I thought it would be an interesting opportunity to see if I could actually redefine what the instrument was." In hindsight, we might file this album alongside similar solo efforts of the time—Anthony Braxton's *For Alto* (1968) or Derek Bailey's *Solo Guitar* (1971)—were it not for the fact that Frith hadn't heard any of them. Bailey had already made his impression on the Cow guitarist in person, and with no money to buy records now that he was finished with university, Frith hadn't caught Bailey's Incus platter.

In the three weeks before the session, Frith woodshedded to refine the techniques he'd already discovered and to find a few more. He decided to make each piece a minimally planned improvisation with a given technical limitation—a set of etudes. With his headstock pickup and the two on the body of the instrument, he could produce three channels of sound independently controlled with volume pedals. He could further vary the sound by adding distortion to one of the body pickups, allowing for one clean and one fuzz channel. Each of these three channels could then be assigned to a specific spot in the stereo field. There are very few plucks on the record; Frith plays almost every short, pitched note by tapping directly on the fingerboard, which makes sound in both directions of the string, or just one if the other hand mutes a side. Sustained sounds came from bows of various sorts and a glass prism. He often attached a capo at the twelfth fret

Figure 3.3 Fred Frith, c. 1975.
PHOTOGRAPH BY SULA NICHOLS.

to divide the strings in half, creating one independent harp for each hand. Fascinated by David Toop's use of alligator clips on the strings, Frith used those too—if he put one between the two body pickups, he had three independently resonating lengths on a single string (if the capo was attached). He held this instrument in the conventional manner, resting on one knee rather than laid out flat, for all but one of the pieces. The exception, "No Birds," was made with two flat guitars simultaneously (both with headstock pickups).[61] Remarkably, Frith added no overdubs to *Guitar Solos* and minimal signal processing beyond the usual (a little distortion and tape delay).[62]

This solo album was extraordinary not only for the astonishing precision and originality of Frith's technique, but for his *détournement* of an instrument whose entire history had been governed by a simple rule: you pluck it and it goes twang. No plucks or twangs here. Many years later, he explained, "*Guitar Solos* is really a set of proposals. It's saying, 'What would happen if this? And how far can I go with that?' In a sense, it gave me a certain kind of geography to travel through, for many years afterwards, before I'd exhausted those particular sets." Writing in the *NME*, Charles Shaar Murray called it "a totally revolutionary album" and "an undeniable landmark in the history of rock guitar."[63]

One might be tempted to hear the dark and ruminative passages of the album's moving final track in light of the turmoil in Frith's home life. His marriage had been deteriorating almost from the moment it had begun, and certainly since they had moved to London two years earlier. For White, her husband's commitment—there's that word again—to Henry Cow and the creative life of the artist had overtaken the private life they had created together. She recalls, "From my perspective on the outside, it was as though the private friendships were becoming more and more music-based. So those of us who weren't involved in music were not exactly of no value, but certainly of no interest." In response, she threw herself into her work, but that meant that she was out all day, and Frith was out all evening—and often all night. "It was almost like a clique at school—you're either in our gang, or you're not, and if you don't follow all the things that we think are important . . . , just forget being around, really." She felt increasingly unwelcome at the Walmer Road house.

For his part, Frith was coming to terms with the band's collective decision to get serious on relocating to the city. What did that actually mean? "That means to live it. So then we start living it and that calls into question everything else. And I didn't have the experience or knowledge or gumption to really understand how to deal with that." His account of this transformation complements that of his former spouse. "We [Cows] had this really intense life . . . and then we went home. You see what I mean? Going home had the feeling of going to the office and our life was actually our work together. And that obviously didn't do our relationships any good at all. . . . Living a strange existence as a newly married, living in our nice little apartment. It felt completely alien to me." Things took a turn for the worse when White became pregnant in late 1973, about the same time that Frith and Cooper began having sex. Although White was well aware of a certain pattern in their marriage, she nursed a hope that the child would renew Frith's commitment to a shared life together. However, the guitarist continued to pursue his music-world passions; as the due date approached in July, he absorbed himself in the preparation and recording of *Guitar Solos* and Newman's *Fine Old Tom*. Although, by force, it pulled them together temporarily, the stillbirth of the child on July 29 ultimately shattered the union. The grief over this loss persisted for years; acutely, it made the autumn very difficult, and Frith and White eventually separated after the Christmas holiday at the end of 1974.

They Didn't Have Office Parties

I linger on the details of this trauma because Henry Cow's response to it exemplified a manner of emotional nonexchange that would endure until its last days. As Hodgkinson phrased it, "Rehearsal would end, and I'd go home. We didn't share domestic." Reflecting on the nonevent that was the birth of Ben Greaves in September 1973, he continued, "We didn't have office parties. . . . We didn't play a special birthday concert in a way that perhaps the Ex [a Dutch anarchist punk band] might have done if somebody in the Ex had produced a baby, for example. Sort of idealized, communal band. We didn't do that shit." The very word *bourgeois* alone was an epithet that could win an argument. Cutler, who prized personal discipline and the pragmatic virtues of poverty, surely didn't share domestic, nor did Cooper, for whom that sphere had always been marked by the history of women's oppression. With Hodgkinson, the disdain for the bourgeois was further cut with the formality of his social background: "I went through the English upper-class training, where at thirteen you go to Winchester and they tell you, 'You're a man. You don't cry.' And then you have to try to unlearn that."

For all these reasons, Henry Cow held themselves together in an ongoing state of tension. "If people had problems and didn't say anything about them, then they were left alone," Cutler explained. "So the collective made no more demands of its members than it was already making." Humor, in the form of wordplay, released that tension but also detoured the group around zones of serious emotional exchange. "We were English, after all," Frith quipped. In a 1988 conversation, three members of the group pondered these issues and the summer that brought them into focus.

Hodgkinson began, "But there were still things that we never took in— say, like when you were suffering a lot with your relationship with Liza and so forth, and that whole period, I mean there was no way that anything like that could be taken into the group. It was a whole level of reality that was going on. And the fact that later you weren't suffering, and that everything was much better, still meant that this failure was somehow still there and part of our history, and would again—as a failure—would be part of a later failure, if you see what I mean. . . ."

"Do you think it could have been otherwise," Cutler asked, "or could be otherwise if the same kind of events were to happen again? I mean, don't you think that, in fact, to a certain extent, what gets characterized as people's private, personal lives is something which they maybe don't want encroached upon?"

Frith answered, "Yes, that's exactly right, but in terms of Henry Cow, the separation was often very difficult to make, because to survive we had to adopt a certain lifestyle, and we had to become very communal in order to keep going."

"That's right."

"In the early days. And that certainly put a lot of strain on people's relationships outside of the group."

Hodgkinson interjected, "Yeah, but the separation . . . you can't choose, you know. I mean, if I arrive at a rehearsal and I'm so upset that I'm in tears, then I've failed to make the separation. The group doesn't choose, as it were—it's reality that chooses."

"Well, yes," Cutler agreed, "but the nature of the relations in the group chooses. The nature of the relations in the group would mean either people would come up to you and put their arm around your shoulder and say 'Tim, what's the problem, what's the matter,' which we would never have done."

"Right."

"I don't think we ever softened up in that way."

Frith added, "I don't think that's . . . I think that happened, but whenever it happened, it happened at a moment that was precisely that amount too late, which enabled the gesture to be misinterpreted. Because I can remember that happening to me—I can remember you saying precisely that to me at a moment when I was having a hard time, and me, because it didn't come earlier, being deeply suspicious of your motives. And that kind of thing was going on all the time—I mean, I think we often were making the gestures, but in a way that was not communicating or too late, or . . ."

"Yeah, yeah."

". . . strange tension, or . . ."[64]

Strange tension, indeed. This conversation outlined a topic that would play an increasingly large role in the band's affairs—namely, the transformation (or failed transformation) of their arts of living, and how these arts of living would relate to their transformations of art making or collective labor. We will return later to this kind of torqued intimacy that the group cultivated in its communal affairs, but it was the summer of 1974 when Henry Cow's contraviviality emerged in particularly conspicuous fashion.

In the midst of this very painful mess, Henry Cow expelled Lindsay Cooper from the band. Although she returned about seven months later, the expulsion was final at the time.[65] The Cows came to this decision for three reasons, only one of which they shared publicly when asked. The first directly concerned Frith and White's unraveling marriage. Because "commitment" demanded so much of band members, Frith often seemed to spend more time with Cooper (and his other comrades) than he did at home, aggravating the wound of his infidelity and putting his bandmates and friends, most of whom had also known Liza for years, into a difficult position—especially when she turned up at the Walmer Road house and confronted the group. "You cannot just ostracize me!" she shouted in one Cow's memory. Therefore, as Cutler recounts, the band and other associates surmised, "For Fred's sake, as much as anybody else's, we need to make a clearing here and Lindsay is going to have to pay the bill for it." Although they may have thought it was necessary at the time, none of the Cows are proud of how they handled this situation. "I think she got a bad time from us," Greaves comments.

The second reason had to do with Cooper's commitment: she was slacking off. Greaves, in particular, questioned her work ethic in presenting a case for dismissal. "His grounds for it were the well-known fact that Lilly didn't rehearse and showed up three hours late for everything," Cutler recalled. According to Hodgkinson, Cooper's superior sight-reading abilities contributed to a strange pattern of getting *worse* the more she played a piece. We might also surmise that the extraction of her wisdom teeth, and the changed embouchure that resulted, created new problems of the sort that demanded extensive and focused solo practice, which would have been impossible during the weeks of heavy rehearsals and touring that inaugurated her first tenure in Henry Cow. Regardless, in the band's view, she was not performing up to the standard they expected.

Finally, the men cast out Cooper because they had grown both suspicious of and unfulfilled by their new position as a rising band in the rock industry, and they wanted off the carousel. This observation represented their public explanation for Cooper's departure. Greaves explained to a journalist at the time, "We wanted to continue as a quartet because we decided we'd wasted enough time and potential. . . . We were going to stop and take time to do things as we wanted. Which is what we did, consolidating the band."[66] Most of all, they needed the freedom to write new music, and in their view of the time, Cooper was not involved in that process. After signing with Virgin, Cutler explained, "Hundreds of problems suddenly arose, we never had time to do anything, we were always behind ourselves with basic commitments, we didn't have time anymore to write material, to work on material the way that we used to, to construct sets the way we used to. Everything got too hurried."[67] For Frith, their late-summer "consolidation" would help them return to their improvisational approach to single gigs, "doing less gigs, but making sure that the gigs we do are really worked out. I think that is our most critical area. We got into the way of working as a rock group and as a result we suffered from it."[68]

Attacking the Circles of Certainty

In consolidating the band, they had to address a clear but difficult question: what is to be done? In his notebooks, Hodgkinson attempted to summarize what they had learned from recent experiences, and then created a kind of "mission statement" for their next stage.[69] The rock press colludes with the record companies, two arms of a larger music industry that generates profit through the commodification of music. In 1974, rock operates by stunning audiences with volume and repetition, wringing the energy out of them "in a great storm about nothing." Listeners leave a concert not only depleted but also in thrall to the fantasy of capitalist success that has been played out in ritual form onstage: the spectacle of a great rock star who appears to have "women, money, freedom, clothes." Rock fans might aspire to this model of powerful subjectivity, but the model itself is part and parcel of the oppressor. Meanwhile, the actual musicians, "far from being 'free,' have their time spent for them by managers intent on milking the profit out of every second" (it's hard not to think of Beefheart and the DiMartino brothers here).

However, Hodgkinson writes, "Every type of communication has 2 faces: what it is under capitalism & what it could be. Each face struggles constantly & furiously to maintain its own truth." Despite the eviscerations of the industry, rock still harbors a dangerous core from earlier moments in its history—rock as an *action* rather than a passive spectacle. He has in mind the anger and rebelliousness of the genre, not simply minor frustrations but a "rage against dehumanization."

Henry Cow's music will "take the dynamic elements of popular culture & sharpen them against lethargy & silence (products of paternalism, economic, social, political, cult[ural] domination)." It will become a "means of liberating people & enabling them to participate in the historical process." Paraphrasing Paulo Freire, Hodgkinson wants to "transform the world; the world is a problem, not a given"; he wishes to "attack the circles of certainty, by example," and emphasizes "the importance of us [Henry Cow] entering into *dialogue* w. audiences, public, & other musicians."

According to Hodgkinson, musicians can create this dialogue through both open improvisation and written music. With improvisation, they offer dialogue between musicians; between musicians and the audience; between musicians and the "material" environment (in response to environmental sound, lighting, and the history of the concert premises and the expectations associated with them); and between members of the audience, in the form of listeners asking each other what the heck is going on, or half the crowd booing while the other half cheers. Using written music, they put individual pieces into dialogue with each other through the sequencing of a set to create surprise or a sense of irony. They also might create dialogical meaning through the presentation of their written music, which can express a freedom from existing forms and a struggle to present new ones, as opposed to the slick packages of the rock industry.

Most importantly, Hodgkinson noted, Henry Cow can write music that is "structured as a dialogue," referring to the simple sonata form, which is still insufficient because it models a false "resolution" of opposing forces instead of a "progressive" struggle with contradiction. True dialogical compositions are "problematic," "hazardous," and "alive," but more importantly, they are *non*-modal, *non*-serial, *non*-cyclical, and *non*-hypnotic/repetitive, because all of these qualities communicate little more than stasis and acceptance.

Now that is quite a mouthful, but two aspects of this analysis and program should not escape notice. First, Hodgkinson's terms suggest that Henry Cow's mode of engagement, musically and socially, is improvisational. The world is a problem, unfinished, requiring intervention; the band forges its relationship with that open-ended world not in theory but through action, where surprise and resistance from the material lead to response, adaptation, dialogue, and awareness. Even composing is hazardous; it is risky; its outcomes are unforeseen. The band wishes to restore provisionality to the world by attacking its ideological veneer of certainty. They are on an improvisational quest for uncertainty. Stanley Cavell might add, "That it *can* be an adventure means that the world is still, however corrupted, knowable, and the truth of it publishable, and hence that both the truth and the world have a chance."[70] The second point I wish to highlight is the explicit critique of compositional styles previously employed by Henry Cow—*no cycles*, which had been enjoyed by everybody in the band, but particularly Cutler and Frith. (Of course, they did indulge in modal jams in the early days, but that style of good-time rockin' had been purged long before.)

It would be dangerous to attribute notes in the surviving documents of a single member to the entire group, especially when some members— Greaves, Frith—began to feel uneasy with the increasingly explicit political tenor of Henry Cow's public persona. As a matter of fact, the paper trail shows that Greaves had little to say to journalists on the matter of the music industry, capitalism, or critique. But other evidence from this time indicates that these matters were shared concerns in the group, or at least had been discussed in band meetings or during rehearsal. When Steve Lake referred to the "cyclic" moods of *Unrest*, Hodgkinson quickly objected, "Cycle? Oh, I think not. For me that suggests mathematical, repetitive, very much non argumentative type structures."

Cutler said, "It's a closed system, you can't get anywhere in a cycle. A lot of rock albums do use that form, and often it's introduced into a very dubious philosophical concept. Always fairly fatalistic in that you can't get out of it."

Apparently, the drummer offered another view on cycles, based on the changing seasons and life and death—all cycles, "but the point is that is always comes back and it's changed."[71] (Cooper, too, was involved in the conversation, but it is difficult to ascertain her contribution from the published text.)

Dialogic composition—that is, the type that "progresses" and struggles with contradiction—is not what Cutler described in a conversation with Shaar Murray in August: "Often Fred's music gets changed a lot after we've started to play it. We'll cut bits out, we'll put bits in, we'll rearrange it, we'll intercut it with other pieces of material. A lot of it works as musical blocks rather than as whole pieces of music."[72] Indeed, Hodgkinson's analysis would seem to complicate severely the continuing use of precisely those compositional techniques at which Frith excelled: Fred frags and links between them (everybody knew that he had no problems as an improviser). The guitarist's comments to Kenneth Ansell ten years later support this interpretation: "We ended up coming to the conclusion that it's actually more effective for an improvised piece to start in space and end in space than for it to attach itself to any sort of structure. When it is attached it's no longer improvisation of any real kind; it becomes an effect."[73]

If Frith was feeling self-conscious about where his musical talents lay, then that would be an excellent reason to begin composing a large-scale, scored work for thirty musicians—nobody would mistake *that* as lacking struggle. And, in fact, this is exactly what he did in the late summer, telling Ansell that he was writing a piece for as many Virgin-affiliated artists as he could get (but he hadn't approached any of them yet).[74] It appears that he wanted to go even more tubular than Oldfield had done the year before. In addition to Virgin's main man, Frith envisioned Henry Cow, Cooper, Dave Stewart (Egg/Hatfield and the North), Wyatt and Dagmar Krause (Slapp Happy) on vocals, a big section of horns ("including most of [Dudu Pukwana's] Spear, certainly Lol [Coxhill] I hope"), and even Edgar Froese of Tangerine Dream. "There's going to be five girl singers but Dagmar's going to be the lead singer." In keeping with Henry Cow's then-fresh analysis of the music business, he wanted to keep things provisional and unpackage the artists from their commodity form. "All the people I use are involved in a group/product thing but I'm trying to sweep them out of it if you like, put them into a context where they're not having to do their product," he explained. In the end, nothing came of these plans, although they extended in some form all the way until spring 1976.[75] But Frith's account of his plans in the contemporary press is an important indication of how the band conceived of "writing" during the consolidation period in the summer of 1974.

In the second week of September 1974, after a break of many weeks for composing and recovery, the band rented a cottage and rehearsal space in Yorkshire; they had booked a nine-concert tour of Holland on their own earlier in the summer, and even though they had cast out Cooper and didn't have any polished new music, they decided to press onward and find some solution. Hodgkinson recounts, "We've suddenly, as it were, given ourselves some new problems to solve. What do we do without Lindsay and what do we do that's not like being on the Beefheart tour?" Problems, yes, but in retrospect these felt like good problems—challenges or opportunities. In 2012, when we discussed his positive memories of this week of rehearsals and the tour that followed, Hodgkinson said, "I have a vague memory of a cottage. We had a nice rehearsal room. Plenty of light. It was probably very cheap. It was probably a very sensible thing to do. Got us away from everybody else."

I replied, "Everybody living together again. Just like the old days."

"Yeah. Also, four boys."

"The boys are back together."

"The boys are back together. No girls."

A long pause. "No women," I answered.

Built into that long pause seemed to be the mutual recognition of a certain loose pattern or arrangement that had always exerted a pull on Henry Cow, but perhaps only became apparent for the first time once a woman became part of the band, only to be dismissed six months later. ("That was Henry Cow to a T," said Dagmar Krause on learning later of this episode.) Remember this moment, when the concrescence of what we might call the "independent men's group" inside the band first became apparent—we will return to it in greater detail later in the band's history.

(As it happened, the boys would have female company in the Netherlands, because Sarah Greaves had rejoined the troupe in her old role as sound engineer; Charles Fletcher's experience on the Beefheart tour had convinced him that he did not have the expertise to continue in that role. Fletcher would continue to help out the Cows now and then when they were in London, but the second Sarah era at the mixing desk had begun. Balchin, still hoping to get a crack at the task, was disappointed enough to stay away from the group until the following summer.)

Hodgkinson's record of a band meeting on the first day of these York rehearsals gives a good summary of their conclusions and plans after some months of consolidation and analysis:

1   Bulk of rehearsals to take place in halls, not Walmer Rd.
2   No more "written-free" linked sets
3   Free music no longer playin[g] around with techniques, but using them to effect
4   Sound radically worked on for written music as well. getting shot of irrelevancies
5   Concentration, purposiveness
6   Written sets, & sets *freely* using written music
7   Rehearsing stuff y're not performing & vice-versa
8   Decided to keep a log of equipment repairs & check all plugs/wires/ [screws?] systematically

Domestic was out ("no girls"?): not even the kind that would attach to Walmer Road. The written music would now be "radically worked on," and free playing would likewise come out of concentration and purposiveness. Improvisation would no longer serve simply to link together written material, but it could become a way to "use" written music.

What did this combined "use" of writing and improvisation sound like in practice on the Dutch tour? The only new material they had were sketches of what would eventually become the first few minutes of Hodgkinson's sixteen-minute-long piece, "Living in the Heart of the Beast," which he had begun to compose in late July. They decided to use each short fragment of his written music as the basis of a collectively composed development: a fragment became the thematic source material for an unaccompanied solo (clarinet, acoustic guitar, bass), or a solo that developed that material over "expansions" of precomposed, repeating accompaniment. The group interspersed these textures with two long, flat blocks of free playing that Cutler later termed "suspensions": in the first, they all contributed droning, long sounds (the drummer rolling with mallets on large glass bowls he had brought along for this purpose), and in the second they began by dropping objects on their instruments, and then extending freely the broken textures that resulted.

Although Henry Cow usually played freely improvised music for their second set, they were having such a good time with this challenge in Holland that they frequently repeated it. (Though not exclusively: a live recording of their fine performance in Halsteren has them playing a short second set of completely improvised music; Greaves delivered some impromptu prose poetry on the subject of Vinko Globokar.) "My memory of that tour is super positive," Frith recalls. "There were a couple of these late tours where we were just being radical in our approach to performance and material. We were no longer like a band that was having to do the stuff from its record. . . . And suddenly the possibilities for performance were hugely expanded, and it was intense." Frith wasn't alone in having positive memories of the Holland concerts in 1974—all of the Cows enjoyed the new ways of playing together that they'd discovered. Hodgkinson employed his clarinet often, and Frith had added the acoustic guitar to his palette. (On this tour, and indeed every other one in Europe, Frith would leave his headstock pickup and second amplifier at home; it was too much extra equipment to haul.)

The year following Henry Cow's tour with Faust had seen the band facing many challenges, some they had created themselves and others that had been thrust in front of them. Surveying these trials of late-1973 to late-1974, I would point to two patterns. The first is the attraction of hazard: they enjoyed risks and, despite the disappointments of *The Tempest* and the Beefheart tour, they remained confident enough in their creative skills to continue seeking uncertainty (provided that they could feel "consolidated" and theoretically grounded when they met it). Going into the studio in February with a only one side of material and a brand new member had ultimately led to an album they were proud of, even if it had been painful in the making. And their equally extreme solution to the Dutch tour—they generated an entirely new method of working collectively, when the easy option would have been to cancel after a crucial member of the band had been dismissed just a few weeks earlier—had brought them great gratification and renewed their faith in the band's improvisational skills.

In both of these cases, the band acquired the view that struggle, hardship, and contention not only weren't incompatible with aesthetic success but in fact might even be necessary for it—and this realization contributed to the second pattern revealed in the events of 1974. The stance of continually testing the world and each other, of building up the discipline of the band through trials, had begun to spill over into their arts of everyday living. In conversation with Frith and Hodgkinson some years later, Cutler reasoned,

> I think it must have been to do, not just with personalities, but actually to do with the structure of the group in the early days which, while it was a strength in one way, that it kept us very much on the point, and made us put up with fairly extraordinary hardships in a physical way and in a . . . you know, relationships were crashing right, left . . . but we carried on, didn't we? And that was a strength, but at the same time, that shell, that hardness that was responsible for driving us in that way, in the end I think was one of the contributory factors to us being unable to deal with the last straws.[76]

At this stage, Henry Cow's characteristic contraviviality had carried them through, even if the price of that armor was a certain loss of emotional sensitivity to individual, private hardships. As 1974 drew to a close, the band encountered a whole new set of relationships and problems to throw themselves up against: an environment for new ways of living with-but-against each other and cultivating a cultural politics to match.

4   Death to the Individual:
Slapp Happy | 1974–75

In a quick five months beginning in November 1974, Henry Cow recorded an album as the backing band to the pop group Slapp Happy, merged with that group to create an expanded seven-member Cow, made a new Henry Cow record with this expanded membership, shed two of the recently added musicians in a painful split, and retained Dagmar Krause, a new front person who would become, in the words of Tim Hodgkinson, the band's "jewel in the crown" for the next three years. To break apart this bewildering and dense sequence of events, it will be necessary to back up once again and trace a heterophonous path through London and West Germany, beginning this time, as with Faust, in Hamburg.

Dagmar Krause was born in 1950 in a middle-class suburb of that city. Although her parents had met and married in Gdansk some years earlier, they had settled in Hamburg after the war as part of a federal housing program. In their culturally rich, bourgeois household, Krause's elder sister, Ursula, was encouraged to take an interest in visual art, while Krause was gently pushed toward music. Although she received piano lessons only after begging her parents for them, she was always a naturally gifted musician, and her father—an organ builder—encouraged her appreciation of the great German composers. Seated in front of the family's radio in the late 1950s and early 1960s, Dagmar also heard the new sounds coming over the airwaves from Cologne. "For me," she later recalled, "it was a mixture of Bach, Mozart, and Stockhausen." Owing in part to her father's line of work, Olivier Messiaen made a substantial impression, as well.

Family and friends recognized Dagmar's vocal talents from an early age. She remembers, "Maybe at the age of five I realized that I could sing, and throughout my childhood and adolescence people would always ask me to sing for them; in my neighborhood, at school, and at home." When she was a bit older, at age fourteen, a classmate of Ursula's named Horst Runkel brought his guitar over and taught Dagmar about the blues. By this time, the family had acquired a record player, and Dagmar's listening stretched to include her sister's jazz LPs. With Horst, Dagmar explored the blues repertoire, singing in English, choosing her favorite songs, and learning to improvise over chord changes.

Soon, the pair decided to take their act on the road. A few years older than Krause, Runkel asked her parents if he could take Dagmar to a singing competition at a nearby youth club. They assented; she won. Krause was a natural, captivating performer who loved the attention that came with singing in clubs. Within a few months, Krause and Runkel were frequenting open-mic venues in Hamburg's Reeperbahn. Dagmar vividly recalls their first entree into this seedy world of entertainment: "All I remember is a full club with guys sitting at long wooden tables and big beer glasses which were shining like golden lanterns. It was smokey and very noisy. And I was thinking, 'God almighty, what have I got myself into? Nobody will even hear me!'" But the spectacle of an elfin, fifteen-year-old German woman passionately singing a murder ballad from the great American songbook was enough to quiet the crowd. "I started to sing, and—I'm not kidding you—it didn't take any time. You could hear a pin drop in that place." On finishing the song, Krause was awarded with a roar of applause—a confidence builder at any age.

A producer in the audience that night introduced himself after Krause's performance, comparing her favorably to a singer she had never heard of: Lotte Lenya. When Krause's mother gifted her a Lenya record for her birthday, Krause didn't hear much in common with her own voice, but she was captivated by the compositions of Kurt Weill—was this classical music, pop, or jazz? In any case, this producer soon arranged for Krause to record "St. Louis Blues" with the St. John's Big Band in Hamburg, and she subsequently appeared with the band at various functions around town, including a song contest at the Musikhalle, Hamburg's most prestigious live venue.

But Dagmar was still only sixteen years old, and becoming a professional singer didn't seem to be a sufficiently stable career choice. When she finished secondary school, she enrolled in a nurse training course, and then found a job at a doctor's surgery. She still performed here and there. Sometime in 1968, Krause paid a visit to Hamburg's Jazzhouse, where a local band called the City Preachers hosted an open-mic night. Dagmar asked to sing "Frankie and Johnny," and then basked in another pin-drop moment. A few days later, she was invited to join the City Preachers by their front man, John O'Brien-Docker.

Encompassing as many as seventeen different members, the City Preachers had been founded a few years earlier by Hamburger Marianne Therstapen and O'Brien-Docker, a transplanted Irishman who was the band's leader until 1969. Although the lineup of the ensemble was always shifting, certain regulars eventually emerged; along with O'Brien-Docker, these included vocalists Sybille Kynast and Inga Rumpf, bouzouki player Michael Laukeninks, and guitarists Eckart Kahlhofer and Götz Humpf. They played what could be described as "international folk"—German, Spanish, Yiddish, African American, and Balkan roots musics and protest songs, often sung in German. By 1967, Anglo-American "beat" music had become the common currency of youth culture across Europe, and, like many non-Anglophonic groups, the City Preachers contended with the commonly-held view that the English language was the only suitable tongue for pop.[1]

For Krause, joining an existing band was both exciting and taxing. They were a known group and had already released some records, and this success meant that Krause could quit her job and live the dream of performing music full time. The City Preachers toured Germany regularly, and soon after Krause joined, they entered the studio to record the album *Der Kürbis, die Traumtänzer, und das Transportproblem,* a soundtrack of sorts for a television movie of the same title that starred the band and aired on German television in 1969. Touring and recording: these were totally new experiences for Krause. The exhilaration they produced was tempered, however, by the physical and psychological exhaustion that came with being part of a group, complete with power struggles and emotional intrigue of all sorts. Moreover, Krause was still searching for her own artistic identity: "I didn't really know who I was musically and I didn't have a 'box' I fitted into. Other band members had found their niche much earlier, and I hated the pressure of being pinned down by any genre that was accessible within this set up. . . . In what area of music? I couldn't say that it was in jazz—not really. I couldn't say it was in pop music, really. I didn't know where it was."

But while Krause cast about for a musical sense of self, others in the band tussled over an economic sense of ownership, and, in January 1969, O'Brien-Docker was forced out of the City Preachers.[2] Inga Rumpf, who had been something of a featured singer in the group until this moment, soon began to take greater aesthetic control by pushing their sound toward African American vernacular styles, writing and singing in English with greater frequency. (With her smoky wail, Rumpf was compared in the press to Janis Joplin.) In the flux of these changes, various group formations came into existence and tested loyalties. "It was a complete nightmare," Krause later recalled.

In the midst of this nightmare, in 1970, however, she did record a notable duo collaboration with Rumpf called *The I.D. Company* ("I" for Inga,

"D" for Dagmar). Each artist wrote the material for one side of the record, and they were accompanied by Frank St. Peter (sax, flute), who led a group of studio musicians. Rumpf's side serves up three tracks of Indian-flavored, bluesy psychedelia. Krause's material, on the other hand, is the kind of lunar voyage that reminds one how fortunate we are that a few record execs smoked dope in the late 1960s: how else could this music have slipped through the cracks? Singing in both English and German, she turns her backing band into an exploratory, low-energy free jazz proposition. The musicians lope and flutter around Krause's voice, delivered with a lightness of tone that might surprise listeners more familiar with the gutsy chest voice of her Henry Cow years. "I was writing songs with no conventional song structure," she would later remember, and, indeed, there are no song forms to speak of, nor is there conventional harmony, and the band settles into pulse-based rhythms only very rarely. What these four tracks *do* offer are free-form, multitracked vocals layered on top of each other (or played backwards) and frequent synthesizer whines, whooshes, and zaps. Taciturn tunes such as "Dünne, gläserne Frauen" and "He's out Now" give St. Peter the chance to register some lovely flute soloing, while the more insectile ramblings provide a platform for serious skronk. "While it wasn't a wholly successful venture," Krause concludes, "it showed a bit more where I might be heading and connected with my past."

I.D. Company was released by Hör Zu Black Label, a subsidiary of Hör Zu records, which was in turn a subsidiary of Electrola. *Hör Zu* was a popular television listings magazine, and their main recording arm had licensed the German releases of LPs by the Beatles, Beach Boys, Pink Floyd, and the Rolling Stones (not to mention Mantovani and von Karajan). The Black Label was aimed at more adventurous listeners. Because it was a discount imprint—and therefore had no studio budget—Black Label released compilations or licensed reissues of previously recorded music. It offered up an odd miscellany of out jazz, avant-garde composition, American psychedelia, European rock, historical artists, and a few novelty records. This catalogue illustrates an important point about the stylistic mixing that was such an important part of the post-1967 moment—namely, that this mixing did not just occur in musical settings (or, "inside" of musical sound), but also in the systems of production and distribution of musical objects. By marketing the likes of Stockhausen and Alice Coltrane alongside Vanilla Fudge and compilations of international folksong, Hör Zu Black Label attempted to cultivate an audience with wide-ranging tastes.

For a time, Krause continued to work with Rumpf in one version of the City Preachers. By 1970, Krause was increasingly marginalized in the group, who, in their new soul-oriented style, wanted her to sing more like Aretha Franklin. Krause couldn't (and didn't want to, anyway), so she simultaneously quit and was fired from the band. In 1971, she participated in a "comeback" album of sorts, *Back to the City*, which also included old Preachers with some new faces (but without Rumpf). Released by Hör Zu, the record had been slapped together: Krause recalls that the musical material had all been prerecorded, so she entered the studio to track vocals by herself for just two songs ("Frankie and Johnny" and "Old Shanty Town"). The trauma of the final months of the City Preachers imprinted itself on Krause's throat: she lost her voice. A specialist examined her and concluded that her vocal cords were fine, but that she should undergo voice therapy; it eventually proved to be successful.

A Troubadour with Revoxes: Anthony Moore

When Krause got together for a meeting with a musician friend in 1971, she was also making contact for the first time with a new gang, whose faces crowded into the frame, but just barely: Anthony Moore, Peter Blegvad, David Larcher, Werner Nekes, Uwe Nettelbeck, Faust, Simon Draper, Henry Cow. Krause's appointment with that nameless musician occurred at a shared flat that was home to a gaggle of filmmakers, artists, and intellectuals. Among them, the art historian Rainer Crone was writing his PhD dissertation on Andy Warhol at the University of Hamburg; he had already, in 1970, published the first catalogue raisonné of Warhol's work, and would go on to publish many more works on the American artist.[3] Krause clicked with this crowd, and soon moved in with them. She began to date Crone, who came from a well-off background and introduced Krause to a strata of society that was quite new to her—art collectors, publishers, and filmmakers. "We were seventies, left-wing, political [people]; everyone was studying. . . . I was going to school, then, to sit my baccalaureate, working, partying, watching lots and lots of films, and generally having an amazing life. . . . I had bought a spinet at that point, so I was now starting to write songs in my little room. It was an exciting time. I met so many amazing people then." This hip crowd led her to hipper music (with apologies to the City Preachers): Jimi Hendrix, the Doors, Jefferson Airplane, and so on.

The leading figures of German experimental cinema—Werner Nekes, Klaus Wyborny, Dore O.—came through the Hamburg apartment. On one occasion in 1971, Wyborny arrived to screen his latest project, bringing with him an Englishman named Anthony Moore, who had been living in Hamburg and making soundtracks for many of these filmmakers. He was an intense guy armed with a Revox. Krause fell in love.

Born in 1948, Moore had grown up in transit, shuttling about with his adventurous parents between the United Kingdom, Cyprus, and Malawi. His father was a teacher of physical education; he settled the family for several years during the 1950s in Letchworth Garden City, where he had been offered a permanent job at St. Christopher School, a Quaker, progressive, vegetarian institution. The clincher was the school's additional job offer to Moore's mother, who became the head of one of their residential houses. Eventually, they sent Anthony to boarding school in Lyme Regis, Dorset, where he sang madrigals and goofed off. After school, he chose art college over university, attending St. Alban's School for his foundation year in 1967–68, then enrolling at the Newcastle College of Art and Design in 1968. There, Moore pursued Indian and Celtic music, the guitar, alcohol, and other substances with great ardor, but not art or design. He soon dropped out and hitched a ride from Edinburgh to Oban, where he caught a ferry to the Inner Hebrides and ended up on the small island of Iona. The few dozen residents there received him with kindness, sensing correctly that their young visitor was in a fragile state of transition. He stayed for four tranquil months, working on the grounds of the Abbey (disputed birthplace of *The Book of Kells*) in exchange for meals and a place to sleep in the cloister.

At about the time Moore began to grow restless, there sounded a thunderous knock on the Abbey door late one night. He opened it to find a "monstrous figure," long-haired and formidably hirsute with a satchel full of high-end cameras: David Larcher, the photographer and filmmaker, who had been documenting druidic stone formations across the islands. He stayed for a while, and the two had a good time constructing musical instruments and talking philosophy.

A few months after this meeting, Larcher invited Moore to create the soundtrack for *Mare's Tail*, a sprawling classic of nonnarrative cinema. The filmmaker's patron, Alan Power, had temporarily donated his empty house in Kew Gardens, where Larcher developed film by hand and hung it up to dry in the garden. The large, rent-free domicile was also a luxury for Moore, who had space to collect instruments and equipment. Tape recorders became a fascination: "Suddenly, I found myself with three or four tape machines, and that possibility of dubbing, looping, running simultaneous loops, cutting, forwards-backwards speech—the whole manipulation of magnetic tape—completely took me over. That became my instrument: tape." With this instrument (usually a pair of Revox quarter-inch reel-to-reel decks), Moore made music that sounded a bit like Terry Riley; it combined drones, repeating consonant loops, and other manipulations to create clear textures and clearly audible processes. (Riley's *A Rainbow in Curved Air* had made an impression, as had the Deutsche Grammophon release of Stockhausen's *Gesang der Junglinge* and *Kontakte*.)

At a screening of *Mare's Tail* at the London Film Festival in 1969, Moore met another filmmaker, Massimo Bacigalupo, who had a trunkload of Stan Brakhage films and a desire to bring them to the people. Twenty-one years old, Moore was up for anything, so the pair hopped the ferry to Calais and flipped a coin: south to Italy or north to Scandinavia? North. They traveled from town to town, phoning ahead to arrange screenings at the local theater or film co-op. In the course of the tour, Bacigalupo introduced Moore to Werner Nekes, a major figure in West German experimental cinema, and Nekes asked Moore to create music for his films. After finishing up other commitments for a few weeks, Moore returned to Hamburg, "a troubadour with Revoxes."

Again, Moore found himself in a luxurious position: "Werner had a loft-like, big space, and the deal was simply that I could live there . . . forever, more or less. And in return, I would produce sound. That was the beginning of a collaboration that went on for years." His scores for Nekes and others were in the same aesthetic vein as his music for Larcher had been. "The work is informed by the medium, and the medium is tape. One thing you do with tape is make loops"—loops running simultaneously at different speeds, drifting apart and resynchronizing in ever-shifting patterns that explore combinatoriality and permutation. In Hamburg, he worked with three or four tape machines, his trusty Revoxes from England plus one or two UHER 4400 Report Stereo decks. "I was very interested in the idea of repetition, very curious about the notion of how something could at the same time stand still and move." Accordingly, Moore focused on complex textures instead of complex melodies, which held little interest for him. He created material for his loops by recording acoustic instruments or generating electronic sound with oscillators and ring modulators.

Rather than performing on a concert stage, Moore presented his works at film screenings, either with a stereo mix of the final soundtrack or by mixing loops on the spot during the projection. Soon after he met Krause at one of these events, he met another important figure for the future, Uwe Nettelbeck, who heard Moore's music at a screening and offered to help him get a record deal.

As with Rumpf and Krause's *I.D. Company*, Moore's first record was positioned in a genre field that was undergoing a serious reshuffling around 1971. Nettelbeck had planned to take Moore to Deutsche Grammophon, the high-end classical imprint, but an executive in the company listened to the tape of what would become Moore's *Pieces from the Cloudland Ballroom* and suggested instead that they release it on Polydor, their pop label. The suit had a point. Whatever the sonic similarities that obtained between Moore's music and that of the minimalists, there were still significant differences in their modes of production. The younger composer had spent his entire musical life working directly with tape, off the page. Unlike Riley, La Monte Young, Philip Glass, or Steve Reich, Moore did not pursue advanced compositional training, and therefore he never conceptualized his practice in terms of traditional concert performance. The most obvious precedent of electronic repetition and delays, Riley's *A Rainbow in Curved Air* (1968), is thus a good comparison and a good contrast: it had succeeded with the same blissed-out, adventurous rock audience that might be interested in Moore's music, but it had been made in a very different way. The sonic material Moore used was always discontinuous and partial, built up without reference to real-time presentation in any way, while Riley effectively recorded a live concert, a single virtuoso performance on his electronically extended organ.

This little decision—Deutsche Grammophon or Polydor?—thus symbolized a major problem in musical aesthetics in the early 1970s, namely, that advanced music was being written by young people who had not chosen any of the established forms of professional accreditation. Where does this music belong? Moreover, they were doing so without a score. Of course, some jazz had knocked down the importance of the written score a few notches by 1970, but it was also firmly established as a serious modern art form; scholarship drew attention to its harmonic structure and motivic development, and no one doubted the credentials of jazz musicians as "serious" musicians. The days of the Ornette doubters were long past.

The other groups of this era who were moving into nonscored sonic exploration came, one way or another, from accredited traditions. In AMM, for example, Eddie Prévost and Keith Rowe had been gigging jazz musicians in the early 1960s, and Cornelius Cardew was as properly trained as one could get. Likewise, the musicians in Musica Elettronica Viva were Yale graduates

Figure 4.1 Anthony Moore in Faust's studio, Wümme, c. 1971.
PHOTOGRAPH BY SHERIDAN COAKLEY.

in composition; all the minimalists were university music students. Many of the composers of the AACM had been conventionally trained well enough to play in US Army bands. With Moore, however, and an increasing number of rock experimentalists, all we have is a stack of records and a bunch of film screenings: this constituted his education.

Moore received Polydor's standard contract during those years: three albums in three years. Apparently energized by the support of his new friends at Polydor, Moore worked quickly at Faust's studio in Wümme (Nettelbeck had put him in touch). He later recalled, "They were a little bit shocked when I delivered the three albums in about three months, and got the advance for each one there and then. . . . So that probably didn't start me off on a very good relationship with the company!" The first side of *Pieces from the Cloudland Ballroom* (the first album) was devoted to "Jam Jem Jim Jom Jum," a twenty-one-minute work representative of Moore's style at this time, thoroughly imbued with the repetitive and cyclic logics of magnetic tape. The tracks consists of three male and two female voices, along with a rich, baritone-range bell sound that originated with an Fsus4 chord played on the piano and later subjected to variable filtering. The singers essentially intone the same chord for the entire piece. At any given moment, each performer sings one of the syllables from the title, followed by "ba" for a repeating number of beats: "Jem-ba-ba, Jem-ba-ba," and so on. But their phrases are all of different lengths: at any given moment, one singer is repeating a phrase in three beats (as in the example in the previous sentence), one in five, one in seven, one in nine, and one in eleven. The result is a chaotic kind of chanting—but it's fast, at more than 160 beats per minute. After 3,465 beats, the cycles resynchronize at their lowest common multiplier and the piece concludes.

In addition to these changes in meter, Moore generates variation in a number of other subtle ways, through microtonal and timbral inflection, swaps of who is singing which pitch and which syllable, and placement of each voice in the stereo field. Some singers get a case of the giggles toward the end of the track, and their near-breakdowns lighten the mood as the piece concludes. Those yuks highlight what is, for me, the distinctive charm of the recording; I hear them as the levity of a young artist who has hit on a musical style that is utterly fresh but achieved without jumping through any of the expected hoops leading to the front edge of musical history—all Moore needed was a record collection, cool friends, two Revox decks, and inspiration.

Moore followed up *Pieces from the Cloudland Ballroom* with *Secrets of the Blue Bag*, which had a more chamber music and less tape-loop feel. In its relentless exploration of the first five steps of the diatonic scale, the record reminds one of Tom Johnson's contemporaneous work. But Polydor was getting nervous: these albums were not selling. Moore recalls, "By the time they got the third one [*Reed, Whistle, and Sticks*, 1972], which was me dropping sticks on the floor for forty-five minutes, that freaked them out a little bit."

I Think They Want Us to Make Pop Music: Slapp Happy

By the time *Blue Bag* was released, Moore and Krause had left Hamburg and moved to Sligo, Ireland. They had visited a friend who lived in the countryside outside of Dublin, and fell for the romance and pastoral beauty of rural Ireland. Along with his close friend, Peter Blegvad, Moore was a fan of the romantic poets, and Sligo was Yeats territory. Moore and Krause were presumably living off of the advance he had received from Polydor, but that doesn't mean they were living particularly well. Plus, Krause was now pregnant. Sheepishly, Moore recalls, "I remember the feeling that it was really unkind of me to expect her to live in a really small cottage which had no running water . . . ; we used to get it from a stream. And the toilet arrangements were somewhat primitive, as well, involving a spade and a walk halfway up the mountain." But the dirt-floored cottage did have electricity, and Moore had brought his electronics and loudspeakers; he was working on a mystical sound garden in the countryside, with tape loops triggered by photocells positioned in the trees.

Meanwhile, Krause was miserable. And lonely. Her days in Hamburg had been lively, filled with cafe conversations about culture and politics, but in Sligo, she led a comparatively solitary life, surrounded by Irish country hippies who baked their own bread and whispered rumors of liberation. Her English, though good enough to sing "Frankie and Johnny," was not sufficient for conversation. This huge change occurred in the blink of an eye. "I left my country, my language, my family and friends. I had no income of my own and I was pregnant. My feeling of independence was vanishing— and there I was in Ireland," she later remembered. Following a threatened miscarriage after digging in the garden, Krause was forced to stay in the wretched cottage, burning peat to stay warm and fending off morning sickness (she hated the smell of peat). Moreover, she and Moore were constantly being reshuffled by trips and visits from friends. "The pace of life was completely relentless," Krause says. "We were pretty much always on the move, never stayed for long anywhere, not even in Sligo. Peter was coming, then Anthony's brother came once to visit." David Larcher and his family also came to stay at one point, but the main visitor was Blegvad. "Peter was always there," recalled Krause. "There was much music and songwriting going on, drinking and philosophizing."

Writing what? "Pop songs," Blegvad answers. "Three-chord stuff. How hard can it be, you know? We'd been in a band together at school, enjoyed 'jamming' as recreation. At this point, the whole thing was a bit of a joke: 'we'll take the piss out of pop.'"[4] Polydor had grown weary of Moore's experiments, and had pressured Nettelbeck to bring them something that would actually sell. Charismatic and persuasive, Nettelbeck took this request in stride. "The situation is somewhat dire," Moore recalls him saying. "Why don't we try to offer them something more palatable? Could you imagine doing something like that?" According to Blegvad, "Uwe, in discussion with Anthony, said, 'You know, I think they want us to make *pop music—commercial pop music.*' And Anthony said, 'That's no problem. I'll call my friend, Peter, in England. We used to play guitar together, as a kind of recreational diversion. We would write several songs in a single evening,

Figure 4.2 Peter Blegvad, 1973. PHOTOGRAPH BY DAVID LARCHER.

just for fun. It's no problem!' So, you know, in a spirit of naive, can-do optimism, he called me up."

Blegvad was a few years younger than Moore; born in New York City to an American mother and Danish father (both bohemian artist-intellectuals), he moved around as a child, from New York to Paris to Connecticut to London, where they relocated in 1966. Everything about Blegvad was puckish except for his size: six-foot seven, so tall that even the army wouldn't draft him. He attended grammar school at St. Christopher School in Hertfordshire, where Moore's parents were employed, students wrote the laws, and there was little pressure to attend classes. Blegvad recalls, "As a consequence I have almost no O- or A-levels, and had almost no education [*laughter*]."[5] Although Blegvad did not do well in school and had problems staying motivated, he loved English literature, and devoured the novels and books of poetry given to him by his teacher, Peter Scupham. He also had a healthy interest in popular music and played guitar in bands with his classmates. His most important musical connection, however, wasn't made with a fellow student, but rather with Moore, who returned regularly to visit his parents on breaks and holidays. He and Blegvad became fast friends, bonding over music, drinking, and drugs, and goofing around in an early version of Slapp Happy. After finishing school, Blegvad enrolled in a double course in English literature and fine arts at Exeter University, but he was having trouble staying focused on his studies, so it wasn't a difficult decision to postpone his coursework for a week or two for quick trips to Hamburg to record.

The first such trip came in spring 1972, when Blegvad and Moore met up to record Slapp Happy's first single, "Just a Conversation" backed with "Jumping Jonah." Blegvad recalls, "The first time I went to Hamburg Anthony and I considered this recording deal a one-off, a bizarre fluke. . . . Uwe Nettelbeck, who was in on the joke, had got some money from Polydor . . . , and they were total squares, responsible adults, straights. We would go to the office on Milchstrasse (i.e., Milk Street) near the Alster in the most elegant part of town and pretend to be polite, but we were mocking them. Callous youth!"[6] For "Just a Conversation," the pair worked up a revision of a ballad that Moore had written as part of the soundtrack for Larcher's *Mare's Tail*. Blegvad again: "Without thinking too hard we wrote 'It was just a conversation / In Grand Central Station / One day . . .' That seemed to fit. So what rhymes? How about 'I'd lost my occupation, didn't have no destination anyway . . .'—and in between we'll just stand around the microphone talking, we'll improvise a conversation. Brilliant! So that was 'Just a Conversation' written, done, took twenty minutes![7] When it came time to put the tunes on tape, they capitalized on Nettelbeck's connections by going out to Wümme to use Faust's studio. Because they were only two, they asked Faust's rhythm section to back them up for the date, so they were joined by Zappi Diermaier on drums and Jean-Hervé Peron on bass. This was Moore's and Blegvad's next good fortune: freed up from the noisy experiments of Faust, Diermaier and Peron really cut loose, grooving effortlessly underneath the straightforward harmonic progressions of Slapp Happy.

After first laying down all the instrumental parts for the two songs, it came time to track the lead vocal. Krause remembers, "I was just there, supporting Peter and Anthony and having fun listening to them recording the song, . . . and rolling around the floor in fits of laughter." Blegvad continues, "So when it came to adding the vocal to the single, Anthony and I stood around the microphone and tried to sing. And Uwe said very quickly, 'This is not going to work.' And we said, 'Well, god, we should have thought of that before, because now we've made the music. The music sounds pretty good. What are we going to do?'" Krause picks up the story: "[Uwe] suddenly turned to me and said, 'Look Dagmar, this isn't working,' as they were still playing around in front of the mic. Uwe said, 'Dagmar, you're a singer, you must go and sing.' I said, 'No, I don't sing anymore. I can't sing.' He said, 'Of course you can, Dagmar! Just give it a go.'"

In this instant, Slapp Happy changed from a goof—"or, if it was a joke, it wasn't a mean joke," Blegvad clarifies—into something else entirely unforeseen. Krause's voice possessed a levity and grace that was shot through with world-weary Lenyiana. With Blegvad singing, Slapp Happy was just a vehicle for quirky songs, fronted by a "bad Dylan impression," as he told me. But Krause's accented English promised some kind of underspecified complexity in these musically anodyne songs.

The freshly formed trio assumed that Nettelbeck would take the single to Polydor and return with bad news, so they were as surprised as anyone to learn that the execs had given them a record deal. "The straights, the suits at PolyGram, to their credit, knew they didn't know diddly about what might sell," Blegvad writes.[8] It was off to Sligo for Moore and Krause, and Blegvad returned to his final year at Exeter, which was now increasingly broken up by trips to Ireland and Hertfordshire to write the material for what would become the band's first album. Once they had an LP's worth of material ready, Nettelbeck booked another session in Wümme in the late spring of 1972. Moore points out, "And then . . . I destroyed Peter's academic career at Exeter University by flying him over just before his finals." By this point, Krause was five months pregnant.

The album they recorded was called *Sort Of*. It combined tossed-off, feel-good tunes like "Just a Conversation" with more introspective songs about love and loneliness. Blegvad supplies lead vocals for four of the album's bluesiest tracks, adopting a kind of gonzo style and African American locution; the lyrics of these songs ("Paradise Express," "Tutankhamun," "I Got Evil," and "Mono Plane") lean toward the absurd. Krause sings the rest of the songs with occasional support from Blegvad, who adopts a more relaxed, spoken style in these cases. Indeed, the interplay between these two voice types calls to mind nothing more strongly than the sweet side of the Velvet Underground, an association also made by listeners at the time. Aside from the German-accented female lead vocals and the American sprechstimme accompaniment, Slapp Happy often used the same jangly, unadorned guitar sound as the VU. One good example is "Blue Flower." One could easily mistake the guitarist for Lou Reed, and the high, insistent piano likewise calls the Velvets to mind. The lyrics, too, seem to offer some Reedish imagery ("Superstar in your own private movie," "Your boots are high-heeled and shining bright"), and Diermeyer's steady, unembellished drums might have been supplied by Maureen Tucker in another universe. One key difference is Peron's funky, melodic bass playing, which is one of the whole album's most pronounced virtues. The other standouts on *Sort Of* include "Heading for Kyoto" and "Small Hands of Stone." The former yields space to Peron and Diermaier, whose gleeful groove matches perfectly with the text's wacky story of Buddhist monks returning home from their holiday by train. "Small Hands of Stone," a delicate tune about impossible love, unfolds over Moore's languorous and surprising chord progression in the piano and bass; it's really the only piece on the record that breaks with conventional song forms.

Moore and Krause's child, Max, was born in Hertfordshire in September 1972. The addition complicated things, but not much, not yet. Max was still just a baby when Slapp Happy returned to Wümme in late 1972 to record their second album. Again, they used Diermaier and Peron as their rhythm section, and again the songs were quirky and surprising. But the music was getting more ambitious. "We were snobs about pop music," Blegvad remembers. "Anthony was more interested in making modern classical music. . . . We loved pop, but we were conflicted, we thought pop was dumb. Now I think there was more art in those funny little songs than in dropping sticks for three-quarters of an hour, but what did we know?" Indeed, most the songs on this second LP were also more artful than the ones on *Sort Of*. On the musical side, Moore had expanded the band's stylistic frame of reference by dropping in some Latin percussion here, or a tango or waltz rhythm there; many of the songs are more formally and harmonically complex, too. Krause sings all of them. But even more striking was Blegvad's new lyrical approach. The jokey character studies aren't totally absent ("Michelangelo" offers many choice couplets, including "He delineates saints on a sepia ground / His temper like his paints is albumen bound"), but overall the tone is more serious, and the poetry more ambitious and lengthy. Bob Dylan's influence is palpable, and Blegvad even cribs an entire Rimbaud verse for one song, "Mr. Rainbow."

The Douanier Rousseau Sound: Commercially Unsuccessful

Moore and Blegvad grew fond of calling their approach "the Douanier Rousseau sound," a reference to the self-taught nineteenth-century artist who painted exotic scenes of jungle life without ever leaving France. They

Figure 4.3 Slapp Happy, 1973: Dagmar Krause, Anthony Moore, and Peter Blegvad.

cultivated their naivete and wore it proudly like a badge. Polydor was not impressed. The company chose not to release the second record, and had also dropped Faust in an early-1973 housecleaning episode. (This second Slapp Happy album, recorded with Faust, would eventually be released for the first time by Chris Cutler's Recommended Records in 1980, under the title *Acnalbasac Noom.*) Moore and Krause returned to England for a while, and Blegvad joined up with David Larcher and his family, who were touring Europe in their truck. Sometime during the summer months, Draper invited Henry Cow to the office to hear a cassette of Slapp Happy's unreleased album. The band loved it and urged Draper to sign them. Greaves says, "I was a fan from the first day that Simon played it for us. . . . Stupendous lyrical quality, basic essential melodies and melodic structures—I mean, it was the perfect pop group." Draper, too, was hooked by the recording, but had his usual misgivings about Krause's German accent in the context of the Anglo market. He says, "I loved the tracks with Peter singing, because it sounded to me like Lou Reed or something. Very Velvet Undergroundy. I had the idea of the sort of record they might make, which was not the record they did make." Once again, Ian MacDonald probably played some role in bringing Draper to the edge of signing Slapp Happy. In the *New Musical Express*, he published a review of *Sort Of*, which had been released in the United Kingdom. Although he offered cool praise for their debut ("the enterprise has its charm"), MacDonald vouched strongly for the new album: "Blegvad and Moore have really got down to it and have written and recorded a solo-record for Daggi that is very exceptional. At the moment, contractual difficulties are preventing it from finding a release, but when it does, grab it with both hands."[9] Robert Wyatt loved Slapp Happy, as well, and certainly advocated for their signing.

The contractual difficulties were cleared later in 1973, when Draper gave Slapp Happy a deal. They couldn't move quickly, because Blegvad, Moore, Krause, and Max took off for the summer to accompany Larcher in a caravan to Turkey. He was making his next epic film, *Monkey's Birthday*, and had called on the services of many friends. In a Bedford van, Slapp Happy and child took off across Europe, through Austria, Hungary, and into Romania, where, after a pause of some weeks, the caravan pushed on to Thessaloniki, then into Turkey. They spent several weeks there searching for dervishes, recording musicians and soundscapes, and shooting film. Moore's and Krause's time in Istanbul ended traumatically, when an unfamiliar guest stole the cash they had been given by the patron Alan Power to pay their way back to England. After days of worried wrangling and unfruitful trips to the British embassy, a Turkish merchant who overheard one of Moore's frantic phone calls gave them a generous gift to cover the return journey. Krause later recalled that the trip helped to solidify her growing realization that she could only be happy singing in front of an audience: Slapp Happy needed to pursue new opportunities that might lead in this direction.[10]

Once back in England, Slapp Happy booked time at Nova Studios in London to record a new version of their song "Casablanca Moon," which Virgin wanted to release as a single. Cutler played drums on the session, but his active, flowing style overwhelmed the writing, and the band decided to record it again with less distinctive studio players.

Soon thereafter (in early 1974), Slapp Happy decamped to the Manor to record their second LP a second time. "Virgin thought the unreleased Slapp Happy record was a good demo, but too crude for radio, so we re-recorded the same songs with swisher production," Blegvad explains.[11] Peron again contributed basslines, and the rest of the band was filled out by session musicians, including Comus's Roger Wootton, who created new arrangements for most of the songs. Although Wootton orchestrated the new versions with great ambition (tabla, mandolin, violin, cello, trumpet, saxophone, congas), the rhythmic feel of the second recording does not match the casual virtuosity of the Faust players. When Virgin released it, they titled this version *Slapp Happy*. Blegvad later recalled the reaction from Henry Cow: "Well, it's OK, the songs aren't bad, but it's really a missed opportunity. You made a conventional pop record and you could have done something more."[12] As we will see, this criticism stuck with Moore and Blegvad and contributed to their compositional development in 1974. But they had found a new fan in Wyatt, who had recorded the fine solo album *Rock Bottom* for Virgin earlier that year and exerted a strong influence on the label and associated journalists like Macdonald, Lake, and John Peel. Krause recalls that Wyatt invited Slapp Happy to his house that spring, when they became good friends. "That was a big thing in those times," Krause says. "His support meant a lot to us."

Peel also took notice, inviting Slapp Happy to perform on his BBC program in late June, when they were joined by Wyatt, Frith, Cooper, Geoff Leigh, Mongezi Feza, and others. (They played "A Little Something" and "Me and Parvati," from *Slapp Happy/Acnalbasac Noom*, then two new ones called "Europa" and "War is Energy Enslaved.") "More giggles from Slapp Happy," Peel muttered after their short set. Indeed, the band's publicity for their Virgin debut that summer played out like a long, exasperated giggle. They spent the first thirty minutes of a *Melody Maker* interview "arguing about the validity of interviews,"[13] according to Lake. "Why should anybody want to talk to me, or read about me?" Moore asked. (A few months later, he hadn't yet found his answer. "'It's very difficult though,' says Moore to no one in particular. 'What the hell are we meant to talk about?' 'Don't start on that track again,' says Blegvad, cutting him off.")[14] In this profile, as well as one that appeared the next month in *New Musical Express*, he cultivated a sense of impending failure. For example, he told James Johnson about the band's befuddling relationship with Blackhill Enterprises, their new management company. "We had this extraordinary meeting where they sat us down and said, 'Now we have to discuss your image.' I mean man, it was so bizarre. They went on for an hour and Peter and I were sitting there open-mouthed trying to understand this language they were talking."[15] Blegvad openly mocked the rituals and tropes of the celebrity/band feature article. While relating the story of his and Moore's alcohol-soaked, drugged-up adolescence, he told his interlocutor, "We pinned my pet goldfish to a tree when it died and read the Tibetan Book of the Dead over its miserable orange carcass. We also used to slit each other open with razors. It was the weirdest relationship, man." "We were great kids," Moore agreed.[16]

In an interview many years later, Blegvad explained that nobody in his milieu at this time would ever explicitly court success. "Young people took prosperity for granted, so we made a show of shunning it. I remember thinking about 'experimental art' a lot, but I don't think I gave much thought to 'commercialism.'"[17] So now, once Moore had, in the words of Blegvad, "succumbed to the globular mass called pop music, which was waving pound notes in his face," they expressed their bemusement and indignation with the British popular music press whenever given the chance. The features, of course, had been arranged to promote Slapp Happy's new album, but Moore took the opportunity to express his wish that Virgin had never released it, noting that the music was already two years old. He was much more excited about their newest songs, perhaps hoping that they would soon lead the band to produce "material that's so weird we'll be back in the comparitively [*sic*] safe situation of what they call commercially unsuccessful."[18] He and Blegvad's attitude toward the music press was summed up in the title of Erskine's *NME* feature, "We're Definitely not the Kind of Thing That'd Interest Readers of *NME*."

The track that Moore *wanted* to discuss, "Europa," was an important transition step between the material they'd been writing over the last few years and what they would come to create with Henry Cow later in 1974. Slapp Happy recorded it at a session in mid-May at London's Nova Studios, with backing musicians chosen from among their new friends at Virgin. Aside from its unusual instrumentation (xylophone, glockenspiel, vibraphone, brass, bassoon, oboe, guitar, piano, organ, and bass guitar) and inventive arrangement, "Europa" offered intricacies that signaled a new kind of compositional ambition. Hewing closely to the syllabic rhythm of Blegvad's poetry, Moore changes meter frequently and plays with melodic contours that accentuate the surprises therein. A masterpiece of misdirection, Greaves's melodic bassline stutters its way onto and off of the beat; it's a Cow line, through and through. Meanwhile, Krause has added an edge to the lighter vocal style of Slapp Happy's two previous albums. The near naivety of those collections gives way in "Europa" to a tighter, more controlled delivery, with flamboyantly rolled Rs that suggest comparisons to Lenya. Blegvad had also made a stylistic departure in his lyrics. The poetry in *Sort Of* or *Slapp Happy*, though uniformly clever, stayed within more common themes like the lovers' dialogue, or less common but still modest character studies of a spy on the run ("Casablanca Moon") or a great artist ("Michelangelo"). By contrast, "Europa" considers "the Occidental Accident," or what had happened to a continent that developed its rational capacities at the cost of other mystical modalities: "She cannot call her myths her own; / lupine nipples squirted infant Rome, / But Reason turned the Beast to stone."

Many years later, Moore told me, "The piece was a dramatic shift. In a sense, the mischievous Slapp Happy, in which I would write kitschy waltzes and tangoes, and Peter would overlay them with subversive and pornographic lyrics, as a kind of ghastly mixture, starts to transform into a more musically developing style." The B side, "War (Is Energy Enslaved)" was just as important. Again, Moore penned a tightly controlled accompaniment to Blegvad's poetry; with a constant eighth-note pulse, individual phrases expand and contract to follow the length of each line. The verses string together bars of uneven meters with a vocal melody that hovers around the fifth scale degree before marching inexorably to the tonic at the end of every second line. The overall effect is claustrophobic, with the rhyming couplets coming relentlessly, one after another, with barely a moment to take another breath. This crowded verbosity makes the instrumental breaks arrive with a sense of great relief. The "chorus," too (if one can call it that), steadies itself in a few bars of 4/4, despite its angularity and syllabic displacement ("Upon her spoon this mot-to, wonderfully defined: 'Violence completes the partial mind'").

"War" is a jewel of many splendid intricacies. One comes at the first instrumental break, when Leigh plays a jittery soprano sax line that Moore employs to explore shifting durations for the same succession of pitches; another is Cutler's simple but highly effective variation between the first and second verses: in the first, he beats time on the ride cymbal in eighth notes, but in the second, he halves the speed into quarters, which fall serenely on or off the beat as the meter changes underneath. (Cutler took over from Gong's Pierre Moerlen when "War" was recorded a second time, in November 1974; I refer to this second recording here.) Blegvad's poetry offers marvelous imagery. As a fetus, war is a knot of fear, then a hateful baby banging its spoon against its plate; she grows up to shake her gory locks and lead pilgrims on a destructive march in the name of peace and fame. Although the entire song is written in tight, rhyming couplets (AA), Blegvad alters the scheme for the final four lines (ABAB), thereby delivering the terminal message with a twist of the knife: "They gut huts with gusto / Pillage villages with verve / War does what she has to / People get what they deserve."

But the star of this little two-minute epic was Krause, who delivers her opening lines ("Thunder and herbs") like a rotten-mouthed ghoul: sinister, cruel, and angry. She seems to have embodied the evil of the subject matter, personifying war as a kind of mythological shrieker. Still in her head voice, Krause's delivery is clipped, almost sneering. Gone is the naif of "Little Girl's World."

Everybody loved the recordings from the Nova sessions, especially Tim Hodgkinson. He was particularly taken with Krause. "She didn't just sing. She inhabited what she did. She was there, in it, *as* somebody." He was most struck by how she seemed to put their Brechtian theoretical inclination into sparkling practice. "For me, she was the real successor to the Lotte Lenya generation, in terms of her 'Brechtianism.' There were other singers who were making good money doing Brecht stuff [at the time], but Dagmar put them all in the shade." Virgin, however, was surprised by this new direction, at least according to Blegvad at the time. "No, no," protested Al Clarke of Virgin. "I wasn't at all surprised because I thought that 'Europa' was what you were sort of aiming at."[19] Surprised or not, Virgin decided not to issue the single, but recognized that the material had potential on an album. Blegvad told the *NME* interviewer, "We've stopped producing single material now and so our whole relationship to what we're doing is altering—it's a whole new band, and it's the only way that we can continue to work in a medium which (and here he begins emphasising his points, beating his fist on the table) *consistently compromises* you."[20] For Slapp Happy, then, the way forward necessitated getting serious and trying to produce material that tested the limits of their creative powers *inside of pop forms*, rather than merely testing the limits of the music industry's tolerance for their antics. This shift in focus was significant, because it meant that Moore and Blegvad would not only set themselves to new writing challenges, but would also require the services of a musically talented groups of collaborators to help them realize their pop art songs on tape.

Good Alchemy: Slapp Happy and Henry Cow

Sometime in the early autumn of 1974, the two groups met for a long, boozy meeting at Walmer Road. As the slow afternoon passed into night, the topic of discussion was Slapp Happy's upcoming recording session for their second Virgin album. They wanted Henry Cow to serve as their new backing band. Moore told a journalist at the time, "By that time there was no alternative as far as I was concerned really. On a very simple level there was material written that was post-'Europa' which had to be executed using a musical vocabulary greater than Peter or I could handle; a lot of work had developed up to three months before with Henry Cow in mind."[21] Earlier that year, Moore and Krause had moved to a farmhouse called Thieves Bridge in Norfolk, where they wrote much of the material for the new album with frequent visits from Blegvad and occasional drop-ins by members of Henry Cow. Although they were excited by the new direction their work was taking, there remained some questions about the future of the project. Moore was resolutely set against live performance, but his bandmates had different desires. Indeed, Blegvad recalls that he and Krause even considered taking dance lessons in order to work up surrealistic cabaret routines for Slapp Happy songs. Krause explains, "At that time, we were all a bit apprehensive about live work. Peter and I would have thrown ourselves into it, I think. But Anthony wasn't ready." Collaborating with Henry Cow on an album of new material might loosen up this impasse and push the group into a new mode of activity. "Well, this could lead anywhere," Blegvad thought. "I was in awe of Henry Cow. I thought they were a fantastic band. So the idea that they might want to collaborate with us, I just found very exciting." Although they had some reservations about the austerity of their new friends—"All these serious [conversations] . . . . we found them quite hilarious," remembers Krause—they were heartened to learn that the Cows had senses of humor, too.

From the Cows' perspective, the prospect of working on an album of Slapp Happy's music was more energizing for some than it was for others.

Figure 4.4 and 4.5 Slapp Happy and Henry Cow, likely discussing their merger, in Jack Balchin's squat, Walmer Road, late 1974. COURTESY OF JACK BALCHIN.

Fred Frith had reservations about their lyrical flamboyance—"too 'pataphysical and all that crap," as Jack Balchin put it. But he liked the musical challenges of arrangement, and he was quickly swept up by Krause's charisma. In our interviews, he was explicit about his early intentions to go beyond providing musical accompaniment for Slapp Happy and acquire the vocalist for his own group. "I was thinking about what that could bring to us, to have a singer like that. Already I was thinking in those terms." And as a child of late Impulse! and Béla Bartók, Hodgkinson lacked a pop sensibility that would have made the collaboration more rewarding for him. There just wouldn't be much for him to do: Moore already played piano well, and there were limits to how much clarinet they could drop on the album. But Greaves loved the idea, and had already been inspired to pen the tune "Bad Alchemy," which would end up on *Desperate Straights*. "I was *in*

Slapp Happy," he told me. Meanwhile, the more technically minded Cows, such as Cutler and Frith, enjoyed Moore's expertise and imagination in the areas of tape loops, recording studios, and the mechanics of sound itself.

They recorded *Desperate Straights* at the Manor between November 11 and 26. For the most part, they hashed out arrangements on the spot. Recording engineer Simon Heyworth took an active role in the creative process; instead of the usual practice of capturing tracks dry and then sculpting the sound with effects at the mixing stage, he worked with the musicians to find the right sounds as they went, and they monitored the wet mix in their headphones. In some cases, Heyworth surreptitiously caught a performance on tape, as occurred with the title track, which was a casual waltz by Moore on piano and Cutler on drums. Because he had turned on only a single microphone in some distant corner of the studio (echoes of Faust), the song feels like a bit of overheard lounge music. It also sounds like filler. There are many wonderful songs on the album, but Slapp Happy squeezed their abundant ideas into short durations. As a result, they needed a few more expansive and straight-forward time killers to get them over the thirty-minute mark. Another of these was "Caucasian Lullaby," an eight-minute multitracked etude concocted by Cutler and Moore that directed Hodgkinson to lie under the piano and resonate the strings above with slowly ascending chromatic scales on his clarinet.

Although *Desperate Straights* featured a few boisterous rockers such as "A Worm Is at Work" and "Strayed," the predominance of cabaret waltzes and more genteel piano-and-winds textures lends the album a certain Weimar flair. Overall, the lyrics mine the dark matter of "Europa." In this writer's opinion, the compositional standouts include Moore's shambolic madrigal "The Owl," and Greaves's "Bad Alchemy," which tumbles its way through expanding and contracting meters in a mad race through the labyrinth.

A few years later, Cutler wrote, "*Desperate Straights* was a joy & a revelation," and everybody agreed. They liked it so much, in fact, that they began to consider the possibility of merging the two groups permanently. "I think it was just so damned exciting," Greaves recalls. "The intellectual level of those people was pretty high. For Chris to match wits . . . with Anthony and Peter, it was pretty high level of communication." To be sure, the Cows would have been impressed by Krause's familiarity with Adorno, Brecht, Weill, and Eisler; Blegvad's formidable knowledge of avant-garde poetics and situationism; and Moore's hands-on expertise in tape manipulation and electronics. Moreover, Hodgkinson explains, "It shows that we are looking around for new problems to take on," after the Beefheart debacle

Figure 4.6 Henry Cow and Slapp Happy, merged, 1975. PHOTOGRAPH BY
DAVID LARCHER.

and the risky tour through Holland earlier that autumn. Spirits were high,
and Slapp Happy called on David Larcher to create slick new publicity photos of the new large group.

It is important to understand that the merger between these two groups
was not an action directed toward a predictable outcome. Although the
riskiness of the idea certainly worried him, Hodgkinson was also thrilled by
the possibilities. "It wasn't going to be like for a weekend," he explained. "It
was like a no-holds-barred, open-ended merge with these people. That was
completely fucking insane. Great idea."

Likewise for Krause, the absurdity of the idea could not obviate its value
as experiment. "A merger—to me it seemed ridiculous, to be honest," she
said. "I couldn't see [it], because Slapp Happy and Henry Cow's approach to
music seemed to be poles apart, and Peter and Anthony were big personalities. I couldn't see Henry Cow being able to deal with that."

"But if it was so absurd, how did it happen?" I asked.

"Well, no. . . . Great and wonderful new things come out of absurdity. And it was do-able, as well. It was a do-able thing, if we could get it past the record company. Sell them the idea, you know. . . . And in fact we could pool our artistic resources and see what we could come up with. . . ."

"So you liked that idea?"

"Yeah, why not? But it would be certainly a tryout, and if it didn't work, we could have gone our separate ways again. And that's what happened ultimately, but not as we expected. But whatever happens, you have to be open to new ideas—that was the thing, wasn't it?"

A tryout, to discover what is possible, what could be accomplished, what an uncertain future might hold. The musicians made their move into contingency with a view to playing a part in a future that remained unknowable but navigable, given appropriate awareness and adaptability. They did not seek a magical transcendence—no, it would take sharp analysis and diligence to turn that uncertainty into opportunity. As Hodgkinson explained to an interviewer in 1975, "The qualities of the two approaches which we were involved in before might eventually, through hard work, arrive at a new synthesis; but this is not something that is immediate."[22]

Once they decided to go for it, they needed to decide how they would handle their name. Acting on a suggestion from the label, they referred to *Desperate Straights* as the creation of "Slapp Happy / Henry Cow," while the upcoming Henry Cow album would become the product of "Henry Cow / Slapp Happy." For his part, Cutler articulated a more conclusive understanding to Kenneth Ansell: "It is no longer valid to speak of Henry Cow and Slapp Happy as two separate entities, it creates confusion. If you abolish these two identities then you can see what advantages there are for all of us as musicians."[23]

Reflecting back many years later, however, Moore was adamant that the two identities were never abolished, the merger was never complete. "I never thought of the two of us as one," he explained. The misunderstanding had much to do with very different way that the two groups conducted their affairs. For Moore, major life or career transitions were rarely formalized. "I don't know about Peter or Dagmar, [but] I've more or less never made a decision in my life. Stuff just happens." Support for his interpretation can again be found in Ansell's draft text, which refers to the "next release" (i.e., after *Desperate Straights* and the HC/SH album that was being recorded at the time of his writing), which would include all new music written after the fusion; in other words, the amalgamation would be complete only after the second album had been recorded and credited to "HC/SH."

In spite of the shared sense of enterprise, significant differences in temperament and personality persisted. As individuals, the members of Henry Cow could be comedians. Together, as an organization, they were more dour, especially in comparison with Slapp Happy, who had hardly been an organization at all. "The idea of having meetings was something totally new," Moore explains. "Slapp Happy never had a 'meeting.'" Krause, Moore, and Blegvad might have shared some chuckles about their new comrades, even though they had great respect and admiration for Henry Cow. Blegvad, for sure, found some of the meetings taxing. In his notebook at the time, he wrote, "How devastating the boredome [sic] is! After 40 minutes unravelling the divergent interpretations of the word 'learning' my ears begin to belch steam. But that is how these people 'work' & work it is—committed, never wavering—a hardy, admirable conglomerate. But how devastating!"

One of the central problems they were laboring on collectively was how to address social issues in their music. Over the long winter, the merged groups debated several positions on this question, and, indeed, the late spring and summer of 1975 saw a proliferation of theoretical and political texts by different members of Henry Cow. In response to Hodgkinson's formulation of the problem—"explicit statements vs. setting up so people discover it for themselves"—Blegvad advocated strongly for aesthetic integrity over political directness.[24] He wrote, "But we make *music*. The didactic potential of a work is [seldom] not the [major] exclusive concern of the composer. That his music be 'pertinent & constructive' is splendid but that it be 'beautiful'—a well-proportioned vehicle for his energies—is essential."[25] He went on to compare their music to a cry issuing forth from a deep pit; the message might be coherent, but the pit's acoustics "make coherence impossible." An audience's hostility to their work was the result of the distorting conditions of its production. Some members of Henry Cow would further develop this latter idea in the months to come, but they would stake out a more conflicted and antagonistic position on the value of beauty alone in their statements of 1975.

The earliest, most public, and most enduring of these statements was a publicity booklet produced by Cutler and Blegvad to celebrate and explain the merger. They worked on it in December and January, and probably had it printed in February 1975 to accompany the release of *Desperate Straights*.[26] Sixteen pages long, the booklet contains artwork by Blegvad, as well as publicity photos of the bands, separate and then together, and relevant discographies. The first couple of pages are devoted to a timeline of the bands' significant artistic work prior to the merger; the history of Slapp Happy and Henry Cow mixes and mingles therein, lending a teleological air to the chronology: all roads led to the merger. Significant events from the recent past appear to have been chosen and framed in such a way as to emphasize a collaborative sensibility (working with Faust, Ottawa Music Company, the ballets, Cabaret Voltaire, Ray Smith).

Cutler further articulated this emphasis in the enthusiastic annotations he added along the margin of the chronology. For example, next to an entry on the formation of the Ottawa Music Company, he wrote, "Death to the Individual! There must be more communal projects, more interpenetration, & sharing of knowledge & experience, as opposed to jealous guarding of abilities & techniques as a monopoly commodity, a sales gimmick to ensure consistent marketing."[27] Cooper later explained, "That's caused a great furore. . . . What we were really attacking was bourgeois individualism, which is a very destructive force. People have been alienated from one another and feeling they must amass as much property as possible to protect them from everyone else, doing things at the expense of other people rather than doing things together with other people. It's that sort of individualism that's dangerous."[28] According to the booklet, therefore, the merger wasn't simply an aesthetic decision motivated by the pleasures of fresh musical partners or new creative problems. It was also a pooling of resources, knowledge, and experience.

But to what end? There was more than one possible answer: Slapp Happy could find opportunities to perform, or Henry Cow could grow more accessible and reach a larger audience. In either of these cases, however, Virgin Records might have been understood as a useful collaborator. And that is how Simon Draper, for one, recalls his attitude to the whole idea: "I thought *Desperate Straights* was one of the best records we'd ever been involved in. The fact that they were merging, I would have thought, 'What an exciting proposition.' I don't remember there being any antipathy towards the group at any time, really. There might have been a certain amount of indifference, because some people didn't love them, just found the music too strange." Despite their growing reputation as "difficult" or "serious," Henry Cow had still garnered more press attention than Slapp Happy, and their experience on the road, if it could help convert Slapp into a touring band, would only have been viewed as useful from a promotional perspective. On the other hand, Krause's magnetism might greatly improve Henry Cow's buttoned-up concert style. Draper explains, "There wasn't anyone [in Henry Cow] who stood out, really, like that. Fred was pretty self-effacing, head down." Virgin, then, had good reason to support the new project.

But that isn't how some members of Henry Cow remember it. Although Greaves and Hodgkinson have no memories of strong objections from Virgin, Cutler and Frith recall that the company were displeased: they still wished to transform Slapp Happy into a viable pop outfit, and they feared that Henry Cow would pull them off that path to greater riches by encouraging instead their oddball tendencies. The merger, of course, would make this latter outcome much more likely, so "they accepted it, but they weren't happy about it," according to Cutler.

These conflicting memories of Virgin's reaction represent not so much a riddle to be solved as a clue about the evolution in Henry Cow's collective thinking about power, commerce, and their roles as public intellectuals. As Cutler told Ansell a few years later, "We didn't suddenly 'come out' as politicos. . . . We were developing too, it was part of our progress."[29] Regardless of whether Virgin *actually* approved of the merger or not, the band line on the episode would become more firmly established by the summer of 1975. The texts that Cutler, Hodgkinson, and Frith produced during these months indicate a more direct answer to the question "To what end?" They would not be sharing resources, knowledge, and experience with Slapp Happy in order to help the latter play live concerts, or to take Henry Cow's music—for its own sake—to a broader audience. No, the goal later that year was to educate audiences about the wretched conditions of their lives under the capitalist mode of production. We will investigate and explicate these texts at greater length in the next chapter, but for the moment, it is sufficient to note that Virgin Records quickly came to symbolize the capitalist culture industries, and therefore served as a target for full-throated critiques in the years to come. Although Draper might have supported the collaboration, or—just as likely—Virgin was simply moving in a new direction that made Henry Cow peripheral to their interests, the strength of the band's convictions later in 1975 might have retrospectively colored their perceptions of how the record company reacted to the merger in late 1974.

As playful as it was earnest ("1972: Peter sells waves on the Côte d'Azur"), the *Desperate Straights* booklet nevertheless registered this ambivalence regarding Virgin by both claiming a home in the debased popular music field and denouncing that field's politically regressive tendencies. Next to a chronology entry marking Henry Cow's appearance at the Bath International Music Festival, Cutler added, "The trap of believing in the desirability of being accepted by the straight music world—imagine us actually WANTING to take their side—to accept the scraps of approval & the status of intriguing pets!"[30] Yet if pop was the side Henry Cow chose, then they made the choice with some revision in mind. On the final page of the booklet, the authors clarified their mission: "Our field is not doomed to glorifying the Superman, the Banal & the Great Escape—it is as *possible* to be pertinent, critical & constructive in this as in any other field—but it is not yet as *usual*. Our aim is to make it so."[31]

Although the booklet prominently presents a disclaimer on page one that "all views herein expressed are those of h. cow/slapphappy [*sic*]," this document offered one of the first emblems of uneasiness inside the group about how to express themselves to the outside world. Hodgkinson, for example, agreed with the political analysis of the pop commodity and thought that the authors expressed it better than he could have done, but he was troubled by the "slight heaviness" and mythology of the portrayal. Further evidence of differing positions appears in the booklet itself. "Slapp Happy confess they did not believe anything of consequence could be produced in the field of rock music," Cutler wrote in one annotation. "It is true that at this point they were incapable of consequent action, taking as their model the image of the 'with it' pop group promulgated by the media—i.e. ignorant, self-involved, sloths. Death to the individual!"[32] A few months later, when the merged group began doing interviews with journalists, Cutler told Steve Lake, "I think their [Slapp Happy's] attitudes are in the process of changing." Picking up on the slightly ominous tone of reeducation, Frith added, "Ven zey come back from Siberia zey will think very differently."[33]

In Praise of Learning New Material

When *Desperate Straights* was released in March, it garnered mixed reviews. In the *Guardian,* Robin Denselow called it "one of the strangest new releases in months," but thought that it did "mark the beginnings of what could become a strange and interesting new rock form."[34] In the *NME,* Pete Erskine devoted many words to describing the music and lyrics, and concluded his appraisal by suggesting that the album was so good that only a few souls would be brave and/or cool enough to follow Slapp Happy off the beaten path: "Don't tell me. You just bought the new Dylan album. Honestly . . . you make me laugh."[35] But not every critic was so kind. Unique among reviewers, Lake listened to *Desperate Straights* more as a Henry Cow endeavor than a Slapp Happy one. He called it a "cul-de-sac" for the former, even it represented a step forward for the latter; the exploratory improvisations that he enjoyed so much on *Unrest* were missing here. He concluded that the "noble words" so nobly spoken in the publicity materials—that it was possible to be pertinent, critical, and constructive in the rock field— were "unfortunately unsupported by the nature of the music."[36]

By the time these reviews appeared, however, the merged group had already been through an entirely new adventure: recording a second merged album with Henry Cow in the lead. Hodgkinson struggled with a new problem in the lead-up to this recording. Now that they were combining with Slapp Happy, he had to rethink some basic issues of instrumentation and texture in "Living in the Heart of the Beast." "You nurture this piece over months for the band that you totally invested in, and [then] the band becomes something else." Most significant was the addition of Krause, a serious singer who would need to have something to do, which meant that somebody would have to write words for her. It had been more than a year since Henry Cow regularly performed "Nine Funerals" (and much longer for "I Came to See You Today" and "Rapt in a Blanket"), and, furthermore, "Beast" was a fifteen-minute piece that would require a lot of verbiage. Blegvad was the natural choice, and the group was already struggling to figure out how to integrate him into the larger unit, so Hodgkinson asked him to write lyrics for the work.

Years later, Blegvad recalled, "I remember feeling tested, and that I had to prove myself, and I *wanted* to prove myself. . . . I just respected them so much, I wanted to bring something that they would be knocked out by, and what I came up with was my usual brand of automatic writing. It was a very dreamy, little scenario, which you couldn't really read as a political allegory." The political allegory, it turned out, would be a crucial element of the new album, which the band titled *In Praise of Learning* after the poem by Berthold Brecht. Some notes from Blegvad's journal of the time suggest the specific themes and messages that Hodgkinson asked him to explore—a "sense of self in impotence," the need for a new language, and the fact that "destiny does not rule—in action you escape limiting sense of limitations."[37] In his first version, a pair or small group of protagonists (the "we" is otherwise unspecified) venture into the bowels of a living machine (or dynamo), "our descent intending overhaul." Lacking manual or map, they hope to learn something of its operations. Because they have no plan, they come to their understanding of the dynamo through a mystical event: "if nothing else at first our fear / may irritate a filament to glowing / & the friction between yes & no / ignites & details of the dynamo / come clear."[38]

"No," Hodgkinson said when he saw these lyrics. "I realized immediately that I wanted something else and I thought, 'Okay, I did "Nine Funerals." This is just the same kind of job, just bigger.'" From his perspective, Blegvad's text posed two related problems. The first, as Blegvad pointed out, was that it was too artful, its meaning too inscrutable. Blegvad clearly struggled with this question after finishing *Desperate Straights*; in one jotting, he considers the relative value of lyrics on their own terms versus their possible function as "mere" ornament.

In addition to these matters of presentation, Hodgkinson disagreed with the substance of Blegvad's lyrics. He noted this disagreement in interviews a few months later and in 1976. "The ideological differences gradually emerged. Well, perhaps not so gradually. As far as I was concerned, they mainly concerned Peter as a lyricist," he told Angus Mackinnon of *Sounds*.[39] After some weeks of critical reflection, Hodgkinson had come to the conclusion that Blegvad's lyrics offered a politically cynical complacency in comparison with what he regarded as the committed optimism of the new Henry Cow album. Of this latter, he explained, "Feelings, the conditions of life, thoughts, and actions affect the music; I think it's a positive change that 'Desperate Straights' didn't have—'Desperate Straights' is . . . a kind of circus, a mode of survival, trying to be happy in a desperate situation. 'In Praise of Learning' is political and positive."[40] Moreover, in his view, the lyrical style of *Desperate Straights* presented an epochal condensation that reflected current conditions but did not wrestle with the problems of creating a new language that could aid social transformation.[41] While Slapp Happy offered the presentational style of the commodity (however cynical or sarcastic), Henry Cow sought the dialogue of "true" communication that went beyond present conditions.

Hodgkinson devoted most of a one-hundred-page notebook to working out the compositional and lyrical themes of "Beast." The text offers up a mix of Marxist humanism, linguistics, and the situationism rendered explicit in the first line. Overall, it outlines a change of consciousness in a protagonist who starts as an individual, subjective "I" and ends as the communist "we" of collective revolution. The first section, which runs to 1:35, opens with a *j'accuse* about the society of the spectacle ("Situation that rules your world (despite all you've said)"); the addressee of this statement is probably the rock rebel, who, despite all s/he said about freedom and liberation, remains imprisoned in an industrialized entertainment complex that provides only opiates of emotional commodities.[42] "I would strike against it," the protagonist responds, "but the rule displaces." Here, Hodgkinson refers to the many naturalized rules—of language, economic exchange, law—that divorce subjects from their historical conditions, simplifying reality and imposing upon it "a fiat of accomplished truth," as George Steiner put it in a line copied into the composer's notes.[43] The deceptions of nationalist wars, histories of great men, mass culture commodities, and (in the next section) alcohol ("histories of marching together . . . , United with heroes"; "Tales told by idiots in paperbacks"; "he hurls a wine glass") paper over the real contradictions in society, leaving the protagonist in despair over his or her "different destiny," that is, obscurity, alienation, and endless toil.

In section 2 (1:35–6:10), the "I" becomes a "we," as the protagonist now realizes the shared, reciprocal systems of exchange for "words, coins, movements." Although words have grown desiccated and language continues to divide people by replacing actor-to-actor communication with mystification, the protagonist ignites a spark of hope by questioning the status quo: "Sere words . . . who has used them how?" Hodgkinson develops this distrust in the next stanza, which he referred to in his notes as the "Steiner position" or the "Rimbaud position" (I take this to mean Steiner's explication of Rimbaud). For Steiner, the French poet "strove to restore to language a fluid, provisional character," one that might approach incantation—"conjuring up the unprecedented,"[44] which Hodgkinson would prefer over the "toothless" language that paralyzes us within "loops of care." Hodgkinson's Rimbaudian poet, therefore, is "rushing to find where there's a world of liquid syntax." Hurling his wine glass at a mirror, he regards himself in the shards; alienated, he separates from his own image, and therefore from the social structure that is concretized there ("I am not I"). "He's changed." Crucially, the poet's final gesture is to pull himself out of despair by advancing from word to deed: "hunting the eye of his own storm."

For Hodgkinson, this resolve nonetheless remains false, because although the poet has recognized his own alienation and the shared nature of language, he has not yet connected them to the social mode of production. The third section of "Beast" dramatizes this final step. The "we"—now a communist we with a historical consciousness—has gained awareness of their economic and linguistic conditions: "We were born to serve you all our bloody lives / labouring tongues we give rise to soft lies." Surveying the modern city, "high in offices," the protagonists now see clearly how it has been organized to "kill all encounter" and to abstract its functions from "all human intent." Armed with their new knowledge, they can now fight for the future and take destiny into their own hands, as the rousing end of the work makes clear ("Now is the time to begin to go forward"). The abstract poetics of the first two and one-half sections give way in the fourth to a more direct style impelling action.

Meanwhile, Cutler revealed himself to be an adroit lyricist when he shared "Beautiful as the Moon—Terrible as an Army with Banners." The song's lyrical themes suggest that the band—or at least its lyricists—had discussed and agreed on the message they wished to convey to listeners, even if Cutler's poetic text develops that message through drawing a connection between the Christian apocalypse and communist revolution. Both turn on the collapse of first days and last days: the new era (of God's reign or the workers' paradise) can only begin once the last days ("Days erased" / Dies Irae) begin. Like "Beasts," "Banners" begins with a desolate scenario ("Careworn & all alone") that nonetheless harbors hope for a different future—though unfurled, Venus is an old communist symbol of class revolt that appears at the darkest moments before dawn. Cutler employs the imagery of death and ghosts ("souls ungraved") to portray a haunted world of lies, where we have "unlearned" the crimes of economic exploitation and linguistic reification. Like Charon, he exhorts the "Daemon" to rise up at a "Rose Dawn" and "seize the morning." In these "last days" of the old world, the science of Marxism will see the workers through the "Glass maze" that has pulled them out of history. As in Hodgkinson's lyrics, consciousness about language—verbal or musical—and its subsequent revitalization are important steps toward revolution ("Love solves worlds—with words"), but the final stage will necessitate action, not discourse ("Time solves words—by deeds"). For Cutler, the future presents both an ending of the old and a beginning of the new. Extremely dense with mythological figures and poetic turns of phrase, his text made up in beauty what it may have lacked in directness.[45]

When Hodgkinson shared the vocal part of "Beast" with Krause, she protested, "I can't sing that! This is too difficult!" But she would in fact learn the part over a few weeks in January, working on her own and then meeting with Henry Cow (sans Moore and Blegvad) to rehearse the next day at Walmer Road. Although Krause was also struggling to master the tricky time signatures of "Banners," she and the band devoted the lion's share of their rehearsal time to the very long and very complicated "Beast" score. Hodgkinson recalls that he and his bandmates were impressed by Krause's work ethic and her seriousness; when she heard something like "That's great, Dagmar," she would often respond, "No, it's not right. I can do better."

Soon enough, the other members of Slapp Happy joined the practice sessions; Moore handled the piano part that Hodgkinson had written for him, and Blegvad did his best with some second guitar parts, but concern about his role in the merged group was beginning to set in.

"I'm dead weight," Blegvad remembers thinking. "They're just pulling me along, because . . . everything I was trying to do—learning by rote these incredibly fiddly guitar parts—anyone else there could have done it better." And aside from "Beasts," there was little else for Moore and Blegvad to do—concentrating his attention solely on Krause, Frith hadn't written extra parts for them on "Banners." Indeed, Greaves puts the situation in stark terms: "We didn't rehearse with Slapp Happy for *In Praise of Learning*. We *ignored* Slapp Happy for *In Praise of Learning*."

In February, the groups decamped to The Manor to record. Although they had spent much of their time since *Desperate Straights* revising and rehearsing "Banners" and "Beasts," both pieces were forbidding challenges to commit to tape. Because they could not yet play it all the way through from start to finish, Henry Cow recorded "Beast" in short sections, building it up as they went along. To ameliorate the issue of Moore and Blegvad's relative underparticipation in the album that was taking shape, the merged group had already decided to hold back "War" from the *Desperate Straights* sessions and place on the new album instead—the song's Brechtian themes and Krause's Mother Courage performance seemed like a better fit for *In Praise of Learning* anyway. But despite this attempt at rebalancing the representation of personnel, Greaves thinks that the pieces were already moving into place for a certain endgame of the merger: "I think then it was out in the open, wasn't it? . . . We needed Dagmar. We didn't need Anthony and Peter—they couldn't play anything!"

Greaves might be understating their musical competence; Hodgkinson has recalled that Moore, in particular, was a strong contributor to the two cuts of improvisation on the album, "Beginning: The Long March" and "Morning Star," though Blegvad's only positive memory of the entire session is of Cutler flashing him a thumbs-up when he slipped a bluesy guitar lick into a more abstract group texture. In any case, the improvisations allowed the group to experiment with Dolby DBX, the new noise-reduction system that had been installed at the Manor. Though not everybody loved the sound, DBX made it possible to overdub many takes without accruing too much tape noise. "The Long March" calls to mind Faust's fuzzier electronic passages; the six-minute track presents a series of ambient hums and loops frequently punctuated with clangorous, percussive interruptions that give way to a series of episodes for winds, violins, radios, and, eventually, a massed collection of superimposed wails. The second improvisation, "Morning Star," proceeds in a manner more reminiscent of the Spontaneous Music Ensemble: quicksilver exchanges between guitar, clarinet, bass, and drums. As in the other piece, loops and manipulations of the recording tape speed provide contrast to the "live" improvised passages.

The improvisations shared another element, bassoon, because Cutler had contacted Lindsay Cooper and invited her to participate as a session musician.[46] As far as he can remember, he acted unilaterally out of a sense that she would be a strong stabilizing force at the Manor.[47] And how had Cooper spent the preceding few months? "In tears, I think, mainly. I was thrown out of the group for that period. I got a job doing music for theatre," she told an interviewer some years later.[48] Although she had a few other freelance gigs during the Slapp Happy period—recording with Egg, Comus, and Hatfield and the North, and performing with Geoff Leigh's Radar Favourites—the Manor date would have meant good money and a chance to hang out with old and new friends (her datebook records a number of appointments with Krause, Moore, and Blegvad in March, which coincided with the onset of serious concerns about the merger).

Though he received no criticism or grumbling from his bandmates, the independence with which Cutler made the decision to bring back Cooper— no meetings, no discussions—suggests that the cohesion of the group had loosened somewhat during their time at The Manor. Indeed, Frith's overall memory of the session was of noninvolvement: he contributed "Banners" and played his parts on "Beast," but he didn't feel creatively invested in the project. Greaves, too, had focused his attention elsewhere. "I was spiritually in Slapp Happy already, I think. I'd jumped ship."

No Solid Base of General Theoretical Agreement

After they finished mixing *In Praise of Learning*, the two groups returned to London for rehearsals at Walmer Road, and eventually traveled in late March to St. Christopher School, where Moore's parents still worked as tutors. The students and staff were away on Easter break, so Henry Cow and Slapp Happy had the run of the place, sleeping in the vacant dorm rooms and cooking massive pots of lentils in the school kitchen. They had to prepare for the future: tours, new music, new plans.[49] They rehearsed in the gymnasium, a dank, unheated cavern so frigid they could barely play their instruments—a "nightmare," in Frith's memory. In Cutler's words, "We went into that rehearsal with the intention of being a band. We came out of the rehearsal with two people gone, Dagmar in Henry Cow, and the merged band a thing of the past."

The problems were many. Moore was a reluctant performer, and had never conceived of his musical practice in a live concert setting. And Henry Cow's music was difficult. "He's not a chops player; he's a conceptualist, and a very interesting one," Frith explains. Henry Cow, on the other hand, might have been too set in its ways to incorporate or respond creatively to what Moore might have contributed. "We weren't particularly listening to him conceptually, and he wasn't able to do the thing musically." Meanwhile, Blegvad was having trouble learning those intricate guitar parts, and had begun making wild proposals for performance art routines to make himself useful.

Skeptical from the beginning, Hodgkinson no longer suspended his judgment of the union once the groups were in Letchworth. The problem, he noted in a journal entry dated March 14, was the following: "We are in a weak position as there is no solid base of general theoretical agreement on crucial social/aesthetic issues." What was the point of playing Slapp Happy songs in their live set? His notes indicate a certain discomfort with the possibility of assuming an ironic or dramatic stance on stage; perhaps one of the ideas circulating at the time was to stage the Slapp Happy material as a kind of circus or festival inside the Cow set. Hodgkinson wrote, "Does it involve assuming a role, as of S's [Slapp Happy's?] 'charlatan' or 'ring-master'— denying yr. own knowledge . . . : a piece of theatre." In light of Henry Cow's increasing confidence and sincerity coming out of the *In Praise of Learning* material, Blegvad's lyrics likely seemed too ironic by comparison. In addition to staging the songs "as dramatic postures taken in reaction to the 'becomings' of 'free' music," Hodgkinson noted other options: totally fragmenting the songs and then superimposing them, or just keeping the Cow and Slapp material completely separate. The principle guiding these attempts at integration came from Theodor Adorno, whose *Philosophy of Modern Music* had just been translated into English in 1973; in his notes, Hodgkinson copied out a directive: "to play music which 'absorbs the contradiction evident in its relationship to reality into its own consciousness of form.'" By struggling to integrate the "commercialism" of Slapp Happy's pop side with the "criticism" of Henry Cow's technically advanced practice, the artists would negate their social conditions and move to a new dialectical arrangement.

Beyond Hodgkinson's reservations based on theoretical analysis, the groups were having trouble at the practical level, because the newest Slapp

Happy songs weren't working in live performance; as the rehearsals wore on, the number of tracks that could conceivably work in the set dwindled down to "Bad Alchemy" alone, which, as a Greaves song, didn't require Blegvad and Moore anyway. One solution to this surprising dearth of material was to play older Slapp songs, but such an option felt like a step backward to the composer and lyricist.

Moreover, Blegvad was having trouble committing fully to the new organization. "Instinctively, . . . I was against the old order, against authority. But revolutionary movements tend to be extremely authoritarian affairs! You gotta toe the line! I couldn't take it seriously."[50] However, as Henry Cow had demonstrated with Cooper nearly a year before, commitment had to be taken seriously. As the musicians went over plans for touring in the summer and beyond, Blegvad was concerned about retaining the freedom to visit his girlfriend after she moved to New York City. Could he sign on for only nine months, and then see where things stood? The proposal did not meet with sympathy.

As Moore and Blegvad gradually realized that their days were numbered, they behaved recklessly. On one occasion, they tried to preempt their own dismissal by showing up at a meeting completely drunk, acting abominably and concluding their performance by rising and shouting, "We fire ourselves!" After unwisely driving off into the night, they returned to the meeting to rejoin the group. Blegvad asks, "This kind of behavior—to someone like Tim Hodgkinson, who was very methodical and committed and clear, what could he have made of this? Did he think, 'Ah, this is an interesting new energy coming into the fold?' I don't think so."

Henry Cow eventually concluded that Blegvad wasn't ready for primetime. He recalls, "I think the exact word was 'flippant.' And though I could be charming while defending myself, they said, let's not be beguiled by that, let's see beyond the performance to what he's actually saying. Which was nothing. Or 'Please fire me.' So they invited me to leave."[51] It was almost certainly Hodgkinson who delivered the sentence. "Tim knew how to do it," Krause explains. "He was brought up at Winchester to do just that—to lead. . . . The leader can do the axe-job." Later, Hodgkinson would explain to a journalist that Henry Cow's critiques of Slapp Happy essentially destroyed the group.[52]

As the group struggled with these intractable issues over the dying gasps of a bitter winter, the emotional skies grew darker by the day. The marriage of Krause and Moore was quickly disintegrating; in her eyes, it wasn't just their ever more obvious incompatibility—"We were just not suited to living together. Right person, wrong time"—but also her incipient alienation from the institution itself: "People regard you as a couple, especially women, because men are regarded as the dominating part of the relationship. It becomes an incredible struggle for the woman to be looked upon as herself for what she's doing, not the child-minder who also entertains the husband's friends. Although neither Anthony nor I wanted it, we just became victims of conditioning."[53] Amid the confusion, anger, and despair, she and Frith began an affair. Though he was only two-and-a-half years old, Max might have sensed this psychic distress, or it might have been the unforgiving climate and general lack of emotional security offered by Henry Cow. In any case, he was unhappy during the St. Christopher sojourn, and couldn't have cared less about rehearsal schedules and live set ideas. Krause, therefore, had to respond to her own ambivalent sensitivities, and to competing claims on her emotional attention from different directions. And Moore's suffering, Max's distress, and Frith's affections were only part of the story. It was becoming increasingly obvious that Krause's future lay not with Slapp Happy but with Henry Cow, whose home base at Walmer Road, wretched as it may have been, appeared rock solid in comparison with the years she had spent shuttling back and forth to Hamburg, Letchworth, Norfolk, Tuscany, Istanbul, and Sligo. And there was no doubting the Cows' commitment to live performance; with them, she would sing for audiences, and the material the Cows had already written for her fortified a growing sense of commitment and dedication on her part.

Meanwhile, as Moore recalls, "I went back again and again, for more punishment." Indeed, even before the groups had arrived in Letchworth in late March, Krause and Max had stayed in the family's apartment above the Blackhill offices in Westbourne Park while Moore began living in his converted lorry that had been parked in front of the Henry Cow house in Notting Hill. He believed in the idea that one's suffering might produce a more profound art. "And that idea is some part of the ideology of the group—you put your bourgeois feelings to one side, and you get on with the work. Obviously, it's a hard thing to take. But if anybody would look at it and say, 'Well, why did you hang around? Why didn't you just walk away weeks, months, before?' Well it's because I took the thing seriously." Indeed, commitment seemed to be a persistent theme shared by these artists as the collaboration deepened and then turned sour. In light of the dilettantism of the earlier Slapp Happy, we might interpret Moore's newfound earnestness as an indication of Henry Cow's charisma, or the power of their developing sense of purpose. The sincerity and complexity of the *Desperate Straights* material, Moore has come to realize, "smells of Henry Cow," though his admiration for Brecht, Weill, and Eisler surely also played its part. But as we have already seen, the qualities of sincerity, commitment, and seriousness came wrapped up with the emotional hardness that Henry Cow had grown, like a carapace, in the previous few years.

Greaves was the exception, and he suffered a nervous breakdown one night in Letchworth that necessitated a trip to the hospital. Admittedly, he had been weakened by an overdose of hard work in the weeks before, when he finally finished writing the song that would later be titled "Kew. Rhone." in 1976. But the vulnerability and openness that often made him the favorite of outsiders also led him to experience acutely the misery in other corners of the group. Reflecting back on this difficult moment, he recalls the distinct feeling that it was a dubious milestone of sorts, when he began separating from the group just as it was about to enter its golden period. "This is not what I signed up for, not what we should be doing," he thought. But in true Henry Cow fashion, he was back at work the next day, no questions asked.

By the time Moore and Blegvad were out of the picture, it was already obvious that Slapp Happy had also met its end (even though the pair would continue to use the name in the next few months).[54] Sarah Greaves remembers, "And then it was a question of, 'Do we keep Dagmar?' and I just said, 'Yes!' because she's just absolutely perfect for this. I thought it was astonishing, her range that could go from Lotte Lenya on the one hand, right the way to Diana Ross. I thought she had the most extraordinary range." Indeed, both Greaveses loved the idea of adding a vocalist, and argued strongly for it; for John, Krause might help keep Henry Cow from indulging in the more abstract sorts of avant-gardism that had grown to feel a bit tiresome to him over the years. The rest of the group were excited by her powerful musical personality—she had "image potential," as Balchin put it. Hodgkinson explains, "As a person, as a being, she was radiant and very captivating. Her sort of sexual ambiguity as well . . . : her boyishness in terms of her sort of stance and the way she sang, she would just kinda stand there and deliver. She didn't wiggle. I've seen people ruin music with wiggling."

As for Simon Draper and Virgin, the split met with as little attention as had the merger three months earlier. Draper said, "In 1975, we were struggling to transform ourselves. We wanted to become a bigger and better record company. . . . They would have been peripheral to our future." By this time, it was becoming distinctly possible that they would remain a one-hit company; *Tubular Bells* was still doing great, and Tangerine Dream was selling well, but none of the other smaller-sized acts had hit it big, and the company was now actively seeking some bigger fish.

After the split, several things happened in quick succession. First, Cooper traveled to Letchworth on April 4 to rejoin the band; they had liked having her around again during part of the *In Praise of Learning* sessions, and the group had probably come to the conclusion that it was feasible once again, now that Frith and White's marriage had reached its terminus. (Cooper had certainly gotten over it: immediately on her return, she hit on Dagmar ardently but without success.) Second, the headline type on the cover was changed from *Henry Cow / Slapp Happy* to just *Henry Cow*. Ray Smith had created a third stocking for the sleeve in a smooth, bold red that announced the band's politics as explicitly as did the lyrics printed on the back. But he was not pleased with the type; he wanted the cover to go unadorned. When Henry Cow disagreed, Smith asked to credit himself under a pseudonym, but they refused, and he therefore went uncredited. (They added a quotation at the end of the credits, attributed to John Grierson: "Art is not a mirror, it is a hammer.") Third, the ensemble departed St. Christopher School and reconvened for rehearsals at a Virgin warehouse on Avonmore Place in Kensington. Why? Richard Branson had persuaded Robert Wyatt to come out of his retirement from public performance to do two large concerts in Paris and London. Wyatt finally agreed, and chose Henry Cow as his backing band. It was a huge opportunity, and this is where we will begin the next chapter.

But first, we must mark the end of Anthony Moore's significant involvement in this story. The split from his wife, his old band, and his new band took their toll. On his departure from Henry Cow in April, he took a quick job from Alan Power, editing sixteen-millimeter film for *Monkey's Birthday*, which would be finished later that year. With the money he made, Moore bought a ticket to New York City, where he followed his experimental film contacts and soon played tapes of his pieces for Frederic Rzewski and Philip Glass. He also researched the Frankfurt School sociologists in the New York Public Library; he had surely encountered Adorno texts during his time in Hamburg, but his interest was probably renewed by the discussions about art and politics that Henry Cow had been having that spring. He also looked into Eisler, returning with the composer's fine song, "On Suicide," to give to Krause. (Frith's arrangement would feature in many of Henry Cow's concerts in the years to come.)

Moore's return to London provoked quite a scene. He spent the evening before at a bar in the newly opened World Trade Center, which began "an alcoholic voyage of pioneering duration and intensity," in the words of Peter Erskine. "Upon arrival at JFK he purchased a bottle of vodka and swallowed an air sickness tablet that just happened to be mescaline. On the plane he drank the bottle of vodka, visited the lavatory and went into a series of brief comae." Disembarking at Heathrow the next morning, he "bellowed educated obscenities" before greeting Blegvad, and they retired to the lounge for screwdrivers; soon thereafter, Moore collapsed while shouting invective at the bartender. "The barman informed Moore of his intention of calling 'the law,' whereupon Moore propped himself up on one shoulder countering with 'The Law? *What* law? The only law is that of the sacrosanct individual!'" The police arrived and hauled him off. Meanwhile, Blegvad traveled separately into London to get help but also to procure more fuel for the fire. He showed up to the police station with a bag of liquor and was promptly arrested. Eventually, somebody from Virgin bailed them out, and they then made their way to the Henry Cow / Robert Wyatt concert at the New London Theatre on Drury Lane. At intermission, Moore pulled Blegvad to the piano on stage and played him a new song, "Johnny's Dead," that he had written in New York; they recorded it later that year, the first step in a solo pop career that would culminate in the fine 1979 album *Flying Doesn't Help.* Anyway, upon leaving a post-concert party, Moore and Blegvad's driver was stopped and charged with drunk and disorderly conduct. I am not making this up.[55]

5   Europa | 1975–76

There is a common feeling among the musicians, crew, and fans of Henry Cow that they hit their stride artistically, politically, and organizationally during the second half of 1975; it might have been the most rewarding and successful stretch in the band's ten-year history. The tension and conflict of the Slapp Happy episode had produced not only disappointment but also a certain propulsion. As John Greaves put it, "We were all very excited, genuinely, about the prospect of this collaboration, which got justified in various ways afterwards, and then the collapse of it, as inevitable as it was, was very emotionally charged." In Tim Hodgkinson's memory, these emotions coalesced into a form of revolutionary optimism, "a sort of continuing, surging, positive feeling. . . . Within our little world it was a way of being high on revolution, whereas before it had been . . . a more labored connection between theory and practice, perhaps."

The positive surge ran through a *Melody Maker* interview with Fred Frith, Chris Cutler, and Dagmar Krause in April 1975. Although he recognized the rotten state of the status quo, Cutler said, "instead of moaning about it and saying how dreadful and terrible everything is, it'd be better to try and get some perspective on it and get hold of some dialectical materialist attitudes and do some work."[1] When Steve Lake offered his opinion that *In Praise of Learning* was a dark and melancholy record, he was met with cries of frustration, shocked at "the new look Henry Cow, positively overflowing with a vibrant optimism." Cutler emphatically insisted that people can take control of their future if they get involved. "It's too late for pessimism and despair—they're too popular." To help move their audience to involvement, he explained, Henry Cow would make optimistic records and play optimistic concerts.

With "Living in the Heart of the Beast" and "Beautiful as the Moon—Terrible as an Army with Banners," they had two new cornerstones for their live set. In May and June, they would perform to the largest and most supportive audiences of their career, and they would garner a laudatory critical reception for their newest release. Moreover, they would establish their autonomy from Virgin as a touring band with new equipment, loyal crew members, and a new base of operations in Battersea. As we will see, these specific, day-to-day developments emboldened the more theoretically minded members to sharpen their analyses of cultural politics.

Once more, Cooper would be contributing solidly to the musical dynamic, and, for the first time, the group could feature a frontperson in the form of Krause, a new avenue of explicit communication with the audience. In Hodgkinson's memory, "I think it came from the fact that we now had a singer—it's like 'politics in command,' a Maoist statement. Internalized revolution: actually live it. Don't just read about it and talk about but see if you can actually get it into the fabric of how you live." In addition to this fortitude that Krause's position seemed to foster, Henry Cow also gained a projective personality in concert. Previously, as Frith puts it, "we weren't exactly showboating." But, he continues, "when we had Dagmar, she provided the kind of emotional center of the group and we responded to that. So that was a huge change. In a way we were able to use her and from that point of view to channel ourselves. She had charisma." Indeed, for the next few years, they presented a striking face in performance, owing to the frank beauty and stark androgyny of several band members.

Sterner Measures Will Have to Be Taken

Many new forces were folded into the arrangement in the middle of 1975, but I will begin with the theoretical developments of this period. Soon after the release of *In Praise of Learning*, Cutler told Kenneth Ansell, "Everything about it—the title, the cover, the quote 'Art is not a mirror, it is a hammer'—is an embodiment, a statement of the ethos of Henry Cow at that time."[2] Like Grierson's hammer, their music would be a tool for intervening in the world, not simply a reflection of the status quo. They were working, Cutler told one interlocutor, "towards a change in the system. In the whole political climate and environment. . . . Certainly action against inaction. Against the generally declining social climate in which we all live, which is getting blacker and Right-er all the time, because [capitalism] is collapsing. . . . Sterner measures will have to be taken, you'll see."[3] To the extent that their musical activities were representations—that is, "mirrors"—of a better world, they were invalid; but, according to Hodgkinson, a piece such as "Living in the Heart of the Beast" was "validly invalid" because its art was a prelude to "action" in "life."[4]

The addition of Krause to Henry Cow spurred them to clarify and strengthen the presentation of their cultural politics. Lyrically, of course, implicit theories of social action in music had to become explicit. But interpersonally, she also pushed the group into taking strong public positions. Frith explained, "She wanted to sing words with a political point to them. She was a lot more political than many of the people already in the band, myself for instance."[5] In an interview that ran in the July 19, 1975, issue of *NME*, Krause said, "I do not want to play a game. I want a very intense feeling, to make me bring out what is on my mind, and *that* will always be very much to do with real human needs. First we must become aware of what is oppressing us."[6] For Krause, much of that oppression owed to the rigid expectations of heterosexual marriage—confined to the house and minding her child, she told an interviewer, "took over from my being human." In Henry Cow, she explained, the musical roles were more fluid. "It was a very *humane* way to work, and in this different social atmosphere, the emotions became much clearer in what I wanted to say." From this perspective as a parent and woman, Krause put a new spin on one of Henry Cow's central ongoing concerns: to encourage people to take back control of their lives from the exploitive powers that oppressed them. "If we could take our lives in our own hands," she said, "not just women but men as well, then society really would look different from the way it looks now."

The seizure of one's life, however, would come about only through hard work, struggle, and committed study (if not "sterner measures"). Although this idea functioned as a general ethos since 1972 and as an explicit aspect of the band's politics since 1974, it gained a new prominence around the time of *In Praise of Learning*. Indeed, Brecht's poem exhorted its readers, those who "must prepare to take command now," to "study from bottom up, / for you who will take the leadership, / it is not too late!" This education would not come easily, however, and the group seemed to be drawn to the notion of prolonged struggle as a necessary path to a better world. As journalist Angus MacKinnon noticed in writing his profile of the group immediately after their split with Slapp Happy, the phrase *it's only a beginning* came up often in their conversation.[7] As indicated by the title "Beginning: The Long March," at least some members of Henry Cow found inspiration in the legend of Mao's leadership of the Red Army during its darkest hour—the path would be long and painful but might lead to a final victory.

One cannot dismiss the romance of this image; according to Hodgkinson, "Chou En-Lai, Mao Zedong, they seemed to be kind of hip dudes. We didn't know about all this bad shit—I mean, well, we didn't *want* to know about it, we *could've* known about it, of course. . . . And the great story of the Long March, and Mao walking all day and then sitting up in his tent with his candle studying and writing all night—writing the theory of the revolution." Sounds like a musician on tour! This romance seemed to have gripped equally Cutler, Hodgkinson, Frith, and Krause. "Dagmar's sinophilia knows no bounds," Cooper wrote a friend in December 1975. "She's started throwing the I Ching between examinations of handling contradictions among the people."[8] Frith recalls his own attraction to Chinese revolutionary poetry and the worker's posters collected by his girlfriend, Sue Steward, who was still working at Virgin.

The Maoist practice of self-criticism provided another new inspiration for the Cows in 1975, one that further resonated with Krause's feminist rearticulation of the Cow's analytic into personal terms. Cutler later explained, "Our response to a lot of this broadening out of social concerns focused itself on a kind of Maoism; we pinned ourselves to Mao—because of the rhetoric of the cultural revolution, criticism and self-criticism and so on . . ."

Hodgkinson added, "Yeah, because Maoism was exactly the point at which macropolitics seemed to have a way into micropolitics; it almost proposed a morality, as it were, a way of good thinking or something, or like 'how should one be' in a particular situation. That seemed to be much more coming from Mao than the older ideas."

"It seemed to me, thinking about it afterwards—not at the time, of course—that our embracing of all that was very much to do with an unconscious comprehension of the lack of personal . . . well, the emotional side of things and that kind of contact between us. . . . And it wasn't dogmatic Maoism. . . . It was much more that there seemed a possibility of breaking through the personality shells, which I don't think we really did, actually."[9]

Mao, therefore, did not simply serve as role model of someone who maintained hope in the midst of a hopeless struggle; he also seemed to provide a means of negotiating personal matters—the "micropolitics"—within a group that had established its sphere of activity as somewhat independent of emotional exchange.[10] In a personal analysis of the group's internal dynamic dating from 1981, Hodgkinson noted the currency inside the group of Mao's famous observation: "A revolution is not a dinner party, or writing an essay, or painting a picture, or doing embroidery; it cannot be so refined, so leisurely & gentle, so temperate, kind, courteous, restrained & magnanimous." But, as he continued in his commentary, "By defining our activity as revolutionary we license ourselves to engage in bitter power-struggles in the name of revolutionary criticism & correct ideology."[11]

As they had done semipublicly in the late summer of 1974, Henry Cow spent the second half of 1975 clarifying their theoretical basis. But unlike the year before, when their thinking about the music industry, audiences, and their own musical practice trickled out in scattered interviews or other press outlets, 1975 saw the band attempting to write and present a formal statement. The vehicle would be a full-page advertisement for a tour in late 1975. Hodgkinson, Cutler, and Cooper submitted drafts for review by the band, and Frith also seems to have drafted a short text. (There is no evidence that this statement was shared with his bandmates, and the drafts by Cutler and Cooper do not seem to have survived.) The "Ho Chi Minh style lang[uage]" of Cutler's submission led Frith to question its suitability, and Cooper's was agreed to be more appropriate for a program note, once revised.[12]

Hodgkinson's statement received the most commentary. It begins by declaring that Henry Cow's music is intended for working people before arguing for a revitalization of *freedom* and *progress*. Rock presents freedom in the figure of the rapist, "the freedom of the Individual to indulge his libido at the cost of others, a freedom which *necessarily* rests on the *un*freedom of others."[13] We are taught, Hodgkinson writes, that freedom is a kind of escape from responsibility, manifest in rock culture as the obsession with drugs. Music figures progress, on the other hand, as the progress of a career or the fetish of success.

> Let us speak of Freedom, not for some but for *all*, a freedom which we can only learn to develop when the relations of property & oppression are swept away. A freedom based on the recognition of the *Communist* Individual, who embraces hir social nature, as a strength, and draws from it.

> When we speak of Progress, we will not mean progress rooted in the needs & ambitions of a class elite, who benefit, & a mass who serve, but one forged by people who collectively revolutionize their society & their culture; people who understand that knowledge must replace fatalism if men & women are to wrest their futures from the uncon[s]cious forces of History.

In place of bourgeois freedom and progress, Henry Cow's music will strive toward "a joy stemming from Action & Commitment, a joy which integrates both feeling & understanding." They wished to foment a social joy, wherein individuals who had been divided by capitalism could recognize their common cause with all oppressed peoples. "We will have a meaningful Progress

& Freedom only when we work collectively & *informedly* to determine our own future."

As one might expect, other members of the band debated Hodgkinson's manifesto at some length. Cooper's minutes of the meeting capture the overall reaction:

Greaves: T's lang alienating

Frith: Both [Cutler's and Hodgkinson's] too long

Hodgkinson: Disagree

Frith: Reservations about T's passage about drugs etc. communicates fact that it is provocative rather than provoking

Krause: Necessity for warmth. found C+T too cold—C harsh

Greaves: Content music be provocative / lang as appr[opriate] veh[icle]—C's on the way there

Frith: Some unnecessarily ornate. . . .

Greaves: Imp[ortant] to put across a human way cf John Berger

Frith: But Berger avoids trap of being didactic—C+T come over as being in elevated position.—one is hyperconscious of the writer. Should be an absence of sloganism—T's full of sloganism—imp[ortant] x [not] to rely on last generation of communists for language

Hodgkinson: Lang revitalised [because of] context

Cooper: Disagree—too obj[jective] and exp[licit] argument—process of writing should be more vital

Frith: Felt closer to C's writing

Cutler: Emotionally must win people over—intellectually must antagonize them. Fundamental way of relating is affective—leads to/produces cognitive reaction.

In his own draft statement, Frith struck a friendlier balance between the intellectual position of the group and the language they might use to communicate it; his comments are also more directly concerned with the conditions of the rock industry and address fans in a more straightforward manner. He explains that since the Beefheart tour, "we have learnt to accept even less what people tell us can or cannot be done. Specifically, we have brought our activities more under our own control, we have continued to develop a more and more collective approach to what we do; and we have renewed our strength and commitment with regard to our beliefs and our music." Like Hodgkinson (and, presumably, Cutler and Cooper), he criticizes the image of "freedom" presented by "so-called rock culture." "Such freedom, like the abuse of drugs, is no more than an escape from, and a refusal to face, real conditions in the real world," he writes.

> It is not enough merely to comment on conditions that we recognise either in our personal lives or in society. To be aware of a contradiction should be to try and expose it, and to change it. Our music is for all people who are dissatisfied with their conditions and want to change them. . . .
>
> Our music represents an ongoing, collective critical process of thought and feeling—it is not finished.
>
> Our music is a celebration—let ends begin.[14]

Although Frith's involvement in and contribution to these conversations about the mission of the band seem clear enough on the evidence, he has expressed to me serious reservations: "The tone that Henry Cow adopted to speak to the press with in the period between *Unrest* and post–*In Praise of Learning* was incredibly pompous and arrogant. That was the feeling I got from it. If I read that stuff, I think, 'These humorless bastards!'"

Rock Music Is for Everyone

It turned out that none of these statements saw the light of day. According to a note by Cutler in 1981, the band had planned to take their full-page worth of advertising guaranteed by the Virgin contract to publish some version of these commentaries. "A music-paper strike put paid to the ad if I recall. . . . We were on tour in France at the time. Then Virgin cut our advertising budget."[15] Nonetheless, the surviving drafts by Hodgkinson and Frith, not to mention other statements in the press from this time, throw a spotlight on the matter of audiences and how Henry Cow conceived of their relationship with them.

As artists, they resisted the image of rebellious outsiders. "So much art has been based on the romantic picture of the individual *against* the society," Cutler told *Time Out*'s John Fordham. "But . . . creative activity is a *collective* thing, you're drawing on the community even if you work alone."[16] At the same time, however, it would be disingenuous to overstate their power to speak for that community, aware as they were that revolutionary social change would come from the working classes, not artists. Frith told Ansell, "Although our relationship to the working class, or the working class struggle, or trade unions or any actuality in that sense is very removed—we needn't pretend that we were a working class band—the statements that we are making bear a direct relation to it."[17] We can surmise that the direct relation to which Frith referred consisted of the many forms of musical dialogue that Hodgkinson had listed in 1974—those that spring up within and through open improvisation, and those that can be modeled inside of written compositions. As Cutler made clear in a broadcast interview with the BBC's Derek Jewell following the release of *In Praise of Learning*, such dialogues extended to their recorded work: "It is necessary with this record and with this music to actually become involved in it—because it lives, because it's unfinished, because there are relationships which one only notices [on a] fourth, fifth, tenth listening, and because they do all relate in a deliberate and conscious way."[18]

So even though Henry Cow, as musicians, would endeavor to extend and revise the techniques and vocabularies of musical sound, they would do so always with a view to wider social relations. In their minds, this close attention to their audience set them apart from some of their contemporaries in free improvised music. As Hodgkinson told Fordham, "The free players' model is an ideal of themselves, and ultimately of society—which is why they attach great significance to the act of playing, whether the audience like it or not. It's a very anarchistic view—an individualism which to me is suspect."[19] Frith, too, found the politics wanting. Although Derek Bailey remained a very inspiring and influential figure for the Cow guitarist, Frith commented, "he appears to enjoy a music where everyone is free to do as they want without getting in each other's way." "This seems to be the opposite of what we're trying to do. Derek also says that he's happy to play whether anyone shows up or not. That's something that we'd totally disagree with."[20] For the Cows, rock could lead to a direct engagement with questions of the social, evident in their fascination with the genre's collective production practices (rather than its myths of racial transcendence or dodgy claims to sexual liberation) and in their construal of the rock audience as a participatory, demotic grouping. Free improvisation, in their view, sought a hermetic purity that led them away from larger groups of listeners.

They felt similarly about their colleagues in more "classical" experimentalism. In a discussion about the problems of the capitalist music industry, Gerard Nguyen asked Hodgkinson if he had heard of Brian Eno's Obscure Records. Founded in 1975, the label had released recordings of works by composers such as Christopher Hobbs, Michael Nyman, John Cage, John Adams, and John White; their best-known LPs were Gavin Bryars's *The Sinking of the Titanic* and Eno's *Discreet Music*. Given Eno's prior membership in the Scratch Orchestra and Portsmouth Sinfonia, Nguyen might have thought that Hodgkinson would have a great interest in the unusual, genre-hopping label. Instead, the composer replied, "Yes, but it has nothing to do with us. We are a rock band, and we need to be in an area where people will promote our records, put them in stores where people can buy them, as rock music. . . . We believe that rock can do something; we do not want to make avant-garde music for a small minority, because rock music is for everyone."[21] He wasn't the only band member who held to this populist interpretation of rock: Frith told another journalist in early 1976, "The largest audiences are within rock and we want to reach as large an audience as possible."[22]

These comments indicate that, unlike the experimentalisms of the concert hall or jazz club, rock had not yet established a strong narrative for or anxiety about audience abandonment in the 1970s. To be sure, however, the British critical reception of German rock represented but one example of a stratified, intellectual, self-conscious connoisseurship inside rock culture, and of course one might say that rock's entire raison d'être owed to its high-status distinction from a debased and feminized "pop." These fault lines were thrown into relief in a group dialogue on the subject of MOR (middle-of-the-road) pop in the November 16, 1974, issue of *Melody Maker*. Although the conversation by Shusha Guppy, Barry Blue, and Francis Rossi ranged widely across subjects in commercial pop, a sampling of the questions asked by moderator (and rock critic) Chris Welch lays bare the anxieties then plaguing rock:

"Doesn't MOR mean a negation of progress?"
"Doesn't middle of the road mean mediocrity?"
"Don't people who listen to [MOR] prefer things to be conservative and safe?"
"Does rock still have the strength of a movement that it used to have?"
"You don't see MOR as a threat to rock music?"

"Isn't MOR the easy way out, for listeners?"

"Is there an element of snobbery in the dismissal of MOR?"

"Isn't MOR a compromise?"

"Doesn't the industry have to create a balance between what will sell anyway, and what is new, fresh and original?"[23]

Welch might have been surprised to find agreement at one point in the discussion with Shusha, the Iranian-born chanteuse who had released several albums of cosmopolitan folk in the 1970s. She even advocated for a kind of corporate-backed patronage for the most progressive and artistic rock bands: "I think the fact that the industry is doing well should help everybody. I really think a lot of the bands, have to be subsidised, there's no doubt about it. Otherwise we'll have nothing that isn't middle of the road."[24]

All told, the scattered discussion in the British press about the possible evaporation of rock audiences or the need to subsidize its most visionary practitioners recapitulated existing anxieties about the commercial basis of the art form. Henry Cow occupied a not entirely predictable position in this discourse. If the general pattern in rock equated paying attention to one's audience with abandoning one's artistic independence, then the Cows appeared not to choose either. "We don't take audience reactions at their face value," Hodgkinson said at the time. "We don't say 'we'd better not play that again because they don't seem to like it.' These things naturally do determine our next move, but not in a one to one way. It might be for instance that we decide we must do whatever it is *more* strongly in order to overcome that resistance."[25] The "audience," therefore, was not a simple category that one engaged in a single way.

Hodgkinson's populist interpretation of the genre—"rock music is for everyone"—spoke both to Henry Cow's outsider status relative to rock (as Cambridge intellectuals, and fans of jazz and contemporary classical music) and to their agonist formulation of the very category: "everyone" was not a unitary place where all agreed but a site of conflict itself. Again in comparison with the free improvisers, Cutler told Ansell, "The compromise that we have made by making records with a commercial company is one that on balance we consider to be more in our own interests at the moment. . . . You have to make allies to achieve what you want to achieve."[26] Rock may have developed a minority, connoisseur audience by the middle of the decade, and it may have been inseparable from the profit interests of the major corporations, but for Henry Cow, the opportunity offered by the sheer number of listeners there far outstripped the alternatives.

Henry Cow, Black Sheep

Contributing to the excitement of the spring months was the infusion of new skills, new ideas, and new personalities into the collective. The first of these, Maggie Thomas, would remain with Henry Cow until its last days. Born in 1947, she was the only child of a Welsh officer in the British Army and a Greek woman whom he married after the liberation of Athens. When Maggie was a baby, dissatisfaction with living in England impelled Thomas père to follow adventure and move his family to Dar es Salaam, Tanzania. Once Maggie turned fifteen years old, they returned to the United Kingdom, and she attended school in St. Leonards-on-Sea.

Within a few years, Thomas was participating in London's underground music scene. Two Americans avoiding the draft had left a box of records at her friend's house, and that collection—Zappa, Dr. John, Sandy Bull, Beefheart, Jefferson Airplane, the United States of America—"changed my whole musical life," she later remembered. Her educational career was a frustrating series of contentious negotiations. After an aborted attempt at an architecture degree at University College London, she enrolled in a course in "problem solving" (effectively industrial design) at Hornsey College of Art in 1967. She was the treasurer of the student union there when they took over the college in the protests of May 1968. (Hornsey had been the site of the most visible student strike in the United Kingdom, and the industrial design course was its crucible.) In the aftermath of those events, the college sacked many of the staff and students. In an unusual turn of events, London's Architectural Association took on the entire degree course, so Thomas ended her student career there. Although she had finished her coursework and passed the final exams, a dispute over fees meant that she left the AA with an education but not a credential.

After her experience in higher education, Thomas left for Europe, hitchhiking across the continent, settling in Morocco for a few months, then Italy for a few months more. She made her way back to London in 1971, and through a chance encounter found herself working at the Manor in the late summer of 1972—cooking and sewing curtains for its many bedrooms or sound absorbing cushions for the studio. During her time there, she grew friendly with Gong, painting part of the cover to their *Flying Teapot* album in early 1973. She continued to work off and on at the studio through 1974. By then, she was looking for a way out: she thought the Manor was being turned from a shambolic country house into something more like a velvet-lined bordello. When Slapp Happy and Henry Cow were on the premises for the *Desperate Straights* sessions, she began a relationship with Cutler, relocating to Shepherd's Bush (and eventually Walmer Road) soon thereafter. Thomas recalls that Hodgkinson expressed a keen interest in her joining Henry Cow's crew, perhaps even as their manager. That never happened—Thomas had zero desire to sit at a desk making phone calls—but she did prize the kinds of hands-on work and problem solving that were valuable on the road, so she joined the group as a cook and roadie.

Thomas knew the Cows needed another crew member, so when she bumped into an old friend, Phil Clarke, at the British Museum, she asked what he might be doing come May. He had been working as a stage manager at Joan Littlewood's Theatre Royal in Stratford, but for whatever reason, he must have been ready for a change, for he appears on the Henry Cow payroll beginning May 1, 1975. In Clarke, the band had found a steady road manager who would remain loyal to the group until the end. He was born in London in 1949, and his mother, Joan, raised him for two years on her own with little family support and no contribution from his father, whom he would never know. However, unable to cope with the conflicting demands of raising a child and earning a living, Joan placed Phil into a Catholic children's home. She stayed in contact with him and declined to give him up for adoption, but he had become a ward of the state.

Clarke experienced an unusual childhood.[27] Even at a young age, he was handsome, intelligent, and articulate, and these qualities impressed the wealthy aristocrats Edward George Hulton and Nika Yurievitch (Lord and Lady Hulton, owners of the *Picture Post*), who chose Clarke to serve as a companion for their younger son, Cosmo. Clark spent school holidays with the family, traveling to Europe with them and learning to speak French in the process. The Hultons even paid for Clarke to attend boarding school, but when they divorced a few years later, they ceased contact with him. After he left school at age fifteen, Clarke worked a number of jobs: tour guide for holidays in France, groundskeeper, stage manager at the Traverse Theatre in Edinburgh. At the time he ran into Thomas, he was back in London.

Once he joined Henry Cow, Clarke made a great fit with Jack Balchin, who remembers, "He did personnel. I did hardware. . . . He had people skills. I was not interested in people skills; I was an animal." A follower of Meher Baba, Clarke took silent days now and then on the road, and routinely presented an even-keeled personality uniquely suited to the position of road manager.

The group also developed protocols to get themselves organized.[28] Of course, they had been holding band meetings for many years, but they pursued a new level of organization in 1975. Hodgkinson would continue to handle finance, while Cutler and Thomas took care of food purchasing and preparation. Balchin was in charge of maintaining the vehicles and assisting with the PA, and Clarke arranged future gigs and tours. Frith planned navigation and estimated the time required for individual journeys, and Greaves coordinated the road crew and rendezvous between the bus and the van (with no walkie-talkies or cell phones, arranging routes and stops for both vehicles was not an easy task). Cooper would keep minutes of the meetings they resolved to hold every week or two. A rotating chairperson set the time and place of these meetings, in which every member of the troupe reported on his or her area of responsibility; anyone was welcome to introduce plans, projects, or criticisms.

Now that Sarah Greaves was handling live sound again, Charles Fletcher could focus on tasks that he felt more qualified to tackle—not just outfitting the vehicles for touring but also joining the crew as a driver and roadie. However, a motorcycle accident in late April ruled out those plans, so he advised Balchin to visit Portobello Road, where his friend, Sula Goschen, worked at the Ceres Bakery.

"Hey darling, Charles has just creamed himself on a motorcycle. You want to be our bus driver? You'd be a great bus driver!" Goschen recalls Balchin asking. Always up for an adventure, she agreed on the spot. Only nineteen years old, Goschen had led a wanderer's life. Born in Surrey to an artist mother and carpenter father, she had spent most of her first five years on the Greek island of Hydra. The family returned to England so that Sula could attend school, but she had little interest in formal education and left the country at age fourteen to work with horses in Ireland. (Her parents were bohemian enough to approve not only this course of action. They also allowed Sula's eleven-year-old sister, Mariora, to appear topless on the famous cover of *Blind Faith*. Sula had been spotted by the photographer, Bob Seidemann, on a train but was not interested in posing nude.[29])

Goschen had returned to London in 1971, working odd jobs and hanging out in the pub rock scene. She had even acquired some experience driving trucks, so when she found herself behind the wheel less than a week later, it was less distressing than it might have been. (More concerning perhaps was the organization's modus operandi: "Jack had warned me: 'Watch out. They have these meetings. I don't know what they're talking about half the time.'") In March, they bought an old school bus and paid Fletcher to improve it for touring. He removed seats at the back and installed six bunks in a double-decker "U" configuration. Between this sleeping area

Figure 5.1 The bus, 1975. PHOTOGRAPH BY SULA NICHOLS.

and the two rows of seats that occupied the front of the vehicle, he set up a modest kitchen, with a propane-powered cooker and storage for produce and dry goods. The band also acquired a new Bedford truck to haul their equipment.

In April, Henry Cow invited Robert Wyatt to join them for a pair of concerts in Paris (May 8) and London (May 21); they began rehearsing later that month. Both had new albums with Virgin to promote: *In Praise of Learning* was released during the second week of May, and Wyatt's *Ruth Is Stranger Than Richard* came out at about the same time. (Greaves had contributed bass to one song on the latter, and Frith composed "Muddy Mouse" and "Muddy Mouth" for Wyatt out of bits from his old Ottawa piece and the music for *The Bacchae*.) Richard Branson was eager to get Wyatt performing again after the great success of his Drury Lane comeback concert in September 1974. Wyatt, however, had developed a set of nerves, compounded by the small embarrassments and large inconveniences of wheelchair-bound travel. But he trusted the Cows, and warmed to the task at hand. Their set would include Henry Cow's "Beautiful as the Moon," "Living in the Heart of the Beast," "Bad Alchemy," "Ruins," "Nirvana for Mice," and "Ottawa Song" (also recycled from Frith's old composition), along with Wyatt's "Gloria Gloom," "Little Red Riding Hood Hits the Road," and the second side of *Ruth Is Stranger Than Richard*, performed as a suite.[30] Wyatt sang with Krause on some of the Henry Cow material, including bits of "Banners" and the final section of "Beast."[31]

The Paris concert was very well received—Wyatt had been a major name there since the Soft Machine days. Cutler remembered, "It was a wild success—the public applauded for about 15 minutes, forcing Richard (Branson) to come back and beg us to do more. Since we didn't know anything more we went out and played an old Soft Machine song, 'We Did It Again.'"[32] According to Frith, the greatest strength of the show was the two vocalists, who "had an extremely magnetic attraction. As a performing duo, they were stunning."[33]

Back in London, the event (at the New London Theatre, Drury Lane) was big enough to garner several lines in the *Melody Maker* gossip column, which listed the stars in attendance (including Julie Christie, Ivor Cutler, and Daevid Allen, among many others). John Fordham, the discriminating critic for *Time Out*, complained that Henry Cow "never seem to really release the enthusiasm for interplay and spontaneity that's central to the music they get their ideas from."[34] He continued, "The band has in fact become a black sheep whichever way it turns; both within rock music, which regards it as self-indulgent, disconnected, joyless and pointless, and within the jazz and improvisational avant garde, which regards it as a watered-down version of innovations that sounded better in their original contexts and the hands of tougher players."

Fordham would subsequently explain his assessment as "bewilderment optimistically veiled as cynicism,"[35] and, indeed, his review was rather positive, given the biting passage quoted above. In fact, Fordham celebrated the evidence that "some really drastic musical pioneering is at last permissible in rock," and he also faithfully reported on the "rapturous audience clamouring for encores."

In the two weeks between the Paris and London concerts with Wyatt, Henry Cow found a handful of gigs in the south of France.[36] The Virgin Agency's contact in Paris, Assad Debs, was supposed to set up a short French tour for Henry Cow after the Théâtre des Champs-Elysées concert. (Although Henry Cow had by then sworn off Virgin for procuring gigs, the Wyatt concerts were large and unusual enough that Virgin's office could indeed help.) In the weeks before the event, however, nothing had materialized; according to Maggie Thomas, Debs told them that he couldn't find any concerts and nobody was interested. Unfazed, the band dispatched Cutler and Thomas to Paris to fix the situation. After an unproductive meeting with Debs, Thomas suggested that they visit Giorgio Gomelsky, the rock impresario and current manager of Magma. Gomelsky had been an important force in galvanizing the British R&B and beat groups, and would continue to exert an influence as one of Polydor's talent scouts and tastemakers on the London scene, until a falling out with the company led him to move to France in 1969. Thomas had made friends with him during her time at the Manor, where Gong had recorded *Flying Teapot* and Magma had recorded *Mëkanïk Dëstruktïẁ Kömmandöh*, both in 1973; Magma had recently returned to the United Kingdom, performing at the Roundhouse in February 1975, when Thomas had caught up with Gomelsky and also made the acquaintance of his business partner and concert booker, Georges Leton.

Gomelsky did not receive the idea with enthusiasm, or at least not at first. "He started off by saying how impossible everything was and our music just wasn't what people wanted," Thomas remembered.[37] As the night wore on, however, he grew increasingly excited; according to Cutler, the tide changed over the course of a long conversation about music, philosophy, and politics. Eventually, Gomelsky rang up Leton and asked him to look into finding gigs for Henry Cow. Leton already knew and admired their music, and he agreed to pursue booking opportunities. In the early 1970s, Gomelsky established a network of youth houses of culture (Maisons des Jeunes et de la Culture), where midlevel bands could perform throughout France. By 1975, he had assembled a reliable, decentralized touring circuit of 120 venues, many of them associated with local socialist and communist parties.[38] Therefore, this fortuitous meeting established Henry Cow on the French underground touring circuit and forged a link to Magma, who enjoyed a large following and commanded much respect among progressive musicians on the continent—at least one of these concerts (in Grenoble) was a shared bill with them.

After the New London Theatre concert on May 21, Henry Cow embarked on a four-date tour of Holland (again, set up through their own contacts, Henk Weltevreden and Jan Smagge), and then returned again to London. They pursued individual projects here and there, but they spent most of their time getting ready for a planned tour of Italy. Some Italian journalists and promoters had heard that the two Wyatt gigs were knockouts, and they invited the combined group to put on a concert in Rome's Piazza Navona on June 27. As with France the month before, the Cows intended to use the big concert as the anchor for a longer tour. Greaves recalls, "Each day, as we were rehearsing, every gig on the list got cancelled—because there'd been storms—until the last day of the rehearsal, when there were two gigs left,

Figure 5.2 Lindsay Cooper, Robert Wyatt, and Dagmar Krause in the Piazza Navona, 1975. PHOTOGRAPH BY SULA NICHOLS.

which would hardly pay for the petrol to get there and back again. And we all said, 'Well, anybody doing anything else? We might as well just go, and see what happens.'" (In addition to storms, several gigs for the Partito Communista Italiano had been canceled because a Lou Reed concert in March had ended in rioting and injuries.[39])

Before leaving on June 19, the Cows packed up their headquarters at Walmer Road: the house was finally facing its end, so everything had to go. In order to address the issue of the disappearing tour, the musicians and crew traveled in the bus to Paris, where they had planned to rendezvous at Leton's home with Balchin and Clarke, who stayed behind to pack up the equipment in the truck. Leton appears to have set them up with gigs in Nantes (21), Paris (22), and Lyon (23), which filled in part of the gap until the Rome gig on the 27th. Balchin and Clarke neglected to tell the rest of the group that the remaining Italian gigs had been cancelled after the bus had started its journey south—Italy sounded nice, and they were afraid the band would want to turn around if they found out that the Piazza Navona gig was all they had.

Expecting at least three concerts, Henry Cow turned up in Rome, where their road manager informed them that there was only one on the books. It had also become clear that the sponsors of the event, the magazine *Muzak* and the countercultural publisher Stampa Alternativa, had turned the concert into something the Cows were not expecting. "We had originally thought that the festival was organized by a left-wing party, and it was only when we'd arrived that we realized that it had nothing to do with that; it was simply to legalize marijuana," Cooper explained to a journalist the following year.[40] According to Charles Shaar Murray, it was the first concert in Rome by an English rock act for nearly a year (Gong played, too).[41]

In spite of the confusion about the cause motivating the event and the disappointing news that they had no further gigs, spirits were high leading up to the concert. Cooper reported to her mother, "Rome is very beautiful and immensely holy, especially at the moment as it's holy year whatever that is. The gigs have been going well—tonight's is in the open air in a big square with fountains and that."[42] Navona certainly was a big square—one of Rome's largest, and on the day of the concert it filled up with tens of thousands of spectators (in my conversations with eyewitnesses, I've heard figures of twenty, thirty, and fifty thousand).

Unfortunately, the concert wasn't very good, according to many who were involved. Facing the indignities of traveling while disabled, Wyatt was not enjoying himself, and Sarah Greaves was having problems with the PA.[43] Balchin had augmented it with extra doodads so that they could

Figure 5.3 Henry Cow performing in the Piazza Navona, 1975. PHOTOGRAPH BY
SULA NICHOLS.

produce enough amplitude to fill out the open-air setting; Greaves's mixing
desk was on a platform in the middle of a sea of listeners, fifty feet away
from the stage. At one point during the gig, the whole system shut down,
sending the crew on a scramble through the crowd to check the cables that
snaked underneath. These mishaps and misgivings were kept out of Shaar
Murray's glowing review in *NME*, which also did much to publicize the line
"Death to the Individual" and contribute to the overly intellectual view of
the band in the British press. As Wyatt commented to the journalist in the
days before the concert, "Fred Frith walked straight past me yesterday. I
think it's got something to do with 'Death to the Individual'; they don't notice people, only buildings."[44]

The Piazza Navona concert made Henry Cow a lot of new friends, which
is exactly what they needed, because they were now stuck in the neighbor-
ing Piazza Farnese with no gigs to sustain them. "Thanks to Chris and Maggie's
ingenuity," Greaves remembers, they "lived off discarded vegetables from

the vegetable market for a week." In fact, there were no gigs to speak of for more than two weeks; the musicians busked on the street for cash and otherwise enjoyed getting to know the neighborhoods of Rome while they scraped by and tried to shake loose some performing opportunities from new contacts in the bustling Italian left.[45] According to a letter from Cooper to her parents postmarked July 11, the band had by then been "reduced to living on the beach there being no gigs to speak of."[46] They were creeping south of Rome toward Magliana, where they had a festival gig on the 12th. They would find two more such opportunities (in Pavia on the 13th and Taranto on the 17th) before heading all the way to Oslo for a concert that had been arranged for the 25th. Though unremunerative, this initial Italian sojourn was revelatory for Henry Cow; it allowed them to forge connections with sympathetic music fans on the left, and introduced them to an entirely new kind of gig. Cutler recalls, "We were invited to these PCI [Partito Comunista Italiano] festivals, the like of which we'd never seen. These were not club gigs, or theater gigs, or rock gigs—but big, open-air, bring-the-family events: political events with red flags flying, organized by the Italian Communist Party. It was a whole new animal." It would take a little while before their Farnese friends found Henry Cow a good string of performing opportunities, but the groundwork had been laid in early July.

The Person with the Cleanest Record: Live Sound

The long journey north—as Greaves put it, "A classic Henry Cow tour: from one gig in southern Italy to the next in Oslo"—took them through Austria, West Germany, and then Denmark. Like the skies, their mood grew darker by the day. In Rome, Sarah Greaves had told her husband that she was leaving him. It had not been an easy tour for the pair, and Sarah's short series of indiscretions with Frith had made the separation inevitable.[47] Apoplectic, John broke down on a rocky beach in Sweden. He pulled it together for the gig at the Henie-Onstad Art Centre in Oslo, after which the band and crew made their way back to London, stopping on the way for one show in Bergen op Zoom before catching a ferry to Ipswich.

On returning home, Sarah was sacked in an echo of the previous summer's events involving Cooper. She recalled, "Chris, Fred, and Tim basically said, 'One of you has got to go, and it's gonna have to be you, because we can't dispense with John.' It was fairly brutal, but inevitable given the circumstances." John has a slightly different memory: "I was completely selfish

Figure 5.4 Sarah Greaves standing at the mixing desk (*at left*), Piazza Navona, 1975.
PHOTOGRAPH BY SULA NICHOLS.

and macho about that, and said, 'I'm more important to this band than you are—you're out.'" Frith, too, regrets his contribution to this wrenching discussion. "I thought I had figured it out, but I had no clue. If I had been John, I would have punched me out, with good reason. I do not have pleasant memories of that conversation."

Sarah's dismissal from the Henry Cow organization was quick and painful; she found a new squat and learned sound engineering with Tom Newman in the studio he had set up on a barge in London's Little Venice. Eventually, she engineered live sound for the Jam Today, the important feminist rock band who were ubiquitous at women's movement demonstrations around London in the late 1970s. Meanwhile, Branson offered John his house to recover in while the young tycoon traveled to Barbados for a few months. In the midst of this enormous upheaval, the Cow visited the BBC's Maida Vale studio to record a Peel session on August 5; the stellar performance that came of it was as good a piece of evidence as any that disturbances in the band's interpersonal relationships did not affect their musical playing in a negative way.

Aside from this impressive set and the emotional disturbance set off by Sarah's dismissal, the band again had to address the live sound issue, a perennial problem that they never fully solved. The relationship between a rock band onstage and the engineer who reinforces their performance is always a vexing and volatile one; it necessarily involves great trust, because the difference between what the musicians hear and what the audience hears can be significant. And if those musicians improvise with electronics, then their momentary judgments about tiny gradations of volume or timbre can be thrown totally off if the engineer makes the wrong adjustments on the fly. As we have already seen in regard to studio recording, Henry Cow were skeptical about the expertise of rock professionals, most of whom had never heard music like theirs. A lack of experience in the industry, therefore, didn't necessarily disqualify a potential engineer, and, indeed, Sarah Greaves had compensated for her technical inexpertise by learning the band's music inside and out so that she would be prepared for its abrupt sonic shifts. But live sound mixing is very difficult to practice, because one needs to experience a variety of concert scenarios to troubleshoot problems—rehearsing sound in the same space simply doesn't prepare one for the vagaries of a concert tour. The size of a hall, the height of its ceiling, the number of reflective surfaces, the position of the stage, the location and angling of the loudspeakers, the arrangement of musicians, the size of the crowd, the volume level of the amplifiers onstage—all these variables shape the sound and produce unpredictable trouble zones in the frequency spectrum that are unique to that specific space.

Henry Cow added another variable to this equation, as Frith explains: "There was a faction in the group who wanted to have the PA behind the stage and not in front. And the logic, which was impeccable, was that if we have the PA behind us we will hear exactly the same as all the audience is hearing and we can mix our sound according to what we actually hear." This arrangement had been pioneered by the Grateful Dead, who had been performing in front of their famous "Wall of Sound" PA system since 1973, and Balchin even recalls trying to talk his way into the Dead's sound check at London's Alexandra Palace in September 1974 so that he could sneak a peek at their setup (he was defeated).

Putting the PA behind the band would not only allow them to hear the same thing as the audience, it would also eliminate the need for monitors, which were muddy and unreliable in those days. The main argument against this setup was the possibility of feedback—anytime a loudspeaker points at the microphone sending it a signal, one risks it. Feedback happened less often than one might think for Henry Cow, but in difficult rooms, the band would give up the approach and bring the loudspeakers out to the front and sides of the stage, using the old, pre-Virgin PA as a monitoring system. On these occasions, they employed postfade monitoring, which meant that any changes in the front-of-house mix were duplicated in the monitor mix. Some found postfade monitoring problematic because instruments that produced a lot of volume onstage (guitar, bass, parts of the drum set) were necessarily softer in the PA mix, which meant that a postfade monitor sound would leave out a major part of what audiences heard.

Charles Fletcher experienced the desire for postfade monitoring as a check on his own performance as much as it was a check on the audience's audition. "Oh, Chris doesn't trust me. He wants to hear what's going out there," he remembers thinking behind the mixing desk. But in the memories of most involved, all of the Cows (and not just Cutler) sought sonic perfection. The general pattern, shared with many bands, was to claim credit for the good gigs and blame the engineer for the bad ones. Goschen recalls that Sarah Greaves came in for much pointed criticism during the summer of 1975, when Henry Cow meetings began to include a period of self-criticism à la Mao. In spite of these criticisms (which often left the engineer in tears), the retrospective consensus was that the "person with the cleanest record," as Hodgkinson put it, was Greaves. Cutler agrees: "My fondest memory was of Sarah. I think we all thought Sarah had really good ears." Women were even rarer as technicians than they were as musicians in rock, which also greatly appealed to the group. Cutler remembers, "It caused the right kind of friction everywhere we went. We'd get these big guys [helping with setup] and then we'd say, 'Do what she says.'"

Her expulsion was unfortunate, then, for several reasons. Balchin saw Greaves's departure as his chance to reoccupy the position he had occasionally held in the past. He had very specific ideas about live mixing. "They talk about how, once they started recording in studios, they started writing music using the studio as an instrument," he explains. "And that was what I liked—that's how I've always felt about doing sound. It is part of the system of music production." In his experience, the band had never entirely exploited this possibility. "It's not just a question of amplifying the bassoon. It's amplifying it so that it sounds not only like a bassoon, but a bassoon that you can give the texture of being in the back of a refrigerator, or sitting in a warm, comfy sofa. . . . And that's what I'd be listening to—when

Figure 5.5 Jack Balchin, 1978. PHOTOGRAPH BY TAKUMBA RIA LAWAL.

Lindsay's playing that bassoon, it can be in both of those locations. . . . That kind of coloration—no one did that." The band held a meeting on August 6 to discuss Balchin's case to handle mixing. He gave them four reasons to trust him with the job: he was close to the music, he knew the equipment, he'd "take the music where it should be going," and he had a real desire to do it. According to Cooper's record, the "job [would] put [him] on similar footing + responsibility w[ith] everyone else." Band members debated how much technical expertise was needed for the job, and also whether Balchin had the personality and communications skills to excel in that role. While some Cows—particularly Frith, Krause, and Hodgkinson—wanted to give Balchin a chance, Cutler was adamant that he was "too emotional" and untrustworthy to do the job, and that he lacked proper communication skills.

In 2012, Balchin told me a story that gives some indication of why Cutler (and, over the years, other members of Henry Cow) questioned his suitability for live sound engineering. The band was on the ferry from Copenhagen to Sweden, and Balchin and Frith were enjoying a beer on the stern of the vessel. Behind them, and close, was a flock of seagulls that cruised near to the ship and waited for handouts from humans. It was a serene, lovely moment until Balchin drained his beer and chucked the empty bottle into the flock. Why did he do it? He has no idea. This mix of impulse, irresponsibility, and irrationality might have been present in the background of discussions about live sound. If Balchin was allowed to handle the mixer, would he suddenly crank the mains until ear-splitting feedback blew out the audience? Would he, like Phil Preston, pass out at the controls after a bottle of brandy and three pints? For an organization as critical and self-conscious as Henry Cow, either possibility likely ruled out Balchin, no matter how loyal and devoted he was in his other roles.

Above all, all parties agree in retrospect that he wanted the live sound reinforcement much louder than the musicians did. He recalls, "I always had a strong notion of what I was listening to and how I wanted to hear it. And every time I would get anywhere near that, there would be Cutler just going fucking nuts. 'Cause the first thing was, it was always louder. In order to get that tranquility in the music, you need to have a bigger dynamic—that was my main thing."[48] Postfade monitoring or having the PA behind the band would severely limit one's ability to achieve this kind of sound, which was based on producing high amplitudes. In the end, Cutler did not relent in his objections, so the band decided to search for a new engineer while also considering Balchin for the job.

To Europe: Autumn 1975

Soon enough, the band hired Neil Sandford, a theatre man who had worked as a lighting engineer at the Traverse Theatre in Edinburgh. They found him through a Virgin connection. Sandford had been on the road with the director/performer Steven Berkoff and percussionist Stomu Yamasht'a, so he was already accustomed to the hardships of touring. Thoughtful and observant, he jumped into the Cow fray right away, judging by the meeting minutes.

After a week or more of rehearsals with their new crew member, the band was again off to Italy in September 1975. Historic political and social shifts were under way in the country. In fact, Henry Cow's Italian years (they would return in 1976, 1977, and 1978) nearly coincided with the height of the fourteen-year stretch of turmoil known as the *Anni di piombo*, "years of lead," during which over twelve thousand acts of terrorism or politically motivated violence were perpetrated.[49] The majority of these incidents took the form of bombing attacks in public spaces, the primary weapon of right-wing groups that sought to discredit the left and to propagate confusion and fear among the public. The rightist forces had a real reason to fear the communists: Italy was the farthest left-leaning country in Europe, and the Partito Communista Italiano (PCI) and Partito Socialista Italiano (PSI) won the local elections in six regions across the north in June 1975. The next summer, the PCI astonished the nation by taking 34 percent of the popular vote in the national election. They soon entered a "historic compromise" with the ruling center-left coalition of the Christian Democrats. This compromise was shattered when the Second Red Brigades, a militant Marxist-Leninist organization critical of it, kidnapped and subsequently killed the president of the Christian Democrats' National Council and former prime minister, Aldo Moro, in the spring of 1978.[50]

But because they took place before tensions arose concerning the historic compromise, the late-summer, small-town festivals customarily organized by the PCI and named after their newspaper, *l'Unità*, assumed a sweet and celebratory vibe during the year of Henry Cow's first visit. And the country was ready for them: for a number of reasons, young Italians had fewer opportunities to hear rock music than many of their European peers. The music had arrived historically late, owing to the Italian music industry's structural inability to respond quickly to changes in the market. Until the 1970s, rock bands often performed only in open-air festivals, because enclosed theaters and clubs were few in number and bureaucratically controlled; the gig season, therefore, lasted only about six months.[51] Furthermore, rock had always been one style among many in the pop field, and, according to Umberto Fiori, was personified by a limited cast of characters (Elvis Presley, Neil Sedaka, Pat Boone, Paul Anka, the Platters, and Harry Belafonte) who were amalgamated indiscriminately and set against Italian light music.[52] Rock never possessed as strong an identity there as it had in other European countries; Fiori notes that listeners didn't even know how to dance to rock—the underground was marked more by rock fashion.

In the early 1970s, the establishment of the European touring circuit for star Anglo bands encountered resistance in Italy, where large numbers of listeners agitated for their right to free rock concerts. This movement, called *Riprendiamoci la musica* (let's take back the music), disrupted concerts by Led Zeppelin in 1971 (Milan), Soft Machine in 1974 (Reggio Emilia and Naples), Traffic the same year (Rome), and Lou Reed in 1975 (Rome).[53] In any case, the left parties held a number of conflicting perspectives on rock. The music was condemned as imperialist, dismissed as an attempt to hegemonize the music of the masses, suspected of producing a false generational conflict in place of the true class differences, or celebrated as the harbinger of a new youth proletariat.[54] In the wake of *musica popolare*, the robust, politicized folksong movement that had begun around 1960, more cosmopolitan popular musics represented an ambivalent politics. Italian rock, for example, moved gradually away from the blues, which, although a symbol of the struggle of oppressed African Americans, also extended the reach of the capitalist culture industries. This avoidance of the blues also helps to explain why the English progressive rock bands (Genesis, Gentle Giant, Yes, King Crimson) were so popular among the Italian record-buying public. As such groups as Area, Canzoniere del Lazio, Premiata Forneria Marconi, and Stormy Six explored Mediterranean folk styles and expanded the rock instrumentarium (mandolin, accordion, violin), they developed an indigenous, local variety of rock.

All of this recent history helps to explain why Henry Cow found such receptive audiences among the Italians. The surging sense of optimism on the left matched what Fiori calls a "music-hunger" for touring, non-Italian rock groups; furthermore, Henry Cow were sufficiently penurious to avoid *Riprendiamoci la musica* actions. Moreover, for Henry Cow, the lack of a rock industry infrastructure was more refreshing than it was disappointing. For example, Cooper told *Liquorice*, "We find it much easier abroad, because they don't have people like Melody Maker and N.M.E. journalists telling them what to think and what music they ought to like. When we were in Italy doing all the Communist Party Festivals, even in very sort of inaccessible [*sic*] districts of Italy, we were actually playing to the whole community—not just to the rock audience, and they really enjoyed it and, I don't suppose for a minute, the word inaccessible [*sic*] entered their minds."[55] The rarity of a foreign rock group performing outside of the largest cities meant that Henry Cow encountered an unjaded, open-minded group of listeners; as Frith told an interviewer a few years later, they were no longer facing rooms of nineteen-year-old men. Greaves, too, remembers, "Ancient old ladies in their black dresses, and the kids, and the goats, I mean, it was the real stuff. They'd never seen a band before, let alone a bunch of weird British people playing this weird music."

New to the band was the multiplicity of left positions in the conversation, far more than just the Soviet model. Henry Cow performed at events organized not solely by the PCI but also the PSI, Partito Radicale, Lotta Continua, and the autonomists. Everyone was discussing their interpretations of Antonio Gramsci, and there was a strong women's movement. In addition to the festivals, these smaller parties hosted all kinds of events; Sandford vividly recalls a rally for abortion rights in Genoa interrupted by a line of police who took the stage shouldering arms and demonstratively loading their rifles ("the most intimidating twenty minutes of my life," he later wrote).[56] Or the gig in Pordenone in which, following the presentation by a panel of activists advocating for a trade union for military conscripts, the crowd of six hundred uniformed young men developed an elaborate masking system to keep the identity of speakers—some of them illegal deserters—hidden from the paparazzi in the balconies. On a different Italian tour some years later, Cooper reported that their PCI-sponsored gig in Pavia was disrupted by marauding activists from Lotta Continua, Avantguardia, and Operaia, who demanded free entry and complained that the PCI controlled the cultural life of their city.[57]

Stormy Six guitarist and musicologist Franco Fabbri later noted, "After the 1975 elections, many local governments (including cities like Milan and Rome, and not just traditional leftist strongholds like Bologna) were ruled by the so-called *giunte rosse*, with PCI and PSI at the height of their collaboration."[58] This transition manifested in pragmatic terms in the institutionalization of progressive music workers into positions in local libraries, theatres, or cultural affairs departments. So even though the open-air Unitá festivals would continue to occupy a central role in the Italy's rock touring infrastructure, a number of enclosed venues gradually became available to bands like Henry Cow. In September, they started their tour in Rome (25), then drove south for feste de l'Unitá in Catania (27) and Milazzo (28), then a Partito Radicale gig in Reggio Calabria (30). After a few days off, they performed in Genoa (October 2), Milan (3), and Rome again (5). Terrible sickness overcame half the band on the beach in Ortobello, sending Phil Clarke to the hospital with suspected meningitis, but the Cow soon traveled to the northeast, playing at events in Pordenone (12) and Udine (13).

Having the bus made all of this possible, because any other form of touring would have required incredible investments in lodging or hospitality from their hosts. With crew, Henry Cow numbered ten, but they often also had fellow travelers. In the summer of 1975, the children came along, a fact that caused little concern for most but that also created some friction between the few parents and the childless in the group. Krause, for example, remembers some of her comrades taking it upon themselves to contribute to the rearing of her son; although the gesture was meant to shore up the communalism of the group, Krause often felt that it betrayed a lack of understanding about the real sacrifices a single mother had to make for her child. She comments, "Really, Max was my responsibility, but it wasn't easy to be a member of Henry Cow and a mother at the same time. I didn't have much support when all is said and done. If it wouldn't have been for Sula, who was very lovely with my son, I couldn't have stayed in Henry Cow for as long as I did." The group added to Goschen's loading and driving responsibilities the charge of childcare, and she wasn't crazy about the idea because it meant that she often had to miss the concerts. The arrangement occasionally caused other organizational problems; band meetings worked best when everybody—crew included—participated, and yet Goschen was often called on to round up the children and get them out of the others' hair at the cost of missing the meeting herself and then being insufficiently informed about the group's plans. The children, then, disrupted business as usual in this artistic milieu, where members were keen to develop healthy forms of collective work but limited in their ability to empathize and compromise with the demands of parenting. "It didn't fit," Krause remarks about parenthood. "There was no understanding at all at that stage, of what it meant to have a child. It was more of a nuisance. . . . Well, a child does cry, a child gets angry, a child might have a tantrum, or just wants to play. There was just no time, allowance, or understanding of that."

In any case, the whole Cow troupe rolled on to France. They played a few big concerts right at the start—the Jazz Pulsations festival in Nancy (October 17), a benefit for the Fourth International's newspaper *Rouge* in Paris (where they caught up with Captain Beefheart on the 18th), and the Massy Jazz Festival (25th, with Ornette Coleman, Archie Shepp, Derek Bailey, and Irène Schweizer). Following these gigs, they retreated to St. Pargoire, a country town outside of Montpellier in southern France, where Goschen's parents kept a house. Her brother, who was living there at the time, made arrangements with the local cinema to allow Henry Cow to rehearse there during the day. A local jazz booker found them gigs in the area—Carmaux (November 2), Toulouse (5), Carcassonne (6), and Montpellier (7)—while Balchin troubleshot the vehicles and Sandford tweaked the PA.

The French experience wrapped up with a scattering of gigs in Rennes (15), Fresnes (16), and Metz (22), but the most memorable was at the Sigma Festival in Bordeaux, where many of the concerts took place in the town's medieval wine caves. The Cows got to catch up with old pals from the Westbrook Brass Band, who were also performing at the festival, but it was Cooper who won the day by receiving an invitation from her idol, the great Cathy Berberian, to turn pages for her pianist.[59] The tomboyish bassoonist, however, had long given up the formal wear of art-music performance, so she donned one of the diva's extra evening gowns much to the merriment of her comrades in the band.

Banners and Beasts

To these adventures in mobile living Henry Cow added others in performance, and they anchored their thrills to the two big cornerstones of the live set during this period, Frith/Cutler's "Beautiful as the Moon—Terrible as an Army with Banners" and Hodgkinson's "Living in the Heart of the Beast." Both composers outlined new territory for collective play. Frith had written "Banners" in 1974; according to a few surviving sketches, he had been messing around with some ingredients of the song on the Beefheart tour, most notably the distinctive rhythmic profile of the "No Sun, No Birds" section (at 0:47 of the CD reissue of *In Praise of Learning*), and the eighth-note, passing-tone stutter at 4:00 (see figure 5.6 and example 5.1). Indeed, the instrumental motive at 4:00, which I consider the heart of the song, is one of the few sketch fragments that Frith identified as "Banners"—it was either the first thing he wrote, or the most important kernel of material. The rest of the song came together in Holland, on the piano of promoter Jan Smagge, with whom Henry Cow stayed during their tour in September.

Scored leanly for piano, bass, and percussion, "Banners" stands out from Frith's other compositions (and, indeed, the rest of the Henry Cow book) for a number of reasons. Frith dispenses with the more intricate counterpoint in favor of a clear and unified texture that sets Krause's voice in heightened relief. He still employs additive rhythms, but the meter changes roll by less conspicuously because the melody often consists of long note values, and, even though Frith's wandering piano line maintains a steady eighth-note pulse throughout, Cutler settles into a recurring beat only here and there. For much of the song, the percussion part stays up on the cymbals, while the kick drum accentuates note changes in the bass. These rhythmically free sections would almost have the feel of recitatives, were it not for Krause's full-bodied singing from the chest. Although "Banners" moves through a few different key areas, Frith avoids functional harmony and strong leading tones; instead, he chooses saturated chords, frequently adding sevenths and ninths. The bass pedal on E and B—the song's predominant feature—further increases tension and power in equal measure.

Frith relaxes this tension in the "Last Days" section (at 2:40) with a lyrical, diatonic vocal melody that provides a nice contrast to the voice's extreme chromaticism and semitonal motion in the rest of the song. Frequently pulling Krause up into her head voice, the calm tune could have been written by Weill in an alternate universe. In the next section (beginning 3:50), he returns to material from the earlier "No Birds, No Sun" passage, extending

Example 5.1 Fred Frith, "Beautiful as the Moon—Terrible as an Army with Banners" (*In Praise of Learning*, track 4, 4:00); transcribed from Frith's notebook, FFA.

Figure 5.6 Fred Frith, "Pigeons" sketch. COURTESY OF FRED FRITH.

it into a gripping chordal pattern that mixes major and minor modes and reestablishes intensity through repetition, a device that he had previously relied on heavily to extend his writing into longer durations—"Nirvana for Mice," "Teenbeat," and "Ruins" all burn through heaps of compositional ideas quickly in the opening minute or two, and then stretch out into a repeating vamp or cycle that becomes the basis for a solo improvisation of several minutes. Frith refines his technique in "Banners" by unifying much of the thematic material in the first four minutes; although it clearly segments into discrete sections, the work is no grab bag of frags.

With the studio version, however, he does not entirely solve the problem of repetition: bracing though it is, the vamping section leads nowhere (even though Greaves and Cutler audibly relished grooving on its alternating pattern of 14 and 13 eighth-notes). Instead, it breaks down into an open improvisation of overdubbed piano parts, as the vamp slowly fades out. In accordance with the iron law of the fade out, here the edit feels like a unsatisfactory solution. In the live version, Frith finds a better one by writing a new melody for the organ and oboe over the top of the vamp, which the composer, from the piano, quickly abandons to take up his guitar and join the ensuing improvisation. It's as if the novelty of the melody distracts us from the breakdown of the work's strong directionality. From the time of the Wyatt concerts all the way until the spring of 1976, Henry Cow often interrupted "Banners" here with a series of arhythmic unison stabs that eventually stuttered into "Nirvana for Mice." They would return to the song later in their set as a kind of lighthouse to lead them out of a storm of open improvisation; once Greaves drifted down to the B pedal, Frith eventually made his way back to the piano and the familiar chordal pattern. Soon thereafter, Cutler would lock in to the "Banners" vamp before signaling a turn to the concluding vocal section, a reprise of the dramatic "Rose Dawn" section with new words. As Greaves would put it many years later, Frith had written "a vocal piece which was neither opera, nor rock, nor song, nor anything else. . . . It was fabulous. It was fresh and new, and nobody had ever done it."

Like Frith, Hodgkinson worked with new compositional techniques in his cornerstone contribution to the set, "Living in the Heart of the Beast." A study of Rudolph Reti's *The Thematic Process in Music* had yielded a new method for organizing his pitch material. Whereas "Amygdala" had required the composer to piece together jigsaw fragments in a craze of counterpoint, "Beast" grew from a more controlled set of thematic materials. Hodgkinson developed four cells (see example 5.2), plus a fifth, referred to as "i," which, the composer noted, had derived from two of the others (a and d, though the precise derivation of a is unclear.) Beyond supplying the pitch content for actual melodic material (the opening run, for example, combines cells a, b, and c), these cells also dictate the larger form of the piece. Hodgkinson used the inversion of the first four pitches of a (A-flat, F, E, D) and the retrograde-inversion of c (A-flat, E-flat, B-flat, D) to form a "root layer" of loosely defined key areas that sound most strongly in the bass and vocal lines. (The key areas are not diatonic.) These four key-area pairs outline the four large sections of the piece (in his sketches, the composer referred to them as movements), and within each section, the tonal center "modulates" in a local manner according to the intervallic content of cell i. On this root layer, Hodgkinson builds a sequence of cells that is repeated within each large section at a different transposition level. This sequence does not precisely dictate the actual melodic content of individual melodies, but it does provide a kind of roadmap for which cell predominates in a given span of a few measures.

Each movement lasts longer than the previous; Hodgkinson called this principle "spiral growth"—like each outer turn around a spiral, every statement of the cellular sequence takes more time to complete as the composer works the material at greater length. As indicated in the example, Hodgkinson eventually eliminated the fourth movement when it became apparent that the piece would grow too unwieldy; it was already fifteen minutes long after three. In addition to this cut, he exercised free judgment in other areas: rhythm, dynamics, and articulation were essentially expressive and not systemized.

Example 5.2 Tim Hodgkinson, "Living in the Heart of the Beast," compositional structure; transcribed from Hodgkinson Notebook 6 (1974). Timings refer to CD reissue.

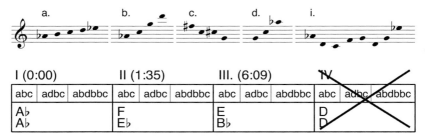

I (0:00)			II (1:35)			III. (6:09)			IV		
abc	adbc	abdbbc	abc	adbc	abdbbc	abc	adbc	abdbbc	abc	adbc	abdbbc
A♭			F			E			D		
A♭			E♭			B♭			D		

There is some jiggery-pokery to how Hodgkinson used his materials. "Beast" challenged him to think globally and integrate parts into sections into wholes, and it taught him how to unify pitch materials to a certain extent, but he also fudged here and there, revised his plans as he got further into the piece, and threw out the major formal plan when it wasn't working out as he had hoped. Most of all, he hadn't developed a musical logic of growing consciousness that could match the radical transformation communicated in the lyrics. In a retrospective report that he wrote in preparation of his next large work, he referred to a number of other faults in "Beast," including the arbitrariness of the series, the "dubious role of percussion," and the "mockery of the finale," which he later speculated might have referred to its excessive repetition and lack of a discrete ending.

But this is what we call *composing*. Hodgkinson expanded his palette and adapted his goals and design to local expressive concerns. Serial techniques created a surfeit of possibilities and problems that Hodgkinson went to work on as they excited his interest. Henry Cow loved performing the piece, which they did with great pride given the difficulty with which they learned it. Through the composition's wide leaps, uncommon intervals, and sparse repetition, Krause, in particular, expanded her musical limits. Greaves reflected in wonder on this "impossible" piece: "Textually, it was extraordinary that anybody could come up with any syllables to fit, so it doesn't really matter whether they're preposterously left-wing or stupidly naive, or just irrelevant. . . . It was original and fabulously creative."

Early in the summer, Virgin released *In Praise of Learning*, and the album garnered reviews in the United Kingdom's three music weeklies. Lake was characteristically unequivocal: "THIS IS THE ALBUM OF THE YEAR."[60] Although he had some qualifications (largely having to do with "Beast" and the overall sound quality of the album), MacDonald also praised the record as "simultaneously the group's most extreme and most accessible album so far."[61] Sounding a familiar theme in Henry Cow's critical reception, MacKinnon wrote, "I only wish I felt 'In Praise of Learning' will reach a wider audience than the group's previous recordings as it's the handful of genuinely excellent people like Cow that go some long way to justifying the existence of an often singularly uninspiring popular music field. You owe them some of your time, at least."[62] In his review in *Let It Rock*, lefty journalist Dave Laing celebrated the band for coming out as politically committed musicians and cast the record as a step "beyond all that" avant-garde cut-up stuff of the first two albums, "pointing a way forward for both avant-garde and 'committed' music in Britain."[63]

A Demonstration of Strength

In the summer of 1975, however, one listener was far more important to Henry Cow than any of these critics, and that listener was the Chilean filmmaker Alejandro Jodorowsky. With two acclaimed films under his belt (*El Topo* [1970] and *The Holy Mountain* [1973]), he was in the middle of planning his next project, a cinematic adaptation of Frank Herbert's *Dune*. As the band would soon discover, he had acquired serious financial backing. In late May, when Henry Cow were back in London, they received a call from Richard Branson: Jodorowsky was coming to dinner that evening, and they were invited.[64] Apparently, the filmmaker was a fan (it's unclear whether he attended the Paris or London concerts with Wyatt, or if he had simply heard their albums), and he wished to discuss their participation in *Dune*. According to Hodgkinson, he said, "'You are the most advanced group in the world and I am the most advanced filmmaker,' or something like that. And . . . so begins a series of peculiar meetings."

The next peculiar meeting occurred in the Piazza Navona, where Jodorowsky sat in the front row of Henry Cow's concert. Afterward, he invited them to his hotel on the square for dinner with him and his valet. Cutler stole the show with his learned and passionate conversational style; he and Jodorowsky sat next to one another, in Greaves's memory, "getting on like a house on fire!" The auteur told them that he wanted Henry Cow, Pink Floyd, and Magma each to provide the music for one of the three planets that featured in the cosmic story. And get this: he would pay them £60,000 (about £580,000 in today's currency).

With the possibility of so much cash, the Cow began discussing the possibility of buying their own communal property. Cutler, Thomas, Cooper, and Balchin had vacated Walmer Road in June, so they were searching for a long-term substitute anyway. Thomas placed a house-wanted advertisement in the *Times*, and soon received a reply from an American businessman who owned a diary farm in Stevenage. The poured-concrete structure was shaped like a cow; I am not making this up. They visited the site in early August. Cutler and Thomas were very excited at the prospect of living together as a group—they could all set up their own recording studio, maintain separate living quarters, and maybe even open a performance venue.

Hodgkinson recalled, "I was very sort of sitting on the fence about living together, you know. I mean, I kind of didn't want to."

"Me too. I didn't want to either," Frith said.

"But I thought I ought to want to."

Cutler interjected, "I can't remember what I thought."

Frith laughed, "Oh, you were all for it."

Hodgkinson said, "That was a bad time, you know—we spent a lot of time and trouble actually finding somewhere, and when we found somewhere I think I, for one, said 'God no.'"[65]

In any case, the opportunity eventually disappeared sometime after the third meeting with Jodorowsky, which Cutler attended alone at the Savoy Hotel in London. Although the two again got along well, it didn't seem to be leading anywhere. Hodgkinson remembers,

> At a point . . . , it became clear that Jodorowsky had gone silent. . . . By then I know that the Pink Floyd were doing one of the planets. I think that Fred said, "Well I suppose I could call." I forget which one of the Floyd that he'd spoken to previously about something, and I think Fred discovered that the Pink Floyd's management had said, "We're not doing one planet, we're doing the whole fucking film." So at this point we thought, ok that's it, doesn't surprise us at all. That's what you expect from these kind of people. I mean, they play golf. That says it all.

It turns out that not even Pink Floyd would get to do the whole fucking film, because Jodorowsky's financial backers lost faith in the project and pulled his funding. The film was never made.[66]

Although the collaboration with Jodorowsky had fallen through, another was in the works that autumn. Henry Cow had shared a bill with Magma a few times, and now they had begun touring on the circuit that had been established by Magma's management, Gomelsky and Leton. By 1975, Magma were the most successful rock outfit in France, and one of the few to enjoy recognition and record sales outside the country. Their music combined an expanded jazz-rock instrumentation with clear references to rhythmically propulsive, neoclassical modernism. Commentaries on the music often mention the influence of late John Coltrane, repeating statements made by drummer/leader Christian Vander in interviews and press releases over the years, but I hear little musical evidence for such a comparison on their best-known work, *Mekanïk Destruktïw Kommandöh*. Nonetheless, that album displays an unusual musical style, with continually shifting, additive rhythms, a dense orchestration, an ambition for extended compositional forms, and a small chorus that intones chantlike melodies in Vander's invented, phonetic language called Kobaïan. Vander had created an elaborate mythology around the band that involved space travel and the future of the human race. As Cutler later explained in a summary of Magma's music, "Their main text, partially translated by Vander, described the purification of a wicked and warring humanity through willing self-sacrifice."[67]

Of all the Cows, Cutler was the least restrained in his enthusiasm for Magma. The festival appearance in Paris on June 22 had made a particularly strong impression; at a concert headlined by Hawkwind, who were to perform last on the bill, Magma's formidable singer, Klaus Blasquiz, took the stage with the rest of his group, grabbed a microphone, and declared, "We are Magma. We hate Hawkwind. We will destroy Hawkwind!" After a short yelp from the vocalist, the band launched into a brilliant, bracing set that brought the audience to a frenzy, according to Cutler. He loved the audacity of the gesture, its momentary posing of a high-stakes problem that the group would have to solve right there on stage. Cutler also admired Vander's invented language and the novelty of his frame of musical reference—by avoiding lyrics in English and giving as much stylistic weight to Carl Orff or Eastern European folk music as he did to the blues, Vander seemed to stake out a position separate from—or even antagonistic to—the US/UK popular music industry. In this way, Magma scratched the same kind of itch that Faust had done.

But anticapitalism is a heterogeneous position, one that has the potential to be rearticulated into the language of anti-semitism. Vander, in fact, had been dogged by whispered accusations of neo-Nazism. Magma's visual imagery seemed to allude to fascist style in the uniformity of their black-leather wardrobe and the atavistic iconography of their logo. Their mythology, with its militaristic stories about the judgment of civilizations and their "purification," strengthened these associations. Furthermore, Vander occasionally expressed Nietzschean themes in the press, as when he told *Melody Maker*'s Steve Lake, "Most people now have too much self-esteem, believing that humans are the highest possible thing. . . . Until you reach the highest state you can get to, you are always nothing compared to the universe."[68] In light of these vague connotations seemingly offered up by Magma, their music—both in composition and performance—evoked fascism in its fetishization of strength, discipline, uniformity, precision, and control. (In fact, one Cow remembers walking to a bar with Vander before a gig somewhere in France and observing him deliver the Nazi salute to passersby, almost as a joke.) This interpretation circulated in the 1970s to a sufficient extent that Cutler would make a passing but direct reference to it in his appraisal of the band in 1979: "Were Magma fascist? Was it true that Christian had learned Hitler's speeches and sometimes declaimed them in Kobaïan at concerts? Rumour and speculation were rife and these as well as the black clothes, the discipline and the 'spiritual radiance' cannot be divorced from their unquestionably progressive cultural position."[69]

But Vander had defended Henry Cow in a very public fashion that autumn. After *Best*'s Hervé Picart called the Cow's music "nothing but sound effects and rehashing of free jazz and other contemporary experimental artists," Vander excoriated the journalist in a vitriolic letter to the editor that October.[70] On October 22, the band held a meeting to debate the question of touring with Magma.[71] Cutler and Leton had suggested that the two bands collaborate on new pieces written for both bands. (In fact, Frith's 1975–76 musical sketchbook includes some jottings of possibilities for a "piece for us and Magma.")[72] Cutler argued strongly for the plan—the two groups had a common enemy (presumably, the press and rock industry), and it was important for Henry Cow to make allies; Sandford and Balchin also seemed open to the idea. Hodgkinson and Cooper were not convinced; why the need for an alliance, and why base that alliance on a "common enemy"? Furthermore, Hodgkinson continued, it would be confusing—it was important for the Cows to make it clear where they stood, and Magma were "putting across a negative, unpleasant ideology." In fact, rather than sharing an enemy, "Magma and us could well also be enemies."

Cutler didn't think that the source of Vander's strength was fascism; instead, he thought that his confused language led to misunderstandings and indefensible ideas. In any case, Greaves said, they should stay in contact with Magma because they were the only band doing anything of value

Figure 5.7 Henry Cow, 1975. PHOTOGRAPH BY SULA NICHOLS.

in the "rotten rock field." Hodgkinson disagreed—what about the Magic Band? Cutler thought that Henry Cow had "advanced" beyond Magma and the Magic Band because they had no leader, but nonetheless they lacked the strength of those groups. Hodgkinson wondered if he was confusing "strength" with "leader." Cutler clarified that he was referring to the example of Magma following Blasquiz's criticism of Hawkwind with a strong set. "We're not strong enough to do that," he said, to which Hodgkinson again disagreed.

He was "dubious about the desire for a demonstration of strength," and disliked its Nietzschean undertones, but Cutler countered that "demonstrated strength lends weight to arguments."

"The weight comes from the argument being right," Hodgkinson responded.

"We are involved in an active struggle, so the display of strength is important—otherwise we would be writing tracts, intellectualizing, and so on. But we are working in an artistic, and therefore emotional, field," Cutler said.

The two continued to debate the place of emotion in music making for a few minutes, with an occasional interjection from Cooper, until Greaves cut in to point out that the purpose of the meeting was to discuss advertising for their upcoming English tour, which concluded the immediate discussion. In the end, Henry Cow decided against touring with Magma.

The Cows often focus on the question of power when they think back on the possible association with Magma. The French band could present a forceful and unified set because their leadership was forcefully unified in the figure of Vander. "I mean, their performances were perfect," Frith explains, but "our strength wasn't in that kind of performance. We had it occasionally with Dagmar in the period doing 'Living in the Heart of the Beast,' but I think we were much more interesting . . . when we were the more experimental." Here, the guitarist uses *experimental* to refer to the kind of risk that comes with *dissipated* intensity, not its opposite. Krause herself expressed a similar preference for the uncertainties of Henry Cow's mode in her criticism of Magma: "It didn't feel as if there was any improvisation in Magma. It was a really well thought-out and completely solid set. To me, it seemed there was nothing left to chance." Again, "solidity" led toward intensity but also away from the unexpected.

When I asked Cutler if he thought Magma represented the "next level" of professionalism that Henry Cow might aspire to, he clarified, "I don't think so, no. We were musically chaotic. We improvised all the time. . . . We were never going to be immaculate like Magma. And . . . they were organized by other people. That wouldn't have been a next level for us." Without a strong leader, Henry Cow was chaotic, improvisational, inefficient—but autonomous. They *weren't* organized by other people, professionally or musically, and this value perhaps remained the one that trumped all others.

Following their long stay on the continent in October and November, Henry Cow planned to return home for a thirty-date tour of the United Kingdom. Clarke had begun putting together the dates before the group left the island, and passed along the handful of leads he already had to one Carol Cruiser, a new acquaintance who was starting her own booking agency. By late November, when the Cows were still in France, it was becoming clear that something was very wrong—having not heard much for several weeks, Clarke pushed Cruiser to produce contracts from the venues. She gave him sixteen of them, but after making a few telephone calls, Clarke determined that the contracts were forged. There was no tour—nothing. It was a known scam at the time to advertise a concert somewhere without gaining a college's approval, and then when the audience and the band showed up on the day of the gig, the institution had no choice but to host the event. Because their reputation was at stake, Clarke scrambled by sending letters to social secretaries at all the universities involved, explaining what had happened and asking if they could go forward with their plans. Only one or two gigs were salvaged.[73] The band did put together a handful of gigs around London in January. The audience for one of them, at Kingston Polytechnic, included the composer Michael Tippett, who was Caroline Ayerst's godfather. In any case, the Cruiser debacle would be the last time Henry Cow considered touring extensively in the United Kingdom; their future would be in Europe.

Time and Space for Everyone

In spite of their continuing frustrations with the British music industry, Henry Cow remained optimistic through the winter holidays. Hodgkinson had begun working in earnest on a large-scale piece that would become his follow-up to "Living in the Heart of the Beast," and Frith was also writing a big piece, though not the one he envisioned in the late summer of 1974.[74] They were playing some of their best live shows in recent memory, and they had forged what would become lasting and important touring networks in France and Italy.[75] In fact, in the minds of most Cows, the short year that began with the Wyatt concerts was the peak of their career together. As we have already seen, their experience with the Italian festivals stood out. Krause remembers, "To play these was completely heavenly and enchanting. . . . Obviously, our music was far from easy listening—no popular music here by any stretch of the imagination. And they were so receptive. . . . all these people standing there and listening and clapping and liking it?"

"It's right," Cutler agrees. "I also look back on this and think, 'That was a great period, for about a year.' When we were in Italy we had a clear run, in part because of the environment: Italian sunshine, summer, big festivals, being treated as comrades, getting up, doing our thing, being generally fit and well fed; and Dagmar absolutely on the case. You can map the fortunes of later Henry Cow through Dagmar's health. As things start to deteriorate, Dagmar gets ill." As it happened, Krause would get ill and stay off a tour in the spring of 1976, perhaps—however unconsciously or subliminally—in response to the surprising announcement by Greaves that he was leaving the band.

Since they returned to London in late November, the bassist had been ping-ponging from Branson's abode to Balchin's squat. Generally adrift, his commitment to Henry Cow had been fading for months. The events surrounding Sarah's expulsion surely hung in the background, but Greaves recalls that he came to his decision simply by observing the very different directions—musical and ideological—he and the Cows were headed in. He later wrote, "The image of Daggie fist raised in Taranto singing 'Now Is the time . . .' was and is extremely powerful. I guess I just wasn't convinced."[76]

In late March, Henry Cow traveled to Hamburg for a one-off gig for the NDR Jazz Workshop that would be Greaves's last. In the weeks before, they had begun rehearsing some newly composed music. One time through passages from Hodgkinson's new piece, which was the most difficult music they'd ever seen, was enough to convince Greaves that it was time to leave. Although he had great respect for Hodgkinson's artistry, his musical preferences were leading him elsewhere. Balchin remembers that "he never felt that the pieces he was writing were Henry Cow music," but other evidence suggests that Greaves's bandmates were less than encouraging, too. In an unpublished account, Hodgkinson wrote, "John feels that he cannot realize his potential inside the group. He writes songs, but they are often rejected by the rest of us as inappropriate, peripheral. He is very close to Peter Blegvad: working with Peter gave him something that he never found in the group."[77]

Written at the emotional low point in the early posthistory of a broken Henry Cow, Hodgkinson's recounting is the most pessimistic of his colleagues, but also the most revealing. He writes,

> John announces that after much thought he has decided to leave the group. What shocks me most is that Fred and Chris regard this as a positive step for him & us. . . . Why does John want to leave? What thoughts occur to us as we listen to him quietly speaking of the other life he will have outside the group? . . . John has always admitted more readily than the rest of us to wanting "straight" success. Now it's coming & he seems to want no part of it. [In apparent parody of the opinions about Greaves: "]John is fundamentally a romantic, a weak character, he can't take it, he can't make the grade, he doesn't struggle enough.["] John is least at home in the language of intellectual cover-up. He is no less insecure than the rest of us but his own working-class background inclines him to express it in different ways. He feels mistrusted, despised, the undeserving butt of criticisms he cannot answer in ways legitimized by the group.[78]

As we will see in the coming history, Hodgkinson attributed much of the group's internal struggle to the problem of repressed emotion and its source in English middle-class social mores, especially those of men. "When a long-standing member leaves a group, this is the clearest sign of a deep contradiction that the group as it was cannot contain," he wrote a the time. He thought that this "emotional concealment & distancing" was "fairly universal" for English men. Although Greaves's working-class background, according to Hodgkinson, allowed him to be less inhibited than the rest of the Cows, it also meant that he possessed little interest in the Maoist discourse that governed the group.

If it had only been dissatisfaction with Henry Cow, then Greaves might have found a way to address the problem inside the group. But he had also been captivated by the process of working with Slapp Happy, and, as Hodgkinson noted above, Blegvad in particular. "I loved him from the moment I set eyes on him," Greaves remembers. "I remember thinking, 'That's the second genius I've met. I'm lucky I've met Fred, and now there's the second one.'" In fact, while we have tended to view the Slapp Happy merger from the perspective of Henry Cow and their acquisition of a vocalist, Greaves offers a parallel narrative that leads to his subsequent, separate collaboration: "We basically stole Dagmar, and that was the object of the exercise. We got Dagmar, and I got my lyricist. I stole Peter from Anthony, killed Slapp Happy stone dead."

The bassist and composer had been writing music for what would eventually become *Kew. Rhone.* (1977) since late 1974, or even earlier if one traces the many permutations of the "Kew. Rhone." melody. Sandford told me that he and Balchin were in the habit of loading the piano at the back of the Bedford truck, so that Greaves could climb up after a Cow gig, lower the gate behind him, and puzzle out his intricate melodies in the dark. A few months after his withdrawal from the band, Greaves traveled to New York, where he reunited with Blegvad and hashed out the rest of the album. Virgin had given them a contract, with a small budget for recording. They produced the record at Carla Bley and Michael Mantler's Grog Kill Studios, in Woodstock, later that summer. (Lisa Herman sang the material admirably, but Greaves and Blegvad had originally asked Krause, who agreed but eventually backed out.)[79]

According to Cutler, Greaves's exit was "a major turning point" for Henry Cow. "That was when the group sort of broke up, for me." This wasn't how they behaved at the time, Cutler clarifies—they were still getting on with it, picking up the pieces and searching for their next problems. "We had an invisible foundation, built on rock pillars, and one of them had just collapsed. That made it tough for whoever replaced John—actually almost impossible. There had been a mechanism, not that we were aware of it—a sort of tolerance—that cushioned our differences; a recognition that the game was worth the candle which, in retrospect, it'd be a bit strong to say it was shattered—but it never really recovered from John's departure." As the warm, welcoming heart of the group, Greaves softened the sharp edges of his colleagues. As Sandford says, "John was the calming influence without whom it all would have fallen apart long before. . . . Nobody disliked him. He had time and space for everyone."

Difficult for everyone, the loss weighed most heavily on Krause. "I should have left at the same time. For me, after that, nothing was ever the same again. Maybe it was sheer coincidence, I don't know. Because we all went through different things, obviously. But I remember that then life became hard for me in Henry Cow. I thought John was such a vital ingredient. Foremost his writing, which I hoped was going to take a greater hold, but as well his personality. I just really liked him a lot and loved his bass playing." Concurring, Frith offered his own observations on Greaves and Krause: "I think we all had a—I certainly ascribe this to myself—a tendency to extreme self-righteousness. . . . John didn't have that and I think Dagmar appreciated that. So when he was gone, that was a very important kind of anchor in the group for a certain kind of normalcy, somebody who actually drank and . . . generally enjoyed himself. . . . I would imagine that it may have been harder for her than it was for us. Not that it was easy for us, but we were busy being pragmatic as usual." As we will see in the next chapter, the Cows had reason to embrace pragmatism with speed: they only had about a month before touring was to begin again.

6   The Roads Leading to Rome | 1976–77

We might venture that the full repercussions of John Greaves's departure from Henry Cow took many months to manifest. In this chapter, we will come to a series of disagreements and turmoils in the group that surely stemmed from several independent causes, among them the loss of Greaves's emotional warmth. Although I will detail some of the local and recent causes of those turmoils, my main interest will be to isolate and describe a specific quality of the band's internal relations that I will call *contraviviality*. This quality calls forth the adversarial associations of any experiment: one tests the world, one tests one's collaborators, one tests oneself. Contraviviality describes an improvisational stance of living that matched the musical form of Henry Cow's modus operandi: to knock the environment about, forcing action.

Greaves was gone, but in the spring and summer of 1976, there were too many new problems to address—the search for a new bassist, a new live double album, the follow-up to *Guitar Solos*, some other personnel changes—for Henry Cow to dwell on the loss. Most pressing was a Scandinavian tour fast approaching. Their contact in Oslo, Frode Holm, had organized a ten-date excursion in Norway, Finland, and Sweden for May. They briefly considered acquiring a new bassist for these concerts, but dropped that plan when Dagmar Krause came down with bronchitis. (It was an unusually hot and hazy spring in London, and respiratory problems were widespread.) Without their vocalist, it made no sense to persevere with the standard set, so the remaining quartet made the drastic choice to scrap what they had and assemble an entirely new improvised piece.

Surprising and inventive, their solution integrated improvisation with tape work in a manner we've come to expect from the group. Prior to the tour, Fred Frith, Tim Hodgkinson, and Lindsay Cooper each created tapes of about ninety minutes. Frith recalls, "We came up with this idea that each of us would have our tape output going through a volume pedal. And that we would all synchronize, press play at the beginning of the concert. And then whenever we felt like bringing the volume pedal down, we would. And we would just improvise. So the idea was that the sequence would always be chronologically intact but then we would hear something different in the sequence every time we did it." The unifying theme was a ritual narrative of genesis and development, and each tape articulated this theme in the terms of a different subject area: language and myth (Hodgkinson), childhood to old age (Cooper), and music/Henry Cow (Frith). The details of Hodgkinson's and Cooper's tapes have been lost, but they both likely contained a fair measure of spoken word. Frith's notes indicate that his tape combined natural sound-effect recordings, folk music, workers' songs, and Henry Cow's back catalogue.

They performed their set of about two hours in the dark or by candle-light; although audiences could not see them clearly during the concert itself, they would learn, with the raising of the lights at the gig's conclusion, that the band had been made up with primitivist face-paint and perhaps costumes (memories are vague on this point). This atavistic masking, of course, took the band back to their earlier historical associations with the Dadaists and futurists, who routinely folded such primitivisms into their avant-garde iconoclasms.

Jack Balchin, who handled live sound for the tour, brought up a recording of birdsong in the PA prior to the band's appearance onstage; someone (probably Chris Cutler) read a short introduction for several of the concerts:

> What we are going to attempt to do tonight is to DRAMATISE our origins, & the history & origins of music itself by creating a world out of SOUND, a world which is self-contained & coherent, & which relates to the material world & the world of the senses only in terms of its SOUNDS—sounds which come from ALL human experience—including imagination. At first this is RITUAL—we draw from the world in order to control it, while in essence we are part of it—but, in as much as we do control it, inasmuch as we organise & reorganise it using a COLLECTIVE Dialectic—then it is DRAMA & it is MUSIC.[1]

Without exception, the music began with drum and pipe. According to a live recording, Chris Cutler kicked off the Trondheim concert with a thunderous strike of his drum and a shriek of Jurassic proportions. His opening wail soon settles into an imitative, avian chirping and then a kind of staccato incantation that reminds one strongly of Magma's Christian Vander. After about a minute, Cooper joins on recorder.

Although Henry Cow repeated this initiatory pairing for every concert, the set was basically an open improvisation. There were two other episodes, however, that they purposefully inserted into each performance, the first being a frenetic blare, led by Frith on tubular bells, that the quartet referred to as the "wedding." It usually popped up about one-third of the way through, in Cutler's memory, and may have originated from a snippet of Eastern European wedding music brought into the mix from Frith's tape. The musicians also concluded every set with an episode called "The March," a lovely snippet of music that had been written by Frith and would stay in the Cow's repertoire for years; it was a very useful musical tool for ending a long improvisation. Sketchbooks indicate that the composer had intended this material for another large-scale work that never came to fruition.

The final distinctive feature of these performances were the text recitations delivered by Cooper and Hodgkinson. Cooper read selections from Adrienne Rich's poetry during the course of the piece, and one undated recording from this tour also reveals her intoning Robin Morgan's "Monster."[2] The delivery of radical feminist texts from a rock stage was distinctive enough in early 1976, but the specifically lesbian themes of Rich's mid-1970s poetry would have charged Cooper's recitative contribution in powerful ways. An explicit cultural politics of lesbian identity had already begun to appear in the folk and singer-songwriter areas, and Pauline Oliveros had, by the mid-1970s, also articulated a lesbian avant-garde practice to the new age side of the late counterculture. But the rock milieu, especially the exploratory rock of Henry Cow's network, remained a strongly masculinist, heterosexual space. As we will see, Cooper's lesbian-identified feminism would develop more explicitly in the Feminist Improvising Group, which she would cofound about a year and a half later. For his part, Hodgkinson seems to have written and spoken his own text that collaged verbiage from a range of religious, literary, and anthropological texts, including those by Thomas Mann, Joseph Campbell, and Elias Canetti.

Cutler later wrote that this tour "cost us a lot of potential popularity in Scandinavia," and the press, though slim, would appear to confirm his assessment.[3] Whether or not the Scandinavian performances measured up to *In Praise of Learning,* they appeared to retreat from the strong and clear message of that record and the tours that immediately followed its release. Although they were searching for a model of music making tied to ritual and fundamentally distinct from the commodity form, and in this way the project was still anticapitalist, one of their comrades on the Italian left might have wondered if the presentation erred on the side of the mystical. "Ritual was the thing," Cutler explains. "And that wasn't remotely to do with politics. If anything, it was prepolitical. . . . These days, music, if it's not for dancing, is for concerts—an object of contemplation. We were trying to make this series of concerts more like rituals, more mysterious, more unaccountable: strange sounds coming out of the dark." To a certain extent, circumstances necessitated the turn away from politics, since the Cows were scrambling to get a show together. But as with the Dutch quartet tour two years earlier, the risk of this improvisational set thrilled the musicians and made a lasting impression. Frith remarks, "I remember it as being one of the most extraordinary tours we ever did. I felt like that we were doing something that was genuinely new by any standards whether we were a rock band or anything else . . . —the whole question about appropriating other peoples' music, you know, all the things that came up later were something to debate. It's all in there."

Another Version of Ourselves

While Henry Cow performed in Scandinavia, Krause attended Maggie Nicols's vocal workshops at Oval House, South London. Her first short year with Henry Cow had been enormously gratifying, but she hadn't been joining in much during the open improvisations. She recalls, "I was sort of thrown into the deep end, really. How brave are you going to be, Dagmar? Are you going to make some sounds? I was constantly trying to see how I could fit in with what was being played." According to Hodgkinson, her character-based approach to singing might have made it more difficult to engage improvisationally: "Dagmar is almost like a Stanislavski-method person. [But] the improvisation isn't giving you any dramatic role in particular, so you have to conceive that yourself and you have got to learn to do that. I think improvisation is very difficult to do. . . . It's a struggle to do something half decent and I think someone like Dagmar would feel that."

In any case, Nicols's vocal class had earned a reputation as a welcoming and productive setting for working on improvisation; like Cooper several years before, Krause figured that she could develop some techniques. Nicols's recollection many years later also indicates that her Oval House sessions offered opportunities for women to support one another. She remembers, "[Krause] was definitely in Henry Cow when she came, and having a hard time. . . . At one point, she was in tears. We got close emotionally, because she needed support from another woman, really. I got that sense.

Cause they were quite hard-line in them days, the Henry Cow men. They were. They've softened immeasurably. I think the women's liberation movement had an impact on that." Nicols's approach centered on breathing exercises as a way to liberate the voice, and Krause came away from the sessions with greater confidence and a more diverse palette of vocal sounds.

As her time in Henry Cow wore on, however, Krause grew skeptical about the "freedom" claims of improvisation. "Maybe I was a reluctant improviser," she speculates, "because when you get to know people quite well, you know immediately how the next improv, what sounds they're going to make. I had problems with that, you see? You'd say, 'Oh, now he's gonna do that.' It became familiar, and I didn't really think what was new that I had to add, and did I actually want to mix with these people?" As this comment suggests, the tension between novelty and predictability emerged as a problem for Krause. "Improvising is great, and it *is* a new language. But, you know, sometimes it felt to me like 'bish, bash, bosh.' I'm sorry, that's what it felt like to me. I couldn't hear anything new after a while, coming out of there. It was never all exactly the same, but it was predictable nevertheless."

These observations raise interesting questions not only about open improvisation as a practice itself but also about the different conditions in which the practice exists. Predictability means one thing in relation to the general musical practice that had arisen in the 1960s—"That saxophonist is simply regurgitating all of Coltrane's licks; it's so predictable." It means something else in the context of a collective or band, where individuals build up a repertoire of sounds, sequences, and techniques in continuous dialogue with their comrades. They forge these sonic relationships over the course of a single set, from night to night, on a four-week tour, over an entire season, year, or even—in the case of Hodgkinson and Frith—most of their adult musical lives. Within this frame of reference, predictability more often means something like, "Lindsay is about to do that honking thing again."

In the jazz-affiliated British free improvisation scene, players did work in stable groupings, but just as frequently they operated as free agents who met up with collaborators for a single concert or short run of dates. (AMM were an important exception to this general rule—they rarely played with others.) The members of Henry Cow, on the other hand, rarely broke off to perform with others on their own. This difference between improvisation as a kind of encounter with other individuals and improvisation as a type of ongoing, collective work was highly significant for some members of the band. For Cutler, the life of the group, exceeding its individual members, "must be held to have had an actual existence and . . . was our great strength if we had any strength."[4] Other great groups, he explained, never realized what they had—Zappa dissolved the Mothers of Invention because he wrongly concluded that his singular musical ego was responsible for the band's success, rather that its collective dynamic.

The Cows also valued the permanence of their collective because they thought it created the conditions for a thorough, empirical exploration of musical possibilities through improvisation. In particular, they thought that group stability enabled an attention toward structure that would otherwise be lacking. Cutler told one journalist at the time, "When you subsequently look at a stretch of our music you can see structure in it—because unlike a lot of the improvising musicians, we're a *regular* group. So a vocabulary and a language builds up."[5] Krause heard the predictability born of repetition as a kind of failure for improvisation, an indication of what that practice might represent to someone coming from the world of song. Some of her colleagues, however, might repeat old material not because they had run out of ideas, but rather because they wished to return to an earlier arrangement of personalities, instruments, and sounds, in order to try out a different solution to the problem posed by that arrangement. They wanted to work with something that was half-known, something at hand that could lead further afield. In 1984, when Trond Garmo noted a few correspondences in Greaves's piano playing on two different recording sessions, Hodgkinson replied, "He probably used the same harmonies for about three years. When you're improvising there's no knowing that you won't actually refer to something that perhaps you are working on at the time—some chord that is in the back of your mind. Why not? If it works—it's still spontaneous, I would say."[6]

Later in the conversation, Garmo asked if Henry Cow used free improvisation to find new sounds. In his subtle response, Hodgkinson clarified how he understood their practice. "The purpose of improvisation is to enable you to explore different sounds. . . . I mean, I don't really like to experiment in front of [the] public. I am taking risks in front of [the] public, but I'm not experimenting, cause I want to give people something that's worth listening to."[7] The composer put the pursuit of new sounds into the service of creating good musical compositions, while the threat of exploration for its own sake could emerge as easily from written composition as it might from improvisation. In Hodgkinson's open improvisation, musicians risk giving a bad performance or generating a musical structure that fails to cohere—one should distinguish this kind of "taking a chance" from other varieties of uncertainty.

Cutler explained in 1980, "We improvised, as it were, collective compositions. This is how we tried to see our improvisations and how we tried to

Figure 6.1 Tim Hodgkinson, 1975. PHOTOGRAPH BY SULA NICHOLS.

realize them although we didn't always succeed."[8] Indeed, Cutler, Hodgkinson, and Frith often described improvisation as a form of collective
composition, a concept that served as the group's bridge between improvisation and recording. In both cases, the musicians searched for sounds
and then worked on that material in the medium itself (be it magnetic
tape or live performance). Moreover, their experience in the recording
studio prepared them to think of improvisation as the combination and
transformation of elements in a sonic texture, often conceived in layers
(or even tracks). In his notes for the first quartet tour in autumn 1974,
Hodgkinson referred to the sections of structured improvisation they had
prepared with the language of tape work: "blocks" and "fades." The plasticity of improvised sound implied here extended to how some Cows thought
of their instruments—recall Frith's goal of "expanding what a guitar can
do"; he conceived of his instrument as a physical site of exploration, indeed
an almost spatial array of possibility. Occasionally, even the live engineer
worked directly on the sound with a view to affecting the emergent composition; Neil Sandford told me, "You could see them struggling to find the
next landing point. And occasionally I'd kick it along by draining all the bass

out of the sound just to make what they were doing so horrible that they had to go somewhere else."

One consequence of the plasticity of Henry Cow's improvisation—or its material (and conceptual) entanglement with the instrument and the recording apparatus—was an interpretation of their work as empirical, pragmatic, unsentimental, and nonexpressive. In a 1981 letter, Frith invoked the concept of expression in relation to his musical practice, but attached the idea to his *instrument*, rather than to himself: "I play the guitar, + I regard everything I've done as part of a logical step by step extension of the guitar's expressive possibilities, + I mean expressive in the broadest possible way. And the process continues. I'm not 'looking' for anything. I'm playing the guitar."[9] Hodgkinson wrote at the time, "We rejected the Cagean philosophy that chance itself can give rise to music of value, & of course we also rejected any individualist or romantic idea of self-expression, or arriving at the essence of Freedom with a capital F, or any religious ideology."[10] As Cutler explained to Fordham in 1976, "There's no magical telepathy—the thing is very practical in that one is responding every second to the material situation being created by everyone else."[11] They weren't bonding directly through sound: those bonds were continually broken, strained, or revised by other players, the felicities of the instrument and audience, or the elaborative and disruptive potentials of tape. For Cutler and Hodgkinson in particular, this arrangement of forces interdicted the transparent assertion of individual identity—the group labored together on a collective sound instead of expressing their musical personalities in concert. In other words, they related to emerging material, not to each other.[12] Cutler explains, "There were certain things that certain people could be relied on to do at some point, but, in practice, I had no sense of personalities when it came to improvising in Henry Cow. I thought 'guitar' rather than 'Fred,' 'organ' rather than 'Tim'—if I thought at all, or distinguished one sound from another. So, I knew that there was agency behind a sound, but that agency didn't really appear to me as agency."

George E. Lewis has labeled this perspective "Eurological."[13] In his view, Cutler, like other European and Euro-American purveyors of musical spontaneity, divorced sound from the individual identity that might have produced it. Afrological improvisation, on the other hand, holds firm the connections between personal history and musical utterance, enabling an expansion of the self through sonic communication. Lewis's analytical distinction can help clarify the particularities of Henry Cow's practice of improvisation and the challenges it posed, for one cannot consistently classify them at either of his heuristic poles. Although the band continually resisted the discourse of personality in a manner akin to the Eurological, they also asserted the importance of history and cultural context in a characteristically Afrological manner by refusing to separate their music from the historical conjuncture that produced it. They discussed these social and cultural circumstances doggedly with each other and in the press. Furthermore, despite their suspicions of the link between sound and person, the group never expressed a wish for the "pure spontaneity" that Lewis pins to the Eurological mode. In fact, they asserted the opposite in their persistent returns to different forms of repetition. Their formative affinities for the Afro-diasporic genres of pop, rock, and jazz endured as cycles, vamps, and loops in their composed and improvised music. As in other Afrological approaches to improvisation, these repetitive techniques provided a springboard for invention.[14]

In his description of the field of "improvised music" that emerges in the 1970s, Lewis emphasizes the continuing salience of the Afrological in that field's staging of intercultural encounter. In a quietly surprising turn, however, he shifts the Afrological's manner of operation away from the reiterative announcement of a kind of personal truth and toward a more provisional imitation of some other form of subjectivity that can be essayed only through invention—a speculation or fictionalization, one might say. This shift has scarcely attracted notice. In improvised music, Lewis writes, the expansion of the self encompasses "not only the formation of individual musical personality but the harmonization of one's musical personality with social environments, both actual and possible."[15] To harmonize one's musical personality with an environment, the author implies, is to deform it in concert with an emerging ensemble of forces, yet unknown: "The possibility of internalizing alternative value systems is implicit from the start. The focus of musical discourse suddenly shifts from the individual, autonomous creator to the collective—the individual as part of global humanity."[16] In Afrological traditions, awareness of one's own positionality in that music leads necessarily to the realization of other positions. Although Lewis doesn't pursue this argument, one might conclude that an improviser who has internalized "an alternative value system" engages in something other than "self-expression." But what does the "internalization" of another value system entail? And what is the nature of this otherness? The example of Henry Cow suggests that the answer has less to do with the movement from one established subjectivity or position to another, and more to do with an otherness within the self that is revealed, worked on, and transformed through improvisation.

In his own view of jazz history, Cutler makes an argument similar to that of Lewis, but he substitutes externalization for Lewis's internalization:

"Well there's this great lie that jazz—especially jazz—is about expressing yourself as if you were such great shakes that it mattered about you expressing yourself," the drummer remarked in an interview in 1980. "What it's really about is working in a group and about constructing music that's got content—that's got something to say. You are not the content. . . . If you go back to the older jazz and the real jazzers like the Coltrane Quartet or even Sun Ra now, nobody's expressing themselves in those groups—everybody is serving the music in a real sense."[17]

These real jazz musicians, for Cutler, succeeded because they humbled themselves and served the music as an external entity, rather than expressing their individuality from the inside out. This variety of self-abnegation, rooted for Cutler in Afrological musics, also differs dramatically from the Cagean model that figures so prominently in Lewis's analysis. Cage's sonic quietism aimed to ready the self for whatever sounds may come, while Cutler's jazz improviser refuses the self to support an emerging musical totality that exceeds the contributions of its individual musicians, and deforms their existing formations of personality.

In a permanent, ongoing group, Cutler reasoned, leadership is shared among all the members at different times, when an individual innovation passes into the "group ontology" to be taken up by others, only to turn around later and pull that original musician in a new direction. This description of the power arrangements improvised by Henry Cow maintains the distinction between individual and group as well as the importance of a single musician's distinctive contribution, but it does so without recourse to the language of personal expression and authentic identity. When Cutler pulls a piezo–contact mike through a pile of chains and then routes that signal through an echo unit, the sound that results might express an agency, but it is not Cutler's alone, and its relationship to his personality is obscure at best.

Lewis critiques the Eurological dismissal of musical personality as one example of the false autonomy of post-Kantian aesthetics, which would claim that a music's validity inheres in structure, not the identity, values, or habits of its creators.[18] Although these responses to the ideology of autonomy have carried great weight in music studies, Cutler and Hodgkinson's scattered comments and writings on the matter of personality, identity, and self-expression illuminate another path that begins from a skepticism about identity rather than its affirmation. Like many Marxist thinkers on aesthetics (most notably Theodor Adorno), they presumed that music, self, and society were inseparable—to investigate one was to investigate the others. The identities, powers, habits, and values of improvisers are never simply the inert conditions for a musical structure but rather themselves undergo mediation through the collective and aesthetic process of creating that structure.[19]

Consider the following exchange in 1988. On the matter of how an ongoing group arrangement transforms the subjectivities of its members, Cutler and Frith discover a certain ambivalence: each developed a new identity through his membership in Henry Cow, but one wished to escape it and one did not.

> **Cutler:** This tiny little self-contained world, in fact, where our internal differences and struggles seemed to be so important . . . wasn't actually quite something that one was glad to escape from. . . . Because by the time the group finished . . . , my experience . . . was very much that there was less and less of what I thought might be "me" left, and more and more of what the "I" that was the member of Henry Cow was, and needed to be, in the context of that group.

> **Frith:** Absolutely. . . . I mean, on the one hand, it was an umbrella from which one didn't particularly want to escape, because it represented a certain weird kind of security. . . . It stopped me from thinking, because I became so, in a way, scared of taking part in discussions in the group that I was happier just to get the discussions over and decide what the line was, and then parrot it, because it was a way to exist. . . . I mean, for me, one of the most important reasons to stop it was because I was completely losing touch with my own thought processes, as if I was rejecting being in the group, while at the same time embracing its superficial aspect of security.

After acknowledging the suffocations of collectivism and the pernicious distortions of personality that might result, Cutler clarified that his point was to open the question of individual identity and its many possible relations to a group identity. Frith's memory of his Henry Cow experience, in contrast, seemed to close this question by detailing the displacement of his original identity by the logic of the group. "But the question I was really asking," Cutler continued, "was: as a result of that, considering getting into a situation like that again—in other words, a permanent group—what kind of consciousness of the problems did you take with you? . . . What made it a thing worth doing again? And what precautions, or what lessons were learned from the old experience that you applied in order to not have all that happen again?"

> **Hodgkinson:** I mean, it seems to me absolutely clear that you get results through being in a permanent group that you can't get any other way.

Frith: Yeah. I mean, there are things that you can do in rehearsal with a fixed number of people over a long-term period that can't be achieved any other way. . . . For me it [became] very clear [when] I was working with Massacre. . . . The biggest frustration with the group was that we . . . would rehearse less and less and leave everything to the gig, and it became very lazy, so that what we had was only the energy of what we could put into the concert, but not the product of having worked before the concert.

Hodgkinson: Well, yes—what you're presenting to people is yourself, your skills, your musical personality. And so much music is put together like that, I mean, the whole pressure is to be like that. . . . That penetrates rock music for economic reasons, because it's not economic to rehearse a lot; you should play a kind of music which can be thrown together quickly, and you know you're good—you know you can carry it off. . . . But you don't get the same results, and you don't forge the new music that way. I think a group has this sort of dialectical relationship between a group and its music, that a group has to find its music, and you can't find the music unless you look for the music. Otherwise what's happening is just everybody's coming with their music.

Hodgkinson did not advance the familiar argument that improvisers play only what they know and therefore cannot create new music. Instead, he argued that social and economic conditions mitigated the radical potential of improvisation to generate new music, and, by extension, new identities. He puts forward the notion that musical individualism itself—"yourself, your skills, your musical personality"—can be the site of significant power relations. In a capitalist society entering its neoliberal stage, the ease with which a contingent group of improvisers could come together and "carry it off" communicates not simply their skill onstage but also their smooth insertion into existing socioeconomic conditions, or the absence of a friction that would attend Hodgkinson's proper dialectic.

In the penetrating analysis of Henry Cow's demise that Hodgkinson wrote in 1981, he developed the same skepticism of identity; it is never a self-evident and transparent quality. "Persons have layered depths. You perceive them through time, layer after layer. For some closely guarded things you must wait years for the rare crisis before truthful admission," he wrote. Identity in a five-year-old group was a very different proposition from identity in a five-week-old one; improvisation could serve as one mode of relation through which to probe, over time, these "layered depths" of an individual identity.

Hodgkinson notes that the group began with white British men of a "largely intellectual middle-class background" who were in the process of being educated for the "professional and technical intelligentsia." (Due to his working-class background, Greaves was the exception, and therefore, as we have seen, his departure gave to Hodgkinson "the clearest sign of a deep contradiction that the group as it was [could not] contain.") For a communist committed to the radical transformation of society, the affirmation or assertion of this class identity was hardly a project to be celebrated—indeed, the telling of this "personal story" might iterate an ideological pattern of class, gender, and race domination. Instead, open improvisation presented opportunities to work on and revise a remnant identity from an unjust, dying world: let ends begin. It was concerned less with delivering the truth about a given self than it was in speculating, fictionalizing, or fabricating a new self with shards of the old one.

I take this kind of improvisational practice to be the rough correlate of disidentification. As Michel Pêcheux explains in his expansion of Louis Althusser, a subject relates to the hail of dominant or majoritarian ideology through one of three modalities.[20] The "good subject" answers the hail unproblematically, magically identifying with the ideological position that has been given to it. The "bad subject," on the other hand, turns against ideological evidentness and imagines itself to have escaped the snares of interpellation, even though its struggle has ultimately been determined by the lines of ideological control. Finally, the disidentifying subject uses the forms issued by ideology without identifying with them; its struggle is *inside* as well as *against*. In musical terms, I understand the good subject to be the idiomatic improviser, which "expresses itself" unproblematically in the pregiven terms of flamenco or Dixieland jazz; the bad subject pursues "nonidiomatic" improvisation, which it construes as a kind of utopian free relation of pure means. But the disidentificatory subject, in the words of José Muñoz, "tactically and simultaneously works on, with, and against a cultural form," which might include stylistic allusion and collision, repetition, and the employment of pre-written structures.[21]

As one mode of relation, improvised music making could be a technique for attending to patterns of exchange in existing genre cultures such as rock, art music, and jazz, and renewing them through the dialectical process of developing a persistent collective art—that is, the play between de- and reformation. And yet, Hodgkinson continues, just as individuals possess many levels of identity, they also relate to one another in many ways at once; improvised music making is but one mode of relation in a concatenated ensemble that would also include collective work, language, and sex. He writes, "The way you become closer to this person itself becomes an unconscious structure. . . . As we turn this way and that shifting our attention & our efforts from one thing to another those parts of ourselves left unattended continue to behave according to the pattern in which we left them." In other words, there exists a danger that a concentration on revolutionizing one's practice in musical improvisation, for example, could cause one to neglect developing an alternative practice of friendship or love. The relationship of self and society might loosen in one domain while hardening in another.

In Hodgkinson's analysis, the implications of this multiplicity of social life—which surely bore the imprint of the socialist feminism that Cooper brought to the group and that Caroline Ayerst brought to their marriage—assumed critical importance in the eventual dissolution of Henry Cow. The original Cambridge trio—Hodgkinson, Frith, Greaves—might have transformed their gender and class identities from a property for expression to a problem for investigation through musical improvisation, but those same identities endured in other aspects of their social lives. The decision to pursue artistic careers brought with it grave fear, owing in Hodgkinson's view to the enormous pressure that their educational institutions and familial units placed on them. Compounding this class guilt, in his view, were their national and gender identities, which inhibited their patterns of emotional and verbal exchange and contributed to a hardened, confrontational contraviviality. Hodgkinson writes, "We . . . are unable to admit feelings of guilt or insecurity to one another, and so we forego the chance to share and understand them together. For these reasons our relationships begin from the start to grow habits of deception, and we are all afraid of one another."[22]

Furthermore, he argued, the core original trio had all turned to marriage as their student days ended, "unable to face the fact of no longer belonging to an institution, and wishing, perhaps, to compensate for the disrespectability of being rock musicians." When two of those unions disintegrated, they were unable to give or receive support from each other, not only because of their buttoned-up class, national, and gender identities, but also because bourgeois marriage had its own conservative expectations about privacy and property that came into conflict with the alternative modes of relation that the band adopted once they grew more serious about their collective work. As middle-class English men aged, intimacy was understood to be a thing shared with a domestic spouse to the exclusion of all others: in Hodgkinson's words, "you are either young enough to have close friends, or you are 'having a relationship' with someone." In an environment of circumscribed intimacies, "one problem for groups, then, is that members are 'attached' without having a ready-made language with which to handle their attachment."

I believe Hodgkinson implicitly refers to collective, open improvisation when he writes about the apparent naturalness of the emotionally stunted conditions created by English men in a capitalist society: "Only when people attempt a different type of relationship, based on a mutual recognition of individual equality and uniqueness, does it begin to seem extraordinary." Indeed, he even characterizes the group as a "refuge" in its early days. "In the act of playing together, particularly of performing together, we find a way of relating to each other which is warm and inclusive without demanding the truth from any of us." In a similar vein, Cutler has written that the band's improvisations "evolved wordlessly and without conflict—as if they belonged to another version of ourselves, more harmonious in spirit."[23] Playing, then, allowed the Cows to refuse their existing identities and collaborate on something yet unknown, even as the existing and the known continued to assert itself offstage.

Although Hodgkinson's analysis of this problem of identities—how and when to shake free of old ones, how and where they channel interactions, how to forge new ones, collectively—remained a private document, my own conversations with band and crew members suggest a widely shared agreement in general terms: the emotional landscape of day-to-day work often grew bleak indeed, but the improvised music rarely suffered, at least not until the final few months. Cooper, for example, effused about the "absolutely wonderful, all-embracing, and extraordinary" experience of touring to a journalist many years later, but also acknowledged the cost of living as though "everything must be called into question, examined, experimented with, changed." Those experiments produced what Cooper called "the walking wounded. . . . I would place Henry Cow squarely in that tradition."[24] Cutler told the same interlocutor, "It was hard, it was Hell, but a lot of the time it was wonderful. We did things, and were satisfied with the results. The principle was that 'an unexamined life is not worth living,' and we were living absolutely 160 percent, and examining most things most of the time."[25]

Hodgkinson's point, however, was that Henry Cow experimented in some domains of the creative life while remaining inattentive and nonexperimental in others; the difference, for him, spelled a fundamental and fatal contradiction. In my own interviews with Cutler (nearly twenty years after he made the comments above), the drummer drew closer to Hodgkinson's more ambivalent appraisal: "If we could have run the band the way we improvised, things would have been much easier, because in our social dealings we never cracked the public/private problem. But improvising was a territory we could negotiate successfully."

Such contradictions mark all cultural politics. For example, many readers will have already arrived at the observation that the opportunity to pull apart one's identity or to refuse some aspects of it accrues to whiteness as an aspect of privilege. Mutatis mutandis, Lewis has offered such an analysis of the downtown New York scene, where critics celebrated the stylistic mobility of white improvisers (i.e., John Zorn), while withholding similar praise for their black confreres (i.e., Anthony Braxton).[26] Although one would wish to account for how the diversities of class background, gender, and sexuality inflected the work of whiteness in this setting, the members of Henry Cow did enact this ambivalent politics: stretching to investigate the power that was sedimented in habit and personality, they exerted a different aspect of that same power. Beyond noting the sense of this critique, and my own agreement with it, I am unsure where else such an analysis might take us. But in his discussion of what I would label as the speculative or fictive dimension of improvised music, Lewis also suggests a more unsettling and promising line of inquiry into the formation and deformation of musical personality. Although the Afrological holds firm a connection to memory and taste in contrast to the myth of pure spontaneity, the history that is invoked arrives already broken, one of "the destruction of family and lineage, the rewriting of history and memory in the image of whiteness."[27] One might say that the very cohesion of personal history that the Afrological wishes to express is that which has only been withheld or taken from it. The broken origin of personhood must be continually improvised anew.[28] This line finds additional momentum and acceleration in Fred Moten's meditations on a blackness defined not by its aspirational relationship to personhood but rather as the antefoundational condition of (white) personhood's existence. For Moten, normative personhood itself is a specialized form of life that one might not have a claim to or a desire for.[29]

What kind of methodological position could emerge from the act of stepping away from the choice to assert or to disassemble subjectivity, when subjectivity is understood to be something "that the black cannot have but by which the black can be had"?[30] That path, I believe, leads to an improvisation of fictiveness and fabulation, in which telling a story in sound about the truth of the self is the same as telling a lie. To improvise is to lie, or to tell the truth about a lie, or to expose the lie of the true self.[31] The Afrological and the Eurological are less opposed approaches to spontaneity than they are tightly braided pathways—complementary, contravivial, asymmetrical—around this shared truth illuminated by the ontological demands of blackness. The self that might be given away or denied through Eurological improvisation can make no rightful claim to an origin, because it is the product of a historical and ontological system that precedes and exceeds it, a system that founds white selfhood on the denial of black humanity.[32] By contrast, the self asserted in Afrological improvisation is already an unstable one bearing the contradictions of double consciousness. For white improvisers seeking to strip away the power relationships sedimented in their identities, it would seem that the Afrological mode harbors the possibility of loosening up these reifications, while the Eurological can do little more than attempt to forget them.

Looking for a Male or Female Bass Player

Prior to embarking on the Scandinavian tour, Henry Cow auditioned two bassists, Uli Trepte and Steve Beresford. Trepte had been on the scene for more than ten years, first as the bassist in Irène Schweizer's free jazz trio, then as a member of the psychedelic, kosmische musik trio Guru Guru. Henry Cow had met him in 1973, when he was filling in on bass for Faust during their UK tour. By the time of his Henry Cow audition, Trepte had been spending much of his year in London, developing a new solo bass/electronics project called Spacebox. A groove-oriented player, he couldn't execute the more difficult compositions of Frith and Hodgkinson, so the potential collaboration never went very far.

Beresford was a different story.[33] A trumpet and piano player in childhood, he had studied music at York University from 1968 to 1971, and even taught for a spell at the grammar school where Frith's father served as headmaster. Under the guiding influence of Wilfrid Mellers, York was perhaps the most progressive music program in the country. (In 1970, Frith had gained acceptance to the doctoral program in composition despite his complete lack of formal music education, a feat that would be scarcely imaginable at any other institution in the United Kingdom.) Although he was always interested and active in many musical genres (especially pop and soul), Beresford soon found free improvisation, producing a handful of concerts at the university for the likes of Evan Parker, Paul Lytton, Derek Bailey, Peter Brotzmann, and Han Bennink. In fact, the music so exhilarated him that he began commuting to London to hear performances at the Little Theatre, where drummer John Stevens had established a weekly evening of free improvisation.

In 1974, he relocated to the city, playing bass in the soul band Roogalator and trumpet in the Portsmouth Sinfonia and founding the improvising group The Four Pullovers. By the time of Henry Cow's auditions, he had quit Roogalator and was concentrating on improvisation. When Frith invited him to audition for the band, Beresford saw it as an opportunity to work on his bass playing. The music wasn't exactly to his taste. A fan of pop, soul, and ska/reggae, Beresford shared little common ground with rock and its discourse, and especially not with the kind of complicated rock that Henry Cow made. "The ideas behind what they were doing were very uninteresting to me. I was listening to . . . it was a great time for Tamla Motown. Those tunes were all in four. It didn't seem to me that you had to play in additive time signatures in order to produce interesting music."

In any case, the band liked his sight-reading but not his improvising, which Beresford describes in retrospect as "low-pitched Derek Bailey pastiche" (the bass guitar is not a common free-improvising instrument). Beresford also remembers that Frith explained that his audition had failed because "none of the women liked me," even though Dagmar was not involved in the audition process and Beresford would soon enjoy a lasting friendship with Cooper at the London Musicians Collective. What became clear was that Beresford and the Cow were not a match.

They found their match in the twenty-year-old cellist, Georgina Born, who had strung her borrowed bass guitar in fifths to fit the tuning of her customary instrument. The third of three children, Born grew up in London mainly with her mother and her second husband. While Born's mother pursued medical training (she eventually trained as a psychoanalyst), Born spent a lot of time with her stepfather, a man of the theater and opera director who encouraged her musical development. She began to play the piano at age five, when a teacher intended for her older brothers took note of Georgina's talent and interest. When she was seven, another piano teacher enrolled her in the Royal College of Music Junior Department, where, every Saturday morning, Born and the other students took lessons on their primary and secondary instrument; received classes in music history, theory, and aural training; had tutorials in chamber music; played in the orchestras; and sang in the choir with their peers. It was a thorough education in Western

art music, even if it exacted its standard psychological price in anxiety over the fear that she had not practiced enough.

From age eleven to fourteen, she attended Godolphin and Latymer grammar school, where she kept up her musical studies augmented with theatre and studio art. An outstanding student, Born won academic prizes and skipped a year. When she finished her third year there, she and her family decided that she needed more music and cello in her life, so she moved to the Central Tutorial School for Young Musicians, where, amid a schedule weighed heavily toward music making, her academics suffered. Another school change followed, this time to Dartington Hall School in Devon, one of Britain's foremost progressive schools. Born had already grown familiar with the area because she had attended the Dartington International Summer School for a year or two, learning about new music and sitting in on composition masterclasses by Peter Maxwell Davies. As a boarder at the year-round school, Born took up studio arts, especially sculpture. After a year and a half, she moved back to London. Working as a restaurant server to support herself, Born returned to the Royal College of Music to finish her pre-eighteen music training while taking A-levels, sang in the Hitones (a jazz-rock group), and played contemporary music in chamber ensembles around London.

At eighteen, Born entered the Royal College of Music as a senior, taking the performance training in cello and piano; but after six months she dropped out, finding the college and course too conservative both musically and culturally. The following year, Born enrolled at Chelsea School of Art for their foundational year, which she enjoyed immensely. Still restless, she decided to prepare for the music entrance exam for Cambridge to study composition, and gained admission to New Hall. However, having secured her place, in May 1976, she answered a distinctive advertisement in *Melody Maker*. Cooper later recalled, "At the time, I thought: 'If only we could find a female bass player, it would be fantastic. . . .' Actually there were female bass players, but they could not read music, and we wanted somebody who is at the same time technically good and who can read their parts."[34] She chose the wording for the advertisement very carefully: "Looking for a male or female bass player." Born responded.

Greaves came to meet her in a pub near the Virgin office on Portobello road, which was significant in her view because he "was the most affable of

---

Figure 6.2 Georgina Born, 1978. PHOTOGRAPH BY TAKUMBA RIA LAWAL.

all of them, and my memory is that it was a kind of handover thing, right? He was keen to find somebody who could do the thing, cause he wanted to get out. . . . My first contact was slightly exciting and also quite affable. I say that because, had I met taciturn Fred or scary Chris, I'm not sure I would have been so into it!" The rest of the Cows were on tour in Scandinavia, so Born had a few weeks to learn the music and acclimate herself to the bass guitar. Her conservatory training meant that she had no problem learning the material, but free improvisation was an utterly alien prospect, so when she visited the new rehearsal space in Clerkenwell for her two auditions in June, she learned, like Krause, to swim from the deep end. Before she jumped in, however, she went back to Cambridge to raise the question of deferring her spot in the program for a year, in light of the unusual opportunity to tour Europe and learn about a new kind of music. "We don't hold places at Cambridge," replied the principal. Born later recalled, "It is a scene I never forgot, and I left the room determined to tour with Henry Cow."[35]

As Born says, "This was an organism that was already highly developed. It was like an ecology that someone had to fit into." Indeed, like any group of long standing, Henry Cow had evolved a set of shadow rules and ghost protocols that, to an outsider like Born, expressed themselves in obscure ways. The shock of losing Greaves was still rippling through the group. Later, Cutler explained, "Georgie really came into the band as an outsider, looked at the unquestioned axiomatic positions the rest of us took for granted—and never spoke about—and questioned them all. They may have needed questioning, but I don't think we were in any kind of mood for it." In Krause's memory, however, Born catalyzed an exciting and unpredictable dynamic. Of course it was nice having a third woman onstage to balance the gender split in a public, visible way (Sula Goschen and Maggie Thomas were still crew members), but Born produced new effects inside the band, as well. Krause recalls, "She questioned everything within the group. All that palaver, that nobody found a way to really question effectively, Georgie—being the new woman, and obviously well educated and sure of herself—found no problem in questioning. Maybe that was a problem [for her], but it looked to come quite effortlessly, I felt. And that was a new thing, a new energy in that group, which suddenly tumbled all those certainties into uncertainty."

To Born, Henry Cow offered an unfamiliar experience, beginning with the politics. "By this point in my life, I had never been close to left politics, because my family—my folks—were left-liberal, but not left." The dissonance and disjunctiveness of the written music were no surprise, given her history at Dartington, but she "cannot remember my reaction to the improvisation. I think throughout my—at least the first month in Henry Cow, and probably longer—I just felt, 'Well, I'll join in and explore and do my thing,' but I didn't feel that it was particularly difficult, but nor did I think—ever—I never felt very affirmed in my improvisation, which goes to aspects of the psychology of the group. . . . Nobody ever turned to me and said, 'Oh, that was great.'" Her effect on the band's sound was similar to what Cooper's had been two and a half years earlier: she rendered the scored works with great precision, and the additional timbral possibilities of her cello excited the Cow composers, particularly Hodgkinson.

Audible in her performance of the material that had been written for Greaves was her classical training, which had produced in her a different rhythmic sensibility from that of her predecessor. As one member put it, "She didn't have a natural rhythmic feel at all, and at her worst she could be a bit stiff, but when it was going it was really going."[36] As a result, Henry Cow's sound underwent a second shift away from Afro-diasporic musical vocabularies and toward a pan-European art-music sound. Born's selection as the Cow bassist affirmed Beresford's opinion of the band's music as rather serious and even antipleasure, whatever the backgrounds and musical tastes of its members. You couldn't dance to Henry Cow before, either, but Greaves did play the bass like somebody who had grown up professionally immersed in African American dance music of an earlier generation. He had the boogie disease. Born had also cultivated a love of jazz and rock since her teenage years, listening constantly at home, attending festivals at the Isle of Wight and Glastonbury, and going to concerts at the Roundhouse; yet she possessed a different training, and, like her predecessor, impressed the sound of that training on the band's subsequent musical work.

A New Base for Dissident Musicians

The departure of John Greaves wasn't the only one for the group that spring. At a meeting on April 2, band members told Sandford that they no longer wanted him to mix their live sound, though they did wish him to stay with the organization and perform other tasks if he wanted to. As it happened, he found a few theatre gigs and otherwise spent the hot summer helping a friend renovate his boat. Oddly, nobody can remember why his mixing was not up to snuff, nor can Sandford himself recall the precise circumstances of his departure. Mostly likely, all parties came to realize that Sandford's lack of experience with live sound might be holding them back. Greaves's exit also didn't help: Sandford spent most of his time on the road with Greaves, talking late into the night in the cab of the equipment truck. In any case, the ties binding Sandford to Henry Cow were not entirely severed, as he would play an important role in the Cow's political activities in 1977.

The engineer who replaced Sandford was named Yoel Schwarcz, a stateless Hungarian born Zoltan Fekete. A cloud of mystery surrounded him, at least in the memories of the Cows: he was "a bisexual anarchist," a former "tank commander," an "Israeli paratrooper," with prodigious electrical engineering chops and wise to the ways of the world—the kind of guy who would drink a bottle of whisky to kill a cold and wake up the next morning right as rain. More verifiably, he had founded the folk/classical/rock band Continuum in the late 1960s, improvising on woodwinds and classical guitar.[37] (Cutler had auditioned for this group prior to his involvement with Henry Cow.) After the breakup of his band in the early 1970s, Schwarcz had trained in electrical engineering, then found work with Dolby in London. So he did indeed possess technical credentials. In the six months or so he spent with the band, he designed and built three parametric equalizers and two twelve-band graphic equalizers, which greatly improved their live sound— particularly that of Cooper's bassoon.[38] Despite these gifts, Schwarcz did not fit in well with Henry Cow, and was in the habit of turning the mixing desk over to Balchin in the middle of a tour.

These shifts in personnel caused Henry Cow to postpone a studio recording date, which they had been tentatively planning since late 1975. But they weren't twiddling their thumbs. Cutler was already working on the idea that would become Recommended Records, his later mail-order business for unusual, noncommercial, and hard-to-find recordings. He envisioned a brick-and-mortar shop that could become "a base for dissident musicians."[39] The Cow also had in mind a tour of North America, which would be a first for a Virgin band; unlike Recommended, nothing would come of this possibility. Meanwhile, Cooper had begun to compose music at the urging of her comrades in Henry Cow.

Aside from Greaves's exit and the second quartet tour, the biggest news from the first half of 1976 was the release of a double-LP live recording called *Concerts*. Near the end of the previous year, the band's Norwegian friend Frode Holm, of Compendium Records, had raised the possibility of the release. Huge fans of Soft Machine, Holm and his buddies had established Compendium as a record importing operation in Oslo.[40] During one of his frequent trips to London, Holm had his mind blown by the Cow in concert and immediately resolved to book them at the Henie-Onstad Art

Centre in Oslo, where they performed in July 1975. The hall was wired for sound and had a studio attached, so the band produced an excellent live recording that night, the tape of which later inspired the Compendium crew to publish it as their inaugural release on the store's record label.

The Cow had been considering the live album on Compendium as well as another LP of improvisation for Caroline, Virgin's cheap imprint. Soon these ideas would be merged, however, in a double LP comprising the Oslo set, their August 1975 Peel session, a portion of their New London Theatre concert with Robert Wyatt, and a few other concert tapes of open improvisation. The band took control of the project, overseeing the covers (illustrated and designed by Maggie Thomas), sleeves, mastering, cutting, pressing, and printing. They only had to negotiate the issue of rights in Scandinavia, which Virgin eventually granted to Compendium, provided that Caroline could release the album in the United Kingdom and handle distribution in Europe. *Concerts* was released in the summer of 1976 to wide critical acclaim in the English, American, and continental music press.[41] According to Cutler and Hodgkinson, the process of putting together the double LP themselves helped Henry Cow to realize that they could have been doing things independently the whole time; indeed, their time with Virgin was coming to an end.

At about the time of the release of *Concerts*, Virgin was undergoing a major spring cleaning to keep the company solvent. Virgin's massive success with *Tubular Bells* had allowed it to expand quickly into music publishing and concert booking, but that meant that they had to staff the expansion, often with music-industry personnel possessing little interest or affinity for the music of early oddballs like Gong or Henry Cow. Simon Frith explained, "[Simon] Draper might like Henry Cow's music, [Richard] Branson might be proud to have them on his label, but all Virgin's [booking] agency knew was that they weren't an easy band to place in the cosy commercial world of live music promotion."[42] Moreover, the mail-order side of the business was suffering because the big retailers had gotten up to speed with the abolition of retail price management by selling albums at a discount, as loss leaders. Their share of record sales between 1972 and 1974 rose from 50 to 70 percent.

Mike Oldfield's debut had achieved stunning chart success, staying in the top five (or in the top slot) for most of 1974, and continuing to chart through 1975 and 1976. (*Sounds* still had it at number 23 in their British album charts in February 1977, nearly four years after its initial release.) His sophomore effort, *Hergest Ridge*, also debuted at number 1. However, reflecting back on this time and the changes to come, Simon Draper comments, "What we suddenly realized was that if we didn't have a Tangerine Dream album or a Mike Oldfield album each year, things wouldn't look good." Those early odd-balls gained Virgin a reputation for "intelligent" rock and left-of-center ideals, but they could not sell enough albums to keep a company of its size afloat.[43] As it happened, Draper recalls that he and Branson convened a meeting for all the department heads at Virgin, "and I'd prepared this paper—which I distributed to everybody—saying, 'This is what I think we have to do: we have to drop all these acts, however much we like them, they've all got to go.' I don't remember whether Henry Cow had gone by then, but they would have been on the list." That list would also have included Hatfield and the North, David Bedford, Ivor Cutler, Wigwam, and Lol Coxhill. Moving away from their "progressive" identity, Virgin would now chase trends like everybody else; they began signing and releasing more reggae and pop-rock, with the symbolic final brick in the wall coming in May 1977, when they famously nabbed the Sex Pistols. Fifteen years later, they'd even land the Rolling Stones.

To Europe: Autumn 1976

As we'll see in the next chapter, Henry Cow's business with Virgin would not wrap up until later in 1977. In the meantime, they had a new bassist and a strong desire to return to Europe.[44] Prior to their departure, however, Frith endured an unpleasant dustup in *Melody Maker*, where Steve Lake had reviewed *Guitar Solos 2*, the follow-up to the Cow guitarist's 1974 solo release. He had compiled the project in the early months of the year, once the Carol Cruiser tour had gone up in smoke. For this one—also to be released on Caroline—he solicited tapes from a few of his favorite guitarists: Derek Bailey, Hans Reichel, and G. F. Fitz-Gerald.

Lake's ornery review, titled "Bailey's Academy of Music," used the occasion of the album to opine that "there are quite a lot of guitarists who sound like Derek Bailey."[45] That hit a nerve, because there had long been whispers that Frith had stolen his best stuff from Bailey. Such allegations were all the more absurd because the two guitarists had been friends for quite a while, and Frith had always voiced his admiration in the press.[46] In the face of this cynical, grumpy press environment, Frith and his bandmates longed for the earnest and engaged audiences of Italy and France.

When they did get around to departing, Frith was hauling some extra equipment (a new eight-channel mixer), because he had successfully applied to the Arts Council of Great Britain for a grant earlier that spring. In his application letter, he underlined his financial precarity, "lest you are under any illusions that I can obtain financial backing from more usual business or other channels; or through the group, which only barely makes ends meet."[47] Penury alone was not a qualification for the grant, Frith seemed to be saying, but he wanted the panel to know that the life of a "commercial" musician came in many forms. It was an understandable position to take; the Arts Council had rejected his application in 1973, "as it was felt that earnings from the Jazz/Pop group, Henry Cow, could cover this cost."[48] The 1976 committee membership, which now included Evan Parker, saw the matter differently. In light of the impending release of the second *Guitar Solos*, and its inclusion of Bailey, they concluded that Frith's "connections with 'rock' music would enable him to reach new audiences for improvised music."[49] They awarded him £800. This grant was the last bit of good financial news for quite some time, and it laid the groundwork for Henry Cow's later success with that granting body. Furthermore, Frith's grant was almost certainly the first such award to a rock- or pop-affiliated artist to be granted in the history of the Arts Council.

With new bassist and sound engineer in tow, Henry Cow set off for the continent sometime in late August after a warm-up gig in York on the 20th.[50] Less than a week later, they were in Vevey, outside of Montreux, where they recorded a televised performance after dark. Several days of rehearsal and a couple of Swiss concerts followed, and then the Cow embarked on a baneful sally through Italy, which lasted nearly a month but produced only ten gigs. The trickle of income was overbalanced by a cascade of capital expenditure: both vehicles broke down. Strong aftershocks from the Udine earthquake ruled out two paying concerts in that city and Pordenone. Everyone was starving. There was, as Cooper told her mother in a letter, "nasty dissention [*sic*]" in the group.

In customary Henry Cow style, the halting tour was being assembled in an ad hoc manner, but with less success than they had enjoyed the year before: "massive uncertainties," as Mandy Merck recalls. Along for the first few weeks of the adventure, Cooper's new girlfriend was a nonaligned leftist intellectual and subeditor at *Time Out*. She recalled the band essentially playing for food and accommodation, as they continued to cultivate their ties to the PCI and the Partito Radicale. The latter, in particular, was important to Cooper's continuing education in feminist politics, because it had a good history of advocating for the rights of women, and furthermore, because it had affiliated with Fuori (Fronte Unitario Omosessuale Rivoluzionario Italiano, the United Italian Revolutionary Homosexual Front), the Italian gay liberation activist group. Merck recalls that the Cow stayed on the concrete floor of two Fuori activists in Turin. "I think we thought that was an improvement on the bus. Boy were we living hard." Merck knew some Italian, and helped Cooper better understand the political currents of feminism in that country; in her memory, the Italian feminists loved Cooper. And Italian men were fascinated with her androgynous beauty, according to Merck; she remembers one pulling open Cooper's jacket to ascertain whether she had breasts. (Cooper kicked their car door shut, leaving it dented.) During the Cow's September 24 gig in Taranto, one bold punter walked right up the amphitheater's steps and sat down next to Cooper at the piano as the band performed. When he grabbed her, she finished her musical phrase, gave him a swift punch, and rejoined the band without missing a beat. "The women in the audience were enchanted," Merck recalls. Some days later, in Rome, Cooper appeared on Radio Donna, the Partito Radicale's women's radio show.

Henry Cow returned to London on October 4 and spent the rest of the month there. They took some time off, rehearsed a bit, and played two gigs: one benefit for the Young Communists League at Goldsmith's on the 23rd, and a festival gig in Southend-on-Sea on the 24th. In early November, they hit France hard, with about twenty-five dates between November 9 and December 14. Around November 20, Cooper wrote to her mother, "It's actually not going too badly—no gigs cancelled yet and the 8 we've done so far were all full with v. enthusiastic audiences." But it wasn't all smooth sailing: "We were in Paris last weekend and Mandy and Sue and Wendy (Jack's girlfriend) came, which wasn't a lot of fun for them as we all went 15 miles out of Paris and had a group argument (sound engineer resigned)."[51] (If Schwarcz had indeed resigned, it didn't last—he continues to appear in the meeting minutes for several months.)

What was the band playing? Live recordings from Vevey (August 25), Milan (September 8), Venice (October 2), Paris (November 10, Radio France), Chaumont (November 25), and Orleans (December 13) give a good picture. Almost all of the sets included "Beautiful as the Moon—Terrible as an Army with Banners," "Living in the Heart of the Beast," and two new ones: a Frith arrangement of Phil Ochs's "No More Songs" and Hodgkinson's new large composition, "Erk Gah." A feature for Krause, the Ochs tune gave the Cow a solid lefty crowd-pleaser, and served as a tribute to its composer, who had committed suicide earlier that year. "Erk Gah," which I will detail shortly, borrowed its title from cartoonist Don Martin (*Mad*

Figure 6.3 Passing time at the back of the bus: Lindsay Cooper, Fred Frith, and Sue Steward, 1978. PHOTOGRAPH BY TAKUMBA RIA LAWAL.

Magazine), whose characters used it to express shock and dismay. Frith uttered the line when first presented with Hodgkinson's daunting score, and the name stuck. The band's open improvisations now routinely incorporated the prerecorded tapes they had used on the Scandinavian quartet tour, and the band, too, often employed ostinatos on individual instruments in a manner suggested by tape loops. These improvisations—usually two or three per concert, ranging from ten to twenty-five minutes each—always transitioned seamlessly into composed material. Without exception, "Beautiful as the Moon" opened up in the middle for a long exploration before circling back around into the vamp to close out the song. By later in November, they were opening with a ten-minute improvisation that increasingly offered motivic material from "Erk Gah," before beginning that piece. And every performance included one improvisation that led to "The March," Frith's tune from the Scandinavian tour, often augmented by Krause's vocalization of its beguiling melody. In fact, Krause took on a pronounced role in many of the improvisations, putting the confidence she had amassed in Maggie Nicols's workshops to good use in the form of passionate cries, yelps, and growls.

Although this core of "Beautiful," "Beasts," "Erk Gah," "No More Songs," and "The March" remained fairly consistent, its sequence shifted. And the group folded in older material, most often "Bittern Storm over Ulm," which functioned wonderfully to launch a woodwind duet for Hodgkinson and Cooper. An acoustic respite in the middle of an otherwise electronic set, this duet usually meandered over the course of five minutes toward "The March," which the rest of the band would slowly fade in. They also occasionally tried "Ruins," "Teenbeat," "Nirvana for Mice," Slapp Happy's "Riding Tigers," and an old Greaves song, "Would You Prefer Us to Lie?" In my opinion, Henry Cow was playing some of their finest concerts between the autumn of 1976 and spring of 1977, especially in the case of their open improvisations. This opinion was shared by other observers at the time, including Malcolm Heyhoe, who wrote in March 1977, "Henry Cow are simply one of the most compelling, adventurous and challenging bands working the rock idiom today, and their current results far outstrip all previous efforts of their nine-year history."[52]

The improvisations might have developed in response to the rigor and heft of "Erk Gah," an eighteen-minute, multisectional work fully notated by Hodgkinson and rehearsed by the band since the early summer of 1976. Extensive sketches and revisions documented across several of his notebooks suggest that the vocal melody formed the core of the piece—various changes to instrumentation, voicing, or harmony arranged themselves around a fairly stable part for Krause. One might recall that Hodgkinson had begun his previous large composition, "Beast," before she had joined the band, and he seems to have committed in "Erk Gah" to reversing that arrangement of priority. The five large sections of the music correspond to five marked sections of the text; each of them has a distinct tonal, instrumental, and rhythmic identity, though certain commonalities are shared across sections. In his notes, the composer describes this material as "a wild, shifting, fluid chaos of transient forms," and indeed tonal, textural, and rhythmic elements mutate often throughout the work.

"Erk Gah" | Tim Hodgkinson

I 1   sentenced to death
      it is time
      it is precious breath I've spent:
    all these cold years
    waiting for the choice
    that's never nearer.

2   on the street
I walk past stumbling men
confused by shouting
they're bleeding on the pavement
I walk past a man
who seems slightly pale:
why did I choose the street
that turns cold?

3   rooms have bare walls
that stare at what remains:
how much I've hated
all our wretched tight-lipped differences
building up to breaking-point
or compromise.
once, I felt we could relive our love
but then it became clear
feelings were dead.
then, you ask, why did I choose
this room that turns cold?
why do I choose this way of dying?

4   time comes to lash and destroy in fury:
each moment of time draws me nearer:
I shall not be measured beyond death
and all the darkest time eternal stands
and hurls me forwards:
anguish shall strike these hollow times
shot with fury.

II 1 that I carried a smile was not in doubt;
they were just not sure why

2 running along the street, it's time;
I left them thinking
who was that girl we thought we knew?

3 there was not much to do; fingerprints planted
led to quick arrest and trial: I confessed.

4 one year ago was when it happened:
how hard they try to forget my smile.

III   1   I was flying kites
when I could by trying hard at school:
all summer long, twisting, turning and
marching away on the telegraph poles.
I lay stretched out for miles
saw ten thousand teachers
drag the sky down with fear of failure
and shreds of reason.

2   see in the garden a child:
will tomorrow be the same as today?
the storm of the world crashing
on my lips and eyes and eardrums
cries out to end them all
and dream of nothing.

3   memories made of air
last no longer than seconds

4   voices quickly melt into distances:
fearful the shadows of sound: exiled:
now my friends put on
the cruel masks of the beast.
who would stay to ask them questions,
don't you know that all the human race is dumb?
it never spoke and never will.
I search for my friends
in the monstrous stomach of this silence.
cry for my friends
in the endless spaces:
now I feel them brush my spine with pinions
eyes a blazing frozen flame of avarice,
uncoil from nests in high-up distant trees
that witness nothing.

IV   I break open stars
finding . . . nothing
and again nothing
and again nothing . . .
then one word
in a foreign tongue . . .

<pre>
            one unknown word . . .
            one word

     v   now feel the fire that burns the sun
            by this fire our time will be won
            I believe in humankind.
            self, whose fear, whose darkness lies
            before us: we stand here with open eyes.
            no mere gods shake tyrant halls
            fling thunder and lightning down
            at our side, and make stone sing.
</pre>

The first section summarizes the techniques and imagery in the rest of the piece; the lyrics advance themes that return in later sections (the trial, in II; the optimism of the past, in III; loss and nothingness, in IV; fury, in VI). Each of these four subsections has a distinct musical flavor that foreshadows later material, as well. For example, the opening vocal melody (see example 6.1) begins with a sequence of eleven pitches that will return in section III. Hodgkinson also introduces an oscillating figure that marks the entire piece; often appearing in the voice, this figure has Krause rocking back and forth between two pitches—for example, hear the line that begins "I walk past stumbling men" on the archival recording of the piece on the *Henry Cow Fortieth-Anniversary Box Set* (disc 6, track 2, 1:06); the oscillation motive also appears in the chordal accompaniment on occasion. The other important element that appears in the opening is a rhythmic figure in which successive beats are divided into an increasing or decreasing number of attacks; in other words, acceleration or deceleration takes place inside a steady tempo. This gesture contributes to the overall temporal sophistication of "Erk Gah," which moves through constantly shifting meters and sharply defined rhythmic gestures, often struck in unison passages for drums and xylophone (played by Frith).

Section II, to which the composer referred in his notes as "four short songs," ushers in on a change of timbre and texture—gone are the triads, harmonic clusters, and stacked fifths of the opening movement, replaced here with contrapuntal relations among the various instruments. Although Hodgkinson had only augmented Cutler's kit with parts for xylophone and tubular bells (which is what I think I hear clattering at the start of the section II) in the opening section, the percussion sounds more varied because he isolates individual parts of the drum set—the hi-hat, ride cymbal, or low

Example 6.1 Tim Hodgkinson, "Erk Gah," vocal melody (*HCFABS*, disc 6, track 2, 0:13); transcribed from the score, THA.

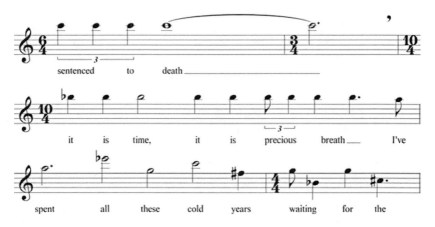

tom—instead of combining them into characteristic rock "gestures." At any rate, all the percussion goes away in section II, when quieter instruments like the cello and flute join saxophone, organ, and guitar in a twelve-tone pitch space that refuses any tonal center. In the section that follows, the music re-centers around E, a tritone up from the B-flat tonal center that was defined at the beginning of the piece (Hodgkinson works with this polarity at every scale of organization). Here, the voice spins out long melodies in a pitch sequence from the first movement; eventually (on *HCFABS*, disc 6, track 3, 1:13 to end), Hodgkinson arrests the sequence on its first two pitches (C and B-flat), which lock into a steady oscillation. Underneath, he modulates the meter and tempo such that Krause's voice remains undisturbed while the rhythms shift erratically underneath—it's a neat trick.

The fourth section, the longest of the piece, is the only one that didn't originate with the voice part. It has a chamber music feel, with many instruments offering atomistic and brittle gestures that cohere at times into unison lines. The composer heavily works the acceleration/deceleration motive in these instrumental sections, and also introduces a new rhythmic motive shared by all but heard frequently in the bass with an oscillating tritone. Section V closes the piece with long tones in the bass that support counterpoint between organ and voice, which offer previously unheard melodic material. After the fixed percussion parts of section IV, Cutler's drumming at the close is freed up to create swells and punctuations of these phrases.

Overall, "Erk Gah" holds little converse with rock convention. It sounds more like modernist chamber music scored mainly for amplified instruments. There is very little repetition and no single drumbeat to speak of, though the metrically modulated vocal oscillation (in section III) that divides the work in half does host some eruptive squeals that call to mind free jazz. The band enjoyed playing the piece, and it stayed in the repertoire for more than a year; eventually, they enjoyed improvising into and out of it, weaving together themes from the piece into looser and somewhat unpredictable textures. When Krause became a less reliable collaborator on tour, Henry Cow pulled apart "Erk Gah" to assemble an instrumental version.

More of the Same: Contraviviality

In mid-September, the band held a meeting in Rome that included a difficult conversation about how they operated, how they made decisions, and how individuals could and should relate to the group. Everybody recalls this painful discussion. Problems that had lain muddied below the waterline now popped up into view, where they bobbed around on the surface of the group, never to be fully submerged again. Some days later, Cooper reported to her mother, "Having a frightful time—many gigs cancelled owing to reasons ranging from local political parties' inefficiency to earthquakes. No money, nasty dissention [*sic*] in group. Georgie is hysterical and Chris as been so severely criticized he's starving us all to death as a punishment."[53]

Henry Cow meetings had always been disputatious and, to some, bewildering. They had flummoxed Slapp Happy, bored Greaves, and often left Balchin, Phil Clarke, and Sula Goschen cold. The elite educational background of some members, not surprisingly, led to occasional outbursts of internal class conflict. "We're the only proles here!" Balchin would yell, according to Goschen. "The rest of you are a bunch of posing wankers!" The ability of Hodgkinson, Cutler, Cooper, Frith, and Krause to wield the language of Marxist analysis set them apart from—and sometimes at odds with—their crew members. Years later, Frith described this analytical language as "a way of retaining the power in the quarters of the people who had the most ability to analyze well. . . . It became almost like a joke, because it was as if they were pupils at a school or something—it became like a school superstructure in which people were being admonished from a schoolteacher's point of view, by the people who had the most command of language."[54]

Although Cutler was certainly not the only one who employed the analytical tools of political economy, he was the one who came in for sustained criticism in the Rome meeting. A few distinct complaints came out at once.

Figure 6.4 Lindsay Cooper, Phil Clarke, Jack Balchin, and Georgina Born in a band meeting, 1978. PHOTOGRAPH BY TAKUMBA RIA LAWAL.

By the mid-1970s, Cutler had developed a personal ethics of making due with what one had without grumbles, working hard and withstanding hardship, cultivating personal discipline, and so on. To some members of the band and crew, this personal ethic could feel intolerant or even censorious; some members, for example, have memories of fierce verbal altercations between Cutler and Greaves over the latter's drinking and smoking. The minutes of a meeting in November 1975 record a discussion on the subject of banning alcohol on gig days. Krause retains an amusing memory of sneaking off in Rome to enjoy cakes secretly with Born, only to be caught by Cutler when he came walking around the corner. "I liked sugar!" she laughs. "And sugar . . . was just a complete no-no. Sugar was so reviled by Chris—equally as reviled as smoking and alcohol at the time, probably." One member of the organization recalls another complaining earnestly during the Rome confrontation, "It is humanly natural to snack!"

Summarizing her own experience with this aspect of life in Henry Cow, Sarah Greaves later explained, "When I left Henry Cow, I started listening to the likes of the Rolling Stones again. I felt it would have been disapproved of somehow. And that would have been Tim and Chris. They were pretty stern and dogmatic in those days."[55] Indeed, Cutler and Hodgkinson were the two most vocal leaders, but they exerted strengths in different ways.

An entrancing and potentially ferocious orator, Cutler could command a room, but Hodgkinson was the more consistent and studied Marxist. I find convincing the following interpretation by Goschen: "Chris is more momentary, more fleeting in his passions. He grabs hold of the essence and ideology of it, and he believes in it, and he expounds it, . . . because he's caught on to something that really speaks to him, and he's not afraid to voice it. Whereas, I think, Tim—he's an academic." Likewise, Krause recalls her own tendency to get swept up in Cutler's dynamism; he had the charisma and language to move people. In my own view, then, Cutler's reputation as "stern" or "dogmatic" had more to do with personal and public presentation than it did with politics. A soft-spoken artist today, the Cutler that many recall from these years accords with John Fordham's description in *Time Out*: "Chris is a disciplinarian, at least when the band presents its public face. He is slight and ascetic-looking, perches on chairs in the lotus position, draws himself up with a long inhalation when he's about to deliver the goods, as if re-balancing some delicate inner equilibrium."[56]

The inhalation was long, presumably, because it would precede a verbal torrent. How Cutler used these torrents—or how the other Cows *thought* he used them—seems to have motivated the Rome confrontation. Although the meeting minutes do not clarify the matter, evidence and interviews suggest that the practice of consensus was at issue. Rather than voting on band matters and accepting the rule of the majority, Henry Cow labored to find or manufacture consensus. "It had to be unanimous," Cutler explains. "On the one hand, this is a recipe for one faction to beat the other faction into submission, but on the other side, you know, it does mean you can hold out." Although Cutler might have advocated most strongly for this type of deliberation, he was not alone, and his comrades tend to blend their memories of his particular verve for consensus building with that of what Born later called the "central committee of Henry Cow—the troika of Chris, Tim and Fred."[57] In either case, the disgruntlement owed to a feeling that an individual or faction was pushing through its own agenda in the guise of the group's. In Neil Sandford's words, "It was an expression of personal will rather than collective will. And that is a very damning comment for a group of people that profess to live by collective consensus. Because they were—Fred, Tim, and Chris . . . —such extreme personalities, with extreme polemical views, that consensus, which I define as the lack of sustained opposition to a proposition, was just not on the agenda."[58]

Troika notwithstanding, Cutler had earned a reputation as "so dominant and so domineering," as Sue Steward put it. In Frith's memory, "We would not do democracy, which was a flawed principle. Instead we would do dictatorship—of the proletariat. Meaning Chris." This dictatorship might have had less to do with Cutler's need for control than it did with his penchant for long-form argument. In practice, Krause recalls, many arguments ended with exhaustion, and Cutler was often the last person talking. In an unpublished memoire of sorts from 1981, Hodgkinson painted what others would find to be an increasingly ordinary scene: "We sit around as Chris lectures us into the darkness about the need for a common language. One by one we are cut off & excluded. . . . His voice drifts on into the night with no audience but himself."[59] Episodes like this one would also lead Krause to remark, "Were we really a collective? What a load of rubbish!"

Responding to the widespread belief among Cows that consensus was a mirage, Cutler maintains, "I think different people in the band have different recollections of how those things went. Some would say, 'Well, in the end, we just gave in. . . .' Others would say, 'We battled it through, and in the end, nobody quite got what they wanted, but we came out with a compromise everyone thought was better than what we started out with.' That would be my position, mostly." Indeed, band and crew members retain almost no memories of specific decisions that Cutler had steered (save the decision to allow Thomas on tour later in autumn 1976, about which more below), although the opposite case—Cutler's desire thwarted by his comrades—can be found in the group's decision not to tour with Magma the previous year.

Regardless of these memory vacillations, there clearly rose a tide of discontent with Cutler that culminated in the Rome meeting. Although specifics have long faded from view, little wisps of evidence and partial memory bear the faintest mark of a feminist response. For some members, beneath the minor complaints about censoriousness and the more serious concerns about consensus lay a mounting distrust with how language was being deployed—to mediate interpersonal relations, to cloak an individual interest in the vestments of the group, to mask personal conflicts in the terms of ideology. Frith explains, "I think I couldn't let go of wanting to be in control. I think I was an undeveloped collective member from that point of view. The group voice didn't seem to me to be any more my voice." For a founding member of the band, this sort of alienation was particularly painful. Moreover, the threat of being found to diverge from the ideologically correct path, "cast as the bourgeois," was but one element in the group's shadow circulation of hopes, fears, alliances, annoyances, and attractions, a flow that was imperfectly routed through the language of political economy and Maoist analysis. As Born later wrote, "What is disappointing, in retrospect, about the experience of the collective—and no doubt attests also to my own deficiencies in communication and cooperation as a truculent young adult on her first major professional adventure—is the incapacity to develop amongst ourselves an open, nuanced and self-interrogating conversation about the politics of the music and of the collectivism, one that would indeed respect and respond to internal differences, and to the 'problems' of gender, of the inevitable hierarchies, of the unkindnesses and stresses of our working life."[60]

Indeed, living together is itself a kind of art that involves subtle dynamics of circulation and recursion. "If you have a language that doesn't actually take that in," Hodgkinson told Frith and Cutler in 1988, "you carry on using that, in a sense, to obscure the situation. . . . People can start to use the language against each other, instead of using it in a social way."[61] In texts from 1981, Hodgkinson recalled the currents that led to the Rome meeting, noting that Cutler had increasingly identified himself with the "correct line" of the band, merging a personal viewpoint with the objective interests of the group. "The other members experience this as a contradiction of increasing intensity. . . . Until now . . . , I mediate between Chris and everyone else, trying to smooth over differences, making sure the boat doesn't rock too far & founder altogether. Now I am caught up in the ground-swell of resistance and forced to admit that our ideological constructions are untrue, and cannot be used by the people for whom they are nominally intended."[62]

Hodgkinson was beginning to consider the possibility that these difficulties were nothing more than struggles for power. "In a borrowed flat in Rome we hold a group meeting at which we confront Chris with the truth about what we are thinking. Chris remains silent & completely withdrawn for what seems like weeks but may be only days. He knows now that the group could exist without him, or does he? He's giving nothing away: his silence means— think it over, and you will come round to the right point of view." In fact, and apparently unbeknownst to all except Thomas, Cutler had consulted the *I Ching*. "The *I Ching* said, 'do nothing, take no action, don't respond, be still' so that's what I did," he says. While Cutler considered the period of silence to be a kind of quasiscientific experiment—"I won't put forward any opinion and I won't insist on anything, and we'll see how it goes"—Hodgkinson viewed it in 1981 as a major turning point in the history of Henry Cow. "My betrayal of Chris will isolate him," Hodgkinson wrote. "Now he will begin to find private spaces outside the group where he may be master in his own house. . . . In this way the seeds for the group's future dissolution are sown."[63] And it wasn't just Hodgkinson who felt the chill; Cutler recalls that he and Frith were not on speaking terms for much of his quiet period, which ended, in his memory, when others began to ask his opinion on matters of daily business. Some Cows felt liberated during Cutler and Thomas's exile, but, always a volatile barometer of the group's emotional climate, Balchin smashed his guitar to pieces on a fountain in the Piazza Farnese.

The unrest continued into the autumn. On October 28, the band met in their Clerkenwell rehearsal space to discuss an upcoming tour of France. According to minutes, a "majority of people in [the] group" didn't want Thomas to come on the tour. Although she had established a reputation as a capable member of the road crew, her bandmates worried that her presence would jeopardize the wounded relationship between Cutler and the rest of the group. The pair had isolated themselves after the Rome rebuke, and the other Cows wished to reestablish their bond with Cutler alone. They also alleged that she had "interfered w. mixing," directly created "tense situations," and only trotted out Cutler's line. Cutler objected that such a move would transform a difficult temporary situation—the extraordinary circumstances of the Italy tour—into a permanent one, but Hodgkinson and Cooper disagreed. The discussion bogged down, and Thomas would indeed join the tour. In her record, Cooper wrote, "More of the same: Georgie left in protest at C's behaviour."

More of the same. An antipathy had grown between Cutler and Born, who, as the newest member of the group, was less acclimated to the usual emotional currents. "She was calling things the way she saw them and then kind of being told, 'We don't talk about that,'" Frith remembers. For her part, Born recalls, "When a difficult issue came up, one could sense that there wasn't a consensus, or that there was a difficult feeling, but it would be swallowed, because neither Fred nor Lindsay would really go out on a limb and stand up to something. And I began to, latterly, and that's when relations got bad, and in the end I just had to bugger off and leave."

"For some reason, [Cutler] never accepted you properly," Hodgkinson later said to Born.

"That's a strong thing to say, but it makes sense," she replied.

"But you know, but did he ever really accept John properly?"

"Hmm," Born said. "I wonder why? We're okay now. He must have just thought I was a kind of amorphous, bourgeois girl."

"'Bourgeois,' yeah. John was 'bourgeois,' you were 'bourgeois.'" He paused and smiled. "John was actually working-class."

"Details!" Born continued, "How did it manifest that I was never accepted?"

Figure 6.5 Contraviviality: Georgina Born, Chris Cutler, and Fred Frith in performance, 1978. PHOTOGRAPH BY TAKUMBA RIA LAWAL.

"I think I just got a sort of gradual feeling, you know. Like maybe after the eleventh time you'd walked out of the room during a conversation, something flickered across his face and I thought, 'Hmm, he doesn't really accept Georgie, does he?'" In fact, Born's frequent temporary departures had other band members wondering whether she would leave the group permanently, especially after the Rome meeting.[64]

Born and Frith recall that the conflict between bassist and drummer also manifested musically in subtle and not-so-subtle ways. Cutler possessed a drumming style that confounded the conventions of a rock rhythm section, but he did settle into occasional grooves with Greaves, particularly on "Teenbeat" and "Beautiful as the Moon—Terrible as an Army with Banners." Frith notes, however, that he and Born never forged a similar kind of rhythmic sympathy, not completely owing to her classical training.

And the improvisations, too, surfaced these disconnections for Born. To take an example from the autumn of 1976, Henry Cow's long set in

Chaumont a few weeks later (November 25), began with a confident, feisty open improvisation that unfolds like a careful collage in real time. Opening with electric sounds of white-noise scrapes, short-out buzzes, and some restive rattling in the percussion, the texture gives way to a series of tape interjections: a Scottish folk song for solo male voice (backward then forward), some Eastern European instrumental folk music, something that sounds like a loop of horse hooves, and a field recording of a children's song. The sonic ideas move around a lot, and there are many of them in the first two minutes; the instrumentalists seem to be emulating the technological apparatus by playing a lot of short repetitive phrases. On bass, Born leads the group forward with a leaping wiggle of a loop, juggling it for about twenty seconds, when Cutler crashes in with an emphatic drum fill leading not quite to a beat but more like a cubist allusion to one.[65] Born comments, "I experienced that as quite aggressive, like Chris basically cutting across what I was doing." To these ears, however, Cutler was responding to that restless wiggle in Born's loop with a surprising answer that pushed the music ahead, both with and against the bass part. They drift into and out of phase with each other—there is no shared beat but instead a kind of shared intention to play as if there were. Born doesn't get too shaken up by the changing currents around her, and the band responds to this momentum with a flurry of intensification. Hodgkinson adds an irregular ostinato of distorted bleeps on the organ, while Cooper soon throws in some flute runs. Suddenly, they're off, into the maelstrom: Hodgkinson turning to saxophone, Frith dropping in samples of shouts and folk music, Cooper onto the piano, Frith to the tubular bells and xylophone, and on and on. Examples such as this ten-minute improvised overture can remind us that for all the turbidity of their imperfect arts of living, the Cow could convert those energies into powerful group music.

Hodgkinson later wrote, "However one may evaluate our music, as artists of being-in-a-group I rate us pretty low."[66] Cutler concurs: "You know, it was a dilemma we never solved. . . . We had no idea how to deal with the psychology of the situation we were in." It would be not only unfair but simply inaccurate to attribute the dysfunction to Cutler, despite the specific complaints that were articulated in the Rome confrontation. Though their drummer may have been the most prolix of the bunch, all the Cows possessed a certain panache for argumentation. Only twenty years old, Born was, in her words, a "truculent young adult"; Cooper and Krause had reputations as astute political quarrelers; Hodgkinson could be as unmovable as a stone; and Frith projected his own sullen disquietude. Of the latter, one bandmate recalled, "Taciturnity is one of his stress reactions, you might say. . . . He felt a lot of tension and reflected a lot of tension, gave out a lot of tension." It's no surprise, then, that Born would diagnose Henry Cow's collectivism with "a kind of distributed autism—attributable to no one in particular—in which the enormous intellectual and human potential of the individuals that composed it . . . were not matched by the quality of the encompassing everyday relationships across the (impossible) totality of The Group."[67]

"But we were a pretty civilized bunch, really," Sarah Greaves would later put it. If Henry Cow's distributed autism sometimes erupted in traumatic moments like the Rome meeting, it also fostered an ongoing mode of relation, contraviviality, that worked like an engine to push them forward. With such a term, I want to name this condition or stance that seems to have contributed positively and productively to the group's musical successes. "Contentment is hopeless, unrest is progress," Cutler wrote in a later lyric.[68] One is reminded of the pugilistic creativity encouraged by Berthold Brecht, of which the Cows were surely familiar. As Anthony Moore explains, "With Henry Cow, . . . those meetings, those discussions, or disagreements, were just another level of toughness that one went through in order to make the music better. Basically, one accepted that you would suffer, and that would feed in in some implicit way, into the musical results, and give it strength and depth." In fact, one might not only tolerate disagreement, but actually seek it out as a tool to help reveal new possibilities for a future agreement that cannot yet be grasped: certainties tumbling into uncertainties, as Krause remarked. And with Henry Cow, those agreements to come often took on surprising or unpredictable shapes, irreducible to the obvious axes of gender, class, or aesthetic sympathies—affinities and repulsions flared up or were forged in contradictory, mutable permutations. For all of the grief that Cutler may have taken in the autumn of 1976, his bandmates continued to respond to his invitations and provocations in the decades to come. For example, Krause explains her continuing involvement with Cutler in the Art Bears, a group that rose partially out of the wreckage of Henry Cow: "The one thing that he never had is any emotional entanglement. When you're right in the middle of something, it's really difficult to be with him. However, on another level, that kept the path clear. . . . You know, everything was judged on a more intellectual level, devoid of emotion. Somehow, it left the path open to start a new venture with the same enthusiasm as you started the venture before."

One more ephemeron of touring might help to capture what I'm trying to get at with *contraviviality*. Jack Balchin remembers a stop on the outskirts

Figure 6.6 Maggie Thomas, 1978. PHOTOGRAPH BY TAKUMBA RIA LAWAL.

of Venice for a few days, probably in 1977. Most of the Cows had gone into the city for pleasure and amusement, but Balchin was deep into a bottle or two of whiskey, with no end in sight and no desire to leave their tiny metal box—nothing pleasurable or amusing about it. Although they had been through years of mutual distrust and exasperation, Cutler and Thomas could tell that Balchin was battling something, so they lured him out of the bus and into the streets for a rambling walk around town. He didn't want to go. "But I was feeling so fragile and dangerous, I thought I'd *better* be helped. I'd feel safer being around someone just in case I'd really fall to pieces. I'm totally grateful for that; I'll never forget it." I do not mean to imply that such touching moments of care and support were rare in the Cow, nor are they especially representative of contraviviality. Instead, I recount this story because of how Balchin introduced it to me in the first place: "Maggie was an amazing woman. I really don't like her, but that doesn't change the fact that she's amazing. We just never hit it off; it's sad. I love her a lot, but she was always . . . *Maggie Thomas*. She saved me once, you know." *Contra* and *vivo*: living against.

Forcing Action

In his review of Henry Cow's Southend concert in October, a critic noted, "The concert was a little dry—their heart is obviously in the new material, which presumably they will be premiering at their London concert next month."[69] They would not, it turns out, premier that material in December, but the critic correctly ascertained their mindset at the time: they wanted new music to play. "I remember there was a restlessness creeping in," Krause recalls, "that one had to change the set: 'It can't be always the same, let's bring in this, let's bring in that.'" And, although there is some ambiguity about it forty years on, a few Cows felt some pressure to deliver new songs for their vocalist, who had been singing the same lines for more than a year (Ochs's "No More Songs" helped in that regard). In her memory, Born's first few weeks with the band in July and August were marked by this desire for novel material.

Clocking in at eighteen minutes or so, Hodgkinson's "Erk Gah" constituted the main hunk of fresh meat. Otherwise, however, their rehearsal in summer 1976 served to bring Born up to speed on the old repertoire. It was no mean feat on her part to learn more than an hour of often very complicated music on a new instrument, but the hours that Henry Cow devoted to practicing old material with her also kept them from developing more new compositions. Moreover, the process of learning the old book often went on with instrumentalists only, so Krause participated in fewer sessions than her comrades; in retrospect, we might see this divided rehearsal arrangement, coming off of Krause's spell during the Scandinavian tour, as the beginning of her separation from the group.

With the encouragement of her bandmates, Cooper began to compose music during these months, but her first piece—which never received a title and didn't remain in the group's repertoire for long—wouldn't be performable until May 1977; she was also concentrating on adding the soprano saxophone to her already wide range of instruments, "because I wanted to learn an instrument which had no classical music connotations."[70]

Also at about this time, Frith's lack of composed production was becoming increasingly apparent. He had authored his last substantial piece, "Beautiful as the Moon," nearly two years before. Bits and bobs like "The March" and his arrangement of "No More Songs" still popped up now and then, but otherwise those two years were marked by discussions in interviews of big, *Tubular Bells*–like orchestral rock compositions that Frith sketched and planned but never completed. Cutler explains, "Tim wrote

'Amygdala.' . . . Two years later he wrote 'Living in the Heart of the Beast,' fiendishly complex and also epic in scope. And I did get the impression that Fred thought this was a model to match. But it wasn't him—and he didn't want to, or he didn't think he could do that. So he did nothing."

In 1981, a few years after the end of the Cow, Frith wrote, "Looking back I would say that Henry Cow was a process for me of realizing that I'm not really a 'composer' at all, though I'd like to have been. I'm pretty uncomfortable with everything I wrote for Henry Cow, though there are nice bits. . . . I feel much happier with improvising, and writing songs and short pieces based on song-form. In this sense I'd say that all my work since 1978 has been stronger and more positive than my Henry Cow WRITING (not talking about performance or collective work which I stand by absolutely)."[71] In his contributions to that performance or collective work, Frith showcased his strengths as an improvisational musician. "Such a machine does *not* solve its problems by thinking, just the opposite: it solves them by forcing action," Ross Ashby wrote of his homeostat device.[72] Likewise for Frith, thought was in the hands: pulling apart material, rearranging it, reconceiving it from different angles. He specialized in tumbling certainties into uncertainties and vice versa: What does "Ruins" sound like when it comes out of an open improvisation with this new little bridge? If "Bittern Storm" ends by kicking up a woodwind duet, how can that eventually lead to "The March"? Again, Ashby: "This is nothing other than 'experimenting': *forcing* the environment to reveal itself."

Every member of Henry Cow was good at forcing the environment to reveal itself, but it was a particular strength of Frith, whose musical intelligence seemed to thrive in conditions of underspecified relation. In this sense, "Ruins" and "Beautiful as the Moon" were anomalies, because the were relatively stable, self-contained, long, and formally set works. Most of the other pieces he contributed to the repertoire—"March," "Solemn Music," "Nirvana for Mice," "Yellow Half-Moon," "Teenbeat"—were practically designed to be taken apart, flipped around, and juxtaposed in new ways in performance.

It is apparent that Frith did not see this kind of musical intelligence in entirely positive terms at the time; as Hodgkinson told an interviewer in 1984, "Fred had this habit of writing big pieces, and then deciding that they didn't hang together and then he sort of took bits out of them."[73] But what may have felt like a failure or inability to produce a large-scale, formally coherent piece of music could instead have simply been another measure of the strength of Frith's improvisative musical personality. The specificity of this way of making music comes into sharper focus when it is compared with what could be called a "blueprint" model: a piece of music that refrains from knocking the environment about and instead simply imposes its will on the world and asks it to comply. This blueprint musical mode was best exemplified by Hodgkinson, a matter attested to by most members of the band. "Tim was the real serious composer of the group," Geoff Leigh told me. "Fred was the musician—his level of musicianship was extraordinary. He wrote a lot more than Tim, but Tim was bringing in the stuff that was more groundbreaking, more difficult to play." Frith himself told Wilton at the time, "I suspect Tim, who has much greater powers of concentration than I have, is much more seriously + deeply involved in those things [i.e., modern compositional techniques] than I am." Though Frith "dabbled with . . . appurtenances of modern music," he did so "strictly on a dilettante, looking-for-effect level I'm afraid."

But in the Cow, relationships among the terms *composition, improvisation,* and *notation* were complex. One of their most distinctive modes of improvisation—what Lydia Goehr calls "improvisation *impromptu*"— consisted in finding the right solution when they were put on the spot (with an unchangeable recording date, a new set of collaborators, or unforeseen performance obstacles). This kind of improvisation is related to but not the same as "improvisation *extempore*," which describes the act of making music up in performance from this moment forward.[74] Being put on the spot, as Goehr explains, is like getting put to the test, and, as we have already seen, the Cows sought out such agonistic situations; if they couldn't find them, they made them. ("Do not suffer in silence: start knocking the env[ironmen]t about, & watch what happens to the discomfort," wrote Ashby.)[75]

And it makes no difference for improvisation *impromptu* whether the right fit involved notation or not: little fragments, bridges, and temporary fix-its moved into and out of notation ad libitum. The Cows' papers are filled with these bridges to nowhere. Furthermore, Cutler didn't read notation, so there were often two kinds of relation to the material going on at once when they rehearsed: the band repeated sections ad nauseam from manuscript while Cutler solved or created metrical puzzles with his appendages. He reasoned that the clash of ear and eye learning in this arrangement pushed him to write drum parts that he never could have arrived at another way. Would that be improvisation or composition? Although Hodgkinson's pieces tended to resist getting pulled apart and revised in performance, they were never immune to that treatment. "Erk Gah" frequently seeded its introductory improvisation with scripted rhythmic interjections by Frith (on xylophone) and Cutler (on drums); these biting unison gestures fore-shadowed some of the rhythmic motives later to come.

Golden Oldies of Yesteryear

When Henry Cow next traveled to Europe in February 1977, it was for a seventeen-date tour of Italy that had been organized by Nick Hobbs.[76] They had met him during their 1974 Beefheart tour, which was the nineteen-year-old's third tour with Van Vliet; he was such a huge fan of Beefheart that he'd skipped school and traveled with the band, eventually working as an unpaid roadie. Finding the Tragic Band less than gripping, he spent more time with Hodgkinson and Cutler, who impressed the youngster with their intensity and eloquence. He liked the music, too, especially once Krause had joined. Hobbs had stayed in touch with Henry Cow, occasionally sleeping at the Walmer Road house when he was in London. A few years later, he was working as a gardener at the Krishnamurti school, in Brockwood Park, when he befriended the rich uncle of an Italian student there. The uncle invited him to work in the office of his factory in Vicenza, where he moved in 1976.

He was still interested in rock, however, and arranged several dates for the Cow in late October. A letter from Hobbs to Hodgkinson, dated November 3, 1976, indicates that he had been pitching himself as a tour administrator for the band—he wanted Hodgkinson to know that he thought Henry Cow were doing important work, and (apparently in reaction to cautions from the elder Cow) getting involved with the organization would not be a waste of time. In fact, in October Henry Cow had agreed that they wanted to employ an administrator to coordinate their business in London while they were on the road; one priority was to establish an alternative gig circuit in England akin to the houses of culture in Holland and France. There the matter rested until March, when, after wrapping up the successful and efficient Italian tour that Hobbs had organized, they took him onto the payroll. Turning down an offer from his boss to manage a new factory in Brazil, Hobbs returned to London and went to work.

He was not accepted by everybody. Cooper voiced serious reservations, while Balchin would have preferred a good mechanic to come along on the road, and Clarke—though he expressed support for the idea of an administrator—was less than welcoming to his new colleague. "He was hell for me," Hobbs explains. They would eventually become friends after the Cows disbanded, but Hobbs's relationship with Balchin remained "a disaster." Although they were rabidly loyal to the band, the stalwart duo of Balchin and Clarke resented the sudden presence of an administrator who appeared (erroneously) to be calling the shots, especially one who came in the form of an "upstart, rather geeky kid," Hobbs explains. They hazed him cruelly. In one memorable trial, they forced the kid to drive the bus from the rehearsal space in Clerkenwell through central London to Clapham in the south. Not only had Hobbs never driven a bus before, he didn't even have a license. "I drove straight through the narrow streets of Soho, amazingly not killing anyone or getting arrested (though I did scratch the paint off someone's car)."[77]

But the first tour that Hobbs booked for the Cow kept them busy every night for seventeen days in a row. The following month, March, took them across France in a week, and they were gone for another month beginning in late April for concerts in Holland and Scandinavia. They were forced to tour heavily because they owed themselves extensive back wages—since summer 1975, everybody in the band and crew earned the same £15 per week (raised to £20 in 1977)—and their equipment and vehicles had persistent upkeep costs. And their sojourns in London—during the Christmas holidays in December, for the first six weeks of 1977, for two weeks in March and three more in April—were further crippled by "appalling difficulties getting gigs," as Cooper noted in the meeting minutes on January 14. Their plans to record a new album had been postponed repeatedly, but even though they had not yet terminated their contract with Virgin, they were still expecting to finance the new recording themselves. That expectation meant that they would need a sizable down payment to secure studio time.

The fifteen-date Holland/Scandinavia tour took the band to a series of low moments; "This tour is making all the others look like a Thomas Cook package holiday," Cooper wrote to her mother.[78] Cutler had to return suddenly to London to be with his terminally ill father, so they cancelled dates until he could rejoin the group. Juggling exhaustion and concern for her son, Krause suffered a breakdown on a ferry in Sweden, screaming at the top of her lungs. "It couldn't have been easy for them, but somehow I just really was at the end of my. . . . I had nothing left in me. I was drained of everything," she remembers. As always, this moment of extremity produced its own small acts of kindness—Balchin giving up his cabin so that Krause could rest by herself, Born watching over Max until his mother was back up to the task—but the group was still riven with nasty divisions exacerbated by their gloomy finances.

In a letter to Merck on May 6, Cooper wrote,

> The group's financial state is really disastrous, and since playing in other countries is only partly to do with playing music to lots of people and a lot to do with keeping various markets ticking over we have to keep touring (though even so, we won't get out of this financial crisis just on gig earnings, it's going to mean loans—not a good idea—or gifts—not likely). The majority of the group is committed to 4-week-maximum tours and I agree that even that is grossly unsatisfactory if there's five of them a year but until the group's practice has been radically transformed (which we are working towards) that may be the only possible interim measure.[79]

They held almost daily meetings to brainstorm economic solutions, but the problem proved intractable.

Henry Cow might have tolerated these travails with greater aplomb had they found a way to put aside time for the creation of new music—the stale repertoire was starting to feel like a family visit gone way too long. "The gigs have really not been going too well," Cooper wrote to Merck in March. "The sooner we stop playing these golden oldies of yesteryear the happier I shall be."[80] In a meeting way back on December 13, Hodgkinson voiced a wish to withdraw "Erk Gah" until he had a chance to rewrite it, but the rest of the Cows insisted that it remain in the set. They thought the rhythm "needs loosening up," and Cutler didn't like how some unison passages were working, but they agreed to keep it on. They also agreed with Hodgkinson's desire to rewrite the lyrics. An old friend from Ottawa Music Company, Jeremy Baines, had written a large piece for them inspired by the gamelan; they also considered working on that, but discovered they had no time in the foreseeable future.[81] Meanwhile, they wanted to rehearse a new Frith/Cutler song ("Joan"), a Frith instrumental (probably an early version of some ideas that Cutler would later call "The Big Tune"), and two Cooper pieces, an instrumental ("Untitled") and a song (unknown). Nonetheless, when they went back out on the road, they took the same repertoire with them. They did premier an early version of "Joan" on February 13 in London, but otherwise the sets appear to be more of the same: "Erk Gah," "Beautiful as the Moon," "Beast," "Ruins," "No More Songs," "The March," "Nirvana for Mice," "Teenbeat," and "Would You Prefer Us to Lie?" They did try "In Two Minds" in Mestre on March 6, but it doesn't show up on any of the other several concert bootlegs from this period. (Occasionally, the set was altered in response to Krause losing her voice.)

Figure 6.7 The storefront at 5 Silverthorne Road, Henry Cow headquarters after 1975. PHOTOGRAPH BY TAKUMBA RIA LAWAL.

In mid-March, Henry Cow again met in London to deliberate on their stagnant live material. Frith thought he had failed in what he'd been trying to do with his instrumental, while Born was dissatisfied with their way of working: they weren't accomplishing what they set out to do. Hobbs chipped in to say that "Erk Gah" was the most interesting part of the set, and "Ruins" was still okay, but "Banners" and "Beast" no longer satisfied him. Furthermore, he said, the band was using free improvisations "irresponsibly," merely as links rather than living, developing music in their own right. Frith concurred that "Banners" and "Beasts" were suffering from overperformance; furthermore, their sets were more ordered and "safe" than they used to be. The next surviving concert recording—from Sweden in early May—testifies that Henry Cow had indeed striven to add new material, including Cooper's first long composition ("Untitled"), another short instrumental (either Frith or Cooper), and a Frith arrangement of Eisler/

Brecht's "On Suicide," which had originally come to the band via Anthony Moore. (In Scandinavia, they seem to have followed this short gem with a cello solo by Born, whose instrument often got swallowed up by the electronics of her comrades in group work.)

In the next chapter, we shall turn to the band's many diverse political projects and musical struggles in 1977. But the main struggle—for survival—would only deepen as the year wore on. Henry Cow's dire financial circumstances created new leakage effects when they tried to address their debt by pursuing more paid gigs instead of taking time off to write new material. Already closely associated with Cutler, Hobbs grew into something of a protégé once he had moved in to 5 Silverthorne Road, Cutler and Thomas's residence that had become the administrative home of Henry Cow. There, Hobbs set to work on the exact tasks he had been hired to accomplish: finding good gigs and planning tours. But for some Cows, this new arrangement introduced a split between the daily intentions and plans of the musicians and their external steering from Silverthorne Road. For example, Cooper complained that when the York International Marxists Group phoned the Cow headquarters to arrange the details for a gig that they'd already mentioned to Frith, Hobbs replied that the band would not play for less than £250. Meanwhile, he booked a show for the Communist Party for only £75, and the CP ended up cancelling.[82] For the nonaligned Cooper, this pecuniary decision was overlaid with ideology, for she was deeply skeptical of the British CP (the IMG was a nonaligned Marxist group); Cutler, as we shall see in the next chapter, tended to support the CP with greater enthusiasm.[83]

For Hodgkinson, Hobbs's organizational activities felt increasingly "exterior" and "institutionalized." "And suddenly the outside starts to determine the inside, instead of the other way around. . . . We were being carried along by external necessities. It was a feeling of disempowerment." In 1981, he noted one concrete example of this disempowerment: "It no longer seems possible to see incoming mail."[84] Though these developments contributed to Hodgkinson's dark worries about the isolation of Cutler from the group, they also fostered doubts of a more fundamental nature. "What about being able to create as you go along? What's happened to improvisation and discovery? Everything's been programmed here." As we get further into 1977, we will see that there were still ample opportunities for discovery and improvisation, but they often arose outside of the band itself.

7 No Joy Anymore | London 1977

In 1977, Henry Cow engaged with cultural politics in London more directly than at any previous point. As we'll see, this engagement brought them into conversation with other sonic activists in their home city, and it also spurred them into new collaborative arrangements as a group and as individuals. Self-organization and DIY continued to serve as guiding ideals, especially once their full separation from Virgin came into view. Conflicts inside the group revealed themselves along gender lines, and by the end of the year, Dagmar Krause would leave the band. The year began, however, with a boost of organizing activity at the intersection of music and radical politics.

Back in the spring of 1976, Henry Cow had befriended some politically minded musicians outside of Stockholm and engaged them in a running debate on the proper form for anticapitalism in music. The Swedes thought Henry Cow's avant-gardism was hopelessly bourgeois, while the Cows castigated the Swedish political songsters for putting socialist lyrics on top of the most banal music product. But they loved the debate, and when the Swedish political song movement produced a documentary film about an alternative festival to counter Eurovision, *We Have Our Own Song*, the Cow (or possibly their former soundperson, Neil Sandford, who had cultivated many contacts there) acquired a copy of the film and arranged a concert, screening, and discussion at the Other Cinema in London on December 19.[1]

A sign-up sheet circulated among attendees, and among the thirty people to sign it were the musicians Steve Beresford (London Musicians Collective), Bob Cubitt (Elevator), Tony Haines (Redbrass), Laurie Baker (People's Liberation Music), Martin King (Elevator); journalists Marion Fudger (*Spare Rib*, also the bassist for the Derelicts), Dave Laing (*Let It Rock*, Rock Writers Coop), Mike Flood Page (Rock Writers Coop), Penny Valentine (*Disc, Sounds*), Ian Hoare (BBC, Rock Writers Coop), and John Hoyland (*Let It Rock*); theatre director Bruce Birchall; and representatives of the Hackney and Islington Music Workshop and the Unity Theatre Folk Club. Consolidated onto one page in Tim Hodgkinson's hand, these interested

A Socialist Festival of Music is being planned for this summer. It'll take the form of a weekend of both performance and discussion aimed at advancing the work of musicians committed to the struggle against capitalism.

The idea arose out of a series of meetings of left-wing musicians and other interested people, sparked off by a showing at the Other Cinema in December of the film 'We've got our own song' – a documentary about the festival staged by radical Scandinavian performers in Stockholm in 1975 as a counter to the Eurovision Song Contest.

At these meetings, we discovered that we shared certain problems. It was generally agreed that:

(i) we have to break down the ways in which musicians are separated from their audiences, through the presentation of music as a commodity in the market; and that

(ii) while individual musicians and groups may develop a connection between their politics and their music, these connections are generally not made clear to a broader community of musicians/listeners, so they remain 'private' and ineffective.

But there were equally clear disagreements about how to approach these problems. Certain questions seemed central:

(a) Can music itself, in the sense of organised sound, have a political content at all?

(b) How important is the accessibility of music — must the music that serves the people be music that most people can easily listen to, understand, dance to, play? Must revolutionary music be revolutionary in form and technique?

(c) Are particular styles or traditions in themselves reactionary or progressive — e.g. is 'folk' always progressive and 'rock' always decadent?

(d) For a Socialist movement, must music serve primarily as a propaganda instrument of some predefined politics? Can music help define a new revolutionary politics?

(e) What claims can be made for the political effectiveness of 'alternative' forms of organisation — such as co-operatives for making records, distribution, touring circuits, etc?

It was felt that a festival – appropriately structured – would provide a forum for socialist musicians to exchange ideas among themselves about these problems, both through critical discussion and through seeing each other at work. It would also aim to involve the audience actively in that process, and it would perhaps bring a number of performers to the attention of a wider audience.

We're now looking for suitable venues – with a view to basing the event in London, but considering the possibility of touring the country. We need support – not just financial help, but advice, clerical work, festival equipment and other resources. Finally, we're exploring the possibility of setting up a co-operative to enable radical music groups to take over their own management, recording and publishing.

To join the project, attend the fortnightly meetings at present held at the Other Cinema (use the back entrance in Scala Street) at 2p.m. on Sundays, 27th Feb., 13th March, etc. * (below). To get on our mailing list, send your name with a donation to cover clerical expenses to the following address:

Music for Socialism,
30 Hornsey Park Road,
London N. 8.

* Among those who have attended the meetings are:

Evan Parker; Peoples' Liberation Music; Frankie Armstrong; Peoples' Record Press; Brian Pearson; Red Brass; 'Art Attacks' magazine; Red Square; Belt and Braces Band; Rock against Racism; Eddie Provost Band; Sidewalk Theatre; Elevator; Unity Theatre Folk Club; Hackney and Islington Music Workshop; Henry Cow; London Musicians' Collective.

parties were invited to a second meeting in January; the provisional title of the group was "Music Against Capitalism."

This name would be one of the first things to go. Ian Hoare recalls himself and others asking, "Can we turn it into something more positive than just simply being 'against'? Rather than 'Rock *Against* Racism,' 'Music *for* something'—and make it something very specific, make it more politically committed." The reference to Rock Against Racism (RAR) was hardly coincidental, as that organization had recently been founded by a group of Socialist Workers Party members and would make a significant contribution to antiracist politics until its demise in 1982. Unlike RAR, which coopted punk and reggae musicians to fight the rising tide of racist nationalism, Music for Socialism (MFS), as they would call the new group, would examine the very relation between music and left politics.

"What is such an organization for? This is the question," Hodgkinson recalls. "There are things we're interested in, there are questions that intrigue us, and it's very interesting just to sit down with a folk singer, a rock musician, and a contemporary composer, . . . all of whom are socialists, and to see what's going on here." Over a series of meetings into February, the participants (who grew to include Evan Parker, Frankie Armstrong, Red Square, Belt and Braces Band, the Eddie Prévost Band, Sidewalk Theatre, and representatives of the People's Record Press and Rock Against Racism) discovered that they shared certain problems, which were enumerated in a February briefing document (see figure 7.1).[2]

This list of problems and discussion points bears the strong imprint of Henry Cow, and indeed Hodgkinson, Lindsay Cooper, and Georgina Born were active in these early meetings. Their experience with left musicians and cultural workers in France, Italy, and Scandinavia had left them wondering why England lacked these strong debates or initiatives for alternative means of production. As Chris Cutler told the *Evening Standard* around this time, in Europe "people have worked out alternative set-ups to fund gigs; there are even co-operative record companies. The cultural climate is more stimulating. Fans are constructively critical. . . . The cultural and political inertia in Britain is so frustrating."[3] Although they rarely played at home anymore, the band had earned a certain credibility among intellectuals on the left. Hoare, a self-described "soul nut" who had published *The Soul Book* in 1975 with

---

Figure 7.1 Music for Socialism, planning document, February 1977. COURTESY OF IAN HOARE.

Clive Anderson, Simon Frith, and Tony Cummings, testifies to their reputation among nonfans such as himself: "Even if you didn't like the music, you respected what they were doing. That was the key thing. I never liked [their music], really—it was hard work for me, to listen to that stuff."

This early planning document also announced a festival to foster critical discussion and creative exchange. Although Hodgkinson seems to have taken a formative role in the early direction of the organization—his surviving notes bear a strong resemblance to the public MFS documents—Henry Cow were soon swept away by their touring commitments, and, by May 1977, the festival organizing committee included no Cows. They were Sue Steward, who had recently quit Virgin in protest of their changed artistic direction in summer 1976; Gerry Fitz-Gerald; Neil Sandford; and Ian Hoare.

The festival, titled simply "Music for Socialism," would take place on May 28 at the Battersea Arts Centre in Wandsworth. About six hundred people attended.[4] Its promotional materials had promised a new type of event, "a kind of conference, with each 'concert' followed by an open discussion on particular aspects of the relationship between socialism and music."[5] The morning began with practical workshops on the guitar, voice, and songwriting, plus a separate space run by the Women's Liberation Music Project where women could experiment alone with instruments and equipment. In the afternoon, the event split into a series of concurrent concert/debate sessions on such topics as women in music, folk traditions and the commercial marketplace, and propaganda versus formal innovation. The animated confab that took place at the final session would dominate the rest of the day's discussion, spilling over into the evening plenary, the next afternoon's sessions, and retrospective accounts of the festival. The agitprop band People's Liberation Music (John Tilbury, Laurie Baker, Geoff Pearce, and Cornelius Cardew) held strongly to the line that music should serve politics; formal experimentation, in their view, was bourgeois affectation. Many in the audience found their performance stiff and dogmatic. According to Ian Walker, the brief time for discussion afterward was initiated by a woman (I believe it was Born) who launched into a tirade against PLM, "screaming that 'their music was devoid of all human content.'"[6]

"Is there anybody from PLM here to answer these charges?" asked the moderator, Hodgkinson. Silence, then howls of derision.

"That's just typical!" said Geoff Leigh, "They're professional politicians. They've probably gone off to address another meeting." The discussion turned to Red Balune's Dada performance, which featured one artist dancing with a broom. Cardew, returning to the hall to answer his critics, asked,

"If musicians started playing brooms, what kind of music would the people have?" Over Leigh's exasperated protests, Cardew went on to explain that music should serve the politics, and not vice versa. In PLM's proper, pro-letarian socialism, Cardew later explained, a strong political theory dic-tates how music must serve the workers' struggle.[7] Bourgeois, reformist socialisms—the Communist Party of Great Britain in their "Moving Left Revue" and the Socialist Workers Party in Rock Against Racism—deny the bourgeois character of popular music, which had been a powerful weapon in US and British imperialism; pop's "ideological heart is slavery and degradation." Given that it was the middle of 1977, the conversation inevitably turned to punk, which Cardew later called a "fascist cult associ-ated with self-mutilation, exhibitionism and the glorification of decay and despair."[8]

Although Cardew thought that PLM's set "showed the historical continu-ity and international breadth of proletarian revolutionary music," most of the audience held the opinion that Irish Republican songs from the nine-teenth century could not speak well to the current crisis. Moreover, in the words of Cutler, "The quality of their performance was wooden and devoid of musical interest."[9] In an extended critique published later that summer, Cutler wrote that PLM's uptight musicianship might fly at a demonstration, but its deficiencies were obvious in a concert setting; they had not adjusted their practice to its context. Furthermore, PLM could have engaged in self-criticism about the fiasco, but instead they defended their position, and did so theoretically instead of empirically. "And there is where their *theory* collapses," Cutler wrote. "Here then is Cornelius Cardew defending his rotten perfor-mance because he says it has 'correct theory.' He ignores the affective aesthetic aspects of what he does, yet it is only these which validate his work."[10]

For an improviser who tested his environment as a fundamental mode of orienting himself, any choice to restrict oneself to the theoretical do-main was fatally flawed. And the particular flaw of PLM's set—not attending to the specificities of the performance setting and changing their practice accordingly—mirrored the general error in Cardew's approach to music and politics. Cutler averred that we must "draw our analysis from the real con-tradictions and interrelations of our political and social environment and not superimpose an analysis . . . onto whatever situation we are in." In their actual historical circumstances, musicians can only struggle *against capi-talism* (Cutler was clearly opposed to MFS's earlier name change), and that meant working inside of contradictions and in tension with the popular music industry.

The day concluded with a plenary performance and debate to pull together the major threads of the day's discussions. Although Tim Souster's group, odB, also appeared on the bill that evening, many in attendance seem to have concluded that the whole shebang was Henry Cow's show. One participant, Warshaw, later wrote that he heard people asking about the band all day long. "I began to wonder whether this was really the Henry Cow show with support. . . . I'm afraid we just have to live with the fact that in 1977, in addition to size of following, number of LPs and success of image promotion, wattage does count. Anyone who wheels in all that equipment *must* be important," he wrote.[11] (Beresford also raised an eyebrow at Henry Cow's "mountains of complex electronic equipment."[12]) As emcee for the night, Hoare even apologized for the appearance that Henry Cow had been given star billing ahead of their many comrades in attendance, but, he explained, "All yesterday people were ringing up and all they wanted to know was 'When are Henry Cow due on?'"[13]

The festival continued the next day at Oval House, where representatives of the Musicians Union joined rock journalists Dave Laing, Simon Frith, and Gary Herman to discuss the music industry, broadcasting, the significance of punk, "alternative" record labels, and the future of MFS. The Bicycle Thieves, Dave Holland, and the Workers' Music Association Choir all gave performances, and they also screened a film on Pierre Boulez and *Sex Pistols Number 1* by Julien Temple.[14] As Walker reported, the day's arguments centered on punk and new wave, with Simon Frith concluding, "Punks tell us more about the record business than they do about unemployed kids."[15] Subsequent publications by Frith, Laing, Hoare, and Herman likewise show that these journalists and critics maintained a skeptical view of the revolutionary potential or working-class credentials of punk.

In his introduction to a print forum on the MFS festival in *Musics* later that summer, Hoare reminded readers that the event was an experimental format to encourage discussion, clarify differences, and survey a heterogeneous field of performers considered "noncommercial" by the industry.[16] He invited several participants to share their impressions of the festival and suggest how similar events might be better organized in the future. Remarkably, only one contributor—Jack Warshaw—commented on the near complete absence of black musics at the gathering (Jackson Kanjela being the one exception). No soul, no reggae, no dub, no funk, and hardly any jazz. These absences represented equally the social, intellectual, and musical circuits of the organizers as well as the race blindness in these corners of the British left. In place of a sustained critique of the race discourse of the event, there was some of the expected anti-intellectual griping about "too much talk, too little music," and more specific commentary on the formal, auditorium setting that might have hampered the free flow of ideas. A few participants—Beresford, Leigh, and Kim Green of the Bicycle Thieves—questioned the apparent divergence between the music (and musicians) on offer and the "real" working classes.

The Musicians Union (MU) had provided support to the Festival, and their rock organizer, Mike Evans, roamed the premises on Saturday, distributing a flyer making the case for the MU as the only organized voice for musicians in the UK.[17] Representing them on the Sunday sessions, Brian Blane urged all socialists to joint the MU and agitate for change from inside the organization, a process that would necessitate interaction with the Union's more reactionary members. Despite a warm reception to his speech, he reported, none of his points were taken up during the general discussion. It's likely that few in attendance saw the MU as an active ally in their struggles; the orchestral, dance band, and wind band musicians who constituted its traditional membership had a far greater record for rank-and-file solidarity than did itinerant jazz, rock, or improvised music artists. (Nonetheless, the archive of the central London branch of the MU reveals that Cardew, Pearce, Baker, Beresford, and Nicols were vocal participants in the London Branch during the 1970s, and Hodgkinson and Cooper regularly attended meetings and occasionally stood for election to become delegates to the Trade Union Conference or members of the District Council.)[18]

As Leon Rosselson noted, the formation of a correct party line was not the goal; unfortunately, he continued, the political and musical divisions among many of the acts might be even greater than anticipated.[19] After just a few meetings in January, MFS had agreed to set aside direct theoretical discussion of socialism and music in favor of practical planning for the festival. The problem with this decision, Cutler later noted, was that, without a clear political theory, it was impossible to evaluate whether individual musicians should be invited to perform, and therefore almost everyone considered was given a spot on the event. Therefore, they had to plan parallel sessions, which barred any single attendee from assembling an overall picture of the contradictions and patterns. So the next step in MFS's plan—take what they had learned in the festival and begin to move toward concrete policies—had been rendered problematic. Cutler held that PLM garnered the most attention at the event because they were the only group who came with a clear and strong political theory.

The only concrete proposal to appear after the event came from Nick Hobbs. (Though the political theory may have been clear in Cardew's case, his essay was light on specifics.) Alternative institutions in the United Kingdom—the Musicians Union, the Jazz Centre Society, the London Musicians Collective, the Bristol Musicians Co-operative—"have limited functions and seem unable to offer a lead to musicians who are critical of the system," Hobbs wrote.[20] While the United Kingdom offered a surfeit of apathy, the Italian and Scandinavian cases had shown Henry Cow that it was possible for audiences to support politically and artistically progressive music. The industry's domination of popular music meant that even independent musical movements like punk would be quickly coopted. Instead, Hobbs advocated for what Berthold Brecht called "functional transformation," in which the intelligentsia not only supplies the production apparatus with progressive material, but also transforms that means of production toward socialism.[21] In Hobbs's terms, "Taking over the means of production is a revolutionary step. If a group of musicians own their own means of production . . . the responsibility falls into *their* hands whether to continue capitalist economic relations or not."[22] Therefore, MFS had to continue to expand its numbers to give it financial strength, then acquire recording and amplification equipment for the benefit of all members. The organization also needed to set up a record company and alternative network for the presentation of live music, and they needed to pressure the Arts Council of Great Britain to support politically and artistically progressive music.

Hobbs was advocating for the same position of artistic self-determination that had been sought previously by a number of jazz musicians—the Jazz Artists Guild, Jazz Composers Guild, Association for the Advancement of Creative Musicians, Jazz Composers Orchestra Association/New Music Distribution Service, and the Sun Ra Arkestra (the last of which Cutler would surely have known about, since he was a huge fan). Similar precedents in the rock field are exceedingly difficult to summon. Hobbs did not indicate any knowledge of these organizations, but the Jazz Composers Orchestra's trip to London in August was covered in MFS's first proper newsletter, where the unnamed author detailed its history (and that of the Jazz Composers Guild).

In the meetings that followed the May 28 festival, MFS constituted itself as an organization. Hodgkinson drafted a statement of aims and a constitu-

Figure 7.2 Nick Hobbs and Chris Cutler, working at home on Silverthorne Road, 1978.
PHOTOGRAPH BY TAKUMBA RIA LAWAL.

STATEMENT OF AIMS APPROVED AT THE MEETING
OF JUNE 25th.

1) The broad aim of this organisation is to advance the struggle
of the working class through musical work.

2) Recognising that this struggle cannot be resolved under the
present system, we aim to reject the individualist and commercial
criteria with which Capitalism defines and legitimizes musical
work, and place our services
work, and place our capabilities at the service of the struggle of
the working class towards Socialism.

3) At the same time we recognise that music serves definite
class interests and that there are many different kinds of music,
and many different ways in which music can be developed in
support of a class struggle which in itself takes many forms.
Therefore we shall not be seeking to impose an absolute definition
of what Socialist music is, but we shall try to discover the
conditions under which different kinds of music are revolutionary.

4) We aim to criticize and advance the relationships between
music workers under Capitalism, their relations with other
cultural workers, with the public, with the broad labour movement
and with the left political parties.

5) NOTE: the phrase ' and their cultural policies ' was
considered too central to this Statement of Aims to stay as a
subsection of Para. 4, and proposals for the wording of a new
paragraph 5 will be discussed at the July 31st. meeting.

6) To these ends we shall attempt, among other things;

> To promote and document events that open up
> debate on Socialist theory and practice in music.
> and that break down the kind of performer/audience
> relationships produced under Capitalism.

> To study the feasibility of setting up co-operatives
> for the distribution and manufacture of records etc.

> To organise the pooling and sharing of information.
> and resources among musicians

> To set up study groups for practical and theoretical
> problems and to investigate the Music Industry

> To promote an independant touring network.

> To lobby for funds to support the working
> activities of this organisation and its members.

> To encourage 100% union membership among
> music workers.

tion, which were revised and adopted later that summer—they appeared in the August newsletter (see figure 7.3).[23] A list of attendees of a meeting on September 4 indicates that the coordinating committee included Nigel Willmott, Neil Sandford, Tony Haynes, Steve Beresford, Ian Hoare, and Georgie Born, and the contact address in these early months was 30 Hornsey Park Road, where Hoare lived with a smattering of leftwing and countercultural figures. Significant was their founding of the MFS *Newsletter*. Willmott, Sandford, and Les Levidov appear to have taken the lion's share of responsibility after the first few issues. The publication, which had existed in the form of a few single-sheet issues, began in earnest in August and became a repository of information and announcements: how to book a benefit gig; solicitations to support the Community Record Press; invitations to community sing-alongs; updates on Rock Against Racism; proposals for Swedish/English rock exchanges; reports on the MU; translation of Swedish song texts; communiqués from the Swedish MFS equivalent, Contact-Net; solicitations for a women's songbook; gig listings; reports from the new Leeds chapter of MFS; and reviews and discussion of various left music events (and a few Henry Cow gigs) around London. They were printing one thousand copies by October.

In the summer and autumn of 1977, the organization programmed two series. The first, "Summer in the City," at Other Cinema, typically paired a film or two with a musical performer, followed by a discussion led by an MFS-affiliated figure. The second, held at the Almost Free Theatre, was called "Words and Music," and featured several performances on each event followed by a more directed debate. Like their previous two public forums, the series embodied the aim to break down the separation between musicians and their audience; this time they set out specific questions for each event and requested that the musicians provide a written statement before their performance. Having previously bogged down on the question of lyrics and their intelligibility, they wanted to unseat the idea that music was merely a delivery system for verbal "content." "By putting forth as debatable issues that which had previously been treated as unquestioned assumptions, we could better focus the discussion and keep it from degenerating from dogmatic assertions as in previous MFS events," wrote Neil Sandford, who took a leading organizational role.[24]

Figure 7.3 Music for Socialism, "Statement of Aims," from the *Music for Socialism Newsletter*, August 1977. COURTESY OF IAN HOARE.

Summer in the City Programs, 1977

JULY 31   **"Rock 'n' Roll"**
The Girl Can't Help It (dir. Tashlin, 1956)
with Shakin' Stevens & the Sunsets

AUGUST 7   **"Black Music in Britain"**
Reggae (dir. Ové, 1971) and
Step Forward Youth (dir. Shabazz, 1976)
with Aswad

AUGUST 14   **"Women and Rock"**
Janis (dir. Alk, 1974)
with Carol Grimes

AUGUST 21   **"Punk"**
The Sex Pistols Number 1 (dir. Temple, 1977) and
The Sex Pistols Riverboat Party (dir. unknown, 1977)
with the Slits, Sham 69

AUGUST 27   **"Songs of Class Struggle"**
Joe Hill (dir. Widerberg, 1971)
with Jack Warshaw

AUGUST 28   **"Macho in Rock"**
Sympathy For the Devil (dir. Godard, 1968)
with Tom Robinson Band

SEPTEMBER 4   **"The Politics of Rock Performance"**
Privilege (dir. Watkins, 1967)
with Dead Fingers Talk

SEPTEMBER 11   **"Chile and the New Song Movement"**
When the People Awake (dir. Beato, 1972) and
El Tigre Salto y Mato, pero Morira . . . Morira (dir. Álvarez, 1973)
with Kelikuri, Jane Machell, and Alvaro

SEPTEMBER 18   **"Jazz: a Tradition of Protest"**
Shorts on Bessie Smith, Duke Ellington, Charlie Parker and Dizzy
Gillespie, and Sonny Rollins
with Johnny Rondo Trio (David Holland, Lol Coxhill, Colin Wood)

Words and Music Events

OCTOBER 24   **Theatre and Music**

How can socialists develop a political music within a theatrical form where the audience is accustomed to treating it as mere entertainment?

with Monstrous Regiment, Estella Schmidt & Co., and Clapperclaw

OCTOBER 25   **Composition**

What are the problems for musical work which tends to be judged as a "finished product"—classical and timeless?

with Michael Nyman, Pete Devenport, Dave Smith,
and Christian Wolff

OCTOBER 26   **Agitational Music**

What are the problems of performing agitational songs in a "gig" situation?

with Hackney & Islington Music Workshop; CounterAct;
and Jack Warshaw, Sandra Kerr, and Ron Elliot

OCTOBER 27   **Voice Styles**

How do individual and traditional styles of singing challenge the constraints of formal music training in bourgeois culture?

with Bob Davenport, Maggie Nicols, John Pole, and Brian Pearson

OCTOBER 28   **Words in Context**

How can music heighten words rather than disguise them? How can songs complement each other so that the whole performance is greater than the sum of its parts?

with Leon Rosselson and Roy Bailey

OCTOBER 29   **Virtuosity**

What musical purpose should virtuosity serve?

with Evan Parker, Paul Rutherford, and Fred Frith

OCTOBER 30   **Improvisation & Structure**

How can new forms of improvisation expand the breadth of what we might consider "music" and "musical structure"?—break down the distinction between "culture" and the rest of life?

with David Toop and Paul Burwell; Heuristic Music;
and the Feminist Improvising Group

Sandwiched between these two series was a conference on the subject of alternative record and tape distribution networks, one of Henry Cow's idées fixes. It took place on October 1–2 at the Oval House.[25] Unfortunately, the band was on tour in Italy and therefore could not attend. Owners or representatives from a handful of small UK labels participated, along with a few independent/socialist bands and collectives. This British contingent, numbering only about a dozen, was dwarfed by their foreign counterparts (Sweden alone had sent about fifteen representatives), an embarrassing showing that had resulted from errors in publicizing the event. The European labels and distributors included SAM, Plattlarngana, and Kontaktnatet (Sweden); LOVE (Finland); DEMOS (Denmark); l'Orchestra Cooperativa (Italy); and Diffusion Alternative (Belgium). A European contact list was started with about fifty names.

Hoare published some preliminary notes on the conference and a follow-up meeting of the MFS coordinating committee in the MFS newsletter. Given their available resources, would a left record and tape distribution network constitute a realistic project? The committee had concluded, in classic left fashion, that "MFS must never fall into the trap of concentrating on recordings at the expense of live music. Our efforts in the record distribution field must be tied in with our attempts to build up alternative venues for socialist performers."[26] Nonetheless, the committee did see the value of canned music, too, and resolved to consider production from the outset, rather than solely distribution. Subsequent issues of the newsletter indicate that they eventually assembled a directory of resources for the production and distribution of records and tapes, a kind of DIY guide for socialist musicians.

Joyless Intellectuals: Music for Socialism and Rock against Racism

In subsequent appraisals of MFS, the group has suffered from comparisons with Rock Against Racism, the successful offshoot of the Socialist Workers Party that lasted until 1982 and is widely agreed to have pulled audiences for punk and reggae away from fascism and toward the left.[27] Supported and coordinated by their SWP sponsors, RAR activists used youth music to achieve commonly held political and social goals. This instrumentalization of popular music toward a predefined political end represented precisely the kind of relationship between music and politics that MFS sought to analyze and question. As Hoare wrote at the time, RAR "put on consider-able numbers of well-intended and often inspiring gigs without asking too many awkward questions about the political-cultural meaning of the 'gig' format itself. . . . Socialists who get involved in this area should be wary of going along with the musicbiz entrepreneurs in the view that the audience are—in the language of the rock elite—'punters,' whose function is merely to turn up with the appropriate stickers and badges and pay for the privi-lege of witnessing their heros [sic] go through their act."[28] Was there an implicit bourgeois politics in the very form of rock spectacle that RAR had employed? This was the kind of question that motivated MFS.

But compared with RAR's striking logo and iconography, the style of its fanzine, *Temporary Hoarding,* and the wattage of its stars (The Clash or Steel Pulse, among many others), MFS could come across as elitist and out of touch with the newest trends in pop music. Such an interpretation mistakes the public statements of some participants (PLM, the folkies) as a "correct line" developed in common by the organization's membership. On the contrary, most of MFS's active members—Sandford, Hoare, Laing, Steward, Herman, Henry Cow—had long worked in the rock field and were eager to produce a theory of popular music's progressive potential. "In fact, highly-politicised people don't really like us," Frith told the *Evening Standard.* "For them it has to be folk, the music of protest. . . . Most of us have a rock background, which is of course highly bourgeois and decadent!"[29] Hodg-kinson retains notes from this period in which he prepared a defense of pop music for his comrades in the Balham branch of the Communist Party of Great Britain, which he had joined earlier in 1977.[30] Many MFS organizers admitted that their struggles to put on "rock" gigs had given them a reputa-tion as "joyless intellectuals," but simply putting on rock gigs as usual might do nothing special to advance the analyses they were interested in.[31]

What RAR possessed that MFS lacked was a disciplined group of young, energetic workers who could devote their time and the Socialist Worker Party's resources to the administration of an organization.[32] With separate fulltime jobs, no office facilities, and no printing capabilities, working musi-cians were too burdened with their own affairs—coordinating gigs, tours, recordings, and publicity—to bring a consistent orderliness to MFS; during the organization's eighteen months of existence, for instance, Henry Cow embarked on more than fifteen tours in the United Kingdom and Europe. Therefore, MFS struggled to develop their conversations into a unified and coherent theory of music and socialism, which was no minor failing. Hodg-kinson called these problems of theoretical clarity and procedural order

both chronic and serious. He wrote, "We readily admit that our organisation is slack but we haven't often admitted that this seriously impedes even
theoretical advance. But continuity seems almost impossible for working musicians: This is the central contradiction of Music for Socialism."[33]
Theoretical advances would come, but it would take a few years for Cutler
and Laing to produce books on issues related to those of MFS; as we'll see,
Cooper published her article, "Women, Music, Feminism—Notes," later in
1977, and Hodgkinson would place several essays in the para-academic and
scholarly press over the next three decades.

Although Music for Socialism would continue publishing their newsletter until the summer of 1978, Henry Cow's involvement in the organization
diminished over the course of the autumn. As we will see, they were touring
again extensively across Europe, fretting about an upcoming recording session, and pursuing their own administrative projects, many of which continued to show up in the pages of the MFS newsletter.

Chief among these was a project called "Music Net," which launched in
January 1978 as a kind of MFS subgroup to continue advancing their interest in an alternative network of venues, promoters, publicity, and personal
contacts.[34] The group's membership included Cutler, Hodgkinson, Hobbs,
Beresford, Haynes, and Cathy Williams and Geoff Leigh (Red Balune); their
contact address, 5 Silverthorne Road, was also Henry Cow headquarters,
suggesting that Hobbs and Cutler had taken a leadership role. The group
thought that a split from MFS was necessary because once the network was
up and running, it would require a full-time administrator, which in turn
would require funds for a salary. Applying to the Arts Council for such a
reason would be hopeless with a name that included the word *socialism*,
ergo "Music Net." They wanted somebody to spend April to September
traveling the country and making contacts with existing small-scale institutions, then write up a report for MFS. This person would also begin applying
for grants to subsidize their work.

A typewritten proposal for Music Net in Hodgkinson's personal archive
evidences a noteworthy narrowing of MFS's more ecumenical scope—
Music Net would work for the interests of many MFS members, but not
folk musicians like Rosselson or doctrinal Marxist-Leninists like PLM. The
proposal concentrated on market representation and sources of support for
"alternative" musics, including possible state subsidy and special relationships with college entertainment committees and other noncommercial
cultural organizations. Strangely, it makes a rather weak appeal for "alternative" musics based on their novelty and "social relevance," but not for how

they actively opposed the capitalist music market, which is how they would have been framed in a MFS meeting. One reason for this reticence might have been that the proposal was to serve as a draft for grant support and therefore had to keep mention of destroying capitalism to a minimum. The anonymous author explains that while art musics (classical and jazz) receive state patronage and folk music gets support in the isolated cell of the folk club, pop and rock live in a world created by the music industry. But some musics enjoy none of these forms of support. "These kinds of music are generally the most experimental. This experiment takes several forms—mainly— improvising music, progressive rock and jazz, and political music."[35]

As the document continues, the reasons for supporting this kind of experimental music get somewhat fuzzy: "If it is worth exploring new musical forms and if there is a case for music which is socially relevant, . . . then experimental music as we are defining it has some considerable importance, and should therefore not be kept out of sight by Market or State cultural considerations." Experimental music "explores new forms," is "socially relevant," and is not necessarily "unpopular"—these were the justifications given for creating, supporting, and consuming experimental music. But this list fails to mention what was perhaps the most important justification for experimentalism from Henry Cow's perspective, which was the way in which it contributed to the functional transformation of a social mode of musical production, moving it toward socialism. As Cutler would write a few years later, "*The politicisation of music* would mean, in our industrial, urban, commodity-alienated context, the *revolutionary transformation of the prevailing relations of production, circulation and consumption.*"[36]

Henry Cow had subscribed to the notion that politically progressive music had to present innovative form, not simply revolutionary content. This difference lay at the heart of their critique of the stale music of PLM or their Swedish friends. To the charge that this approach eventuated in elitist or inaccessible music, they would have responded that the music industry— record companies, concert promotion, and journalism—exerted a deleterious control over the tastes of the public.[37] Their experience in Europe had shown them that more complicated or unusual music could indeed capture the interest of a diverse audience that was less administered by the Anglo entertainment industry. According to Cutler, Henry Cow's revolutionary transformation of production consisted in its refusal of the split between composer and performer (practiced most of all, but not exclusively, in open improvisation), collective authorship, and employment of electronic instruments and the recording process.[38] Through these practices, the band reasoned, they negated the existing relations of art music and commodified popular music, which Cutler called hierarchical, money-mediated, and exploitative. The result was an incremental move toward socialism, within the limits of the possible.

For Henry Cow, these changes in production would also effect changes in reception, as we have already observed. To negate the existing relationships between artist and listener, a relationship mediated by the commodity form, they sought exchanges based on communication rather than consumption (of an LP, a concert experience, or a pop star). Improvisation forged numerous channels of dialogue, but so too did written compositions. Unfamiliar, nonidiomatic, or "difficult" material could confound the "automatic consumption reflex."[39] Above all, Cutler later explained, they worked to engage their audience—"we shall have to be prepared to discuss and to take criticism seriously."[40]

If Henry Cow had been pursuing this politicization of musical production and consumption for many years, the "revolutionary transformation" of circulation had emerged more recently as a topic of intense interest, since the band had become exasperated with Virgin to the point of exploring alternative means of getting their music to its audience. Virgin's early years may have been rhetorically marked by an allegiance to low-sellers with "integrity," but by 1977 it had become obvious to Henry Cow and others that all big record companies only release music that is "worth" releasing, and "worth" was measured by projected sales. There would always be freak successes like *Tubular Bells*, but on the whole companies could not afford to speculate, Cutler pointed out, and therefore the industry pitched against innovative content.[41]

Nonetheless, conversations with their Swedish and Italian comrades had yielded a strong hope for independent production and distribution, and this was exactly the direction that Henry Cow was pointing toward in 1977. Later, Cutler would clarify that "such strategies . . . necessitate, if they are to be revolutionary, a type of independence which is not merely *petty bourgeois*."[42] To the drummer, early Virgin would be an example of a petty bourgeois enterprise, because it attempted to corner the market in unusual music and accumulate wealth through doing so. (A notice for Music Net in 1978 announced their aversion to becoming "New Wave capitalists."[43]) The type of independence Cutler desired "knows itself to be political and provisional, no more than an intermediate cell of resistance (because, after all, it must always find itself in opposition, and thus defined by the thing it opposes)."[44]

Music Net would soon vanish, leaving no trace after April 1978 (and little memory among the Cows today). By then, the situation in Henry Cow had changed considerably, and, probably in response to the organizational chaos and ideological provisionality of MFS as well as the desultory participation of their English associates, Hobbs and Cutler had thrown themselves into two new ventures that closely shadowed the general concerns of Music Net: Rock in Opposition and Recommended Records. I will examine both of these projects in greater detail in the next chapter, but all this MFS hubbub indicates the incredible diversity and energy in London's extraparliamentary left during the 1970s—it was but one DIY organization in a sea of self-starter theory/praxis initiatives situated on the line between culture and politics during these years.[45]

We're Not into Chaos

Though just a sampling, these forums and organizations give a good sense of how musicians and music workers on the left—some "avant-garde" and some not—took concrete steps toward an analysis of their social circumstances and a committed advocacy for their marginalized practice in the 1970s. They thought hard about the relation between contemporary cultural production and radical politics. Ever aloof, the scholarly music disciplines in the United Kingdom had little to say about these latest developments, so music intellectuals outside the academy developed theory and analyses in informal exchanges like these. Hodgkinson's early engagement with Theodor Adorno's writing is one case in point: his notes indicate that he was reading *The Philosophy of Modern Music* soon after it was translated into English in 1973, and the philosopher's complaints about the empty sacralization of "serious music" show up in Hodgkinson's Henry Cow–related texts. And yet, given the tremendous role of LPs in Henry Cow's musical education, as well as the unprecedented creative labor arrangements that the recording apparatus enabled, Hodgkinson and his theoretically inclined bandmates (Cutler and probably Cooper) refused to subscribe to Adorno's totalizing portrayal of the alienation inherent in mechanical reproduction and the musical commodity. Though informal and never published in any accredited or academic forum, these DIY responses to Adorno contributed to the wave of English-language reception of his work in the 1970s.[46]

Of course, punk was the DIY initiative that made the most news in London during these months. Frequently abroad in the second half of 1976 and late winter of 1977, Henry Cow missed punk when it burst out of the gate. "We'd arrive back in Britain, glean half an idea of what was going on, and immediately leave again," Cutler recalls. "Then there was a time when we got back and realized something very different was going on, but we weren't around long enough to absorb it. At least I didn't. And I don't think we really thought it affected us." There was a slow realization that the map Henry Cow had been using to orient themselves on the terrain of cultural politics no longer corresponded to actual conditions. Hodgkinson explains, "Now this map was possibly changing, in that this was not the Communist party or the Trotskyites, the Young Socialists, or the feminists. This was some peculiar new kind of phenomenon which just seemed to kind of erupt from somewhere, and it seemed to have a political content, but it was difficult to kind of pin down what it was. And it was saying—was it nihilist? Negative? In fact, was it fascist? And nobody seemed to have a clear answer to these questions."

Krause experienced her perceptions more clearly: "All I could feel from them was anger." The punks had a new singing style, new fashion, and a new, aggressive stance; they were at most ten years younger than the Cows, but that felt like a generation, she remembers. For Frith, it was a shock to see elements of their own practice gaining wider currency: "We are independent of the music business and we are running our own show. . . . Punk comes along and suddenly everybody is independent of the music business and everybody is running their own show and it has nothing to do with us. . . . We would like people to acknowledge who we were and take our models and idea but I think it was never going to happen given that our rhetoric was so horrendously pompous and rigid, frankly." Frith is certainly correct that the Cow made an ill fit with punk, but it had as much to do with the substance of their commitments as it did with the rhetoric they employed. As Hodgkinson told a pair of Swedish teenagers in 1977, "I mean, you can sort of detect their political ideas. . . . Mostly it's on the level . . . of terrorism or vandalism, just the act of violence—of rebellion—in itself, as a symbol. But on the other hand, there are quite positive tendencies in punk, but they are not the dominant tendencies."[47] Even if the Sex Pistols were "into chaos," there was nothing unpredictable about their career paths. "They're very reactionary, cause they all have managers, and they all get record deals with the capitalist companies, and they all go straight for success and stardom."[48]

As Malcolm McLaren later told Jon Savage, he consumed situationist texts for the pictures, not the theory.[49] The anonymous author of one 1978 situationist pamphlet on music explained, "His shop SEX was opened up in Kings Road, Chelsea which sold T shirts on which were stencilled, 'Be reasonable demand the impossible' . . . (slogans from Paris 1968), which now meant, buy some of my kinky gear . . . and help make me a rich man."[50] Although they have been subsequently cast as knowing situationist avant-gardistes, at the time the Sex Pistols' music sounded like old-time rock 'n' roll, their revolution looked like edgy marketing, and their seizure of the means of production took the form of signing record deals with EMI, A&M, and Virgin.[51] This contradiction suffuses chronicles of the band. Observers refer to their "sociopolitical ideology" or their "assault" on the industry, but they strove to become "rock stars" in a capitalist field "riven with competition," and even hired an exploitative manager.[52] Sounds like the music business. As Savage himself wrote, "The new world looked much like the old world."[53] If their big news was that the industry only valued economic profit and had conservative tastes, then Henry Cow would have greeted it with a yawn. In *Melody Maker*, Cutler told Steve Lake, "Well, of course, 'Anarchy in the UK,' for example, is just utter drivel. Musically, it's merely sub-Who. . . . Lyrically, it's meaningless. . . . It's not even real rebellion. Signing fat contracts outside Buckingham Palace doesn't exactly smack of integrity writ large either."[54] In fact, although he unsparingly criticized the gloomy disposition of PLM at the MFS event, he also admitted, "I agree fundamentally with their conclusion" on punk.[55]

The throwback quality of punk's musical style also puzzled Hodgkinson, who thought it rendered its own politics contradictory—in its nihilism, punk offered a negation of existing bourgeois relations, but the musical form it took merely reaffirmed an earlier moment in cultural history. And punk's chaotic proliferation of signs led one to wonder about the soundness of its political analysis. Hodgkinson says, "Is this left or is it right? I'm not quite sure here. And even if it is intentionally left, are they fucking it up? This thing about trying to make symbols meaningless by wearing, let's say, a swastika. Where does that take you? Is it clear who the enemy is?" As Born told a Swedish journalist, the nihilism and helplessness that punk expressed would not lead anywhere—the music industry simply needed punk to survive the economic crisis of the 1970s.[56]

In addition to the obvious political divergences, the gap between Henry Cow and punk opened wider with respect to musical qualities. The Cow's instrumental virtuosity and their long, complicated written works made a poor match with punk, of course, and their expanded instrumentarium—complete with keys and reeds—was positively decadent by comparison. And punk's timbral raggedness mainly owed to its musicians' lack of training, rather than the open-ended exploration of sound that characterized

Henry Cow's improvisation practice. Furthermore, when Krause became essentially unavailable for touring in autumn 1977, Henry Cow couldn't even relate to punk through its compelling singer. "It certainly made our political message harder for people to grasp," Hodgkinson told an interviewer in 1980. "I think we would have been much more relevant had we not lost Dagmar."[57] Furthermore, those "mountains of complex electronic equipment" prohibited entry into the new wave performance spaces, which usually possessed tiny stages that could scarcely support half of the Cow PA.[58]

Finally, recall that for Henry Cow, "rock is for everyone." Whatever kind of connoisseur their music was actually suited to, the band subscribed to a naïve but expansive and inclusive understanding of the rock audience, one that had been formed through their specific experience on the continent and their memories of the diverse 1967 moment. One of their greatest frustrations had been the way the industry divided audiences and told them what they could or should enjoy. But punk seemed to perform much the same kind of work in reverse. As journalist Jonh Ingham told Savage, "They [early punks] were into it for the clothes and the elitism and as soon as it became Rock 'n' Roll they didn't want to know."[59]

In spite of these serious differences, Henry Cow did attract a limited following among the younger punks. Observing that it was fitting that the Pistols would eventually sign with Virgin, Simon Frith wrote in 1977, "The most ironic thing about the current ideology of punk is how much of it is, in fact, the old ideology of Hippie."[60] In his view, both movements held to the naive idea that there was a kind of pure rock business formation that could reconcile art and commerce without contradiction. Some younger bands looking for models of self-determination or ideological critique had found them in Henry Cow, who recall members of the Buzzcocks, the Fall, Scritti Politti, and Crass showing up at their concerts in 1977 and after.[61] When the Cow wasn't out on the road, Jack Balchin would rent out their PA system and his services as engineer for Rough Trade's London shows. By early 1978, when Frith wrote a summary report for the Arts Council about a Henry Cow tour of the United Kingdom, he could assert, "We feel that a genuine change has occurred in rock audiences over the last year due to the impact of the new wave in rock music."[62]

According to Frith, Bernie Rhodes worked at the garage where Frith took his car to be repaired; sometime in 1976, he mentioned that the Sex Pistols (for whom he served as an early manager) were interested in meeting with him, "because, he suggested, our experience in alternative methods could be useful to them, and we might pick up on their 'different' approach."[63]

The meeting never happened, but he continued to receive updates and soft sells from his acquaintances, Jamie Reid (the graphic designer of the Pistols' iconic imagery) and Sophie Richmond (the manager of Malcolm McLaren's management company, Glitterbest). At one point, Frith reports, a query came through his romantic partner, Sue Steward, who had joined Glitterbest as an assistant: would Frith be interested in producing a Sex Pistols recording? It all remained strictly casual, with Frith insisting that he'd want to hear from the musicians themselves, which he never did. Hodgkinson later commented, "I remember him saying, 'Listen, Pistols want to do a tour of England with us.' And us thinking, 'Sounds like a bit of a set-up job. We're just gonna be massacred.'"

Rock Collectivism and Its Discontents

By the time the Sex Pistols had signed with Virgin in the late spring of 1977, Henry Cow had long been in negotiations to terminate their contract with the company. Some observers have pointed out to me that "getting out of the contract" would be overstating Henry Cow's importance to the label, who were already moving toward XTC, The Motors, and U-Roy, following their decision to drop acts like Henry Cow in the summer of 1976. But to the Cows, the issue assumed critical importance—not simply because a Virgin affiliation contradicted their politics and public stance, but because Virgin's European licensees, such as Dischi Ricordi in Italy, had no motivation to promote a small act such as Henry Cow. Therefore, the band's LPs languished on shelves in the United Kingdom, where they rarely toured, while fans in Holland, Italy, Sweden, and other viable markets had to import copies of their records. Escaping Virgin would mean that they could negotiate new licensing agreements for their back catalogue with more sympathetic European affiliates, not to mention self-releasing any new recordings and licensing those in individual national markets.

In order to axe the band after their summer 1976 housecleaning, Virgin needed to reach a termination agreement with Henry Cow that autumn, but the band was on the road more often than they were back in London, so the meeting kept getting put off. Band records indicate that Draper and Branson had proposed by October 1976 a deal that gave Henry Cow "world rights," presumably to relicense their albums anywhere that Virgin didn't already have agreements in place.[64] This new contract would cancel the old one, and also forgive a debt of £1,200 that Henry Cow owed the company.

For a bunch of hippy communists, the Cows acted shrewdly by hiring a solicitor, James Ware, to review the old contract and represent their interests. Once they sat down with Virgin, the plan was to request that the company provide them with two weeks in a first-class studio, according to their original 1973 contract. If Virgin broke the contract by refusing, Henry Cow would try to reacquire their publishing, to obtain releases to negotiate in new foreign markets, and to have an accountant review their books, sales figures, expenses, and back catalogue stock.

In April 1977, Henry Cow drew up their proposed terms for Virgin, but the two parties wouldn't sign on the dotted line until October. To summarize the termination agreement: Virgin no longer would be obliged to record them, and the band would be free to pursue their own arrangements; Virgin would still pay Henry Cow royalties on its album sales; Henry Cow would take licensing rights to all their albums in the territories where Virgin had not released them (or wherever the company had deleted the stock), subject to royalties paid to Virgin; if Virgin deleted their album in the United Kingdom, rights would revert to Henry Cow, and the band would have the option of buying unused stock at cost; Virgin would grant the band access to all tapes of unreleased recordings, and once recording costs had been repaid, would allow Henry Cow to release them with another company, subject to royalties paid to Virgin; Virgin would not rerelease any albums in any different form without the band's consent; Henry Cow would gain access to old publicity materials, artwork, and masters; Virgin would retain publishing; *Desperate Straights* would not count as a Henry Cow album for the purpose of their agreement.

Even before the Virgin business wrapped up in October 1977, Henry Cow had begun exploring how they could release their new record by themselves. All their associates on the continent would come in handy. For France, they debated setting up their own record company there or signing a deal with another label, such as RCA France, Gratte-Ciel, or a new venture by BYG co-founder, Jean Karakos (Tapioca). In discussions over the course of the year, Karakos emerged as the best bet; in Maggie Thomas's memory, he struck them like a "pirate," and they appreciated his outlaw style (though BYG has since garnered a certain reputation as conducting its affairs in a less than proper way). In Italy, Henry Cow weighed the merits of signing with Cramps or starting their own Italian label. Their own label would be supported by l'Orchestra Cooperativa, which had been founded in 1975 in Milan and embodied Henry Cow's values: they were a workers' cooperative spanning multiple genres and committed to sharing resources and improving the labor conditions for musicians across Italy.[65] By 1977, when Henry Cow joined (probably as the first non-Italian members), l'Orchestra handled their publicity and promotion, contracts, and record distribution. L'Orchestra's Swedish analogue and the leading alternative distribution network in Scandinavia, SAM, could handle the Scandinavian release, and would offer the Cow good terms and even an advance. Meanwhile, at home, they planned on capitalizing on their experience managing the production of *Concerts* by founding their own UK operation; in dire financial circumstances, they sent letters around in the spring and summer soliciting prepayments for the new record, and advertised advanced subscriptions to it in the autumn of 1977.[66] They had reason to believe that their plans for self-production and licensing would pay off. By spring 1977, the *Concerts* LP (1976) had sold about as many copies as had *In Praise of Learning* (1975)—a bit more than ten thousand—but Compendium was actually paying them royalties, which hadn't happened with the Virgin releases for quite a while.[67]

They had initially been planning to record their new album with Tom Newman in the new studio he had set up on a barge on the Regent's canal in Little Venice. He had some money trouble, however, and the Cow would need to come up with a substantial down payment. After a few months of inconclusive fundraising and planning, however, they still didn't have the money, nor did they have a firm idea of what they would record. By June 15, when Henry Cow had a band meeting to discuss, Newman was no longer available—but Sarah Greaves, who had apprenticed herself to Newman in studio engineering since her expulsion from the band, was eager to work with them on a "nonspecialist" basis. There were some concerns about her level of competence (she'd been learning only for a short while), and eventually that plan was scrapped. Frith began investigating Pink Floyd's studio (Britannia Row), and, though it seemed somewhat Manor-like in a lugubrious way, they thought it might be possible.

But in addition to or beyond these administrative details, band members had serious concerns about their schedule and way of working in the summer of 1977. Should they record in July, October, or January? Should they do half the album in July (i.e., "Erk Gah") and half later? Their whole autumn 1977 touring schedule (France, Italy, and maybe Germany) was based on having a new album out in September, so waiting would put them in the stale position of "getting the same music to a wider audience," as Hodgkinson put it in a June 28 meeting. Cutler held the opinion that Henry Cow's problems were material—they had to prioritize getting out of debt, and it wasn't possible to adopt an idealistic approach until their financial problems were solved. Most of his colleagues disagreed. Hodgkinson critiqued the "managerial, product-oriented side of the group" (i.e., Hobbs and Cutler), insisting that it needed to rest on the firm and valid artistic work of the group. Frith complained that Henry Cow wasn't even doing what they always said they did (work collectively); furthermore, they weren't performing well. It would be a mistake to push those problems aside for economic reasons. Joining the fray, Cooper voiced a concern that the band's "means and relations of production" were increasingly reproducing those of bourgeois culture, by which she meant they were just writing music privately, then bringing it into the group and telling the others what to do. Hodgkinson reminded them that the move to individual composition originated in their desire to cease lumping together frags into longer spans of music—the drive for thematic consistency necessitated individual work, but it seemed that a new approach was needed.

Hodgkinson, Frith, and Cooper (and possibly Born, though it's difficult to say) wished to make radical changes in their musical practice toward committed collective work. What might that mean? Frith offered the example of theatre groups working collectively on a theme; Cooper clarified that deprivatization meant everybody in the group working on music and lyrics. For Hodgkinson, the recording of "Erk Gah" needed to avoid becoming a historical document; he wanted them to work on it differently and collectively.

The collective nature of tape work was obvious and had already been demonstrated on the Greasy Truckers LP and the second side of *Unrest*, and earlier in the work of Can and Faust (Miles Davis was certainly a fellow traveler, but Teo Macero cut up those tapes by himself). Nevertheless, I have been surprised to find no evidence of a specific conversation or notes about the restricted ownership of the technological means for such a creative practice. It would seem that magnetic tape offered the most intuitive "next step" beyond the bourgeois individualism of art-music composition, given how Henry Cow had defined the problem, but any good multitrack recording studio lay beyond the means of most rock bands, and collaborative environments like the Radiophonic Workshop remained closed to all but their own employees. There were even recent historical precedents— Motown comes to mind—of a tape-based collaboration that mixed writing, performing, and recording in (initially) small-scale, petty bourgeois arrangements, but perhaps the unashamedly capitalist success of Motown obscured the lessons it might offer about acquiring a studio of one's own. But in any case, Henry Cow seems not to have taken up the argument that the potential of collective tape work could be unleashed only once the tools of the capitalist entertainment industry had become more widely available.

Notes by Hodgkinson dating from this period further clarify the matter of collective creativity vis-à-vis improvisation and composition. In what he called "free music," Henry Cow forged a collective arrangement by improvising a music without constraint, which meant casting off such "cruder unifying principles" as key, mode, meter, tempo, or musical style. "In more general terms," he wrote in his notes, "to *guard against habit*—but only *bad habits*, which are *unconscious* dispositions to play in a way which denies qualities in the music." Meter or mode were fine so long as they were chosen consciously as open problems rather than closed solutions. Those decisions might not be owned by any single individual in the group during performance—they might "generate collectively a musical form, but not a preconceived one."

At the individual level, improvised music "technically and musically surpasses what could be grasped, notated & composed." Because players often work just inside their own technical limits on the instrument, the aleatoric and controlled elements blend at a granular level beyond the reach of notation, Hodgkinson thought. The best collective composition might synthesize this individual work with collective decision-making in real time.

In retrospect, the practice of a distinctive "collective composition" in notation remained underspecified. Hodgkinson, Frith, and Cooper, when they individually wrote new compositions for the band, were quite different from "the composer" figure so central to classical music's ideological division of creative labor; in contrast to that figure, the Cow composers always routed their ideas through the same performing resources, of which they were also a part. This microsocial tension between the individual performers' skills or musical personalities and the new directions a composer might ask them to take produced a dialectical transformation that was collective. And something about pop and rock seemed to lend itself to this collaborative form of authorship—Hodgkinson thought that the move away from the single creator to the pop group effected a "partial or potential collectivization of the production of music, of a type probably unique to this area."[68] And yet, for decades, pairs or trios had been shutting themselves into practice rooms and hashing out tunes; that labor arrangement, counter to Hodgkinson's desire, abetted rather than subverted musical commodity production. One gets the sense that Hodgkinson had something else in mind, such as each member of the group writing their own lines, or alternating authorship of successive sections, or inching along some melodic trail a few beats at a time, with different members suggesting new directions, divergent paths, or analeptic alterations. When pressed for more detail, Hodgkinson recalled "the moment at which Fred and I were in my flat [in 1972], going into different rooms far from one another, and coming back and saying, 'Ah, okay.' Putting the music for *The Bacchae* together. That was kind of a glimpse of what collective composition could be . . . , but with all of us involved, maybe in a recording studio." In the event, Henry Cow never made it to collective notated composition; band members offered their comments on certain sections of "Erk Gah," but that would have been business as usual. Financial stress left them no time to experiment with their collective practice, instead impelling them once again to the (relative) riches of Europe.

But what material were they going to record? Hodgkinson had concluded that the band had underestimated the divergence between Europe, where they'd spent much of their time, and the United Kingdom. It was not simply a matter of there being less money around and less gratifying gigs—he was referring to the ideological and cultural difference.[69] The development uppermost in his mind was punk, "which puts us on the spot both economically and ideologically." Economically, punk was now taking over the audience and the press space, while, ideologically, its popularity clearly expressed a grassroots demand. But Hodgkinson's analysis of punk's content, he said, "leads me to the position that there are fascist elements in it which are dominant over the progressive elements, and both of these are ideologically against and clearly differentiated from the previously dominating musical culture, which corresponds much more to the 'soft' form of bourgeois hegemony." If they presented an "avant-garde rock" album as a well-intentioned socialist alternative, he reasoned, they won't get anywhere.

Therefore, he proposed that Henry Cow record an antifascist album with a newly lyricized "Erk Gah." A clear antifascist position would explain what they're doing and critique the rightist elements in punk. Born was concerned about this critical stance—how would their meaning come through, and won't it come across as negative? Hodgkinson proposed a clear album cover with lyrics and an explanation of their decision. He had even begun to sketch out this statement: "Our stand is not to hit-out at the nearest target, to REVEL in violence and brutality and promote anarchy. This is just acting out the *bourgeois* fantasy of the unbridled BEAST."[70] Cooper pointed out that antifascism could be a unifying force on the left, which was already mobilizing against it. Born remained unconvinced that they could provide a good enough alternative for punk audiences. Siding with Hodgkinson and criticizing Born, Cutler insisted that they take a clear stand against fascism. Born remained unmoved: Cutler's analysis wasn't based on knowing anything about punk, which hadn't made statements that bore out his reading.

Frith and Krause agreed that Henry Cow might want to withhold a judgment on punk. Frith went on to note that the music press had stopped characterizing the Cow as "avant-garde" after *IPOL*, when it began to emphasize the political dimension of the band's work instead. Therefore, making an antifascist record wouldn't be a big jump. More importantly, however, Frith cautioned his bandmates against believing that they could be a musical alternative to punk, because it was simply wrong to think that their music would be popular were it not for punk. Instead, he said, Henry Cow should be trying to engage in dialogue those working in punk. Cooper, too, contended that they should be fighting fascism, not punk, while Born agitated for a confrontation with the Sex Pistols. Frith's opinion: it wouldn't work. In any case, they all agreed to work on ideas and lyrics for the second side of the record, and to hold in abeyance further discussion of the sleeve.

The strongest side-two possibility they had going was "Joan," a five-minute Frith composition to lyrics by Cutler. The song sandwiched a dark, syncopated rumble between slower, guitar-led verses. Although the text setting flowed naturally (and there was a lot of text in the early version), "Joan" has the feel of a patchwork of two frags. Until he revised them at the end of the year, Cutler's lyrics presented a somewhat opaque narrative about a car crash; strangely, the Cows referred to this song as "Joan" nearly a year before the text had been changed into a first-person statement from Joan of Arc.

The Orckestra

Amid the great uncertainties about their repertoire, political position, financial troubles, and recording plans in 1977, Henry Cow found a fascinating new problem to grab on to and work: a merger with the Mike Westbrook Brass Band (MWBB) and folk singer Frankie Armstrong. They had a history together: recall that Westbrook, Lol Coxhill, and Phil Minton had chipped in for Henry Cow's Rainbow Theatre concert in October 1973, and the MWBB had staged a (previously agreed) sabotage of the Cows' set at the Sigma Festival in 1975, when they marched in from the side in homage to Charles Ives. Krause had worked with Minton in Maggie Nicols's voice workshops in spring 1976, and the three of them had even performed as the ensemble Voice. Finally, the Cows who had been working with MFS in early

1977 were likely running into Armstrong quite a lot, since she was an active folk musician on London's left and increasingly involved in the women's movement. They had all appeared separately on a benefit bill in 1976, and when the invitation came to appear on the Moving Left Revue benefit for the Communist Party of Great Britain on March 13, they seized the opportunity to develop a show that combined their talents.[71]

Westbrook had long enjoyed a reputation as a composer friendly to free jazz and the avant-garde, even if he was more inspired by Ellington than by Coleman. He kept a big band going through most of the 1960s; its members included not only John Surman but future AMM members Keith Rowe, Lawrence Sheaff, and Lou Gare.[72] "There was a major sea change in my work in the early 1970s," he explains, when his big projects wound up and he became more interested in community involvement and alternative theatre. The Brass Band came out of this period. "It was a very Utopian notion. Just get a few people together and play without having to worry about PA's and venues and the whole cumbersome process. We played discos, factories and geriatric wards as well as Arts Centres," he later commented.[73] Although Coxhill had been an early contributor, the band soon settled into the formation it maintained for several years: Mike Westbrook (piano, euphonium), Kate Westbrook (tenor horn, piccolo, voice), Dave Chambers (saxophones), Phil Minton (trumpet, voice), and Paul Rutherford (trombone, euphonium). Rutherford was a leading light of London's free improvisation movement as well as an outspoken member of the Communist Party. Mobile and committed to the street, the Brass Band played all kinds of music, including hymns, marches, jazz standards, early music, folk songs, pop classics, and original settings of Brecht and Blake. Their stylistic range— for which they received as much grief from jazz purists as Henry Cow did from rock ones—and their political slant made them a natural match for the Cows. Armstrong made sense, too: a veteran of the second folk revival, she had been a member of the Critics Group (with Ewan McColl and Peggy Seeger), where she honed her iron voice and Marxist politics.[74] By 1977, she had three solo albums and many collaborations already in the can.

Held at the Roundhouse, the Moving Left Revue lasted three and a half hours and presented a wide range of material: Westbrook originals, jazz classics, traditional tunes, pop standards, Brecht/Weill collaborations, and Henry Cow songs.[75] According to most eyewitness accounts (and a partial bootleg recording), the audience gave a warm reception to the "Henry Cow/Mike Westbrook Occasional Orchestra and Big Band, Featuring

Frankie Armstrong," and Steve Lake gave them a favorable review in *Melody Maker*.[76] Even that paper's folk-music editors, in praising Armstrong, enthused that "the revue must be regarded as the most adventurous project undertaken by a folk singer."[77]

A few weeks later, Armstrong remarked, "I can hardly believe it all, it incorporates such an amazing range of music. . . . We had a fantastic time."[78] Almost all the musicians agreed with Born's assessment: "Fantastic fun and a great gig." Born particularly appreciated Westbrook's sense of musical space in his arrangements, which gave her an opportunity to play the cello without getting overrun by the electronics of her bandmates. The Brass Band musicians, though "spellbinding" (in Cooper's memory), were more difficult to integrate into Henry Cow's music than vice versa; the combined groups lacked the kind of rehearsal time that would be required to play learn something like "Living in the Heart of the Beast." But Westbrook's music was much less fiddly, and Armstrong's often modal folksongs allowed the Cow plenty of room to create a droning bed of noise.

With such a fun program that highlighted the diversity of musical approaches on the left, the combined group shortened its name to the Orckestra and put together a follow-up gig, organized by the Jazz Centre Society, on June 26 in the Regent's Park Open-Air Theatre. They tweaked their repertoire—keeping the same general balance of rock, jazz, cabaret, folk, and pop—and spent more time (three days) rehearsing for this one. Rutherford worked out some arrangements of Armstrong's songs using the lighter instruments in Henry Cow. And Westbrook expanded one of his Blake songs, "Holy Thursday," into a twenty-minute version for the extended group once he had more time to consider the Cows' instrumentarium. "That was exciting because I was able to try all sorts of things," he told a journalist at the time. "I'd never written for a cello, so I did a cello accompaniment for a song, which was played beautifully. Then there was the electric bassoon and all kinds of possibilities with such a line-up."

But the rehearsals weren't entirely smooth, either. In fact, the Brass Band's drummer, Trevor Tomkins, walked out of the first session and never returned. As a more conventional jazz man, he could not abide the Cows' approach to rhythm. Westbrook explains, "In jazz, because of its origins in dance, we always have a pulse to relate to. . . . But they may have quite systematically rejected the notion of any kind of swing or rhythmic momentum at all as being something decadent." The Cows' irregular rhythms were "totally alien to our way of writing and thinking about music." Accordingly,

Figure 7.4 Dagmar Krause singing with the Orckestra at Regents Park, London, June 26, 1977. Visible behind her are Kate Westbrook, Paul Rutherford, Phil Minton, and Chris Cutler. PHOTOGRAPHER UNKNOWN; COURTESY OF CHRIS CUTLER.

the Henry Cow material that was taken up by the Orckestra remained those big tunes that could be blown largely in unison, *Ascension*-style, or cycles-n-solos: Frith's "D-tune" (a new frag), the 21-beat cycle from "Nirvana for Mice," the middle part and final chorus of "Beautiful as the Moon," the "Teenbeat" tune, and a new piece, "La citta futura." This latter was a skeletal structure created by Cutler as a feature for Born on the cello. Basically, she improvised over a series of repeating quarter-note chords in a steady pulse; the band repeated a single chord for several iterations (anywhere from four to twenty, it seems) before shifting up a semitone. Its title is a reference to Antonio Gramsci.

The Regent's Park gig was not the Orckestra's finest moment. Balchin remembers "some really beautiful moments, and some acute despair," the latter owing to major live sound issues after driving straight back from a Cow gig the previous night in France. But the critics seemed to like it: *Melody Maker*'s Maureen Paton called it "spectacularly imaginative excursion into (virtually) uncharted seas."[79] But Ronald Atkins hit the nail on the head when he wrote, "In general, the group sounded rather like the Westbrook band augmented by a rhythm section."[80] The Cows could never scratch together the time and focus either to write a large piece for the Orckestra or to put together solid new arrangements of their existing compositions. Frith recalls this sharp feeling of a missed opportunity. As Balchin puts it, "The idea of being able to merge the two groups of musical voices and abilities—yeah, great idea. . . . The potential's there. Certainly at points of the time when Cows were playing along with the Westies' music, you could see a glimmer of something. [But] it never, *ever* worked." According to the minutes of a Henry Cow meeting on July 18, 1977, Westbrook had phoned Nick Hobbs to share his dissatisfaction with the Orckestra playing mainly MWBB material. He also didn't like how Henry Cow were often the only ones really playing their own works in concert, and he urged them to come up with arrangements of some of their shorter pieces—even with the expected paucity of rehearsal time, the MWBB could get something together if they had written parts and tapes to work from.

In the end, the impossibility of serious rehearsal time sunk the ensemble. Although they played four more events that year, and six concerts in 1978, most of their "rehearsals" took place in a rush during Henry Cow's sound checks, which the Brass Band and Armstrong—not used to playing with electronics or amplified instruments—found interminable.[81] Some Cows also developed particularly strong bonds with Chambers and Rutherford, and when they left the group in a 1978 personnel change, a faction of the group grew less excited about continuing.[82]

Reflecting back, Westbrook remarks, "I wouldn't want to say that it was just easy—it wasn't. It wasn't totally personally easy, either. This was not a cosy love-in, at all. . . . They were working towards splitting up during that period." Nonetheless, like so many Henry Cow projects, the suffering in this one also created some new openings. Hanging out with Frith in the Orckestra, Armstrong gave him tapes of folk music from Bulgaria and other parts of Eastern Europe, which would strongly inform the guitarist's next compositional phase. Born and Cooper would continue performing with Westbrook into the 1980s, and Phil Clarke served as his manager after Henry Cow broke up. Working with a bigger group of instruments after several years with the Brass Band had whetted Westbrook's appetite for large ensembles, and he would move on almost immediately to his next large project, *The Cortege*. "I got a lot out of it. I found it quite liberating to be part of a big ensemble like that. I didn't mind that it wasn't fantastically together. I thought it was about something important," he later remarked. Although the gigs were sometimes haphazard, the Cows enjoyed their two short tours with the rest of the Orckestra, whose easy bonhomie lightened the mood during some dark, contentious days.

Shifting but Inescapable Fences: Late 1977

In the lead-up to the Moving Left benefit, Henry Cow had a conversation about their relationship to the Communist Party of Great Britain (CPGB), who had asked them to do a tour to benefit the party.[83] Hodgkinson was highly motivated to encourage the party to support "progressive culture," but Cooper worried that they were merely seizing an opportunity: "The CP is fond of coopting people outside the party, partly in order to help recruitment," she protested. Cutler didn't get it—they never had qualms about working for the PCI, and everybody already knew that they were communists. But Cooper responded that communism isn't synonymous with the CP, and Frith agreed that there was a difference between the CPGB and PCI, which embraced a wider area of culture and functioned as more of a mass party. Cooper's opinion, made clear in letters throughout that year, was that Cutler "thinks all CP s are always right."[84] She wanted to know why they didn't play gigs for other parties and nonparty left groups; it appeared to her that Henry Cow couldn't establish a basis for discussion of political gigs because they didn't share a group line on specific parties and affiliations, nor did they all have solid political positions.[85] Born, in particular, expressed a desire to learn more during her time in Henry Cow. Less than a year after this meeting, she would write, "I'm not as certain + definite about most political areas."[86]

"Do you want each person to state their political views?" asked Clarke, perhaps incredulously. No, Cooper replied, but an exchange of information might help them evaluate possible gigs better. "Perhaps we could all read the *British Road to Socialism*?" This question produced a long discussion about the CP's latest document, which the band agreed to on their own. (The tour never materialized, but the reasons are unclear.)

Henry Cow followed the MFS Battersea festival with a run of concerts in the United Kingdom, beginning with a five-date tour of the southwestern United Kingdom with Red Balune, which gave them a chance to reconnect with Geoff Leigh and Cathy Williams. They also played three concerts around London with their new friends in Etron Fou Leloublan, a French band they had met earlier that year. In between, they appeared at the Brighton Contemporary Festival of Arts, an interesting week of events that featured a string of the Cow's longtime associates: Derek Bailey, Ivor Cutler, Ron Geesin, Evan Parker, Lol Coxhill, Gerry Fitz-gerald, and Lumiere et Son.

But Henry Cow returned to Italy in September bereft of a singer. Krause had been warning them since the spring that her son, Max, would be starting school in September, and therefore she could join them on the road only with great difficulty. Anthony Moore did not customarily lend much assistance in child rearing, so she faced an impossible situation. Moreover, her physical health tended to reflect back the entire group's emotional health. In the summer of 1977, the latter was not good and getting worse. Accordingly, Krause fell ill with a mixture of exhaustion and laryngitis. Her doctor told her not to work until the third week of September, but the band already had gigs booked, so they agreed to tour without her and then decide what to do when they got back to London.

No singer meant assembling an instrumental set. That autumn, the main components were "Ruins," "Teenbeat," "Bittern Storm," "Nirvana for Mice," "The March," and sections of "Erk Gah" woven into improvisations. They also had a few new ones, including a ninety-second bear of an instrumental by Cooper and a short arrangement of Thelonious Monk's "Jackie-ing" that they had held over from their Orckestra experience. To these standalone pieces, they added about five new Fred Frags, including a few scavenged from one of his unfinished bigger compositions earlier in the year, as well as a duo for sax and bassoon in counterpoint over a slowly moving cantus firmus and high-energy, rolling drums.

A jotting in one of Frith's notebooks at the time suggests how he viewed the frags in relation to what the Cow needed at the time: "what kind of piece is required by Henry Cow at present time—1) short, contained, simple (as antidote to long, unwieldy blocks of material[)]. 2) limited instrumentation (as counter to constant distracting multi-instrumental changes[)]. 3) non-virtuoso—to stop people listening to the external factors of music production + help them hear the music[.] 4) breaking new ground—to counter feeling of staleness + encourage new exchanges of ideas."[87] The frags, then, weren't simply long pieces that failed to cohere or develop. Instead, Frith wanted to "limit length" and "limit speed" in each individual snippet.

The most fully realized of the new works was Hodgkinson's four-and-a-half-minute "Viva Pa Ubu," a nasty little rocker with a roiling bass part. Beefheartian in its unruly counterpoint, the song throws out surprising unisons and changes of direction without losing coherence, probably because Hodgkinson repeats some sections and phrases more often than he would have done in a piece like "Erk Gah." The quicksilver propulsion of the verse sections gives way to a more relaxed, almost grand chorus built on Born's low C pedal, which soon starts creeping up the scale, only to drop down to the C for another go. When they performed it that autumn, they sometimes only played this chorus section, which announced the name of the song with a broad "Viva, Pa Ubu!" Hodgkinson wanted the singing to sound like a mob of workers seizing their revenge, and in concert he and Frith usually belted out the words together. By the time Henry Cow recorded the song in January 1978, Hodgkinson had written lyrics for the verse sections, too; they imagine a kind of reckoning for the unscrupulous financier at the hands of a sneering crowd. For the studio recording, Hodgkinson got as many mouths as he could fit around the microphone to sing along.

Their first autumn 1977 tour consisted of about fourteen gigs, anchored by well-paying appearances at the Como Festival and the Lugano Festival, where some adventurous programmer put together a day of concerts featuring works by John Cage, Christian Wolff, Dieter Schnebel, and Henry Cow.[88] Henry Cow's performance in Lugano fell on the day of a Swiss referendum to legalize abortion in the first trimester, and they inserted into one of their improvisations a reading of Brecht's poem, "Paragraph 218," which he wrote to protest a German antiabortion measure in the 1920s. Other socialist festivals in Italy helped to fill out the schedule, and the Cow particularly enjoyed a string of dates with Etron Fou Leloublan. October took them to the Nancy Jazz Pulsations Festival (with the Orckestra), back to the United Kingdom for a few dates outside of London, and then, in November, to France, where they spent more than two weeks but only played a handful of gigs. The financial situation might not have been great, but they enjoyed the comforts of staying with good friends in "a house of fading aristocratic proportions" in Angers, where they rehearsed, played basketball, ate and drank well, and awaited news on gigs, recording studios, and the state of their vehicles' disrepair.[89] Sula Goschen had moved to California several months earlier, so the crew consisted of a new roadie, Bernie Guest, as well as Clarke, Thomas, and Balchin, who had finally achieved his goal of mixing their live sound.

In late November, they broke into post-Franco Spain. Cutler and Thomas had made the Spanish connection the previous summer when they were traveling around Barcelona. At a big summer festival in Calella, they heard a Spanish band called Suck Electrònic Enciclopèdic, who played a kind of cosmic rock with multiple synthesizers among its seven members. Cutler and Thomas introduced themselves afterward to Suck E.E.'s leader, Jordi García, raising the question of a tour in the country later that year. García would eventually set up five dates in Spain for November. According to the contemporary testimony of several Cows, as well as their Spanish hosts, the gigs were well attended, well paying, and enthusiastically received.[90] A journalist who covered the Cow extensively, Francesc X. Puerto, later described their impact to an interlocutor: "That night a door was opened and as I stood on the threshold I knew I wanted to hear more of what was on the other side—there were other independent bands in Europe exploring uncharted maps."[91]

On these tours of the second half of 1977—Italy, France, Germany, Spain—the band's numerous open improvisations sounded lighter, less dense, and less mediated by electronic interventions (I hear no more pre-recorded tapes, for example). Solos and smaller chamber groups rose up in the sets more often than in the past, including some wonderful new passes through "Ruins" for Frith. But with no Krause, the sets sound more fragmented, with no big hunks such as "Erk Gah" or "Beautiful as the Moon," nor any straight-ahead belters like "No More Songs." Some instrumental attempts at finding such gravitas, like "The Big Tune," sound more ponderous than weighty. Cutler sums it up thus: "I think the program was pretty much a couple of old warhorses and some scraps—almost exercise pieces, short fragments, not anything very substantial. Except from Lindsay."

In her various reports home, Cooper described a group that was frequently ill, tired, and hungry: "wasted time, lost money and bad temper."[92] Due to the number of gigs that failed to materialize, long gaps in their performing schedule opened up, and, although they found good audiences and some new energy in their first swings through Spain and Germany (Freiburg, Munich, and Hamburg), too many concerts fell off the schedule, contributing to their financial woes. More than one witness has described a bleak emotional landscape among members of the band, which, Cooper reported, was drinking more than usual;[93] "tout rien, tout rien, tout rien," Frith intoned endlessly, in the memory of one observer.[94] Thomas hopped off the bus in Spain because she had had enough of the bad vibes. By this point in their long career, Henry Cow had many admirers in Europe, and they would occasionally welcome visitors onto the bus after concerts or during off-days. But, in Krause's memory, the discord inside the group made it difficult to host outsiders: "Visitors didn't fit in on the bus. Nobody fitted in except the group." One of those visitors, an idealistic young American named Chris Wangro, had found the atmosphere welcoming (or bracing) enough to join the troupe as a roadie off and on for several months after their show in Rennes on November 8. He recalls, "Air shared in close quarters was tinged with internal tensions, tensions that were personal & sexual & philosophical & hard to pinpoint. Alliances and estrangements creating shifting but inescapable fences, yet these were *sub rosa*, hushed."[95]

To Underline the Gender Thing

Among the sub rosa fences that Wangro might have divined was a barrier that was emerging along gender lines in 1977. Hodgkinson wrote in 1981: "The impact of the women who join the group is particularly strong. Emotional & sexual relationships begin in the group. There is a new turmoil of affection & rejection, jealousy & conflict. . . . At the same time the solidarity of the men is broken. The women's relationships with them differentiate each from the others: the old boy's club mentality is broken down; to be replaced by a more sophisticated ideology which manages to encompass 'feminism.'"[96] Although he is correct to register the turmoils of the heart—I count a good ten unique pairings inside the band, some reported in these pages, some not—Hodgkinson might overstate the impact of the women in antagonizing gender arrangements. In our discussion of Cooper's expulsion from the group in 1974, we lingered briefly on what I called the "independent men's group," a situation that we might say constituted the default settings of the band. It was there before Henry Cow even began—defined, as such things always are, in relation to its other: one of the cofounders says he joined a band to attract girls, and the other to escape them.[97] It was there in the early days, with Frith's desire to avoid getting forced into accepting a girl singer and all that this might have implied. It was there in the Virgin honeymoon, when Steve Lake, scrambling to explain their use of makeup and costumes in 1972, called the Cow "a decidedly human and heterosexual quintet in these times of transvestism and implied deviation."[98] It was there in the post-Greaves era, when some in the London Musicians Collective saw the band's intimidating PA and gruff roadies as all but confirming a stereotypical kind of rock masculinity. Said Steve Beresford, "I thought there was a machismo that hid behind feminism there. Certainly, my failed audition as their bass player was all explained in terms of the fact that none of the women in the band liked me. But this was explained to me by Fred Frith." And it was there, just the other day, when Nick Hobbs insisted, "I don't think it's a very useful way of looking at Henry Cow. I think there were two highly articulate men in the band, Chris and Tim, [who were] highly argumentative. But everybody in the band was kind of also very argumentative and stubborn in their own ways. . . . I wouldn't want to underline this gender thing. I don't think it's very fruitful or accurate."

But if we did underline this gender thing, we would merely be following the example of many in the band who analyzed gender as an important category for understanding their experience of power, language, emotion, and other relations inside and outside the group. In a notebook she kept during 1976–77, Krause expressed some anger about her male bandmates, who thought of themselves as "this highly developed creation, separate [from] a female species," according to the singer. Compensating for their "under-developed emotional lives," she wrote, the men wielded a "rational pater-nalistic pretense," which they apparently used to "ridicule" her in meetings. She even wondered if she had to withdraw from the group because of this treatment.[99]

But it was Cooper who had been the strongest, most public voice of feminism in Henry Cow. She wrote a biting critique of *NME* journalist Kate Phillips's profile of Krause in a letter to the editor of that magazine in August 1975. Cooper took the journalist to task for her sexist language ("Mrs. Moore") and for how she misrepresented Henry Cow's critique of individualism, a critique that had special value for 50 percent of the popu-lation.[100] She published a more substantial piece on music and feminism in *Musics* in October 1977. Titled "Women, Music, Feminism—Notes," Cooper's essay surveyed a range of issues, but concentrated on how music structured (rather than merely reflected) the social position of women.[101] Any informed reader would have surmised that she was a member of Henry Cow. She contended that the popular music programs on the BBC and the commercial stations "are aimed specifically at housewives with all male disc jockeys playing monotonous pop music" to match the monotony of domes-tic labor.[102] And outside the home, female workers are more likely than men to be employed in "environments where music is used to create superficial-ity and a false sense of well-being," such as hotels, restaurants, and super-markets.[103] Musical discourse routinely positions women as "emotional," wrote Cooper, and the ideology of romantic love that had been the subject of so much music since at least the twelfth century served to preserve the sexist institution of monogamy and to privatize the emotional life of the people. The gender discourse of opera and cock rock spoke for itself.

Cooper went on to consider the history of women making music before summarizing the problems that remained to be addressed. Interestingly, she spun some issues that had been of general interest to her bandmates into areas of specific concern for women. For instance, the fracture and policing of genre boundaries, she wrote, "pose particular questions for women. For example, should they get involved in 'commercial' music where they will have more of a mass impact, or in 'non-commercial' music where they can possibly make better music and get less sexist treatment?"[104] In commercial music, the mystification and inequality of the star system runs counter to feminism's antielitist politics, she wrote, while "non-commercial" music—that is, Henry Cow—"must constantly struggle against the monopoly control of record distribution and live performance and therefore at least begin with a narrow and usually non-working class and non-female audience."[105] Furthermore, the politically progressive men whom one might find in those noncommercial settings might not uniformly share feminist views. "Working with men who are also critical of the existing structure can be a struggle—sexism doesn't necessarily disappear among progressive men—and its extinction may be more easily discussed than achieved."[106] Nonetheless, Cooper argued against a stylistically narrow understanding of "women's music," advocating instead for pluralism and a lasting engagement with musical practices that had been marked as masculine. "Men do use rhythm, technology, improvisation to express the same power and sexual dominance which oppresses women, but if women react by restricting themselves to melodic and acoustic forms rather than also using other elements in a non-oppressive way . . . they perpetuate the old definitions of themselves," she wrote.[107] (In private correspondence, Cooper more clearly stated her disdain for "relentlessly harmless accoustic [sic]/folk."[108])

In a later essay in *Leveller*, Cooper discussed rock music in particular, noting that the European reaction against Anglo-American cultural imperialism had produced a number of political rock bands (most of them Henry Cow associates: Stormy Six, Magma, the Swedes, Univers Zero). "The number of women musicians involved can be counted on the strings of one guitar, and the audiences are predominantly male," she wrote, "but the collective, unmacho approach of most of the European political groups is making more than cosmetic changes in the music and its performance."[109] The real changes, according to Cooper, were taking place in the all-women bands. (Naming none, she presumably meant the Jam Today, among others.)

Written a few years after she had joined Henry Cow, these articles allowed Cooper to express her own analyses of music culture without the distorting or alienating filter of the rock press. Almost always present, that filter became conspicuous in its absence when interviews appeared in fanzines such as *Liquorice* or *Atem*. Cooper told *Liquorice*'s Malcolm Heyhoe and Irena Krumb, "It does tend to happen when we do interviews as a group that Dagmar and I say very little. And when we do say things they tend not to be written up in the interview. . . . Very quickly, particularly if it's a man interviewer, which it generally is, a sort of dialogue builds up between the men and it's very difficult for me and Dagmar to break into that."[110] When

Cooper was free of these structures, she spoke eloquently about the varieties of sexism in rock culture, her own role in a "non-commercial" band, Henry Cow's political views, and the example she might set for other female instrumentalists and composers.

It is difficult to ascertain whether she praised all-female bands in *Leveller* because of the different experience she had endured in Henry Cow. "In any situation where you work with men, a kind of power structure emerges," she told *Atem*'s Gerard Nguyen in April 1978. "It is particularly visible in Henry Cow, since not only is work divided, but furthermore the men have been in the group much longer, and their musical ideas were already clear when I arrived. It is of course even truer for Georgie."[111] But does she mean the work was divided unequally? Do the men have more power because of their seniority in the organization, the clarity of their musical ideas, or their gender identities? The ambivalent logic of this statement can be generalized to stand in for many of Cooper's retrospective statements on the band, which communicate a subtle analysis that never settles on an easy judgment. Yes, other Cows had clearer musical ideas when Cooper joined, but that's because they are encouraged as young men to develop musical personalities and take risks with authorship. Yes, these structures of seniority would exist in an all-woman band, too, but they grew inseparable from gender patterns in this case. Yes, the men spoke more in interviews, but that's because they got asked all the questions in a rock culture that only recognized male agency. Yes, all rock culture was sexist, but Henry Cow's corner of that culture was more welcoming than most parts of "straight" society. And above all, her bandmates got her composing: "They encouraged me, maybe a bit too much!"[112] Indeed, Cooper told two Italian journalists in early 1977 that she had noticed recently a tendency to express more "feminine creativity" in the band.[113]

Given Cooper's strong feminism, the political awareness of her colleagues, the undeniable workings of the independent men's group, and the relative prevalence of women-only spaces in the mid-1970s, it isn't surprising that there formed an independent women's group in Henry Cow, though it was hardly a stable grouping and probably consisted of a few isolated conversations (as well as shared joking among all in the group). Krause explains, "We started to set up a group-within-a-group at some point. We were looking at examining the inner workings of Henry Cow and how it affected our creativity. It was meant to be a feminist cell within." In the memory of most Cows, Cooper and Born participated in these conversations, and Maggie Thomas firmly recalls Mandy Merck, Goschen, and Hodgkinson also taking part in

Figure 7.5 Lindsay Cooper and Chris
Cutler, 1978. PHOTOGRAPH BY TAKUMBA
RIA LAWAL.

whatever fleeting exchanges took place. (Hodgkinson confirms that he took a great interest, because he and Caroline Ayerst had attended many meetings on socialist feminism and other left concerns.) Thomas insists that she did not participate; women's solidarity thus was not taken for granted, and there was a range of positions on feminism in the group.

Krause's position, for example, shifted. Although she was involved initially, "I remember rejecting this idea of being a separate entity, because I felt that our group, Henry Cow, would fall to pieces—which at that time, I didn't see as an option, because Henry Cow was a stronger force, and it was what makes us go out on the road and do music." In her letters to Merck in autumn 1976, Cooper made several references to Krause's skepticism on the woman question. "She doesn't like to discuss common problems + talk with women, she thinks it should all be talked about en groupe with the boys."[114]

Born has adamantly maintained that no such subgroup existed. She later wrote, "This has been attributed to a period in which I was in the group, but I never experienced it. Indeed I would question that it ever existed: we may have debated such a thing, but it never developed."[115] Although she isn't the only one to have no memory of it (Balchin never noticed and didn't care), most of her bandmates do indeed recall the development, including Cutler, Frith, Hodgkinson, Thomas, Hobbs, and Krause. In our interviews, Thomas made clear that she thought the group was frivolous, and Hodgkinson expressed skepticism shortly after the band folded: "Gradually the women bring into the group a new struggle against ideological & linguistic structures they identify as repressive. But their actual critique stops short of the heart of the matter and leaves us with the project of merely excluding patronising and sexist elements in the group's language and behaviour. At this time the group is divided in itself: there is, temporarily[,] a women's group within the group. Members of the original group occasionally look back with nostalgia to the unity of the past."[116] Hodgkinson may have been referring to some ongoing disagreements on the perennial question of who should do the washing up. (That isn't just a bad joke: both Cooper and Krause discuss conflicts related to this question in their private documents.) But in a more serious and less dismissive vein, he was also referring to the privatized nature of romantic, emotional, and even familial attachments inside the group, which reproduced bourgeois norms of privacy and obstructed their other revolutionary openings from taking shape. In his final analysis of Henry Cow's dissolution, he would maintain that their inability to revolutionize their "arts of living" (including but not limited to romantic and emotional relationships) was responsible for the failure of the collective.

Born has identified "an aching retrospective desire that Henry Cow should have supported a politics of gender appropriate to the group's political ambitions, which are then projected onto the women in the group—perhaps in itself a sign of a certain capacity to overwrite their (our, my) actual experiences."[117] In other words, Born is saying, for some members and observers of Henry Cow, there *should have been* an independent women's group in the band, because such a feminist practice of women-only spaces would fit in well with the band's politics. Irrespective of the group's actual existence in the memories of most of its participants, we would do well to consider Born's greater point, that real differences among the women in the group prevented any kind of automatic solidarity. I have already touched on some of these divergences, including differences in sexual orientation, varied relationships with the men and each other, and distinct positions on feminism itself. They extended all the way down to quotidian matters of personal style: Krause points out that the Cow women—herself, Cooper, Goschen, Thomas—usually wore trousers and dungarees. "No! Georgie was wearing skirts. . . . So there was this feminine element coming, this type of femininity we had sort of denied. From the androgynous idea, we had a 'real woman' in there!"

Krause's experience also highlighted the specificities of her maternal struggles, which were shared with nobody else in the band after Greaves's departure. "Other people could focus a lot more on all the other people that were floating in and out, but I had a child. My energy had to go somewhere else when I wasn't working." Long tours were difficult for everyone, but they placed a unique burden on a single mother of a toddler. In her memory, few of the Cows showed any sensitivity to this responsibility (though they discussed boarding school for Max or a permanent minder—Krause's objections and the prohibitive cost quickly ruled out these options).[118] However, Krause recalls that Hodgkinson voiced an interest in assisting with Max's upbringing, and her memory helps to flesh out a picture of what he had in mind when he wrote that the feminists' "actual critique stops short of the heart of the matter." Krause recalls an incident when Hodgkinson disciplined Max on tour. "He said, 'We're all a collective, and we all take on parental roles. We share the parental roles here.' I said, 'And do you share it when I'm going home with Max, when the tour is over? Where are you then?'" In Krause's memory, Hodgkinson's parental responsibility was altered or asserted selectively. In the end, as we shall see, some combination of the Cows' unsatisfactory attempts at childcare and Krause's desire to keep the matter private would eventually contribute to her departure from the band.

Someone Else Can Clean Up This Mess: Feminist Improvising Group

Another important development in 1977 brings us back to Lindsay Cooper's opinion on women's separatism. When Val Wilmer asked the bassoonist how she reconciled her feminist politics with her decision to play music with men, her reply stressed the importance of her aesthetic principles and the power of professionalism:

> Many feminists must be saying about people like me: "They have chosen to play with men." This is not the case. What is important is having chosen to be a professional musician. . . . When you decide to be a musician, you inevitably face the problem of whether you will play with men. . . . I would never say that I absolutely would not do it. Even if I found a women's group that is successful and with which I could make a living— in fact I do not think it's possible. Many of the musicians with whom I like to play are men and I have learned enormously . . . with them. Those with whom I worked in Henry Cow are considerably less sexist than the other musicians that I knew.[119]

Nonetheless, women-only groups could offer exciting possibilities for musicians struggling with a male-dominated music industry, Cooper asserted elsewhere, especially "when practical and economic difficulties, lack of confidence and isolation from each other and means of making music can stop women singing/playing *at all*."[120] These obstacles were particularly acute in the case of improvised music, she noted.[121] Poised between integrative and separatist strategies, Cooper would move toward the latter as the decade wore on. "I'm not interested in any sort of feminism that doesn't have a streak of separatism in it. It would be extremely reactionary for any feminist politics not to be profoundly autonomous," she told Hannah Charlton in 1979.[122]

Her two interests—in a women's group and one of improvisers—would come together in autumn 1977. After a meeting of the Central London Branch of the Musicians Union, Cooper and Nicols discussed the dearth of women in free improvisation, and eventually resolved to put together a women-only group. Like Cooper, Nicols was a radical feminist and noted improviser on the European scene, and both were active in MU politics and the Women's Sub-Committee of the Central London Branch. At some point in the late summer, Nicols pointed out to the organizers of Music for Socialism that "Summer in the City" didn't have many female performers, and they urged her to put something together for the next series, "Words and Music." To join them in the new group, they invited Born; Corine Liensol, a trumpeter and activist who had performed with Jam Today; and Cathy Williams, a pianist from the anarchist theatre/music collective, Red Balune. As detailed in chapter 6, Nicols had been leading workshops on singing and improvisation since about 1970, usually at the Oval House in South London, so the group began as a focused workshop/consciousness-raising session for the five musicians. They discussed the gender stereotypes that had been pushed upon them in their daily lives and turned them into characters to play with in performance. To the musicians' surprise, they had been assigned a name: Feminist Improvising Group.

"That gig was all about bringing one's life into the performance," Cooper later told Wilmer. "So Maggie was being a harassed mother, Corine was being the irritating child."[123] (Liensol, who was black and disabled, often felt infantilized.) Born "had a sort of secretary persona for that gig, and I had the actual dress that I used to wear for classical music concerts, long since vanished. And Cathy was a sort of vampish image, I seem to remember. The gig was really about playing with images of women." Taking place at the Almost Free Theatre on October 30, the concert began with a brilliant bit of improvisation by Nicols. The previous performer had been Paul Burwell, who worked at the time with environmental installations and a lot of water. As a consequence, the stage was very wet after his act. "And he was going to clean it all up," Nicols remembers. "I said, 'No, don't clean it up!' And then of course we went on, and I went on with a mop," cursing the nerve of these male musicians who make a big mess and don't bother to tidy up afterward. Nicols then began to build anticipation for the "important middleclass lady musicians" offstage, as two reviewers put it; Cooper and Born appeared in a burst of virtuosic duets before all got busy with washing up and preparing dinner (smashing plates and cutting onions). Williams had also come onstage, "adding some glittery and confused poetic imprecations." And it went on, reportedly exploring themes of claustrophobia, anger, bewilderment, and grinding irritation. Their final words before leaving the stage, delivered with a rhetorical mic drop, were, "Someone else can clear up this mess."[124]

Like the many FIG concerts that followed, the group's premiere was funny, theatrical, and stylistically diverse. As with contemporaneous groups such as the Art Ensemble of Chicago, London's Alterations, and John Zorn's ensembles in New York, FIG routinely mixed in references to all kind of idiomatic musics in their improvised pastiche. The MFS decision to name the group "FIG" in its publicity materials pushed the group to take on a kind of confrontational, agitprop stance; Nicols explains, "We claimed it, and then we worked with it. 'Okay, you call us feminist? You want to see feminist?'" The feminism they gave their audiences included not only these ironic presentations of female stereotypes but also short sketches about the sexism in everyday life, mocking parodies of demeaning language in popular music, and even readings of extracts from feminist magazines.[125]

Space prohibits a fuller consideration of this important group, but they went on to play dozens of concerts until their last show at the Institute of Contemporary Arts in 1982. In the first stage of their existence, they envisioned a flexible pool of collaborators who would come together in different combinations. In February 1978's *Musics*, Born published an announcement: "Our aim is to enlarge and open up this group of women musicians interested in improvisation; to set up a loose contact network so that they can get together for gigs and projects in different combinations as they come up; and we hope that this can become more than that, a means of general communication between the now isolated few women working in this area."[126] Born later reported that her notice netted nothing more than a single gig in Norwich, but, nevertheless, the group did expand over the years to include pianist Irène Schweizer, vocalist/saxophonist Sally Potter, saxophonist Angèle Veltmeijer of Jam Today, vocalist Françoise Dupety, trombonist/violinist Annemarie Roelofs, and Frankie Armstrong.[127] By late 1978, they had jettisoned the open pool policy, and the group settled into a core of Cooper, Born, Nicols, Schweizer, Potter, and Liensol (who also departed the group eventually).

This detour through the Feminist Improvising Group not only provides some further detail into the cultural politics among the women of Henry Cow in its final years but also serves as a fitting example of how individual Cows had begun to cultivate social, political, and musical ties outside of the band in 1977. For example, in her comments to a journalist, Born indicated that she measured her experience in FIG to some degree against that of Henry Cow: "It's very different working in an all-women group. The whole approach is honest and open and in many ways we are more prepared to listen to each other, to be more sensitive to what other musicians are doing. In a mixed group, when you are playing with men, there is an element of competition. . . . In an all-woman band we are released from that kind of pressure."[128] In addition to their activities in FIG, Born and Cooper had become regulars at the LMC, gigging occasionally with improvisers such as Beresford and Bailey, and in the Campiello Band of Michael Nyman.[129] And Cooper moved further into London's feminist arts and culture scene, hanging out with friends in the *Screen*-centered film world, *Spare Rib* editors and writers, and feminist theatre (Women's Theatre Group and Monstrous Regiment). Frith played a few concerts at the LMC, too, and was circulating through new scenes that had been opened up to him by Steward, his girlfriend of several years. Along with his housemates at 5 Silverthorne Road, Cutler was getting more involved in Music Net / Recommended Records, which would become a major project in the years to come. This gradual loosening, slight but significant, would contribute to fractures that would be revealed in early 1978.

No Joy Anymore: Dagmar Krause's Departure

But the most serious case of a Cow leaving the herd came with Krause's departure from the band in autumn 1977. She reached the decision in Hamburg while recovering from the trials of touring during the summer of 1977. Like so many events, her departure from Henry Cow was overdetermined. Most important was the insurmountable challenge of motherhood in a city where she enjoyed neither extended family support nor the affluence necessary to hire domestic assistance. Absent any feasible shared parenting arrangement or the desire to pull Max out of school, Krause would be rooted in London for the foreseeable future. And, although everybody in Henry Cow was feeling restless with their old live material, Krause longed for more stuff with extended vocals. And by February or March 1977, she was feeling constrained by the lyrics: "Certainly they limit my expression; the words are restrictive, and I interpret them as one would a pamphlet," she commented in an Italian magazine.[130] She maintains that she loved singing "Erk Gah," but the little new music that was trickling into their set was largely instrumental, including Cooper's first composition (a long one without vocals), "Half the Sky," the Fred frags, and "La citta futura." Merck had authored some lyrics about the Stammheim deaths of the Baader-Meinhof revolutionaries, probably for one of Cooper's unfinished pieces, but they never saw the light of day. Hodgkinson's "Viva Pa Ubu," had singing, of course, but it was meant to sound more barroom than concert hall.

Krause's experience in the Orckestra exacerbated her dissatisfaction—she didn't enjoy the collaboration as much as her bandmates did. The instrumentalists could dig into all that fun new material throughout 1977, but the Westbrook band already had a singer, so Krause was obliged to share the mic. Literally: she sang "Alabama Song" with Kate Westbrook, and when the latter jokingly elbowed her German costar to the side during one concert, the gesture did not go down well. Krause did not appreciate the light touch that the Westbrooks brought to Brecht and Weill. "It was already an ironic song," she explains. "The irony shouldn't be over-emphasized in its delivery. The British are very keen on expressing it as a bit of fun and a joke." Mike Westbrook also recalls a confrontation with Krause over these songs: "She suddenly attacked me, quite strongly, over our treatment of the Brecht/Weill material. I approach that material just as I approach any material . . . : as a vehicle to do your thing. . . . I think she thought it was perhaps unserious, the way we approached things." For Krause, there was an added element of national allegiance; "They were messing about with my culture," she said.

These concerns over tone combined with Krause's insufficient airtime at the concerts themselves. Her feature, "Erk Gah," was too daunting for the skilled musicians of the MWBB, who declined to dedicate the considerable rehearsal time it required for what could turn out to be only a handful of concerts. That didn't leave much for Henry Cow's singer. "I sing one minute: 'On Suicide.' I sing 'Beautiful as the Moon,' which is a little longer, but it wouldn't have been the full version. And then I come on at the end for 'Alabama Song.' Do you get the gist of it?" she asked me. In between, of course, was up to one hundred minutes of non-Krause performance. "For me, it was painful and humiliating."

As she had begun to do in regard to Henry Cow gigs, Krause waffled about participating in some of the Orckestra concerts. Such waffling was met by exasperation in some quarters. The uncertain origin of her malaise—apart from maternal pressures, unfulfilled desires for new songs, and unwanted collaborations—might also be traced to the contraviviality that was starting to shade into a less productive, ordinary kind of ill humor. According to Krause, the relentlessly analytical, antiemotional discourse of criticism and self-criticism that had become the common language of the group for so long had alienated each of the members from the others. She was still an emotionally sensitive artist, but found no solace there. "Ultimately, I felt that I didn't belong there anymore. I felt there was, for me, no joy anymore. . . . There was no kindness, no friendship. There was just the group, and what it had to do next, and trying to say the right thing," she recalls.

Despite the delicacy of Krause's physical and emotional health, the rest of Henry Cow was not given to special considerations. In Born's words, "At the time, I had no idea what it would be like to tour with a small child, but now it makes perfect sense. . . . The idea—however fond I am of Tim, just

Figure 7.6 Dagmar Krause, 1975. PHOTOGRAPH BY SULA NICHOLS.

to take an example—the idea that Tim or Chris would understand what it would be to have a child, and tour with a child as a woman, I don't know." The conditions that she might have required to continue working with the group professionally, such as a private dressing room and hotel accommodation, proper supervision for her child, and consistently high-quality vocal amplification, lay far beyond the horizon of imagination for a group so committed to the equal sharing of ascetic circumstances. As Born recalls, "She was giving all the signs at the time—she showed how fragile she was, all the time—and she was incessantly ambivalent about being there on tour and performing."

"But . . . I was able to blank out a lot of that stuff, because I didn't want to see it," Hodgkinson adds.

"Yeah, that's what I'm trying to say, is that at the time . . . there was irritation and bafflement, and not understanding that this was intrinsically her. So we all said, 'Well, she's ill again.'"

Frith concurs: "I'm sure that some part of us must have been aware of [the strains she faced], but we never cut her any kind of slack, emotionally, for that. It was inevitable. How could she possibly have stayed?" Frith thinks that a big part of the denial—that she was having problems, that they couldn't face them—owed to their quiet agreement that she made a huge difference in their stage presentation, and they needed her. He said, "She was the front person, people loved her. We were not stupid. . . . When she was there, she was the very center of attention." And in the face of the "irritation and bafflement" that Born describes, Krause was an open book. "Everybody was tired, basically, but I'm always an easy target. . . . I'm too open, I say too much, I lay myself bare. They say nothing about themselves, they keep everything under their breath and up their sleeve, and hold tight. I let everything [out], right here I am. I've done it to you [i.e., the author], so let's just see how that turns out." I interpret this statement to mean that there were mutual frustrations on the subject of emotional expression.

In any case, Hodgkinson recalls that practical matters required them to begin rehearsing an instrumental set. "Everybody was thinking, you know, 'She's going to drop out, isn't she? We're in a real fix.' And then somebody said, 'Maybe we should do an instrumental set.' And then you sort of think, 'Ah. . . . That sort of means that Dagmar is out.'" While still in Italy in late September, they decided to begin searching for a new singer. "Now that it's official I can also reveal that Dagmar has been sent the golden handshake," Cooper wrote on September 21.[131] In Hodgkinson's memory, it was he who did the axe job by calling Krause. The show had to go on. "We were nothing if not pragmatic when it came down to the bottom line," Frith admits. "In spite of all the rhetoric, when it came down to it we made whatever decisions we had to make in order to keep the band on the road." In the immediate future, that meant telephoning Klaus Blasquiz of Magma to see if he was available (apparently he was not), and then placing some advertisements for a singer in *Melody Maker* and the Music for Socialism newsletter. They held auditions in late October, but the names of the invitees and whatever transpired in Clerkenwell are lost to history.

The band issued a press release (authored by Cutler) on October 26: "Henry Cow are presently working as an instrumental group. Dagmar

Krause, as a result of progressive physical exhaustion, is no longer able to tour with us because our schedules and the conditions in which it is necessary for us to work make it impossible for her to fully recover her health." Graciously, Cutler added, "Dagmar is irreplaceable."[132] Krause's poor health was a partial screen, of course: yes, she was tired and sick from the road, but these physical symptoms were outward manifestations of her deeper dissatisfaction with the band and its manner of operation. As more than one former Cow notes, Cutler may have been unwilling to acknowledge a bourgeois indulgence such as emotional crisis, perhaps another measure of the band's failure to accommodate the needs of every one of its members. Surprisingly, Henry Cow continued their perfunctory search for a singer as late as February 1978. As we'll see in the next chapter, however, October was hardly the end of the story for Krause and the Cows.

Before turning to the final chapter of this history, I must note again the economic duress in which the band found itself by the summer of 1977. In mid-June, with only one or two approaching gigs on the schedule for almost three months, they forecast a deficit of £2,500 in back wages by September 9 (£16,550 in 2017), plus another £3,300 in existing debts. They discussed going on the dole, but because "Henry Cow" as their "employer" had never been able to afford national insurance stamps for contribution cards, social services would be impossible.[133] Nor would loans offer much relief, because they already owed so much that it would be quite a long time before they could realistically repay any new debts. Their only hope, as far as they could see, would come in the form of gifts or long-term loans. To Frith fell the ghastly task of asking for money from the richest people they knew (Richard Branson, Mike Oldfield, and the Sex Pistols), but it is quite unlikely that the requests were ever issued. Miraculously, their disaster was averted when emergency relief came from a source they were not expecting: the Arts Council of Great Britain.

8   Henry Cow Always Had to Be Henry Cow | 1978

In the summer of 1977, Henry Cow received a substantial grant from the Arts Council of Great Britain (AC) that would go far in helping them stay afloat into 1978. The AC had known about them for several years—recall that Fred Frith had applied for an individual artist grant in 1974 (denied), and tried again with success in April 1976. One month later, their old friend and mentor Tim Souster from Cambridge, who was now teaching at Keele University and serving on the Arts Council Music Panel, had put Henry Cow's name forward for the Contemporary Music Network (CMN), the Arts Council's innovative program for presenting new music outside of London. The scheme devoted AC funds to paying for fees and travel for a performing group to tour the provinces, while the regional arts councils and local presenting bodies would pick up accommodation and subsistence costs. Essentially, CMN subsidized contemporary music concerts outside of London, where it was more difficult to assemble a paying audience.

Initiated by the council's Annette Morreau in 1970, the CMN had a history of rather ecumenical support across contemporary composed music, jazz, and free improvisation, the latter owing to the early advocacy of concert presenter Victor Schonfield, as well as to Morreau's respect for Evan Parker (who joined the Music Panel's Jazz Subcommittee in 1976 and the Music Panel proper in 1977).[1] The selection process for the CMN was somewhat convoluted.[2] The AC had taken over stewardship of the British section of the International Society for Contemporary Music (ISCM) in the early 1970s, and that body would put together an advisory panel every year to recommend ensembles for the CMN to the AC, who would also solicit a list from its Jazz Subcommittee (the implication being that the ISCM did not do "jazz"). Souster served on both the Music Panel and the ISCM committee. The ISCM's advisory panel for the CMN met on August 6 to discuss the nominations, then forwarded their list to the Music Panel.[3]

Henry Cow was classified as "jazz" in the Music Panel's deliberations, but they were a nominee of the ISCM (through Souster), not the Jazz Subcommittee. In other words, insofar as "rock" snuck into the AC's music funding in 1976, it did so through Henry Cow's associations with high-art contemporary music, live electronics, and tape work—not through associations with any of the Afro-diasporic musical forms that were otherwise defining the popular music landscape in the North Atlantic. Almost certainly the first rock band to receive AC funding, Henry Cow were therefore also a socially conservative choice, removed as they were from these more overtly raced vernacular musics.[4] (For their CMN tour, which would take place in February 1978, Tim Hodgkinson requested a fee of £500 for each of the nine concerts; along with money for travel reimbursement, two weeks of rehearsals, and administrative costs, it shaped up to be a remunerative run of gigs.[5])

By the summer of 1977, therefore, the music administrators at the AC had been interacting with Henry Cow for over a year. In fact, music director John Cruft had even attended the Cow's Battersea Town Hall concert in February, reporting in an internal memo that "after a slowish start," the band "carried its audience" of 450 to 500 listeners. Cruft thought they were "very skillful," and was particularly impressed by Lindsay Cooper's multi-instrumentalism.[6] This appraisal may have been remembered on June 30, when, at the summer meeting of the ISCM British section, the committee discussed Henry Cow's severe financial difficulties. Noting that their relationship with Virgin had effectively ended, Souster "pointed out that because of the gloomy economic situation, commercial record companies were not prepared to invest large sums of money in this sort of experimental music, which he thought to be of very high quality."[7] Ian Carr attested to their popularity abroad. Persuaded, the committee "urged the council to help as generously as possible."

It's unclear how Henry Cow had the idea to apply for a grant independent of their upcoming CMN tour. Nick Hobbs had sent a proposal, with budgets, projected earnings, and a list of capital repairs and purchases totaling over £32,000 (that's a lot of money).[8] He included everything, from urgent needs such as the phone bill, back wages, and outstanding debts to vehicle repairs, new and repaired PA equipment, and new musical instruments for everybody in the band. Somewhat audaciously, he explained how their collective compositional process necessitated a basic recording studio (cost: £9,660, about £64,000 in 2017).

They didn't get everything they asked for, but they did receive a sizable award. Cruft actually recommended to his colleagues on the finance committee and the AC that they award Henry Cow £14,500, which would cover the amounts they requested for outstanding debts, back wages, vehicle repairs, a new PA, upgraded microphones, and a new mixer.[9] "I realise that this will create a sizeable precedent," Cruft wrote, "but think it appropriate that such a creative Music organisation be funded in a way already considered acceptable in the Drama allocations." Not entirely meeting Cruft's recommendation, the AC eventually awarded Henry Cow £7,000 total in July, to address the pressing needs for vehicle repairs, PA upgrades, and back wages. Combined with the nearly £5,000 they were to receive for the nine-date CMN tour, this sum pulled the Cow most of the way out of debt. But by the time the tour came around in February, it would turn out, the band had come apart. First, however, they would travel to Sunrise Studios, in Kirchberg, Switzerland, finally to record the new album they had been planning for over a year.

Etienne Conod founded Sunrise in 1975; he had been in a band of the same name that had recently split up after about a year of too few gigs. With a small inheritance from his father, Conod bought a former meat factory in the tiny town of Kirchberg, about an hour outside Zurich. With a Revox tape deck and a single Sennheiser dummy-head microphone, he started a business recording band demos. He charged by the song, and also provided advice to fledgling bands on how to cut a record themselves. "Record deals? No way," he explains. "I'm a hippy. I'm against record companies. . . . I'm kind of a lefty revolutionary—quote-unquote—type of guy at the time." This renegade streak no doubt endeared Conod to the Cows, but by the time they arrived to inspect the studio, he had also upgraded his facilities with a sixteen-track Ampex tape recorder. With a few new microphones, a new mixer, and some construction work to divide up the ground floor of the building, he had put together a more serious studio.

Henry Cow's new friends in the German band Embryo probably recommended Sunrise when the Cows met them during their short swing through West Germany in late 1977. They also heard about Conod through their old comrade, Anthony Moore, who had worked at the studio for about a month writing compositions and arrangements with Dieter Meier. That material was never released, but Moore enjoyed a good rapport with Conod, and wanted to help the studio succeed by sending bands to record there. Henry Cow visited in early December. Conod recalls, "They arrived at night, and they were all very tired, and it was winter, and they came . . . it was otherworldly. They were like researchers in the North Pole, coming into the warm—frozen, and hungry and thirsty, and not having slept, and poor, and everything: and they look ripped off, and smelly. But nice eyes! . . . I was fascinated." Henry Cow liked what they saw at the studio, and they liked Conod, so they booked two weeks of recording time in January.

While they were in Kirchberg, Henry Cow also met Jean Karakos, who had flown there with a tape of the Orckestra's Paris gig from November. They evaluated it for possible release (not good enough), and discussed financial arrangements for releasing Henry Cow's forthcoming album. Karakos promised them a huge advance.[10]

Back in London for the holidays, the Cows had their work cut out for them. They had scheduled two weeks of recording time beginning on January 15, but Hodgkinson wanted to write new antifascist lyrics for "Erk Gah," and the rest of the band—primarily Frith and Cooper—were tasked with generating music for the other side of the record. Although nobody mentioned it to me explicitly, they were probably also thinking that some open improvisation would work on the second side, as it had on their previous two studio productions.

Hodgkinson remembers, "I was upping the priority of the politics, partly because of just what was going on—the punk thing, the whole antiracist movement, Rock Against Racism, the antifascism movement in England. . . . I created this huge problem by rewriting the text for 'Erk Gah' in what I imagined was a much more effectively political vein." He rushed to finish these new lyrics and presented them to his bandmates in early January: they rehearsed on January 2 then had a meeting on the 4th. Chris Cutler's diary is succinct but helpful:

4 Tim's lyrics all day

Fred outburst

5 Tim's lyrics standoff

commission me

Frith bursted out on the subject of Hodgkinson's new text, which he thought was "generic, forced, wooden, [and] self-consciously revolutionary." Worst of all: the lyrics reminded him of Cornelius Cardew's zombie rock music. "I was one of the people who was the most uncomfortable with them," Frith later recalled, but he was joined in this opinion by Cooper and possibly Georgina Born and Dagmar Krause. Their negative opinion had to do with aesthetics, not politics, and it is one that Hodgkinson now shares in retrospect.

Although accounts differ about the extent to which he voiced reservations, Cutler maintains that he was assigned the problematic project of authoring new lyrics for "Erk Gah." He says, "What I remember at the time is saying, 'It can't be done,' but being tasked to 'Go home and give it a try' anyway. . . . But I . . . had no serious problem with them; he'd worked hard on them and they were what he wanted to say. As a lyricist I had to respect that. Anyway, the piece was twenty minutes long and I was given maybe a week to do it all. So I didn't start. It made no sense." Instead, Cutler generated several short texts for songs and handed them out to everybody when they boarded the bus on the 9th. "Everybody can write settings for these," he told them. "We've got five days before we're in the studio." His thinking was pragmatic: they'd had a good experience with *Desperate Straights* a few years before, songs could be practical given their time constraints, and Krause had already been contracted as a guest artist to record "Erk Gah," so would need something else to sing.

As trying as they might have been for most, these conditions were ripe for Frith to exercise his talents and experience. Songs are short, liberating him from the formal demands of more extended writing and showcasing his gift for generating evocative miniatures. The form took him back to his folk-club days, and it also connected directly to his developing interest in Eastern European folk music. Most of all, these circumstances gave Frith risky opportunities for getting out of a jam, given the many uncertainties that needed to be converted into certainty by the end of the month. He already had two songs in the bag: "Joan" and "In Two Minds," which the band had played at least once as an instrumental in concert earlier that year. In the five days leading up in Kirchberg, in moments seized between driving spells and two Swiss gigs, Frith contributed three more originals, "Riddle," "Moeris, Dancing," and "Maze," the last of which the band had been working on for about a year.

Henry Cow began working at Sunrise on January 15 with great trepidation. Progress was slow, and they lacked a clear plan. Cooper felt "completely unequal to contributing anything to this record at all. Who knows what we're going to put on it—I think the idea of the moment is that everyone turns out songs and lyrics prestissimo."[11] Krause flew in to the studio on the 15th, joining what Cooper called "anguished discussions" about the contents of the album. Krause loved singing "Erk Gah," but she thought the new lyrics were too labored. Hodgkinson had trouble accepting his colleagues' disapproval, and, according to Cooper, "he argued long and bitterly for its retention on the album."[12] He was defeated: "We argued about it right down to the point where we were actually in the studio and I saw that I was in a minority of one, so we said, 'OK we'll put together an album of songs.'"[13] His capitulation gave way to an uneasy cooperation: he wasn't sure that it would work, but he'd go along for now. Cooper, meanwhile, expressed serious doubts about her ability to write new songs, and her letters indicate that she got off to a slow start.

Studio Democracy and Its Opposite

Given Henry Cow's many conversations about collective composition over the previous year or so, the new manner of collaboration they forged at Sunrise was surprising and contradictory. As we've seen, the band had construed group work in a number of ways, including open improvisation, where a musical piece could emerge through collective decision making; spontaneous work on preorganized materials, like the "Beast" segments in the first quartet tour or the tape interactions of the second quartet tour; co-composition, as when they wrote material together for *the Bacchae* or *Desperate Straights*; technologically enhanced collective exploration, such as their improvisations for the Greasy Truckers benefit; and tape work, which had featured on all of their studio albums. Occasionally, this collectivism produced strategies that seem misguided in retrospect, like that of the Cows arrayed around the Manor's mixing desk, each fader drawn by its own finger. But even the strangeness of this image communicates the extent to which they struggled to discover new forms of authorship and performance within the historical and material conditions of their time.

In Kirchberg, however, some members of the band would come to new realizations about the recording studio and how to work within it. Frith, Cutler, and Hodgkinson discussed this sea change a decade later. Frith commented, "The thing that strikes me as most extraordinary about what we did [before Sunrise] was the fact that we were so hands on, all of us—which is, in my experience since then, extremely counterproductive." When everybody operates their own fader, he explained, nobody had an ear out for the whole; moreover, Cutler added, "Everybody wanted to be audible, but nobody wanted to be ostentatiously loud." These compromises make the music suffer, Frith said, "It sounds like a bunch of people who've basically taken a soft option in order to avoid having any distinctive characteristics."

"Right," said Hodgkinson, "and the producer would say things like, 'Well . . .'"

"'Take the bass out.'"

"Exactly. 'Just don't use the bass for these parts.'"

"Yes, and those are the kinds of things that we now do as a matter of course," said Frith. "In those days I think a suggestion of that kind would have caused a major political problem in the group."

The result, in Hodgkinson's phrase, would be a "committee sound," a kind of conservative aesthetic compromise. A single, unified point of audition and artistic decision making—a producer—"would've definitely helped us in that respect," Frith said. Sensing an inconsistency, Hodgkinson reasoned, "But we didn't want a producer, just like we didn't want a manager. . . . There is a real contradiction: one of the things we thought about a lot was this idea about collective work, and of course, that would suggest that everybody should be all hands-on on the desk."

Although the producer presented a kind of impasse in Hodgkinson's political theorization, the centralized approach to recording practice it symbolized led Frith and Cutler more unproblematically to new aesthetic terrain. Not to imply that they were rushing out on their own, however: in fact, the band had discussed the very possibility the previous spring, when they concluded that "there is nothing wrong with one or two people mixing things—in fact can be better."[14] The new problem, they would learn, was that an innovative creative practice rooted firmly in the studio's capabilities would not necessarily lead to a new or "revolutionary" creative practice for the group. Rather, it could foster atomization and alienation along with its original kind of excitement.

Its ink barely dry on the page, the music's recent vintage forced Henry Cow to arrange much of the material on the fly, direct to tape. There was no time for group rehearsals to work out parts. "So we are basically constructing the music track by track," Frith later explained. "Which is more like the second side of *Unrest* than anything else that we've done, except that there are written parts. . . . So it becomes much less of a tight process where everybody's communally involved, it becomes a process which is somewhat socially fragmented." To fabricate a hypothetical example, Frith might record a scratch track of himself playing a sequence of chords on the guitar to establish the harmony, tempo, and rhythms for Krause, who then would learn the melody and lyrics, eventually recording her vocal on top. Meanwhile, Frith might break up the voicing of the harmonies for alto sax, bassoon, and flute, which Hodgkinson and Cooper could record, one at a time, while monitoring his original guitar track. Then Cutler might overdub some drum parts, and they would finally mute the original guitar, leaving the song in its final form.

Of the eleven scraps and songs they had to record, Frith contributed five, all of which had probably been written before their arrival at Kirchberg. (While there, he'd also write, with Cooper, a sixth, "The Dividing Line.") In other words, he was more ready to jump into the recording process than the other Cows. Frith remembers, "I've just written a whole bunch of material in a hurry and we're already putting it on tape in a hurry, and I'm really intensely going for it—and I'm in charge. And Chris is kind of right there, also in charge. In a way, I think we kind of took over the whole thing." Recalling some uncharacteristic aggression from the mild-mannered Hodgkinson, as well as some pushback from Born, Frith later said, "I was probably being very autocratic and just going for it. So the chances are, they were both mirroring something that they were getting out of me, which was negative energy of some description. So I'm prepared to own that—I can only imagine."

Although their relations with Hodgkinson, Born, and Cooper might have been deteriorating over the course of the session, Frith and Cutler really hit it off with Conod, who recalls, "With Chris and with Fred, we did intuitively work in that field. Both not coming from the intellectual but from the playful and from the intuitive approach." Foremost in his memory as leaders during the session, Conod loved their energy and curiosity, their way of knocking around in the studio to shake loose new creative possibilities. "Nothing was given. There was a lust for chaos and the creative way of going about things," he later commented. Late into the night they would work, and just when Conod thought he could creep away for some sleep of his own, he'd hear a whisper from Cutler: "Pssst, Etienne! Let's work on the drum sound!"

As busy as the session may have been for those three, there was "not all that much for the others to do half the time," Frith recalls. "I just remember working my butt off. But it's possible that the others who were not doing so much of the work were actually upstairs talking about shit." Frith may think now that he was "behaving badly," but Hodgkinson later remarked, "I have no memory of Fred conducting himself in any way that I would want to criticize during those sessions." According to Hodgkinson, Frith was very likely keeping the group from running out of time; with his numerous guest spots in the previous years, Frith had accrued some fluency with recording technique, and was therefore in a position to drive the session.

But his opinion of Frith's individual behavior notwithstanding, Hodgkinson was less charitable in his description of the overall labor arrangement during the sessions: "It was like a factory." Cooper and Born agreed with his assessment, adding more than a dash of alienation. In a letter to Mandy

Figure 8.1 Fred Frith, 1978. PHOTOGRAPH BY TAKUMBA RIA LAWAL.

Merck during the session, Born wrote, "Linz and me swallow fear and prejudice re our use in this disc, finding it very hard . . . we're pretty much session people, though she's got a piece on, and I've got a raunchy bass part or two, maybe 5 mins out of the 40. Actually, it's basically a Fred Frith . . . and Chris Cutlery Production!"[15] And Cooper reported feeling "very pissed off with it all because I and my instruments have been grossly underused."[16]

But in spite of their mates' discontent with the technical process of writing on tape, Cutler and Frith found the experience to be transformative. Frith later said, "That was a profound moment in my life."

Cutler said, "Me too."

Frith continued, "It was like suddenly understanding what a studio could do and what it was for. . . . This was a way to work where the individual as an instrumentalist suddenly became completely unimportant; you were suddenly dealing with the sound and atmosphere of a song, and what the material needed."

"And also this thing of laying it down track by track," Cutler added. "Of course . . . we knew that people put down backing tracks, . . . but we absolutely wouldn't ever do it."

"It was because 'the group' had to be 'there,'" Hodgkinson said.

"Yeah, that was the thing."

Hodgkinson continued, "The group, as a 'thing,' was like a sort of membrane between us and the sound. I mean, when you did those Art Bears things in Kaleidophon [studio], there wasn't a group. You were actually creating the music."

Frith: "Yes, we were outside of it."

"Whereas, Henry Cow always had to be Henry Cow, with everybody there."

The Art Bears to which Hodgkinson referred was a new band—comprising Frith, Cutler, and Krause—that would be formed once Henry Cow decided to break up just days after these Sunrise sessions. In his contribution to this illuminating exchange on technique, efficiency, and creativity, Hodgkinson seems to be saying that the streamlined, efficient, and novel studio practices of Art Bears, whatever their many virtues and forceful results (see the marvelous *Winter Songs*), did not actually address the problems of collective work in the recording studio (the worst of which might have been a "committee sound"), because Art Bears weren't a "group" in the same way Henry Cow had been. They were more of what we might call a "project-based" ensemble: light, efficient, flexible.

The group, "with everybody there," was more of a lumbering beast, and Frith and Cutler were doing nothing more in Kirchberg than trying to corral it in the right direction. Yet it is difficult not to conclude that this correction of Henry Cow's dysfunctional and subproductive studio practice also effected a kind of normalization of their errant experiments in collective creation. Those experimental ventures had been clumsy, slow, inefficient, and inconclusive. The escape from or solution to these various obstructions, in the form of "best practices" or efficiencies, represented a resolution of certain problems, but only on the surface; beyond this surface lay an abjuration of problematization itself. Such a doubled effect must be heard in the chuckle that opens Frith's first post–Henry Cow solo album, *Gravity* (1980), a brilliant title whose irony references the carefree music therein as well as the ponderous concerns of the band reflected in its rearview mirror. Its meaning was understood well by the radio interviewer who introduced his guest in 1980 thus: "Since the breakup of Henry Cow, Mr. Frith has vigorously avoided the clumsy, impersonal monolithic rock group, and chosen the path of being a mobile independent musician, which has left him free to choose what he wants to do and when he wants to do it."[17] That chuckle. It says, "I am free, life is good, don't take yourself too seriously." Henry Cow did not chuckle. Relieved of obstructions, Frith found a remarkable mobility: the barriers had been removed and the world was no longer a problem.

There arose other conflicts at Sunrise. Hodgkinson, for example, lost his temper viciously with both Frith and Cutler. He wasn't convinced, either through argument or in practice, that their decision to record an album of songs constituted anything less than a step backward in terms of form. "Why are we playing this stuff? This is, like, The Who!" he later remarked, probably in reference to the vaguely "Baba O'Riley"–esque "In Two Minds." "I felt we had a political and aesthetic responsibility: we needed to always go beyond what we'd done before. And I thought 'Erk Gah' went beyond what *I'd* done before, and I thought, in terms of compositions, it went beyond what *the group* had done before." Many of the songs, however, did not leave him with the same impression. ("For Fred and me, it was definitely a step forward," Cutler told me.) In Hodgkinson's memory of 1981, Cutler had been pushed to his limit by these outbursts and expressed a wish to get free of the group.[18]

Meanwhile, Born felt actively excluded from the unfolding creative process, the discussions about the direction of the band, and the technological apparatus that was making it possible. "There were all these intense discussions and decisions being taken in that kitchen, and I know—and it's not a huge reproach—but I wasn't party to them," she later explained. More than one participant in the January Sunrise sessions noted to me that Born seemed insecure about her role during those weeks, and it cannot have been easy to experience the weird world of the recording studio for the first extended time in these trying circumstances. One Cow recalls finding a postcard she had written but left out in the studio detailing her anger at how the men in the group were dominating the technology. (For his part, Frith recalls making an early start on some mornings with tutorials on the mixing desk with Born. "Who knows how I was telling her how the studio worked, I was probably patronizing as hell," he says. Born remembers no such tutorials.)

Through all of this turmoil, Cutler soldiered on in the excitement of his synergy with Frith and Conod. "I had no idea that there was so much unhappiness rumbling away underneath," he comments. "That was all being discussed in the kitchen when I wasn't there—and Fred wasn't there, and Dagmar probably wasn't there." Among the topics up for discussion in that kitchen were the new lyrics Cutler had written for the band, which leaned away from the evocative but relatively clear and leftist slant of "Beautiful as the Moon." Hodgkinson's complaint was largely inversional: "Well that was my defense. When he said, 'These lyrics are crap,' I said, 'Yeah, but your lyrics are mystical.'" Born, too, expressed some dismay with the mythological and "adolescent" lyrics in a letter at the time.

Great Terrible Horrorshock Joan of Arc Lyric Controversy

But the main complaint against Cutler's lyrics had to do with his new text for "Joan."[19] He never liked the original lyrics, and the new ones he wrote for the Sunrise sessions celebrated Joan of Arc as an exemplar of charismatic power, of which there were numerous examples in the medieval period, he later explained.[20] Born and Cooper objected strongly, in part because of their skepticism about Cutler stepping into the first-person voice in representing a female character, but also because he figured the female as a mother. The offending line was "I embraced him my breast with Milk swelling / Child of my life: the flames turned my Flesh into Legend." Cooper described the brouhaha over these lyrics with reference to the difficult Rome meeting: "a re-run of the 1976 H. Cow anti-feminist outrage."[21] She quipped, "I did feel it was going a bit far to harp on and on about her maternal relationship with death. . . . We can never escape you see—even if we're out there in chain mail on direct instructions from saints, it's only because we want to give birth to a phallus . . . or death or something." Krause had balked initially at singing these lines, but soon embraced the opinion that maternity should not be rejected so categorically, perhaps in reflecting on her own circumstances. Wrote Born, "We two were both amazed and weakened by Dagmar's complete change of heart over this. She suddenly couldn't get out of her . . . head that women should be glorified in their maternal role, there's nothing to be apologetic or defensive about in that."[22] Unwilling to "coerce" their bandmates with a veto, Born did not wish to employ their rules about consensus to get her way; as a result, she was left with "the cow[,] faced with an obvious and serious feminist-offending content, choosing blythely [sic] to find 'other qualities' in the lyrics, thus let 'em pass."[23]

The women also objected to Cutler's text for "In Two Minds," an antipsychiatric portrait of a troubled young woman trying to make sense of her experiences but whose parents label her struggles as pathological and in need of professional help. For Cooper and Born, Cutler's portrayal of a confused woman sitting in a nightshirt at the kitchen table seemed to offer a pathetic figure. And other lyrics came in for comment from the band's extended circle—Caroline Ayerst, for example, remembers giving Cutler a hard time about the word *carapace* in his lyrics for "Maze": for regular, working people who might be thought of as an audience, such esoteric words functioned to alienate rather than communicate.

The tussles over lyrics, working style, and general emotional ructions left Born and Cooper "feeling wretchedly + desperate about the whole business."[24] In her letter to Merck, Born wrote, "I can assure you that at least our solidarity is a step forward, I'm becoming more definite in my ideas + views; and I felt the others, boys, somewhat more challenged in their fairly traditional power positions as regards opinions and 'political integrity' than usual."[25] Cooper perceived that "the boys seem to be making all the decisions," and even the usually quiet, sympathetic feminist Hodgkinson grew prone to tossing out quite uncomradely jokes. Cooper wrote, "As Tim Hodgkinson celebrated C. P. and H Cow member says, women aren't oppressed they're lazy, so if I don't seize control of everything immediately its my own fault.[26]" Spun round by this poisonous atmosphere, Cooper quickly penned a lyric about "filling her breast not with milk but with rage" that was quickly rejected by Cutler. Always tough but also pragmatic, Cooper nonetheless continued a productive back-and-forth with her male collaborators. "Otherwise my songwriting has met with partial success," she told a correspondent. "Fred and I wrote a song between us ["Dividing Line"] which Chris wrote the words for (it was about men and soldiers and he's allright on that sort of thing)."[27]

Henry Cow left Kirchberg with eleven songs, including older repertoire they had been performing or rehearsing for a while: "Joan," "In Two Minds," and "Viva Pa Ubu." Another of the older ones, Hodgkinson's "Pirate Song," glowed with the same warmth as Eisler's sublime "On Suicide," which the Cow also recorded. Hodgkinson's new song, "Labyrinth," created a musical analogue for Cutler's text about Daedalus, the designer of the Minotaur's labyrinth in Crete. Hodgkinson told Trond Garmo that he wanted to write music that would express the confusion and frustration of dwelling in a labyrinth, where dead ends and false exits make it easy to get lost and difficult to escape. He built his piece in three layers: percussion, mainly clay drums with occasional guiro, cymbal, and bell; chords played on a clean electric guitar; and vocal melody, sung by Krause and supported by a distorted guitar. Each layer has a unique tempo and meter, related to the others through various ratios; when the metrical cycles of the upper layers align temporally,

Figure 8.2 Henry Cow and friends singing Tim Hodgkinson's "Viva Pa Ubu" at Sunrise Studios, January 1978. *From left:* Lindsay Cooper, Fred Frith (*obscured*), Isabelle Bulard, Tim Hodgkinson, Shirley Bennett, Jack Balchin, Georgina Born, and Dagmar Krause.
COURTESY OF THE LINDSAY COOPER ESTATE.

Hodgkinson marks the event with a strike of the bell. He set the melody in a free chromatic style, according to a loose row of pitches that is repeated for each of the three verses. Probably in light of the song's sophisticated temporal layering, Hodgkinson limits the chord sequences to triads with occasional added ninths, but because the harmony moves independently of the melody, several jarring dissonances can be found. To create the piece in the studio, each layer had to be recorded to its own metronome click, independently from the other parts.[28]

Cooper considered "Half the Sky," an instrumental, to be her first proper composition; she divided its five minutes into three parts. In the first, a slow long melody is unspooled in unison by bass, guitar, and bassoon over a crashing beat by Cutler; the line avoids any sense of repetition beyond the descending half-note triplet that comes back four more times in the opening section's thirteen bars. After about a minute, the texture opens up onto a series of slowly changing organ chords (Hodgkinson contributed these), over which Cooper solos on the soprano sax and Frith adds some sustained guitar flourishes. Cooper winds up the section with a trilling counterpoint for clarinet and soprano sax that breaks into a rhapsodic flutter to kick-start the upbeat coda. Cooper's quirky melody in the winds oscillates through some tricky rhythmic changes before transitioning into another series of melodies, mainly in 5/4, for the clarinet and guitar over eighth-note tut-tutting in the bassoon. Episodic in nature, "Half the Sky" revealed Cooper to be an inventive writer of melodies and syncopated accompaniment. In "The Dividing Line," her melody wanders a bit more but does coax an expressive vocal performance from Krause.

Frith's new tunes, "Maze" and "Riddle," both presented long, doom-ridden introductions of either reverbed drum gestures or pensive drones. Sung by Krause and Born, the vocal writing in "Maze" gives off a certain organum feel, with its frequent perfect fifths. Often highly dissonant, both songs share a fraglet heard most clearly in the opening to "Riddle," where it is played by the organ and recorder; the snippet comes back variously in that tune, as well as in "Maze" and "The Dividing Line," where it constitutes—at half-speed—Frith's contribution to the song. Depending on one's perspective, this riddle theme either united the material they had recorded or served as evidence that they were working under duress and with limited time for new ideas.

The rollicking "Moeris, Dancing" best showcased Frith's new direction and interest in eastern European folk music. Basically an instrumental (Krause doubles the acoustic guitar line with nasally "ah's" at the beginning), the piece jumps right into a gem of a fast melody in 15/8; it keeps the listener guessing by alighting off and onto the beat for two quick measures before coming to rest on a long-sustained note that balances the phrase (example 8.1). Fifteen had long been Frith's favorite metrical grouping, but the Balkan flavor of "Moeris" allowed him to explore a new way of organizing the unit. Wisely, he chose to limit the bass motion to a single pedal for the first two bars, and a second for its consequent pair (his score called for more notes), which nicely opens up the texture in a manner reminiscent of "Beautiful as the Moon." As the tune progresses, he adds a strong rhythmic counterpoint with repeating chords on the violin. Cutler's drumming keeps a steady pulse but refrains from strongly marking phrases or sections, which allows the enchanting melody to do all that kind of work. After about a minute, Frith takes us to the "chorus," a slower, grand melody doubled in acoustic and distorted guitars over droning bass, which soon gives way to another series of snaking melodic lines, this time voiced by Frith's violin and acoustic guitar and unadorned by drums, with occasional percussive interjections and hand claps. Another turn to the chorus and return to the opening melodic phrases bring the song to a close, but not quite: Frith appends an odd coda in the form of sustained violin (and probably cello) drones (on

Example 8.1 Fred Frith, "Moeris Dancing," guitar and voice (*Hopes and Fears*, track 12, 0:00); transcribed from the score, FFA.

F-sharp) in three octaves, all of which slide slightly sharp and flat over the course of the coda's two minutes. Meanwhile, one of the bongo tracks from "Labyrinth" tuk-tuks away in the background until the whole texture fades out. (This tape splice worked thematically: Lake Moeris was adjacent to the Ancient Egyptian labyrinth, making a nice pun with Morris Dancing, the English folk style.[29])

So the material that Henry Cow recorded at Sunrise in January 1978, which I will often refer to as *Hopes and Fears* for reasons that will become clear, presented a mixed bag. There was a Henry Cow–style "rock" song ("Joan"); another more conventional rock song ("In Two Minds"); two lieder ("Pirate Song" and "On Suicide"); Cooper's instrumental ("Half the Sky"); a raucous, live-sounding "Viva Pa Ubu"; a folk dance ("Moeris, Dancing"); and the new siblings "Maze," "Riddle," "The Dividing Line," and "Labyrinth." Overall, the instrumentation was lighter than most Henry Cow recordings had been in the past, with often just one or two acoustic instruments playing along with Krause. Cutler had written lyrics that crystallized ancient and medieval themes, with frequent references to confusion, labyrinths, greed, mazes, and fear. Although they skewed toward the abstract and mystical, his explanatory notes share that he often thought about them in terms of struggle and the present historical circumstances.

Very Bizarre Thorny Group Period

Henry Cow left Switzerland at the end of the month and returned to London on January 31. They took cassettes of the mixes and listened at home that night, then reconvened for a meeting at Cooper's flat the next day. Frith remembers, "There was already an atmosphere of foreboding about how this was actually going to pan out. On the one hand, you've got Chris and I, who are quietly excited about it—and at the same time sensitive to the fact that our excitement is not necessarily shared." When they finally reconvened, Hodgkinson announced to Cutler and Frith that he, Cooper, and Born had agreed that the Sunrise material shouldn't be released. The reasons they gave have varied with time and in individual memories: that it was not good enough, that it wasn't hanging together as an album, that it was not what Henry Cow should be doing, that the lyrics were still problematic, and that everybody in the band had not been represented properly in the recordings.

Frith recalls strongly a new dynamic creeping into their exchanges, one that had to do with ownership. "Before that, everything was discussed very openly with no contention about whose songs would be on a record because it was all collectively arranged," he said. "But this obviously felt like something that Chris and I were in control of." Although Hodgkinson and Cooper might have felt some dissatisfaction at not having many of their pieces on the prospective album, the ownership issue seems to have had more to do with individual contributions to the songs that were there (and, as I've noted, both Born and Cooper didn't feel like they'd been able to participate as much as they would have liked). Cutler maintains, however, that if the three didn't actually like the songs, they could have insisted that the material not be released: "The group always had veto power," he told me.

> And the group was perfectly happy to have the material put out. The argument wasn't that it was bad music; the argument was that it wasn't Henry Cow, that "Henry Cow shouldn't be putting out a record like this; it's not what 'the band' should be doing." That's largely why, I think, "the band" broke up on the day we had that meeting. . . . we couldn't agree on who we were any more. Nobody said, "This record shouldn't see the light of day." We'd all worked hard on it and it had been the usual collaborative effort. The assessments came later.

Hodgkinson, however, recalls stating that his reservations were clearly aesthetic: the album was not cutting it (his personal writings from the time support this memory).

Elated at what they had created at Sunrise, Frith and Cutler thought the material was too good to keep under wraps. Cutler said, "I was really responsible for this record, and I don't want to see it go down the sink, so I'll pay for it and take it and put it out."[30] Their bandmates agreed, but wished to keep back "Viva Pa Ubu" and "Half the Sky," because those two pieces were more bovine and wouldn't fit on the proposed record anyway; they wanted them for the real Henry Cow record still to come. That means that they thought the rest—including the Frith songs, Hodgkinson's "Pirate Song" and "Labyrinth," and Cooper's "The Dividing Line"—were *not good*, *not good enough* for Henry Cow, or simply *not suited* to Henry Cow at that moment. Frith received this message "like I got a slap in the face afterwards.

It's like, 'This stuff is not good enough for Henry Cow.'" Hodgkinson recalls that this meeting proceeded through three distinct steps with increasing speed. The first was their voicing of reservations about releasing the project, and the second was agreeing to release what would become *Hopes and Fears* as a separate project. He explains, "As far as I remember, I agree to that. That's much more fatal than anything up to that point. And then very quickly somebody . . . says, 'Well, that sort of more or less means the end of the road for the band.'" Frith's memory of the same moment corroborates this version of events, and also hints that it was he who suggested the split: "And it almost immediately was like, 'Well okay, ciao.' Cause this is what we gotta do now—this is it. I don't want to allow them to drop this, I want to do this." Henry Cow would be no more.

As disputatious as the band had long been, there had never been a difference of opinion so deep. Reflecting on this new factionalism, Cutler reasoned, "That one part of the band could call a meeting after we'd just finished an album and say, 'We can't release this album,' three weeks after another part of the band had called a meeting and said to a major composer, 'We can't record your piece,' indicates a major mismatch. . . . And the prospect of sorting all that out seemed to require more emotional energy and commitment than anyone had left." Hodgkinson recalls feeling "scandalized" by what the band considered next, which was to continue working as a group for six more months so that they could honor the agreements they had already made for tours and concerts, and also so that they could pay final visits to all the friends in Europe who had helped them over the years. Hodgkinson thought they had reached a point of reality by deciding to disband, and they would be betraying that reality by proceeding as if the contradiction had not been exposed. "We are supposed to get up in front of audiences and inspire and encourage them, and we have all this other shit in our hearts," he wrote at the time.[31] It might have been easier for Frith and Cutler to visualize this course of action, because they now had the *Hopes and Fears* material directly in front of them on the horizon. Therefore, a six-month farewell tour for Henry Cow could be conceived as one "project" among others. Hodgkinson explains, "But for me, Henry Cow was the top line, was *the* thing, and I was being asked to do it in a position of absolute falsity."

But he agreed, as did the others. Cutler and Frith called their new project Art Bears. To fill out *Hopes and Fears* (since some tracks had been withheld), they booked a few days in March at London's Kaleidophon and subsequently recorded four more Frith/Cutler songs. Cutler founded a record label, Rē Records (in homage to Sun Ra), to release *Hopes and Fears,* which he did in May 1978. He noted at the time (and since) that it had begun as an album by Henry Cow, who declined to release it as their own.

One may wonder why Born and Hodgkinson allowed Cutler and Frith to publish the Sunrise material, because both expressed sharp dissatisfaction in the years afterward. Hodgkinson told Wilton in 1980, "What they did in fact was to take two or three tracks off and record two or three new tracks in London, stick them on, and invent a group (Art Bears) who recorded the album. . . . From that point things were very, very difficult."[32] He recalls being in a Henry Cow meeting a few weeks later and "overhearing from another room a recording of music that I recognize as Cow music, but it had become something else [i.e., Art Bears music]. . . . I felt like something had been stolen from me." He was referring to one of the Kaleidophon songs ("Terrain," "The Tube," "The Dance," or "Piers") that had been worked on by the whole band, even though it hadn't been recorded at Sunrise; now, it had been taken back and presented as the product of a different group that hadn't previously existed. The emotional impact for Hodgkinson was huge: "I [was] unable to communicate with the 'Art Bears'—the magnitude of their betrayal seem[ed] too enormous," he wrote a few years later.[33]

Likewise, Born felt "dispossessed of my labor," both because some of the Cow material was now going to come out under another name, and because Frith and Cutler had presented this new group as a fait accompli. Born is, in fact, credited on the sleeve of *Hopes and Fears,* and she did, in fact, assent to its release as a non–Henry Cow project; her feeling of dispossession stemmed from the ambiguities of distributed authorship that characterized all rock production: in particular, she had authored her basslines on "Joan" and "In Two Minds," but the compositions were credited to Frith. Moreover, those two songs allowed her to exercise a looser rhythmic approach that she felt otherwise barred from asserting during her time with the band. "I felt so angry," she later explained to Hodgkinson and myself.

"I felt totally powerless in this decision that this stuff would not be released with me in the group that was releasing it. . . . I wasn't given an option to be part of that group."

"Oh right," Hodgkinson said. "Yeah, I can see that."

"This was my first recording fruit playing with the Cows. There had been no other studio recording, you see."

"Oh, god, yeah, that's awful."

"So it was like a fait accompli that this thing would go to this other entity. And suddenly I wasn't part of that entity. Now I don't know if I wanted to be, but I didn't want to have that playing, sort of . . ."

"You'd been erased."

"I was rather erased, which I probably asked for."

"Well, no, I don't think you did."

"I was being pretty difficult."

But she wasn't the only one being pretty difficult, and after this meeting Henry Cow entered what Frith later called a "very bizarre thorny group period." At one point in this "state of living death," Hodgkinson tried to reverse their decision to break up, but in his private account, Frith and Cutler were adamant. According to Jack Balchin, this bizarre period was also one when all the energy and long-term planning for the Henry Cow record label got redirected to Rē, Cutler's label, and another related venture, Recommended, a mail-order business for Cutler's favorite artists. "The dissatisfaction on my part was the fact that when we got out of the Virgin Records deal, the notion of setting up our own label—this was really, really very important, and a fabulous opportunity for us to see if we could do that idea of an independent label—very appealing," Balchin explains. Although Hobbs had once been the paid administrator for Henry Cow, he then appeared to Balchin to be working for Cutler alone, organizing new Cutler projects such as Rock in Opposition and general record company affairs (as a matter of fact, Hobbs did continue to work for and with Cutler for a few years beyond the breakup). Balchin recalls, "It was like Cutler and Hobbs had gone and plotted the whole thing out. And they were going to call it 'Recommended Records.' It *was* going to be Henry Cow's label, and we were going to put out stuff" by like-minded European comrades. Similarly, Hodgkinson noted in 1981, "And from being a collective idea, Rec Rec seems to have become a personal empire."[34]

In Cutler's view, Recommended had always been his idea, collectivized because he was a member of Henry Cow. Some differences of interpretation might be attributed to the confusion among entities: Balchin and Hodgkinson thought the label itself had been a collective enterprise (given the band's extensive research and discussion into self-releasing their music in previous years), while Cutler rightly notes that, having broken up in early February, Henry Cow as a collective entity could not be expected to run a mail-order and distribution service. Moreover, recall that the band had chosen not to release *Hopes and Fears* as a Henry Cow product; therefore, any label constituted to publish that music would have to be independent from Henry Cow itself.

Balchin continues, "Hobbs and Cutler were just really very divisive at that point in time, and . . . it just seemed like the whole idea of taking away those songs from Henry Cow—it was concluded as far as they were concerned, and they came in and just did it." Balchin suspected that Cutler, Frith, and Hobbs were presenting their new venture as the next step in Henry Cow, an impression that others might have gathered in 1978. A public example can be found in the program/magazine that accompanied the Zū Manifestival on October 8, 1978, in New York. The event was Georgio Gomelsky's big introductory splash in the United States, at which he had planned to introduce North American audiences to many progressive musicians from Europe. (Gomelsky flew Frith and Cutler over for the event.) The Zū Magazine and program featured large advertisements for Cutler's Recommended Records, as well as a list of "recommended bands," which states that Henry Cow was "now working as THE ART BEARS (Chris Cutler, Fred Frith, and Dagmar Krause)."[35] A private example can be found in a letter from Hobbs to Morreau after the Arts Council tour, in which he reported "the news of the group's disbandment. There will be a new group—ART BEARS—formed by Chris, Fred and Dagmar. They have already recorded a record—'Hopes and Fears'—and we will send you a copy when it is ready. So, quoting Chris Cutler, the Work goes on."[36] In both of these cases, Art Bears was presented as something like a new version of Henry Cow, rather than a separate project that had defined itself in practice as *not* Henry Cow.

If Cooper experienced the same kind of anger and shock over *Hopes and Fears* as had Hodgkinson, Born, and Balchin, then she left very little evidence for it. (The Cow wasn't touring abroad for seven weeks, so there is a gap in her correspondence.) In any case, she was comfortable enough to accept Cutler and Frith's invitation to add some overdubs on the new Art Bears songs in March. When Hodgkinson received the same invitation, he refused.

Two days after their break-up meeting on February 1, Henry Cow began their nine-date Arts Council tour of the United Kingdom. They played arts centers and universities. If live recordings of their gigs at Warwick University (13th) and Lambeth Town Hall (14th, but not a concert on the funded tour) are any indication, the improvisations on the tour were gripping: lots of space, timbrally varied, and more discursive than what they'd been playing in 1977. In his summary report to the Arts Council, Frith wrote,

> The variety of venues and audiences gave us the chance to experiment in a number of ways, and the improvisation struck us as being very fresh for most of the time. Examples particularly worthy of mention are the introduction to the Manchester concert where we all played wind instruments while moving behind the audience in the echoic chamber formed

Figure 8.3 Henry Cow at the Royal Exchange Theatre in Manchester, February 5, 1978.
PHOTOGRAPH BY TAKUMBA RIA LAWAL.

by the old Exchange—a dramatic and beautiful sound; and the use of tapes at Scunthorpe where we explored various kinds of ethnic music. Perhaps one should also mention our acoustic improvised performance in Bristol cathedral.[37]

As Frith indicates, they reintegrated their prerecorded tapes on occasion, and some squeaky moments evoked the sillier side of the Art Ensemble of Chicago. Frith even reported some theatrical situations, perhaps a return to the early dada days. Their set included an instrumental version of "Erk Gah," plus "Ruins," "Bittern Storm," "Teenbeat," and Cooper's "Half the Sky." They also included a new suite of Fred frags, including a new one called "Van Fleet" (a pun on Don Van Vliet, aka Captain Beefheart), which they combined with an older collection later called "The Big Tune."

Arts Council records show that Henry Cow played to about fifteen hundred people on the tour.[38] Of the eleven groups on the CMN that year,

Figure 8.4 Henry Cow at Hudderfield Town Hall, February 7, 1978. PHOTOGRAPH BY
TAKUMBA RIA LAWAL.

they were among the three most popular in terms of ticket sales, surpassed
only by Fires of London and Gil Evans. At the Bridgwater Arts Centre, they
played three encores. "It was the most successful that we've ever undertaken here on every level—administration, organisation, audience numbers
and consistency of playing," Frith reported.[39] A reviewer for *Sounds* called
their Sheffield performance on February 4 "mesmerizing" and compared
Henry Cow favorably with Throbbing Gristle, Devo, and the Residents,
pronouncing them (strangely) "the ultimate in new Wave."[40] In *Melody
Maker*, Chris Brazier upheld the publication's stalwart reputation for anti-
intellectual dismissal by stating that the group's appeal is "essentially elitist," and their music "a totally inaccessible, endless stream of squeaks and
noises." Nonetheless, he had to admit that "the audience hung earnestly on
every note."[41]

Rock in Opposition (to Crap Music)

While Henry Cow were recording *Hopes and Fears* and touring the United Kingdom, Hobbs was initiating a new venture called Rock in Opposition (RIO), which he viewed as a kind of international network of resistance to the global entertainment industry.[42] The Cow had already brought over Etron Fou Leloublan the previous summer, and when they began planning a similar touring visit for Stormy Six, a theatrical, progressive folk group that dated back to the 1960s and was associated with l'Orchestra Cooperativa, Hobbs expanded on the idea by conceiving a larger touring show for them, Henry Cow, Etron Fou (again), and two other groups they had become friendly with in the course of their European tours: Sammla Mammas Manna, a Swedish folk/free jazz band from Uppsala; and the Belgian Univers Zero, who followed the jazz/classical path of Magma.[43]

"Whereas the rest of Henry Cow were more pessimistic," Hobbs told Kenneth Ansell, he thought they could put together a UK tour of all the bands, or at least have them in London for a week or two, sending them out for individual concerts of two acts. To this end, he spent weeks visiting university student societies and entertainment committees but was ultimately unsuccessful.[44] He did get Stormy Six a few extra gigs, but their MFS event on March 7 only drew forty attendees to the much larger Finsbury Town Hall.[45] The main focus of Hobbs's organizational activity turned out to be a one-day festival for all five bands on March 12 at the New London Theatre. He worked hard at promotion, getting a survey of RIO records favorably reviewed by Maureen Paton in *Melody Maker* and a selection of their songs played by John Peel on the BBC.[46] He also wrote an introduction to the work of Stormy Six for the MFS newsletter, which ran translations of three of their lyrics.[47]

Visitors to the March 12 concert received a Cutler-authored pamphlet that dispensed background information on each of the guest bands and explained the impetus behind the event. (Although RIO was launched by Hobbs, his close working relationship with Cutler meant that the latter also became involved.) London was a curious host for the first RIO festival, he wrote, given that Britain was the "least interested" in such an event. But it had been the missing cultural politics in the British pop music field that had pushed Henry Cow to the continent to begin with, and their touring across Europe was the connecting thread among all the invited acts. "With the international organisation of the music industry (who couldn't care less about culture, only money) the international organisation, the pooling of knowledge, resources & contacts amongst 'uncommercial' rock musicians was inevitable."[48] Realistically noting that the festival was but a "tiny fragment," Cutler expressed a strong hope that the struggle would continue and expand: "This is only a thread of a life & death struggle which wracks the world now—itself will change nothing, but the battle must be fought on all fronts however small—everything must be called into question, examined, experimented with, changed—even the concepts of 'enjoyment' & 'entertainment.'"

The RIO concert was something of a disappointment, with only 444 tickets sold for a hall that held 907.[49] "It failed to interest any more people than those we already knew in advance would be interested in it," Hobbs told Ansell.[50] Although Hobbs had obtained a £1,000 grant from the Arts Council, all the groups lost money on their English visits, an embarrassing outcome for Henry Cow.[51]

Rock in Opposition's raison d'être was easy enough to understand, but its analysis seemed muddled in comparison with past Henry Cow communications, and jazz journalist Dave Gelly had a point when he observed in an Arts Council meeting that its "prime motive appeared to be hatred of recording companies."[52] There was a slippage between aesthetics and political economy in Hobbs's explanatory texts, summarized best in the headline for his first announcement of the project: "ROCK IN OPPOSITION (to crap music)." To Hobbs, crap music was "compromised" commercially or wasn't "culturally serious," "intense[, or] intelligent."[53] In his thinking, any music released by a (non-musician-owned) record company had low aesthetic value: "If we want an irrelevant and vapid culture then the best thing is to leave it to the industry."[54] But good music would seem to require more than just independent production and distribution; Hobbs had in mind the kind of compositionally ambitious rock of the Mothers, Soft Machine, and Captain Beefheart.[55] In other words, Ian Smith's Skrewdriver or a band in the rightist Rock Against Communism might take DIY seriously and seek to seize the means of cultural production, but they would not constitute the kind of "opposition" that Hobbs envisioned.[56] Furthermore, RIO's support from the Arts Council was not entirely consistent with Hobbs's opinion that "the key to progress—to musical progress—can only be found in economic independence; by the bands organising themselves to have complete control at both economic and artistic levels."[57]

But was the progress supposed to be musical or political, or, if both, then what was the nature of their relationship? That was less than crystal clear, but it seems that artistic self-determination and commercial independence had now become the main goals. The sociopolitical side reemerged in December 1978, when the RIO bands met at Sunrise Studios to discuss plans for the organization and to create a constitution.[58] They had decided to admit some new groups (Art Zoyd, Art Bears, Aksak Maboul), which initiated a discussion about their criteria for membership. After much discussion, they decided it would be: (1) "musical excellence," according to the assessment of those already in RIO; (2) a record of working outside the establishment music business; and (3) a "social commitment" to rock. The first two renewed Hobbs's earlier assertions, but the third indicated a principled allegiance to the vernacular, particularly when we consider their ensuing discussion about how to define rock itself.

It's an impossible task, of course, but Cutler reports that they wished to emphasize four elements of rock: (1) its use of modern communications technologies (electronic instruments, the recording studio, records, tape, radio, and mass production); (2) its collective creative process; (3) its low artistic status, which liberates it from historical aesthetic expectations; and (4) its origins in the music of an oppressed people, made universal and appropriated by a mass audience. The genre of rock itself, therefore, seemed to provide a modern left politics otherwise lacking (or underdefined) in RIO's program of artistic and economic autonomy. In any case, RIO never went very far. Bands organized tours for their foreign counterparts here and there, and seven groups met for a second festival in Milan in April–May 1979. A few other festivals soon took place, but disagreements about the mission and future of the organization led to its slow dissolve. The "RIO" name would live on, however, as a kind of stylistic brand with little input or participation from the former Cows.

A major reason Cutler, for one, could let RIO fade away was the comparative success of his other venture, Recommended Records.[59] Recommended built on and superseded a number of earlier efforts that we have already surveyed, including RIO (which, as Hobbs initially reported in November 1977, was to include an importing and mail-order component), Music for Socialism, and Music Net, announcements for which ceased to appear once Rē and then Recommended got going in the spring of 1978. These like-minded initiatives and impulses were all swirling around at the same time; as early as October 1977, Cutler announced that he had imported copies of Samla Mammas Manna's *Klossa Knapitatet* (1974), albums by the Residents (US), "and several other gems" for sale.[60] In November, Thomas had picked up some more stock for him in Spain.

Pragmatic and possessing an impresarial streak (remember Ottawa Music Company, Explorer's Club, Hollywood Thibet, and so on), Cutler valued more highly the goal of a nonindustry distribution network than he did the socialist and cooperative ethos of something like Music for Socialism. What I mean is that the inefficiency of MFS seems to have felt sufficiently like an obstacle that Cutler broke out to work toward the same goal by himself (but with the help of Hobbs, of course). Like RIO, which Hobbs described at the time as a "temporary organization" or "project," Recommended began as a provisional enterprise. Any close look at what we might call his "nonstandard" accounting practices would be enough to convince one that Cutler was not in it for the money. He said as much in the advertisement he placed on the back cover of *Impetus* in 1979 (to raise money for the Faust reissues): "Recommended Records is not a commercial concern and this is not a commercial venture—we are a musical service run by musicians—we began because we realized that if no one else would support us then rather than complaining we should get on and support ourselves." As Born would point out many years later, the petty capitalist aspect of this anticapitalist distribution network is worth noting. Situated somewhere between the arts funding programs of the state and profit-oriented corporate capitalism, small-time operations like Recommended made possible the circulation of experimental and subcommercial (by which I mean small-audience-based) musical material. Indeed, given its early emphasis on Faust and Slapp Happy reissues, Recommended was almost like a shadow Virgin Records—what it could have been if its hippie idealism had been no illusion after all. But also worth noting is Cutler's turn away from modeling utopia (as we might describe one aspect of Henry Cow's practice) toward an "intermediate cell of resistance," which he realized could only ever be defined by what it opposed.[61]

As a business venture, Recommended drew on the social capital that Cutler had accrued as a member of Henry Cow. Its first mailing went out to the entire Henry Cow mailing list, for example. In late February 1978, Cutler traveled to the United States on a trip paid for by Henry Cow; it had been booked, prior to their decision to break up, because the band was planning to tour the United States that autumn. Cutler's task was to make contact with venues, promoters, and other like-minded associates—all of which he did, but to the immediate benefit of Recommended, Rē, and Art Bears, because Henry Cow was already on its way out. Frith recalls, "Many of the things that happened on his fact-finding tour were very instrumental in what happened when I moved to the States, for example, in '78 [after the breakup of Henry Cow]. By then, he'd met people like the Muffins, the Residents, and other connections that became very important to me in my first period in the States." (Cutler also met David Thomas of Pere Ubu, Steve Feigenbaum of Random Radar [and later of Cuneiform Records], and several other important figures in the US scene.) Some members of the band might regard the establishment of these connections through the lens of opportunism, yet they all had given Cutler their blessing to take the trip in the first place, and he would put the distribution network he established to good use later promoting Henry Cow's final album, as well as most subsequent releases by individual Cows.[62]

Dead Band Touring

Once Cutler had returned to the United Kingdom, Henry Cow played a few shows on the island (including the RIO festival), then departed to Europe for what was planned to be a one-month tour, beginning in Bremen and then taking a swing through Sweden and Oslo, all the way to Spain, then back through Paris. Their crew consisted of Thomas, Balchin, Phil Clarke, and Bernie Guest. They played with the Orckestra for three of the Swedish gigs (plus Oslo), which brought in some good money and a bit of cheer on what appears otherwise to have been a trying few weeks. In their Swedish gigs without the Orckestra, Henry Cow played much the same material they had presented on the Arts Council tour, with deliberate but magisterial open improvisations. Unfortunately, multiple and complex breakdowns of the bus engine sucked holes in their finances and morale until April 6, when the vehicle finally gave up back in Bremen. Their next gig was three days later in Barcelona. Unbowed, they used the truck to tow the bus to a ferry, and then dispatched Frith with it to England, where he could procure the necessary major repair on the cheap. Meanwhile, the Brass Band's Phil Minton was still hanging out with the Cows after the Orckestra's run of gigs in Sweden; Hodgkinson impulsively invited him to join the band as it continued on to Spain, and the trumpeter/singer accepted the offer. (Hodgkinson later faced some questioning from Cutler and Frith, who had not been a party to the former's decision to invite Minton.) "I loved Phil, I'd got a hell of a lot out of watching him perform," Hodgkinson recalls. "And he's a tremendously easy person to travel with."

And travel they would: while Frith traversed the North Sea alone with the dead bus, the truck spirited Balchin, Guest, and Minton on to France; the others took an overnight train. They reconvened in the Paris apartment of their friend, Gilles Hugo, and tried to figure out what to do next and how to pay for it (the bus would require serious funds, and they had already spent plenty on repairs and towing to this point). "I look forward to a grossly uncomfortable trip to Spain with resignation and distaste," Cooper wrote to a friend. But she never made it. Word reached her of trouble back in London; Merck had to move to a new apartment and required Cooper's urgent assistance with packing (especially Cooper's own possessions, which languished in Merck's care while Cooper disappeared for weeks on tour). It was a nonnegotiable emergency, and she caught a train back to London immediately.

And the calamity continued. Reaching her limit, Born chose not to continue on to Spain. Balchin, her romantic partner in this period, returned with Born to London. Why? In addition to their festering dissatisfaction with the *Hopes and Fears* proceedings and the acute difficulties of the present situation, they were likely responding to Henry Cow's new status as a dead band touring: Cutler and Hobbs had sent out a press release two or three weeks earlier, announcing the breakup of the group after August. Although the band was "ceasing to operate as a permanent group," Cutler wrote, "the *work* of the group will go on—the group is disbanding *in order that* this work, what we have stood for, can continue."[63] He promised that they would release one more studio album, as well as a few more live records, but "the group is no longer strong enough to carry this weight and we in our turn can no longer, collectively or individually, carry the group— our carapace has turned from strength to weakness—now we have to force ourselves not to hide behind it."[64] Born and Balchin had evidently reached the same conclusion, and had quit the band by April 8. (As with all group communications, Cutler had not volunteered to write this press release, but was assigned the task when nobody else stepped up; as ever, band members had been given the opportunity to alter the press release at the time.)

As we will discuss below, Hodgkinson had serious objections to the tone of the press release, but was "now too weak to argue" about it..[65])

The remaining Cows figured out a plan, sending Clarke and Guest southward in the truck with their equipment and instructions to phone Hugo on reaching Orleans. They called Sue Steward in London, who found Frith in a cinema to give him the news: their bassist, wind player, and sound engineer had bailed out, and the Cow would stomp on with Minton as a temporary member. Frith would have to switch to bass. He got a direct flight to Barcelona. Thomas, Cutler, Hodgkinson, and Minton hopped a train. Meanwhile, when Clarke and Guest called back to Paris, they learned that Hugo had procured a pile of emergency cash to get the band through their Spanish gigs; he sent it with a courier to meet them by the side of the motorway.

When they finally all made it to the l'Aliança Club in Barcelona, Hodgkinson told the crew during load-in that Maggie Thomas should take over mixing duties, since she knew the music best. In her memory, Clarke and

Guest replied, "Uh, huh?" But they didn't put up a big fuss over the decision because another issue soon emerged. Hodgkinson: "So we get ourselves down there to Barcelona, we get into the theatre, and then we can't get the PA to work. Because only Jack knows how it works!" (In anger, Balchin had spurned the band's entreaties for instructions on running the system before he vanished.) Their attempts to fix the problem grew increasingly frantic. "The audience were literally hammering at the doors, and we were trying to figure out how to turn the amps on," Thomas recalls. They finally came to life with a rude burst of feedback, and the doors were thrown open. "If it feeds back, just switch it off and on again quickly," somebody told Thomas in her very short crash course in mixing. The band—rechristened The Lions of Desire for this run of shows—cobbled together their setlist in the dressing room. They relied on some reliable frags, including "D-Tune," the 21's from "Nirvana for Mice," the second vamp from "Terrible as an Army with Banners," the "Teenbeat" tune, the "Ruins" cycle, "The Big Tune," "The March," and "Viva Pa Ubu." To this list they added a few Westbrook numbers such as "Lady Howerd's Coach" and "Wheel of Fortune." Although band lore has it that they even played "Good Golly, Miss Molly," a private tape recording of the gig reveals a rather loose interpretation of the original text (though I do hear Minton scream the words "Good Golly!").[66] Describing the band's affect as "euphoric," Frith recalls that they "had somehow discovered an energy that we hadn't had in a very long time." That energy carried them through seven or eight more shows, and then they returned to London at the end of April.

With a few weeks off, they had some decisions to make: what to do about Cooper, Born, and Balchin? Frith recalls that, after the breakup, a depressing showing for RIO, and the recent Paris calamity, "we somehow pull something out of it which is really special and we feel very good about ourselves for doing it. At that moment, suddenly, the whole energy in the group changes as a result of that." According to Cooper, Hodgkinson asked her to come to a band meeting without Born and Balchin, with whom they no longer wished to work; Born, meanwhile, had urged Cooper to "be strong and don't let them divide us Lilly."[67] Cooper chose to remain with the band; according to Thomas, Balchin also petitioned for readmission but was refused. Thomas would become their new live sound person, spending the break learning the sound system and receiving tutorials from old pals Neil Sandford and Charles Fletcher.

Aside from the matters of social relations, personality, musicianship, and her tenure in the band, Henry Cow viewed Cooper's desertion—a personal emergency requiring immediate attention—as of a different kind than that of Born and Balchin. Those two had bailed on the group in the midst of hardship, interpreted as an unforgivable lapse of commitment at the time when it was most needed. "So un−Henry Cow!" as one crew member said. For her part, Born had been unhappy for some time, and concerns about her reliability had arisen among the rest of the band.[68]

In response to a journalist's inquiry about why Born quit the group, Cutler glibly replied, "It was too hot."[69] Hodgkinson and Frith expressed more ambivalence and regret that they didn't do more to support Born or understand her position in a dissolution process that had begun before she had joined. They all agreed that, for whatever reason, she had never fully integrated into the group. In Born's memory, while everybody else in the group had developed personal strategies for remaining productive and intellectually engaged on the road (such as reading, composing, journaling, or letter writing), she had not been able to find similar ways to cope with the uniquely strange trials of touring. And, she says, "What got to me over the years and months was this kind of absence of these very basic protocols, of kind of human interchange, which didn't seem to be very present much, ever." As we have already discussed, Balchin was smarting from what he perceived as the opportunism of Cutler and Hobbs, though he likely didn't express his criticisms as Born would have. "She could voice things that I could only feel," he later told me.

Day by Day: The Final Tours

The outfit's final two tours took them through France in May and June, and through Italy in July. In France, they had a handful of satisfying gigs with the Orckestra in Paris and Nancy, then a run of about twenty shows that concluded with a five-night stand at the Théâtre Campagne-Première with the Art Ensemble of Chicago. The fees weren't great, but they didn't want to pass up the chance to see the Americans (the groups did not perform together). Frith took over bass duties on the tour, though he did switch over to guitar here and there during the set. With only four musicians, they couldn't play much of the material they'd been performing earlier that year, but they did have versions of the "Ruins" solo, "The March," "The Big Tune," "Viva Pa Ubu," two new Cooper tunes ("Slice" and "Falling Away"), and a Westbrook number held over from the Orckestra, "Virgins of Illinois," which collaged together little English folk tunes on the winds (flute and recorder) before launching into a broad dance in three.[70] They also played two new compositions by Hodgkinson, "Industry" and "On the Raft."

Figure 8.5 Lindsay Cooper, Tim Hodgkinson, and Maggie Thomas take in sun at the death of the bus, 1978. PHOTOGRAPHER UNKNOWN.

In spite of their reduced forces, the band enjoyed itself and thought they were playing well on this tour (as disclosed in Cooper's and Hodgkinson's correspondence). The good cheer may have been related to Born and Balchin's withdrawal from the group, but not directly. As Hodgkinson explains, "I don't think it was their absence that made things better, but I think the crisis that their absence caused made things better." As always, Henry Cow regrouped well after a rupture. Soon enough, however, the band finally lost another long-time companion for good: the bus, newly repaired after the early April breakdown, finally gave up the ghost around Valence in the first days of June. They sold it for scrap. (When the band toured Italy the next month, they traveled in Frith's "horrid little van," in Cooper's words.[71])

In France and Italy, the Cows occasionally welcomed guests for a long open improvisation in the middle of the set. These invitees included Yochk'o Seffer, a Hungarian alto sax player who had played in Magma for a few years but by 1978 had established himself as a composer of jazz-rock. Terje Rypdal, the Norwegian jazz guitarist, as well as Henry Kaiser, an American guitarist, also joined in for two gigs in France. Kaiser, who had been in London visiting his idol, Derek Bailey, wanted to meet Frith, so the Cows invited him to come along for a bit. He had never played with a rock band. "I played part of the show," Kaiser later recalled. "I remember playing 'Ruins.' I remember

Fred was playing bass, and I tried to imitate what Fred did on guitar on the record, having a strong personal affection for what he did on the album." In Orléans, Albert Marcoeur's brass section ambushed the group during their rendition of Westbrook's "The Fortune Song," to the delight of all.

The most significant and lasting guest, however, would be the Dutch improviser Annemarie Roelofs, who would begin playing with the group in June (a live recording from Paris on the 16th contains the sound of her trombone), but who wouldn't join them as a member until the Italy tour in July. They had met her the previous December, when the band performed at the Melkweg in Amsterdam; as was their custom, Cooper and Geoff Leigh (he was around because Red Balune had opened the gig) strolled out through the audience during "Teenbeat," and Roelofs, sitting on the aisle with her trombone at her feet, thought, "Well, this seems like an invitation!" She knew nothing about Henry Cow, and had dropped by the club that night to see a friend who worked there; as it happened, she rose up to meet the strolling horn players and made a strong impression improvising with the group.

A violin student at the Amsterdam Conservatory since 1971, Roelofs had picked up the trombone as a secondary instrument; the institution offered a course in free improvisation—quite rare in those days—so she was exposed to a wide range of contemporary art music practices, from scored chamber music to electronics and improvisation. Her introduction to Amsterdam's nonclassical music world came through improvising on the trombone with salsa bands.

The Cows loved her energy. After the gig, Cooper invited Roelofs to join the next concert of the Feminist Improvising Group, which was to take place the following night at London's Drill Hall, and their new Dutch friend accepted. (European travel was relatively easy for Roelofs because her father was a KLM pilot and she could fly free on standby.) They would have loved to welcome her on the May–June French tour, but she had to prepare her final violin recital at the conservatory at the end of May. In Italy, then, the Cows were a five-piece. They played the same material that they'd been presenting in France, with the addition of a Frith folk tune called "Herring People" (later titled "Waking Against Sleep" on the 1991 CD reissue of *Gravity*). Henry Cow's farewell gig in London was supposed to be a Rock Against Racism benefit in Wandsworth, but the other band, Matumbi, apparently tried to bigtime them at the soundcheck (you know, "You have to take your equipment off the stage when you're done . . ." and that kind of thing), so Henry Cow pulled out at the last minute and stood on the steps of the hall explaining to

Figure 8.6 Annemarie
Roelofs, 1978. PHOTOGRAPH
BY LUCIO BRIGANTI, COURTESY
OF TIM HODGKINSON.

all their London fans that they would not in fact be performing.[72] Their actual
final gig took place in Milan's Piazza del Duomo on July 25; they were joined
onstage by some of their friends in the Stormy Six, playing to thousands.

Just a few days after their Milan farewell, Henry Cow traversed the Alps
to return to Kirchberg and record their final album with Conod. Following
the trauma of the *Hopes and Fears* sessions and their aftermath, the work of
recording what would become *Western Culture* proceeded rather breezily.
It was summertime and the musicians were in good cheer. "I remember the
session as being extremely fun, whereas the Art Bears sessions had been
dark," Frith explains. Putting to work again the studio knowledge they had
gained seven months earlier, the band devoted more time than they ever
had to fine-tuning the sound of individual instruments, often multitracking
them one at a time to maintain clarity and control. They usually added the
drums last. Indeed, *Western Culture* has the most transparent and detailed
sound of any of the Cow's studio records.

In retrospect, however, Hodgkinson was unsatisfied with his own compositional offerings, which he later pegged as "Britten on the hop." "I don't

Example 8.2 Tim Hodgkinson, "Industry," guitar and organ (*Western Culture*, track 1, 0:00); transcribed from the score, THA.

think it's extreme enough—I find it too mild. I think that the actual music is not of the highest quality and whatever sound you get you can't cover that up."[73] In a critical review of his own group's album that ran twenty-five years later, he would lament the absence of Krause, whom he called "the tactile surface of the group's anger."[74] In the void of "simpler certainties" that animated the group's earlier work, he wrote, the band searched in vain for a new direction. It failed to materialize, in Hodgkinson's interpretation, because they could not render in musical terms the personal and political circumstances that were in the process of coming undone. But for Cooper, the album captured her first serious compositional work, and it also provided an opportunity to work with her "big all time fave" Irène Schweizer, who visited the studio to record a fierce piano solo in Cooper's "Gretel's Tale."[75]

On the final album release, Hodgkinson's music appears on side one and Cooper's on side two. Cutler gave each a "suite title": *History and Prospects* for Hodgkinson, and *Day by Day* for Cooper. The former's gaunt opener, "Industry," sees Hodgkinson manipulating stringent melodic strands over relatively simple harmonic supports. He has pointed out in the years since that his *Western Culture* compositions were written for a performing band on the road, and they do exhibit a rough-and-ready quality missing from the more rarefied "Erk Gah." The main melody (see example 8.2), which opens with a falling semitone followed by a perfect fourth, contains twelve notes but is not dodecaphonic; it returns throughout the piece, set in different rhythms and octave displacements, and fragments appear in inversion (hear, for example, the bassoon melody at 2:01 on the CD releases). One common feature is a melodic repetition that generally preserves contour and the distribution of steps and leaps, but alters pitches here and there by a semitone. Hodgkinson maintains unity by preserving the opening gesture of a melody, while the second half of many lines tends to unspool in a less systematic manner. Aside from these melodic characteristics, "Industry" also displays the most extensive effects to be found on *Western Culture*; for example, much of its opening melodic section (0:26–1:08) unfolds over a

Example 8.3 Lindsay Cooper, "Falling Away" (*Western Culture*, track 4, 0:52); transcribed by the author.

strutting bassline doubled by the organ, which has been disabled by Hodg-kinson's wobbly ring modulator.

Although Hodgkinson's second track, "The Decay of Cities," begins with a similarly lengthy melodic ramble on the Spanish guitar (he wrote the piece in Valencia), most of the piece replaces "Industry"-style melodic transformation with an exploration of rhythmic juxtaposition (though he does explore whole-tone collections and modal pitch organization). Many sections—at 2:32, for instance—call to mind Stravinsky. Hodgkinson often builds textures of severe temporal disjunction and mounting tension that release into heavy plateaux, such as the one at 3:43, which opens onto a droning pedal that unifies the scattered rhythmic motives above. Side one's closer, "On the Raft," trades these metrical barbs for an easier 4/4, which supports a variously orchestrated progression of planed chords that had been quite evidently written at the organ.

Cooper's "Falling Away" outpaces the other music on the album in its sophistication and variety. She launches the seven-and-a-half-minute piece with a stretch of counterpoint in three voices that lopes through various drag triplets (Cooper's favorite) over a quarter note pulse supplied by slack strumming. Like Hodgkinson, she tends to build tension throughout a section with shifting modes and contrapuntal complexity, eventually breaking the tension by landing on a more stable pillar. For example, the fast section that begins at 0:52 spins an octatonic collection of four pitches (0134) around a stuttering melody, the unsteady rhythm of which is further undercut by interjections in the bass and contrastive gestures in the bassoon (see example 8.3). At 1:17, this instability yields to a new, unison melody in the guitar and organ, which focuses attention momentarily even as it pushes the music forward. Her characteristic wit can be heard in a number of places on side two, but my favorite is the fluttering, klezmer waltz that begins at 5:30, in the octatonic scale that has been sparring with various modal and diatonic collections for much of the piece.

Example 8.4 Lindsay Cooper, "Gretel's Tale," recorder (*Western Culture*, track 5, 0:59); transcribed from the score, LCA.

The second composition on side two, "Gretel's Tale," is tightly controlled. Cooper writes a series of off-kilter rhythmic lines in counterpoint that "resolve" to more unified harmonies built on C and A-flat—hear at 0:59, for example, the Stravinskian gestures over C, A-flat, and G, (see example 8.4), which return in an altered form at 2:43 (see example 8.5). Here, the composer ingeniously telescopes the meter from 6 to 5 to 4, thereby channeling momentum to the 4/4 bar in G, when Cooper departs whole-tone pitch space for a diatonic collection that establishes the G-F as a V-IV progression in C, also rendering the A-flat as a lowered submediant in retrospect. These two passages frame Schweizer's dazzling piano solo. "Gretel's Tale" is followed by the wan "Look Back," a short bit of pensive and dissonant chamber music for bass, clarinet, violin, and oboe built on a semitone oscillation in the bass. "Half the Sky," which I have already discussed, closed out the side.

The group wouldn't release *Western Culture* until the early autumn of 1979; they set up their own record label, Broadcast, to press and distribute the album. Because Cutler, Frith, and Krause continued to define and expand the Art Bears project, Hodgkinson was effectively in charge of Broadcast. The group had asked *Mad* magazine's Don Martin to design the cover, but he declined. Their old friend Ray Smith also produced a canvas that was never used; it portrayed a modern, industrial city from above, the name "Henry Cow" spelled in the layout of the city's streets. In the end, Cutler designed a cover using what looks like paper cutouts with a prominent hammer and sickle, along with other more abstract motifs of horns and fractures. Coming as the final document of a no-longer-extant band, the record was not widely reviewed; in the *NME*, Andy Gill compared it unfa-

Example 8.5 Lindsay Cooper, "Gretel's Tale" (*Western Culture*, track 5, 2:43); transcribed from the score, LCA.

vorably to the contemporaneously released sophomore effort of Art Bears, *Winter Songs*, which remains to this day a notable artistic achievement.[76]

An End, and Endings

I have no intention of bringing this account of Henry Cow "up to date" by detailing the many projects, musical and otherwise, that band members have initiated in the four decades since its demise. (That information—there's a lot of it—is available online.) Several clear markers—the electoral pivot of 1979/80 (Thatcher/Reagan), the end of the historic compromise in Italy, and the musical transition to postpunk in London's rock field—suggest that the post-1968 collection of social, technical, and institutional arrangements that could host a Henry Cow no longer operated, or no longer operated in the same way. I wish to resist the impulse to chart continuities across such ruptures, even while acknowledging the profound connections and friendships that persist to this day. The world that offered its problems for Henry Cow in 1972 or 1977 differed dramatically from the world of 1982 or 1986; the problems of that world require their own separate books.

The interesting question of whether to draw out continuities or to foreclose their possibility began to make its appearance within three years of Henry Cow's breakup, when Cutler and Hodgkinson collaborated on *The Henry Cow Book*, a 116-page documentary scrapbook and history of the band that the pair produced and published themselves in 1982. The book testifies to Henry Cow's remarkable self-historicizing impulse, especially in the case of Cutler, who made detailed chronologies (often for publicity materials) at significant moments in their history. He also convened Frith and Hodgkinson in 1988 for the invaluable three-way interview that I have excerpted in these pages. (A second self-interview at that time with Cooper and Krause has gone missing in Cutler's archive, an indescribable loss.) These histories culminated in Cutler's release of the *40th-Anniversary Henry Cow Box Set*, a nine-CD / one-DVD set with extensive liner notes, yet more chronologies, and a history of the band that Cutler had written in 1978.[77]

In the 1982 book, they had originally intended to include introductory essays by Hodgkinson and Frith, in addition to Cutler's 1978 memoir that would be reprinted in the 2008 box set. Both texts conveyed an uneasiness with what they perceived to be the mythologizing of their history. For example, Frith feared being represented "as a martyr to a cause, which was an uneasy feeling I got from reading some of Chris's prose. My experience wasn't like that, I'm afraid."[78] His own text focused primarily on their musical practices but took pains to emphasize such "romantic images" as an icy shower in a waterfall in Norway and the many kindnesses of strangers-turned-friends.[79] For his part, Hodgkinson felt that they had a responsibility to their fans and supporters to analyze and share the precise nature of their struggles, lest future groups who might admire Henry Cow be fated to reproduce their failures. (I have drawn on drafts of his essay throughout the present study.) Not surprisingly, his introduction adopted a reserved tone. "It is written from the viewpoint of someone who has been a long time away from this group and who is now rather inclined to see it in a ruthless and unsympathetic light."[80]

In the end, Cutler argued that opinions varied too widely (and perhaps wounds were too fresh) to include anything but a factual accounting of the band's activities, so he chose not to include any individual interpretations of the band's history and its relative success or failure. In the prefatory text that he published instead, he cautioned, "This pamphlet is not an official history, nor does it attempt to give a balanced or considered picture of the *life* of the group. It is, in essence, no more than a collection of contemporary documents (in more or less chronological order), showing: a) what we did, b) what image of ourselves and what 'message' we were trying to get across *about* what we did, c) some public traces of ourselves and of specific projects in which we were involved—often as instigators, d) where we stood."[81] Cutler's preface, then, promised a kind of documentary neutrality even as it asserted its own partiality. The narrative historical prose that takes up ten pages at the end of the book does tend to avoid sustained self-criticism. In his account, the band gradually discovers the decay at the heart of the rock industry and triumphantly escapes it (though not without great struggle).

Hodgkinson's objections went all the way back to the press release that announced the band's split; here, the matter of continuity versus rupture found acute expression. Recall that Cutler wrote, "The *work* of the group will go on—the group is disbanding *in order that* this work, what we have stood for, can continue." Their work, he stated, "is now better pursued in several ways simultaneously and not under the umbrella of 'Henry Cow.'" But Hodgkinson thought that collective labor and group composition *was* the work of "the group," so it was difficult to conceive of a continuation in several simultaneous, individual ways. "It would be a shame if people think that after having tried the collective path, Henry Cow dissolved in order to pursue simultaneous diversity and a change for oneself, for [lightness] and fluidity," he wrote in an open letter to *Atem*'s Gerard Nguyen, who had published Cutler's press release quoted above. "As for myself," Hodgkinson clarified, "I'd like to say that I didn't choose another path; I recognize *simply* that this time we failed."[82]

If Cutler asked Cooper to contribute an essay to *The Henry Cow Book*, then her text does not survive. But at about the time she might have been asked, she told an interviewer that "the group" itself had ceased to operate as such prior to the split anyway. "It did get very tiresome making ourselves out to be 'collective' and to being in political agreement when in fact were weren't either of those things. It was just ridiculous. I think parting company was a very good idea. At the time I was really sad and it took me a while to adjust to it but I'm glad we did it."[83] With the addition of Schweizer, FIG was entering a new phase, and Cooper would soon begin writing her soundtrack to Sue Clayton and Jonathan Curling's film *The Song of the Shirt* (1979). In other words, the rupture of Henry Cow's failure was smudged in Cooper's case by the founding of FIG and her further work in London's feminist avant-garde: the ending of one group was elided by the emergence of another.[84]

The substance of Hodgkinson's "ruthless and unsympathetic" criticism—echoed by Frith in their 1988 conversation—had to do with their arts of living, rather than their musical practices, a perspective with which we will conclude, for it leads well into the afterword on the theory of the avant-garde. As Frith pointed out years later, "I think the only way we could have survived the contradictions of the last two years, which were being dictated by our success, if you like, was by taking the step, that we often discussed but never took, of living together. I think if we'd actually been brave enough to take that on and actually survived it, it could probably have given us the means whereby we could've done the serious work we needed in order to renew our musical commitment, which was, in fact, dying instead."[85] Indeed, the purchase of the Cow palace or another communal living environment would have enabled the same kind of autonomy and singularity of purpose that the bus made possible when they were on the road. It would also have alleviated (but hardly cured) their intractable economic woes.

But Hodgkinson also had another benefit in mind: communal living would have allowed them to problematize their arts of everyday life, which had otherwise preserved bourgeois norms of emotional privacy and family care. Their inability to nurture each other inside the group—a lack, as we've seen, highlighted by Born in addition to Hodgkinson—testified to their maintenance of those norms, a massive blind spot for a group that was so committed in their work to rooting out unconscious musical and technical habits: "Those parts of ourselves left unattended continue to behave according to the pattern in which we left them," he wrote in one draft of his introduction. Unable to notice these patterns or to "find the means and strength to break" them, "we re-enact the same conflicts, the same 'situations' as occur in normal society, but using ideological terms derived from movements which have sought to revolutionize this society." Although the generative energies of contraviviality propelled Henry Cow through many hardships and into bracing artistic territory, the real "strange tension" manifested not among the Cows in their emotional exchanges but in the chasm between their modes of working and their modes of living.

Afterword

The Vernacular Avant-Garde

For time flows on. . . . Methods become exhausted;
stimuli no longer work. New problems appear
and demand new methods.

Berthold Brecht

In researching and writing *The World Is a Problem*, I have felt acutely the need for a new provisional concept of the vernacular avant-garde, which I will sketch and justify in this short theoretical afterword.[1] Briefly and to begin, it names musics made and received outside the mainstream recording/publishing industry and the university/conservatory system, employing a range of techniques and discourses but irreducible to any single hypostatized conception of radicalism. Although they generally resist the profit motive of the entertainment companies and the socio-aesthetic conservatism of academic and state-funded institutions, these diverse and often incompatible musics hardly escape the market or the academy completely. Indeed, they are strongly connected to the former, taking shape within and across myriad genre formations, which meet and mutate by means of recording, not writing. I am more interested in the vernacular avant-garde as a descriptive concept than as a periodization, but it nonetheless appears most distinctly after World War II, when the long-playing vinyl record and the consolidation of a popular music aesthetics issue important material and discursive conditions for its dehiscence.[2] Although the first half of the century produced a range of vernacular modernisms (Louis Armstrong, Umm Kulthum, Bessie Smith, to name some), it offers fewer examples of vernacular avant-gardes.

I have sketched the "question space" of this afterword below:

elite modernism	elite avant-garde
vernacular modernism	vernacular avant-garde

This sketch is more a chart of analytical categories than it is a Bourdieu-style map of social space. To begin with the vertical dimension, I make a distinction between the vernacular and the elite not as a judgment of value or skill but rather as a registration of the real social and economic differences in the production and reception of the music.[3] Ellington and Webern are both modernist, but with *vernacular*, I would wish to signal Ellington's position in the entertainment industry (night clubs, ballrooms) and mass media (radio, recordings, film, television), as well as the collaborative practice of his orchestra. In the horizontal dimension I distinguish between the many cultural performances and forms that translate modernity into aesthetic terms (modernism) and a smaller number that does so in a more radical or critical manner, using any of several contradictory strategies (avant-garde). It is the analytical distinction, rather than the specific formulation of avant-gardism at play, that I will examine here.

Although the term *modernism* works best when describing aesthetic responses to modernization prior to World War II (despite its confusing afterlife as a stylistic marker for some music into the twenty-first century), the *distinction* between something like modernism and something like the avant-garde continues to operate in the last seventy years. For example, compare the Rolling Stones and Faust, both of whom wrangled with their record companies in the early 1970s. Decca merely stood in the way of the Stones realizing their considerable earning power; their escape from the contract and subsequent signing to Atlantic was a simple business decision. But Polydor was a different kind of problem for Faust, who had to grab all they could until the jig was up. The *very idea* of a record company—a business, addressing a market and possessing the capital necessary to manufacture and distribute recordings in quantity—constituted the problem to be negotiated, so Faust could never relate to the institution in as clear and direct a manner as the Stones did. Both of these groups operated in the vernacular register, but Faust's antagonistic, duplicitous, and problematic relationship to Polydor represents an orientation distinct from the mainstream pop music industry, even as it was clearly wrapped up within it—this kind of case is what I would like the vernacular avant-garde to help describe.

One could draw the same distinction between Miles Davis's tussles with Columbia and the artists of the Jazz Composers Guild, who aimed to revise radically how their work would reach its audience. Andreas Huyssen's notion of the avant-garde, characterized by its engagement with the technical apparatus of mass culture and its aim to dissolve the boundary between art and life in a revolutionary praxis, partially muddles the distinction between elite and vernacular, but his artists never actually departed the milieu of fine arts and letters, no matter how much they might have borrowed from popular culture. With the vernacular avant-garde, I wish to focus on artists and musicians coming from and working within the so-called low forms.

Or consider the difference between two signposts from Pauline Oliveros that take us from elite modernism to the vernacular avant-garde. The early work *Sound Patterns* (1962) presents an innovative sonic language unthinkable without electronic music, conveyed by means of a score to the small choral ensemble who performs it. Who does the piece address? The international community of contemporary music listeners who contemplate the work in front of them as they would any other choral piece in the tradition. The *Sonic Meditations* (1970), by contrast, use text instructions to turn any group of people into a provisional musical ensemble, fundamentally revising the arrangement of creative labor. Who does the piece address? Whomever might be participating in it, but especially the woman ensemble, the nonspecialist feminist group for which she wrote it. Although they don't live inside of mass-mediated commercial production, the *Sonic Meditations* still strike me as vernacular because of their everyday means of communication and their local adaptability—they can be taken anywhere and performed by groups of three or one hundred.

I wish to find and define the edges of this concept for the sake of what appear to be necessary analytical distinctions, and not to propose a transhistorical "true spirit" of the avant-garde or some other bold but empty claim. As a general term or historical marker, *avant-garde* has generated many such claims, owing to the underspecification of its object.[4] I aim a little lower: to provide a concept that can help sort, distinguish, and compare various musical avant-gardes, one that is open to local variation even as it remains sensitive to shared impulses.[5]

Descriptive and analytical, the vernacular avant-garde helps to name something, but it isn't an evaluation. It gives nothing to voices shouting that this or that group "deserves" to be included in the history of avant-gardism, simply because it is not an honorific and there is no trophy to claim. The idea of *avant-garde* describes a deeply flawed, broken space, one that is

forever tagged by the European middle class—no matter its many revisions, mutations, and appropriations. The Latin derivation of *vernāculus*—
domestic or native, as in *verna*, a home-born slave—underscores this sense
of familiarity.[6] But critique is no more the present goal than is laudation.
What we need, as Georgina Born pointed out in her first academic publication (following her departure from Henry Cow and enrollment in the PhD
program in anthropology at the University College London), is a careful
analysis of the transformations of the musical field—ranging from art to
pop—in the second half of the century, and a willingness to revise the established discourse of avant-gardism built on a monolithic base of the critical
negation of the market.[7] Self-consciously critical, resistant, and politicized
musics emerge from or create new spaces within the capitalist culture industries, and they link these politics to varied types of formal or technical
innovation. Empirical studies of moments such as these will always rise up
to challenge theoretical work on the avant-garde; there will always be a new
example, a new social or historical arrangement in a particular case that
creates insoluble problems for an already existing theory. The best of these
studies swerve back out from their empirical work to rerender fundamental
questions of avant-garde theory.

Although something rings true in Chris Cutler's observation that the
radical baton of the avant-garde passed from art music to jazz to rock, it
would be equally as difficult to deny his complementary assertion that, by
the time it reached the end of that chain, the term *avant-garde* had become
"little more than a hopeful badge of honour," or even "an off-the-shelf commercial label for general application."[8] And yet, as Cutler notes, words live
in communities of use, which can never be wrong, no matter how perplexing and contradictory. The challenge is to identify and group consistent
problems of a theoretical nature kicked up by art practice, problems that
were once known by a name that might be denied or now used to denote
something else. What is needed is a concept that can group together these
problems and see how they travel to other situations or compare with historically distinct arrangements.

Cutler writes that the European avant-garde of Darmstadt was born facing backward.[9] If that is true, then behind its back grew the more novel
sonic strategies of the Silver Apples and Ornette Coleman, of the AACM
and AMM, of Terry Riley and La Monte Young, of Pauline Oliveros and Max
Neuhaus, of Sun Ra and Alice Coltrane, of John Cale and Annea Lockwood,
of Henry Cow and the Residents, of Christina Kubisch and Brian Eno, of
Derek Bailey and Merzbow, of the Sun City Girls and Suzanne Ciani, which

sprung up and mixed together with such a fervor. As I noted at the outset of this study, such a list all but demands that any account of postwar avant-gardism depart from the literate tradition. Of course, many on this list trained in some version of that very same tradition (piano lessons, military bands, church choir), but the zone where they meet is far more defined by recording than by notation, the composer's pen nudged aside by the needle, the tape head, and the laser.[10] The word *vernacular* can point to or signal this mixed scriptural economy. Standard Western notation isn't gone, of course—Henry Cow used it all the time—but it has assumed a transformed position in relation to improvisation and distinct modes of inscription and exchange that, like traditional oral folk transmission, never leave the domain of sound. This basic quality distinguishes vernacular avant-garde musics from elite formations that look to and borrow from the vernacular without ever joining it.[11]

Even if the new sonic arts—dub, noise, electro-acoustic improvisation, musique concrète, drone, sound art, field recording, installation, turntablism—might grapple with emergent aesthetic possibilities more directly than academic composition's "studiously joyless applications of an exhausted language," the concept of a vernacular avant-garde that I wish to illuminate must eventually be articulated to more than formal and technical characteristics.[12] To be sure, the persistence of institutionalized aesthetic norms issues specific cultural values against which insurgent challengers can define alternatives (often drawing on but renovating those same established vocabularies), but this aesthetic discourse draws only one ordinal point around which avant-gardes might turn.[13] Other factors alter their course, including the emergence of new communications technologies affecting modes of poiesis and sensation, the imaginative proximity of real social change (revolutionary and utopian at one extreme, merely hopeful or prospective at the other), and the encounter with distinct cultures and life experiences wrought by European colonialism.[14] In other words, *avant-garde* operates in "the space between a still usable [aesthetic] past, a still indeterminate technical present, and a still unpredictable [geo-]political future."[15]

Any one of these factors alone cannot explain a given real case, because they interact with each other unevenly. If a historical example would seem to privilege one or two factors, then this heterogeneity can be discovered only through a postpositivist, empirical study that assumes no totalizing causes or explanations.[16] An avant-garde artist or movement might employ any number of strategies—Greenbergian material refinement; Cagean intermedia;

Benjaminian allegory, shock, or innervation; Bürgerian institutional critique; or Brechtian functional transformation. For example, what do we make of the black New York jazz avant-garde of the mid-1960s, which, with the exception of Sun Ra's various keyboards and in contrast to their more composerly confreres in Chicago, had little converse with the new technologies of sense perception (i.e., tape, live electronics, amplification)? In this case, the force of the anti-institutional critique, the attempts at functional transformation, and the explicit utopian or revolutionary discourse seem to counterbalance the unsubstantiality of its Benjaminian strain. And Cutler's desiccated post-war avant-garde, retaining only "homeopathic traces of political engagement" in his exquisite description, conveys the proximal slide in Western Europe and North America away from the imagination of substantial political alternatives—a slide surely accelerated by the elections of Thatcher and Reagan (to pick a moment relevant to Henry Cow), but perhaps now in uncertain reverse given the radical stirrings on the left and right that indicate some returning commitment to the idea of an unpredictable political future (Black Lives Matter, Occupy, but also Brexit, Donald Trump, Marine Le Pen).[17]

The manifestly politicized or critical stances of functional transformation, medium specificity, intermedia, and institutional critique mark the strategies particular to avant-gardes. We have already discussed functional transformation, which works on production and distribution, shifting those operations incrementally toward greater cooperation and equality.[18] It is there in Music Net and Recommended, in Henry Cow's common, meager wage, in the didactic commitments of the AACM, or in the cooperative ethos of the Jazz Artists Guild, Crass, the New Music Distribution Service, the Women's Liberation Music Project, l'Orchestra Cooperativa, the Explorer's Club, the Cartel, or SAM distribution. And it must be distinguished from endeavors such as the Stockhausen Verlag or the Philip Glass Ensemble, which existed to present and promote the work of their namesakes.

Although the vernacular avant-garde has drawn on and advanced discourses of medium specificity, its social basis outside of patronage networks or academe has forced these artists into proliferative, ambivalent relationships with the corporations that administer the production and circulation of recordings. For this reason, even the most austere works of medium specificity that issue from the vernacular—Reynols' *Blank Tapes* comes to mind—are disinclined to claim a pure, aesthetic formalism in response to society's "refusal to permit the arts to be their own justification."[19] Twinned with such projects of critical medium specificity has been a contrary tendency that turns for inspiration outward toward other cultural practices, such as animation (John Zorn), immersive cinema (Velvet Underground / Exploding Plastic Inevitable), dance (Solar Arkestra), meditation (Pauline Oliveros), spiritualism (Alice Coltrane), psychology (Henry Flynt, Catherine Christer Hennix), fantasy literature (black metal), and critical theory (the Red Krayola / Art and Language), to name a few.

The term *vernacular modernism* comes from Miriam Hansen, who argued for the importance of a mass-produced, mass-mediated, and mass-consumed modernism that took new modes of sensory experience to audiences worldwide, where the liberatory impulses and pathologies of the modern—that is, the doubled consequences of shaken gender, ethnic, class, and generational norms—multiplied and ramified unpredictably in local conditions of reception.[20] Vernacular modernist musics in the United States, born of a direct embrace of the electronic apparatus, also developed new pleasures of formal innovation, abstraction, repetition, distortion, and irony to dissociate early- and midcentury pop from the old narratives of authentic communal culture, and to habituate listeners to the uncertain roils and shocks of the new age.[21] These often rural and regional responses to modernization, caught in wax and shellac, complement and twist "traditional accounts of modernism that privilege print, the literary elite, and the bohemian experiences of urban life."[22] Indeed, yet another side of urban modernity, that of the bourgeoning working-class communities in global port cities, would flood the century's shipping channels with another polyglot music vernacular testifying to shifting social, political, and geographical formations.[23] As a musical tradition facing backward, the elite forms of European composition had little to say directly about this emergent reordering of the daily world. Yet new approaches to the "modernism of sensation" have connected musicology's familiar cast of characters in promising ways to the new modes of listening, the new realities of migration and translation, and the exploding reach of the mass media.[24]

The novel sorts of sonic experience emerging since 1945 are too many to number here, but several must be singled out for their audible role in the story of Henry Cow as artists and fans. Musical amplification was nothing new in those years, but its transistorization defined a consumer market and raised the limits of loudness for what a single knob twiddler could accomplish.[25] High volume alone became a compositional property for artists across the musical field, and the problems of amplitude in live bands set off a number of leakage effects for road crews and musicians. Likewise, cheap effects units for live sound greatly increased an electronic musician's range of timbral possibility. Together, loudness and effects fostered a new kind of attraction to abstract or "pure" sound, even for those unfamiliar with the Cagean innovations of the 1950s or the jazz musician's goal of developing one's "own" sound; this privileging of sonic materialism over music's theoretical structures of pitch-space or meter would make an important meeting point for the converging traditions of the late sixties. Effects also played a distinct role in the studio, of course, from early rock 'n' roll to dub.[26] Producers and artists from every corner of elite and vernacular music shared a keen interest in the outer possibilities of magnetic tape, and consumer-grade tape decks in the early 1960s meant that even teenaged nobodies like Anthony Moore could experiment with tape loops just a few years after their institutionally accredited peers.

In all of these cases of mechanical and electronic reproduction since the late nineteenth century, producers as well as consumers keenly drew on the new technologies of auditory experience. With the long-playing vinyl record, the path connecting creation to consumption took more turns, but the example of Henry Cow and friends does indicate that the specific mode of listening to LPs—that is, a pile of them next to the turntable, or traded with friends, with running times well over thirty minutes, a good frequency range, and low noise—had new effects on musical production. Although vinyl was a more expensive material than shellac, especially in the United Kingdom, the overall cost of a single vinyl long-player was lower than a comparable album of three or four 78s.[27] Combined with the postwar economic boom and the particularly rapid expansion of the recording industry, these lower costs meant that more kinds of music made it on to musicians' turntables in the 1960s, where the standardization of the format encouraged a kind of equalizing effect: one LP after another. Certainly, the multi-stylism of Henry Cow or other roughly contemporaneous artists, such as the Feminist Improvising Group, the Art Ensemble of Chicago, Alterations, or John Zorn, would be very difficult to imagine without the recent history of vinyl records. But the effects of vinyl went far beyond multistylism to foster a radical cosmopolitanism and a proleptic temporal imagination.[28]

On one list of borrowed LPs that Tim Hodgkinson kept in the early 1970s there appeared Messiaen's *Chronochromie*, Berio's *Visage*, Coleman's *Free Jazz*, Nonesuch's *Golden Rain* Balinese gamelan compilation, and The Who's *Tommy*. What do these have in common? What *could* they have in common? Such questions seem particularly characteristic of LP listening, and therefore pinned to the postwar arrangement. For another specific set of records—Stockhausen's *Gesang der Jünglinge* and *Kontakte* (1962,

Deutsche Grammophone), Cage's *Cartridge Music* (1963, Time), and Riley's *In C* (1968, Columbia)—the important question for a certain kind of rock listener (Cutler, Moore, Eno) seemed to be, How can I do that? Amateur filmmakers in the 1950s and 1960s asked similar questions in their world, suggesting a formidable wave of nonaccredited-yet-advanced artistic production in the decades after World War II.[29]

Earlier in the century, one subset of the new, modern modes of experience—the new noise of popular musics circulating the globe in cylinders, 78s, LPs, cassettes, CDs, and MP3s—played a critically important role in enabling the imagination and the embrace of remote life experiences, especially those from oppressed classes and regions.[30] Worldwide consumers may have sought a dubious, racialized authenticity in these commodities, but they also reveled in the sensational, "blind encounter with pure mystery."[31] Although such bumptious dislocations characterized all modern listening practices, they assumed a specific meaning for the historical avant-gardes, because this rapidly expanding social imaginary—both enabled by and in revolt against European colonization—had as much to contribute to the avant-garde's critique of institutionalized, autonomous art as did bourgeois art's own internal "unfolding," as Peter Bürger would have it. Against the tunnel vision of such abstract, dialectical models, which claim some kinds of historicity while ignoring others, a revised account of the avant-garde would insist on the crucial role of the imperialist crisis in forming sensational shifts.[32]

The other persuasive critiques of Bürger are many and need not be recapitulated in full here. His assessment of the neo-avant-garde as a kind of empty rehash of the original betrays a miscomprehension of the massive upheavals in politics and culture after 1945, the emergence of new relations of power and resistance, the decline of shock as a viable strategy of negation, the significance of the reparative efforts in the 1950s to reestablish continuities with the radical movements of the 1910s and 1920s, and the novel institutional arrangements of postwar modern and contemporary art.[33] Even the material and social basis of Bürger's historical avant-garde is questionable.[34] But despite his limits, Bürger's notion of the nonorganic artwork and the critique of the autonomous art institution issues a valuable sociological basis for conceiving the avant-garde, one that obviates a merely aesthetic approach that would put forward the term for any mildly unusual or left-of-center music.

Given his Adornian foundation, it is not surprising that Bürger harbors the same weaknesses as the Frankfurt School elder, namely an understanding of popular culture impoverished by a lack of empirical investigation that might determine whether his theoretical models corresponded with material reality. Among the insights he would have found is the variegation of the culture industry, its fragmentation, tension, and change—especially in the decades after the second world war. He would have found surprising endeavors to "negate the category of individual production" and to problematize the isolation of the individual art consumer.[35] The collectivization of cultural production for the mass media need not be reduced to the "false sublations" of the Hollywood assembly line or pulp fiction publishing— there might indeed exist experiments in group authorship that amount to more than the production of cultural commodities and the maintenance of ideological control.[36] He would have noticed continuing forays in montage and chance, mobilized to pull apart the organic work of art and question the durable artist-genius trope. He would have discovered a multiplication of the social axes along which struggles of marginalized, oppressed, or exploited people have advanced, and he would have found surprising reconfigurations of avant-garde practice in the interstices of empire, patriarchy, and white supremacy. He would have considered carefully, as did Born nearly a decade after her departure from Henry Cow, the role of affirmative petty capitalism in fostering aesthetic-political innovation in the popular sphere, perhaps emulating Born's skepticism in 1987 that Recommended Records or other DIY punk productions offered anything other than "aspirations and marketing," or her more sanguine view, twenty-five years later, that petty capitalism "has been one of the key means by which progressive leftist, antiracist, and resistant forms of culture, music, and art have been made possible: have been produced, circulated, and lived."[37] Like Born and other scholars of the late twentieth century art movements, he would have cultivated a sensitivity to emergent postwar labor patterns based on collaboration, communication, and participation that would seem to make similar neo-avant-garde practices less "autonomous from" than "imbricated within" the new spirit of capitalism.[38]

A more sustained empirical inquiry would also ideally alight on the subject of institutions. Bürger had in mind the bourgeois academies and gallery system when he partially defined the avant-garde as that which critiques these institutions, but a survey of the postwar arrangements would need to redefine that term not only in light of the firm establishment of museums dedicated specifically to modern art and the successive ballooning of the global contemporary art complex but also with a certain awareness of how historical movements such as Dada eventuated in different reanimations in the 1950s and 1960s, occasionally at odds with each other over precisely their relation to those institutions.[39] And the neo-avant-garde's commitment to institutional critique within the North Atlantic art world itself occasionally devolved into a kind of solipsism that prevented, ironically, the emergence of a tangible engagement with social and political activisms analogous to the spark shared by surrealism and anticolonial movements.[40]

In music, historical research has documented the unusual situation in postwar France, where there was a pervasive and influential discourse dating to the nineteenth century that intertwined, rather than opposed, avant-gardism and state institutionalization.[41] Likewise in North America, Western Europe, and Latin America something routinely—if perhaps peculiarly—called "the avant-garde" in music found support from the US State Department, universities, private US foundations, and traditional music publishers like Universal and Peters.[42] It would be a different set of sonic artists, with an oblique (but certainly not mutually exclusive) relationship with those postwar musical institutions who most clearly reactivated the institutional critique of Bürger's historical avant-garde, or who attempted to forge new alternative or independent institutions motivated by an aspiration for self-determination or a radical transformation of society.[43] Unburdened by any early twentieth-century history of an oppositional dismantling of its bourgeois institutional frame (save Luigi Russolo, in his way), music was late to develop avant-gardes, but this very tardiness made the conditions ripe for an initial flowering in the wake of Cage and Coltrane.[44]

The specific institutional arrangements of the jazz world would lead avant-gardists there to challenge the influence of the big festivals, the name clubs, the major record companies, and a critical establishment dominated by white journalists and broadcasters.[45] Popular music's embrace of the recorded form meant that the capitalist recording industry would emerge in tandem with the music as its predominant institutional apparatus, one that might be resisted through state-funded alternatives like the US Library of Congress in the 1930s, or through consumption practices like those of the white male collectors who searched for a kind of racial authenticity that would overflow, predate, or transcend the supposedly corrupting influence of the culture industries.[46] Distinctively late-century, experimental listening practices would respond to the sentimental pieties of these noncommercial alternatives by fostering instead an open-source, ethnographic surrealism of impure global pop.[47]

Henry Cow and its associates problematized the record company as an institution in some specific ways. While the group's increasingly antagonistic relationship with Virgin developed from a bizarre position internal to the company itself, their opportunistic cultivation of the publicity and resources of the larger company signaled an awareness of the affirmative possibilities such mass media outlets provided. Likewise, Anthony Moore and Faust seized on the opportunities provided by their contracts with Polydor to explore new working methods and to produce music that would have been prohibitively expensive to create on their own. The clear parallel with Anthony Braxton's Arista period (also in the 1970s) only throws into starker relief the differences in critical reception between Faust, who were celebrated by critics eager to define an unprecedented rock experimentalism, and Braxton, whose own unprecedented forays would be met with a far more ambivalent response from jazz critics caught up in another side of the same racialized discourse of musical innovation.[48] And like the jazz intellectuals of the 1960s (Baraka, Shepp, Spellman, Kofsky), groups such as Henry Cow and Slapp Happy would render the press itself as a problem that required skepticism, scrutiny, disassembly, challenge, or mockery. In this critical stance toward the industry, we find a position inside the vernacular music field that must be distinguished analytically from that of artists— again, like the Stones—who operate unproblematically through these existing channels. Of course, individual musicians commonly oscillate between these positions.

But this sort of anti-institutional politics defined itself against entertainment corporations, not against the notion of institutionalization itself. Indeed, organizations like Ottawa Music Company, the Musicians Cooperative, the London Musicians Collective, Recommended, Rock in Opposition, Music for Socialism, and l'Orchestra Cooperativa aspired to create alternative or oppositional institutions of musical production, distribution, and consumption, even though they routinely grabbed at commercial or state resources to help them establish or maintain their enterprises.[49]

These problems of analysis and interpretation have not concerned theorists in art history who have critiqued and revised Bürger's assessment of the neo-avant-garde, because those later writers had nothing to say about cultural production outside the institutionalized fine arts.[50] (Writers in the history of photography have by necessity proven more adept at moving across fine art and amateur practices than their colleagues in modern painting and sculpture.) Among the most important of these critics, Hal Foster's theory of avant-garde *nachträglichkeit* locks the neo-avant-garde into a tight dialogue with the past that would seem to occlude the precise kind of transverse jumps across the cultural field that the LP era had evidently made possible in music. Although he articulates well the need for "new genealogies of the avant-garde, ones that both complicate its past and pluralize its present," his disciplinary tendencies keep him from enacting that very pluralization.[51] Even the post-Bürgerian critic most beguiled by the possibilities of the postwar avant-garde, Andreas Huyssen, ventured his praise for Andy Warhol, and not for the low arts of advertising itself (not to mention other postwar visual media, such as color television, underground comics, psychedelic light shows, and poster art). Only recently have leading art historians widened their critical grasp to hold the genealogies of folkways, handicrafts, and popular culture in tension with those of advanced fine art practices.[52]

In addition to the long-playing record, the crucial development in music that had no clear analog in the visual arts was the widespread emergence of a popular music aesthetics in the postwar period, beginning first with jazz criticism in the 1940s and reaching an apogee of sorts in rock discourse of the 1960s.[53] Henry Cow intervened in a world where journalists, musicians, and, eventually, scholars closely considered the distinction "between those values only to be found in [rock] and the values which can be found elsewhere."[54] The precise form that this problem took shifted depending on who tackled it. Although rock critics articulated the distinctive energies and forms that made "good rock" good, other intellectuals reflected on how the medium or genre's specific aesthetic qualities mediated larger social and historical questions.[55] A musician might isolate and extend the specific possibilities inherent in his electrified instrument; an aesthetic theorist might highlight the timbral exactitude or instrumental techniques enabled by the recorded format; a political thinker might prize the collective composition inherent in edited improvisation or the music's origins in an oppressed class; a cultural studies scholar might examine the sociological and historical specificities that distinguish rock from, say, folk music.[56]

The relationships among the high arts and mass culture go back a long way and have taken a variety of forms.[57] Nonetheless, one of the main tasks for scholars of the vernacular avant-garde would be to explain the difference, if there is one, between the aestheticist conception of the avant-garde (as that which pursues changing aesthetic standards and continual revisions to the canon, according to Bernard Gendron's gloss of Baudelaire) and the more mundane emergence of new styles kicked up by the commercial marketplace—especially in the capitalist saturation of the postwar epoch. I would contend that there is no such difference if one does not maintain a critical valence for the avant-garde, whether that takes the shape of an imaginative proximity to social change; a questioning of its institutional framing or rewriting of its codes of operation; the exploration of new technologies of perception to entrain new subjectivities; or the functional transformation of production, circulation, and consumption. To posit such a valence would be to make a weak but necessary analytical distinction that would stop short of the plainly ridiculous conclusion that all popular culture dupes its consumers and offers more of the same in the glittering guise of the new.

Among Gendron's valuable contributions is a detailed account of how early rock discourse, like R&B, exhibited a distinct reluctance to attach its aesthetics to notions of political change.[58] In a strange kind of reverse negation, rock offered fun, energy, youth, and kicks—not political commentary.[59] As we've seen, the postwar realignments would generate a plethora of strategies for connecting aesthetic experimentation to the imagination of new social arrangements. An explicit link between rock and "revolution," however, would be only the most obvious turn to an analytically distinct position in cultural politics that I wish to label *avant-garde*. To draw out this distinction is not to suggest that only avant-gardism may lay claim to the political, but rather that its mode of political engagement differs in some way from that of other musics. Early country artists such as Jenny Lou Carson or Hank Williams contributed to a melancholy poetics of displaced rural labor in the midcentury, and therefore addressed a scattered community born of agricultural industrialization. Only a poor critic would miss the implicit political critique in much of this music, or for that matter the more explicit gender critique in Kitty Wells's "It Wasn't God Who Made Honky Tonk Angels." If its politics and status as vernacular modernism seem plain enough, however, this music becomes avant-garde only when it offers a radical vision of the future, an interrogation of its institutional basis, or some functional transformation.

As a term and a concept, the *vernacular* is dangerous.[60] I wish to employ it both carefully and irresponsibly to refer to the everyday arts of regular people who combine established and shared norms with improvisations in response to novel situations.[61] These arts are taught and learned through practice, largely by ear. The word also conveys the local, transitory, situational, adaptable, and translational dimensions of these practices, which dissolve the boundary between art and life in their own specific, processual ways.[62] An avant-garde that is vernacular would pursue emancipatory transformations, but it would turn away from the universalizing and transcendent model of total revolution in political, social, and economic life.[63] The music I want to call *vernacular* does not often ring out in concert halls. One experiences it in nightclubs, bars, DIY venues, dance halls, and improvised spaces such as church basements, cinemas, town halls, lofts, community centers, and various converted outdoor facilities. Above all and most importantly, one listens to it on the radio, the stereo, or the computer. It finds a mixed audience of nonspecialists and connoisseurs—yet the category of "audience" works differently in the vernacular, where the gap between artist and listener is smaller and more fluid than in elite art and performance practices. The vernacular is participatory and circulatory. In any case, its discourse—critical, theoretical, analytical—lives in mass-market music periodicals, newspapers, and, latterly, in specialist, small-run magazines. Historically, scholarly discussion was basically nonexistent. Economically situated in the commercial marketplace as well as small alternative networks, it received little private patronage or state subsidy.[64]

The *vernacular* is close to the *popular*, but I am avoiding the latter because of its ideological overdeterminations.[65] Although many vernacular musics might originate with working people, they are consumed and created by all classes and never function in a transparently "populist" manner. Some vernacular artists might address "their own" communities, while others—Chuck Berry comes to mind—choose to modify their aesthetic practices to address other communities or expand the boundaries of their own. Neither approach is more "authentic" than the other, because the market logics of all modern musics create their own formations of the popular.[66] Furthermore, the class position of artists working in the vernacular avant-garde is just as complex as that of the nineteenth-century avant-garde, which committed itself to the preservation of aristocratic values shed by the bourgeoisie in the face of an ascendant working class.[67] Like that avant-garde, supported by "an elite among the ruling class of that society from which it assumed itself to be cut off," the vernacular avant-garde remains connected to the culture industries by its parasitical relationship to that reproductive apparatus, to private patronage in the form of boutique record labels and "projects" made possible by hipster trust funds, and to private foundations and the state by means of an umbilical cord of grants.[68]

But regardless of these contradictory social positions, the vernacular is no less vernacular when a Cambridge University undergraduate plays it, just as Hindustani vocal music remains Hindustani even when Terry Riley sings it. The same can be said for the art students that populated so many

British pop groups.[69] To insist otherwise, or to bemoan the vernacular's continual recuperation by capitalism, would be to pine for a historically elusive authenticity matching artist to audience.[70] It is precisely such a naturalization of the vernacular concept that necessitates its interrogation and reanimation into a social space accelerated by the commodity form.

The vernacular is *impure* and, though demotic in some broad way described above, not necessarily inclusive. The preceding history reveals just as many fine gradations of taste policing as in cultivated circles, in contrast to the observations of some important early authors who noted how the indifference of the fine arts establishment freed up vernacular craftspeople to experiment unselfconsciously.[71] By the later 1960s, we see the appearance of a pop music critical establishment whose cultivated judgment made unselfconscious invention in that world seem like a thing of the past. Inequalities of opportunity persist; although they were reportedly reduced to eating dog food in one lean period, Faust did just fine enjoying the largesse of a major multinational corporation. Finally, unlike *popular*, which retains a homeopathic trace of the revolutionary masses, I would like *vernacular* to help me understand musicians who are committed to working in pop forms and unabashedly confident about their position within them—artists like Pere Ubu's David Thomas, who recently commented, "'Leveling the playing field' is a euphemism for lowering the level of expectations. I am an elitist. Music is a nearly masonic craft. Self-expression should be left to the professionals—we are uniquely trained and emotionally equipped to bear the bitter disappointment."[72]

In self-consciously advanced musics, however, the vinyl LP dramatically transformed the meaning of training itself by digging a route to professionalization that tunneled under academe. If *The World Is a Problem* cuts through this vernacular mix, its cross section reveals a significant reduction in the importance of formal academic accreditation.[73] Fred Frith, Tim Hodgkinson, and John Greaves may have attended Cambridge, but they weren't there to study music; Lindsay Cooper was apt to mention the work required to *unlearn* her conservatory training. Self-teaching or casual, non-institutionalized pedagogy was the norm.[74] Many vernacular artists did not learn through composition lessons, university seminars, the exchange of scores, or attendance at new music festivals. Although Karlheinz Stockhausen characteristically mistook a historical shift in material conditions for an innovation in personal style, he homed in on this consequential turn when, in 1971, he told a student reporter for Cambridge's *Varsity* newspaper, "The new oral tradition starting with my group players is a complete new development. Up to now we have traded all information on paper; now we have discs. My own recordings are models not for strict imitation but to allow people to get a feeling for the quality we try to achieve."[75]

Frith's presence at an exclusive performance of *In C* by Cornelius Cardew and the gang says more of the immense concentration of social capital at Oxbridge than it does of any formal curriculum in musical composition. For the most part, he learned about contemporary art music the same way he learned about every other kind of music: buying and trading LPs. Jazz and pop enthusiasts had long cultivated a vernacular practice of learning by ear from historical recordings, but the new social and technical arrangements in the postwar decades meant that experiments in tape, electronics, and indeterminacy were reaching the ears of young, adventurous listeners across the social field.[76] Soon enough, a nonaccredited, extrascholarly critical discourse grew up to address this emergent vernacular formation, in periodicals such as *Bells, Microphone, Musics, Impetus, Collusion, Ear, The Improvisor, ReR Quarterly, The Wire, Resonance, Rubberneck, Signal to Noise, Opprobrium, Audion,* and the *Bull Tongue Review.*[77] These outlets underscore the difference between the "low" or "popular" and the vernacular, which explicitly signals "the performance of translation, the desire to make a dialect."[78]

By tracking this vernacularization, we contribute to "a local and contingent articulation of the vernacular, . . . rather than a universalizing and essentializing conception" that would refuse the signs of historical change and pin that concept conclusively to an ever abundant populism—a black one, in most US music studies.[79] Rethinking the vernacular in response to how it is getting repracticed would yield a concept that "need not be defined in reaction to a similarly fixed notion of high culture, and would, moreover, be immune to the high/low class and race binaries that currently animate the cultivated/vernacular distinction."[80] Although I am less bullish than is George E. Lewis about the immunity of this new vernacular to rebarbative class and race binaries, we agree that the creaky opposition of high and low fails to describe the postwar maelstrom of recombinative sonic practices. Chris Corsano and Bill Orcutt's *The Raw and the Cooked* (2012) and Matana Roberts's *Coin Coin* (2011–) both suggest as vexed a relation with "low" as they do with "high"; the binary itself has been displaced.

In this sense, one has the impression that the mixed mess of the postwar vernacular avant-garde bears some special relationship to all of twentieth-century black performance, for which the operative terms of (European) avant-garde analysis—autonomy, mass culture, critique, high/low, resistance, telos—were always already inadequate, ill-fitting, apposite, and out-from-outside (even if they could not be completely ignored).[81] Since the vernacular practices of black, brown, beige, and white avant-garde musicians in the last seventy years *all* appear to overflow the analytical containers we might already have for them, any theoretical formulation resulting from the present conceptual definition would do well to draw on critical work that thinks through blackness as the surplus of the production of the modern—even though it is doubtless imperative to think beyond the black-white binary. Indeed, the postwar arrangements adumbrated here would seem to unite, historically, two forces—the avant-garde and blackness—that Fred Moten joins isomorphically by underlining their shared production and consumption of a surplus.[82] The teleological philosophy of history embedded in the avant-garde—the future is in the present—was built through prior spatial operations of constraint, mobility, and displacement that are also racial. Those racial operations haunt the avant-garde most conspicuously in its manifestations of primitivism—the past is in the present.[83] Likewise, the vernacular, put into opposition with the modern, lags behind, belatedly awaiting cultivation.[84] Its redoubled recrudescence in the postwar period as an avant-garde lends some material specificity to Moten's description of the black radical tradition as "anticipatory critique or future anterior maneuver" and illustrates powerfully what he refers to as the "blackness of blackness, the doubleness of blackness, the fucked-up whiteness of the essence of blackness."[85] This avant-garde leads from behind, from the audience, where "the new universal is listening."[86]

I will wrap up this farewell ramble by discussing why music, of all the arts, provides a special perspective for spinning out some reflections on the vernacular avant-garde—especially music in the commodified commercial landscape of the last century. This afterword has oscillated carelessly between listener and maker, or fan and artist, because those positions are closer to each other in vernacular musical practices than they are in elite ones (the new universal is listening).[87] Compare them with Hansen's vernacular modernists, however. The classical Hollywood cinema mass-produced new sensory experiences for regular viewers around the world, but those people weren't the ones making the films. Even within the demotic and contrary cinematic traditions surveyed by David E. James, the participatory oscillation of roles that we find in vernacular music is greatly diminished. "Socially disenfranchised groups are especially disenfranchised in respect to a medium such as film, whose dominant practice is so integrally industrialized and capital-intensive."[88] Film's high production costs and collaborative necessities have meant that there is no cinematic equivalent of learning new songs by ear or by trading records, playing them over and over, and figuring them out yourself—a consumption process that flows into vernacular production. Video enables a roughly analogous process, but the historical exceptionalism of microcinemas for DIY production and participatory viewing only underscores the absence of these practices in the dominant gallery- and museum-centered lineage of that newer medium.[89] Although theater and television also offer more opportunities than film did for this type of creative circulation, recorded music's easy and early commodification has produced a more saturated diffusion into the everyday lives of regular listeners.

This participatory circulation distinguishes music's "user experience" in its vernacular mode (and one could say the same for dance). But music possesses another quality that sets it apart from the visual arts, namely, a conceptual coherence across the range of its manifestations, from its highest elite forms of art music to its most devalued bubblegum pop or abject, talent-show catastrophes.[90] The academic music disciplines match the continuity and consistency of this field; to study music's low forms has not meant a departure from music studies itself (notwithstanding the enormous contributions from African American studies, sociology, and cultural studies). Even the special cases of advertising jingles and background music, which surely raise specific and irreducible questions of analysis, do not fall below or outside of the field of music studies.

Compare this practical coherence with the visual field, in which a turn to the low arts—advertising, crafts, industrial design—has also meant a disciplinary shift away from art history to American studies, folklore, or material/visual culture, all of which seem to remap the coordinates of experience in a manner categorically different from those used for fine arts spectatorship. I mean to highlight only this discontinuity of field, not its ideological valences. (Warhol rigorously investigated but did not eliminate it.) The study of ambient visualities implied in the disciplinary schism between art history and visual culture has an analogue in the emergence of a sound studies distinct from musicology, but there are limits to the comparison. In the visual domains, a shift away from fine-art objects and spectatorship toward the "low forms" would seem to require a disciplinary shift away from art history itself.[91] Not so in music, where reformulation and renewal around novel disciplinary fundamentals—such as listening—were not necessary for the study of nonelite musical forms. Those reformulations did occur and continue to do so, but not in order to clear a disciplinary space for pop, rock, blues, folk, and so on.

Of course, each art cultivates specific modes of existence. Music is no exception. But by comparing it with these other artistic modes, I'm suggesting that music has a particular gravitational pull in the vernacular. Thomas Crow's important study, *The Long March of Pop*, frequently turns to music to ease its stunning sweep from gallery to folk art. (Or take poetry: its low form *is* the musical lyric.) I mean to note that it isn't some kind of blinkered elitism keeping art historians of the neo-avant-garde, for example, from engaging vernacular aesthetic production, but rather the specific formation of the vernacular in their discipline, which rests on a fundamental and formative distinction between fine art and kitsch, even if innovative research in modern and contemporary art moves across that line with increasing frequency.[92]

In this afterword, I have tried to think with ideas that have popped up during a long writing process. Many of those ideas whip past and slide around a negative space that appears to be crowding in on ongoing conversations about avant-gardes in the postwar period. I would like call that negative space the "vernacular avant-garde," to recognize the collective significance of these disparate traditions of music-making by gathering them into a common field of reference.[93] Inspired by my subjects in Henry Cow, I have elaborated this concept with speculation and speed; I want to match their audacity, their sense of urgency, and their method of DIY theorizing: open, improvisational, not yet complete. A concept, not a theory or category, the vernacular avant-garde is built up just enough in these pages to wobble out into the world and cause trouble.[94] A call, it is made to move, to knock the environment about and make some effects.

The second half of the appellation creates many problems, not least of which are its nostalgic connotations. So dominant has been the expectation of critical negation in avant-garde studies that users of the term are continually beholden to the demand that one "either supports or opposes avant-garde ideology: the avant-garde either is or is not an authentic mode of cultural opposition, is or is not dead, is or is not the guiding spirit of this or that current movement."[95] The systematic relation between these two warring poles—negation and recuperation—both signals and reproduces, in academic discourse, the fundamental contradiction of the avant-garde:

that it is a product of bourgeois culture but tries to negate it. Commentators in search of further exemplification of this formalism, so impervious to ill-fitting evidence or historical explanation, will view any new statement on the avant-garde as nothing more than a mapping of territory soon to be coopted—dead already as its very condition of being.[96] But for those of us who do not see the avant-garde as the mere instantiation of a structural opposition, the contingencies and inconsistencies of historical cases militate strongly for the continual revision of the concepts we use to make sense of the cultural field, interrupting the structure of so much avant-garde discourse, a cycle of negation, disputation, recuperation, and failure that Paul Mann has termed "theory-death." The theory-death of the avant-garde promises nothing but collapse. Every rebirth brings its own exhaustion; every resistance its own neutralization; every beginning, its own ending. Here is another.

Notes

Preface

1 Mackenzie Wark, *The Beach Beneath the Street: The Lives and Times of Situationism* (London: Verso, 2011), 5.
2 William James, *Pragmatism* (New York: World Publishing Company, [1907] 1967), 33.

Introduction

1 David Toop, *Into the Maelstrom: Music, Improvisation, and the Dream of Freedom: Before 1970* (New York: Bloomsbury, 2016), 6.
2 A number of important studies of genre have recently appeared; see Eric Drott, "The End(s) of Genre," *Journal of Music Theory* 57, no. 1 (2013): 1–45; Robin James, "Is the Post- in Post-Identity the Post- in Post-Genre?" *Popular Music* 36, no. 1 (January 2016): 21–32; and David Brackett, *Categorizing Sound: Genre and Twentieth-Century Popular Music* (Oakland: University of California Press, 2016).
3 Michael Nyman, *Experimental Music: Cage and Beyond*, 2nd ed. (Cambridge: Cambridge University Press, 1999).
4 As Matei Calinescu has shown, theorist Angelo Guglielmi had already marked a similar distinction between the politicized, historical avant-garde and a more ideologically neutral, experimentalist "rearguard" by 1964, in his *Avanguardia e sperimentalismo* (Milan: Feltrinelli, 1964); see Calinescu, *Five Faces of Modernity: Modernism, Avant-Garde, Decadence, Kitsch, Postmodernism* (Durham, NC: Duke University Press, 1987), 121–22. Thanks to Bernard Gendron for pointing out this passage to me.
5 See, however, Tamara Levitz, "Yoko Ono and the Unfinished Music of 'John and Yoko,'" in *Impossible to Hold: Women and Culture in the 1960s*, edited by Avital H. Bloch and Lauri Umansky (New York: New York University Press, 2005), 217–39; Elizabeth Lindau, "Art Is Dead. Long Live Rock! Avant-Gardism and Rock Music, 1967–99," PhD diss., University of Virginia, 2012; Bill Martin, *Avant Rock: Experimental Music from the Beatles to Bjork* (Chicago, IL: Open Court, 2002); Stephen Graham, *Sounds of the Underground: A Cultural, Political, and Aesthetic Mapping of Underground and Fringe Music* (Ann Arbor: University of Michigan Press, 2016); and Tim Lawrence, *Hold On to Your Dreams: Arthur Russell and the Downtown Music Scene, 1973–1992* (Durham, NC: Duke University Press, 2009).

6   John Fordham, "Not with a Mirror . . . but a Hammer," *Time Out*, January 30–February 5, 1976, 11.

7   Bernard Gendron, *Between Montmartre and the Mudd Club: Popular Music and the Avant-Garde* (Chicago, IL: University of Chicago Press, 2002); Phil Ford, *Dig: Sound and Music in Hip Culture* (Oxford: Oxford University Press, 2013).

8   Tony Palmer, *Born under a Bad Sign* (London: William Kimber, 1970), 19. Palmer appears unaware of the writing of musicologist Wilfrid Mellers, who had been investigating popular music as early as 1964; Wilfrid Mellers, *Music in a New Found Land: Themes and Developments in the History of American Music* (London: Barrie and Rockliff, 1964).

9   Ian MacDonald, "Faust: The Sound of the Eighties," *New Musical Express*, March 3, 1973; he refers to William Mann, "The Beatles Revive Hopes of Progress in Pop Music," *Times* (London), May 29, 1967.

10 Richard Taruskin, *The Oxford History of Western Music* (New York: Oxford University Press, 2005).

11 Ed Pinsent, "Merzbow," *Sound Projector* 5 (1998): 6–7; Jing Wang, "Considering the Politics of Sound Art in China in the 21st Century," *Leonardo Music Journal* 25 (2015): 73–78.

12 Georgina Born, "On Musical Mediation: Ontology, Technology and Creativity," *Twentieth-Century Music* 2, no. 1 (March 2005): 7–36. See also Chris Cutler, *File under Popular: Theoretical and Critical Writings on Music* (London: November Books, 1985).

13 Ornette Coleman, liner notes to *Dancing in Your Head*, A&M SP-722, 1977.

14 George E. Lewis, *A Power Stronger than Itself: The AACM and American Experimental Music* (Chicago, IL: University of Chicago Press, 2008), 360.

15 Daniel Belgrad, *The Culture of Spontaneity: Improvisation and the Arts in Postwar America* (Chicago, IL: University of Chicago Press, 1998).

16 Sabine M. Feisst, "John Cage and Improvisation: An Unresolved Relationship," in *Musical Improvisation: Art, Education, and Society*, edited by Gabriel Solis and Bruno Nettl (Urbana: University of Illinois Press, 2009), 38–51.

17 You Nakai, "On the Instrumental Natures of David Tudor's Music," PhD diss., New York University, 2016; Jeremy Grimshaw, *Draw a Straight Line and Follow It: The Music and Mysticism of La Monte Young* (New York: Oxford University Press, 2012); Martha Mockus, *Sounding Out: Pauline Oliveros and Lesbian Musicality* (New York: Routledge, 2008); William Marotti, "Challenge to Music: The Music Group's Sonic Politics," in *Tomorrow Is the Question: New Directions in Experimental Music Studies*, edited by Benjamin Piekut (Ann Arbor: University of Michigan Press, 2014), 109–38; John Tilbury, *Cornelius Cardew (1936–1981): A Life Unfinished* (Harlow, UK: Copula, 2008); Branden W. Joseph, *Beyond the Dream Syndicate: Tony Conrad and the Arts After Cage* (New York: Zone Books, 2008).

18 G. Lewis, *Power Stronger than Itself*; Andrew Raffo Dewar, "Searching for the Center of a Sound: Bill Dixon's *Webern*, the Unaccompanied Solo, and Compositional Ontology in Post-Songform Jazz," *Jazz Perspectives* 4, no. 1 (2010): 59–87; Ekkehard

Jost, *Free Jazz* (New York: Da Capo Press, 1975); Paul Steinbeck, *A Message to Our Folks: The Art Ensemble of Chicago* (Chicago, IL: University of Chicago Press, 2017); John Stevens, *Search and Reflect: A Music Workshop Handbook* (London: Rockschool, [1985] 2007).

19 Jay Keister, "'The Long Freak Out': Unfinished Music and Countercultural Madness in 1960s and 1970s Avant-Garde Rock," *Volume!* 9, no. 2 (2012), http://volume.revues.org/3413?gathStatIcon=true#tocto1n1 (accessed December 29, 2016).

20 On friction, see Joseph, *Beyond the Dream Syndicate*, 35–40. The 1960s was hardly the first decade to produce serious conundrums about shared authorship; see, for example, Tamara Levitz, *Modernist Mysteries: Perséphone* (New York: Oxford University Press, 2012).

21 See Benjamin Piekut, "Not So Much a Program of Music as the Experience of Music," in *Merce Cunningham: CO:MM:ON TI:ME*, ed. Joan Rothfuss (Minneapolis: Walker Arts Center, 2017), 113–29.

22 Morton Feldman, "Liner Notes" (1962), in *Give My Regards to Eighth Street Street: Collected Writings of Morton Feldman* (Cambridge, MA: Exact Change, 2000), 3–7; on Cage, see Benjamin Piekut, "When Orchestras Attack! John Cage Meets the New York Philharmonic," in *Experimentalism Otherwise: The New York Avant-Garde and Its Limits* (Berkeley: University of California Press, 2011), 20–64; and Branden W. Joseph, "HPSCHD—Ghost or Monster?," in *Mainframe Experimentalism: Early Computing and the Foundation of the Digital Arts*, edited by Hannah B. Higgins and Douglas Kahn (Berkeley: University of California Press, 2012), 147–69.

23 Tony Palmer, "The Road to Nowhere," *London Magazine*, July 1967, 85–89.

24 Michael Parsons, "Sounds of Discovery," *Musical Times* 109, no. 1503 (May 1968): 429–30.

25 Parsons, "Sounds of Discovery," 430.

26 Victor Schonfield, "Arts in Society: Sergeant Pepper's Favourite Composer," *New Society*, September 7, 1967, 331.

27 Cornelius Cardew, "Sitting in the Dark," *Musical Times* 109, no. 1501 (March 1968): 233–34.

28 "Cornelius Cardew," interview, *International Times*, February 2–15, 1968; see also Michael Parsons, "Michael Parsons Writes about the Music of Cornelius Cardew," *Listener*, November 30, 1967, 728–29.

29 The Generation of Music 3 program, Wigmore Hall, June 2, 1962.

30 Stanley Sadie, "Carrying Improvisation to Its Logical End," *Times* (London), August 4, 1967.

31 Tim Souster, "Sounds of Discovery," *Financial Times*, May 21, 1968.

32 John Lewis, "So What Do You Want from Your Music—Security?" *Time Out*, December 8–14, 1972, 38–39; see also Max Harrison's appraisal of the Spontaneous Music Ensemble, "Crossing the Great Musical Divide," *Record Collector*, November 1971.

33 Michael Walters, "The Open-Ended Music Company," *Sounds*, October 24, 1970; see also John Cruft, letter to the editor, *Musics* 8 (July 1976): 3.

34 Miles Kington, "Trip Beyond Jazz's Outermost Fringe," *Times* (London), November 30, 1967.

35 Stanley Myers, "Shock Tactics," *Spectator*, May 31, 1968.

36 Alan Rich, "Jazz and Classical Styles Converging," *New York/World Journal Tribune*, April 23, 1967.

37 Russell Unwin, "Nothing Like a Bit of the Ol' Boulez," *Cream* 2, no. 1 (May 1972): 7.

38 Unwin, "Nothing." Unwin published often on high/low interactions during these years; see also Russell Unwin, "Rock and the Classics—continued . . ." *Melody Maker*, March 13, 1971; Russell Unwin, "The New, Spiritual Era of Stockhausen," *Melody Maker*, May 29, 1971.

39 "Cornelius Cardew, AMM, and the Path to Perfect Hearing," *Jazz Monthly*, May 1968, 10–11, at 10.

40 Loraine Alterman, "This Is Not Here," *Melody Maker*, October 23, 1971.

41 Karl Dallas and Steve Lake, "Stockhausen: Free as a Bird," *Melody Maker*, April 24, 1976.

42 Michael Zwerin, "The Soft Machine," *Down Beat* 35, no. 14 (July 11, 1968): 21, 40; for a similarly wide field of critical reference, see Robert Greenfield, "Sun Ra and Europe's Space Music Scene," *Rolling Stone*, January 7, 1971, 17–18, in which the author compares Sun Ra to other cosmic artists, including Stockhausen, Keith Tippett's Centipede, Pink Floyd, and the Scratch Orchestra.

43 Gendron, *Montmartre.*

44 Eric Drott, *Music and the Elusive Revolution: Cultural Politics and Political Culture in France, 1968–1981* (Berkeley: University of California Press, 2011), 73–81.

45 All by Tim Souster: "Long and Loud," *Listener*, May 2, 1968; "The Velvet Underground," *Listener*, July 4, 1968; "Pop Form," *Listener*, October 10, 1968; "Pre-Christmas," *Listener*, December 12, 1968; "Notes on Pop Music," *Tempo* 87 (winter 1968–69): 2–6; "Goodbye Cream," *Listener*, March 20, 1969; "A New Dylan," *Listener*, June 5, 1969; "Through the Sound Barrier," *Observer Magazine*, October 5, 1969; "Down Abbey Road," *Listener*, November 13, 1969.

46 Souster, "Through the Sound Barrier."

47 Although it is surely related to this discursive formation in a general sense, Charles le Vay's "A Guide to Avant Garde Rock" (*Let It Rock*, February 1974, 22–24) constructs its project quite differently, with no references to other traditions or any sense of "convergence."

48 Victor, "Rule Britannia?" *Down Beat* 35, no. 14 (1968): 24–25, 32, at 32; see also Vic Schonfield, "Free Jazz in Britain," *Music Maker*, November 1967, 22.

49 Victor Schonfield, "Total Improvisation," *International Times*, March 28, 1969, 15; see also Colin Wood, "How We Differ," *Musics* 1 (April–May 1975): 31.

50 Evan Parker, "Speech to the SPNM Forum on 'Music In the Future,'" *Musics* 1 (April–May 1975): 13.

51 Joseph, *Beyond the Dream Syndicate*, 104–110.

52 Richard Williams, "Jazz/Rock: A Personal Opinion," *Melody Maker*, February 7, 1970. See also Kevin Fellezs, *Birds of Fire: Jazz, Rock, Funk, and the Creation of Fusion* (Durham, NC: Duke University Press, 2011).

53 Williams, "Jazz/Rock"; see also Steve Lake and Karl Dallas, "Rocking the Avant-Garde," *Melody Maker*, April 24, 1976.

54 Richard Williams, "Derek Bailey: Feeding the Post-Cage Ear," *Melody Maker*, July 10, 1971; Russell Unwin, "Where Pop and Classics Meet . . . ," *Melody Maker*, June 27, 1970; Souster, "Long and Loud."

55 Dallas and Lake, "Stockhausen"; Michael Zwerin, "A Lethal Measurement," *Village Voice* (New York), January 6, 1966.

56 Harrison, "Crossing the Great Musical Divide."

57 Richard Williams, "Classical Musicians Have a Lot to Learn," *Melody Maker*, July 25, 1970.

58 Russell Unwin, "What's Wrong with Our Music Colleges?" *Melody Maker*, August 29, 1970.

59 Benjamin Piekut, "Indeterminacy, Free Improvisation, and the Mixed Avant-Garde: Experimental Music in London, 1965–75," *Journal of the American Musicological Society* 67, no. 3 (fall 2014): 769–824.

60 Piekut, "Indeterminacy"; see also Samuel Dwinell, "Blackness in British Opera," PhD diss., Cornell University, 2016.

61 Allan Jones, "Ruth, Richard, and Robert . . ." *Melody Maker*, June 14, 1975.

62 Piekut, "Indeterminacy."

63 Steve Lake and Karl Dallas, "Prophet, Seers, and Sages," *Melody Maker*, April 24, 1976.

64 Lewis, "So What Do You Want?," 38–39.

65 George E. Lewis, review of *Northern Sun, Southern Moon*, by Mike Heffley, *Current Musicology* 78 (fall 2004): 84.

66 Ronald Atkins, untitled interview with Victor Schonfield, *Guardian*, November 24, 1970.

67 Atkins interview.

68 Fred Moten, *In the Break: The Aesthetics of the Black Radical Tradition* (Minneapolis: University of Minnesota Press, 2003), 32.

69 Maureen Mahon, *Right to Rock: The Black Rock Coalition and the Cultural Politics of Race* (Durham, NC: Duke University Press, 2004).

70 Evan Rapport, "Hearing Punk as Blues," *Popular Music* 33, no. 1 (January 2014): 39–67.

71 The following discussion surveys the British reception of krautrock; for general introductions to the genre, see David Stubbs, *Future Days: Krautrock and the Birth of a Revolutionary New Music* (London: Faber and Faber, 2014); Ulrich Adelt, *Krautrock: German Music in the Seventies* (Ann Arbor: University of Michigan Press, 2016); and Henning Dedekind, *Krautrock: Underground, LSD, und Kosmische Kuriere* (Innsbruck, Austria: Hannibal Verlag, 2008).

72 Charles Shaar Murray, "Gerroff an' Milk It," *New Musical Express*, August 31, 1974, 8; Kenneth Ansell, "Tangerine Dream: Chatting with Edgar Froese and Peter Baumann," *Zigzag* 44 (August 1974): 39; see also the comments of Amon Düül's Renata Knaup-Kroetenshwantz in Peter Erskine, "Never a Duul Moment," *Disc*, July 1, 1972.

73 Michael Watts, "Can: *Tago Mago*," review, *Melody Maker*, January 29, 1972.

74 James Johnson, "Can Can . . . and They Will," *New Musical Express*, February 5, 1972; and Nick Kent, "Can: Ve Give Ze Orders Here," *New Musical Express*, February 16, 1974; Richard Williams, review of *Ege Bamyasi*, by Can, and *Neu!*, by Neu!, *Melody Maker*, November 11, 1972; Gerald O'Connell, "Dream: Alien Rock," *Sounds*, April 6, 1974.

75 Karl Dallas, "Faust and Foremost," *Melody Maker*, June 2, 1973.

76 Peter Erskine, "Canned Music," *Disc*, December 16, 1972.

77 Martin Hayman, "Which Way the Trade Gap?" *Sounds*, December 8, 1973; O'Connell, "Dream: Alien Rock."

78 John Peel, review of *Super*, by Neu!, *Disc*, January 27, 1973.

79 Hayman, "Which Way the Trade Gap?"

80 Williams, review of *Ege Bamyasi* and *Neu!*.

81 Ian MacDonald, "Krautrock: Germany Calling #2," *New Musical Express*, December 16, 1972; Richard Williams, "Is It Euro-Rock Next?" *Melody Maker*, June 13, 1970, 22.

82 Richard Williams, review of *Monster Movie*, by Can, *Melody Maker*, May 30, 1970; Williams, "Is It Euro-Rock Next?"; Duncan Fallowell, "Can: The Heaviest of All?" *Melody Maker*, October 30, 1971, 10. These kinds of comparisons showed up in the French press, too; see Phillippe Paringaux, "Faust," *Rock and Folk*, February 1972.

83 Steve Lake, "Dream Kids," *Melody Maker*, April 6, 1974.

84 Richard Williams, "Roxy Music," *Melody Maker*, February 12, 1972.

85 Jean-Pierre Lentin, "At Last: German Rock Has Arrived!" *Actuel* 27 (January 1973), in *Krautrock: Cosmic Rock and Its Legacy*, trans. Clodagh Kinsella (London: Black Dog, 2009); O'Connell, "Dream: Alien Rock"; Lake, "Dream Kids."

86 Michael Watts, "Karlheinz Stockhausen," *Melody Maker*, March 4, 1972.

87 Miles, "Tangerine Dream," *New Musical Express*, November 29, 1975.

88 Michael Watts, "Amon for All Seasons," *Melody Maker*, 12 December 1970.

89 Miles, "Tangerine Dream."; see also Lake, "Dream Kids."

90 Karl Dallas, "The Ecstasy without the Agony," *Let It Rock*, October 1975, 24–26, at 25.

91 Richard Williams, "Can Do," *Melody Maker*, January 27, 1973.

92 Ian MacDonald, "Krautrock: Germany Calling," *New Musical Express*, December 9, 1972; Miles, "Tangerine Dream."

93 Watts, "Amon for All Seasons."

94 Lentin, "At Last!"

95 Watts, "Amon for All Seasons."

96 Paringaux ("Faust") wrote, "Germany seems to be the only country on the Continent capable of making a really original contribution to what we call rock music"; see also Williams, "Is It Euro-Rock Next?," 22; Michael Watts, "Deutsche Rock," *Melody Maker*, April 15, 1972, 25; Michael Watts, "Can You Dig It?," *Melody Maker*, February 5, 1972; Michael Watts, "Amon Duul: Every Good Thing Goes in Threes," *Melody Maker*, June 24, 1972, 29; and Martin Hayman, "Amon Duul: Community of Lemmings?" *Sounds*, June 24, 1972, 10.

97 MacDonald, "Krautrock: Germany Calling #2"; Lentin, "At Last!"

98 Kent, "Can."

99 Steve Peacock, "Faust: What We All Need?" *Sounds*, July 15, 1972, 6. See also Roy Hollingworth, "Euro Vision," *Melody Maker*, January 20, 1973, 19.

100 Christian Lebrun, "Faust: Rock du Marché Commun," *Best*, June 1972.

101 Lebrun, "Faust."

102 Gerald O'Connell, "Another Time, Another Place," *Let It Rock*, February 1975, 30–31; see also O'Connell, "Dream: Alien Rock."

103 Quoted in Dallas, "Faust and Foremost," 36.

104 Paringaux, "Faust."

105 Johnson, "Can Can." See also MacDonald, "Krautrock: Germany Calling."

106 Rob Young, *All Gates Open: The Story of Can* (London: Faber and Faber, 2018).

107 Fallowell, "Can."; see also Max Bell, "Tangerine Dream: Is This the End of Rock as We Know It?" *New Musical Express*, November 16, 1974.

108 MacDonald, "Krautrock: Germany Calling"; see also Lentin, "At Last!" See also Fallowell, "Can."

109 Watts, "Can You Dig It?"

110 MacDonald, "Krautrock: Germany Calling."

111 Johnson, "Can Can."

112 Dallas, "Faust and Foremost," 36.

113 MacDonald, "Krautrock: Germany Calling."

114 MacDonald, "Krautrock: Germany Calling."

115 Steve Lake, "Milking the Cow," *Melody Maker*, June 22, 1974. The context and tone indicate that the speaker was John Greaves.

116 Ian MacDonald, *Revolution in the Head: The Beatles' Records and the Sixties* (New York: Henry Holt, 1994), 21.

117 MacDonald, *Revolution in the Head*, 21.

118 MacDonald, *Revolution in the Head*, 22.

119 MacDonald, *Revolution in the Head*, 22.

120 MacDonald, *Revolution in the Head*, 23.

121 Peter Blegvad, 1974 Notebook, PBA.

122 I refer to Alfred Jarry, *Exploits and Opinions of Doctor Faustroll, Pataphysician*, trans. Simon Watson Taylor (Boston, MA: Exact Change, 1996), 21. I'm grateful to Charles Curtis for pointing out this correspondence to me.

123 Andrew Pickering, *The Cybernetic Brain: Sketches of Another Future* (Chicago, IL: University of Chicago Press, 2009), 139.

124 For an illuminating study of cybernetics and free improvisation, see David Borgo, *Sync or Swarm: Improvising Music in a Complex Age* (New York: Continuum, 2006).

125 One should also take note of the indeterminate ethics of improvisation advanced in Ashby's thinking: it is hardly a resource limited to the weak in his view, but rather a choice for those with the power to choose among tactics. Another view would note the necessity of improvisation as a tactic for those without the power to choose an alternative. Therefore, the practice of improvisation takes on different meanings in different contexts. I'm grateful to Eric Drott for guiding me to this observation.

126 I've taken this phrase from one of Hodgkinson's notebooks; he was paraphrasing a passage from Paolo Freire, *Pedagogy of the Oppressed*, trans. Myra Bergman Ramos (New York: Herder and Herder, 1970). I am also thinking with and against one of the finest explications of a world navigated through improvisation, Stanley Cavell's *Pursuits of Happiness: The Hollywood Comedy of Remarriage* (Cambridge, Mass.: Harvard University Press, 1981), especially chapter 5, "Counterfeiting Happiness: *His Girl Friday*," 161–88.

127 Tim Hodgkinson, draft introduction to *The Henry Cow Book*, THA.

Chapter 1. You Can't Play This Music at Cambridge (1968–1973)

1 Graham Lock, *Forces In Motion: The Music and Thoughts of Anthony Braxton* (New York: Da Capo, [1988] 1989), 162–74.

2 I base the following on my interviews with Frith, and Alan Barnes, Donald Frith obituary, *Guardian*, April 30, 2000.

3 Christopher Hitchens, *Hitch-22* (New York: Twelve, 2010), 63–64.

4 Bill Milkowski, "The Frith Factor: Exploration in Sound," *Down Beat*, January 1983, 22–25, 61, at 23.

5 Milkowski, "The Frith Factor," 23.

6 Kenneth Ansell, "Dissecting the Cow: An Almost Complete History of Henry Cow," *Impetus* 2 (June 1976): n.p.

7 Rob Young, *Electric Eden: Unearthing Britain's Visionary Music* (London: Faber and Faber, 2010).

8 For more on this center of postwar British modernism, see Philip Rupprecht, *British Musical Modernism: The Manchester Group and Their Contemporaries* (Cambridge: Cambridge University Press, 2015), 252–55.

9 On Bedford, see Christopher Ford, "Bedford Chords," *Guardian*, February 24, 1971; Ian McKenzie, "Bedford Trucking," *Sounds*, January 29, 1977; and Rupprecht, *British Musical Modernism*, 378–407.

10 Roger Smalley, "Musical Party in King's," interview with Norman Bryson, *Varsity* (Cambridge UK), February 1, 1969.

11 Michael Zwerin, "The Soft Machine," *Down Beat* 35, no. 14 (July 11, 1968): 21, 40.

12 I base this list on listings in the *1/- Paper* and Frith's datebook.

13 *1/- Paper* (Cambridge, UK), "Rights of Man," February 28, 1969; Colin Filer, "Beast v. Theatre," *Varsity* (Cambridge UK), March 8, 1969; Jon Chadwick, "Tom Paine," *Varsity* (Cambridge UK), March 1, 1969; "Tom Paine" flyer, THA.

14 Advertisement, *Varsity* (Cambridge UK), January 25, 1969.

15 Anthony Barnett, *UnNatural Music: John Lennon and Yoko Ono in Cambridge 1969* (Lewes, UK: Allardyce, 2016).

16 Nick Tottan, "Avant-garde Concert—A Surprise for Performers?" *Varsity*, February 22, 1969.

17 Chris Walker, "'Worldes Blis' and the Word of New Music," *Granta*, October 1969, 15–16.

18 Tim Souster, "Long and Loud," *Listener*, May 2, 1968, 581.

19 Tim Souster, "Intermodulation: A Short History," *Contact* 17 (summer 1977): 3–6, at 3.

20 I draw these details from Souster, "Intermodulation," and a press release, dated March 1970, in Souster's personal archive (TSA).

21 Frith, quoted in Ansell, "Dissecting the Cow," n.p.

22 These tracks can be found on many of the various *Henry Cow Peel Sessions* bootleg CDs, though in one prominent MP3 collection they have been mistitled. The correct version of "Hieronymo" is over eleven minutes long, while "Poglith" lasts 9:53.

23 Flyer, THA.

24 Ansell, "Dissecting the Cow," n.p.

25 Clive Bell, "Epiphanies," *Wire* 212 (October 2001): 106.

26 Nigel Stafford-Clark, "Age of Gilt—Don't Look Back," *Varsity* (Cambridge UK), June 7, 1969.

27 *1/- Paper* (Cambridge, UK), "Rock . . . ," n.d. [October 2, 1970?]; Tony Wilson, "Fairport and Henry Cow Concert," *Varsity* (Cambridge UK), November 14, 1970.

28 Liebe Klug, "Dancers and the Dance," *Varsity* (Cambridge UK), 75, no. 1, n.d. [January 15, 1972].

29 "Henry Cow" promotional leaflet, n.d. [after February 1971], FFA. Klug mentions the work by name in "Dancers and the Dance." The title comes from a painting by Paul Klee; Greaves had visited a Klee retrospective at the Museum of Modern Art in summer 1970, and returned to Cambridge with postcards of two Klee works, *With the Yellow Half-Moon and Blue Star* and *Dance Monster to My Soft Song*.

30 Frank Perry, email communications with the author, October 2016. I am grateful to Perry for sharing tapes of his rehearsal with Henry Cow.

31 James Cannon, "Henry Cow / Christ's Theatre," *Varsity* (Cambridge UK), May 8, 1971.

32 Greaves, quoted in Ansell, "Dissecting the Cow," n.p.

33 Chris Cutler, Fred Frith, and Tim Hodgkinson, unpublished conversation, 1988, cassette, CCA.

34 Classified advertisement, *Melody Maker*, September 11, 1971.

35 I am grateful to Aymeric Leroy for sharing with me transcripts of his interviews with members of Louise.

36 For the following account of the Ottawa Music Company, I am relying on programs in Henry Cow personal archives, my interviews with the Cows, and an extensive set of email communications between participants in the group and Aymeric Leroy, who graciously shared them with me.

37 Chris Cutler, liner notes, HCFABS, I:4.

38 Cutler, liner notes, HCFABS, I:4.

39 The original *Henry Cow Fortieth Anniversary Box Set* is now sold out, but Cutler intends to release a new box of complete works, ReR HC51, in 2019.

40 The "fast 13s" call to mind what we could term the "fast 11s" in Soft Machine's "Hibou, Anemone and Bear."

41 Frith, liner notes, *HCFABS*, I:6.

42 Hear the Peel session recording, collected on *HCFABS*, disc 1 at 2:14, or the *Leg End* version, at 1:53.

43 Hodgkinson, liner notes, *HCFABS*, I:4.

44 Henry Cow, "For the Attention of the Social Secretary," n.d. [1972], THA.

45 "Henry Cow," n.d. [late 1972], CCA.

46 "A Message from Henry Cow," *Bacchae*, Arts Theatre Cambridge, May 8–13, 1972.

47 See Nicholas de Jongh, "A Critical Discovery," *Guardian*, May 10, 1972; Charles Lewsen, "The Bacchae," *Times* (London), April 28, 1972; and Mike Sternberg, "Euripides at the Arts," *Varsity* (Cambridge UK), May 13, 1972.

48 On Bailey's setup during these years, see Martin Davidson, liner notes to Derek Bailey, *Domestic and Public Pieces*, Emanem 4001, 1995; and Ben Watson, *Derek Bailey and the Story of Free Improvisation* (London: Verso, 2004), 188–192.

49 G. F. Fitz-Gerald, *Mouseproof*, LP, UNI Records UNLS 115, 1970.

50 Leigh's instrumental range was one reason that Henry Cow chose him instead of their friend Clive Bell, who also would soon relocate to London but who only played the flute.

51 The title for "Guider" was taken from a newspaper headline about a UFO sighting; Traverse Theatre Club, July programme, FFA.

52 I am grateful to Leibe Klug for clarifying some details of these performances in email correspondence, October 2016.

53 For the "First Hollywood Theme," hear at 0:27 of "With the Yellow Half-Moon and Blue Star: Demi-lune jaune" on *HCFABS*, disc 1. Cutler has lightly edited the complete recording. For the "Second Hollywood Theme," hear "With the Yellow half Moon and Blue Star: Chorale flautando" on *HCFABS*, disc 1.

54 Hear this section on "With the Yellow Half Moon and Blue Star: Cycling over the Cliff," *HCFABS*, disc 1.

55 Cutler, quoted in *HCFABS*, 1:8.

56 Cutler, liner notes, *HCFABS*, I:11.

57 Balchin also recalls doing the same to his own room next door, in a house he shared with Angela Stewart Park, among others.

58 Ian MacDonald, "Ayers / Cabaret Voltaire," *New Musical Express*, October 14, 1972.

59 MacDonald, "Ayers / Cabaret Voltaire."

60 Explorer's Club 3 program, May 4, 1973, CCA.

61 Explorer's Club 2 program, April 27, 1973, CCA.

62 Tim Hodgkinson, Notebook 2, n.d. [1972], THA.

Chapter 2. Faust and the Virgins (1973)

1 The following account draws on my interviews with Simon Draper, Sue Steward, and Tom Newman, as well as Simon Draper, afterword to Terry Southern, *Virgin: A History of Virgin Records* (Axminster, UK: A Publishing Company, [1996?]), 240–56;

Paul Philips, "Draper: Interesting People Make Interesting Records," *Music Week*, November 5, 1977; Simon Frodsham, "Professional Virgin," *West London Observer*, November 29, 1974; Richard Branson, *Losing My Virginity: How I Survived, Had Fun, and Made a Fortune Doing Business My Way* (New York: Crown, [1998] 2007), 77; Steve Peacock, "Tale of Two Virgins," *Sounds*, May 4, 1974; Louis Barfe, *Where Have All the Good Times Gone? The Rise and Fall of the Record Industry* (London: Atlantic Books, 2005), 265–68; Rosalind Morris, "Brisk, Brash and Branson," *Guardian*, January 22, 1970.

2   Morris, "Brisk, Brash and Branson."

3   Morris, "Brisk, Brash and Branson."

4   Morris, "Brisk, Brash and Branson."

5   Maurice Corina, "Record Men Drop RPM: Cut-Price War Expected," *Times* (London), June 27, 1969.

6   Virgin advertisement, *Student* 2, no. 4 (spring 1970): n.p. The first advert in *Melody Maker* appeared on August 1, 1970.

7   Branson, *Losing My Virginity*, 77.

8   Branson, *Losing My Virginity*, 59.

9   Branson, *Losing My Virginity*, 78.

10 Laurie Henshaw, "Import Records," *Melody Maker*, November 13, 1971, 29.

11 Virgin advertisement, *Melody Maker*, May 1, 1971.

12 See, for example, Mark Plummer, "The Rise and Rise of Richard Branson," *Melody Maker*, May 27, 1972, which calls attention to obscure German bands (i.e., Faust).

13 For surveys of krautrock, see David Stubbs, *Future Days: Krautrock and the Birth of a Revolutionary New Music* (London: Melville House, 2015); and Ulrich Adelt, *Krautrock: German Music in the Seventies* (Ann Arbor: University of Michigan Press, 2016).

14 See the introduction for a survey of this literature.

15 Henning Dedekind, *Krautrock: Underground, LSD, und Kosmische Kuriere* (Innsbruck, Austria: Hannibal Verlag, 2008), 203–5.

16 Michael Heatley, *John Peel: A Life in Music* (London: Michael O' Mara Books, 2004), 79.

17 Julian Cope, *Krautrocksampler*, 2nd ed. (London: Head Heritage, [1995] 1996), dedication.

18 Ian MacDonald, "Krautrock: Germany Calling #3," *New Musical Express*, December 23, 1972.

19 Karl Dallas, "Faust and Foremost," *Melody Maker*, June 2, 1973, 36.

20 This synopsis draws on Tom Doyle, "Faust: Hans Joachim Irmler," *Sound on Sound*, July 2010, http://www.soundonsound.com/sos/jul10/articles/faust.htm; Andy Wilson, *Faust: Stretch Out Time: 1970–1975* (London: The Faust Pages, 2006); Faust, *Faust: The Wümme Years, 1970–73*, liner notes, ReR Megacorp ReR FB1, 2000; Christian Lebrun, "Faust: Rock du Marché Commun," *Best*, August 1972.

21 Wilson, *Faust*.

22 On the Coop, see Helmut Herbst, "New German Cinema, 1962–83: A View from Hamburg," in *West German Filmmakers on Film: Visions and Voices*, ed. Eric Rent-

schler (New York: Holmes and Meier, 1988), 225–34; article originally written in 1983.

23 Helmut Salzinger, "Raus Klainer Röhl: Der mißglückte Versuch, die Redaktion von 'konkret' zu besetzen," *Die Zeit* (Hamburg), May 16, 1969, http://www.zeit.de/1969 /20/raus-klainer-roehl (accessed December 10, 2016).

24 Joe Boyd, *White Bicycles: Making Music in the 1960s* (London: Serpent's Tail, 2006), 178.

25 Uwe Nettelbeck, interview with Chris Cutler, liner notes to Faust, *Faust: The Wümme Years*, 33.

26 Wilson, *Faust*, 20.

27 Virgin press release, reprinted in Wilson, *Faust*, 95–96.

28 The following account of Graupner's activities with Faust draws on Kurt Graupner interview with Cutler, liner notes to *Faust: The Wümme Years*.

29 Liner notes to Faust, *Faust: The Wümme Years*, 26.

30 Liner notes to Faust, *Faust: The Wümme Years*, 26.

31 Virgin press release, reprinted in Wilson, *Faust*, 95; Dallas, "Faust and Foremost."

32 Graupner interview, 26.

33 Quoted in Karl Dallas, "Faust and Foremost," 36.

34 Ralph Ellison, "The Golden Age, Time Past," in *The Jazz Cadence of American Culture*, ed. Robert G. O'Meally (New York: Columbia University Press, 1998), 454.

35 Peter Blegvad and Co., "Faust Manifesto," available at http://faust-pages.com /publications/faust.manifesto.html (accessed December 10, 2016).

36 This press release is available on the Faust Pages website, but I believe it has been mistakenly dated there to March 1971. The content of the document makes clear that it was written later, likely September or October 1971.

37 "Statt Musik Kampf mit der Technik," *Hamburger Abendblatt*, November 24, 1971.

38 Jean-Hervé Peron, interview with Chris Cutler, in liner notes to Faust, *Faust: The Wümme Years*.

39 Irmler, interview with Cutler, liner notes to *Faust: The Wümme Years*. This incident contributes to a bigger story about the rock infrastructure in Germany during these years: it didn't exist yet. Bands had to perform in halls or gymnasiums that weren't really built for this kind of music, so the electricity was always off or inconveniently accessible. For more on this point, see Dedekind, *Krautrock*, 143–44.

40 Philipe Paringaux, "Faust," *Rock and Folk*, February 1972; my translation.

41 Paringaux, "Faust."

42 Nettelbeck interview, 36.

43 G. B., review of *So Far*, by Faust, *Melody Maker*, April 7, 1973; Christian Lebrun, "Faust: Rock du Marche Commun," *Best*, June 1972; Ian MacDonald, review of *So Far*, by Faust, *New Musical Express*, April 14, 1973.

44 John Peel, "Faust," *Disc*, June 10, 1972. See also Steve Peacock, "Faust: What We All Need?" *Sounds*, July 15, 1972, 6.

45 Nettelbeck interview, 36.

46 Nettelbeck interview, 36.

47 "In the Manor to Which They Are Accustomed," *Melody Maker*, January 22, 1972, 27.

48 "Experience of a Virgin," *Sennet* (London Student), February 27, 1974.

49 Nettelbeck interview, 37.

50 Cope, *Krautrocksampler*, 24.

51 "Virgin Success," *Music Week*, undated clipping, THA.

52 "Deleted: The LP that Was TOO Popular," *Melody Maker*, June 30, 1973.

53 Richard Williams, review of *The Faust Tapes*, *Melody Maker*, June 9, 1973.

54 Ian MacDonald, review of *The Faust Tapes*, *New Musical Express*, May 26, 1973.

55 MacDonald, "Krautrock: Germany Calling #3."

56 Ian MacDonald, "Common Market Rock," *New Musical Express*, April 28, 1973.

57 Nettelbeck interview, 35.

58 Ian MacDonald, "Faust: The Sound of the Eighties," *New Musical Express*, March 3, 1973.

59 MacDonald, "Faust: The Sound of the Eighties."

60 Dallas, "Faust and Foremost."

61 The quote is from my interview with Draper; he confirmed MacDonald's role in an email communication, June 19, 2014.

62 The following account draws on P. Philips, "Draper"; Draper, "Afterword"; Frodsham, "Professional Virgin"; and "Experience of a Virgin," *Sennet*.

63 Draper, "Afterword," 243.

64 White Noise has become something of a cult classic. Formed by South African David Vorhaus and British composers Delia Derbyshire and Brian Hodgson of the BBC's Radiophonic Workshop, White Noise released their debut, *An Electric Storm*, in 1969.

65 Peacock, "Tale of Two Virgins."

66 P. Philips, "Draper."

67 Peacock, "Tale of Two Virgins."

68 Peacock, "Tale of Two Virgins."

69 Branson, *Losing My Virginity*, 77; Peacock, "Tale of Two Virgins." On Branson's opportunistic business ethics and more, see Tom Bower, *Branson* (London: Fourth Estate, 2000).

70 Jean Fernandez (Barclay International) to Geoff Leigh, January 10, 1973, CCA.

71 Lebrun, "Faust."

72 This conversation was reconstructed by Leigh in my interviews with him.

73 Tim Hodgkinson, unpublished interview with Trond Einar Garmo, January 16, 1984, THA.

74 I've taken this dialogue from an interview with Henry Cow that appeared in a Rockenstock program on the Manor from 1973; the clip has been posted to YouTube: https://www.youtube.com/watch?v=u2wIUw9AW9k (accessed December 20, 2016).

75 "Experience of a Virgin," *Sennet*, 25.

76 Contract in THA.

77 Steve Lake, "HENRY COW: It Cud Not Happen to a Better Band!" *Melody Maker*, October 6, 1973.

78 Geoff Leigh, liner notes to *HCFABS*, 1:34.

79 Chris Cutler, Fred Frith, and Tim Hodgkinson, unpublished conversation, 1988, cassette, CCA.

80 I've taken this dialogue from my interview with Hodgkinson.

81 See, for example, Frith and Hodgkinson's comments in Kenneth Ansell, "Dissecting the Cow: An Almost Complete History of Henry Cow." *Impetus* 2 (June 1976): n.p.

82 Hodgkinson interview.

83 There are ten different takes edited together, which gave the piece half of its name.

84 P. Philips, "Draper." The phrase "a minor milestone in contemporary rock" is from an untitled clipping (from *Let It Rock*), THA.

85 Frodsham, "Professional Virgin."

86 Mike Oldfield, Tubular Bells program, Queen Elizabeth Hall, June 25, 1973, THA.

87 "Henry Cow," Virgin press release, n.d., THA.

88 Marcus O'Dair, *Different Every Time: The Authorized Biography of Robert Wyatt* (London: Serpent's Tail, 2014), 186–87.

89 "The Henry Cow File," *Melody Maker*, February 9, 1974.

90 The source of this information is the Tim Hodgkinson notebooks (THA), particularly his notes on the insurance policy some months later, and "The Henry Cow File."

91 *Darts* (University of Sheffield Union of Students), unsigned review of *Leg End*, by Henry Cow, October 1973; *South Westerner*, unsigned review of *Leg End*, by Henry Cow, October 6, 1973; Roger Blaikie, review of *Leg End*, by Henry Cow, *Cracker* 39, October 19, 1973; Steve Peacock, review of *Leg End*, by Henry Cow, *Sounds*, October 20, 1973; Nick Simmons, Review of *Leg End*, by Henry Cow, *King's News* (Cambridge), November 1973; *SINE Student Magazine*, unsigned review of *Leg End*, by Henry Cow, January 1974, clipping, FFA; William A. Murray, review of *Leg End*, by Henry Cow, *Time Out*, September 21, 1973.

92 Unsigned review of *Leg End*, by Henry Cow, *Morning Star*, November 6, 1973; see also Murray, review of *Leg End*; unsigned review of *Leg End*, by Henry Cow, *HiFi for Pleasure*, December 1973.

93 S. J. K., review of *Leg End*, by Henry Cow, *Coventry Evening Telegraph*, September 25, 1973.

94 H. K., review of *Leg End*, by Henry Cow, *Disc*, September 29, 1973.

95 Manfred Gillig, "The Henry Cow Legend," *Sounds* (Germany) 7 (1974): 48–49.

96 John Hoyland, review of *Leg End*, by Henry Cow, *Let It Rock*, November 1973.

97 Unsigned review of *Leg End*, by Henry Cow, *Records and Recording*, December 1973; Howell Llewellyn, review of *Leg End*, *Evening Echo*, undated clipping, THA; Fred Dellar, review of *Leg End*, by Henry Cow, *Hi-Fi News*, November 1973.

98 Ian MacDonald, review of *Leg End*, by Henry Cow, *New Musical Express*, September 22, 1973.

99 Steve Lake, review of *Leg End*, by Henry Cow, *Melody Maker*, September 22, 1973.

100 Lake, "HENRY COW."

101 Lake, "HENRY COW."

102 Lake, "HENRY COW."

103 Ian MacDonald, "Faust: Sturm und Drang and Scenes of Wild Abandon," *New Musical Express*, June 2, 1973.

104 They performed on March 1, 1973, and May 22, 1973; see "Keeping It Peel," BBC website, http://www.bbc.co.uk/radio1/johnpeel/artists/f/faust/ (accessed December 29, 2016). For a review of one London concert, see Karl Dallas, "Faust," *Melody Maker*, June 16, 1973.

105 Peron interview, 16.

106 It is quite likely that Faust did not actually play seventeen gigs; in at least one documented case, they bowed out of a concert in Wolverhampton. See Anthony Sawford, "Henry Cow," *Music Scene*, undated clipping, CCA.

107 Steve Lake reported PA problems in his review: "Faust/Henry Cow," *Melody Maker*, October 6, 1973.

108 Graupner interview.

109 Lake, "Faust/Henry Cow"; see also Ian MacDonald, "Faust: We're Just Trying to Be Here Now," *New Musical Express*, November 3, 1973.

110 On this topic, see also Howard Fielding, "Faust," *Sounds*, October 23, 1973.

111 Cope, *Krautrocksampler*, 26.

112 Cope, *Krautrocksampler*, 25.

113 Sawford, "Henry Cow"; Fielding, "Faust." In his account of the first time he saw Henry Cow in September 1973, Peter Blegvad noted that Frith "was as talented a comedian as he was a guitarist"; HCFABS, 1:36.

114 Sawford, "Henry Cow."

115 Leigh, liner notes to HCFABS, vol. 1.

116 Fred Frith, interviews with the author; and Hodgkinson to Ayerst, October 31, 1973, CAA.

117 The following account is based on my interviews with the band and its crew, but, more importantly, on a detailed setlist prepared by Frith for the event, written on the back of the program and still in his personal files, as well as Hodgkinson's own setlist for the same event.

118 David Gale, "Lumiere and Son," http://www.strengthweekly.com/lumiere-son/ (accessed August 2, 2014). Gale had attended the Royal College of Art film school with Afreda Benge, who was the romantic partner of Robert Wyatt. It is likely that Wyatt made the connection between Henry Cow and Lumiere and Son. I'm grateful to Hilary Westlake for clarifying this in an email of August 3, 2014.

119 Rose English, oral history interviews with Anna Dyke, 2005–6, British Library Sound collection.

120 There is more than one version of this story; in another, Peron offered to wear half his clothes in response to the threat of receiving only half their desired payment.

121 Simon Frith, "Ugly, Vulgar, Insulting—Zappa Scores!," *Let It Rock*, November 1973; Ian MacDonald, "Faust: Faust IV (Virgin)," *New Musical Express*, October 13, 1973.

122 Cutler, liner notes to *HCFABS*, 1:24.

123 Blegvad, liner notes to *HCFABS*, 1:36.

Chapter 3. Contentment Is Hopeless, Unrest Is Progress (1974)

1 Tim Hodgkinson to Caroline Ayerst, October 31, 1973, CAA.

2 Hodgkinson to Ayerst, November 5, 1973, CAA.

3 Henry Cow advertisement, *Melody Maker*, October 27, 1973.

4 Hodgkinson to Ayerst, November 21, 1973, CAA.

5 Hodgkinson to Ayerst, November 5, 1973.

6 Kenneth Ansell, "Dissecting the Cow: An Almost Complete History of Henry Cow," *Impetus* 2 (June 1976): n.p.

7 Hodgkinson to Ayerst, October 31, 1973. Cutler notes that in his own interpretation, the conclusion marked *nature*'s revolt.

8 Tim Hodgkinson Notebook 3, 1973, THA.

9 Hodgkinson to Ayerst, October 31, 1973.

10 I based this observation on Frith's sketches for the project.

11 Nicholas de Jongh, "The Tempest," *Guardian*, November 1, 1973.

12 Henk Weltevreden, interview with the author, March 29, 2016.

13 Steve Lake, "Henry Cow," *Melody Maker*, December 29, 1973. See also a brief mention in Chris Welch, "The Year of Pop," *Melody Maker*, December 29, 1973. Another profile appeared in the German *Sounds*: Doug Case, "Henry Cow," *Sounds* 5, no. 11 (1973): 31–32.

14 "The Henry Cow File," *Melody Maker*, February 9, 1974.

15 Steve Lake, "Chris Cutler," *Melody Maker*, March 30, 1974.

16 Ian MacDonald, review of Camel, Henry Cow, Global Village Trucking Company, and Gong, *Live at Dingwall's Dance Hall*, *New Musical Express*, March 23, 1974.

17 Some notes in Hodgkinson's journal indicate that Henry Cow might have been considering an invitation to Ritual Theatre to appear on the Explorer's Club series.

18 Ansell, "Dissecting the Cow."

19 For this biographical text, I am relying on Sally Potter, interview with the author, April 27, 2012; Lindsay Cooper, oral history interviews with Val Wilmer, July 14, 1992, Oral History of Jazz in Britain, British Library; Mandy Merck, interview with the author, May 6, 2012; Dale Smoak, "Lindsay Cooper Interview," *Cadence* 16 (1990): 5–10; "A Young Lady's Vision: Lindsay Cooper," *Bad Alchemy* 2 (1985): 13–21; and Lindsay Cooper, *The Road Is Wider Than Long: Travels with MS*, unpublished manuscript, LCA; Clive Bell, interview with the author, April 15, 2012; and Colin Wood, interview with the author, May 3, 2012; Lindsay Cooper, datebooks, LCA.

20 Cooper, *Road Is Wider Than Long*, n.p.

21 Cooper, *Road Is Wider Than Long*, n.p.

22 Cooper oral history.

23 "Henry Cow File"; on Comus, see Jeanette Leech, *Seasons They Change: The Story of Acid and Psychedelic Folk* (London: Jawbone, 2010), 127–30.

24 On Nicols, see Maggie Nichols [Nicols], "The Strength of Tomorrow," in *'68, '78, '88: From Women's Liberation to Feminism*, ed. Amanda Sebestyen (Bridport, UK: Prism Press, 1988), 175–84.

25 Lindsay Cooper and Dagmar Krause, "Talking till the Henry Cow Comes Home," interview with Malcolm Heyhoe and Irena Krumb, *Liquorice*, June 1976, 9.

26 Cooper oral history.

27 Cooper oral history. Though limited, a feminist discourse was emerging in the mainstream British rock press, much of it coming from Yoko Ono. For example, see Michael Watts, "Lady of Pain," *Melody Maker*, January 27, 1973, 28–29; and Loraine Alterman, "YOKO: How I Rescued John from Chauvinism," *Melody Maker*, September 22, 1973. See also a three-page spread on women in rock, called "Dialogue," in *Melody Maker*, November 10, 1973.

28 Smoak, "Lindsay Cooper Interview," 7.

29 To this day, the Cows wince when they hear the flubs sprinkled throughout the recording.

30 Chris Cutler, untitled notes on *Unrest*, n.d., n.p., CCA.

31 Simon Draper, quoted in "Experience of a Virgin," *Sennet* (*London Student*), February 27, 1974.

32 Cutler, untitled notes on *Unrest*.

33 Cutler, untitled notes on *Unrest*.

34 Cutler, untitled notes on *Unrest*.

35 Mike Barnes, *Captain Beefheart: The Biography* (London: Omnibus Press, 2000).

36 Steve Ingham, review of Captain Beefheart concert, Leeds, UK, *Contact* 9 (autumn 1974): 26–28.

37 Steve Lake, "Milking the Cow," *Melody Maker*, June 22, 1974.

38 Chris Cutler, Fred Frith, and Tim Hodgkinson, unpublished conversation, 1988, cassette, CCA.

39 Lake, "Milking the Cow."

40 Cutler, in *HCFABS*, 1:25

41 Ansell, "Dissecting the Cow," n.p.

42 Cutler, in *HCFABS*, 2:13.

43 For this summary, I am drawing on reviews in the following sources, some undated clippings: n.a., *Darts* [Sheffield], n.d., FFA; Steve Lake in *Melody Maker*, June 15, 1974; Barry Levine in *Morning Star* (London), June 25, 1974; n.a., *Hifi for Pleasure*, August 1974; n.a., *Records and Recording*, August 1974; Jenny Dawson in *Stratford Express*, June 29, 1974; Carl Anthony in *Audio*, August 1974; n.a. in [Glasgow] *Sunday Mail*, (Glasgow), July 28, 1974; S. W., in *Derby Evening Telegraph*, June 12, 1974; n.a. in *Record and Radio Mirror*, June 29, 1974; n.a. in *South Wales Echo*, (Cardiff), July 6, 1974; Rick Peckham in *The Mid Sussex Times*, June 13, 1974; n.a. in *Times*, n.d.; John Sivyer in *Watford Observer*, July 9, 1974; n.a., "For Minority Tastes," *Blackpool Gazette and Herald*, June 28, 1974; Ian MacDonald in *New Musical Express*,

June 8, 1974; Howell Llewellyn in *Evening Echo Southend*, July 1974; Keith Altham in *Look Now*, August 1974; n.a. in *Malvern Gazette*, n.d.; n.a. in *Oxford Review*, June 15, 1974; Steve Peacock, in *Sounds*, July 13, 1974.

44 Sivyer, review of *Unrest*.

45 *Records and Recording*, unsigned review of *Unrest*.

46 "For Minority Tastes."

47 Sivyer, review of *Unrest*.

48 *Records and Recording*, unsigned review of *Unrest*.

49 Levine, review of *Unrest*.

50 Lake, review of *Unrest*

51 Neil Spencer, "Triumphal Re-entry of the Magic Gladiators," *New Musical Express*, June 15, 1974. Spencer's comments clearly irked Henry Cow: Hodgkinson copied them out verbatim into his notebook for further processing.

52 Chris Cutler, letter to the editor, *New Musical Express*, June 29, 1974.

53 Charles Shaar Murray, "Gerroff an' Milk It," *New Musical Express*, August 31, 1974, 8.

54 Lake, "Milking the Cow."

55 Spencer, "Triumphal Re-entry."

56 Fred Frith, "Great Rock Solos of Our Time," *New Musical Express*, October 12, 1974.

57 Frith, "Great Rock Solos," October 12, 1974.

58 Frith, "Great Rock Solos of Our Time," *New Musical Express*, October 19, 1974.

59 Frith, "Great Rock Solos of Our Time," *New Musical Express*, December 14, 1974.

60 On Vorhaus, see David Ellis, "David Vorhaus and Kaleidophon Studio," *Electronics and Music Maker*, June 1981, 74–76.

61 "No Birds" was the final line in a Captain Beefheart poem that was printed on the back of *Mirror Man* (it was also a line from "Beautiful as the Moon"). Frith gave a copy of *Guitar Solos* to Captain Beefheart when he saw him in Paris in 1975; John French, Beefheart's longtime drummer, later told Frith that Beefheart had handed the album to him and said, "Check it out—he's ripping me off."

62 For more on the production, see Bill Milkowski, "The Frith Factor: Exploration in Sound," *Down Beat* 50, no. 1 (January 1983): 22–25, 61.

63 Charles Shaar Murray, review of *Guitar Solos*, *New Musical Express*, November 30, 1974, 22–23. See also Steve Lake, review of *Guitar Solos*, *Melody Maker*, February 22, 1975, 42.

64 Cutler, Frith, and Hodgkinson conversation.

65 A jotting in one of Hodgkinson's notebooks specifies the date September 1, which, if it wasn't the date of the expulsion, was perhaps the date Cooper fell off the Cow payroll (such as it was).

66 Ansell, "Dissecting the Cow," n.p.

67 Ansell, "Dissecting the Cow," n.p.

68 Ansell, "Dissecting the Cow," n.p.

69 I am summarizing notes in Notebook 6, a document titled "notes to be considered," and an untitled document in the THA. The three sources are different drafts working with the summarized ideas.

70 Stanley Cavell, *Pursuits of Happiness: The Hollywood Comedy of Remarriage* (Cambridge, Mass.: Harvard University Press, 1981), 177.

71 Lake, "Milking the Cow."

72 Shaar Murray, "Gerroff an' Milk It."

73 Kenneth Ansell, "Fred Frith: Balancing the Axe," *Wire* 6 (1984): 23–26.

74 Ansell, "Dissecting the Cow," n.p.

75 In February 1976, Dave Laing reported that a new Frith work for a twenty-person orchestra was slated for an April premiere; Dave Laing, "In Praise of Henry Cow," *Sounds*, February 6, 1976.

76 Cutler, Frith, and Hodgkinson conversation.

Chapter 4. Death to the Individual: Slapp Happy (1974–75)

1 Werner Sillescu, "Vom Protestsong zum Soul," *Hamburger Abendblatt*, February 12, 1967.

2 "City Preachers machen lustig weiter," *Hamburger Abendblatt*, January 28, 1969.

3 Crone provides a curriculum vitae of sorts in Rainer Crone, "What Andy Warhol Really Did," *New York Review of Books*, February 25, 2010.

4 Peter Blegvad, "The Bleaching Stream," interview with Kevin Jackson, *Journal of the London Institute of 'Pataphysics* 3 (September 2011): 21.

5 Blegvad, "Bleaching Stream," 16–17.

6 Blegvad, "Bleaching Stream," 22.

7 Blegvad, "Bleaching Stream," 22.

8 Blegvad, "Bleaching Stream," 23.

9 Ian MacDonald, "Slapp Happy: Sort Of," *New Musical Express*, April 14, 1973.

10 Lindsay Cooper and Dagmar Krause, "Talking till the Henry Cow Comes Home," interview with Malcolm Heyhoe and Irena Krumb, *Liquorice*, June 1976, 5.

11 Blegvad, quoted in "The Bleaching Stream," 36.

12 Blegvad, "Bleaching Stream," 36.

13 Steve Lake, "Happy Trails," *Melody Maker*, May 11, 1974.

14 Peter Erskine, "We're Definitely not the Kind of Thing That'd Interest Readers of *NME*," *New Musical Express*, October 26, 1974.

15 James Johnson, "Blatant Eccentrics Get Record Deal," *New Musical Express*, June 8, 1974.

16 Lake, "Happy Trails."

17 Ed Pinsent, "Numinous Objects: An Interview with Peter Blegvad of Slapp Happy," *Sound Projector* 8 (2000): 16–18, at 18.

18 Johnson, "Blatant Eccentrics Get Record Deal."

19 Erskine, "We're Definitely not the Kind of Thing That'd Interest Readers of *NME*."

20 Erskine, "We're Definitely not the Kind of Thing That'd Interest Readers of *NME*."

21 Kenneth Ansell, "Dissecting the Cow: An Almost Complete History of Henry Cow," *Impetus* 2 (June 1976): n.p.

22 Ansell, "Dissecting the Cow."

23 Ansell, "Dissecting the Cow."

24 Tim Hodgkinson, Notebook 4, 1974–75, n.p.

25 Peter Blegvad, 1974 notebook, n.p., PBA. The brackets and additions in bold are in Cutler's hand.

26 Steve Lake, review of *Desperate Straights*, by Slapp Happy / Henry Cow, *Melody Maker*, March 8, 1975.

27 *Slapp Happy / Henry Cow* promotional booklet, 1975, 2, THA.

28 Lindsay Cooper and Dagmar Krause, "Talking till the Henry Cow Comes Home," interview with Malcolm Heyhoe and Irena Krumb, *Liquorice*, June 1976, 8–9.

29 Kenneth Ansell, "Henry Cow," *Impetus* 9 (1979): 377.

30 *Slapp Happy / Henry Cow* promotional booklet, 1975, 4, THA.

31 This paragraph was quoted in more than one press account of the album at the time.

32 *Slapp Happy / Henry Cow* promotional booklet, 1975, 3, THA.

33 Steve Lake, "How Now, Henry Cow?" *Melody Maker*, April 5, 1975.

34 Robin Denselow, review of *Desperate Straights*, by Slapp Happy / Henry Cow, *Guardian*, April 1, 1975.

35 Pete Erskine, review of *Desperate Straights*, by Slapp Happy / Henry Cow, *New Musical Express*, February 22, 1975.

36 Lake, review of *Desperate Straights*.

37 Peter Blegvad Notebook 1974, n.p., PBA. Although these notes appear on a page that contains the first draft of Blegvad's "Apricot" (later set and recorded on *Kew. Rhone.*), they closely match the themes that Hodgkinson eventually elaborated in "Beast," which suggests to me an unlikely shared provenance for these two compositions.

38 Blegvad Notebook 1974, n.p., PBA.

39 Angus Mackinnon, "Tiptoeing through the Cow/Slapps," *Sounds*, May 3, 1975, 40.

40 Hodgkinson, quoted in [Gerard Nguyen], "Atem Raconte l'Histoire (presque) Complete de Henry Cow," *Atem*, September 15, 1976, 19.

41 Tim Hodgkinson Notebook 6, 1974, n.p., THA.

42 Hodgkinson Notebook 6, n.p.

43 George Steiner, *Language and Silence: Essays on Language, Literature, and the Inhuman* (New Haven, CT: Yale University Press, 1967), 345. In this passage, Steiner is actually referring to the socialist realism of Stalin, which Hodgkinson understands to be the same kind of authoritarian regime as advanced capitalism in Western Europe.

44 Steiner, *Language and Silence*, 27.

45 I draw on clarifications made in Chris Cutler, unpublished interview with Trond Garmo, London, January 19, 1984.

46 She was not coming back as a permanent member at this time. In his Notebook 4, Hodgkinson noted on March 25 (i.e., after recording *In Praise of Learning*) that they needed to take some instruments off of the band's insurance policy in preparation for their upcoming tours. Among them was Cooper's oboe.

47 Her diary indicates that she was at the Manor February 20–23 and February 25–March 2, LCA.

48 Lindsay Cooper, interviewed by anonymous journalist, London Musicians Collective, January 14, 1982, British Library, Michael Gerzon Collection, C236/1566.

49 They definitely planned to tour together: Chris Wangro possesses a poster advertising a gig (that never took place) for both Slapp Happy and Henry Cow on May 23, 1975, at Rasa in Utrecht. The Cow would eventually play this date on their own.

50 Blegvad, "Bleaching Stream," 41.

51 Blegvad, "Bleaching Stream," 44.

52 [Nguyen], "Atem Raconte l'Histoire." This history of the band was essentially reprinted from Kenneth Ansell's series in *ZigZag* and *Impetus*, but it interpolated material that apparently came from a new interview with Hodgkinson.

53 Cooper and Krause, "Talking," 6.

54 News of the split was announced in *Melody Maker*, April 19, 1975. See also "Moore of the Same," *Disc*, August 16, 1975; Kate Phillips, "Johnny's Dead," *New Musical Express*, August 16, 1975.

55 Peter Erskine, "Annals of Excess," *New Musical Express*, June 7, 1975.

Chapter 5. Europa (1975–76)

1 Steve Lake, "How Now, Henry Cow?" *Melody Maker*, April 5, 1975.

2 Kenneth Ansell, "Henry Cow," *Impetus* 9 (1979): 377.

3 Lake, "How Now, Henry Cow?"

4 Tim Hodgkinson Notebook 6, n.p., THA.

5 Kenneth Ansell, "Dissecting the Cow: An Almost Complete History of Henry Cow," *Impetus* 2 (June 1976): n.p.

6 Kate Phillips, "Watching the Trains Go By," interview with Dagmar Krause, *New Musical Express*, July 19, 1975.

7 Angus MacKinnon, "Tiptoeing through the Cow/Slapps," *Sounds*, May 3, 1975. See also "Henry Cow: Serieuze en boeiende muziek," source unknown, likely May 1975; clipping in THA.

8 Lindsay Cooper to Mandy Merck, December 2, 1975, MMA.

9 Chris Cutler, Fred Frith, and Tim Hodgkinson, unpublished conversation, 1988, cassette, CCA.

10 In one musician's sketchbook appear lyric ideas on the theme: "China, China you've been our light / don't lose your sight now / don't lose the fight."

11 Tim Hodgkinson, draft introduction to *The Henry Cow Book*, THA.

12 Henry Cow meeting minutes, Notebook 1, November 1, 1975, St. Pargoire, France, THA.

13 Reprinted in Chris Cutler and Tim Hodgkinson, eds., *The Henry Cow Book, 1968–78* (London: self-published, 1981), 56.

14 Written in Fred Frith, 1975 datebook, FFA.

15 Cutler and Hodgkinson, *Henry Cow Book*.

16 John Fordham, "Not with a Mirror . . . but a Hammer," *Time Out*, January 30–February 5, 1976, 11.

17 Ansell, "Dissecting the Cow," n.p.

18 Chris Cutler, interview with Derek Jewell, BBC Radio 3, ["mid-1975"], transcript. I am grateful to Trond Einar Garmo for sharing this document with me.

19 Fordham, "Not with a Mirror," 11.

20 Fordham, "Not with a Mirror," 11.

21 [Gerard, Nguyen], "Atem Raconte l'Histoire (presque) Complete de Henry Cow," *Atem*, September 15, 1976, 20, translation by Andrew Zhou.

22 Dave Laing, "In Praise of Henry Cow," *Sounds*, February 7, 1976, 44.

23 "Who Buys Records by John Denver, Charles Aznavour, and Peters and Less?," *Melody Maker*, November 16, 1974, 26–28.

24 "Who Buys Records," 28.

25 Fordham, "Not with a Mirror," 11.

26 Ansell, "Dissecting the Cow," n.p.

27 I am grateful to Nuala Sheehan for sharing these details of Clarke's life with me.

28 Tim Hodgkinson, Notebook 5, 1975–76, n.p., THA, and subsequent meeting minutes.

29 David Brown, "How 'Botticelli's Angel' Went from Shock Album Cover to Movie Extra," *Times* (London), March 1, 2014.

30 I am basing this list on a live recording of the Rome concert.

31 Charles Shaar Murray, "The Roman Spring of Mr. Wyatt," *New Musical Express*, July 19, 1975.

32 Chris Cutler, in liner notes to HCFABS, 1:27.

33 See Alain Pons, "Wyatt and Cow," *Best*, June 1975, 18; and Pierre Lattès, "Mechamment Rock," *Charlie Hebdo*, May 15, 1975, 15.

34 John Fordham, "Above the Herd," *Time Out*, May 30–June 5, 1975, 9.

35 Fordham, "Not with a Mirror," 10; see also Angus Mackinnon, "Robert Wyatt," *Sounds*, May 31, 1975.

36 In the Henry Cow 40th Anniversary CD Box Set, Cutler has included an impressive chronology of Cow gigs, but it is, as he notes, incomplete. In my own study of the band's accounts and various member datebooks, I've determined that the chronology is the least accurate for the gigs from the second half of 1975. If the band performed in any cities beyond those I've listed in the text, then they were not paid for them, or the extremely careful Hodgkinson made some omissions in the accounting. I've done my best to correct where I can in the text, but there are doubtless still concerts that have slipped through the cracks.

37 Maggie Thomas, email communication with the author, June 24, 2015.

38 Archie Patterson, "Georgio Gomelsky Interview," in *Eurock: Music and Second Culture Post Millennium* (Portland, OR: Eurock Publications, 2013), 14–31.

39 Roman Waschko, "Rome Concert by Lou Reed Results in Riot, Injuries," *Billboard*, March 1, 1975, 4, 49.

40 [Nguyen], "Atem Raconte l'Histoire," 19; my translation from the French.

41 Charles Shaar Murray, "Robert Wyatt, Henry Cow," *New Musical Express*, July 19, 1975.

42 Lindsay Cooper to Alison and Lew Cooper, June 28, 1975, LCA.

43 Marcus O'Dair, *Different Every Time: The Authorized Biography of Robert Wyatt* (London: Serpent's Tail, 2014), 225.

44 Shaar Murray, "Robert Wyatt, Henry Cow."

45 It is possible that they played here and there for nothing more than a meal, but Hodgkinson's meticulous bookkeeping shows no income from concerts between the Rome gig and Magliana on the 12th.

46 Lindsay Cooper to Alison and Lew Cooper, July 11, 1975, LCA.

47 John Greaves discusses this event in Peter Blegvad, ed., *Kew. Rhone* (Axminster, UK: Uniformbooks, 2014), 116.

48 Balchin's subsequent career as a live sound engineer for This Heat, The Swans, Laibach, and Test Department garnered him a reputation as a very loud mixer. See Byron Coley, "This Heat: Head Birth in the Year Zero," Rock's Back Pages, December 2015, http://www.rocksbackpages.com/Library/Article/this-heat-head-birth-in -the-year-zero (accessed December 19, 2016).

49 Pierpaolo Antonello and Alan O'Leary, introduction to *Imagining Terrorism: The Rhetoric and Representation of Political Violence in Italy, 1969–2009*, ed. Pierpaolo Antonello and Alan O'Leary (London: Legenda, 2009), 1.

50 Donald Sassoon, *Contemporary Italy: Economy, Society and Politics, since 1945*, 2nd ed. (London: Longman, 1997).

51 Umberto Fiori, "Rock Music and Politics in Italy," *Popular Music* 4 (1984): 261–77.

52 Fiori, "Rock Music"; Gianmario Borio, "Key Questions of Antagonistic Music Making: A View from Italy," in *Red Strains: Music and Communism Outside the Communist Bloc*, edited by Robert Adlington (London: The British Academy and Oxford University Press, 2013); and Franco Fabbri, "Orchestral Manoevres in the 1970s: L'Orchestra Co-Operative, 1978–1983," *Popular Music* 26, no. 3 (2007): 409–27.

53 Borio, "Key Questions"; see also Paul Bompard, "Top Italian Promoter Sees Hope for Rock," *Billboard*, April 2, 1977, 60.

54 Fiori, "Rock Music," 265.

55 Lindsay Cooper and Dagmar Krause, "Talking till the Henry Cow Comes Home," interview with Malcolm Heyhoe and Irena Krumb, *Liquorice*, June 1976, 7.

56 Neil Sandford, "You Couldn't Make It Up: Life on the Road in the 1970s," n.d., unpublished memoir. Thank you to Neil for sharing this document with me.

57 Lindsay Cooper to Mandy Merck, February 21, 1977, MMA.

58 Fabbri, "Orchestral Manoevres," 419.

59 Lindsay Cooper, *The Road Is Wider Than Long: Travels with MS*, unpublished memoir, n.d., LCA.

60 Steve Lake, review of *In Praise of Learning*, by Henry Cow, *Melody Maker*, July 5, 1975.

61 Ian MacDonald, review of *In Praise of Learning*, by Henry Cow, *New Musical Express*, June 7, 1975.

62 Angus MacKinnon, review of *In Praise of Learning*, by Henry Cow, *Sounds*, May 31, 1975.

63 Dave Laing, review of *In Praise of Learning*, by Henry Cow, *Let It Rock*, September 1975.

64 Cooper recorded this as June 2 in her datebook, LCA.

65 Cutler, Frith, and Hodgkinson, unpublished conversation.

66 On Pink Floyd's possible involvement, see "Floyd: Dune to Work!," *Melody Maker*, January 24, 1976, 10. David Lynch resuscitated the project some years later, but his *Dune* (1984) bore little relation to Jodorowsky's vision.

67 Chris Cutler, "Magic Magma," *Sound International*, May 1979, 13.

68 Steve Lake, "Parlez Vous Magma?" *Melody Maker*, December 15, 1973.

69 Cutler, "Magma Magic." Cutler is well aware of the reasons for the widespread distrust of Magma's politics; he simply does not hear the music to be communicating those political values.

70 Hervé Picart, "L'énigme Henry Cow," *Best*, August 1975, 22; "Magma / Hervé Picart, une 'joute' mémorable . . . ," *Best*, October 1975, available at http://robert.guillerault.free.fr/magma/textes/1975/best_87.htm.

71 Here I am summarizing the conversation as it was recorded by Cooper in the Henry Cow meeting minutes, Notebook 1, October 22, 1975, Paris, France, THA. Direct quotes are taken from these pages, with abbreviations spelled out and grammar filled in.

72 Fred Frith Musical Notebook 1, 1975–76, FFA.

73 "Taking Off," *Melody Maker*, December 6, 1975.

74 Frith shared his intentions in Ansell, "Dissecting the Cow," and in Laing, "In Praise of Henry Cow."

75 Miles, "Henry Cow," *New Musical Express*, February 7, 1976; Ian Adams, "Henry Cow," *Sounds*, December 13, 1975, 34.

76 John Greaves, liner notes to HCFABS, 1:19.

77 Hodgkinson, draft introduction for *The Henry Cow Book*.

78 Hodgkinson, draft introduction for *The Henry Cow Book*.

79 On *Kew. Rhone.*, see Blegvad, *Kew. Rhone.*

Chapter 6. The Roads Leading to Rome (1976–77)

1 Chris Cutler and Tim Hodgkinson, eds., *The Henry Cow Book, 1968–78* (London: self-published, 1981), 51.

2 In the summer of 1976, Krause told an interviewer that she and Cooper were considering setting Morgan's poetry to music; see Lindsay Cooper and Dagmar Krause, "Talking till the Henry Cow Comes Home," interview with Malcolm Heyhoe and Irena Krumb, *Liquorice*, June 1976, 4.

3   Cutler and Hodgkinson, *Henry Cow Book,* 98. See A S-W, "Vill fönya, förändra," *Upsala Nya Tidning* (Uppsala, Sweden), May 20, 1976; Sivert Bramstedt, "Engelska Henry Cow blev röriga på scen," *Dagens Nyheter* (Stockholm), May 21, 1976. Markku Tuuli, "Henry Cow: Etsii Vaihtoehtoja," *Katso* (Finland), May 9, 1976, was written before the band actually left London, and includes no information about their performances in Finland.

4   Chris Cutler, unpublished interview with Nick Wilton, October 20, 1980; I am grateful to Trond Einar Garmo for sharing this transcript with me.

5   John Fordham, "Not with a Mirror . . . but a Hammer," *Time Out,* January 31, 1976, 10.

6   Tim Hodgkinson, unpublished interview with Trond Einar Garmo, January 16, 1984, typescript in THA.

7   Hodgkinson interview.

8   Cutler interview.

9   Fred Frith to Nick Wilton, January 6, 1981. I am grateful to Trond Einar Garmo for sharing a copy of this letter with me.

10 Tim Hodgkinson notebook 7, 1975–76, n.p.

11 Fordham, "Not with a Mirror," 10.

12 See Gary Peters, *The Philosophy of Improvisation* (Chicago, IL: University of Chicago Press, 2009), especially chapter 2.

13 George E. Lewis, "Improvised Music after 1950: Afrological and Eurological Perspectives," in *The Other Side of Nowhere: Jazz, Improvisation, and Communities in Dialogue,* ed. Daniel Fischlin and Ajay Heble, 131–62 (Middletown, CT: Wesleyan University Press, 2004); originally published in 1996.

14 James Snead, "On Repetition in Black Culture," *Black American Literature Forum* 15, no. 4 (winter 1981): 146–54.

15 Lewis, "Improvised Music after 1950," 150.

16 Lewis, "Improvised Music after 1950," 150.

17 Cutler interview.

18 Lewis, "Improvised Music after 1950," 157.

19 For more on music and social mediation in improvised contexts, see Georgina Born, "After Relational Aesthetics: Improvised Music, the Social, and (Re)Theorizing the Aesthetic," in *Improvisation and Social Aesthetics,* edited by Georgina Born, Eric Lewis, and Will Straw, 33–58 (Durham, NC: Duke University Press, 2017).

20 Michel Pêcheux, *Language, Semantics, and Ideology* (New York: St. Martin's, 1982).

21 José Esteban Muñoz, *Disidentifications: Queers of Color and the Performance of Politics* (Minneapolis: University of Minnesota Press, 1999), 12.

22 Tim Hodgkinson, draft introduction to *The Henry Cow Book,* THA.

23 Cutler, liner notes to HCFABS, 1:9. One might quibble with the phrase "without conflict," since the staging of musical conflict was something that Henry Cow excelled at, as Cutler himself writes in HCFABS, 1:9. We will return to this idea later in the chapter.

24 Patrick Wright, "Resist Me. Make Me Strong," *Guardian Weekend,* November 11, 1995, 41.

25 Wright, "Resist Me," 41.

26 George E. Lewis, *A Power Stronger Than Itself: The AACM and American Experimental Music* (Chicago, IL: University of Chicago Press, 2008); see also Tim Lawrence, "Pluralism, Minor Deviations, and Radical Change: The Challenge to Experimental Music in Downtown New York, 1971–85," in *Tomorrow Is the Question: New Directions in Experimental Music Studies*, ed. Benjamin Piekut (Ann Arbor: University of Michigan Press, 2014), 63–85.

27 Lewis, "Improvised Music after 1950," 149.

28 Fred Moten, *In the Break: The Aesthetics of the Black Radical Tradition* (Minneapolis: University of Minnesota Press, 2003).

29 Fred Moten, "Blackness and Nothingness (Mysticism in the Flesh)," *South Atlantic Quarterly* 112, no. 4 (fall 2013): 737–80; thanks to Marcus Boon for pointing me to this text.

30 Moten, "Blackness and Nothingness," 749.

31 See Tracy McMullen, "Subject, Object, Improv: John Cage, Pauline Oliveros, and Eastern (Western) Philosophy in Music," *Critical Studies in Improvisation / Études critiques en improvisation* 6, no. 2 (2010), http://www.criticalimprov.com/article /view/851/1918 (accessed June 29, 2017); see also Vijay Iyer, "Exploding the Narrative in Jazz Improvisation," in *Uptown Conversation: The New Jazz Studies*, edited by Robert G. O'Meally, Brent Hayes Edwards, and Farah Jasmine Griffin (New York: Columbia University Press, 2004), 393–403.

32 Nahum Dimitri Chandler, "Originary Displacement," *boundary 2* 27, no. 3 (2000): 249–86. I am grateful to Fumi Okiji for directing me to this essay and for explicating its stakes in her wonderful chapter, "Double Consciousness and the Critical Potential of Black Expression," in *Jazz as Critique: Adorno and Black Expression Revisited* (Stanford, CA: Stanford University Press, 2018).

33 For this biographical sketch, I am drawing on my own interview with Beresford, as well as Jon C. Morgan, "Steve Beresford Signals for Tea," *Coda* 286 (1999): 16–19; and Julian Cowley, "Game for a Laugh," interview with Steve Beresford, *Wire* 218 (2002): 24–29.

34 [Gerard Nguyen], "Lindsay Cooper," *Atem* 12 (April 1978): 19.

35 Georgina Born, liner notes to *HCFABS*, 2:33–34.

36 For her part, Born has expressed the opinion that the band as a whole didn't groove, owing partially to Cutler's drumming. She later recalled feeling the absence of African American musical aesthetics in Henry Cow's music; see Georgina Born, "On Music and Politics: Henry Cow, Avant-Gardism and Its Discontents," in *Red Strains: Music and Communism Outside the Communist Bloc*, edited by Robert Adlington (Oxford: Oxford University Press, 2013), 57.

37 Yoel Schwarcz, interview with Easy Livin, May 2006, Prog Archives, http://www .progarchives.com/forum/forum_posts.asp?TID=23236 (accessed August 18. 2016).

38 A parametric EQ allows the sound engineer to sweep through a frequency range— say, 400 to 2,000 hertz—and boost or attenuate specific bands of varying size; it

helps a technical listener to sculpt the sound in much more flexible way than a regular EQ would allow.

39 Kenneth Ansell, "Dissecting the Cow: An Almost Complete History of Henry Cow," *Impetus* 2 (June 1976): n.p.

40 This description of the company draws from Holm's writing at the Compendium Records website, compendiumrecords.wordpress.com, accessed June 8, 2016.

41 Dave Laing, review of *Concerts,* by Henry Cow, *Sounds,* June 19, 1976; Steve Lake, review of *Concerts,* by Henry Cow, *Melody Maker,* September 11, 1976; Robert Kainer, review of *Concerts,* by Henry Cow, *The Lamb* 11 (1977); Miles, review of *Concerts,* by Henry Cow, *New Musical Express,* August 7, 1976; Scott Isler, review of *Concerts,* by Henry Cow, *Trouser Press,* October–November 1976, 32. Clipping files for the band also contain reviews from Norway, Sweden, and Italy.

42 Simon Frith, "Punk—Hippies with Short Hair," *Leveller,* November 1977, 20–21, at 22.

43 "'I'm Broke' Says 'Bells' Producer," *Disc,* March 22, 1975.

44 Henry Cow announced Born's joining in a press release on July 27; Virgin Information, "Henry Cow New Member and Plans," CCA.

45 Steve Lake, review of *Guitar Solos 2,* by Fred Frith, *Melody Maker,* July 31, 1976.

46 The Raver, *Melody Maker,* December 8, 1973; "Udder News," *Melody Maker,* January 5, 1974, 10. For Frith's response, see Fred Frith, letter to the editor, *Melody Maker,* August 14, 1976. Frith continued to be bothered by what I would call "genre-based sniping." For example, following a profile in *Down Beat* in January, 1983, a reader wrote in to say that all Frith's "innovations" had been pioneered by Bailey and Keith Rowe, two figures "unknown to the world of fringe rock fashions." For jazz loyalists like this one, the big dumb rock stars (even the fringe ones) could only ever steal from "the *real* innovators on guitar." See Giancarlo Tantini, letter to the editor, *Down Beat,* April 1983, 9.

47 Fred Frith, grant application, April 18, 1976, Arts Council of Great Britain, Music Panel, Jazz Sub-committee, AC 51/91 2/1.

48 Arts Council of Great Britain, Music Panel, Jazz Sub-committee, minutes, 16th meeting, June 12, 1973. ACGB 51/91 1/3.

49 Arts Council of Great Britain, Music Panel, Jazz Sub-committee, minutes, 27th meeting, May 5, 1976, ACGB 51/91 2/1.

50 Although Born thinks that her first gig with Henry Cow was at Vevey on August 25, Frith recorded in his diary that there were "not many people" at the gig in York; since they'd been there the whole week rehearsing, my guess is that Born is misremembering the concert itself as another rehearsal. Sula Goschen did not drive on this tour; those duties were taken over by Nigel Brown.

51 Lindsay Cooper to Mandy Merck, December 20, 1976, MMA.

52 Malcolm Heyhoe, "Henry Cow," *New Musical Express,* March 12, 1977, 52.

53 Lindsay Cooper to Ms/r Cooper, September 22, 1976, LCA.

54 Chris Cutler, Fred Frith, and Tim Hodgkinson, unpublished conversation, 1988, cassette, CCA.

55 Skepticism and denunciation of the Stones as hedonistic capitalists was not unknown at the time—see Dave Laing, "Radicals to Reactionaries?," *Let It Rock*, November 1973, 37–38.

56 Fordham, "Not with a Mirror," 10–11.

57 Georgina Born, liner notes to HCFABS, 2:38.

58 As Paul Steinbeck has shown, the Art Ensemble of Chicago operated by consensus with greater success, which also distinguished them from their fellow bands in the AACM; Paul Steinbeck, *A Message to Our Folks: The Art Ensemble of Chicago* (Chicago, IL: University of Chicago Press, 2017), 162–63.

59 Hodgkinson, draft introduction.

60 Born, liner notes to HCFABS, 2:39.

61 Cutler, Frith, and Hodgkinson, unpublished conversation.

62 Hodgkinson, draft introduction.

63 Hodgkinson, draft introduction.

64 Lindsay Cooper to Mandu Merck, November 30, 1976, MMA.

65 This moment can be heard on HCFABS, vol. 7, "Chaumont 1," at 2:20.

66 Tim Hodgkinson, "[The Whithering (*sic*) of Other Sspects of Life]," unpublished notes, [1981?], THA.

67 Born, liner notes to HCFABS, 2:39.

68 The line is from "Maze," which began its life as a Henry Cow tune but ended up as one by the Art Bears.

69 Miles, "Henry Cow: Southend," *New Musical Express*, November 13, 1976.

70 Dale Smoak, "Lindsay Cooper Interview," *Cadence* 16 (1990): 6. She would later add the sopranino, too.

71 Frith to Wilton, October 16, 1981.

72 Andrew Pickering, *The Cybernetic Brain: Sketches of Another Future* (Chicago, IL: University of Chicago Press, 2009), 139.

73 Hodgkinson interview.

74 Lydia Goehr, "Improvising *Impromptu*, or, What to Do with a Broken String," in *The Oxford Handbook of Critical Improvisation Studies*, ed. George E. Lewis and Benjamin Piekut(New York: Oxford University Press, 2106), 1:458–80.

75 Pickering, *Cybernetic Brain*, 139.

76 For the following brief sketch, I am relying on my interview with Hobbs, an interview with Cutler in the liner notes to HCFABS; a letter from Hobbs to Hodgkinson, November 3, 1976, THA; and Henry Cow meeting minutes from autumn 1976 through spring 1977.

77 Nick Hobbs, liner notes to HCFABS, 2:30.

78 Lindsay Cooper to Alison and Lew Cooper, May 4, 1977, LCA.

79 Lindsay Cooper to Mandy Merck, May 6, 1977, MMA.

80 Lindsay Cooper to Mandy Merck, March 23, 1977, MMA.

81 Jeremy Baines, interview with Aymeric Leroy, n.d. I am grateful to Leroy for sharing this transcript with me.

82 Lindsay Cooper to Mandy Merck, May 4, 1977, MMA.

83 Henry Cow meeting minutes, Notebook 3, February 8, 1977, London, THA.

84 Hodgkinson, draft introduction.

Chapter 7. No Joy Anymore: London 1977

1 David Thyrén, "The Alternative Eurovision Song Contest in Sweden, 1975," in *A Cultural History of the Avant-garde in the Nordic Countries, 1950–1975*, edited by Tania Ørum and Jesper Olsson (Leiden: Brill, 2016), 831–40.

2 "MUSIC FOR SOCIALISM, February 1977," typed document/mailer in THA. Some of these questions were raised infrequently but consistently in the mainstream and alternative rock press; see, for example, Richard Williams, "The Trip," *Melody Maker*, September 12, 1970; Richard Williams, "The Revolt against the Business Establishment," *Melody Maker*, September 19, 1970; Mike Evans, "Rank 'n' File Rockanroll," *Cream* 18 (November 1972): 18–20; John Hoyland, "Who Owns the Music?" *Cream* 22 (March 1973): 8–9; and Mick Farren, "Rocking on within the System," *Cream* 23 (April 1973): 8–9.

3 Charles Catchpole, "Rock Prophets Scorn Success," *Evening Standard*, March 23, 1977.

4 Ian Hoare, "Music for Socialism," *Wedge* 1 (summer 1977): 25–26; see also Robert Shelton, "Socialist Music Festival," *Times* (London), May 30, 1977. For a more detailed account of this festival and its aftermath, see Benjamin Piekut, "Music for Socialism, London 1977," *Twentieth-Century Music*, forthcoming.

5 "Music for Socialism, Battersea Arts Centre," flyer, THA. See Phil McNeill, "Revolution Planned for May 28," *New Musical Express*, May 28, 1977.

6 Ian Walker, "Whole Lotta Shakin' Goin' On," *Leveller* 7 (July/August 1977): 18–20. See also Malcolm Heyhoe, "Music for Socialism" review, *New Musical Express*, June 18, 1977.

7 Cornelius Cardew, untitled report, *Musics* 13 (August 1977): 12–13.

8 Cardew, untitled report, 13; Cardew's colleague in PLM and the Progressive Cultural Association, Geoff Pearce, repeated the argument in greater detail in untitled report, *Musics* 13 (August 1977): 15–16.

9 Chris Cutler, untitled report, *Musics* 13 (August 1977): 17.

10 Cutler, untitled report, 17.

11 Jack Warshaw, untitled report, *Musics* 13 (August 1977): 10.

12 Steve Beresford, untitled report, *Musics* 13 (August 1977): 18.

13 Walker, "Whole Lotta Shakin,'" 18–20.

14 The Temple documentary was swapped in for a different film that had been advertised.

15 Walker, "Whole Lotta Shakin,'" 19.

16 Hoare, "Music for Socialism," 9.

17 Musicians Union, untitled report, *Musics* 13 (August 1977): 11. Cooper's motion that the MU provide support for the festival was carried on January 18, 1977; minutes of the Central London Branch Meeting of the Musicians Union, January 18, 1977, archives of the Musicians Union, University of Stirling, Scotland.

18 Musicians Union archive, University of Stirling, Scotland.

19 Leon Rosselson, untitled report, *Musics* 13 (August 1977): 12.

20 Nick Hobbs, untitled report, *Musics* 13 (August 1977): 14–15.

21 Walter Benjamin, "The Author as Producer," in *Understanding Brecht*, trans. Anna Bostock (London: Verso, [1934] 1998), at 93; see also Christopher Ballantine, "Towards an Aesthetic of Experimental Music," *Musical Quarterly* 63, no. 2 (1977): 224–46.

22 Hobbs, untitled report.

23 "Statement of Aims Approved at the Meeting of June 25th," *Music for Socialism Newsletter*, August 1977, 1.

24 [Neil Sandford], "Words and Music," *Music for Socialism Newsletter*, December 1977, 4; see also Les Levidov, "Words and Music—An Overview," *Music for Socialism Newsletter*, December 1977, 11, 13.

25 Tim Hodgkinson, "Thoughts on the Conference," *Music for Socialism Newsletter*, November 1977, 5–6.

26 Ian Hoare, "Record and Tape Distribution: The First Steps," *Music for Socialism Newsletter*, November 1977, 7.

27 Ian Goodyer, *Crisis Music: The Cultural Politics of Rock Against Racism* (Manchester, UK: University of Manchester Press, 2009).

28 Ian Hoare, "The Politics of Rock Performance," *Music for Socialism Newsletter*, November 1977, 10. See also the "Art Attacks" section of *Wedge* 2 (April 1978): 30: "And maybe it's also time that music started to do more than "support" campaigns in the way that RAR does (eg tried to develop the kind of political role that Henry Cow have found in their tours of France and Italy)."

29 Fred Frith, quoted in Catchpole, "Rock Prophets Scorn Success."

30 Tim Hodgkinson, Notebook 9, 1976–77, n.p., THA

31 See the exchange on rock in *Music for Socialism Newsletter*, February 1978, 3.

32 Goodyer, *Crisis Music*, chapters 2–3. Cofounder Dave Widgery later wrote of this "hard-headed political organization"; David Widgery, quoted in Simon Frith and John Street, "Rock against Racism and Red Wedge: From Music to Politics, from Politics to Music," in *Rockin' the Boat*, ed. Reebee Garofalo (Boston, MA: South End Press, 1992), 70.

33 Hodgkinson, "Thoughts on the Conference," 6. See also Gary Herman and Ian Hoare, "The Struggle for Song: A Reply to Leon Rosselson," in *Media, Politics, and Culture: A Socialist View*, ed. Carl Gardner (London: Macmillan, 1979), 51–60.

34 "Music Net," *Music for Socialism Newsletter*, February 1978; and "Art Attacks."

35 "Music Net," typescript, April 2, 1978, 1, THA.

36 Chris Cutler, "'Progressive' Music, 'Progressive' Politics?" in *File under Popular: Theoretical and Critical Writings on Music* (London: November Books, 1985), 151. This essay was written in 1981 or 1982.

37 For a charge of elitism, see S. B., "Yes, It's All Very Clever but . . . . . Henry Cow at Leeds," *Leeds Music News*, December 1977.

38 Cutler, "'Progressive' Music," 152.

39 Cutler, "'Progressive' Music," 156.

40 Cutler, "'Progressive' Music," 156.

41 Cutler, "'Progressive' Music," 153.

42 Cutler, "'Progressive' Music," 154.

43 "Music Net," 7.

44 Cutler, "'Progressive' Music," 154.

45 For an earlier survey, see John Hoyland, "Up against the Business," *Let It Rock*, May 1973, 27; and Hoyland, "Still up against the Business," *Let It Rock*, July 1973, 31–32.

46 Martin Jay, *The Dialectical Imagination: A History of the Frankfurt School and the Institute of Social Research, 1923–1950* (Berkeley: University of California Press, 1973); Rose Rosengard Subotnik, "Adorno's Diagnosis of Beethoven's Late Style: Early Symptom of a Fatal Condition," *Journal of the American Musicological Society* 29, no. 2 (1976): 242–75; Ballantine, "Towards an Aesthetic," 224–46.

47 Tim Hodgkinson, interview with *Resignation* [Sweden], [May 1977?], typescript, THA.

48 Hodgkinson interview.

49 Jon Savage, *England's Dreaming: Anarchy, Sex Pistols, Punk Rock, and Beyond* (New York: St. Martins, 1991), 30.

50 [David Wise], "The End of Music," 1978, Revolt against Plenty, available at http://www.revoltagainstplenty.com/index.php/recent/216-the-original-copy-of-the-end-of-music.html (accessed September 5, 2016).

51 Savage, *England's Dreaming*; Greil Marcus, *Lipstick Traces: A Secret History of the Twentieth Century* (Cambridge, MA: Harvard University Press, 1989).

52 The quotes are from Savage, *England's Dreaming*: "socio-political ideology" (225); "assault" (205); "rock stars" (225); "riven with competition" (208); "exploitative manager" (226).

53 Savage, *England's Dreaming*, 221.

54 Steve Lake, "Cow: Moving Left . . . ," *Melody Maker*, April 16, 1977.

55 Cutler, untitled report, 17.

56 Georgina Born, quoted in "Musiken är ingen spegel—den är en hammare," *Dagens Nyheter* (Stockholm), May 18, 1977.

57 Tim Hodgkinson, unpublished interview with Nick Wilton, October 1, 1980, typescript; I am grateful to Trond Einar Garmo for sharing a photocopy of this interview with me.

58 Beresford, untitled report.

59 Savage, *England's Dreaming*, 278.

60 Simon Frith, "Punk—Hippies with Short Hair," *Leveller*, November 1977, 20.

61 After their time in Henry Cow, Born and Balchin both became more involved in London's postpunk scene.

62 Fred Frith, "Henry Cow: English Tour 1978," n.d. [March 1978], ACGB 51/309 40.

63 Fred Frith, letter to the editor, *Melody Maker*, August 11, 1979.

64 Henry Cow meeting minutes, Notebook 3, October 17, 1976, THA.

65 Franco Fabbri, "Orchestral Manoevres in the 1970s: L'Orchestra Co-Operative, 1978–1983," *Popular Music* 26, no. 3 (2007): 409–27.

66 Advertisements in *Music for Socialism Newsletter*, November 1977. See also Chris Cutler, letter sent to advances, July 29, 1977, CCA.

67 Sales figures come from an internal planning document, "Loans for the Next Record," which is undated but was probably written in May or June 1977, CCA.

68 Tim Hodgkinson, "Some Important Distinctive Points about Pop-Music," Notebook 9, 1976–77, THA.

69 The following three paragraphs are based on meeting minutes from June 15, 1977; and Hodgkinson's Notebook 9.

70 Hodgkinson Notebook 9.

71 I'm drawing on Lake, "Cow: Moving Left . . ."; press releases for the Orckestra in various personal archives; and my interviews with participants.

72 Michael Shera, "Mike Westbrook and His Orchestra," *Jazz Journal* 19, no. 1 (1966): 10–11.

73 Duncan Heining, "Mike Westbrook: Is This Man Britain's Greatest Living Composer?," *Avant* 1 (1997): 22–23.

74 Westbrook discusses the jazz grumblers in Andy Duncan, "Mike Westbrook, Part 1," *Impetus* 4 [1976?]: 169–72.

75 I'm basing this list on a press release in CCA, reviews of the concert, and a live bootleg recording.

76 Steve Lake, "Cow Orchestra," *Melody Maker*, March 19, 1977, 23. See also Paul Bradshaw, "Blake, Brecht, Coltrane, Jazz, Folk, Rock: All from One Band!!" *Challenge*, May 1977; and photos in *The Morning Star*, March 14, 1977. See also an advance profile: Alan Slingsby, "Music to Challenge Big Business With," *Morning Star*, March 3, 1977.

77 "Unlikely Alliance Encores," *Melody Maker*, April 30, 1977, 58.

78 "Unlikely Alliance Encores," 58.

79 Maureen Paton, "Cow Orchestra," *Melody Maker*, July 2, 1977, 17.

80 Ronald Atkins, "The Orckestra," *Guardian*, June 27, 1977

81 In addition to the two London concerts, in 1977 the Orckestra played Milan (September 16), Modena (September 17), Nancy (October 15), and Paris (November 20). In 1978, they performed in Stockholm (March 28), Norrkoping (March 30), Gothenberg (April 2), Oslo (April 4), Paris (May 17), and Nancy (May 18).

82 Kenneth Ansell, "Henry Cow," *Impetus* 9 [1978?]: 375–78.

83 Henry Cow meeting minutes, Notebook 3, February 8, 1977, THA.

84 Lindsay Cooper to Mandy Merck, September 21, 1977, MMA.

85 Cooper said as much in Franco Bolelli and Peppo Delconte, "Henry Cow: L'avventura é solo cominciata," *Gong*, April 1977, 11.

86 Georgina Born to Mandy Merck, n.d. [January 1978], MMA.

87 Fred Frith, unnumbered notebook, [1977], n.p.

88 The SEM Ensemble was among the performing groups on the event.

89 Lindsay Cooper to Mandy Merck, November 15, 1977, MMA.

90 I am grateful to Juanjo Sanchez for sharing documents related to Henry Cow in Spain. For press coverage, see Antonio de Miguel, "Henry Cow: Los Marginados del Rollo Asaltan España (Ya Era Hora!)," *Disco Express*, November 11, 1977; Jordi Tardà, "Henry Cow en Barcelona," *Disco Express*, December 16, 1977; Francesc X. Puerto, "Henry Cow," *Star*, n.d.; Francesc X. Puerto, "Henry Cow Concerts," *Star*, January 1978; "Francesc X. Puerto, "Henry Cow," *Popular 1*, January 1978; "Vuelve a Visitarnos Henry Cow," *Disco Express*, March 31, 1978.

91 Juanjo Sanchez, "Henry Cow in Barcelona (1977): Memories by Francesc X. Puerto," unpublished interview in the author's possession, n.d.

92 Lindsay Cooper to Mandy Merck, November 12, 1977, MMA.

93 Lindsay Cooper to Mandy Merck, October 3, 1977, MMA.

94 Chris Wangro, liner notes to HCFABS, 2:49.

95 Wangro, liner notes, 2:48–49.

96 Tim Hodgkinson, draft introduction to *The Henry Cow Book*, THA.

97 Chris Cutler, Fred Frith, and Tim Hodgkinson, unpublished conversation, 1988, cassette, CCA.

98 Steve Lake, "HENRY COW: It Cud Not Happen to a Better Band!" *Melody Maker*, October 6, 1973.

99 Dagmar Krause, untitled notebook, n.d. [1976–77], DKA.

100 Lindsay Cooper, letter to the editor, *New Musical Express*, August 16, 1975.

101 Lindsay Cooper, "Women, Music, Feminism—Notes," *Musics* 14 (October 1977): 16–19.

102 Cooper, "Women, Music, Feminism," 16.

103 Cooper, "Women, Music, Feminism,"17.

104 Cooper, "Women, Music, Feminism,"18.

105 Cooper, "Women, Music, Feminism,"18.

106 Cooper, "Women, Music, Feminism,"18.

107 Cooper, "Women, Music, Feminism,"19.

108 Lindsay Cooper to Mandy Merck, May 4, 1977, MMA.

109 Lindsay Cooper, "Rock around the Cock," *Leveller*, October 1978, 12.

110 Lindsay Cooper and Dagmar Krause, "Talking till the Henry Cow Comes Home," interview with Malcolm Heyhoe and Irena Krumb, *Liquorice*, June 1976, 7. Born later commented, "There was an unspoken imperative among the guys to protect the Cow's image, and that probably meant making sure that Dagmar and I didn't speak often because we were deemed unreliable or 'emotional.' I was anyway reticent, and didn't feel I understood enough to communicate what we were about."

111 [Gerard Nguyen], "Lindsay Cooper," *Atem* 12 (April 1978): 20; translated by Aymeric Leroy.

112 [Nguyen], "Lindsay Cooper."

113 Cooper, quoted in Bolelli and Delconte, "Henry Cow," 12; translated by Amanda Recupero.

114 Lindsay Cooper to Mandy Merck, November 30, 1976, MMA.

115 Georgina Born, "On Music and Politics: Henry Cow, Avant-Gardism and Its Discontents," in *Red Strains: Music and Communism outside the Communist Bloc*, edited by Robert Adlington (Oxford: Oxford University Press, 2013), 55.

116 Hodgkinson, draft introduction.

117 Born, "On Music and Politics," 56.

118 Henry Cow, meeting minutes, Notebook 3, February 27, 1977, Sauve, France, THA.

119 Val Wilmer, "Ici Londres," *Jazz*, March 1979, 28–29, 70, at 28; translation by the author.

120 Cooper, "Women, Music, Feminism," 19.

121 Cooper, "Women, Music, Feminism," 18.

122 Hannah Charlton, "No Apologies," *Melody Maker*, December 8, 1979.

123 Lindsay Cooper, oral history interviews with Val Wilmer, July 14, 1992, Oral History of Jazz in Britain, British Library.

124 Susan Hemmings and Norma Pitfield, "The Feminist Improvising Group," *Musics*, December 1977, 20.

125 This description comes from my own listening to Cooper's extensive cassette archive of FIG performances, as well as Nicolas Soames, "FIG on a Gig," *Guardian*, September 29, 1978.

126 Georgie Born, "Some Notes on the Feminist Improvising Group," *Musics* 16 (February 1978): 5.

127 Born reports the disappointing outcome to her announcement in an unpublished interview with Hannah Charlton; her comment was edited out of the final version that ran in *Melody Maker*. Typescript in the unprocessed papers of the London Musicians Collective at the London College of Communication. Personnel come from a one-sheet in LCC papers.

128 Quoted in Soames, "FIG on a Gig."

129 Born also recalls playing in the Penguin Café Orchestra, either before or during her time in Henry Cow.

130 Krause, quoted in Bolelli and Delconte, "Henry Cow," 12; translated by Amanda Recupero.

131 Cooper to Merck, September 21, 1977.

132 Henry Cow press release, October 26, 1977, CCA.

133 Henry Cow meeting minutes, Notebook 3, June 15, 1977, London, THA; and International Society for Contemporary Music, British Section, meeting minutes, June 30, 1977, ACGB 51/272 2/1.

Chapter 8. Henry Cow Always Had to Be Henry Cow (1978)

1 For more on the backstory, see my "Indeterminacy, Free Improvisation, and the Mixed Avant-garde: Experimental Music in London, 1965–1975," *Journal of the American Musicological Society* 67, no. 3 (fall 2014): 769–824.

2   See "The Contemporary Music Network: A Discussion," *Tempo* 119 (December 1976): 7–14.

3   ISCM meeting minutes, September 28, 1976, ACGB 51/46; see also scrap dated August 6, 1976, which lists the jazz nominations; ACGB 51/309 40.

4   See also Dick Witts, "Cow Milks Maid Experiment," *New Manchester Review*, January 27, 1978.

5   I'm summarizing correspondence between Henry Cow and the AC during this period, all which can be found in the ACGB archives.

6   Tony Wills to John Cruft and Annette Morreau, February 10, 1977, ACGB 51/309 40.

7   ISCM, UK section, meeting minutes, June 30, 1977, ACGB 51/46.

8   Nick Hobbs to Annette Morreau, June 30, 1977, ACGB 1/3793

9   John Cruft to Secretary General, July 11, 1977, ACGB 1/3793.

10 Liner notes to Henry Cow, *Concerts*, ReR HC5&6, [1976] 2006.

11 Lindsay Cooper to Mandy Merck, January 14, 1978, MMA.

12 Lindsay Cooper to Mandy Merck, January 16, 1978, MMA.

13 Tim Hodgkinson, unpublished interview with Nick Wilton, October 1, 1980, typescript; I am grateful to Trond Einar Garmo for sharing a photocopy of this interview with me.

14 Henry Cow meeting minutes, Notebook 3, April 1, 1977, THA.

15 Georgina Born to Mandy Merck, [January 1978], MMA.

16 Lindsay Cooper to Mr. and Mrs. Cooper, January 27, 1978, LCA.

17 Fred Frith, interview on Vassar College radio [interviewer unknown], April 16, 1980, recording in author's possession.

18 Tim Hodgkinson, draft introduction to *The Henry Cow Book*, THA.

19 The phrase "Great Terrible Horrorshock" is Born's; Born to Merck, [January 1978].

20 Art Bears, *Hope and Fears Booklet* (London: self-published, 1978).

21 Lindsay Cooper to Susan Hemmings, [January 1978], LCA.

22 Born to Merck, [January 1978].

23 Born to Merck, [January 1978].

24 Lindsay Cooper to Mandy Merck, [January 1978], MMA.

25 Born to Merck, [January 1978].

26 Lindsay Cooper to Susan Hemmings, [January 1978], LCA.

27 Cooper to Hemmings, [January 1978].

28 For this description, I've borrowed heavily from Garmo's excellent analysis in Trond Einar Garmo, *Henry Cow: En analyse av avantgarderock* (Trondheim, Norway: Skrifter fra Musikkvitenskapelig Institutt, 2001), 143–48. I am grateful to Thomas Hilder for his translation of this text.

29 Garmo, *Henry Cow.*

30 Chris Cutler, interview with Trond Einar Garmo, January 19, 1984, digital recording in author's possession. I am grateful to Trond Einar Garmo for sharing this recording with me.

31 Hodgkinson, draft introduction.

32 Tim Hodgkinson, unpublished interview with Nick Wilton, October 1, 1980, typescript; I am grateful to Trond Einar Garmo for sharing a photocopy of this interview with me.

33 Tim Hodgkinson, draft introduction.

34 Tim Hodgkinson, draft introduction.

35 "Recommended Bands," *Zū Magazine*, n.d. [September 1978], 9. See also John Walters, "Walters," *ZigZag*, April–May 1978, 37: "They are to reform as 'The Art Bears.'"

36 Nick Hobbs to Annette Morreau, April 19, 1978, ACGB 51/309 40.

37 Fred Frith, "Henry Cow: English Tour 1978," n.d. [March 1978], ACGB 51/309 40. The cathedral concert was a free gig after their Arnolfini show the night before. The dean of the cathedral was an old Cow fan.

38 They ran advertisements in *Melody Maker* and *Sounds*, and garnered several advanced publicity stories.

39 Frith, "Henry Cow: English Tour 1978."

40 Bob Watson, "Henry Cow," *Sounds*, February 18, 1978.

41 Chris Brazier, "Henry Cow," *Melody Maker*, February 25, 1978. Brazier's nasty review received a rebuke in the next issue from P. R. Kelly, letter to the editor, *Melody Maker*, March 11, 1978.

42 For more on RIO, see *Impetus* 9 (1979), a special issue dedicated to the collective, and Archie Patterson, "Rock Began in Opposition to *Mainstream Culture* . . . ," in *Eurock: Music and Second Culture Post Millennium* (Portland, OR: Eurock Publications, 2013), 7–13; and Karl Dallas, "Fighting the System Europe-wide," *Melody Maker*, April 15, 1978.

43 Kenneth Ansell, "Nick Hobbs: Instigator," *Impetus* 9 (1979): 372–73.

44 Kenneth Ansell, "Rock in Opposition," *Impetus* 7 (1978): 282–83.

45 Les Levidov, "Stormy Six Concert," *Music for Socialism Newsletter*, April 1978, 14.

46 Maureen Paton, "Revolution in the Studio," *Melody Maker*, January 7, 1978; Peel and BBC were reported by Walters, "Walters," 36–37.

47 Nick Hobbs, "Rock in Opposition (to Crap Music)," *Music for Socialism Newsletter*, February 1978, 4–5.

48 Rock in Opposition program, New London Theatre, March 12, 1978, THA.

49 Arts Council of Great Britain, Music Panel, Jazz Sub-committee meeting minutes, May 19, 1978, ACGB 51/37.

50 Ansell, "Nick Hobbs," 372.

51 Hobbs, "Rock in Opposition," 15.

52 Arts Council of Great Britain, Music Panel, Jazz Sub-committee meeting minutes, September 8, 1978, ACGB 51/37.

53 On commercial compromise, see Hobbs, "Rock in Opposition," 8; on cultural seriousness, intensity, and intelligence, see Hobbs, "Rock in Opposition," 14–15.

54 Hobbs, "Rock in Opposition," 15.

55 Hobbs, "Rock in Opposition," 8.

56 Graham White, "The Ians in the Audience: Punk Attitude and the Influence of the Avant-Garde," in *Avant-Garde Performance and Material Exchange: Vectors of the Radical*, edited by Mike Sell (New York: Palgrave Macmillan, 2010), 188–206.

57 Ansell, "Nick Hobbs," 372–73.

58 Chris Cutler, "Postscript—Chris Cutler Brings RIO Up to Date," *Impetus* 9 (1979): 395, 411.

59 The nomenclature of these projects can be confusing. Rē Records was the label Cutler formed to release Art Bears material; Recommended was his mail order and record import business, which expanded in 1979 into reissuing out-of-print albums by Cutler's favorite artists, such as Faust, Slapp Happy, and Sun Ra, as well as new albums by RIO artists such as Univers Zero and Art Zoyd; in 1988, he combined these operations into ReR Megacorp.

60 "Klossaknapitatet [sic]," *Music for Socialism Newsletter*, October 1977, 2.

61 Chris Cutler, "'Progressive' Music, 'Progressive' Politics?" in *File under Popular: Theoretical and Critical Writings on Music* (London: November Books, 1985), 154.

62 In the years after 1978, it would become apparent that Henry Cow royalty payments were getting mixed up with Recommended accounts until, with Cutler's assistance, Hodgkinson disambiguated their affairs and established separate books for Henry Cow, disbursing royalty checks to this day to the nineteen musicians and crew members who had spent longer than three months with the band. Hodgkinson divides these payments according to the number of months each member had spent with the organization. See "Henry Cow Time-Based Shares," n.d., FFA.

63 Henry Cow press release, March 15, 1978, CCA.

64 The press release resulted in a reasonably wide coverage in the British music press.

65 Hodgkinson, draft introduction.

66 Thank you to Juanjo Sanchez for sharing this tape with me.

67 Lindsay Cooper to Susan Hemmings, [April 1978], LCA.

68 These concerns were alluded to in Kenneth Ansell, "Henry Cow," *Impetus* 9 (1979): 375–78; and in private documents at the time.

69 Chris Cutler, quoted in Ansell, "Henry Cow," 376.

70 Cutler's eventual release of this tune on HCFABS fades out before it reaches the main tune.

71 Lindsay Cooper to Susan Hemmings, [July 1978?], LCA.

72 This story was related to me by Cutler and Thomas, and is corroborated by Steven Ashworth, letter to the editor, *Melody Maker*, July 15, 1978.

73 Hodgkinson interview.

74 Tim Hodgkinson, review of Henry Cow, *Western Culture* (CD rerelease), *Resonance* 9, no. 2 (2002): 34.

75 Lindsay Cooper to Susan Hemmings, n.d. [August 1978], LCA.

76 Andy Gill, review of Henry Cow, *Western Culture*, and Art Bears, *Winter Songs*, *New Musical Express*, February 16, 1980.

77 Cutler wrote the text to aid Andy Ortmann in preparing "Eine Henry Cow-Story," *Hanni Manni: Kritik der Ware Popmusik* 6 (November 1978).

78 Fred Frith to Tim Hodgkinson, September 10, 1981, THA.

79 An excerpt of this text is published in *HCFABS*.

80 Hodgkinson, draft introduction.

81 Chris Cutler, "Prefatory," in *The Henry Cow Book* (London: self-published, 1982), 3.

82 Hodgkinson, letter draft to Gerard Nguyen, n.d. Original in French—thank you to Andrew Zhou for this translation. This letter would be published in *Atem* in response to their publication of Cutler's farewell press release in issue 12 (April 1978).

83 Lindsay Cooper, interview with Nick Wilton, November 27, 1980.

84 For more on Cooper and film, see Mandy Merck, "Composing for the Films," *Screen* 25, no. 3 (1984): 40–54.

85 Chris Cutler, Fred Frith, and Tim Hodgkinson, unpublished conversation, 1988, cassette, CCA.

Afterword

Epigraph: Berthold Brecht, "Against George Lukacs," in *Aesthetics and Politics* (London: Verso, [1977] 1980), 82.

1 Although characters and events from the preceding account will feature in the following, this afterword is more concerned with speculation than it is with wrapping up or reframing the story of Henry Cow alone.

2 If we accept Chris Cutler's three successive modes of "musical memory systems" (biological/folk, written/art, phonographic/popular), then the vernacular avant-garde would coincide with that later stage of the phonographic, which begins in the late nineteenth century; Chris Cutler, "Necessity and Choice in Musical Forms, Concerning Musical and Technical Means and Political Needs," in *File under Popular: Theoretical and Critical Writings on Music* (London: November Books, 1985), 19–38.

3 In my view, a text such as Alfred Appel, Jr., *Jazz Modernism: From Ellington and Armstrong to Matisse and Joyce* (New York: Knopf, 2002), overlooks these crucial differences, while H. Wiley Hitchcock, *Music in the United States: A Historical Introduction*, rev. ed. (Englewood Cliffs, NJ: Prentice Hall, 1974) does not.

4 Paul Mann, *The Theory-Death of the Avant-Garde* (Bloomington: Indiana University Press, 1991).

5 David Cottington, "The Formation of the Avant-Garde in Paris and London, c. 1880–1915," *Art History* 35, no. 3 (2012): 596–621; see also Gianmario Borio, "Avant-garde als pluralistisches Konzept: Musik um 1968," in *Rebellische Musik: Kulturwandel und gesellschaftlicher Protest um 1968*, ed. Arnold Jacobshagen and Markus Leniger (Cologne, Germany: Dohr, 2007), 15–33; and Fred Orton and Griselda Pollock, "Avant-Gardes and Partisans Reviewed," *Art History* 4, no. 3 (1981): 305–27.

6 I'm grateful to Esther Leslie for helping to define this point with her question at the Darmstadt International Summer Courses in 2018.

7 Georgina Born, "Modern Music Culture: On Shock, Pop and Synthesis," *New Formations* 2 (summer 1987): 51–78.

8 Chris Cutler, "Thoughts on Music and the Avant-Garde: Considerations of a Term and Its Public Use," in *Musik-Avantgarde: Zur Dialektik von Vorhut und Nachhut*, ed. Hanns-Werner Heister, Wolfgang Martin Stroh, and Peter Wicke (Oldenburg: BIS-Verlag, 2006), 71.

9 Cutler, "Thoughts on Music," 61.

10 Chris Cutler, *File under Popular* (London: November Books, 1985).

11 Cutler, "Necessity and Choice," 36.

12 The "studiously joyless" formulation is from David Toop, *Into the Maelstrom: Music, Improvisation, and the Dream of Freedom: Before 1970* (London: Bloomsbury, 2016), 19.

13 Perry Anderson, "Modernity and Revolution," *New Left Review* 1, no. 144 (March–April 1984): 104–5.

14 P. Anderson, "Modernity and Revolution," 104–9; George Yúdice, "Rethinking the Theory of the Avant-Garde from the Periphery," in *Modernism and Its Margins: Reinscribing Cultural Modernity From Spain and Latin America*, ed. Anthony L. Geist and José Monleón (Minneapolis: University of Minnesota Press, 1999), 61. James M. Harding, "From Cutting Edges to Rough Edges: On the Transnational Foundations of Avant-Garde Performance," in *The Ghosts of the Avant-Garde(s): Exorcising Experimental Theater and Performance* (Ann Arbor: University of Michigan Press, 2013), 136–58.

15 P. Anderson, "Modernity and Revolution," 105. I do not share Anderson's opinion that World War II "destroyed" these coordinates. Instead, it destroyed the specific, European arrangements that had conditioned the appearance of the historical avant-gardes half a century earlier. As general theoretical axes, Anderson's coordinates (augmented by Yúdice's addendum) can do more analytical work than he allows.

16 Yúdice, "Rethinking the Theory," 63.

17 Andreas Huyssen, "Back to the Future: Fluxus in Context," in *Twilight Memories: Marking Time in a Culture of Amnesia* (New York: Routledge, 1995), 197–98. On the capacity of radicalism to harbor right and left positions, see Mike Sell, *The Avant-Garde: Race, Religion, War* (New York: Seagull, 2011). For an apposite example of a different articulation of culture and politics, outside of the capitalist west, see Tamara Levitz, "Experimental Music and Revolution: Cuba's Grupo de Experimentación Sonora del ICAIC," in *Tomorrow Is the Question: New Directions in Experimental Music Studies*, ed. Benjamin Piekut (Ann Arbor: University of Michigan Press, 2014), 180–210.

18 Walter Benjamin, "The Author as Producer," in *Understanding Brecht*, trans. Anna Bostock (London: Verso, [1934] 1998), 85–103.

19 Reynols, *Blank Tapes*, Trente Oiseaux TOC002, CD, 2000; Clement Greenberg, "Towards a Newer Laocoön," *Partisan Review* 7 (July–August 1940): 301. It is unknown whether Reynols were familiar with Kunsu Shim's *Secret Garden* (1993), a contemporary work that similarly thematized blank magnetic tape.

20 Miriam Bratu Hansen, "The Mass Production of the Senses: Classical Cinema as Vernacular Modernism," *Modernism/Modernity* 6, no. 2 (April 1999): 59–77; Miriam Bratu Hansen, "Fallen Women, Rising Stars, New Horizons: Shanghai Silent Film as Vernacular Modernism," *Film Quarterly* 54, no. 1 (autumn 2000): 10–22. It is not without irony that Hansen has provided such a springboard for my thinking on the vernacular avant-garde, because she was responding to a cinema studies discourse that privileged avant-garde film as the only true register of that medium's engagement with modernity. In other words, I am attempting to reconceive a term that she wanted to push aside.

21 Edward P. Comentale, *Sweet Air: Modernism, Regionalism, and American Popular Song,* (Urbana: University of Illinois Press, 2013).

22 Comentale, *Sweet Air,* 8.

23 Michael Denning, *Noise Uprising: The Audiopolitics of a World Musical Revolution* (New York: Verso, 2015).

24 Benjamin Steege, *Helmholtz and the Modern Listener* (Cambridge: Cambridge University Press, 2012), 215–51; Brigid Cohen, *Stefan Wolpe and the Avant-Garde Diaspora* (Cambridge: Cambridge University Press, 2012); Carolyn Abbate, "Wagner, Cinema, and Redemptive Glee," *Opera Quarterly* 21, no. 4 (2005): 597–611; Christopher Chowrimootoo, "Reviving the Middlebrow, or: Deconstructing Modernism from the Inside," *Journal of the Royal Musical Association* 139, no. 1 (2014): 187–93; Thomas Patteson, *Instruments for New Music: Sound, Technology, and Modernism* (Oakland: University of California Press, 2016).

25 Benjamin Piekut, *Experimentalism Otherwise: The New York Avant-Garde and Its Limits* (Berkeley: University of California Press, 2011), epilogue; Kyle Devine, "Imperfect Sound Forever: Loudness Wars, Listening Formations and the History of Sound Reproduction," *Popular Music* 32, no. 2 (May 2013): 159–76.

26 Peter Doyle, *Echo and Reverb: Fabricating Space in Popular Music Recording, 1900–1960* (Middletown, CT: Wesleyan University Press, 2005); Albin J. Zak III, *I Don't Sound Like Nobody: Remaking Music in 1950s America* (Ann Arbor: University of Michigan Press, 2010); Michael Veal, *Dub: Soundscapes and Shattered Songs in Jamaican Reggae* (Middletown, CT: Wesleyan University Press, 2007).

27 Richard Osborne, *Vinyl: A History of the Analogue Record* (Aldershot, UK: Ashgate, 2012).

28 Christopher Ballantine, "Modernism and Popular Music," *Journal of the Royal Musical Association* 139, no. 1 (2014): 200–204; Motti Regev, *Pop-Rock Music: Aesthetic Cosmopolitanism in Late Modernity* (Cambridge: Cambridge University Press, 2013). See also David Grubbs, *Records Ruin the Landscape: John Cage, the Sixties, and Sound Recording* (Durham, NC: Duke University Press, 2014).

29 David E. James, "The Idea of the Amateur," in *The Most Typical Avant-Garde: History and Geography of Minor Cinemas in Los Angeles* (Berkeley: University of California Press, 2005), 137–64; Jonas Mekas, *Movie Journal: The Rise of the New American Cinema, 1959–1971,* second ed., edited by Gregory Smulewicz-Zucker (New York: Columbia University Press, 2016), 138–42; and Annette Michelson,

"Film and the Radical Aspiration," in *The New American Cinema: A Critical Anthology*, ed. Gregory Battcock (New York: Dutton, [1966] 1967), 83–102.

30 Yúdice, "Rethinking the Theory," 62–63; Denning, *Noise Uprising*.

31 David Novak, "The Sublime Frequencies of New Old Media," *Public Culture* 23, no. 3 (2011): 614.

32 Yúdice, "Rethinking the Theory"; Coco Fusco, "The Other History of Intercultural Performance," *Drama Review* 381, no. 1 (spring 1994): 143–67.

33 Dietrich Scheunemann, "From Collage to the Multiple: On the Genealogy of Avant-Garde and Neo-Avant-Garde," in *Avant-Garde/Neo-Avant-Garde*, ed. Dietrich Schneunemann (Amsterdam: Rodopi, 2005), 15–48; Branden W. Joseph, *Random Order: Robert Rauschenberg and the Neo-Avant-Garde* (Cambridge, MA: MIT Press, 2003); Hubert van den Berg, "On the Historiographic Distinction between Historical and Neo-Avant-Garde," in *Avant-Garde / Neo-Avant-Garde*, ed. Dietrich Schneunemann (Amsterdam: Rodolpi, 2005), 63–74; Benjamin Buchloh, "Theorizing the Avant-Garde," *Art in America* 72, no. 10 (1984): 19, 21; Hal Foster, "What's Neo about the Neo-Avant-Garde?," *October* 70 (autumn 1994): 5–32; Terry Smith, *What Is Contemporary Art?* (Chicago, IL: University of Chicago Press, 2009).

34 Art historian David Cottington makes this clear in a single devastating paragraph in "Formation of the Avant-Garde," 598. For a more theoretical, affirmative revision of Dada and surrealism, see Gavin Grindon, "Surrealism, Dada, and the Refusal of Work: Autonomy, Activism, and Social Participation in the Radical Avant-Garde," *Oxford Art Journal* 34, no. 1 (March 2011): 79–96.

35 Peter Bürger, *Theory of the Avant-Garde* (Minneapolis: University of Minnesota Press, 1984), 50–54.

36 Hansen, "Mass Production," 69. Patrick Nickleson, "The Names of Minimalism: Authorship and the Historiography of Dispute in New York Minimalism, 1960–1982," PhD diss., University of Toronto, 2017.

37 Born, "Modern Music Culture," 71; Georgina Born, "On Music and Politics: Henry Cow, Avant-Gardism and Its Discontents," in *Red Strains: Music and Communism outside the Communist Bloc*, ed. Robert Adlington (Oxford: Oxford University Press, 2013), 64.

38 Gavin Grindon, "Poetry Written in Gasoline: Black Mask and Up Against the Wall Motherfucker," *Art History* 38, no. 1 (February 2015): 174–75; Huyssen, "Back to the Future," 197.

39 Grindon, "Poetry Written in Gasoline."

40 Jayne Wark, *Radical Gestures: Feminism and Performance Art in North America* (Montreal: McGill-Queen's University Press, 2006), 21.

41 Georgina Born, *Rationalizing Culture: IRCAM, Boulez, and the Institutionalization of the Musical Avant-Garde* (Berkeley: University of California Press, 1995).

42 Amy C. Beal, *New Music, New Allies: American Experimental Music in West Germany from the Zero Hour to Reunification* (Berkeley: University of California Press, 2006); Jann Pasler, "The Political Economy of Composition in the American University, 1965–1985," in *Writing through Music: Essays on Music, Culture and*

Politics (New York: Oxford University Press, 2008), 318–65; Martin Iddon, *New Music at Darmstadt: Nono, Stockhausen, Cage, and Boulez* (Cambridge: Cambridge University Press, 2013); Luis Eduardo Herrera, "The CLAEM and the Construction of Elite Art Worlds: Philanthropy, Latinamericanism and Avant-Garde Music," PhD diss., University of Illinois at Urbana-Champaign, 2013. But see also Levitz, "Experimental Music and Revolution."

43 Branden W. Joseph, *Experimentations: John Cage in Music, Art, and Architecture* (New York: Bloomsbury Academic, 2016); David W. Bernstein, ed. *The San Francisco Tape Music Center: 1960s Counterculture and the Avant-Garde* (Berkeley: University of California Press, 2008); Edwin Prévost, *No Sound Is Innocent: AMM and the Practice of Self-Invention, Meta-Musical Narratives, Essays* (Matching Tye, UK: Copula, 1995); Martha Mockus, *Sounding Out: Pauline Oliveros and Lesbian Musicality* (New York: Routledge, 2008); Jeremy Grimshaw, *Draw a Straight Line and Follow It: The Music and Mysticism of La Monte Young* (New York: Oxford University Press, 2012); George E. Lewis, *A Power Stronger Than Itself: The AACM and American Experimental Music* (Chicago, IL: University of Chicago Press, 2008); Hannah Higgins, *Fluxus Experience* (Berkeley: University of California Press, 2002); John Tilbury, *Cornelius Cardew (1936–1981): A Life Unfinished* (Harlow, UK: Copula, 2008); Tara Rodgers, *Pink Noises: Women on Electronic Music and Sound* (Durham, NC: Duke University Press, 2010); Andrew Raffo Dewar, "Handmade Sounds: The Sonic Arts Union and American Technoculture," PhD diss., Wesleyan University, 2009; John F. Szwed, *Space Is the Place: The Lives and Times of Sun Ra* (New York: Da Capo, 1998); Joanna Demers, *Listening Through the Noise: The Aesthetics of Experimental Electronic Music* (New York: Oxford University Press, 2010); David Novak, *Japanoise: Music at the Edge of Circulation* (Durham, NC: Duke University Press, 2013); Trevor Barre, *Beyond Jazz: Plink, Plonk, and Scratch: The Golden Age of Free Music in London, 1966–1972* (London: Book Refinery, 2015); Mike Heffley, *Northern Sun, Southern Moon: Europe's Reinvention of Jazz* (New Haven, CT: Yale University Press, 2005); Jennie Gottschalk, *Experimental Music since 1970* (New York: Bloomsbury, 2016); Michael E. Veal and E. Tammy Kim, eds., *Punk Ethnography: Artists and Scholars Listen to Sublime Frequencies* (Middletown CT: Wesleyan University Press, 2016).

44 Huyssen, "Back to the Future," 203.

45 Eric Porter, *What Is This Thing Called Jazz? African American Musicians as Artists, Critics, and Activists* (Berkeley: University of California Press, 2002); Scott Saul, *Freedom Is, Freedom Ain't: Jazz and the Making of the Sixties* (Cambridge, MA: Harvard University Press, 2003); Iain Anderson, *This Is Our Music: Free Jazz, the Sixties, and American Culture* (Philadelphia: University of Pennsylvania Press, 2007); Eric Drott, "Free Jazz and the French Critic," *Journal of the American Musicological Society* 61, no. 3 (fall 2008): 541–82; Franya Berkman, *Monument Eternal: The Music of Alice Coltrane* (Middletown, CT: Wesleyan University Press, 2010); and Michael Heller, *Loft Jazz: Improvising New York in the 1970s* (Oakland: University of California Press, 2017).

46 Benjamin Filene, *Romancing the Folk: Public Memory and American Roots Music* (Chapel Hill: University of North Carolina Press, 2000); Krin Gabbard, "Revenge of the Nerds: Representing the White Male Collector of Black Music," in *Jammin' at the Margins: Jazz and the American Cinema* (Chicago, IL: University of Chicago Press, 1996), 199–232. See also the classic account of race and commercialism in LeRoi Jones, *Blues People* (New York: Morrow Quill Paperbacks, 1963).

47 Novak, "Sublime Frequencies."

48 Ronald Radano, "Critical Alchemy: Anthony Braxton and the Imagined Tradition," in *Jazz among the Discourses*, ed. Krin Gabbard (Durham, NC: Duke University Press, 1994), 189–216;

49 Or note the role of the BBC's Radiophonic Workshop for experimenting with and popularizing the latest electronic music techniques in the postwar years; Louis Niebur, *Special Sound: The Creation and Legacy of the BBC Radiophonic Workshop* (Oxford: Oxford University Press, 2010).

50 Hal Foster, "What's Neo?"; Buchloh, "Theorizing the Avant-Garde," 19, 21.

51 Foster, "What's Neo?," 10n10.

52 Elissa Auther, *String, Felt, Thread: The Hierarchy of Art and Craft in American Art* (Minneapolis: University of Minnesota Press, 2009); T'ai Smith, *Bauhaus Weaving Theory: From Feminine Craft to Mode of Design* (Minneapolis: University of Minnesota Press, 2014); Thomas Crow, *The Long March of Pop: Art, Music, and Design, 1930–1995* (New Haven, CT: Yale University Press, 2014); and Julia Bryan-Wilson, *Fray: Art and Textile Politics* (Chicago, IL: University of Chicago Press, 2017).

53 Bernard Gendron, *Between Montmartre and the Mudd Club: Popular Music and the Avant-Garde* (Chicago, IL: University of Chicago Press, 2002); Phil Ford, *Dig: Sound and Music in Hip Culture* (New York: Oxford University Press, 2013).

54 I've nicked this famous phrase about art (not rock) from Clement Greenberg, "Avant-Garde and Kitsch," *Partisan Review* 6 (fall 1939): 34–49.

55 Lester Bangs, *Psychotic Reactions and Carburetor Dung: The Work of a Legendary Critic: Rock 'n' Roll as Literature and Literature as Rock 'n' Roll*, ed. Greil Marcus (New York: Knopf, 1987).

56 Fred Frith, *Guitar Solos*, Caroline C 1508, 1974; Cutler, *File under Popular*; Tim Hodgkinson, various notebooks and unpublished essays, THA; themed issue, Folk or Popular? Distinctions, Influences, Continuities, *Popular Music* 1 (1981).

57 Gendron, *Between Montmartre and the Mudd Club*.

58 Gendron, *Between Montmartre and the Mudd Club*, 216–18; see also Brian Ward, *Just My Soul Responding: Rhythm and Blues, Black Consciousness, and Race Relations* (Berkeley: University of California Press, 1998).

59 Comentale, *Sweet Air*, 160–204.

60 One of the word's old usages was to describe a slave born on the master's estate. The more carefree connotations of *local* in the term are therefore also imbued with the possibility of confinement. Houston Baker and Robert O'Meally have emphasized this lexical history to imprint the term with a distinct tie to black US history.

61 Ralph Ellison, quoted in Robert G. O'Meally, "On Burke and the Vernacular: Ralph Ellison's Boomerang of History," in *History and Memory in African-American Culture*, ed. Genevieve Fabre and Robert G. O'Meally (New York: Oxford University Press, 2004), 248. Although John Kouwenhoven's influential early formulation found the vernacular expressed most clearly in the useful items of industrial design—in other words, in the crafting and use of nonaesthetic objects—everyday, "low" discourse on nonelite forms of music, fashion, film, and design regularly displays a finely tuned aesthetic sense; John Kouwenhoven, *The Beer Can by the Highway: Essays on What's American about America* (Garden City, NJ: Doubleday, 1961).

62 Hansen, "Mass Production," 59.

63 Homi Bhabha, "Unsatisfied: Notes on Vernacular Cosmopolitanism," in *Text and Nation: Cross-Disciplinary Essays on Cultural and National Identities*, ed. Laura García-Moreno and Peter C. Pfeiffer (London: Camden House, 1996), 195.

64 Prizes like Henry Cow's Arts Council grant were exceedingly rare, and the youth ministries of France and Holland, though state supported, served many purposes beyond the presentation of popular music.

65 Hansen, "Mass Production," 59.

66 Simon Frith, "Art Ideology and Pop Practice," in *Marxism and the Interpretation of Culture*, ed. Cary Nelson and Lawrence Grossberg (Urbana: University of Illinois Press, 1988), 461–75. For a different perspective, see Fred Ho's conception of the "popular avant-garde," explicated in Kevin Fellezs, "Enter the Voice of the Dragon: Fred Ho, Bruce Lee, and the Popular Avant-Garde," in *Yellow Power, Yellow Soul: The Radical Art of Fred Ho*, ed. Roger N. Buckley and Tamara Roberts (Urbana: University of Illinois Press, 2013), 35–53.

67 Greenberg, "Avant-Garde and Kitsch"; T. J. Clark, "Clement Greenberg's Theory of Art," *Critical Inquiry* 9 (September 1982): 139–56.

68 Greenberg, "Avant-Garde and Kitsch," 38.

69 Simon Frith and Howard Horne, *Art into Pop* (London: Methuen, 1987).

70 Cornel West bemoans the vernacular's continual recuperation by capitalism in a paper quoted by O'Meally, "On Burke and the Vernacular," 250. See also Thomas Crow, "Modernism and Mass Culture," in *Modernism and Modernity*, ed. Benjamin H. D. Buchloh, Serge Guilbaut, and David Solkin (Halifax: Press of the Nova Scotia College of Art and Design, 1983), 215–64.

71 O'Meally, "On Burke and the Vernacular"; Kouwenhoven, *Beer Can*.

72 David Thomas, "LAist Interview: David Thomas of Pere Ubu," interview with Bobzilla, LAist, October 8, 2009, http://laist.com/2009/10/08/laist_interview_david_thomas_of_per.php (accessed September 5, 2016).

73 A reviewer of *Leg End* expressed a wish that Henry Cow "avoid the grooves of Academe"; *HiFi for Pleasure*, December 1973.

74 This point is not the same as saying that the vernacular allows anybody to be a star artist, because it offers no escape from the uneven processes of sorting performed by circumstances of region, race, class, and cultural or social capital.

75 Karlheinz Stockhausen, interview with John Banks, *Varsity* (Cambridge University), May 8, 1971.

76 Georgina Born, "On Musical Mediation: Ontology, Technology and Creativity," *Twentieth-Century Music* 2, no. 1 (2005): 7–36.

77 Such a discourse was a natural successor to the nascent popular music aesthetics examined in Gendron, *Between Montmartre and the Mudd Club*.

78 Bhabha, "Unsatisfied," 202.

79 Lewis, *Power Stronger Than Itself*, 367.

80 Lewis, *Power Stronger Than* Itself, 367.

81 Lewis, *Power Stronger Than Itself*, 353–88; Fred Moten, *In the Break: The Aesthetics of the Black Radical Tradition* (Minneapolis: University of Minnesota Press, 2003), 25–84; Guthrie P. Ramsey, *Race Music: Black Cultures from Bebop to Hip-Hop* (Berkeley: University of California Press, 2003), 96–130; Houston A. Baker, Jr., *Blues, Ideology, and Afro-American Literature: A Vernacular Theory* (Chicago, IL: University of Chicago Press, 1984).

82 See Moten, *In the Break*, 32–33, and Fred Moten, "Not in between: Lyric Painting, Visual History, and the Postcolonial Future," *The Drama Review*, 47 no. 1 (Spring 2003): 127–48.

83 Moten, *In the Break*, 40–41.

84 Moten, *In the Break*, 70.

85 Moten, "Not in between," 135; Moten, *In the Break*, 70.

86 Moten, "Not in between," 135; I was led to this crucial passage and its meaning by Jordan Musser, "Black Creation: On the Popular Avant-Gardism of Linton Kwesi Johnson's Dub Poetry," unpublished manuscript.

87 Antoine Hennion, "An Intermediary between Production and Consumption: The Producer of Popular Music," *Science, Technology, and Human Values* 14, no. 4 (autumn 1989): 400–24.

88 James, *Most Typical Avant-Garde*, 16.

89 Julia Bryan-Wilson, "'Out to See Video': EZTV's Queer Microcinema in West Hollywood," *Grey Room* 56 (summer 2014): 56–89.

90 Like dance, which ranges from the classical ballet to everyday social dancing, music's sweep from esoteric to quotidian involves no categorical break in how we comprehend the practice; for one example of such a study, see Danielle Goldman, *I Want to Be Ready: Improvised Dance as a Practice of Freedom* (Ann Arbor: University of Michigan Press, 2010). But again, I think music's long history of domestication and privatization via the commodified forms of sheet music and recordings distinguishes it from dance.

91 Again, the history of photography stands as an important exception.

92 Bryan-Wilson, *Fray*; Crow, *Long March of Pop*; Branden W. Joseph, *Beyond the Dream Syndicate: Tony Conrad and the Arts after Cage* (Cambridge: Zone Books, 2008).

93 I've drawn inspiration and this formulation from James's elaboration of the "minor cinemas" of Los Angeles in *The Most Typical Avant-Garde*.

94 For a useful summary of the differences among concept, theory, and category, see Colin Koopman and Tomas Matza, "Putting Foucault to Work: Analytic and Concept in Foucaultian Inquiry," *Critical Inquiry* 39 (summer 2013): 817–40.

95 Mann, *Theory-Death*, 18.

96 See, for instance, Mann, *Theory-Death*, 17.

Bibliography

Interviews by the Author

Caroline Ayerst, London, April 18, 2012.

Sarah (Greaves) Baker Smith, Cambridge, UK, February 18, 2012; telephone interviews, April 14, 2012, and October 12, 2016.

Jack Balchin, Scappoose, OR, October 7–8, 2012.

Clive Bell, London, April 15, 2012.

Steve Beresford, London, April 13, 2012.

Peter Blegvad, London, December 11, 2011.

Georgina Born, Cambridge, UK, February 19–20, 2012.

Georgina Born and Tim Hodgkinson, Cambridge, UK, February 21, 2012.

Jane Colling, London, July 13, 2013.

Etienne Conod, Zürich, March 26, 2016.

Chris Cutler, Croydon, UK, May 14, 21–23, 2012.

Chris Cutler and Maggie Thomas, Toulouse, France, June 29, 2013.

Simon Draper, Petersfield, UK, May 10, 2012.

Franco Fabbri, Skype interview, July 20, 2015.

Steve Feigenbaum, telephone interview, August 10, 2016.

Charles Fletcher, London, February 5, 2012.

Fred Frith, Oakland, CA, November 8–9, 12, 14, 2011; Skype interview, January 20, 2012; Basel, Switzerland, April 7–9, 11, 2012.

Simon Frith, Newcastle upon Tyne, UK, April 1, 2016.

John Greaves, Paris, February 16–17, 2012; telephone interview, May 10, 2012.

Ian Hoare, London, July 23, 2013.

Nick Hobbs, Skype interview, April 4, 2012.

Tim Hodgkinson, Brixton, UK, March 21–25, April 3–4, 2012; telephone interview, April 6, 2012; Brixton, UK, April 22–23, 2012; Skype interview, August 13, 2016.

Henry Kaiser, telephone interview, September 15, 2016.

Dagmar Krause, Chiltern Hills, UK, February 2–4, 2012; Chiltern Hills, UK, April 21, 2012.

Dave Laing, London, July 24, 2013.

Geoff Leigh, Hastings, UK, December 8–9, 2011.

Richard Leigh, London, April 25, 2012.

Mandy Merck, London, May 6, 2012.

Phil Minton, London, May 5, 2012.

Anthony Moore, Cologne, Germany, April 19, 2012; Skype interview, August 29, 2014.

Annette Morreau, London, September 24, 2016.

Phil Newell, telephone interview, August 3, 2014.

Tom Newman, telephone interview, January 14, 2012.

Sula (Goschen) Nichols, Carmel, CA, October 5, 2012.

Maggie Nicols, London, March 22, 2012; Drefach Felindre, Wales, May 15, 2012.

David Perry, Shrewsbury, Wales, March 30, 2016.

Sally Potter, London, April 27, 2012.

Andrew Powell, Skype interview, August 4, 2014.

Bill and Vicky Ridgers, London, March 25, 2016.

Annemarie Roelofs, Frankfurt, Germany, May 27, 2012.

Neil Sandford, Teddington, UK, April 24, 2012.

Victor Schonfield, London, April 20, 2012, and July 17, 2013.

Ray Smith, Tintinhull, UK, April 16, 2012.

Sue Steward, London, May 18, 2012.

Maggie Thomas, Caudeval, France, June 16–18, 2013.

Liza (White) Tonner, Skype interview, June 8, 2015.

David Toop, London, May 7–8, 2012.

Chris Wangro, Woodstock, NY, July 25, 2012.

Henk Weltevreden, Rotterdam, Netherlands, March 29, 2016.

Mike Westbrook, Skype interview, August 7, 2014.

Veryan Weston, Welwyn Garden City, UK, March 26, 2012.

Cathy Williams, telephone interview, May 19, 2012.

Colin Wood, telephone interview, May 3, 2012.

Archives and Personal Collections

Arts Council of Great Britain (ACGB).

Ayerst, Caroline. Personal archive (CAA).

Blegvad, Peter. Personal archive (PBA).

British Library Sound Collection, British Library.

Colling, Jane. Personal archive.

Cooper, Lindsay. Personal archive (LCA).

Cutler, Chris. Personal archive (CCA).

Frith, Fred. Personal archive (FFA).

Hoare, Ian. Personal archive.

Hodgkinson, Tim. Personal archive (THA).

Laing, Dave. Personal archive.

Merck, Mandy. Personal archive (MMA).

Musicians Union, University of Stirling, Scotland.

Oral History of Jazz in Britain, British Library.

Souster, Tim. Personal archive (TSA).

Books, Articles, and Musical Albums

1/- Paper (Cambridge, UK). "Rights of Man." February 28, 1969.

1/- Paper (Cambridge, UK). "Rock . . ." n.d. [October 2, 1970?].

Abbate, Carolyn. "Wagner, Cinema, and Redemptive Glee." *Opera Quarterly* 21, no. 4 (2005): 597–611.

Adams, Ian. "Henry Cow." *Sounds*, December 13, 1975, 34.

Adelt, Ulrich. *Krautrock: German Music in the Seventies*. Ann Arbor: University of Michigan Press, 2016.

Alterman, Loraine. "This Is Not Here." *Melody Maker*, October 23, 1971.

Alterman, Loraine. "YOKO: How I Rescued John from Chauvinism." *Melody Maker*, September 22, 1973.

Altham, Keith. Review of *Unrest*, by Henry Cow. *Look Now*, August 1974.

Anderson, Iain. *This Is Our Music: Free Jazz, the Sixties, and American Culture*. Philadelphia: University of Pennsylvania Press, 2007.

Anderson, Perry. "Modernity and Revolution." *New Left Review* 1, no. 144 (1984): 96–113.

Ansell, Kenneth. "Dissecting the Cow: An Almost Complete History of Henry Cow." *Impetus* 2 (June 1976): n.p.

Ansell, Kenneth. "Fred Frith: Balancing the Axe." *Wire* 6 (1984): 23–26.

Ansell, Kenneth. "Henry Cow." *Impetus* 9 (1979): 375–78.

Ansell, Kenneth. "Nick Hobbs: Instigator." *Impetus* 9 (1979): 372–73.

Ansell, Kenneth. "Rock in Opposition." *Impetus* 7 (1978): 282–83.

Ansell, Kenneth. "Tangerine Dream: Chatting with Edgar Froese and Peter Baumann." *Zigzag* 44 (August 1974): 39–43.

Anthony, Carl. Review of *Unrest*, by Henry Cow. *Audio*, August 1974.

Art Bears. *Hope and Fears Booklet*. London: self-published, 1978.

Ashworth, Steven. Letter to the editor. *Melody Maker*, July 15, 1978.

A S-W. "Vill fönya, förändra." *Upsala Nya Tidning* (Uppsala, Sweden), May 20, 1976.

Atkins, Ronald. "The Orckestra." *Guardian*, June 27, 1977.

Atkins, Ronald. Untitled interview with Victor Schonfield. *Guardian*, November 24, 1970.

Auther, Elissa. *String, Felt, Thread: The Hierarchy of Art and Craft in American Art*. Minneapolis: University of Minnesota Press, 2009.

Bad Alchemy. "A Young Lady's Vision: Lindsay Cooper." 2 (1985): 13–21.

Baker, Jr., Houston A. *Blues, Ideology, and Afro-American Literature: A Vernacular Theory*. Chicago, IL: University of Chicago Press, 1984.

Ballantine, Christopher. "Modernism and Popular Music." *Journal of the Royal Musical Association* 139, no. 1 (2014): 200–204.

Ballantine, Christopher. "Towards an Aesthetic of Experimental Music." *Musical Quarterly* 63, no. 2 (1977): 224–46.

Bangs, Lester. *Psychotic Reactions and Carburetor Dung: The Work of a Legendary Critic: Rock 'n' Roll as Literature and Literature as Rock 'n' Roll.* Edited by Greil Marcus. New York: Knopf, 1987.

Barfe, Louis. *Where Have All the Good Times Gone? The Rise and Fall of the Record Industry.* London: Atlantic Books, 2005.

Barnes, Alan. Donald Frith obituary. *Guardian*, April 30, 2000.

Barnes, Mike. *Captain Beefheart: The Biography.* London: Omnibus, 2000.

Barnett, Anthony. *UnNatural Music: John Lennon and Yoko Ono in Cambridge 1969: Account of the Circumstances Surrounding Their Appearance at the Natural Music Concert.* Lewes, UK: Allardyce, 2016.

Barre, Trevor. *Beyond Jazz: Plink, Plonk, and Scratch: The Golden Age of Free Music in London, 1966–1972.* London: Book Refinery, 2015.

Beal, Amy C. *New Music, New Allies: American Experimental Music in West Germany from the Zero Hour to Reunification.* Berkeley: University of California Press, 2006.

Belgrad, Daniel. *The Culture of Spontaneity: Improvisation and the Arts in Postwar America.* Chicago, IL: University of Chicago Press, 1998.

Bell, Clive. "Epiphanies." *Wire* 212 (October 2001): 106.

Bell, Max. "Tangerine Dream: Is This the End of Rock as We Know It?" *New Musical Express*, November 16, 1974.

Benjamin, Walter. "The Author as Producer." In *Understanding Brecht*, translated by Anna Bostock, 85–103. London: Verso, [1934] 1998.

Benton, Michael. "Never a Duul Moment." *Melody Maker*, June 2, 1973.

Beresford, Steve. "Game for a Laugh." Interview with Julian Cowley. *Wire* 218 (2002): 24–29.

Beresford, Steve. Untitled report. *Musics* 13 (August 1977): 18.

Berkman, Franya. *Monument Eternal: The Music of Alice Coltrane.* Middletown, CT: Wesleyan University Press, 2010.

Bernstein, David W., ed. *The San Francisco Tape Music Center: 1960s Counterculture and the Avant-Garde.* Berkeley: University of California Press, 2008.

Best. "Magma / Hervé Picart, une 'joute' mémorable . . ." October 1975, no. 87. Available at http://robert.guillerault.free.fr/magma/textes/1975/best_87.htm.

Bhabha, Homi. "Unsatisfied: Notes on Vernacular Cosmopolitanism." In *Text and Nation: Cross-Disciplinary Essays on Cultural and National Identities*, edited by Laura García-Moreno and Peter C. Pfeiffer, 191–207. London: Camden House, 1996.

Blackpool Gazette and Herald. "For Minority Tastes." June 28, 1974.

Blaikie, Roger. Review of *Leg End*, by Henry Cow. *Cracker* 39 (October 19, 1973).

Blegvad, Peter. "The Bleaching Stream." Interview with Kevin Jackson. *Journal of the London Institute of 'Pataphysics* 3 (September 2011): 7–79.

Blegvad, Peter, ed., *Kew. Rhone.* Axminster, UK: Uniformbooks, 2014.

Bolelli, Franco, and Peppo Delconte. "Henry Cow: L'avventura é solo cominciata." *Gong*, April 1977, 11.

Bompard, Paul. "Top Italian Promoter Sees Hope for Rock." *Billboard*, April 2, 1977, 60.

Borgo, David. *Sync or Swarm: Improvising Music in a Complex Age*. New York: Continuum, 2006.

Borio, Gianmario. "Avantgarde als pluralistisches Konzept: Musik um 1968." In *Rebellische Musik: Kulturwandel und gesellschaftlicher Protest um 1968*, ed. Arnold Jacobshagen and Markus Leniger, 15–33. Cologne, Germany: Dohr, 2007.

Borio, Gianmario. "Key Questions of Antagonistic Music Making: A View from Italy." In *Red Strains: Music and Communism outside the Communist Bloc*, edited by Robert Adlington, 175–91. London: The British Academy and Oxford University Press, 2013.

Born, Georgina. "Modern Music Culture: On Shock, Pop and Synthesis." *New Formations* 2 (summer 1987): 51–78.

Born, Georgina. "On Musical Mediation: Ontology, Technology and Creativity." *Twentieth-Century Music* 2, no. 1 (2005): 7–36.

Born, Georgina. "On Music and Politics: Henry Cow, Avant-Gardism and Its Discontents." In *Red Strains: Music and Communism outside the Communist Bloc*, edited by Robert Adlington, 55–64. Oxford: Oxford University Press, 2013.

Born, Georgina. *Rationalizing Culture: IRCAM, Boulez, and the Institutionalization of the Musical Avant-Garde*. Berkeley: University of California Press, 1995.

Born, Georgie. "Some Notes on the Feminist Improvising Group." *Musics* 16 (February 1978): 5.

Bower, Tom. *Branson*. London: Fourth Estate, 2000.

Boyd, Joe. Uwe Nettelbeck obituary. *Guardian*, February 12, 2007.

Boyd, Joe. *White Bicycles: Making Music in the 1960s*. London: Serpent's Tail, 2006.

Brackett, David. *Categorizing Sound: Genre and Twentieth-Century Popular Music*. Oakland: University of California Press, 2016.

Bradshaw, Paul. "Blake, Brecht, Coltrane, Jazz, Folk, Rock: All from One Band!!" *Challenge*, May 1977.

Bramstedt, Sivert. "Engelska Henry Cow blev röriga på scen." *Dagens Nyheter* (Stockholm), May 21, 1976.

Branson, Richard. *Losing My Virginity: How I Survived, Had Fun, and Made a Fortune Doing Business My Way*. New York: Crown, [1998] 2007.

Brazier, Chris. "Henry Cow." *Melody Maker*, February 25, 1978.

Brown, David. "How 'Botticelli's Angel' Went from Shock Album Cover to Movie Extra." *Times* (London), March 1, 2014.

Bryan-Wilson, Julia. *Fray: Art and Textile Politics*. Chicago, IL: University of Chicago Press, 2017.

Bryan-Wilson, Julia. "'Out to See Video': EZTV's Queer Microcinema in West Hollywood." *Grey Room* 56 (summer 2014): 56–89.

Buchloh, Benjamin. "Theorizing the Avant-Garde." *Art in America* 72, no. 10 (1984): 19, 21.

Burdor, John. "Commander Hugh Hodgkinson." Obituary. *Independent* (London), January 28, 1996. Accessed September 9, 2016. http://www.independent.co.uk/news/people/obituary-commander-hugh-hodgkinson-1326449.html.

Bürger, Peter. *Theory of the Avant-Garde*. Minneapolis: University of Minnesota Press, 1984.

Calinescu, Matei. *Five Faces of Modernity: Modernism, Avant-Garde, Decadence, Kitsch, Postmodernism*. Durham, NC: Duke University Press, 1987.

Cannon, James. "Henry Cow / Christ's Theatre." *Varsity* (Cambridge UK), May 8, 1971.

Cardew, Cornelius. "Cornelius Cardew." Interview. *International Times*, February 2–15, 1968.

Cardew, Cornelius. "Sitting in the Dark." *Musical Times* 109, no. 1501 (March 1968): 233–34.

Cardew, Cornelius. Untitled report. *Musics* 13 (August 1977): 12–13.

Case, Doug. "Henry Cow." *Sounds* 5, no. 11 (1973): 31–32.

Catchpole, Charles. "Rock Prophets Scorn Success." *Evening Standard*, March 23, 1977.

Cavell, Stanley. *Pursuits of Happiness: The Hollywood Comedy of Remarriage*. Cambridge, MA: Harvard University Press, 1981.

Chadwick, Jon. "Tom Paine." *Varsity* (Cambridge UK), March 1, 1969.

Charlton, Hannah. "No Apologies." *Melody Maker*, December 8, 1979.

Chowrimootoo, Christopher. "Reviving the Middlebrow, or: Deconstructing Modernism from the Inside." *Journal of the Royal Musical Association* 139, no. 1 (2014): 187–93.

Clark, T. J. "Clement Greenberg's Theory of Art." *Critical Inquiry* 9, no. 1 (September 1982): 139–56.

Cohen, Brigid. *Stefan Wolpe and the Avant-Garde Diaspora*. Cambridge: Cambridge University Press, 2012.

Coleman, Ornette. Liner notes to *Dancing in Your Head*, by Ornette Coleman. A&M SP-722, 1977, LP.

Coley, Byron. "This Heat: Head Birth in the Year Zero." *Rock's Back Pages*, December 2015. Accessed December 19, 2016. http://www.rocksbackpages.com/Library /Article/this-heat-head-birth-in-the-year-zero.

Comentale, Edward P. *Sweet Air: Modernism, Regionalism, and American Popular Song*. Urbana: University of Illinois Press, 2013.

"Contemporary Music Network: A Discussion." *Tempo*, no. 119 (December 1976): 7–14.

Cooper, Lindsay. Letter to the editor. *New Musical Express*, August 16, 1975.

Cooper, Lindsay. "Rock around the Cock." *Leveller*, October 1978, 12.

Cooper, Lindsay. "Women, Music, Feminism—Notes." *Musics* 14 (October 1977): 16–19.

Cooper, Lindsay, and Dagmar Krause. "Talking till the Henry Cow Comes Home." Interview with Malcolm Heyhoe and Irena Krumb. *Liquorice* 6 (June 1976): 4–9.

Cope, Julian. *Krautrocksampler*. 2nd ed. London: Head Heritage, [1995] 1996.

Corina, Maurice. "Record Men Drop RPM: Cut-Price War Expected." *Times* (London), June 27, 1969.

Cottington, David. "The Formation of the Avant-Garde in Paris and London, c. 1880–1915." *Art History* 35, no. 3 (June 2012): 596–621.

Crone, Rainer. "What Andy Warhol Really Did." *New York Review of Books*, February 25, 2010.

Crow, Thomas. "Modernism and Mass Culture." In *Modernism and Modernity: The Vancouver Conference Papers*, edited by Benjamin H. D. Buchloh, Serge Guilbaut, and David Solkin, 215–64. Halifax: Press of the Nova Scotia College of Art and Design, 1983.

Crow, Thomas. *The Long March of Pop: Art, Music, and Design, 1930–1995.* New Haven, CT: Yale University Press, 2014.

Cruft, John. Letter to the editor. *Musics* 8 (July 1976): 3.

Cutler, Chris. *File under Popular: Theoretical and Critical Writings on Music.* London: November Books, 1985.

Cutler, Chris. Letter to the editor. *New Musical Express,* June 29, 1974.

Cutler, Chris. "Magic Magma." *Sound International,* May 1979, 13.

Cutler, Chris. "Postscript—Chris Cutler Brings RIO Up to Date." *Impetus* 9 (1979): 395, 411.

Cutler, Chris. "Thoughts on Music and the Avant-Garde: Considerations of a Term and Its Public Use." In *Musik-Avantgarde: Zur Dialektik von Vorhut und Nachhut,* edited by Hanns-Werner Heister, Wolfgang Martin Stroh, and Peter Wicke, 52–73. Oldenburg, Germany: BIS-Verlag, 2006.

Cutler, Chris. Untitled report. *Musics* 13 (August 1977): 16–18.

Cutler, Chris, and Tim Hodgkinson, eds. *The Henry Cow Book, 1968–78.* London: self-published, 1981.

Dagens Nyheter (Stockholm). "Musiken är ingen spegel—den är en hammare." May 18, 1977.

Dallas, Karl. "The Ecstasy without the Agony." *Let It Rock,* October 1975, 24–26.

Dallas, Karl. "Faust." *Melody Maker,* June 16, 1973.

Dallas, Karl. "Faust and Foremost." *Melody Maker,* June 2, 1973.

Dallas, Karl. "Fighting the System Europe-wide." *Melody Maker,* April 15, 1978.

Dallas, Karl, and Steve Lake. "Stockhausen: Free as a Bird." *Melody Maker,* April 24, 1976.

Darts (University of Sheffield Union of Students). Unsigned review of *Leg End,* by Henry Cow. October 1973.

Dawson, Jenny. Review of *Unrest,* by Henry Cow. *Stratford Express,* June 29, 1974.

Dedekind, Henning. *Krautrock: Underground, LSD, und kosmische Kuriere.* Innsbruck, Austria: Hannibal Verlag, 2008.

de Jongh, Nicholas. "A Critical Discovery." *Guardian,* May 10, 1972.

de Jongh, Nicholas. "The Tempest." *Guardian,* November 1, 1973.

Dellar, Fred. Review of *Leg End,* by Henry Cow. *Hi-Fi News,* November 1973.

Demers, Joanna. *Listening through the Noise: The Aesthetics of Experimental Electronic Music.* New York: Oxford University Press, 2010.

de Miguel, Antonio. "Henry Cow: Los Marginados del Rollo Asaltan España (Ya Era Hora!)." *Disco Express,* November 11, 1977.

Denning, Michael. *Noise Uprising: The Audiopolitics of a World Musical Revolution.* New York: Verso, 2015.

Denselow, Robin. Review of *Desperate Straights,* by Slapp Happy / Henry Cow. *Guardian,* April 1, 1975.

Devenport, Pete. Untitled report. *Musics* 13 (August 1977): 11–12.

Devine, Kyle. "Imperfect Sound Forever: Loudness Wars, Listening Formations and the History of Sound Reproduction." *Popular Music* 32, no. 2 (May 2013): 159–76.

Dewar, Andrew Raffo. "Handmade Sounds: The Sonic Arts Union and American Technoculture." PhD diss., Wesleyan University, 2009.

Dewar, Andrew Raffo. "Searching for the Center of a Sound: Bill Dixon's *Webern*, the Unaccompanied Solo, and Compositional Ontology in Post-Songform Jazz." *Jazz Perspectives* 4, no. 1 (2010): 59–87.

Disc. "'I'm Broke' Says 'Bells' Producer." March 22, 1975.

Disc. "Moore of the Same." August 16, 1975.

Disco Express. "Vuelve a Visitarnos Henry Cow." March 31, 1978.

Doyle, Peter. *Echo and Reverb: Fabricating Space in Popular Music Recording, 1900–1960.* Middletown, CT: Wesleyan University Press, 2005.

Doyle, Tom. "Faust: Hans Joachim Irmler." *Sound on Sound*, July 2010. http://www.soundonsound.com/people/faust-hans-joachim-irmler.

Draper, Simon. Afterword to *Virgin: A History of Virgin Records*, by Terry Southern, 240–56. Axminster, UK: A Publishing Company, [1996?].

Drott, Eric. "The End(s) of Genre." *Journal of Music Theory* 57, no. 1 (2013): 1–45.

Drott, Eric. "Free Jazz and the French Critic." *Journal of the American Musicological Society* 61, no. 3 (fall 2008): 541–81.

Drott, Eric. *Music and the Elusive Revolution: Cultural Politics and Political Culture in France, 1968–1981.* Berkeley: University of California Press, 2011.

Duncan, Andy. "Mike Westbrook, Part 1." *Impetus* 4 [1976?]: 169–72.

Dwinell, Samuel. "Blackness in British Opera." PhD diss., Cornell University, 2016.

Ellis, David. "David Vorhaus and Kaleidophon Studio." *Electronics and Music Maker,* June 1981, 74–76.

Ellison, Ralph. "The Golden Age, Time Past." In *The Jazz Cadence of American Culture,* edited by Robert G. O'Meally, 448–56. New York: Columbia University Press, 1998.

Erskine, Peter. "Annals of Excess." *New Musical Express*, June 7, 1975.

Erskine, Peter. "Canned Music." *Disc*, December 16, 1972.

Erskine, Peter. "Never a Duul Moment." *Disc*, July 1, 1972.

Erskine, Peter. Review of *Desperate Straights*, by Slapp Happy / Henry Cow. *New Musical Express*, February 22, 1975.

Erskine, Peter. "We're Definitely Not the Kind of Thing That'd Interest Readers of *NME*." *New Musical Express*, October 26, 1974.

Eshelman, Clayton. "The Sanjo Bridge." *Sparrow* 2 (November 1972).

Evans, Mike. "Rank 'n' File Rockanroll." *Cream* 18 (November 1972): 18–20.

Fabbri, Franco. "Orchestral Manoeuvres in the 1970s: L'Orchestra Co-Operative, 1978–1983." *Popular Music* 26, no. 3 (October 2007): 409–27.

Fallowell, Duncan "Can: The Heaviest of All?" *Melody Maker*, October 30, 1971, 10.

Farren, Mick. "Rocking on within the System." *Cream* 23 (April 1973): 8–9.

Faust. *Faust: The Wümme Years, 1970–73.* ReR Megacorp ReRFB1, 2000, 5 CD box set.

Feldman, Morton. "Liner Notes." In *Give My Regards to Eighth Street: Collected Writings of Morton Feldman*, edited by B. H. Friedman, 3–7. Cambridge, MA: Exact Change, 2000. Originally written in 1962.

Fellezs, Kevin. *Birds of Fire: Jazz, Rock, Funk, and the Creation of Fusion*. Durham, NC: Duke University Press, 2011.

Fellezs, Kevin. "Enter the Voice of the Dragon: Fred Ho, Bruce Lee, and the Popular Avant-Garde." In *Yellow Power Yellow Soul: The Radical Art of Fred Ho*, edited by Roger N. Buckley and Tamara Roberts, 35–53. Urbana: University of Illinois Press, 2013.

Feisst, Sabine M. "John Cage and Improvisation: An Unresolved Relationship." In *Musical Improvisation: Art, Education, and Society*, edited by Gabriel Solis and Bruno Nettl, 38–51. Urbana: University of Illinois Press, 2009.

Fielding, Howard. "Faust." *Sounds*, October 23, 1973.

Filene, Benjamin. *Romancing the Folk: Public Memory and American Roots Music*. Chapel Hill: University of North Carolina Press, 2000.

Filer, Colin. "Beast v. Theatre." *Varsity* (Cambridge UK), March 8, 1969.

Fiori, Umberto. "Rock Music and Politics in Italy." *Popular Music* 4 (1984): 261–77.

Fitz-Gerald, G. F. *Mouseproof*. UNI Records UNLS 115, 1970, LP.

Ford, Christopher. "Bedford Chords." *Guardian*, February 24, 1971.

Ford, Phil. *Dig: Sound and Music in Hip Culture*. New York: Oxford University Press, 2013.

Fordham, John. "Above the Herd." *Time Out*, May 30–June 5, 1975, 9.

Fordham, John. "Not with a Mirror . . . but a Hammer." *Time Out*, January 30–February 5, 1976, 10–11.

Foster, Hal. "What's Neo about the Neo-Avant-Garde?" *October* 70 (autumn 1994): 5–32.

Freire, Paulo. *Pedagogy of the Oppressed*. Translated by Myra Bergman Ramos. New York: Herder and Herder, 1970.

Freni, Nicolle. Untitled report. *Musics* 13 (August 1977): 16.

Frith, Fred. "Great Rock Solos of Our Time." *New Musical Express*, October 12, 1974.

Frith, Fred. "Great Rock Solos of Our Time." *New Musical Express*, October 19, 1974.

Frith, Fred. "Great Rock Solos of Our Time." *New Musical Express*, December 14, 1974.

Frith, Fred. *Guitar Solos*. Caroline C 1508, 1974, LP.

Frith, Fred. Letter to the editor. *Melody Maker*, August 14, 1976.

Frith, Simon. "Art Ideology and Pop Practice." In *Marxism and the Interpretation of Culture*, edited by Cary Nelson and Lawrence Grossberg, 461–75. Urbana: University of Illinois Press, 1988.

Frith, Simon. "Punk—Hippies with Short Hair." *Leveller*, November 1977, 20–21.

Frith, Simon. "Ugly, Vulgar, Insulting—Zappa Scores!" *Let It Rock*, November 1973.

Frith, Simon, and Howard Horne. *Art into Pop*. London: Methuen, 1987.

Frith, Simon, and John Street. "Rock against Racism and Red Wedge: From Music to Politics, from Politics to Music." In *Rockin' the Boat: Mass Music and Mass Movements*, edited by Reebee Garofalo, 67–80. Boston, MA: South End Press, 1992.

Frodsham, Simon. "Professional Virgin." *West London Observer*, November 29, 1974.

Fusco, Coco. "The Other History of Intercultural Performance." *Drama Review* 38, no. 1 (spring 1994): 143–67.

Gabbard, Krin. "Revenge of the Nerds: Representing the White Male Collector of Black Music." In *Jammin' at the Margins: Jazz and the American Cinema*, 199–232. Chicago, IL: University of Chicago Press, 1996.

Garmo, Trond Einar. *Henry Cow: En analyse av avantgarderock*. Trondheim, Norway: Skrifter fra Musikkvitenskapelig Institutt, 2001.

G. B. Review of *So Far*, by Faust. *Melody Maker*, April 7, 1973.

Gendron, Bernard. *Between Montmartre and the Mudd Club: Popular Music and the Avant-Garde*. Chicago, IL: University of Chicago Press, 2002.

Gennari, John. *Blowin' Hot and Cool: Jazz and Its Critics*. Chicago, IL: University of Chicago Press, 2006.

Gillig, Manfred. "The Henry Cow Legend." *Sounds* (Germany) 7 (1974): 48–49.

Goehr, Lydia. "Improvising *Impromptu*, or, What to Do with a Broken String." In *The Oxford Handbook of Critical Improvisation Studies*, edited by George E. Lewis and Benjamin Piekut, 1:458–80. New York: Oxford University Press, 2016.

Goldman, Danielle. *I Want to Be Ready: Improvised Dance as a Practice of Freedom*. Ann Arbor: University of Michigan Press, 2010.

Gomelsky, Georgio. "Georgio Gomelsky Interview." Interview with Archie Patterson. In *Eurock: Music and Second Culture Post Millennium*, 14–31. Portland, OR: Eurock Publications, 2013.

Goodyer, Ian. *Crisis Music: The Cultural Politics of Rock against Racism*. Manchester, UK: University of Manchester Press, 2009.

Gottschalk, Jennie. *Experimental Music since 1970*. New York: Bloomsbury, 2016.

Graham, Stephen. *Sounds of the Underground: A Cultural, Political, and Aesthetic Mapping of Underground and Fringe Music*. Ann Arbor: University of Michigan Press, 2016.

Green, Kim. Untitled report. *Musics* 13 (August 1977): 12.

Greenberg, Clement. "Avant-Garde and Kitsch." *Partisan Review* 6 (fall 1939): 34–49.

Greenberg, Clement. "Towards a Newer Laocoön." *Partisan Review* 7 (July–August 1940): 296–310.

Greenfield, Robert. "Sun Ra and Europe's Space Music Scene." *Rolling Stone*, January 7, 1971, 17–18.

Grimshaw, Jeremy. *Draw a Straight Line and Follow It: The Music and Mysticism of La Monte Young*. New York: Oxford University Press, 2012.

Grindon, Gavin. "Poetry Written in Gasoline: Black Mask and Up Against the Wall Motherfucker." *Art History* 38, no. 1 (February 2015): 174–75.

Grindon, Gavin. "Surrealism, Dada, and the Refusal of Work: Autonomy, Activism, and Social Participation in the Radical Avant-Garde." *Oxford Art Journal* 34, no. 1 (March 2011): 79–96.

Grubbs, David. *Records Ruin the Landscape: John Cage, the Sixties, and Sound Recording*. Durham, NC: Duke University Press, 2014.

Hamburger Abendblatt. "Statt Musik Kampf mit der Technik." November 24, 1971.

Hansen, Miriam Bratu. "Fallen Women, Rising Stars, New Horizons: Shanghai Silent Film as Vernacular Modernism." *Film Quarterly* 54, no. 1 (autumn 2000): 10–22.

Hansen, Miriam Bratu. "The Mass Production of the Senses: Classical Cinema as Vernacular Modernism." *Modernism/Modernity* 6, no. 2 (April 1999): 59–77.

Harding, James M. "From Cutting Edges to Rough Edges: On the Transnational Foundations of Avant-Garde Performance." In *The Ghosts of the Avant-Garde(s): Exorcising Experimental Theater and Performance*, 136–58. Ann Arbor: University of Michigan Press, 2013.

Harrison, Max. "Crossing the Great Musical Divide." *Record Collector*, November 1971.

Harron, Mary. "Dialectics Meet Disco." *Melody Maker*, May 26, 1979, 17.

Hayman, Martin. "Amon Duul: Community of Lemmings?" *Sounds*, June 24, 1972.

Hayman, Martin. "Which Way the Trade Gap?" *Sounds*, December 8, 1973.

Heatley, Michael. *John Peel: A Life in Music*. London: Michael O'Mara Books, 2004.

Heffley, Mike. *Northern Sun, Southern Moon: Europe's Reinvention of Jazz*. New Haven, CT: Yale University Press, 2005.

Heining, Duncan. "Mike Westbrook: Is This Man Britain's Greatest Living Composer?" *Avant* 1 (1997): 22–23.

Heller, Michael. *Loft Jazz: Improvising New York in the 1970s*. Oakland: University of California Press, 2017.

Hemmings, Susan, and Norma Pitfield. "The Feminist Improvising Group." *Musics* 15 (December 1977): 20.

Hennion, Antoine. "An Intermediary between Production and Consumption: The Producer of Popular Music." *Science, Technology, and Human Values* 14, no. 4 (autumn 1989): 400–24.

Henry Cow. *Henry Cow: Fortieth-Anniversary Box Set*. ReR Megacorp RERHCBOX2a-c, 2009, 9 CDs and 1 DVD.

Henshaw, Laurie. "Import Records." *Melody Maker*, November 13, 1971, 29.

Herbst, Helmut. "New German Cinema, 1962–83: A View from Hamburg." In *West German Filmmakers on Film: Visions and Voices*, edited by Eric Rentschler, 225–34. New York: Holmes and Meier, 1988. Article originally written in 1983.

Herman, Gary, and Ian Hoare. "The Struggle for Song: A Reply to Leon Rosselson." In *Media, Politics, and Culture: A Socialist View*, edited by Carl Gardner, 51–60. London: Macmillan, 1979.

Herrera, Luis Eduardo. "The CLAEM and the Construction of Elite Art Worlds: Philanthropy, Latinamericanism and Avant-Garde Music." PhD diss., University of Illinois at Urbana-Champaign, 2013.

Heyhoe, Malcolm. "Henry Cow." *New Musical Express*, March 12, 1977, 52.

Heyhoe, Malcolm. "Music for Socialism." *New Musical Express*, June 18, 1977.

HiFi for Pleasure. Unsigned review of *Leg End*, by Henry Cow. December 1973.

HiFi for Pleasure. Unsigned review of *Unrest*, by Henry Cow. August 1974.

Higgins, Hannah. *Fluxus Experience*. Berkeley: University of California Press, 2002.

Hitchcock, H. Wiley. *Music in the United States: A Historical Introduction*. Rev. ed. Englewood Cliffs, NJ: Prentice Hall, 1974.

Hitchens, Christopher. *Hitch-22: A Memoir*. New York: Twelve, 2010.

H. K. Review of *Leg End*, by Henry Cow. *Disc*, September 29, 1973.

Hoare, Ian. "Black Music in Britain." *Music for Socialism Newsletter*, November 1977, 4.

Hoare, Ian. "Music for Socialism." *Musics* 13 (August 1977): 9.

Hoare, Ian. "Music for Socialism." *Wedge* 1 (summer 1977): 25–26.

Hoare, Ian. "The Politics of Rock Performance." *Music for Socialism Newsletter*, November 1977, 10.

Hoare, Ian. "Record and Tape Distribution: The First Steps." *Music for Socialism Newsletter*, November 1977, 7.

Hobbs, Nick. "Rock in Opposition (to Crap Music)." *Music for Socialism Newsletter*, November 1977, 8.

Hobbs, Nick. "Rock in Opposition." *Music for Socialism Newsletter*, February 1978, 4–5.

Hobbs, Nick. Untitled report. *Musics* 13 (August 1977): 14–15.

Hodgkinson, Tim. "Thoughts on the Conference." *Music for Socialism Newsletter*, November 1977, 5–6.

Hollingworth, Roy. "Euro Vision." *Melody Maker*, January 20, 1973.

Hoyland, John. "How Do Music and Socialism Connect?" *Comment*, June 11, 1977, 200.

Hoyland, John. Review of *Leg End*, by Henry Cow. *Let It Rock*, November 1973.

Hoyland, John. "Still up against the Business." *Let It Rock*, July 1973, 31–32.

Hoyland, John. "Up against the Business." *Let It Rock*, May 1973, 27.

Hoyland, John. "Who Owns the Music?" *Cream* 22 (March 1973): 8–9.

Huyssen, Andreas. "Back to the Future: Fluxus in Context." In *Twilight Memories: Marking Time in a Culture of Amnesia*, 191–208. New York: Routledge, 1995.

Iddon, Martin. "The Haus That Karlheinz Built: Composition, Authority, and Control at the 1968 Darmstadt Ferienkurse." *Musical Quarterly* 87, no. 1 (2004): 87–118.

Iddon, Martin. *New Music at Darmstadt: Nono, Stockhausen, Cage, and Boulez.* Cambridge: Cambridge University Press, 2013.

Ingham, Steve. Review of Captain Beefheart concert, Leeds, UK. *Contact* 9 (autumn 1974): 26–28.

Irmler, Hans-Joachim. Interview with Ralf B. *Ptolemaic Terrascope* 29 (2000): n.p.

Isler, Scott. Review of *Concerts*, by Henry Cow. *Trouser Press*, October–November 1976, 32.

James, David E. *The Most Typical Avant-Garde: History and Geography of Minor Cinemas in Los Angeles.* Berkeley: University of California Press, 2005.

James, Robin. "Is the Post- in Post-Identity the Post- in Post-Genre?" *Popular Music* 36, no. 1 (January 2016): 21–32.

Jay, Martin. *The Dialectical Imagination: A History of the Frankfurt School and the Institute of Social Research, 1923–1950.* Berkeley: University of California Press, 1973.

Jazz Monthly. "Cornelius Cardew, AMM, and the Path to Perfect Hearing." May 1968, 10–11.

Johnson, James. "Blatant Eccentrics Get Record Deal." *New Musical Express*, June 8, 1974.

Johnson, James. "Can Can . . . and They Will." *New Musical Express*, February 5, 1972.

Jones, Allan. "Ruth, Richard, and Robert . . ." *Melody Maker*, June 14, 1975.

Jones, LeRoi. *Blues People.* New York: Morrow Quill Paperbacks, 1963.

Joseph, Branden W. *Beyond the Dream Syndicate: Tony Conrad and the Arts after Cage.* New York: Zone Books, 2008.

Joseph, Branden W. *Experimentations: John Cage in Music, Art, and Architecture*. New York: Bloomsbury Academic, 2016.

Joseph, Branden W. "HPSCHD—Ghost or Monster?" In *Mainframe Experimentalism: Early Computing and the Foundation of the Digital Arts*, edited by Hannah B. Higgins and Douglas Kahn, 147–69. Berkeley: University of California Press, 2012.

Joseph, Branden W. *Random Order: Robert Rauschenberg and the Neo-Avant-Garde*. Cambridge: MIT Press, 2003.

Jost, Ekkehard. *Free Jazz*. New York: Da Capo Press, 1975.

Kainer, Robert. Review of *Concerts*, by Henry Cow. *Lamb* 11, 1977.

Keister, Jay. "'The Long Freak Out': Unfinished Music and Countercultural Madness in 1960s and 1970s Avant-Garde Rock." *Volume!* 9, no. 2 (2012). Accessed December 29, 2016. http://volume.revues.org/3413?gathStatIcon=true#toc to1n1.

Kelly, P. R. Letter to the editor. *Melody Maker*, March 11, 1978.

Kent, Nick. "Can: Ve Give Ze Orders Here." *New Musical Express*, February 16, 1974.

Kington, Miles. "Trip Beyond Jazz's Outermost Fringe." *Times* (London), November 30, 1967.

Klug, Liebe. "Dancers and the Dance." *Varsity* (Cambridge UK) 75, no. 1, n.d. [January 15, 1972]: 10.

Koopman, Colin and Tomas Matza. "Putting Foucault to Work: Analytic and Concept in Foucaultian Inquiry." *Critical Inquiry* 39 (summer 2013): 817–40.

Kouwenhoven, John. *The Beer Can by the Highway: Essays on What's American about America*. Garden City, NJ: Doubleday, 1961.

Krause, Dagmar. "Watching the Trains Go By." Interview with Kate Phillips. *New Musical Express*, July 19, 1975.

Krautrock: The Rebirth of Germany. Directed by Benjamin Whalley. BBC Four, 2009.

Laing, Dave. "In Praise of Henry Cow." *Sounds*, February 6, 1976.

Laing, Dave. *One-Chord Wonders: Power and Meaning in Punk Rock*. Milton Keynes, UK: Open University Press, 1985.

Laing, Dave. "Radicals to Reactionaries?" *Let It Rock*, November 1973, 37–38.

Laing, Dave. Review of *Concerts*, by Henry Cow. *Sounds*, June 19, 1976.

Laing, Dave. Review of *In Praise of Learning*, by Henry Cow. *Let It Rock*, September 1975.

Laing, Dave. "'The World's Best Rock Read': Let It Rock 1972–75." *Popular Music and Society* 33, no. 4 (October 2010): 449–63.

Lake, Steve. "Chris Cutler." *Melody Maker*, March 30, 1974.

Lake, Steve. "Cow: Moving Left . . ." *Melody Maker*, April 16, 1977.

Lake, Steve. "Cow Orchestra." *Melody Maker*, March 19, 1977, 23.

Lake, Steve. "Dream Kids." *Melody Maker*, April 6, 1974.

Lake, Steve. "Faust/Henry Cow." *Melody Maker*, October 6, 1973.

Lake, Steve. "Happy Trails." *Melody Maker*, May 11, 1974.

Lake, Steve. "Henry Cow." *Melody Maker*, December 29, 1973.

Lake, Steve. "HENRY COW: It Cud Not Happen to a Better Band!" *Melody Maker*, October 6, 1973.

Lake, Steve. "How Now, Henry Cow?" *Melody Maker*, April 5, 1975.

Lake, Steve. "Milking the Cow." *Melody Maker*, June 22, 1974.

Lake, Steve. Review of *Concerts*, by Henry Cow. *Melody Maker*, September 11, 1976.

Lake, Steve. Review of *Desperate Straights*, by Slapp Happy / Henry Cow. *Melody Maker*, March 8, 1975.

Lake, Steve. Review of *Guitar Solos*, by Fred Frith. *Melody Maker*, February 22, 1975, 42.

Lake, Steve. Review of *Guitar Solos 2*, by Fred Frith. *Melody Maker*, July 31, 1976.

Lake, Steve. Review of *In Praise of Learning*, by Henry Cow. *Melody Maker*, July 5, 1975.

Lake, Steve. Review of *Leg End*, by Henry Cow. *Melody Maker*, September 22, 1973.

Lake, Steve. Review of *Unrest*, by Henry Cow. *Melody Maker*, June 15, 1974.

Lake, Steve, and Karl Dallas. "Prophet, Seers, and Sages." *Melody Maker*, April 24, 1976.

Lake, Steve, and Karl Dallas. "Rocking the Avant-Garde." *Melody Maker*, April 24, 1976.

Lentin, Jean-Pierre. "At Last: German Rock Has Arrived!" In *Krautrock: Cosmic Rock and Its Legacy*, edited by Nikolaos Kotsopoulos, 184–89. Translated by Clodagh Kinsella. London: Black Dog, 2009. Originally published in *Actuel* 27 (January 1973).

Lattès, Pierre. "Mechamment Rock." *Charlie Hebdo*, May 15, 1975, 15.

Lawrence, Tim. *Hold On to Your Dreams: Arthur Russell and the Downtown Music Scene, 1973–1992*. Durham, NC: Duke University Press, 2009.

Lebrun, Christian. "Faust: Rock du Marché Commun." *Best*, August 1972.

Leech, Jeanette. *Seasons They Change: The Story of Acid and Psychedelic Folk*. London: Jawbone, 2010.

le Vay, Charles. "A Guide to Avant Garde Rock." *Let It Rock*, February 1974, 22–24.

Levidov, Les. "Chile and the New Song Movement." *Music for Socialism Newsletter*, November 1977, 10–11.

Levidov, Les. "Songs of Class Struggle." *Music for Socialism Newsletter*, November 1977, 9–10.

Levidov, Les. "Stormy Six Concert." *Music for Socialism Newsletter*, April 1978, 14.

Levidov, Les. Untitled report. *Musics* 13 (August 1977): 13–14.

Levidov, Les. "Words and Music—An Overview." *Music for Socialism Newsletter*, December 1977, 11, 13.

Levine, Barry. Review of *Unrest*, by Henry Cow. *Morning Star* (London), June 25, 1974.

Levitz, Tamara. "Experimental Music and Revolution: Cuba's Grupo de Experimentación Sonora del ICAIC." In *Tomorrow Is the Question: New Directions in Experimental Music Studies*, edited by Benjamin Piekut, 180–210. Ann Arbor: University of Michigan Press, 2014.

Levitz, Tamara. *Modernist Mysteries: Perséphone*. New York: Oxford University Press, 2012.

Levitz, Tamara. "Yoko Ono and the Unfinished Music of 'John and Yoko.'" In *Impossible to Hold: Women and Culture in the 1960s*, edited by Avital H. Bloch and Lauri Umansky, 217–39. New York: New York University Press, 2005.

Lewis, George E. "Improvised Music after 1950: Afrological and Eurological Perspectives." In *The Other Side of Nowhere: Jazz, Improvisation, and Communities in*

Dialogue, ed. Daniel Fischlin and Ajay Heble, 131–62. Middletown, CT: Wesleyan University Press, 2004. Originally published in 1996.

Lewis, George E. *A Power Stronger Than Itself: The AACM and American Experimental Music*. Chicago, IL: University of Chicago Press, 2008.

Lewis, George E. Review of *Northern Sun, Southern Moon*, by Mike Heffley. *Current Musicology* 78 (fall 2004): 84.

Lewis, John. "So What Do You Want from Your Music—Security?" *Time Out*, December 8–14, 1972, 38–39.

Lewsen, Charles. "The Bacchae." *Times* (London), April 28, 1972.

Lewsen, Charles. "The City: Royal Court." *Times* (London), November 13, 1974.

Lindau, Elizabeth. "Art Is Dead. Long Live Rock! Avant-Gardism and Rock Music, 1967–99." PhD diss., University of Virginia, 2012.

Llewellyn, Howell. Review of *Unrest*, by Henry Cow. *Evening Echo Southend*, July 1974.

Lock, Graham. *Forces in Motion: The Music and Thoughts of Anthony Braxton*. New York: Da Capo, [1988] 1989.

MacDonald, Ian. "Ayers / Cabaret Voltaire." *New Musical Express*, October 14, 1972.

MacDonald, Ian. "Common Market Rock." *New Musical Express*, April 28, 1973.

MacDonald, Ian. "Faust: Faust IV (Virgin)." *New Musical Express*, October 13, 1973.

MacDonald, Ian. "Faust: The Sound of the Eighties." *New Musical Express*, March 3, 1973.

MacDonald, Ian. "Faust: Sturm und Drang and Scenes of Wild Abandon." *New Musical Express*, June 2, 1973.

MacDonald, Ian. "Faust: We're Just Trying to Be Here Now." *New Musical Express*, November 3, 1973.

MacDonald, Ian. "Krautrock: Germany Calling." *New Musical Express*, December 9, 1972.

MacDonald, Ian. "Krautrock: Germany Calling #2." *New Musical Express*, December 16, 1972.

MacDonald, Ian. "Krautrock: Germany Calling #3." *New Musical Express*, December 23, 1972.

MacDonald, Ian. Review of *The Faust Tapes. New Musical Express*, May 26, 1973.

MacDonald, Ian. Review of *Greasy Truckers Live at Dingwalls Dance Hall*, by Camel, Henry Cow, Global Village Trucking Company, and Gong. *New Musical Express*, March 23, 1974.

MacDonald, Ian. Review of *In Praise of Learning*, by Henry Cow. *New Musical Express*, June 7, 1975.

MacDonald, Ian. Review of *Leg End*, by Henry Cow. *New Musical Express*, September 22, 1973.

MacDonald, Ian. Review of *So Far*, by Faust. *New Musical Express*, April 14, 1973.

MacDonald, Ian. Review of *Unrest*, by Henry Cow. *New Musical Express*, June 8, 1974.

MacDonald, Ian. *Revolution in the Head: The Beatles' Records and the Sixties*. New York: Henry Holt, 1994.

MacDonald, Ian. "Slapp Happy: Sort Of." *New Musical Express*, April 14, 1973.

MacKinnon, Angus. Review of *In Praise of Learning*, Henry Cow. *Sounds*, May 31, 1975.

MacKinnon, Angus. "Robert Wyatt." *Sounds*, May 31, 1975.

MacKinnon, Angus. "Tiptoeing through the Cow/Slapps." *Sounds*, May 3, 1975, 40.

Mahon, Maureen. *Right to Rock: The Black Rock Coalition and the Cultural Politics of Race*. Durham, NC: Duke University Press, 2004.

Malvern Gazette. Unsigned review of *Unrest*, by Henry Cow. n.d.

Mann, Paul. *The Theory-Death of the Avant-Garde*. Bloomington: Indiana University Press, 1991.

Mann, William. "The Beatles Revive Hopes of Progress in Pop Music." *Times* (London), May 29, 1967.

Marcus, Greil. *Lipstick Traces: A Secret History of the Twentieth Century*. Cambridge, MA: Harvard University Press, 1989.

Marotti, William. "Challenge to Music: The Music Group's Sonic Politics." In *Tomorrow Is the Question: New Directions in Experimental Music Studies*, edited by Benjamin Piekut, 109–38. Ann Arbor: University of Michigan Press, 2014.

Martin, Bill. *Avant Rock: Experimental Music from the Beatles to Bjork*. Chicago, IL: Open Court, 2002.

McKenzie, Ian. "Bedford Trucking." *Sounds*, January 29, 1977.

McNeill, Phil. "Revolution Planned for May 28." *New Musical Express*, May 28, 1977.

Mead, Stephen. Letter to the editor. *New Musical Express*, November 9, 1974.

Megahey, Alan. *A School in Africa: Peterhouse; Education in Rhodesia and Zimbabwe, 1955–2005*. Oxford: Macmillan, 2005.

Mekas, Jonas. *Movie Journal: The Rise of the New American Cinema, 1959–1971*. Second ed., edited by Gregory Smulewicz-Zucker. New York: Columbia University Press, 2016.

Mellers, Wilfrid. *Music in a New Found Land: Themes and Developments in the History of American Music*. London: Barrie and Rockliff, 1964.

Melody Maker. "Deleted: The LP That Was TOO Popular." June 30, 1973.

Melody Maker. "Dialogue." November 10, 1973.

Melody Maker. "Floyd: Dune to Work!" January 24, 1976.

Melody Maker. "The Henry Cow File." February 9, 1974.

Melody Maker. "In the Manor to Which They Are Accustomed." January 22, 1972, 27.

Melody Maker. "Taking Off." December 6, 1975.

Melody Maker. "Udder News." January 5, 1974, 10.

Melody Maker. "Unlikely Alliance Encores." April 30, 1977, 58.

Melody Maker. "Who Buys Records by John Denver, Charles Aznavour, and Peters and Less?" Dialogue. November 16, 1974, 26–28.

Merck, Mandy. "Composing for the Films." *Screen* 25, no. 3 (1984): 40–54.

Michelson, Annette. "Film and the Radical Aspiration." In *The New American Cinema: A Critical Anthology*, edited by Gregory Battcock, 83–102. New York: Dutton, 1967. First version written in 1966.

Miles. "Henry Cow." *New Musical Express*, February 7, 1976.

Miles. "Henry Cow: Southend." *New Musical Express*, November 13, 1976.

Miles. Review of *Concerts*, by Henry Cow. *New Musical Express,* August 7, 1976.

Miles. "Tangerine Dream." *New Musical Express*, November 29, 1975.

Milkowski, Bill. "The Frith Factor: Exploration in Sound." *Down Beat* 50, no. 1 (January 1983): 22–25, 61.

Mockus, Martha. *Sounding Out: Pauline Oliveros and Lesbian Musicality*. New York: Routledge, 2008.

Morgan, Jon C. "Steve Beresford Signals for Tea." *Coda* 286 (1999): 16–19.

Morning Star (London). Unsigned review of *Leg End*, by Henry Cow. November 6, 1973.

Morris, Rosalind. "Brisk, Brash and Branson." *Guardian*, January 22, 1970.

Moten, Fred. *In the Break: The Aesthetics of the Black Radical Tradition*. Minneapolis: University of Minnesota Press, 2003.

Muñoz, José Esteban. *Disidentifications: Queers of Color and the Performance of Politics*. Minneapolis: University of Minnesota Press, 1999.

Murray, William A. Review of *Leg End*, by Henry Cow. *Time Out*, September 21, 1973.

Music for Socialism Newsletter. "Klossaknapitatet [sic]." October 1977, 2.

Music for Socialism Newsletter. "Music Net." February 1978.

Music for Socialism Newsletter. "Statement of Aims Approved at the Meeting of June 25th." August 1977, 1.

Musicians Union. Untitled report. *Musics* 13 (August 1977): 11.

Myers, Stanley. "Shock Tactics." *Spectator*, May 31, 1968.

Nakai, You. "On the Instrumental Natures of David Tudor's Music." PhD diss., New York University, 2016.

Nettelbeck, Uwe. "Besonders wertvoll–nicht in Oberhausen." *Die Zeit* (Hamburg), April 5, 1968. Accessed December 10, 2016. http://www.zeit.de/1968/14/besonders -wertvoll-nicht-in-oberhausen.

[Nguyen, Gerard]. "Atem Raconte l'Histoire (presque) Complete de Henry Cow." *Atem* 6 (September 15, 1976): 11–22.

[Nguyen, Gerard]. "Lindsay Cooper." *Atem* 12 (April 1978): 18–22.

Nichols [Nicols], Maggie. "The Strength of Tomorrow." In *'68, '78, '88: From Women's Liberation to Feminism*, edited by Amanda Sebestyen, 175–84. Bridport, UK: Prism Press, 1988.

Nickleson, Patrick. "The Names of Minimalism: Authorship and the Historiography of Dispute in New York Minimalism, 1960–1982." PhD diss., University of Toronto, 2017.

Niebur, Louis. *Special Sound: The Creation and Legacy of the BBC Radiophonic Workshop*. Oxford: Oxford University Press, 2010.

Novak, David. *Japanoise: Music at the Edge of Circulation*. Durham, NC: Duke University Press, 2013.

Novak, David. "The Sublime Frequencies of New Old Media." *Public Culture* 23, no. 3 (2011): 603–34.

O'Connell, Gerald. "Another Time, Another Place." *Let It Rock*, February 1975, 30–31.

O'Connell, Gerald. "Dream: Alien Rock." *Sounds*, April 6, 1974.

O'Dair, Marcus. *Different Every Time: The Authorized Biography of Robert Wyatt*. London: Serpent's Tail, 2014.

Olzak, April. "Would You Believe That the Bass-Player on Many of Those Motown Classics Is a 38-Year-Old Mother of Three?" Profile of Carol Kaye. *Melody Maker*, August 18, 1973, 49.

O'Meally, Robert G. "On Burke and the Vernacular: Ralph Ellison's Boomerang of History." In *History and Memory in African-American Culture*, edited by Genevieve Fabre and Robert G. O'Meally, 244–60. New York: Oxford University Press, 1994.

Ortmann, Andy. "Eine Henry Cow-Story." *Hanni Manni: Kritik der Ware Popmusik* 6 (November 1978).

Orton, Fred, and Griselda Pollock. "Avant-Gardes and Partisans Reviewed." *Art History* 4, no. 3 (1981): 305–27.

Osborne, Richard. *Vinyl: A History of the Analogue Record*. Aldershot, UK: Ashgate, 2012.

Oxford Review. Unsigned review of *Unrest*, by Henry Cow. June 15, 1974.

Palmer, Tony. *Born under a Bad Sign*. London: William Kimber, 1970.

Palmer, Tony. "The Road to Nowhere." *London Magazine*, July 1967, 85–89.

Paringaux, Philipe. "Faust." *Rock and Folk*, February 1972.

Parker, Evan. "Speech to the SPNM Forum on 'Music in the Future.'" *Musics* 1 (April–May 1975): 12–13.

Parsons, Michael. "Michael Parsons Writes about the Music of Cornelius Cardew." *Listener*, November 30, 1967, 728–29.

Parsons, Michael. "Sounds of Discovery." *Musical Times* 109, no. 1503 (May 1968): 429–30.

Pasler, Jann. "The Political Economy of Composition in the American University, 1965–1985." In *Writing through Music: Essays on Music, Culture, and Politics*, 318–65. New York: Oxford University Press, 2008.

Paton, Maureen. "Cow Orchestra." *Melody Maker*, July 2, 1977, 17.

Paton, Maureen "Revolution in the Studio." *Melody Maker*, January 7, 1978.

Patterson, Archie. "Rock Began in Opposition to *Mainstream Culture* . . ." In *Eurock: Music and Second Culture Post Millennium*, 7–13. Portland, OR: Eurock Publications, 2013.

Patteson, Thomas. *Instruments for New Music: Sound, Technology, and Modernism*. Oakland: University of California Press, 2016.

Peacock, Steve. "Faust: What We All Need?" *Sounds*, July 15, 1972.

Peacock, Steve. "Tale of Two Virgins." *Sounds*, May 4, 1974.

Peacock, Steve. Review of *Leg End*, by Henry Cow. *Sounds*, October 20, 1973.

Peacock, Steve. Review of *Unrest*, by Henry Cow. *Sounds*, July 13, 1974.

Pearce, Geoff. Untitled report. *Musics* 13 (August 1977): 15–16.

Pêcheux, Michel. *Language, Semantics, and Ideology*. New York: St. Martin's, 1982.

Peckham, Rick. Review of *Unrest*, by Henry Cow. *Mid Sussex Times*, June 13, 1974.

Peel, John. "Faust." *Disc*, June 10, 1972.

Peel, John. Review of *Super*, by Neu! *Disc*, January 27, 1973.

Peters, Gary. *The Philosophy of Improvisation*. Chicago, IL: University of Chicago Press, 2009.

Phillips, Kate. "Johnny's Dead." *New Musical Express*, August 16, 1975.

Philips, Paul. "Draper: Interesting People Make Interesting Records." *Music Week*, November 5, 1977.

Picart, Hervé. "L'énigme Henry Cow." *Best*, August 1975, 22.

Pickering, Andrew. *The Cybernetic Brain: Sketches of Another Future*. Chicago, IL: University of Chicago Press, 2009.

Piekut, Benjamin. *Experimentalism Otherwise: The New York Avant-Garde and Its Limits*. Berkeley: University of California Press, 2011.

Piekut, Benjamin. "Indeterminacy, Free Improvisation, and the Mixed Avant-Garde: Experimental Music in London, 1965–1975." *Journal of the American Musicological Society* 67, no. 3 (fall 2014): 769–824.

Piekut, Benjamin. "Music for Socialism, London 1977." *Twentieth-Century Music*, forthcoming.

Piekut, Benjamin. "Not So Much a Program of Music as the Experience of Music." In *Merce Cunningham: CO:MM:ON TI:ME*, edited by Joan Rothfuss, 113–29. Minneapolis: Walker Arts Center, 2017.

Pinsent, ed. "Merzbow." *Sound Projector* 5 (1998): 6–7.

Pinsent, ed. "Numinous Objects: An Interview with Peter Blegvad of Slapp Happy." *Sound Projector* 8 (2000): 16–18.

Plummer, Mark. "The Rise and Rise of Richard Branson." *Melody Maker*, May 27, 1972.

Pons, Alain. "Wyatt and Cow." *Best*, June 1975, 18.

Porter, Eric. *What Is This Thing Called Jazz? African American Musicians as Artists, Critics, and Activists*. Berkeley: University of California Press, 2002.

Prévost, Eddie. *No Sound Is Innocent: AMM and the Practice of Self-Invention, Meta-Musical Narratives, Essays*. Matching Tye, UK: Copula, 1995.

Puerto, Francesc X. "Henry Cow." *Popular* 1, January 1978.

Puerto, Francesc X. "Henry Cow Concerts." *Star*, January 1978.

Radano, Ronald. "Critical Alchemy: Anthony Braxton and the Imagined Tradition." In *Jazz among the Discourses*, edited by Krin Gabbard, 189–216. Durham, NC: Duke University Press, 1995.

Ramsey, Guthrie P. *Race Music: Black Cultures from Bebop to Hip-Hop*. Berkeley: University of California Press, 2003.

Rapport, Evan. "Hearing Punk as Blues." *Popular Music* 33, no. 1 (January 2014): 39–67.

Records and Recording. Unsigned review of *Leg End*, by Henry Cow. December 1973.

Record and Radio Mirror. Unsigned review of *Unrest*, by Henry Cow. June 29, 1974.

Records and Recording. Unsigned review of *Unrest*, by Henry Cow. August 1974.

Regev, Motti. *Pop-Rock Music: Aesthetic Cosmopolitanism in Late Modernity*. Cambridge: Cambridge University Press, 2013.

Reynols. *Blank Tapes*. Trente Oiseaux TOC002, CD, 2000.

Rich, Alan. "Jazz and Classical Styles Converging." *New York / World Journal Tribune*, April 23, 1967.

Rodgers, Tara. *Pink Noises: Women on Electronic Music and Sound*. Durham, NC: Duke University Press, 2010.

Rosselson, Leon. Untitled report. *Musics* 13 (August 1977): 12.

Rupprecht, Philip. *British Musical Modernism: The Manchester Group and Their Contemporaries*. Cambridge: Cambridge University Press, 2015.

Sadie, Stanley. "Carrying Improvisation to Its Logical End." *Times* (London), August 4, 1967.

Salzinger, Helmut. "'Raus Klainer Röhl': Der mißglückte Versuch, die Redaktion von 'konkret' zu besetzen." *Die Zeit* (Hamburg), May 16, 1969. Accessed December 10, 2016. http://www.zeit.de/1969/20/raus-klainer-roehl.

Sandford, Neil. "Jazz: A Tradition of Protest." *Music for Socialism Newsletter*, November 1977, 11.

Sandford, Neil. "Macho in Rock." *Music for Socialism Newsletter*, November 1977, 10.

[Sandford, Neil]. "Words and Music." *Music for Socialism Newsletter*, December 1977, 4.

Sassoon, Donald. *Contemporary Italy: Economy, Society, and Politics since 1945*. 2nd ed. London: Longman, 1997.

Saul, Scott. *Freedom Is, Freedom Ain't: Jazz and the Making of the Sixties*. Cambridge, MA: Harvard University Press, 2003.

Savage, Jon. *England's Dreaming: Anarchy, Sex Pistols, Punk Rock, and Beyond*. New York: St. Martins, 1991.

S. B. "Yes, It's All Very Clever but . . . . . Henry Cow at Leeds." *Leeds Music News*, December 1977.

Scheunemann, Dietrich. "From Collage to the Multiple: On the Genealogy of Avant-Garde and Neo-Avant-Garde." In *Avant-Garde / Neo-Avant-Garde*, edited by Dietrich Scheunemann, 15–48. Amsterdam: Rodopi, 2005.

Schonfield, Vic. "Free Jazz in Britain." *Music Maker*, November 1967, 22.

Schonfield, Victor. "Arts in Society: Sergeant Pepper's Favourite Composer." *New Society*, September 7, 1967, 331.

Schonfield, Victor. "Cornelius Cardew, AMM, and the Path to Perfect Hearing." *Jazz Monthly*, May 1968, 10–11.

Schonfield, Victor. "Rule Britannia?" *Down Beat* 35, no. 14 (1968): 24–25, 32.

Schonfield, Victor. "Total Improvisation." *International Times*, March 28, 1969, 15.

Schwarcz, Yoel. Interview with Easy Livin. May 2006. Prog Archives. Accessed August 18, 2016. http://www.progarchives.com/forum/forum_posts.asp?TID=23236.

Sell, Mike. *The Avant-Garde: Race, Religion, War*. New York: Seagull, 2011.

Sennet (London; current *London Student*). "Experience of a Virgin." February 27, 1974.

Shaar Murray, Charles. "Gerroff an' Milk It." *New Musical Express*, August 31, 1974, 8.

Shaar Murray, Charles. Review of *Guitar Solos*, by Fred Frith. *New Musical Express*, November 30, 1974, 22–23.

Shaar Murray, Charles. "Robert Wyatt, Henry Cow." *New Musical Express*, July 19, 1975.

Shaar Murray, Charles. "The Roman Spring of Mr. Wyatt." *New Musical Express*, July 19, 1975.

Shelton, Robert. "Socialist Music Festival." *Times* (London), May 30, 1977.

Shera, Michael. "Mike Westbrook and His Orchestra." *Jazz Journal* 19, no. 1 (1966): 10–11.

Simmons, Nick. Review of *Leg End*, by Henry Cow. *King's News* (Cambridge, UK), November 1973.

SINE Student Magazine. Unsigned review of *Leg End*, by Henry Cow. January 1974. Clipping, FFA.

Sivyer, John. Review of *Unrest*, by Henry Cow. *Watford Observer*, July 9, 1974.

S. J. K. Review of *Leg End*, by Henry Cow. *Coventry Evening Telegraph*, September 25, 1973.

Slingsby, Alan. "Music to Challenge Big Business With." *Morning Star*, March 3, 1977.

Smalley, Roger. "Musical Party in King's." Interview with Norman Bryson. *Varsity* (Cambridge UK), February 1, 1969.

Smith, Terry. *What Is Contemporary Art?* Chicago, IL: University of Chicago Press, 2009.

Smith, T'ai. *Bauhaus Weaving Theory: From Feminine Craft to Mode of Design.* Minneapolis: University of Minnesota Press, 2014.

Smoak, Dale. "Lindsay Cooper Interview." *Cadence* 16 (1990): 5–10.

Snead, James. "On Repetition in Black Culture." *Black American Literature Forum* 15, no. 4 (winter 1981): 146–54.

Soames, Nicolas. "FIG on a Gig." *Guardian*, September 29, 1978.

Souster, Tim. "Down Abbey Road." *Listener*, November 13, 1969.

Souster, Tim. "Goodbye Cream." *Listener*, March 20, 1969.

Souster, Tim. "Intermodulation: A Short History." *Contact* 17 (summer 1977): 3–6.

Souster, Tim. "Long and Loud." *Listener*, May 2, 1968, 581.

Souster, Tim. "A New Dylan." *Listener*, June 5, 1969.

Souster, Tim. "Notes on Pop Music." *Tempo* 87 (winter 1968–69): 2–6.

Souster, Tim. "Pop Form." *Listener*, October 10, 1968.

Souster, Tim. "Pre-Christmas." *Listener*, December 12, 1968.

Souster, Tim. "Sounds of Discovery." *Financial Times*, May 21, 1968.

Souster, Tim. "Through the Sound Barrier." *Observer Magazine*, October 5, 1969.

Souster, Tim. "The Velvet Underground." *Listener,* July 4, 1968.

South Wales Echo (Cardiff). Unsigned review of *Unrest*, by Henry Cow. July 6, 1974.

South Westerner. Unsigned review of *Leg End*, by Henry Cow. October 6, 1973.

Spencer, Neil. "Triumphal Re-entry of the Magic Gladiators." *New Musical Express*, June 15, 1974.

Stafford-Clark, Nigel. "Age of Gilt—Don't Look Back." *Varsity* (Cambridge UK), June 7, 1969.

Steege, Benjamin. *Helmholtz and the Modern Listener.* Cambridge: Cambridge University Press, 2012.

Steinbeck, Paul. *A Message to Our Folks: The Art Ensemble of Chicago.* Chicago, IL: University of Chicago Press, 2017.

Steiner, George. *Language and Silence: Essays on Language, Literature, and the Inhuman.* New Haven, CT: Yale University Press, 1967.

Sternberg, Mike. "Euripides at the Arts." *Varsity* (Cambridge UK), May 13, 1972.

Stockhausen, Karlheinz. Interview with John Banks. *Varsity* (Cambridge UK), May 8, 1971.

Stubbs, David. *Future Days: Krautrock and the Birth of a Revolutionary New Music.* London: Faber and Faber, 2014.

Subotnik, Rose Rosengard. "Adorno's Diagnosis of Beethoven's Late Style: Early Symptom of a Fatal Condition." *Journal of the American Musicological Society* 29, no. 2 (1976): 242–75.

Sunday Mail (Glasgow). Unsigned review of *Unrest*, by Henry Cow. July 28, 1974.

S. W. Review of *Unrest*, by Henry Cow. *Derby Evening Telegraph*, June 12, 1974.

Szwed, John F. *Space Is the Place: The Lives and Times of Sun Ra*. New York: Da Capo, 1998.

Tantini, Giancarlo. Letter to the editor. *Down Beat*, April 1983.

Tardà, Jordi. "Henry Cow en Barcelona." *Disco Express*, December 16, 1977.

Taruskin, Richard. *The Oxford History of Western Music*. New York: Oxford University Press, 2005.

Thomas, David. "LAist Interview: David Thomas of Pere Ubu." Interview with Bobzilla. *LAist*, October 8, 2009. Accessed September 5, 2016. http://laist.com/2009/10/08/laist_interview_david_thomas_of_per.php.

Thyrén, David. "The Alternative Eurovision Song Contest in Sweden, 1975." In *A Cultural History of the Avant-garde in the Nordic Countries, 1950–1975*, edited by Tania Ørum and Jesper Olsson, 831–40. Leiden: Brill, 2016.

Tilbury, John. *Cornelius Cardew (1936–1981): A Life Unfinished*. Harlow, UK: Copula, 2008.

Toop, David. *Into the Maelstrom: Music, Improvisation, and the Dream of Freedom: Before 1970*. London: Bloomsbury, 2016.

Tottan, Nick. "Avant-Garde Concert—A Surprise for Performers?" *Varsity* (Cambridge UK), February 22, 1969.

Tudor, David. "From Piano to Electronics." Interview with Victor Schonfield. *Music and Musicians*, August 1972, 24.

Tuuli, Markku. "Henry Cow: Etsii Vaihtoehtoja." *Katso* (Finland), May 9, 1976.

Unwin, Russell. "The New, Spiritual Era of Stockhausen." *Melody Maker*, May 29, 1971.

Unwin, Russell. "Nothing Like a Bit of the Ol' Boulez." *Cream* 2, no. 1 (May 1972): 7.

Unwin, Russell. "Rock and the Classics—Continued . . ." *Melody Maker*, March 13, 1971.

Unwin, Russell. "What's Wrong with Our Music Colleges?" *Melody Maker*, August 29, 1970.

Unwin, Russell. "Where Pop and Classics Meet . . ." *Melody Maker*, June 27, 1970.

van den Berg, Hubert. "On the Historiographic Distinction between Historical and Neo-Avant-Garde." In *Avant-Garde / Neo-Avant-Garde*, edited by Dietrich Scheunemann, 63–74. Amsterdam: Rodolpi, 2005.

Veal, Michael E. *Dub: Soundscapes and Shattered Songs in Jamaican Reggae*. Middletown, CT: Wesleyan University Press, 2007.

Veal, Michael E., and E. Tammy Kim, eds. *Punk Ethnography: Artists and Scholars Listen to Sublime Frequencies*. Middletown, CT: Wesleyan University Press, 2016.

Walker, Chris. "'Worldes Blis' and the Word of New Music." *Granta*, October 1969, 15–16.

Walker, Ian. "Whole Lotta Shakin' Goin' On." *Leveller* 7 (July/August 1977): 18–20.

Walters, John. "Walters." *ZigZag*, April–May 1978, 37.

Walters, Michael. "The Open-Ended Music Company." *Sounds*, October 24, 1970.

Wang, Jing. "Considering the Politics of Sound Art in China in the 21st Century." *Leonardo Music Journal* 25 (2015): 73–78.

Ward, Brian. *Just My Soul Responding: Rhythm and Blues, Black Consciousness, and Race Relations*. Berkeley: University of California Press, 1998.

Wark, Jayne. *Radical Gestures: Feminism and Performance Art in North America*. Montreal: McGill-Queen's University Press, 2006.

Warshaw, Jack. Untitled report. *Musics* 13 (August 1977): 10.

Waschko, Roman. "Rome Concert by Lou Reed Results in Riot, Injuries." *Billboard*, March 1, 1975, 4, 49.

Watson, Bob. "Henry Cow." *Sounds*, February 18, 1978.

Watson, Ben. *Derek Bailey and the Story of Free Improvisation*. London: Verso, 2004.

Watts, Michael. "Amon Duul: Every Good Thing Goes in Threes." *Melody Maker*, June 24, 1972.

Watts, Michael. "Amon for All Seasons." *Melody Maker*, December 12, 1970.

Watts, Michael. "Can: *Tago Mago*." Review. *Melody Maker*, January 29, 1972.

Watts, Michael. "Can You Dig It?" *Melody Maker*, February 5, 1972.

Watts, Michael. "Deutsch Rock." *Melody Maker*, April 15, 1972.

Watts, Michael. "Karlheinz Stockhausen." *Melody Maker*, March 4, 1972.

Watts, Michael. "Lady of Pain." *Melody Maker*, January 27, 1973, 28–29.

Wedge. "Art Attacks." 2 (April 1978): 30.

Welch, Chris. "The Year of Pop." *Melody Maker*, December 29, 1973.

White, Graham. "The Ians in the Audience: Punk Attitude and the Influence of the Avant-Garde." In *Avant-Garde Performance and Material Exchange: Vectors of the Radical*, edited by Mike Sell, 188–206. New York: Palgrave Macmillan, 2011.

Williams, Richard. "Can Do." *Melody Maker*, January 27, 1973.

Williams, Richard. "Classical Musicians Have a Lot to Learn." *Melody Maker*, July 25, 1970.

Williams, Richard. "Derek Bailey: Feeding the Post-Cage Ear." *Melody Maker*, July 10, 1971.

Williams, Richard. "Is It Euro-Rock Next?" *Melody Maker*, June 13, 1970.

Williams, Richard. "Jazz/Rock: A Personal Opinion." *Melody Maker*, February 7, 1970.

Williams, Richard. Review of *Ege Bamyasi*, by Can, and *Neu!*, by Neu! *Melody Maker*, November 11, 1972.

Williams, Richard. Review of *Monster Movie*, by Can. *Melody Maker*, May 30, 1970.

Williams, Richard. "The Revolt against the Business Establishment." *Melody Maker*, September 19, 1970.

Williams, Richard. "Roxy Music." *Melody Maker*, February 12, 1972, 9.

Williams, Richard. "The Trip." *Melody Maker*, September 12, 1970.

Willmott, Nigel. "Rock 'n' Roll." *Music for Socialism Newsletter*, November 1977, 4.

Wilmer, Val. "Ici Londres." *Jazz*, March 1979, 28–29, 70.

Wilson, Andy. *Faust: Stretch Out Time: 1970–1975*. London: The Faust Pages, 2006.

Wilson, Tony. "Fairport and Henry Cow Concert." *Varsity* (Cambridge UK), November 14, 1970.

[Wise, David]. "The End of Music." 1978. Revolt against Plenty. Accessed September 5, 2016. http://www.revoltagainstplenty.com/index.php/recent/216-the-original-copy-of-the-end-of-music.html.

Witts, Dick. "Cow Milks Maid Experiment." *New Manchester Review*, January 27, 1978.

Wood, Colin. "How We Differ." *Musics* 1 (April–May 1975): 31.

Wright, Patrick. "Resist Me. Make Me Strong." *Guardian Weekend*, November 11, 1995, 41.

Young, Rob. *Electric Eden: Unearthing Britain's Visionary Music*. London: Faber and Faber, 2010.

Young, Rob. *All Gates Open: The Story of Can*. London: Faber and Faber, 2018.

Yúdice, George. "Rethinking the Theory of the Avant-Garde from the Periphery." In *Modernism and Its Margins: Reinscribing Cultural Modernity from Spain and Latin America*, edited by Anthony L. Geist and José Monleón, 52–80. Minneapolis: University of Minnesota Press, 1999.

Zak, Albin J., III. *I Don't Sound Like Nobody: Remaking Music in 1950s America*. Ann Arbor: University of Michigan Press, 2010.

Zū Magazine. "Recommended Bands." n.d. [September 1978], 9.

Zwerin, Michael. "A Lethal Measurement." *Village Voice* (New York), January 6, 1966.

Zwerin, Michael. "The Soft Machine." *Down Beat* 35, no. 14 (July 11, 1968): 21, 40.

Penman — Anado , LRB